TRADE-MARKS

Legal and commercial aspects with particular attention to chemicals, chemical specialties and allied products, including a list of trade-mark and trade-name products and their suppliers

by

H. BENNETT, F.A.I.C.

Technical Director, Glyco Products Company, Inc.

1949

CHEMICAL PUBLISHING CO., INC.

BROOKLYN N. Y.

PRINTED IN THE UNITED STATES OF AMERICA

Preface

Since a good trade-mark is of great importance in merchandising a product, it has been felt that a book outlining the principles of trade-mark selection would be highly useful.

Buyers, sellers, manufacturers, lawyers and others will welcome this book which gives a comprehensive list of trade-mark products. Much of the information given has never been published before.

Although all the necessary information for the registration of trade-marks in the United States Patent Office is given, it is strongly advised that the registration is handled by an attorney experienced in this field. Suggestions made by him will often save time, money and effort and prevent possible lawsuits.

The writer has had many years of experience in coining trade-marks and hopes that this experience will be helpful to others. Some of the material used is taken from *Trade-Names* by Cousins and Wadsworth, with the kind permission of the Harlequin Press Co.

The author is extremely grateful to A. J. Nydick, registered patent attorney, for his scrutiny of the legal aspects of the manuscript before publication.

H. Bennett

Table of Contents

Introduction

Makers' names and trade-marks have been used for thousands of years, but the modern system of trade-marks was introduced in the United States about 1865. The first federal legislation on trade-marks was passed in 1870. This act, providing for the registration of trade-marks, was later repealed, and trade-marks were protected by an act of 1905, as amended in 1906, until July 1947, when the Lanham Act became effective.

Trade-Mark protection is of value not only to the manufacturer and vendor but also to the consumer. The consumer can easily remember the name and will get a product which is usually of a uniform and satisfactory quality. The advertising of the manufacturer fixes the trade-mark in the mind of the consumer. It promotes and simplifies reordering.

The naming of a new product is not as simple as it may appear at first glance. The name must be an entirely new one in the field concerned. Because of the many thousands of names now registered, it is not too easy to find a name that is suitable and does not bear some resemblance to a name already in use. Generally, a preliminary list of names is drawn up and this is weeded out until only a very few names are left. Even these may not be acceptable because conscious or subconscious analogies are drawn from existing names and thus a resemblance follows in the new names selected.

Four different ways of finding or coining original names are given in this book. Different types of available names are discussed in detail so that a provisional decision can be made in selecting the type of name particularly suitable to cover a definite product.

In practice, once a trade-mark is selected, usually it is not changed. A product or its package can be varied or improved, but the trade name remains unaltered.

The difference between a good and a poor trade-mark is often equivalent to the difference between a mediocre and a highly successful business.

LEGAL ASPECTS

Rules of Practice in Trade-Mark* Cases

The following rules governing the registration of trade-marks and other marks in the Patent Office, and other proceedings in the Patent Office relating to marks, have been adopted and promulgated under the authority of the Trade-Mark Act of 1946, effective July 5, 1947, and other authority, after publication of proposed rules and a hearing, and consideration of all material and arguments submitted.

In view of the novelty of many of the provisions of the Trade-Mark Act of 1946, it is recognized that changes may be required in these rules from time to time. It is respectfully requested that practitioners working under these rules promptly inform the Patent Office of any proposed changes that appear to be desirable.

These rules were published in the Federal Register for June 19, 1947.[1]

CASPER W. OOMS
Commissioner of Patents.

* The difference between a trade-mark and trade name is that the first refers to a product manufactured and/or sold by a particular firm and the second designates a firm or house which makes or sells the product. However, in this book this distinction is not always made, but the two terms are sometimes used interchangeably.

[1] In the Federal Register and in the Code of Federal Regulations these rules are Part 100 of Title 37 and the individual rules, there called sections, are numbered with 100 prefixed to the numbers here used, with the decimal point following the 100.

1. GENERAL INFORMATION

1.1 **All communications to be addressed to Commissioner of Patents.** All letters should be addressed to "The Commissioner of Patents, Washington 25, D. C."

1.2 **Business to be transacted in writing.** All business with the Patent Office should be transacted in writing. Personal appearance is unnecessary. The action of the Office will be based exclusively on the written record. No recognition will be given to any alleged oral promise, stipulation, or understanding in relation to which there is disagreement or doubt.

1.3 **Business to be conducted with decorum and courtesy.** Applicants and their representatives will be required to conduct their business with the Patent Office with decorum and courtesy. Papers presented in violation of this requirement will be submitted to the Commissioner and will be returned by his direct order. Complaints against Examiners and other employees must be made in communications separate from other papers.

1.4 **Separate letters.** A separate letter should, in every instance, be written in relation to each distinct subject of inquiry.

1.5 **Identification of pending application or registered mark.** A letter relating to a pending application should identify it by the name of the applicant and the serial number and filing date of the application. A letter relating to a registered trade-mark should identify it by the name of the registrant and by the number and date of the certificate.

1.6 Times for taking action expiring on Sunday or holiday. Where the last day for taking any action falls on Sunday or on a holiday within the District of Columbia, the action may be taken on the next succeeding secular or business day.

1.7 Inquiries. The Patent Office cannot undertake to respond to inquiries whether certain trade-marks have been registered, or, if so, to whom, or for what goods; nor can it give legal advice or advice as to the registrability of a specified mark or the nature and extent of the protection afforded by the law, except as questions may arise in connection with pending applications. Information of a general nature may be furnished either by answering the inquiry or by providing or calling attention to an appropriate publication.

2. FEES AND PAYMENT OF MONEY

2.1 Fees and charges. The following is the schedule of fees and charges to be paid to the Patent Office:

(*a*) On filing each original application for registration of a mark in each class on either the Principal or the Supplemental Register.................. $25.00

(*b*) On filing each application for renewal in each class 25.00

(*c*) On filing each application for renewal in each class after expiration of the registration, additional.... 5.00

(*d*) On filing notice of claim of benefits of the act of 1946 for a mark to be published under section 12 (*c*) thereof.............................. 10.00

(*e*) On filing notice of opposition or petition for cancellation 25.00

(*f*) On appeal from the Examiner of Trade-Marks to the Commissioner......................... 25.00

(*g*) On appeal from the Examiner of Interferences to the Commissioner......................... 25.00

(*h*) For issuance of a new certificate of registration following change of ownership of a mark or correction of a registrant's mistake............... 10.00

(*i*) For certificate of correction of registrant's mistake 10.00

(*j*) For filing disclaimer, amendment, surrender, or cancellation after registration. 10.00

(*k*) For manuscript copies, for every one hundred words or fraction thereof. 0.10

(*l*) For comparing other copies, for every one hundred words or fraction thereof. 0.05

(*m*) For certification of copies in any case, additional 1.00

(*n*) For each additional registration or application which may be included under a single certification, additional 0.50

(*o*) For recording every assignment or other paper not exceeding six pages. 3.00

For each additional two pages or less. 1.00

For each additional registration or application included, or involved in one writing, where more than one is so included or involved, additional 0.50

(*p*) For abstracts of title:

For the search, one hour or less, and certificate 3.00

Each additional hour or fraction thereof. 1.50

For each brief from the digest of assignments of two hundred words or less. 1.00

(*q*) For title reports required for Office use. 1.00

(*r*) For a single printed copy of statement and drawing 0.10

(*s*) For certificate that trade-mark has not been registered, search and certificate (for deposit in foreign countries only). 3.00

(*t*) For certified copies of certificates of registration:

For each copy of printed statement and drawing 0.10

For each grant (certificate of registration). . . . 1.00

For the certification. 1.00

For each additional registration which may be included under a single certification, additional 0.50

If renewed, for copy of each certificate of renewal 1.00

(*u*) For photostat copies of records and papers, per sheet 0.20

(*v*) For photoprints of drawing.................... 0.20

(*w*) For making drawings, when they can be made by the Patent Office, the cost of making the same, minimum charge.............................. 5.00

(*x*) For correcting drawings, 20 cents for photoprint of uncorrected drawing, and the cost of making correction, minimum charge for making the correction 1.00

2.2 **Method of payment.** All payments of money required for Patent Office fees must be made in United States specie, Treasury notes, national bank notes, post office money orders or postal notes payable in Washington, D. C., or certified checks. Money orders and certified checks must be made payable to the Commissioner of Patents. If sent in any other form the Office may delay the credit until collection is made. Remittances from foreign countries must be payable and immediately negotiable in the United States for the full amount of the fee required. Money sent by mail to the Patent Office will be at the risk of the sender; letters containing money should be registered.

2.3 **Refunds.** Money paid by actual mistake or in excess, such as a payment not required by law, will be refunded, but a mere change of purpose after the payment of money, as when a party desires to withdraw his application for the registration of a mark or to withdraw an appeal, will not entitle a party to demand such a return. Amounts of ten cents or less will not be returned unless specifically demanded, nor will the payer be notified of such amount; amounts over ten cents but less than one dollar may be returned in postage stamps, and other amounts by check.

3. RECORDS AND PUBLICATIONS OF THE PATENT OFFICE

3.1 **Printed copies of registered marks available.** After a mark has been registered, printed copies of the statement, with a copy of the drawing, will be furnished by the Patent Office upon the payment of the fee therefor.

3.2 **Registration files open to public inspection.** After a mark has been registered, or published for opposition, the file of the application and all proceedings relating thereto are available for public inspection and copies of the papers may be furnished upon paying the fee therefor.

3.3 **Assignment records open to public inspection.** The assignment records are open to public inspection and copies of any assignment recorded may be obtained upon payment of the fee therefor. An order for a copy of an assignment should give the liber and page of the record. If identified only by the name of the applicant and serial number, or by the name of the registrant and registration number, an extra charge will be made for the time consumed in making a search for such assignment.

3.4 **Certified copies.** Copies of records, books, papers, or drawings belonging to the Patent Office relating to marks and copies of certificates of registration, authenticated by the seal of the Patent Office and certified by the Commissioner, or in his name by a chief of division duly designated by the Commissioner, will be furnished by the Patent Office to any person entitled thereto upon payment of the fee for the copies and for the authentication certificate.

3.5 **Official Gazette.** The Official Gazette of the United States Patent Office is published weekly and contains, in addition to the material relating to patents, information relating to trade-marks, including the text or digest of opinions in trade-mark cases. It includes:

(*a*) A list of marks published for opposition, with a reproduction of and information concerning each mark.

(*b*) A list of marks registered on the Principal Register and under the act of 1905.

(*c*) A list of registrations cancelled.

(*d*) A list of marks registered on the Supplemental Register and under the act of 1920, with a reproduction of and information concerning each mark.

(*e*) A list of registrations renewed.

(*f*) A list of marks republished under section 12 (*c*) of the Trade-Mark Act of 1946, with a reproduction of each mark.

(*g*) A list of registrations amended, surrendered, disclaimed, or corrected in accordance with section 7 (*d*), (*f*) and (*g*) of the act with a statement of any change in the registration.

Single copies and subscriptions are sold by the Superintendent of Documents, Government Printing Office, Washington, D. C. Part of the trade-mark material is reprinted separately in a trade-mark leaflet which may be purchased or subscribed to separately.

3.6 **Annual trade-mark index.** An annual index of trade-marks registered is published, and sold by the Superintendent of Documents.

3.7 **Pamphlet of trade-mark laws and rules.** Pamphlet copies of trade-mark laws and rules, and of general information concerning trade-marks, are furnished without charge by the Patent Office.

4. ATTORNEYS AND REPRESENTATION BY ATTORNEYS

4.1 **Applicants may be represented by an attorney.** The owner of a trade-mark may file and prosecute his own application for registration of such trade-mark, or he may be represented by an attorney or other person authorized to practice in trade-mark cases. The Patent Office cannot aid in the selection of an attorney or agent.

4.2 **Persons who may practice before the Patent Office in trade-mark cases.** Attorneys at law in good standing admitted to practice before the Supreme Court of the United States, the United States Court of Customs and Patent Appeals, or the highest court of any State or Territory of the United States or of the District of Columbia, and persons registered to practice in the United States Patent Office in patent cases (Patent Rule 17) may practice before the Patent Office in trade-mark cases.

Attorneys at law. No register of attorneys who may practice before the Patent Office in trade-mark cases is maintained, and no application by an attorney at law for admission to practice is required. A statement in the power of attorney, or in an accompanying paper, of the bar to which the attorney at law is admitted is required, and recognition is limited to each case.

Attorneys and agents registered at the Patent Office. Persons or firms, including attorneys at law, who are registered to practice before the Patent Office need only specify the registration number in the power of attorney.

Special recognition. No persons other than those hereinabove mentioned will be permitted to practice before the Patent Office in trade-mark cases unless specially and formally recognized by the Commissioner of Patents, but any person may appear for himself in a proceeding to which he is a party, or for a firm of which he is a member, or for a corporation or association of which he is an officer and which he is authorized to represent, if such firm, corporation, or association is a party to the proceeding.

Refusal of recognition for cause. Persons entitled to be recognized under this rule may, nevertheless, be refused recognition for cause.

4.3 **Professional conduct.** Attorneys at law and other persons appearing before the Patent Office in trade-mark cases must conform to the standards of ethical and professional conduct generally applicable to attorneys before the courts.

4.4 **Advertising.** The use of display advertising, circulars, letters, cards, and similar material to solicit trade-mark business, directly or indirectly, is forbidden as unprofessional conduct, and any person engaging in such solicitation, or associated with or employed by others who so solicit, shall be refused recognition to practice before the Patent Office or suspended or excluded from further practice.

The use of simple professional letterheads, calling cards, or office signs; simple announcements necessitated by opening an office, change of association, or change of address, distributed to clients and friends, and insertion of professional cards, listings in common form (not display) in a classified telephone or city directory, and listings and professional cards with biographical data in standard professional directories are not prohibited.

(This rule does not come into effect until Jan. 1, 1948, and until that date old trade-mark Rule 11 is still in force.)

4.5 **Signature and certificate of attorney.** Every paper filed by an attorney at law or other recognized person representing an applicant or party to a trade-mark proceeding in the Patent Office must be signed by such attorney or person, except papers which are required to be signed by the applicant or party (such as the application itself and affidavits required of applicants or registrants). When an applicant or party is represented by a firm such papers must carry the signature of an individual member of the firm in addition to the firm name. The signature of an attorney at law or other person to a paper filed by him, or the filing of any paper by him, constitutes a certificate by him that he has read the paper; that he is authorized to file it; that to the best of his knowledge, information, and belief it is well founded in law and fact; and that it is not interposed for delay.

4.6 **Suspension or exclusion from practice.** The Commissioner of Patents may, after notice and opportunity for a hearing, suspend or exclude, either generally or in any particular case, from further practice before the Patent Office any person, attorney, or agent shown to be incompetent or disreputable, or guilty of unethical or unprofessional conduct or gross misconduct, or who refuses to comply with the rules and regulations, or who shall, with intent to defraud in any manner, deceive, mislead, or threaten any applicant or prospective applicant or other person having immediate or prospective business before the Patent Office, by word, circular, letter, or in any other manner. The reasons for any such suspension or exclusion shall be duly recorded.

(See R. S. 487; 35 U.S.C. 11 for review of the Commissioner's action by the District Court of the United States for the District of Columbia.)

4.7 **Power of attorney or authorization.** Before any attorney at law or other recognized person will be allowed to take action in any case or proceeding, a written power of attorney or authorization must be filed in that particular case or proceeding.

A substitute or associate attorney may be appointed by an

attorney only upon the written authorization of his principal; but a third attorney appointed by the second will not be recognized.

4.8 **Correspondence held with attorney.** When an attorney or other recognized person shall have filed his power of attorney or authorization, duly executed, the correspondence will be held with him. Double correspondence with an applicant and his attorney, or with two attorneys, will not be undertaken. If more than one attorney be appointed, correspondence will be held with the one last appointed unless otherwise requested.

4.9 **Revocation of power of attorney.** A power of attorney or authorization may be revoked at any stage in the proceedings of a case upon notification to the Commissioner; and, when it is so revoked, the Office will communicate directly with the applicant or with such other attorney as he may appoint. An attorney or agent will be notified of the revocation of his power of attorney or authorization.

6. APPLICATION FOR REGISTRATION

6.1 **Parts of application.** A complete application for registration comprises:

(*a*) A written application (see Rules 7.1 to 8.8);

(*b*) A drawing of the mark (see Rules 9.1 to 9.5);

(*c*) Five specimens or facsimiles (see Rules 10.1 to 10.3);

(*d*) The required filing fee (see Rule 2.1 (*a*));

(*e*) A certified copy of the registration in the country of origin if the application is based on such foreign registration pursuant to section 44 (*e*) of the act (see Rule 7.9).

6.2 **Application must be complete to receive filing date.** An application will not be accepted and filed for examination unless all the required parts specified in Rule 6.1, complying with the rules and regulations relating thereto, are received, but minor informalities may be waived subject to subsequent correction. If the papers and parts are incomplete or so defective that they cannot be accepted as a complete application, the applicant will be notified and the papers and fee held 6 months for completion if possible, return to the applicant, or other disposition. If not completed in

6 months, a new application must thereafter be filed. The drawing, specimens, or fee of an unaccepted application may be applied to a later application.

6.3 **Serial number and filing date.** Complete applications will be numbered as received, and the applicant will be informed of the serial number and filing date of the application. The filing date of the application is the date on which the complete application is received in the Patent Office in acceptable form.

6.4 **Designation of representative by foreign applicant.** If the applicant is not domiciled in the United States, he must designate by a written document filed in the Patent Office the name and address of some person resident in the United States on whom may be served notices or process in proceedings affecting the mark and to whom all official communications will be addressed unless the applicant is represented by an attorney or other recognized person. If this document does not accompany or form part of the application, it will be required and registration refused unless it is supplied.

6.5 **Papers not returnable.** After acceptance of the application the papers will not be returned for any purpose whatever. If the applicant has not preserved copies of the papers the Office will furnish them on the usual terms.

6.6 **Use of old drawing in new application.** In an application filed in place of an abandoned or rejected application, or in an application for reregistration (Rule 31.1), a new complete application is required, but the old drawing, if suitable, may be used. The application must be accompanied by a request for the transfer of the drawing, and by a permanent photographic copy, or an order for such copy, of the drawing to be placed in the original file. A drawing so transferred, or to be transferred, cannot be amended.

6.7 **Application confidential prior to publication.** No information respecting the filing of an application for the registration of a trade-mark, or the subject matter thereof will be given, prior to publication under Rule 15.1, without authority of the applicant, unless it shall, in the opinion of the Commissioner, be necessary to the proper conduct of business before the Patent Office. Decisions of the Commissioner in applications and proceedings relating thereto are published or available for inspection or publication.

7. THE WRITTEN APPLICATION

7.1 **Application must be in English.** The written application must be in the English language and plainly written on but one side of the paper. Legal size paper, typewritten double spaced, with at least a 1½ inch margin on the left-hand side and top of the page, is deemed preferable.

7.2 **Application to be signed and sworn to by applicant.** The written application must be made to the Commissioner of Patents and must be signed and verified (sworn to) by the applicant or by a member of the firm or an officer of the corporation or association applying.

Re-executed papers may be required when the application has not been filed in the Patent Office within a reasonable time after the date of execution.

7.3 **Requirements for application—Statement.** The written application shall include a request for registration and shall specify:

(*a*) The name of the applicant;

(*b*) The citizenship of the applicant; if the applicant be a partnership, the names and citizenship of the general partners or, if the applicant be a corporation or association, the state or nation under the laws of which organized;

(*c*) The domicile and post office address of the applicant;

(*d*) That the applicant has adopted and is using the mark shown in the accompanying drawing;

(*e*) The particular description of goods on or in connection with which the mark is used;

(*f*) The class of merchandise according to the official classification (if the number and title of the class are not known to the applicant, they may be left blank, in which case they will be filled in by the Patent Office and applicant informed thereof);

(*g*) The date of applicant's first use of the mark as a trade-mark on or in connection with goods specified in the application;

(*h*) The date of applicant's first use of the mark as a trade-mark on or in connection with goods specified in the application in commerce which may lawfully be regulated by Congress, specifying the nature of such commerce;

(*i*) The mode or manner in which the mark is used on or in connection with the particular goods specified.

This part of the written application is called the statement.

7.4 **Requirements for application—Declaration.** The written application must also include averments to the effect that the applicant or other person making the verification believes himself or the firm, corporation, or association in whose behalf he makes the verification to be the owner of the mark sought to be registered; that the mark is in use in commerce which may lawfully be regulated by Congress, specifying the nature of such commerce; that no other person, firm, corporation, or association, to the best of his knowledge and belief, has the right to use such mark in commerce, either in the identical form thereof or in such near resemblance thereto as might be calculated to deceive, that the drawing and description truly represent the mark sought to be registered; that the specimens or facsimiles show the mark as actually used in connection with the goods; and that the facts set forth in the statement are true.

This part of the written application is called the declaration.

7.5 **Description of mark.** A description of the mark, which must be acceptable to the Examiner of Trade-Marks, may be included in the statement, and must be included if required by the Examiner.

7.6 **Identification of prior registrations.** Prior registrations of the same or similar marks owned by the applicant should be identified in the written application.

7.7 **Power of attorney, domestic representative.** The power of attorney or authorization of agent (Rule 4.7) and the appointment of a domestic representative (Rule 6.4) may be included as a paragraph or paragraphs in the written application.

7.8 **Use by predecessor or by related companies.** If the first use, the date of which is required by paragraph (*g*) or (*h*) of Rule 7.3, was by a predecessor in title, or by a related company (sections 5 and 45 of the act), and such use inures to the benefit of the applicant, the date of such first use may be asserted with a statement that such first use was by the predecessor in title or by the related company as the case may be. The Office may require further details and additional proof showing that such use inures to the benefit of the applicant.

Where the mark sought to be registered is legitimately used by one or more related companies at the time of the filing of the application, the declaration (Rule 7.4) must recite exceptions to the averment of the exclusive right to use the mark, stating the nature of such related companies and, if practicable, the names and addresses.

7.9 **Omission of allegation of use by foreign applicants.** The allegation that the mark is in use in commerce which may lawfully be regulated by Congress, required by Rule 7.4, and the statements of the dates of the applicant's first use, required by Rule 7.3(*g*) and (*h*), may be omitted in the case of an application, filed pursuant to section 44(*e*) of the act, for registration of a mark duly registered in the country of origin of a foreign applicant, provided the application when filed is accompanied by a certified copy of the registration in the country of origin and said registration is then in full force and effect. A sworn translation of the registration, if not in the English language, may be required after the application is filed.

Such allegation and statement may also be omitted in the case of an application claiming the benefit of a prior foreign application in accordance with section 44(*d*) of the act, provided that the application states the date and country of the first foreign application and a certified copy of the foreign application and a sworn translation of the same, if not in English language, are filed before the registration is granted, but the registration will not be granted until the mark has been registered in the country of origin of the applicant.

In such cases the description of goods or services shall not exceed the scope of that covered by the foreign registration or application.

8. THE WRITTEN APPLICATION (continued)

8.1 **Proof of distinctiveness under section 2** *(f)*. When registration is sought under section 2 (*f*) of the act and the claim of distinctiveness is based on substantially exclusive and continuous use of the mark by the applicant for a period of 5 years preceding the filing of the application in commerce which may lawfully be regulated by Congress, the written application shall include in the declaration a statement to that effect; but proof of such exclusive and continuous use and further evidence showing that the mark has become distinctive may be required.

If the allegation of distinctiveness is not based on substantially exclusive use over a 5-year period, as specified in the preceding paragraph, but is based on other facts and circumstances, proof of distinctiveness must be submitted separately and should accompany the application.

8.2 **Concurrent use.** In the case of an application claiming concurrent use, the applicant shall also specify in the statement any concurrent use by others, designating their names, addresses, and registrations or applications, if any, the goods in connection with which and the areas in which such concurrent use exists, the mode of such use, the periods of such use, and the goods, area, or mode of use for which the applicant desires registration; and the claim of exclusive use made in the declaration shall be made with the stated exceptions.

8.3 **Service mark.** In the case of an application for the registration of a service mark, the written application shall specify and contain all the elements required by the preceding rules for trade-marks, but shall be modified to relate to services instead of to goods wherever necessary.

8.4 **Collective mark.** In the case of an application for registration of a collective mark, the written application shall specify and contain all applicable elements required by the preceding rules for trade-marks, but shall, in addition, specify the class of persons entitled to use the mark, indicating their relationship to the owner

or address or other extraneous matter should not appear upon the face of a drawing, within or without the marginal line.

(*f*) *Linings for color.* Where color is a material feature of a mark as used, the color or colors employed should, if feasible, be illustrated in the drawing by means of the conventional linings as shown in the following color chart for draftsmen:

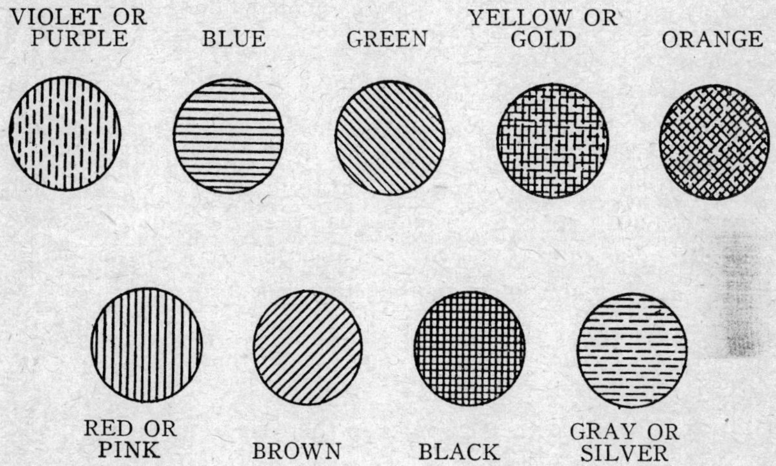

9.3 **Transmission of drawings.** Drawings transmitted to the Patent Office should be sent flat, protected by a sheet of heavy binder's board, or should be rolled for transmission in a suitable mailing tube to prevent mutilation. They should never be folded.

9.4 **Informal drawings.** A drawing not executed in conformity with the foregoing rules may be accepted for purpose of examination, but the drawing must be corrected or a new one furnished, as required, before the mark can be published or the application allowed. The necessary corrections will be made by the Patent Office upon applicant's request and at his expense. Substitute drawings will not be accepted unless they have been required by the Examiner or correction of the original drawing would require that the mark be substantially entirely redrawn.

9.5 **Patent Office may make drawings.** The Patent Office.

at the request of applicants and at their expense, will make drawings if facilities permit.

10. SPECIMENS

10.1 **Specimens.** The five specimens of a trade-mark shall be specimens of the trade-mark as actually used on or in connection with the goods in commerce, and shall be duplicates of the actually used labels, tags, or containers, or the displays associated therewith or portions thereof, when made of suitable material and capable of being arranged flat and of a size not larger than the size of the drawing.

10.2 **Facsimiles.** When, from the mode of applying or affixing the trade-mark to the goods, or from the manner of using the mark on the goods, or from the nature of the mark, specimens as above stated cannot be furnished, five copies of a suitable photograph or other acceptable reproduction, not larger than the size specified for the drawing and clearly and legibly showing the mark and all matter used in connection therewith, shall be furnished.

10.3 **Specimens or facsimiles in the case of a service mark.** In the case of a service mark a specimen or facsimile as specified in Rules 10.1 and 10.2, of the mark as used in the sale or advertising of the services shall be furnished unless impossible from the nature of the mark or the manner in which it is used, in which event, some other representation acceptable to the Commissioner must be submitted.

12. EXAMINATION OF APPLICATION AND ACTION BY APPLICANTS

12.1 **Action by Examiner.** Applications for registration will be examined or caused to be examined by the Examiner of Trade-Marks, and, if the applicant is found not entitled to registration for any reason, he will be so notified and advised of the reasons therefor and of any formal requirements or objections and will be given such information and references as may be helpful in the further prosecution of the application.

12.2 **Period for response.** The applicant has 6 months from the date of mailing of any action by the Patent Office to respond thereto. Such response may be made with or without amendment and must include such proper action by the applicant as the nature of the action and the condition of the case may require.

12.3 **Re-examinations.** After response by the applicant, the application will be re-examined or reconsidered, and if the registration is again refused or formal requirements insisted upon, but not stated to be final, the applicant may respond again.

12.4 **Final action.** On the first or any subsequent re-examination or reconsideration the refusal of the registration or the insistence upon a requirement may be stated to be final, whereupon applicant's response is limited to an appeal or to a compliance with any requirement made.

12.5 **Abandonment.** If an applicant fails to respond, or to respond completely, within 6 months after the date an action is mailed, the application shall be deemed to have been abandoned.

12.6 **Revival of abandoned applications.** An application abandoned for failure to respond may be revived as a pending application if it is shown to the satisfaction of the Commissioner that the delay was unavoidable. A petition to revive an abandoned application must be accompanied by a verified showing of the causes of the delay, and by the proposed response, unless the same has been previously filed.

12.7 **Suspension of action by Patent Office.** Action by the Patent Office may be suspended upon request of the applicant for good and sufficient cause and for a reasonable time specified. Only one suspension will be granted by the Examiner, and any further suspension must be approved by the Commissioner.

12.8 **Express abandonment.** An application may be expressly abandoned by filing in the Patent Office a written declaration of abandonment signed by the applicant himself or, if assigned, by the assignee.

13. AMENDMENT OF APPLICATION

13.1 **Amendments to statement.** The statement may be amended to correct informalities, or to avoid objections made by the Patent Office, or for other reasons arising in the course of examination. No amendments to the dates of use will be permitted unless such changes are supported by affidavit by the applicant and by such showing as may be required by the Examiner.

Additions to the description of goods or services will not be permitted unless the mark was in actual use on all of the goods or services proposed to be added by the amendment at the time the application was filed and unless the amendment is accompanied by additional specimens (or facsimiles) and by a supplemental affidavit by the applicant in support thereof, alleging said facts.

Amendment of the declaration will not be permitted. If that filed with the application be faulty or defective, a substitute declaration must be filed.

13.2 **Amendments to description or drawing.** Amendments to the description or drawing of the mark may be permitted only if warranted by the specimens (or facsimiles) as originally filed, but may not be made if the nature of the mark is changed thereby.

13.3 **Amendment to recite concurrent use.** An application may be amended in the Examiner's discretion so as to be treated as an application for a concurrent registration, provided the application as amended satisfies the requirements of Rule 8.2.

13.4 **Form of amendment.** In every amendment the exact word or words to be stricken out or inserted in the statement must be specified and the precise point indicated where the deletion or insertion is to be made. Erasures, additions, insertions, or mutilations of the papers and records must not be made by the applicant or attorney.

When an amendatory clause is amended, it must be wholly rewritten so that no interlineation or erasure will appear in the clause, as finally amended, when the application is passed to registration. If the number or nature of the amendments shall render it otherwise difficult to consider the case or to arrange the papers for printing or copying, or when otherwise desired to clarify the record, the Examiner may require the entire statement to be rewritten.

13.5 Amendment to change application to different register. An application for registration on the Principal Register may be changed to an application for registration on the Supplemental Register and vice versa by amending the application to comply with the rules relating to the requirements for registration on the appropriate register, as the case may be. Unless the written application as originally filed was sufficient for registration on the register to which converted, the date of filing such amendment will be considered the filing date of the application so converted. Only one such conversion will be permitted after an action by the Examiner.

14. FEDERAL LABEL APPROVAL

14.1 Federal label approval required in certain cases. Whenever an application is filed for the registration of a trademark which is either a part of or associated with a label for a product which, under the provisions of an act of Congress, cannot be lawfully sold in the commerce specified in the written application without prior approval of the label by a designated Government agency, a copy of such label and its certification must be made of record in the application before allowance in cases specified by this rule.

Types of labels for which prior approval must be secured and copies of which must be filed as indicated above are set forth in the following schedule:

Labels for meat products (Class 46) which are subject to Federal inspection, must be approved by the Meat Inspection Division, Bureau of Animal Industry, Department of Agriculture.

Labels for wines (Class 47) and for distilled alcoholic liquors (Class 49) must be approved by the Federal Alcohol Administration.

15. PUBLICATION AND ALLOWANCE

15.1 Publication in Official Gazette. If, on examination or re-examination of an application for registration on the Principal Register, it appears that the applicant is entitled to have his mark registered, the mark will be published in the Official Gazette for opposition.

15.2 **Allowance of application.** If no notice of opposition is filed within the time permitted, Rules 20.1 and 20.2, and no interference is declared, the applicant will be duly notified of the allowance of his application, and a certificate of registration may be issued as provided in Rule 29.1.

Certificates are normally issued on the fourth Tuesday after the Thursday following the date of the notice of allowance.

15.3 **Marks on Supplemental Register published only upon registration.** In the case of an application for registration on the Supplemental Register the mark will not be published for opposition but the applicant will be notified of the allowance of his application if it appears, after examination or re-examination, that he is entitled to have the mark registered, and a certificate of registration may be issued as provided in Rule 29.1. The mark will be published in the Official Gazette when registered.

15.4 **Jurisdiction over published or allowed applications.** After publication or allowance the Examiner may exercise jurisdiction over an application by special authority from the Commissioner.

Amendments may be made after the allowance of an application if the certificate has not been printed, on the recommendation of the Examiner approved by the Commissioner, without withdrawing the allowance.

16. CLASSIFICATION

16.1 **Classification of goods and services.** There is established, for convenience of administration, the following classification of goods and services. Such classification shall not limit or extend the applicant's rights.

Class	Title
1	Raw or partly prepared materials
2	Receptacles
3	Baggage, animal equipments, portfolios, and pocketbooks

Class	Title
4	Abrasive, detergent, and polishing materials
5	Adhesives
6	Chemicals, medicines, and pharmaceutical preparations
7	Cordage
8	Smokers' articles, not including tobacco products
9	Explosives, firearms, equipments, and projectiles
10	Fertilizers
11	Inks and inking materials
12	Construction materials
13	Hardware and plumbing and steam-fitting supplies
14	Metals and metal castings and forgings
15	Oils and greases
16	Paints and painters' materials
17	Tobacco products
19	Vehicles
20	Linoleum and oiled cloth
21	Electrical apparatus, machines, and supplies
22	Games, toys, and sporting goods
23	Cutlery, machinery, and tools, and parts thereof
24	Laundry appliances and machines
25	Locks and safes
26	Measuring and scientific appliances
27	Horological instruments
28	Jewelry and precious-metal ware
29	Brooms, brushes, and dusters
30	Crockery, earthenware, and porcelain
31	Filters and refrigerators
32	Furniture and upholstery
33	Glassware
34	Heating, lighting, and ventilating apparatus
35	Belting, hose, machinery packing, and non-metallic tires
36	Musical instruments and supplies
37	Paper and stationery
38	Prints and publications
39	Clothing

Class	Title
40	Fancy goods, furnishings, and notions
41	Canes, parasols, and umbrellas
42	Knitted, netted and textile fabrics, and substitutes therefor
43	Thread and yarn
44	Dental, medical, and surgical appliances
45	Soft drinks and carbonated waters
46	Foods and ingredients of foods
47	Wines
48	Malt beverages and liquors
49	Distilled alcoholic liquors
50	Goods not otherwise classified
55	Services (temporary)

16.2 **Plurality of goods or services comprised in single class may be covered by single application.** A mark may be registered on a single application for a plurality of goods, or for a plurality of services, comprised in a single class, provided the particular description of each of the goods or services be stated and the mark has actually been used on or in connection with all of the goods, or in connection with all of the services specified.

16.3 **Original application must be limited to goods or services comprised in a single class.** When a single application is filed to register a mark for both goods and services or for goods or services in a plurality of different classes, registration will be refused, and the applicant will be required to restrict the application to goods or services comprised in a single class.

16.4 **Applications may be combined.** When several applications have been filed by the same applicant for registration on the same register of the identical mark on goods in different classes, or services in different classes, and each of the applications has been allowed, a single certificate based on such several applications may be issued. For the purpose of issuing such single certificate, a copy of the written applications, combined as a single application eliminating unnecessary repetition, must be filed in one of such applications.

The issuance of any original certificate may be suspended upon request of the applicant, for a period not exceeding 6 months to permit such consolidation.

18. CONTESTED OR INTER PARTES PROCEEDINGS

18.1 **Contested or inter partes proceedings.** Contested or inter partes cases or proceedings comprise (*a*) interferences between pending applications or between registrations and pending applications, which are instituted by the Examiner of Trade-Marks, (*b*) opposition proceedings, which are instituted on the filing of a notice of opposition against a mark published for opposition, (*c*) cancellation proceedings, which are instituted on the filing of a petition to cancel a registration, and (*d*) concurrent use proceedings which are instituted upon giving notice to the users named in an application to register as concurrent user.

19. INTERFERENCES

19.1 **Interferences.** Whenever application is made for registration on the Principal Register of a mark which so resembles a mark previously registered by another, or for the registration of which another has previously made application, as to be likely, when applied to the goods or when used in connection with the services of the applicant, to cause confusion or mistake or to deceive purchasers, an interference may be declared to exist. An interference will not be declared between two applications or an application and a registration unless the junior party alleges in his application a date of use prior to the filing date of the senior party. No interference shall be declared between an application and the registration of a mark the right to the use of which has become incontestable, nor with respect to registrations or applications to register on the Supplemental Register.

19.2 **Preliminary to interference.** Before the declaration of interference, all preliminary questions must have been settled by the Examiner of Trade-Marks and the interfering marks which are to form the subject matter of the controversy must have been decided to be registrable, and at least one of them must have been published in the Official Gazette.

The Examiner of Trade-Marks may require an applicant to put his application in condition for publication or allowance, within a time specified, not less than 30 days, in order that an interference may be declared. If any such applicant fails to put his application in condition for publication or allowance within the time specified, the declaration of interference will not necessarily be delayed, but after final judgment the application of such applicant will be held for revision or restriction, subject to interference with other applications or registrations.

Whenever it shall be found that two or more parties whose interests are in conflict are represented by the same attorney, the Examiner of Trade-Marks shall notify each of said parties and also the attorney of this fact.

19.3 **Declaration of interference.** An interference is declared and instituted by the mailing of notices of interference to each of the parties by the Examiner of Interferences, which notices shall have been prepared by the Examiner of Trade-Marks. The notices shall be sent to all the parties, in care of their attorneys, if they have an attorney of record, and if one of the parties is a registrant, a notice shall also be sent to him or his assignee of record. The notice to each party shall give the name and address of the adverse party and of his attorney, if any, together with the serial number and date of filing and publication, if published, of each of the applications or registrations involved.

19.4 **Motions to dissolve interference.** Motions to dissolve an interference upon the ground that no interference in fact exists, or that there has been such irregularity in declaring the same as will preclude a proper determination of the right of registration, or that an applicant's mark is not registrable, and all other motions of a similar character, shall contain a full statement of the grounds relied upon and shall be made not later than 40 days after the notices of interference have been mailed. Such motions, if in proper form, will be transmitted to the Examiner of Trade-Marks for determination, and the parties will be so notified. If the motion is not in proper form or if it is not brought within the time specified and no satisfactory reason is given for the delay, it will not be considered, and the parties will be so notified. Transmitting such a motion for determination will act as a stay of proceedings pending the determination of the motion.

19.5 **Decision on motion to dissolve.** The decision of the Examiner of Trade-Marks upon a motion for dissolution will be binding upon the Examiner of Interferences unless reversed or modified on appeal. Appeal may be taken to the Commissioner from a decision granting a motion to dissolve. No appeal may be had from a decision denying a motion to dissolve, but the question may be reviewed by the Commissioner on appeal from the final decision of the Examiner of Interferences.

19.6 **Burden of proof.** The party whose application or registration involved in the interference has the latest filing date is the junior party and will be regarded as having the burden of proof.

Motions to shift the burden of proof shall be made within 40 days from the mailing of the notices of interference and will be determined by the Examiner of Interferences. No appeal from the decision on such motion will be entertained, but the matter may be reviewed by the Commissioner on appeal from the final decision of the Examiner of Interferences.

19.7 **Motion to add.** An applicant or registrant involved in an interference may, not more than 40 days after the notices of interference have been mailed, bring a motion to add to the interference any other application or registration which he may own. The procedure affecting such motion will be the same as that hereinabove set forth on motions to dissolve.

19.8 **Adding party to interference.** If, during the pendency of an interference, another case appears involving substantially the same registrable subject matter, the Examiner of Trade-Marks may request the suspension of the interference for the purpose of adding said case. Such suspension will be granted as a matter of course by the Examiner of Interferences if no testimony has been taken. If, however, any testimony has been taken, a notice for the proposed new party disclosing the issue in interference and the names and addresses of the interferants and of their attorneys, and notices for the interferants disclosing the name and address of the said party and his attorney, shall be prepared by the Examiner of Trade-Marks and forwarded to the Examiner of Interferences, who shall make such inquiries as are deemed necessary to determine the question of admissibility of the new party. If the Examiner of Interferences be of the opinion that the interference should be suspended and a new party added, he shall prescribe the terms for such suspension.

20. OPPOSITION

20.1 **Time for filing notice of opposition.** Any person who believes that he would be damaged by the registration of a mark upon the Principal Register may, upon payment of the required fee, oppose the same by filing a verified notice of opposition in the Patent Office within 30 days after the publication (Rule 15.1) of the mark sought to be registered.

20.2 **Extension of time.** A request to extend the time for filing a notice of opposition must be received before the expiration of 40 days from the date of publication. Any such request must show good cause for the extension and specify the period of extension desired.

20.3 **Notice filed by attorney.** An unverified notice of opposition may be filed by a duly authorized attorney, but such opposition will be null and void unless verified by the opposer within 30 days after such filing, or within such further time after such filing as may be fixed by the Commissioner upon request made before the expiration of said 30 days.

20.4 **Contents of notice of opposition.** The notice of opposition must allege facts tending to show why the opposer would be damaged by the registration of the opposed mark and state the specific grounds for opposition. A duplicate copy of the notice of opposition and two specimens (or facsimiles) of the mark as actually used by the opposer, if there be such, shall be filed.

20.5 **Institution of opposition.** When a notice of opposition is filed, the Examiner of Trade-Marks shall inform the party filing the same of the receipt thereof and, if regularly filed, shall transmit it to the Examiner of Interferences.

The Examiner of Interferences shall prepare a notice disclosing the name and address of the opposer, and of his attorney, if he has such, and designate a time, not less than 30 days from the date of such notice, within which answer must be filed. Copies of this notice shall be forwarded to the parties in care of their attorneys, if they have attorneys of record. The duplicate copy of the notice of opposition and one of the specimens (or facsimiles), if there be such, shall be forwarded with the notice to the party against whom the opposition is filed.

21. CANCELLATION

21.1 **Time for filing petition for cancellation.** Any person who believes that he is or will be damaged by a registration may, upon payment of the required fee, apply to the Commissioner to cancel said registration. Such petition may be made at any time in the case of registrations on the Supplemental Register or under the act of 1920, or registrations under the act of 1881 or the act of 1905 which have not been republished under section 12(*c*) of the act (Rule 30.1), and in cases involving the grounds specified in section 14(*c*) and (*d*) of the act. In all other cases such petition must be made within 5 years from the date of registration of the mark under the act of 1946 or from the date of republication under section 12(*c*) of the act.

21.2 **Petition for cancellation.** The petition to cancel must allege facts tending to show why the petitioner believes he is or will be damaged by the registration, state the specific grounds for cancellation, and indicate the respondent party to whom notice shall be sent. The petition must be verified by the petitioner. A duplicate copy of the petition, an abstract of title of the mark sought to be cancelled or an order for a title report for Office use, and two specimens (or facsimiles) of the mark actually used by the petitioner, if there be such, shall be filed with the petition.

A petition to cancel filed by the Federal Trade Commission under section 14(*c*) or section 14(*d*) of the act need not show or allege that the petitioner is or will be damaged, and a fee is not required for filing such petition.

21.3 **Notice of filing of petition.** When a petition for cancellation is filed, it shall be transmitted to the Examiner of Interferences, who shall make examination thereof to determine if it is formally correct. If he be of the opinion that the petition is defective as to form, he shall so advise the party filing the same and set a time for correcting the informality.

When the petition is correct as to form, the Examiner of Interferences shall prepare a notice disclosing the name and address of the petitioner and of his attorney, if he has such, and designate a time, not less than 30 days from the date of the notice, within which an answer must be filed. Copies of this notice shall be forwarded to the registrant as well as to his attorney if there be such, and to the petitioner. The duplicate copy of the petition for cancellation and one of the specimens (or facsimiles), if there be such, shall be forwarded with the notice to the registrant whose registration is sought to be cancelled.

22. APPLICATION FOR REGISTRATION AS CONCURRENT USER

22.1 **Application to register as concurrent user.** An application for registration as a lawful concurrent user will be examined in the same manner as other applications for registration. When it is determined that the mark is ready for publication or allowance, except for questions relating to concurrent registration, the applicant may be required to furnish as many copies of his written application, specimens and drawing, as may be necessary. The Examiner of Trade-Marks shall prepare notices for the applicant and for each applicant, registrant, or user specified in the application for registration as a concurrent user. Such notices for the specified parties shall give the name and address of the applicant and of his attorney, if any, together with the serial number and filing date of the application.

The notices shall be sent by the Examiner of Interferences to each of the parties, in care of their attorneys, if they have attorneys of record, and if one of the parties is a registrant, a notice shall also be sent to him or his assignee of record. A copy of the application shall be forwarded with the notices to the parties specified in the application. An answer to the notice is not required in the case of an applicant or registrant whose application or registration is specified in the application to register as concurrent user but a statement may be filed if desired; an answer is required in the case of other parties specified in the application to register as concurrent user and a time, not less than 30 days from the date of the notice, within which such answer must be filed will be designated in the notice.

Subsequent proceedings shall follow the practice in interferences, the applicant for concurrent registration, or the one having the latest filing date if there be more than one such applicant, having the burden of proof in the first instance.

23. PROCEDURE IN CONTESTED OR INTER PARTES PROCEEDINGS

23.1 **Federal Rules of Civil Procedure.** Except as otherwise provided, procedure and practice in contested or inter partes proceedings shall be governed by the Rules of Civil Procedure for the District Courts of the United States wherever considered applicable and appropriate.

Any junior party in an interference, the opposer in an opposition proceeding, the petitioner in a cancellation proceeding, and the applicant to register as a concurrent user, shall be deemed to be in the position of plaintiff, and the other parties to such proceedings in the position of defendants with respect thereto. The notice of opposition and the petition to cancel, and the answers thereto, correspond to complaint and answer; there are no equivalent pleadings in interferences and in concurrent use proceedings when no answer is required, the issues in such cases being determined by the respective applications or registrations involved. The taking of testimony and the final hearing correspond to trial, and the assignment of times for taking testimony and for final hearing to setting a case for trial.

23.2 **Undelivered Office notices.** When the notices sent by the Patent Office to any registrant are returned to the Office undelivered, or when one of the parties resides abroad and his representative in the United States is unknown, additional notice may be given by publication in the Official Gazette for such period of time as the Commissioner may direct.

23.3 **Service of papers.** Every paper filed in the Patent Office in contested cases, including appeals, must be served upon the other parties as provided by Patent Rule 154(*b*) except the notices of interference (Rule 19.3), the notice of opposition (Rule 20.5), the petition for cancellation (Rule 21.3), the notices of a concurrent use proceeding (Rule 22.1), and the copies of the testimony (Rule 23.6), which are mailed by the Patent Office. Proof of such service must be made before the paper will be considered by the Office. A statement signed by the attorney, attached to or appearing on the original paper, when filed clearly stating the time and manner in which service was made will be accepted as prima facie proof of service.

23.4 **Assignment of times for taking testimony and of date of final hearing.** Times will be assigned for the taking of testimony in behalf of each of the parties, and no testimony shall be taken except during the times assigned. If there be more than two parties to an interference, the times for taking testimony will be so arranged that each shall have an opportunity to prove his case against prior parties, to rebut their evidence, and to meet the evidence of junior parties.

The times will ordinarily be assigned in the notices sent by the Patent Office in interferences and in concurrent use proceedings, and in a notice sent after the answers have been filed in cases of opposition and cancellation. The time for final hearing will be set in the same notices. If either party desires an extension of the time assigned to him for taking testimony he may apply therefor as provided in Patent Rule 154(*d*).

23.5 **Testimony in contested or inter partes cases.** Testimony in contested or inter partes proceedings shall be taken and filed in accordance with the provisions of Patent Rules 154 to 161, inclusive, and these rules shall apply to trade-mark cases.

23.6 **Copies of testimony.** In addition to the original transcripts of the testimony, three or more copies of the record of each party must be filed, two for the use of the Patent Office and one for each of the opposing parties. These records may be submitted either in printed or typewritten form. They must include the testimony presented by the party filing the same, and shall be certified to as being true copies. Each record must contain an index of the names of the witnesses, giving the pages where their examination and cross-examination begin, and an index of the pages where exhibits are offered in evidence and of the pages where copies of papers and documents introduced as exhibits are shown when such exhibits are copied in the record; the names of the witnesses must appear at the top of the pages over their testimony, and the pages must be consecutively numbered.

The copies of the record for the party in the position of plaintiff must be filed not less than 70 days before the day for final hearing and in the case of parties in the position of defendants not less than 50 days.

When the copies of the record are submitted in printed form, they shall be printed in 11-point type and adequately leaded; the paper must be opaque and unglazed; the size of the page shall be 7⅝ by 10¼ inches; and the size of the printed matter shall be 4⅙ by 7⅙ inches. Twenty-five additional copies for the United States Court of Customs and Patent Appeals, should appeal be taken, may also be filed; if no such appeal be taken, the 25 copies will be returned to the party filing them.

When the copies of the record are submitted in typewritten form, they must be clearly legible copies on opaque, unglazed, durable paper 8½ by 11 inches in size. The typing shall be on one side of the paper, in not smaller than pica type; and double-spaced with a margin of 1½ inches on the left-hand side of the page. The sheets shall be bound at their left edges in a volume or volumes of convenient size provided with covers. Multigraphed or otherwise reproduced copies conforming to the same standards specified for typewritten copies will be accepted as typewritten.

The testimony of any party failing to supply copies of his record as specified may be refused consideration.

23.7 **Allegations in application not evidence on behalf of**

applicant. The allegation of dates of use in the application for registration of the applicant or registrant cannot be used as evidence in behalf of the party making the same.

23.8 **Motions.** Motions shall be made in writing and shall contain a full statement of the grounds therefor. Oral hearings will not be held on motions except on order of the Examiner having jurisdiction. Briefs in support of or in opposition to motions shall be filed on dates set by the Examiner of Interferences and, if not so filed, consideraiton thereof may be refused.

Petitions for reconsideration or modification of the decision must be led within 20 days after the decision or before the time for appeal expires.

Appeal must be taken, in the case of such decisions as are appealable, within the time limit set in the decision, or within 20 days if no time limit is set.

24. PROCEDURE IN CONTESTED OR INTER PARTES PROCEEDINGS (continued)

24.1 **Briefs at final hearing.** Briefs at final hearing shall be submitted in printed form, except that where not in excess of 30 typewritten pages, and in any other case where satisfactory reason therefor is shown, they may be submitted in typewritten form. If submitted in printed form, they shall be the same in size and the same as to page and print as is specified for printed copies of testimony. Typewritten briefs shall conform to the requirements for typewritten copies of testimony, except that legal size paper may be used and the binding and covers specified are not required. The brief of a party in the position of plaintiff shall be filed not less than 40 days, and that of a party in the position of a defendant not less than 20 days, prior to the hearing. Reply briefs, if filed, shall be due not less than 10 days before the hearing.

24.2 **Final hearing.** Final hearings will be held by the Examiner of Interferences at the time stated in the notice. If either party in a contested case appears at the proper time, he will be heard. If the Examiner of Interferences is prevented from hearing the case at the time specified for the hearing, a new assignment will be made, or the case will be continued from day to day until heard. Unless otherwise permitted, oral arguments will be limited to one-half hour for each party. Petitions for rehearings or modifications of the decision must be filed before the time for appeal expires.

Hearings may be advanced or adjourned, as far as is convenient and proper, to meet the wishes of the parties and their attorneys.

24.3 **New matter suggested by Examiner of Trade-Marks.** If, during the pendency of a contested or inter partes case, facts appear which in the opinion of the Examiner of Trade-Marks render the mark of any applicant involved unregistrable, the attention of the Examiner of Interferences shall be called thereto. The Examiner of Interferences may suspend the proceeding and refer the case to the Examiner of Trade-Marks for his determination of the question of registrability, and the proceeding shall be dissolved or continued in accordance with such determination. The consideration of such facts by the Examiner of Trade-Marks shall be inter partes.

24.4 **Failure to take testimony.** Upon the filing of an affidavit by any party in the position of a defendant, that the time for taking testimony on behalf of any party in the position of plaintiff has expired and that no testimony has been taken by him and no other evidence offered, an order may be entered that such party show cause within a time set therein, not less than 10 days, why judgment should not be rendered against him, and in the absence of a showing of good and sufficient cause judgment may be rendered as by default.

24.5 **Amendment of application or registration during proceedings.** An application involved in a contested proceeding may not be amended, nor may a registration be amended or disclaimed in part, except upon the written consent of the other party or parties and the approval of the Examiner of Interferences, or except upon motion duly brought and considered.

24.6 **Surrender or cancellation of registration.** If a registrant involved in a contested proceeding applies to surrender or cancel his registration, under section 7(*d*) of the act, and such action is permitted, the proceeding may be terminated or continued on such terms as may be appropriate.

24.7 **Abandonment of application, abandonment or disclaimer in whole of mark, concession of priority.** If an applicant involved in a contested proceeding files a written abandonment of the application, or abandonment of the mark, or if a registrant applies to disclaim the mark in whole under section 7(*d*) of the act and such disclaimer is permitted, or if a party to an interference files a written concession of priority, judgment may be entered against said party; the proceeding will not be dismissed or dissolved at the request of said party unless with the consent of the other parties.

26. APPEALS

26.1 **Ex parte appeals to the Commissioner from the Examiner of Trade-Marks.** Every applicant for the registration of a mark may, upon final refusal by the Examiner of Trade-Marks, appeal to the Commissioner in person upon payment of the prescribed fee. A second refusal on the same grounds may be considered as final by the applicant for purpose of appeal. Appeal may also be taken to the Commissioner from the refusal by the Examiner of Trade-Marks to accept an affidavit filed under section 8 of the act or to renew a registration.

26.2 **Time and manner of ex parte appeals.** Such appeal must be taken within 6 months from the date of the action appealed from and must be accompanied by a statement of the reasons therefor. The Examiner shall, within 30 days therefrom, furnish the Commissioner with a written statement of the grounds of his decision, supplying a copy to the applicant. The date for hearing will be fixed by the Commissioner in each case and the brief of the appellant shall be due on or before the day of the hearing. Cases which have been heard and decided by the Commissioner will not be reopened except by his order.

26.3 **Appeal to the Commissioner from decision of Examiner of Interferences.** Any party of an interference, opposition, cancellation, or a concurrent use proceeding may appeal, stating the reasons therefor, from the final decision of the Examiner of Interferences to the Commissioner in person within the time limit, not less than 30 days, prescribed in the decision, or, if no time limit is prescribed, within 30 days, upon payment of the prescribed fee. The date for hearing will be fixed by the Commissioner in each case. Appellants shall file briefs not less than 40 days before the hearing, and appellees shall file briefs not less than 20 days before the hearing; reply briefs, if filed, shall be due not less than 10 days before the hearing. Briefs and hearings on appeal shall be subject to Rules 24.1 and 24.2 insofar as applicable.

26.4 **Appeal to court.** Any applicant for registration, any registrant who has filed an affidavit under section 8 of the act, or any party to an inter partes proceeding, who is dissatisfied with the decision of the Commissioner, may appeal to the United States Court of Customs and Patent Appeals or may proceed under section 4915, Revised Statutes (U. S. Code, title 35, sec. 63), as in the case of applicants for patents, under the same conditions, rules and procedure as are applicable in the case of patent appeals or proceedings.

(See Patent Rules 148 to 150 and rules of the United States Court of Customs and Patent Appeals.)

27. PETITION TO THE COMMISSIONER

27.1 **Petition to the Commissioner.** Petition may be filed with the Commissioner from any repeated action or requirement of the Examiner of Trade-Marks which is not subject to appeal and in other appropriate circumstances. Such petition, and any other petition which may be filed, must contain a statement of the facts involved and the point or points to be reviewed. Briefs or memoranda, if any, in support thereof should accompany or be embodied in the petition. The Examiner may be directed by the Commissioner to furnish a written statement setting forth the reasons for his decision upon the matters averred in the petition, supplying a copy thereof to the petitioner. Oral hearing will be granted only in the discretion of the Commissioner. No fee is required for such a petition. The mere filing of a petition will not stay the period of 6 months for replying to an Examiner's action as provided in Rule 12.2 nor act as a stay of other proceedings.

29. CERTIFICATE

29.1 **Certificate.** When the requirements of the law and of the rules have been complied with, and the Patent Office has adjudged a mark registrable, a certificate will be issued to the effect that the applicant has complied with the law and that he is entitled to registration of his mark on the Principal Register or on the Supplemental Register as the case may be. The certificate will state the date on which the application for registration was filed in the Patent Office, the act under which the mark is registered, the date of issue and the number of the certificate. Attached to the certificate and forming a part thereof will be a copy of the drawing of the mark and a printed copy of the written statement and declaration. A notice of the affidavit requirement of section 8(*a*) of the act (Rule 32.1) will be attached to the certificate.

Certificates are numbered in consecutive order, those issued under the acts of 1905 and 1920 continuing the series of numberings heretofore employed; those issued under the act of 1946 begin with number 500,001.

30. REPUBLICATION OF MARKS REGISTERED UNDER 1905 ACT

30.1 **Republication requirements.** A registrant of a mark registered under the provisions of the acts of 1881 or 1905 may, at any time prior to the expiration of the period for which the registration was issued or renewed, upon the payment of the prescribed fee, file an affidavit setting forth those goods stated in the registration on which said mark is in use in commerce which may lawfully be regulated by Congress, specifying the nature of such commerce, and stating that the registrant claims the benefits of the Trade-Mark Act of 1946. An abstract of title or an order for a title report for Patent Office use shall accompany the affidavit.

Such marks may, in lieu of republication under this rule, be reregistered in accordance with Rule 31.1 at the option of the registrant.

30.2 **Republication in Official Gazette.** A notice of the claim of benefits under the act of 1946 and a reproduction of the mark will then be published in the Official Gazette as soon as practicable. The republished mark will retain its original registration number.

30.3 **Notice of republication.** A notice of such republication of the mark and of the requirement for the affidavit specified in section 8(*b*) of the act (Rule 32.1) will be sent to the registrant.

30.4 **Not subject to opposition; subject to cancellation.** The republished mark is not subject to opposition on such publication in the Official Gazette but is subject to petitions to cancel as specified in Rule 21.1 and to cancellation for failure to file the affidavit specified in Rule 32.1.

31. REREGISTRATION OF MARKS REGISTERED UNDER PRIOR ACTS

31.1 **Reregistration of marks registered under acts of 1881, 1905 and 1920.** Trade-marks registered under the act of 1881, the act of 1905 or the act of 1920 may be reregistered under the act of 1946, either on the Principal Register, if eligible, or on the Supplemental Register, but a new complete application for registration must be filed complying with the rules relating thereto, and such application will be subject to examination and other proceedings in the same manner as other applications filed under the act of 1946.

See Rule 6.6 for use of old drawing.

32. CANCELLATION FOR FAILURE TO FILE AFFIDAVIT DURING SIXTH YEAR

32.1 **Cancellation for failure to file affidavit during sixth year.** Any registration under the provisions of the act of 1946 and any registration republished under the provisions of section 12(*c*) of the act (Rule 30.1) shall be cancelled at the end of 6 years following the date of registration or the date of such republication, unless within 1 year next preceding the expiration of such

6 years the registrant shall file in the Patent Office an affidavit showing that said mark is still in use or showing that its nonuse is due to special circumstances which excuse such nonuse and is not due to any intention to abandon the mark.

32.2 **Requirements for affidavit.** The affidavit required by Rule 32.1 must:

(*a*) Be executed by the registrant after expiration of the 5-year period;

(*b*) Identify the certificate of registration by the certificate number and date of registration;

(*c*) Recite sufficient facts to show that the mark described in the registration is still in use, specifying the nature of such use, or recite sufficient facts to show that its nonuse is due to special circumstances which excuse such nonuse and is not due to any intention to abandon the mark; and

(*d*) Be accompanied by an abstract of title or an order for a title report for Office use.

32.3 **Acknowledgment of receipt of affidavit.** The registrant will be notified by the Examiner of Trade-Marks of the receipt of the affidavit and, if satisfactory, of its acceptance.

32.4 **Reconsideration of affidavit.** If the affidavit is insufficient, the registrant will be notified of the reasons by the Examiner. Reconsideration of such refusal may be requested within 6 months from the date of the mailing of the notice. The request for reconsideration must state the reasons therefor; a supplemental or substitute affidavit required by section 12(*c*) of the act cannot be considered unless it is received before the expiration of 6 years from the date of the registration, or from the date of republication.

See Rules 26.1, 26.2 and 26.4 for appeal.

32.5 **Time of cancellation.** If no affidavit is filed, the registration will be cancelled forthwith by the Commissioner after the end of the 6th year, and a notice of the cancellation will be sent to the registrant. If the affidavit is filed but is refused, cancellation of the registration will be withheld pending further proceedings.

33. AFFIDAVIT FOR INCONTESTABILITY

33.1 **Affidavit for incontestability.** The affidavit required by section 15 of the act for acquiring incontestability for a mark registered on the Principal Register or a mark registered under the act of 1881 or 1905 and republished under section 12(*c*) of the act (Rule 30.1) must

(*a*) Be signed by the registrant;

(*b*) Identify the certificate of registration by the certificate number and date of registration;

(*c*) Recite the goods or services stated in the registration on or in connection with which the mark has been in continuous use for a period of 5 years subsequent to the date of registration or date of republication under section 12(*c*) of the act, in commerce which may lawfully be regulated by Congress and is still in use in commerce, specifying the nature of such commerce;

(*d*) Specify that there has been no final decision adverse to registrant's claim of ownership of such mark for such goods or services, or to registrant's right to register the same or to keep the same on the register;

(*e*) Specify that there is no proceeding involving said rights pending in the Patent Office or in a court and not finally disposed of;

(*f*) Be filed within 1 year after the expiration of any such 5-year period.

The registrant will be notified of the receipt of the affidavit.

33.2 **Combined with other affidavits.** The affidavit filed under section 15 of the act for the purpose of acquiring incontestability may also be used as the affidavit required by section 8, provided it also complies with the requirements and is filed within the time limit specified in Rules 32.1 and 32.2.

In appropriate circumstances the affidavit filed under section 15 of the act may be combined with the affidavit required for renewal of a registration (see Rule 35.3).

34. CORRECTION, DISCLAIMER, SURRENDER, ETC.

34.1 **New certificate on change of ownership.** In case of change of ownership of a registered mark, a new certificate of registration may be issued in the name of the assignee for the unexpired part of the original period, at the request of the assignee. The assignment must be recorded in the Patent Office and the request must be accompanied by the required fee and by an abstract of title or an order for a title report for Office use.

34.2 **Surrender, cancellation, disclaimer in whole.** The Commissioner may permit any registration to be surrendered or cancelled, or any registered mark to be disclaimed in whole, upon application by the registrant. Application for such action must be signed by the registrant and must be accompanied by the required fee, and by an abstract of title or an order for a title report for Office use.

34.3 **Amendment and disclaimer in part.** The Commissioner may permit any registration to be amended or any registered mark to be disclaimed in part, upon application by the registrant. Application for such action must specify the amendment or disclaimer and be signed by the registrant, and must be accompanied by the required fee and by an abstract of title or an order for a title report for Office use. The certificate of registration or, if said certificate is lost or destroyed, a certified copy thereof, must also be submitted in order that the Commissioner may make appropriate entry thereon and in the records of the Office. The registration when so amended must still contain registrable matter and the mark as amended must be registrable as a whole, and such amendment or disclaimer must not involve such changes in the registration as to alter materially the character of the mark.

Changes in the description of goods other than in the nature of deletions will not be permitted except under the provisions of Rule 34.5. No amendment seeking the elimination of a disclaimer will be permitted.

A printed copy of the amendment or disclaimer shall be attached to each printed copy of the registration.

34.4 **Correction of Office mistake.** Whenever a material mistake in a registration, incurred through the fault of the Patent Office, is clearly disclosed by the records of the Office, a certificate stating the fact and nature of such mistake, signed by the Commissioner and sealed with the seal of the Patent Office, shall be issued without charge and recorded and a printed copy thereof shall be attached to each printed copy of the registration certificate and such corrected certificate shall thereafter have the same effect as if the same had been originally issued in such corrected form, or in the discretion of the Commissioner a new certificate of registration may be issued without charge.

34.5 **Correction of mistake by registrant.** Whenever a mistake has been made in a registration and a showing has been made that such mistake occurred in good faith through the fault of the applicant, the Commissioner may issue a certificate of correction, or in his discretion, a new certificate upon the payment of the required fee, provided that the correction does not involve such changes in the registration as to require republication of the mark.

Application for such action must specify the mistake for which correction is sought and the manner in which it arose, show that it occurred in good faith, be signed by the applicant, and be accompanied by the required fee and by an abstract of title or an order for a title report for Office use.

A printed copy of the certificate of correction shall be attached to each printed copy of the registration.

35. TERM AND RENEWAL

35.1 **Term of original registrations and renewals.** Registrations under the act of 1946, whether on the Principal Register or on the Supplemental Register, remain in force for 20 years, and may be renewed for periods of 20 years from the expiring period unless previously cancelled, disclaimed in whole, or surrendered.

Registrations under the acts of 1905 and 1881 remain in force for their unexpired terms and may only be renewed in the same manner as registrations under the act of 1946.

Registrations under the act of 1920 which were issued on or

before January 5, 1928, expire on January 5, 1948, and such registrations issued after January 5, 1928, expire 20 years from their date of issue. Such registrations cannot be renewed unless renewal is required to support foreign registrations and in such case may be renewed on the Supplemental Register in the same manner as registrations under the act of 1946.

35.2 **Period within which application for renewal must be filed.** An application for renewal may be made by the registrant at any time within 6 months before the expiration of the period for which the certificate of registration was issued or renewed, or it may be made within 3 months after such expiration on payment of the additional fee required.

35.3 **Requirements of application for renewal.** The application for renewal must be accompanied by:

(*a*) An affidavit by the registrant stating that the mark is still in use in commerce which may lawfully be regulated by Congress, specifying the nature of such commerce. This affidavit must be executed not more than 6 months before the expiration of the registration.

(*b*) The required fee, including the additional fee required in the case of a delayed application for renewal.

The affidavit and the fee must accompany the application for renewal and therefore must be filed within the period provided for applying for renewal. If defective or insufficient, they cannot be completed after the period for applying for renewal has passed; if completed after the initial 6-month period has expired but before the expiration of the 3-month delay period, the application can be considered only as a delayed application for renewal.

The application for renewal must also include:

(*c*) An abstract of title or an order for a title report for Office use.

(*d*) If the applicant is not domiciled in the United States, the designation of some person resident in the United States on whom may be served notices or process in proceedings affecting the mark.

(*e*) If the mark is registered under the act of 1920, a verified showing that renewal is required to support foreign registrations.

35.4 Refusal of renewal. If the application for renewal is incomplete or defective, the renewal will be refused by the Examiner of Trade-Marks. The application may be completed or amended in response to a refusal, subject to the provisions of Rules 12.2 and 35.3.

See Rules 26.1 and 26.2 for appeal.

36. ASSIGNMENT OF MARKS

36.1 Requirements for assignments. A mark which has been registered or a mark for which an application for registration has been filed shall be assignable with the good will of the business in which the mark is used, or with that part of the good will of the business connected with the use of and symbolized by the mark.

Such assignments shall be by instruments in writing duly executed. Acknowledgment as provided by section 11 of the act shall be prima facie evidence of the execution of an assignment and when recorded in the Patent Office the record shall be prima facie evidence of execution. No assignment will be recorded unless it has been executed and unless:

(*a*) The certificate of registration is identified in the assignment by the certificate number (the date of registration should also be given), or, the application for registration shall have been first filed in the Patent Office and the application is identified in the assignment by serial number (the date of filing should also be given);

(*b*) It is in the English language or, if not in the English language, accompanied by a sworn translation;

(*c*) The fee for recording is received; and

(*d*) An appointment of a resident agent is made in case the assignee is not domiciled in the United States. The appointment must be separate from the assignment and there must be a separate appointment for each registration or application assigned in one instrument.

The date of record of the assignment is the date of the receipt of the assignment at the Patent Office in proper form and accompanied by the full fee for recording.

36.2 **Action may be taken by assignee of record.** Any action which may or must be taken by a registrant or applicant may be taken by the assignee, provided the assignment has been recorded, and unless such assignment has been recorded no assignee will be recognized.

36.3 **Certificate of registration may issue to assignee.** The certificate of registration may be issued to the assignee of the applicant, but the assignment must first be entered of record in the Patent Office as of a date not later than the fourth Thursday before the date the certificate of registration is to bear. See Rule 15.2.

38. UNPROVIDED FOR AND EXTRAORDINARY CASES

38.1 **Cases not specifically defined.** All cases not specifically defined and provided for by these rules will be decided in accordance with the merits of each case under the authority of the Commissioner, and such decision will be communicated to the interested parties in writing.

38.2 **Commissioner may suspend certain rules.** In an extraordinary situation, when justice requires and no other party is injured thereby, any requirement of these rules not being a requirement of the statute may be suspended or waived by the Commissioner.

39. AMENDMENT OF RULES

39.1 **Amendments to rules will be published.** All amendments to these rules will be published in the Official Gazette and in the Federal Register.

39.2 **Publication of notice of proposed amendments.** Whenever required by law, and in other cases whenever practicable, notice of proposed amendments to these rules will be published in the Federal Register and in the Official Gazette. If not published with the notice, copies of the text will be furnished to any person requesting the same. All comments, suggestions, and briefs received within a time specified in the notice will be considered before adoption of the proposed amendments which may be modified in the light thereof.

Oral hearings may be held at the discretion of the Commissioner.

40. TIME OF TAKING EFFECT

40.1 **Effective date of rules.** These rules, except Rule 4.4, shall take effect on July 5, 1947, and shall apply to all applications for registration, registrations, and proceedings under and subject to the act of 1946. Applications filed prior to July 5, 1947, and still subject to the acts under which said applications were filed shall be prosecuted and certificates granted in accordance with the act under which filed and the rules thereunder in effect immediately prior to July 5, 1947.

These rules shall apply to contested or inter partes proceedings instituted on or after July 5, 1947, and also to further inter partes action in such cases pending on July 5, 1947, except to the extent that in the opinion of the Commissioner their application to a particular case pending when these rules take effect would not be feasible or would work injustice, in which event the rules in effect immediately prior to July 5, 1947, shall apply to such case.

Rule 4.4 shall take effect on January 1, 1948.

41. APPLICATIONS PENDING ON JULY 5, 1947

41.1 **Conversion of pending applications to act of 1946.** Applications for registration filed before July 5, 1947, and pending in the Patent Office on and after that date may be amended, if practicable, to bring them under the provisions of the act of 1946.

41.2 **Requirements of amendment.** Such amendment must supply the facts required by these rules to be included in the statement of an original application which are not contained in the statement on file, supported by a supplemental affidavit including any required averments which are not contained in the original declaration. The amendment is subject to all rules relating to or affecting amendments and must not be inconsistent with the original statement and declaration. The amendment may take the form of a substitute written application and in any case the Examiner may require the amended application to be rewritten.

The entire filing fee required for an original application under the act of 1946 must be paid, but the filing fee previously paid will be considered as part payment of such filing fee.

For the purpose of proceedings in the Patent Office, the date of filing the amendment will be considered as the filing date of the application; for the purpose of contested proceedings, the applicant may be permitted to rely on the filing date of his original application, provided the mark was registrable under the act on which the original application was based.

41.3 **Applications which cannot be amended.** An amendment to bring an application under the act of 1946 will not be considered:

(*a*) If the application is abandoned at the time the amendment is filed;

(*b*) If the application is under rejection or other action by the Examiner and the appropriate response thereto is not received within the time for response, in which case the mere filing of the proposed amendment will not avoid abandonment of the application;

(*c*) If filed after the notice of allowance has been sent; and

(*d*) In any other case if, from the nature of the particular amendment or the condition of the application, it is not practicable.

FORMS FOR TRADE-MARK CASES

1 Application for trade-mark registration by an individual, Principal Register

2 Application for trade-mark registration by a firm, Principal Register

3 Application for trade-mark registration by a corporation, Principal Register

6 Application for trade-mark registration claiming concurrent use, Principal Register

9 Application for service mark registration, Principal Register
12 Application for collective mark registration, Principal Register
13 Application for certification mark registration, Principal Register
16 Application for trade-mark registration, Supplemental Register
19 Application for trade-mark registration based on foreign registration or application
21 Application for renewal of registration by an individual
25 Affidavit under section 8
26 Affidavit under section 12(*c*)
27 Affidavit under section 15
28 Combined affidavits under sections 8 and 15
31 Notice of opposition
32 Petition for cancellation of trade-marks
33 Appeal from the Examiner of Trade-Marks to the Commissioner in ex parte cases
34 Appeal from the Examiner of Interferences to the Commissioner in contested or inter partes proceedings
35 Assignment of application for registration
36 Assignment of registered mark

The following forms illustrate the manner of preparing applications for registration of marks and various papers in trade-mark cases, to be filed in the Patent Office. Applicants and other parties will find their business facilitated by following them. These forms should be used in cases to which they are applicable. A sufficient number of representative forms are given which, with the variations indicated by the notes, should take care of all the usual situations. In special situations such alterations as the circumstances may render necessary may be made provided they do not depart from the requirements of the rules or the statute. Before using any forms the pertinent rules and sections of the statute should be studied carefully.

1. APPLICATION FOR TRADE-MARK REGISTRATION BY AN INDIVIDUAL, PRINCIPAL REGISTER

To the Commissioner of Patents:

(Statement)

................, a citizen of .... residing at
(name) (citizenship)
.... and doing business at .... has adopted and is using the trade-mark shown in the accompanying drawing for .... in Class ....
(particular description of goods) (number and title of Class)
and presents herewith five specimens (or facsimiles) showing the trade-mark as actually used in connection with such goods, the trade-mark being applied to (1) .... and requests that the same be registered in the United States Patent Office on the Principal Register in accordance with the Act of July 5, 1946.

The trade-mark was first used on (2) .... and first
(date)
used in commerce (3) .... which may lawfully be regulated by Congress on ....
(date)

(Declaration)

Applicant being duly sworn, deposes and says that he believes himself to be the owner of the trade-mark, which is in use in commerce (3) .... and that no other person, firm, corporation or association, to the best of his knowledge and belief, has the right to use such trade-mark in commerce which may lawfully be regulated by Congress, either in the identical form thereof or in such near resemblance thereto as might be calculated to deceive, that the drawing and description truly represent the trade-mark sought to be registered, that the specimens (or facsimiles) show the trade-mark as actually used in connection with the goods, and that the facts set forth in the statement are true.

(Power of Attorney)

The undersigned hereby appoints .... of .... State of .... Registration No. .... (4)................ his attorney (or agent) to prosecute this application for registration with full power of substitution and revocation, to transact all business in the Patent Office connected therewith, and to receive the certificate.

. . . .
(signature)

State of . . . .
County of . . . . } ss

Before me personally appeared . . . . to me known to be the person described in the above application for registration, who signed the foregoing instrument in my presence, and made oath before me to the allegations set forth therein, on the . . . . day of . . . ., 19. . . . . .

. . . .
(notary public)

Notes:

(1) Insert: "the goods"; "the containers for the goods"; "displays associated with the goods," and/or, "tags or labels affixed to the goods," as the case may be.

(2) State the date on which the trade-mark was first used as a trade-mark whether or not in commerce which may lawfully be regulated by Congress.

(3) Specify kind of commerce, such as: "among the several states"; "in commerce between foreign nations and the United States"; or specify other commerce which may lawfully be regulated by Congress, as the case may be.

(4) If the attorney is not registered on the Patent Office Register the power of attorney or separate paper must recite the bar to which he has been admitted to practice as required by Rule 4.2.

If the applicant is not domiciled in the United States a domestic representative must be appointed, see Form 19 for appropriate paragraph.

2. APPLICATION FOR TRADE-MARK REGISTRATION BY A FIRM, PRINCIPAL REGISTER

To the Commissioner of Patents:

(Statement)

. . . . a firm domiciled in . . . . ,
(firm name) (domicile)
doing business at . . . . and composed of the fol-
(business address)
lowing members . . . . all citizens of
(names of firm members)
. . . . has adopted and used the trade-mark
(citizenship of firm members)
shown in the accompanying drawing for . . . . in
(particular description of goods)

Class .... and presents herewith five speci-
(number and title of Class)
mens (or facsimiles) showing the trade-mark as actually used in connection with such goods, the trade-mark being applied to .... and requests that the same be registered in the United States Patent Office on the Principal Register in accordance with the Act of July 5, 1946.

The trade-mark was first used on .... and first
(date)
used in commerce .... which may lawfully be regulated by Congress on ....
(date)

(Declaration)

.... being duly sworn, deposes and says that he is a member of the firm of ...., the
(firm name)
applicant named in the foregoing statement, that he believes that said firm is the owner of the trade-mark, which is in use in commerce .... and that no other person, firm, corporation or association, to the best of his knowledge and belief, has the right to use such trade-mark in commerce which may lawfully be regulated by Congress either in the identical form thereof or in such near resemblance thereto as might be calculated to deceive, that the drawing and description truly represent the trade-mark sought to be registered, that the specimens (or facsimiles) show the trade-mark as actually used in connection with the goods, and that the facts set forth in the statement are true.

(Power of Attorney)

The undersigned hereby appoints .... of .... State of .... Registration No. .... its attorney (or agent) to prosecute this application for registration with full power of substitution and revocation, to transact all business in the Patent Office connected therewith, and to receive the certificate.

....
(firm name)

By....................
(full signature of member of firm)

State of . . . .
County of . . . . } ss

Before me personally appeared . . . . to me known to be the person described in the above application for registration, who signed the foregoing instrument in my presence, and made oath before me to the allegations set forth therein, on the . . . . day of . . . ., 19 . . . . . .

. . . .
(notary public)

Note: See Form 1 for appropriate notes.

3. APPLICATION FOR TRADE-MARK REGISTRATION BY A CORPORATION, PRINCIPAL REGISTER

To the Commissioner of Patents:

(Statement)

. . . . a corporation (1) duly organized under the laws of . . . . located
(state or country under which organized)
at . . . . and doing business at
(location of corporation)
. . . . has adopted and used the trade-mark
(business address)
shown in the accompanying drawing for . . . .
(particular description of goods)
in Class . . . . and presents herewith five
(number and title of Class)
specimens (or facsimiles) showing the trade-mark as actually used in connection with such goods, the trade-mark being applied to . . . . and requests that the same be registered in the United States Patent Office on the Principal Register in accordance with the Act of July 5, 1946.

The trade-mark was first used on . . . . and
(date)
first used in commerce . . . . which may lawfully be regulated by Congress on . . . .
(date)

(Declaration)

. . . ., being duly sworn, deposes and says
(name of affiant)

that he is the .... of ....,
(official title) (corporation (1) name)
the applicant named in the foregoing statement, that he believes that said corporation (1) is the owner of the trade-mark which is in use in commerce .... and that no other person, firm, corporation or association, to the best of his knowledge and belief, has the right to use such trade-mark in commerce which may lawfully be regulated by Congress either in the identical form thereof or in such near resemblance thereto as might be calculated to deceive, that the drawing and description truly represent the trade-mark sought to be registered, that the specimens (or facsimiles) show the trade-mark as actually used in connection with the goods, and that the facts set forth in the statement are true.

(Power of Attorney)

The undersigned hereby appoints .... of .... State of .... Registration No. .... its attorney (or agent) to prosecute this application for registration with full power of substitution and revocation, to transact all business in the Patent Office connected therewith, and to receive the certificate.

....
(name of applicant)

By....................
(full signature of officer)

....
(official title)

State of .... }
County of .... } ss

Before me personally appeared .... to me known to be the person described in the above application for registration, who signed the foregoing instrument in my presence, and made oath before me to the allegations set forth therein, on the .... day of ...., 19......

....
(notary public)

Notes:

(1) If applicant is an association, the word "association" should be substituted for the word "corporation."

See Form 1 for other applicable notes.

6. APPLICATION FOR TRADE-MARK REGISTRATION CLAIMING CONCURRENT USE, PRINCIPAL REGISTER

To the Commissioner of Patents:

(Statement)

. . . ., a citizen of . . . . residing
(citizenship)
at . . . . and doing business at . . . .
has adopted and is using the trade-mark shown in the accompanying drawing for . . . . in Class . . . .
(particular description of goods) (number)
. . . . and presents herewith five specimens (or
(title of Class)
facsimiles) showing the trade-mark as actually used in connection with such goods, the trade-mark being applied to (1) . . . . and requests that the same be registered in the United States Patent Office on the Principal Register in accordance with the Act of July 5, 1946, for the goods stated above for the area comprising (2) . . . .

The trade-mark was first used by applicant on (3) . . . .
(date)
and first used by applicant in commerce (4) . . . .
which may lawfully be regulated by Congress on . . . .
(date)

(Exceptions to claim of exclusive use)

The following exceptions to applicant's claim of exclusive use are specified:

By . . . . located and doing business at . . . .
. . . . and using the mark . . . .
(description of the mark and Registration
. . . . in connection with the following
No., or application, Serial No., if any)
. . . . the mark being used as follows
(particular description of goods or services)
. . . . in the territory embracing the states
(mode of application or use)
of . . . . from . . . . to . . . . ;
(date) (date)
and,

By . . . . located and doing business, etc.

(Declaration)

Applicant being duly sworn, deposes and says that he believes himself to be the owner of the trade-mark which is in use in commerce (4) .... and that no other person, firm, corporation or association, to the best of his knowledge and belief, has the right to use such trade-mark in commerce which may lawfully be regulated by Congress, either in the identical form thereof or in such near resemblance thereto as might be calculated to deceive, except for the specified exceptions, that the drawing and description truly represent the trade-mark sought to be registered, that the specimens (or facsimiles) show the trade-mark as actually used in connection with the goods, and that the facts set forth in the statement are true.

(Power of Attorney)

(Use Power of Attorney and Verification of Form 1.)

Notes:

(1) Insert "the goods"; "the containers for the goods"; "displays associated with the goods," and/or, "tags or labels affixed to the goods," as the case may be.

(2) Describe the area for which registration is desired.

(3) State the date on which the trade-mark was first used as a trade-mark whether or not in commerce which may lawfully be regulated by Congress.

(4) Specify the kind of commerce, such as: "among the several states"; "in commerce between foreign nations and the United States"; or specify other commerce which may lawfully be regulated by Congress, as the case may be.

See Forms 2 and 3 for style of application by a firm and by a corporation.

9. APPLICATION FOR SERVICE MARK REGISTRATION, PRINCIPAL REGISTER

To the Commissioner of Patents:

(Statement)

.... a citizen of .... residing at
(name of applicant) (citizenship)
................and doing business at .... has adopted and is using the service mark shown in the accompanying drawing (1) for .... in Class ....
(particular description of services) (number and

.... and presents herewith (2) ....
title of Class)
showing the service mark as actually used in connection with the sale or advertising of such services; the service mark being used as follows: .... and requests
(mode of application or use)
that the same be registered in the United States Patent Office on the Principal Register in accordance with the Act of July 5, 1946.

The service mark was first used on (3) ....
(date)
and first used in the sale or advertising of services and the services rendered in commerce (4) .... which may lawfully be regulated by Congress on ....
(date)

(Declaration)

Applicant being duly sworn, deposes and says that he believes himself to be the owner of the service mark, which is in use in commerce (4) .... and that no other person, firm, corporation or association, to the best of his knowledge and belief, has the right to use such service mark in commerce which may lawfully be regulated by Congress either in the identical form thereof, or in such near resemblance thereto as might be calculated to deceive; that the drawing (if any) and description truly represent the service mark sought to be registered; that (5) .... show the service mark as actually used in connection with the sale or advertising of services, and that the facts set forth in the Statement are true.

(Power of Attorney)

(Use Power of Attorney and Verification of Form 1.)

Notes:

(1) If drawing is not possible, see Rule 9.1, insert description of the mark instead of reference to the drawing.

(2) If specimens (or facsimiles) are not possible, see Rule 10.3, state the nature of other representation furnished.

(3) State the date on which the mark was first used as a service mark whether or not the services were rendered in commerce which may lawfully be regulated by Congress.

(4) Specify kind of commerce, such as: "among the several states"; "in commerce between foreign nations and the United States"; or specify other

commerce which may lawfully be regulated by Congress, as the case may be.

(5) Insert: "the specimens (or facsimiles)" or, state nature of other representation furnished.

See Forms 2 and 3 for style of application by a firm and by a corporation.

12. APPLICATION FOR COLLECTIVE MARK REGISTRATION, PRINCIPAL REGISTER

To the Commissioner of Patents:

(Statement)

.... an association (1) duly organized under
(name of applicant)
the laws of .... located at ....
(state or country under which organized) (location of
.... and doing business at .... has
association(1)) (business address)
adopted and is exercising legitimate control over the use of the collective mark shown in the accompanying drawing for ....
(particular
.... in Class .... and presents
description of goods) (number and title of Class)
herewith five specimens (or facsimiles) showing the collective mark as actually used in connection with such goods by members of such organization, the collective mark being applied to (2) .... and requests that the same be registered in the United States Patent Office on the Principal Register in accordance with the Act of July 5, 1946. The collective mark is used in connection with the goods to indicate (3) ....

The collective mark was first used on (4) .... and
(date)
first used in commerce (5) .... which may lawfully be regulated by Congress on ....
(date)

(Declaration)

.................., ... of ....,
(name of affiant) (official title) (association (1) name)
the applicant named in the foregoing statement, being duly sworn, deposes and says that he believes said association (1) is the owner of the collective mark which is in use in commerce (5) .... and that, to the best of his knowledge and belief, no other person, firm, corporation or association has the

right to authorize the use of, and no person, firm, corporation or association other than members has the right to use, such collective mark in commerce which may lawfully be regulated by Congress either in the identical form thereof or in such near resemblance thereto as might be calculated to deceive, that the drawing and description truly represent the collective mark sought to be registered, that the specimens (or facsimiles) show the mark as actually used in connection with the goods, and that the facts set forth in the statement are true.

(Power of Attorney)

(Use Power of Attorney and Verification of Form 3.)

Notes:

(1) Or cooperative or other collective group or organization.

(2) Insert: "the goods"; "the containers for the goods"; "displays associated with the goods," and/or "tags or labels affixed to the goods," as the case may be.

(3) Membership in the organization or other appropriate statement.

(4) State the date on which the mark was first used as a collective mark whether or not in commerce which may lawfully be regulated by Congress.

(5) Specify the kind of commerce, such as: "among the several states"; "in commerce between foreign nations and the United States"; or specify other commerce which may lawfully be regulated by Congress, as the case may be.

See Forms 1 and 2 for style of application by an individual and by a firm, and Form 9 for style of application for service mark.

13. APPLICATION FOR CERTIFICATION MARK REGISTRATION, PRINCIPAL REGISTER

To the Commissioner of Patents:

(Statement)

.... a corporation (1) duly organized under
(name of applicant)
the laws of .... located at
(state or country under which organized)
.... and doing business at ....
(location of corporation) (business address)
has adopted and is exercising legitimate control over the use of the certification mark shown in the accompanying drawing for
.... in Class .... and presents
(particular description of goods) (number and title of Class)
herewith five specimens .... showing the cer-
(or facsimiles)

tification mark as actually used in connection with such goods by persons duly authorized by applicant, the certification mark being applied to (2) .... and requests that the same be registered in the United States Patent Office on the Principal Register in accordance with the Act of July 5, 1946. The certification mark is used upon the goods to indicate (3) ....

The certification mark was first used on (4) ....
(date)
and first used in commerce (5) .... which may lawfully be regulated by Congress on ....
(date)

(Declaration)

.... being duly sworn, deposes and says that
(name of affiant)
he is the .... of .... the
(official title) (corporation (1) name)
applicant named in the foregoing statement; that he believes that said corporation (1) is the owner of the certification mark which is in use in commerce (5) .... and that to the best of his knowledge and belief, no other person, firm, corporation or association, has the right to authorize the use of such mark and that no person, firm, corporation or association other than those duly authorized by applicant has the right to use the mark in commerce which may lawfully be regulated by Congress either in the identical form thereof or in such near resemblance thereto as might be calculated to deceive, that the drawing and description truly represent the certification mark sought to be registered, that the specimens (or facsimiles) show the certification mark as actually used in connection with the goods, that the applicant itself is not engaged in the production or marketing of goods with which the mark is used, and that the facts set forth in the statement are true.

(Power of Attorney)

(Use Power of Attorney and Verification of Form 3.)

Notes:

(1) If applicant is an association, the word "association" should be substituted for the word "corporation."

(2) Insert: "the goods"; "the containers for the goods"; "displays associated

with the goods," and/or, "tags or labels affixed to the goods," as the case may be.

(3) Insert a statement that the mark certifies regional or other origin, material, mode or manufacture, quality, accuracy or other characteristic of such goods, or that the work or labor on the goods was performed by a member of a union or other organization, or other appropriate statement.

(4) State the date on which the mark was first used as a certification mark whether or not in commerce which may lawfully be regulated by Congress.

(5) Specify kind of commerce, such as: "among the several states"; "in commerce between foreign nations and the United States"; or specify other commerce which may lawfully be regulated by Congress, as the case may be.

See Forms 1 and 2 for style of application by an individual and by a firm and Form 9 for style of application for service mark.

16. APPLICATION FOR TRADE-MARK REGISTRATION, SUPPLEMENTAL REGISTER

To the Commissioner of Patents:

(Statement)

................, a citizen of .... (citizenship) residing at .... and doing business at .... has adopted and is using the mark shown for .... (particular description of goods) in Class .... (number and title of Class) and presents herewith five specimens (or facsimiles) showing the mark as actually used in connection with such goods, the mark being applied to (1) .... and requests that the same be registered in the United States Patent Office on the Supplemental Register in accordance with the Act of July 5, 1946.

The mark was first used on (2) .... (date) and first used in commerce (3) .... which may lawfully be regulated by Congress on .... (date), and has been in lawful use in such commerce upon or in connection with the goods for the year preceding the filing of this application. (4)

(Declaration)

Applicant being duly sworn, deposes and says that he believes himself to be the owner of the mark, which is in use in commerce (3) .... and that no other person, firm, corporation or association to the best of his knowledge and belief, has the right to use such mark in commerce which may lawfully be regulated by Congress, either in the identical form thereof or in such near resemblance thereto as might be calculated to deceive, that the drawing (if any) and description truly represent the mark sought to be registered, that the specimens (or facsimiles) show the mark as actually used in connection with the goods, and that the facts set forth in the statement are true.

(Power of Attorney)

(Use Power of Attorney and Verification of Form 1.)

Notes:

(1) Insert: "the goods"; "the containers for the goods"; "displays associated with the goods," and/or "tags or labels affixed to the goods," as the case may be.

(2) State the date on which the trade-mark was first used as a trade-mark whether or not in commerce which may lawfully be regulated by Congress.

(3) Specify kind of commerce, such as: "among the several states"; "in commerce between foreign nations and the United States"; or specify other commerce which may lawfully be regulated by Congress, as the case may be.

(4) If appropriate, substitute for last clause: "and applicant has begun the use of such mark in commerce between the United States and .... (specify foreign country) ...." In the latter instance a separate showing should be submitted to the effect that domestic registration is required as a basis for foreign protection of said mark.

See Forms 2 and 3 for style of application by a firm and by a corporation.

See Forms 9, 12 and 13 for style of application for service, collective and certification marks.

19. APPLICATION FOR TRADE-MARK REGISTRATION BASED ON FOREIGN REGISTRATION OR APPLICATION

To the Commissioner of Patents:

(Statement)

................, (name) a citizen of .... (citizenship) residing at .... and doing business at .... has adopted and is using the trade-mark shown in the accompanying drawing for .... (particular description of goods) in Class .... (number and title of Class) and presents herewith five specimens (or facsimiles) showing the trade-mark as actually used in connection with such goods, the trade-mark being applied to (1) .... and requests that the same be registered in the United States Patent Office on the Principal (2) Register in accordance with the Act of July 5, 1946.

Such trade-mark has been registered in ....
(country)
Registration No. .... dated .... and said registration is now in force and effect. (3)

(Declaration)

Applicant being duly sworn, deposes and says that he believes himself to be the owner of the trade-mark, which is in use as a trade-mark and that no other person, firm, corporation or association, to the best of his knowledge and belief, has the right to use such trade-mark in commerce which may lawfully be regulated by Congress, either in the identical form thereof or in such near resemblance thereto as might be calculated to deceive, that the drawing and description truly represent the trade-mark sought to be registered, that the specimens (or facsimiles) show the trademark as actually used in connection with the goods, and that the facts set forth in the statement are true.

(Domestic Representative)

.... whose postal address is ....,
(street)
................, ... is designated as applicant's
(city) (state)
representative on whom notices or process in proceedings affecting the mark may be served.

(Power of Attorney)

The undersigned hereby appoints .... of .... State of .... Registration No. ....(4) .... his attorney (or agent) to prosecute this application for registration with full power of substitution and revocation, to transact all business in the Patent Office connected therewith, and to receive the certificate.

....
(signature)

.....................}
.....................} ss

Before me personally appeared .... to me known to be the person described in the above application for registration, who signed the foregoing instrument in my presence, and made oath before me to the allegations set forth therein on the .... day of .... 19.....

.....................(5)
(notary public)

Notes:

(1) Insert "the goods"; "the containers for the goods"; "displays associated with the goods," and/or "tags or labels affixed to the goods," as the case may be.

(2) Or, "Supplemental," if appropriate.

(3) If the right of priority of an application filed in a foreign country is claimed, the following paragraph should be substituted:

"Application for registration of said trade-mark has been filed in .... (country) on ...., (date) Registration No. .... dated ...., and a right of priority based on this application is claimed."

If the registration has not yet been granted the registration number and date in this substitute paragraph may be left blank for subsequent insertion.

(4) If the attorney is not registered on the Patent Office Register the power of attorney or separate paper must recite the bar to which he has been admitted as required by Rule 4.2.

(5) If made in a foreign country the oath may be taken before any diplomatic or consular officer of the United States or before any official authorized to administer oaths in the foreign country concerned whose authority shall be proved by a certificate of a diplomatic or consular officer of the United States.

See Forms 2 and 3 for style of application by a firm and by a corporation.

See Forms 9, 12 and 13 for style of application for service, collective and certification marks.

21. APPLICATION FOR RENEWAL OF REGISTRATION BY AN INDIVIDUAL

To the Commissioner of Patents:

(Application)

...................., a citizen of (1) .... (citizenship) residing at .... (address) and doing business at .... (business address) requests that Certificate of Registration No. .... granted to .... on .... which he now owns as evidenced by the accompanying (2) .... be renewed (3) in accordance with the provisions of section 9 of the Trade-Mark Act of July 5, 1946.

The renewal fee of $25.00 (4) is presented herewith.

(Affidavit)

Applicant, being duly sworn, deposes and says that he is the owner of Registration No. .... and that the mark described therein is still in use in commerce (5) .... and that the facts recited in the application are true.

(Power of Attorney)

The undersigned hereby appoints .... of ....State of .... Registration No. ....(6) ...., his attorney (or agent) to prosecute this application for renewal with full power of substitution and revocation, to transact all business in the Patent Office connected therewith, and to receive the certificate.

....
(signature)

State .... }
County of .... } SS

Before me personally appeared .... to me known to be the person described in the above application for renewal, who signed the foregoing instrument in my presence, and made oath before me to the allegations set forth therein, on the .... day of .... 19....

....
(notary public)

Notes:

(1) If applicant is not domiciled in the United States, a domestic representative must be designated. See Form 19 for appropriate language for such designation.

(2) Abstract of title, or, title report, as the case may be.

(3) If the registration sought to be renewed is registered under the Act of March 19, 1920, here insert "on the Supplemental Register" and add the following paragraph:

"Renewal of Registration No. .... is necessary to support Registration No. .... registered in .... on ...."
(foreign country) (date)

(4) If the application is a delayed application for renewal, the fee is $30.00.

(5) Specify the kind of commerce, such as: "among the several states"; "in commerce between foreign nations and the United States"; or specify other commerce which may lawfully be regulated by Congress, as the case may be.

(6) If the attorney is not registered on the Patent Office Register, the power of attorney or separate paper must recite the bar to which he has been admitted as required by Rule 4.2.

25. AFFIDAVIT UNDER SECTION 8

To the Commissioner of Patents:

........................, being duly sworn, deposes and says that he is the owner of Registration No. ...., dated ....(1), as evidenced by the accompanying (2) ....; that the mark described therein is still in use (3) ....

(Power of Attorney)

The undersigned hereby appoints .... of .... State of .... Registration No. .... (4) .... his attorney (or agent) to file this affidavit, with full power of substitution and revocation, and to transact all business in the Patent Office in connection therewith.

....
(signature)

State of ....
County of .... } ss

Before me personally appeared .... to me known to be the person described in the foregoing affidavit, who signed the said affidavit in my presence, and made oath before me to the allegations set forth therein on the ....day of .... 19.....

....
(notary public)

Notes:

(1) If the mark has been republished under the provisions of subsection (*c*) of section 12 of the Trade-Mark Act of 1946, add the following:
"and republished ...."
(date of republication)

(2) Abstract of title, or, title report, as the case may be.

(3) Recite sufficient facts to show that the mark is still in use and indicate the nature of such use, or, if the mark is not being used, recite sufficient facts to show that non-use is due to special circumstances which excuse such non-use and is not due to any intention of the owner to abandon the mark.

(4) If the attorney is not registered on the Patent Office Register, the power of attorney or a separate paper must recite the bar to which he has been admitted as required by Rule 4.2.

26. AFFIDAVIT UNDER SECTION 12 (*c*)

To the Commissioner of Patents:
Registration No. . . . .
Dated . . . .
Act of . . . .
To . . . .
(registrant)

. . . ., being duly sworn, deposes and says that he is the owner of Registration No. . . . ., above identified, as evidenced by the accompanying (1) . . . .; that said registration is now in force; that the trade-mark described therein is in use in commerce (2) . . . . on each of the following goods named in said registration, ... and claims the benefits of the Trade-Mark Act of 1946 for said trade-mark.

(Power of Attorney)

(Use Power of Attorney and Verification of Form 25.)

Notes:
(1) Abstract of title, or, title report, as the case may be.
(2) Specify the kind of commerce, such as: "among the several states"; "in commerce between foreign nations and the United States"; or specify other commerce which may lawfully be regulated by Congress, as the case may be.

27. AFFIDAVIT UNDER SECTION 15

To the Commissioner of Patents:

. . . ., being duly sworn, deposes and says that he is the owner of Registration No. . . . ., dated . . . . (1), that the mark described in said registration has been in continuous use in commerce (2) . . . . for five consecutive years, from . . . . to . . . ., subsequent to the date of registration (or republication), on or in connection with the following . . . .
(particular description of goods or services)
stated in the registration and that said mark is still in use in com-

merce (2) ....
.............................; that there has been no final decision adverse to affiant's claim of ownership of such mark (3) .... or his right to register the same, or keep the same on the register, and, that there is no proceeding involving said rights pending in the Patent Office or in a court and not finally disposed of.

(Power of Attorney)

(Use Power of Attorney and Verification of Form 25.)

Notes:

(1) If the mark has been republished under the provisions of subsection (*c*) of section 12 of the Trade-Mark Act of 1946, add the following:

"and republished ...."
(date of republication)

(2) Specify the kind of commerce, such as: "among the several states"; "in commerce between foreign nations and the United States"; or specify other commerce which may lawfully be regulated by Congress, as they case may be.

(3) Insert: "for such goods," or "for such services," as the case may be.

28. COMBINED AFFIDAVITS UNDER SECTIONS 8 AND 15

To the Commissioner of Patents:

......................, being duly sworn, deposes and says that he is the owner of Registration No. ...., dated .... (1), as evidenced by the accompanying (2) ....; that the mark described therein has been in continuous use in commerce (3) .... for five consecutive years, from .... to ...., subsequent to the date of registration, on or in connection with the following ...., stated in
(particular description of goods or services)
the registration; that the mark is still in use in commerce (4) .....
....; that there has been no final decision adverse to affiant's claim of ownership of such mark (5) ...., or his right to register the same, or keep the same on the register, and, that there is no proceeding involving said rights pending in the Patent Office or in a court and not finally disposed of.

(Power of Attorney)

(Use Power of Attorney and Verification of Form 25.)

Notes:

(1) If the mark has been republished under the provisions of subsection (*c*) of section 12 of the Trade-Mark Act of 1946, add the following:

"and republished ...."
(date of republication)

(2) Abstract of title, or, title report, as the case may be.
commerce between foreign nations and the United States"; or specify other commerce which may lawfully be regulated by Congress, as the case may be.

(3) Specify the kind of commerce, such as: "among the several states"; "in

(4) Recite sufficient facts to show that the mark is still in use and indicate the nature of such use, or, if the mark is not being used, recite sufficient facts to show that non-use is due to special circumstances which excuse such non-use and is not due to any intention of the owner to abandon the mark.

(5) Insert: "for such goods," or, "for such services," as the case may be.

31. NOTICE OF OPPOSITION

To the Commissioner of Patents:

In the matter of an application for the registration of a trade-mark for .... Serial No. ....
(particular goods) (number and date of application)
by ...., ...,
(name of applicant) (location or residence of applicant)
which was published on page .... of the Official
(volume, number)
Gazette of ...., I ....,
(date of the Official Gazette) (name of opposer)
residing at ...., believe I would be
(residence or location of opposer)
damaged by such registration, and I hereby oppose the registration of said trade-mark.

The grounds for opposition are as follows:

(Here state the specific grounds of opposition and facts tending to show why the opposer believes he would be damaged by the proposed registration.)

Two specimens of the mark as used by me are attached hereto.

................, being duly sworn (or affirmed), deposes
(name of opposer)
and says that he is the party of that name mentioned in the foregoing notice of opposition, that he has read and signed the same and knows the contents thereof, and that the same is true of his

own knowledge, except as to the matters therein stated to be alleged upon information and belief, and as to those matters he believes it to be true.

. . . .
(signature of opposer)

State of . . . . }
County of . . . . } ss

Subscribed and sworn to (or affirmed) before me this . . . . day of . . . .

. . . .
(notary public)

32. PETITION FOR CANCELLATION OF TRADE-MARKS

To the Commissioner of Patents:

In the matter of Trade-Mark Registration No. . . . ., (number of registration) registered . . . ., by . . . ., (date of registration) (name of registrant) of . . . ., I, ..., (residence or location of registrant) (name of petitioner) residing at . . . ., deem myself damaged (residence or location of petitioner) by said registration, and hereby petition for cancellation thereof.

The grounds for cancellation are as follows:

(Here state the specific grounds for cancellation and facts tending to show why the petitioner believes he is or will be damaged by the registration.)

Two specimens of the mark as used by me are attached hereto.

. . . ., being duly sworn (or affirmed), deposes and says that he is the party of that name mentioned in the foregoing petition for cancellation, that he has read and signed the same and knows the contents thereof, and that the same is true of his own knowledge, except as to the matters therein stated to be alleged upon information and belief, and as to those matters he believes it to be true.

. . . .
(signature)

State of .... }
County of .... } ss

Subscribed and sworn to (or affirmed) before me this .... day of ....

....
(notary public)

33. APPEAL FROM THE EXAMINER OF TRADE-MARKS TO THE COMMISSIONER IN EX PARTE CASES

(Heading, Application or Registration)

To the Commissioner of Patents:

I hereby appeal to the Commissioner from the decision rendered ...., 19...., by the Examiner of Trade-Marks in the matter of my (1) ....

....

The following are assigned as reasons of appeal: (Here should follow an explicit statement of the alleged errors in the decision of the Examiner of Trade-Marks.)

....
(name of applicant)

....
(signature)

Note:

(1) Insert one of the following applicable clauses: "application for registration, Serial No. ...., filed .... 19....," or "application for renewal of registration No. ...., dated ....," or "affidavit filed under Section 8 of the Trade-Mark Act of July 5, 1946, in Registration No. ...., dated ...."

34. APPEAL FROM THE EXAMINER OF INTERFERENCES TO THE COMMISSIONER IN CONTESTED OR INTER PARTES PROCEEDINGS

(1) .... }
v. } (3) ....
(2) .... } No. ....

To the Commissioner of Patents:

I hereby appeal to the Commissioner from the decision rendered ...., 19...., by the Examiner of Interferences in the above identified proceeding. The following are the points of the decision on which appeal is taken: (Here should follow an explicit statement of the alleged errors in the decision appealed from.

....
(name of appellant)

....
(signature)

Notes:

(1) Name of party in position of plaintiff.

(2) Name of party in position of defendant.

(3) Type (Interference, Opposition, Cancellation or Concurrent Use) and identification number of proceeding.

35. ASSIGNMENT OF APPLICATION FOR REGISTRATION

Whereas ...., of the city of ...., county of .... and State of ...., has adopted and used in his business a trade-mark for which he has filed application for registration, Serial No. .... dated .... 19...., in the United States Patent Office; and

Whereas ...., of the city of ...., county of .... and State of ...., is desirous of acquiring said mark:

Now, Therefore, To All Whom It May Concern:

Be it known that for and in consideration of the sum of .... dollars and other good and valuable consideration to him paid, the receipt of which is hereby acknowledged, said .... by these presents does sell, assign, and transfer, unto the said .... the entire right, title, and interest in and to the said trade-mark and the good will of the business in connection with which the mark is used, (1), and the Commissioner of Patents is requested to issue the certificate of registration of said mark to said assignee.

State of .... }
County of .... } ss

Personally appeared before me the said .... and

acknowledged the above instrument as his free act and deed this .... day of ...., 19.....

.... (notary public)

Note:

(1) Or this phrase may read in appropriate circumstances: "that part of the good will of the business connected with the use of and symbolized by the mark."

36. ASSIGNMENT OF REGISTERED MARK

Whereas ...., of the city of ...., county ...., and State of ...., has adopted and used in his business a trade-mark, which is registered under No. ...., dated ...., 19...., in the United States Patent Office; and

Whereas ...., of the city of ...., county of ...., and State of ...., is desirous of acquiring said mark:

Now, Therefore, To All Whom It May Concern:

Be it known that for and in consideration of the sum of .... dollars and other good and valuable consideration to him in hand paid, the receipt of which is hereby acknowledged, said .... by these presents does sell, assign, and transfer, unto the said .... the entire right, title, and interest in and to the said trade-mark and the registration thereof, No. ...., together with the good will of the business in connection with which the said mark is used (1) ....

.... (signature)

State of ....
County of .... } ss

Personally appeared before me the said ....

and acknowledged the above instrument as his free act and deed this .... day of ...., 19.....

....
(notary public)

Note:
(1) Or the last phrase may read in appropriate circumstances:
"that part of the good will of the business connected with the use of and symbolized by the mark."

NEW TRADE-MARK LAW ("Lanham Act")

EFFECTIVE JULY 5, 1947

[PUBLIC LAW 489—79TH CONGRESS]

[CHAPTER 540—2D SESSION]

[H. R. 1654]

AN ACT

TO PROVIDE FOR THE REGISTRATION AND PROTECTION OF TRADE-MARKS USED IN COMMERCE, TO CARRY OUT THE PROVISIONS OF CERTAIN INTERNATIONAL CONVENTIONS, AND FOR OTHER PURPOSES

Be it enacted by the Senate and House of Representatives of the United States of America in Congress assembled,

TITLE I—THE PRINCIPAL REGISTER

SEC. 1. The owner of a trade-mark used in commerce may register his trade-mark under this act on the principal register hereby established:

(*a*) By filing in the Patent Office—

(1) A written application, in such form as may be prescribed by the Commissioner, verified by the applicant, or by a member of the firm or an officer of the corporation or association applying, specifying applicant's domicile and citizenship, the date of applicant's first use of the mark, the date of applicant's first use of the mark in commerce, the goods in connection with which the mark

is used and the mode or manner in which the mark is used in connection with such goods, and including a statement to the effect that the person making the verification believes himself, or the firm, corporation, or association in whose behalf he makes the verification, to be the owner of the mark sought to be registered, that the mark is in use in commerce, and that no other person, firm, corporation, or association, to the best of his knowledge and belief, has the right to use such mark in commerce either in the identical form thereof or in such near resemblance thereto as might be calculated to deceive: *Provided,* That in the case of every application claiming concurrent use the applicant shall state exceptions to his claim of exclusive use, in which he shall specify, to the extent of his knowledge, any concurrent use by others, the goods or services in connection with which and the areas in which each concurrent use exists, the periods of each use, and the goods and area for which the applicant desires registration;

(2) A drawing of the mark; and

(3) Such number of specimens or facsimiles of the mark as actually used as may be required by the Commissioner.

(*b*) By paying into the Patent Office the filing fee.

(*c*) By complying with such rules or regulations, not inconsistent with law, as may be prescribed by the Commissioner.

(*d*) If the applicant is not domiciled in the United States he shall designate by a written document filed in the Patent Office the name and address of some person resident in the United States on whom may be served notices or process in proceedings affecting the mark. Such notices or process may be served upon the person so designated by leaving with him or mailing to him a copy thereof at the address specified in the last designation so filed. If the person so designated cannot be found at the address given in the last designation, such notice or process may be served upon the Commissioner.

Marks Registrable on the Principal Register

SEC. 2. No trade-mark by which the goods of the applicant may be distinguished from the goods of others shall be refused registration on the principal register on account of its nature unless it—

(*a*) Consists of or comprises immoral, deceptive, or scandalous matter; or matter which may disparage or falsely suggest a connection with persons, living or dead, institutions, beliefs, or national symbols, or bring them into contempt, or disrepute.

(*b*) Consists of or comprises the flag or coat of arms or other insignia of the United States, or of any State or municipality, or of any foreign nation, or any simulation thereof.

(*c*) Consists of or comprises a name, portrait, or signature identifying a particular living individual except by his written consent, or the name, signature, or portrait of a deceased President of the United States during the life of his widow, if any, except by the written consent of the widow.

(*d*) Consists of or comprises a mark which so resembles a mark registered in the Patent Office or a mark or trade name previously used in the United States by another and not abandoned, as to be likely, when applied to the goods of the applicant, to cause confusion or mistake or to deceive purchasers: *Provided,* That the Commissioner may register as concurrent registrations the same or similar marks to more than one registrant when they have become entitled to use such marks as a result of their concurrent lawful use thereof in commerce prior to any of the filing dates of the applications involved and the Commissioner of a court on appeal determines that confusion or mistake or deceit of purchasers is not likely to result from the continued use of said marks under conditions and limitations as to the mode or place of use or the goods in connection with which such registrations may be granted which conditions and limitations shall be prescribed in the grant of the concurrent registrations thereof; and concurrent registrations may be similarly granted by the Commissioner with such conditions and limitations when a court has finally determined that more than one person is entitled to use the same or similar marks in commerce. The Commissioner shall give not less than 30 days' written notice to all applicants, registrants, and users specified by any of the parties concerned of any application for concurrent registration and of the time and place of the hearings thereon. When the Commissioner decides to grant a concurrent registration the proposed registration shall be published in the *Official Gazette* of the Patent Office and the application shall be subject to opposition as hereinafter provided for other applications to register marks. Concurrent registrations may be ordered by a court in an action under the provisions of section 4915, Revised Statutes, under such conditions and limitations as the court considers proper in accordance herewith.

(*e*) Consists of a mark which, (1) when applied to the goods of the applicant is merely descriptive or deceptively misdescriptive of them, or (2) when applied to the goods of the applicant is primarily geographically descriptive or deceptively misdescriptive of them, except as indications of regional origin may be registrable under section 4 hereof, or (3) is primarily merely a surname.

(*f*) Except as expressly excluded in paragraphs (*a*), (*b*), (*c*), and (*d*) of this section, nothing herein shall prevent the registration of a mark used by the applicant which has become distinctive of the applicant's goods in commerce. The Commissioner may accept as prima facie evidence that the mark has become distinctive, as applied to the applicant's goods in commerce, proof of substantially exclusive and continuous use thereof as a mark by the applicant in commerce for the 5 years next preceding the date of the filing of the application for its registration.

Service Marks Registrable

SEC. 3. Subject to the provisions relating to the registration of trade-marks, so far as they are applicable, service marks used in commerce shall be registrable, in the same manner and with the same effect as are trade-marks, and when registered they shall be entitled to the protection provided herein in the case of trade-marks, except when used so as to represent falsely that the owner thereof makes or sells the goods on which such mark is used. The Commissioner may establish a separate register for such service marks. Applications and procedure under this section shall conform as nearly as practicable to those prescribed for the registration of trade-marks.

Collective and Certification Marks Registrable

SEC. 4. Subject to the provisions relating to the registration of trade-marks, so far as they are applicable, collective and certification marks, including indications of regional origin used in commerce, shall be registrable under this act, in the same manner and with the same effect as are trade-marks, by persons, and nations, States, municipalities, and the like, exercising legitimate control over the use of the marks sought to be registered, even though not possessing an industrial or commercial establishment, and when registered they shall be entitled to the protection provided herein in the case of trade-marks, except when used so as to represent falsely that the owner or a user thereof makes or sells the goods or performs the services on or in connection with which such mark is used. The Commissioner may establish a separate register for such collective marks and certification marks. Applications and procedure under this section shall conform as nearly as practicable to those prescribed for the registration of trade-marks.

Use By Related Companies

SEC. 5. Where a registered mark or a mark sought to be registered is or may be used legitimately by related companies, such use shall inure to the benefit of the registrant or applicant for registration, and such use shall not affect the validity of such mark or of its registration, provided such mark is not used in such manner as to deceive the public.

Disclaimers

SEC. 6. The Commissioner shall require unregistrable matter to be disclaimed, but such disclaimer shall not prejudice or affect the applicant's or owner's rights then existing or thereafter arising in the disclaimed matter, nor shall such disclaimer prejudice or affect the applicant's or owner's rights of registration on another application of later date if the disclaimed matter has become distinctive of the applicant's or owner's goods or services.

Certificates

Sec. 7. (*a*) Certificates of registration of marks registered upon the principal register shall be issued in the name of the United States of America, under the seal of the Patent Office, and shall either be signed by the Commissioner or have his name printed thereon and attested by an Assistant Commissioner or by one of the Law Examiners duly designated by the Commissioner, and a record thereof, together with printed copies of the drawing and statement of the applicant, shall be kept in books for that purpose. The certificate shall reproduce the drawing of the mark, contain the statement of the applicant and state that the mark is registered on the principal register under this act, the date of the first use of the mark, the date of the first use of the mark in commerce, the particular goods or services for which it is registered, the number and date of the registration, the term thereof, the date on which the application for registration was received in the Patent Office, and any conditions and limitations that may be imposed in the grant of the registration.

(*b*) A certificate of registration of a mark upon the principal register provided by this act shall be prima facie evidence of the validity of the registration, registrant's ownership of the mark, and of registrant's exclusive right to use the mark in commerce in connection with the goods or services specified in the certificate, subject to any conditions and limitations stated therein.

(*c*) A certificate of registration of a mark may be issued to the assignee of the applicant, but the assignment must first be recorded in the Patent Office. In case of change of ownership the Commissioner shall, at the request of the owner and upon a proper showing and the payment of the fee herein provided, issue to such assignee a new certificate of registration of the said mark in the name of such assignee, and for the unexpired part of the original period.

(*d*) At any time, upon application of the registrant and payment of the fee herein provided, the Commissioner may permit any registration in the Patent Office to be surrendered, canceled, or for good cause to be amended, and he may permit any registered mark to be disclaimed in whole or in part: *Provided,* That the registration when so amended shall still contain registrable matter and the mark as amended shall still be registrable as a whole, and that such amendment or disclaimer does not involve such changes in the registration as to alter materially the character of the mark. The Commissioner shall make appropriate entry upon the records of the Patent Office and upon the certificate of registration or, if said certificate is lost or destroyed, upon a certified copy thereof.

(*e*) Copies of any records, books, papers, or drawings belonging to the Patent Office relating to marks, and copies of certificates of registration, when authenticated by the seal of the Patent Office and certified by the Commissioner, or in his name by a chief of division duly designated by the Commissioner, shall be evidence in all cases wherein the originals would be evidence; and any person making application therefor and paying the fee required by law shall have such copies.

(*f*) Whenever a material mistake in a registration, incurred through the fault of the Patent Office, is clearly disclosed by the records of the Office a certificate stating the fact and nature of such mistake, signed by the Commissioner and sealed with the seal of the Patent Office, shall be issued without charge and recorded and a printed copy thereof shall be attached to each printed copy of the registration certificate and such corrected certificate shall thereafter have the same effect as if the same had been originally issued in such corrected form, or in the discretion of the Commissioner a new certificate of registration may be issued without charge. All certificates of correction heretofore issued in accordance with the rules of the Patent Office and the registrations to which they are attached shall have the same force and effect as if such certificates and their issue had been specifically authorized by statute.

(*g*) Whenever a mistake has been made in a registration and a showing has been made that such mistake occurred in good faith through the fault of the applicant, the Commissioner is authorized to issue a certificate of correction or, in his discretion, a new certificate upon the payment of the required fee: *Provided,* That the correction does not involve such changes in the registration as to require republication of the mark.

Duration

SEC. 8. (*a*) Each certificate of registration shall remain in force for 20 years: *Provided,* That the registration of any mark under the provisions of this act shall be canceled by the Commissioner at the end of 6 years following its date, unless within 1 year next preceding the expiration of such 6 years the registrant shall file in the Patent Office an affidavit showing that said mark is still in use or showing that its nonuse is due to special circumstances which excuse such nonuse and is not due to any intention to abandon the mark. Special notice of the requirement for such affidavit shall be attached to each certificate of registration.

(*b*) Any registration published under the provisions of subsection (*c*) of section 12 of this act shall be canceled by the Commissioner at the end of 6 years after the date of such publication unless within 1 year next preceding the expiration of such 6 years the registrant shall file in the Patent Office an affidavit showing that said mark is still in use or showing that its nonuse is due to special circumstances which excuse such nonuse and is not due to any intention to abandon the mark.

(*c*) The Commissioner shall notify any registrant who files either of the above-prescribed affidavits of his acceptance or refusal thereof and, if a refusal, the reasons therefor.

Renewal

SEC. 9. Each registration may be renewed for periods of 20 years from the end of the expiring period upon the filing of an application therefor accompanied by an affidavit by the registrant stating that the mark is still in use in commerce and the payment of the renewal fee required by this act; and such application may be made at any time within 6 months before the expiration of the period for which the certificate of registration was issued or renewed, or it may be made within 3 months after such expiration on payment of the additional fee herein provided.

An applicant for renewal not domiciled in the United States shall be subject to and comply with the provisions of section 1 (*d*) hereof.

Assignment

SEC. 10. A registered mark or a mark for which application to register has been filed shall be assignable with the goodwill of the business in which the mark is used, or with that part of the goodwill of the business connected with the use of and symbolized by the mark, and in any such assignment it shall not be necessary to include the goodwill of the business connected with the use of and symbolized by any other mark used in the business or by the name or style under which the business is conducted: *Provided,* That any assigned registration may be canceled at any time if the registered mark is being used by, or with the permission of, the assignee so as to misrepresent the source of the goods or services in connection with which the mark is used. Assignments shall be by instruments in writing duly executed. Acknowledgment shall be prima facie evidence of the execution of an assignment and when recorded in the Patent Office the record shall be prima facie evidence of execution. An assignment shall be void as against any subsequent purchaser for a valuable consideration without notice, unless it is recorded in the Patent Office within 3 months after the date thereof or prior to such subsequent purchase. The Commissioner shall keep a separate record of such assignments submitted to him for recording.

An assignee not domiciled in the United States shall be subject to and comply with the provisions of section 1 (*d*) hereof.

Acknowledgements and Verifications

SEC. 11. Acknowledgments and verifications required hereunder may be made before any person within the United States authorized by law to administer oaths, or, when made in a foreign country, before any diplomatic or consular officer of the United States or before any official authorized to administer oaths in the foreign country concerned whose authority shall be proved by a certificate of a diplomatic or consular officer of the United States, and shall be valid if they comply with the laws of the State or country where made.

Publication

SEC. 12. (*a*) Upon the filing of an application for registration and payment of the fee herein provided, the Commissioner shall refer the application of the Examiner in charge of the registration of marks, who shall cause an examination to be made and, if on such examination it shall appear that the applicant is entitled to registration, the Commissioner shall cause the mark to be published in the *Official Gazette* of the Patent Office.

(*b*) If the applicant is found not entitled to registration, the Examiner shall advise the applicant thereof and of the reasons therefor. The applicant shall have a period of 6 months in which to reply or amend his application, which shall then be reexamined. This procedure may be repeated until (1) the Examiner finally refuses registration of the mark or (2) the applicant fails for a period of 6 months to reply or amend or appeal, whereupon the application shall be deemed to have been abandoned, unless it can be shown to the satisfaction of the Commissioner that the delay in responding was unavoidable, whereupon such time may be extended.

(*c*) A registrant of a mark registered under the provisions of the act of March 3, 1881, or the act of February 20, 1905, may, at any time prior to the expiration of the registration thereof, upon the payment of the prescribed fee file with the Commissioner an affidavit setting forth those goods stated in the registration on which said mark is in use in commerce and that the registrant claims the benefits of this act for said mark. The Commissioner shall publish notice thereof with a reproduction of said mark in the *Official Gazette,* and notify the registrant of such publication and of the requirement for the affidavit of use or nonuse as provided for in subsection (*b*) of section 8 of this act. This subsection shall not be subject to the provisions of section 13 of this act.

Opposition

SEC. 13. Any person who believes that he would be damaged by the registration of a mark upon the principal register may, upon payment of the required fee, file a verified notice of opposition in the Patent Office, stating the grounds therefor, within 30 days after the publication under subsection (*a*) of section 12 of this act of the mark sought to be registered. For good cause shown, the time for filing notice of opposition may be extended by the Commissioner, who shall notify the applicant. An unverified opposition may be filed by a duly authorized attorney, but such opposition shall be null and void unless verified by the opposer within a reasonable time after such filing to be fixed by the Commissioner.

Cancellation

SEC. 14. Any person who believes that he is or will be damaged by the registration of a mark on the principal register established by this act, or under the act of March 3, 1881, or the act of February 20, 1905, may upon the payment of the prescribed fee, apply to cancel said registration—

(*a*) Within 5 years from the date of the registration of the mark under this act; or

(*b*) Within 5 years from the date of the publication under section 12 (*c*) hereof of a mark registered under the act of March 3, 1881, or the act of February 20, 1905; or

(*c*) At any time if the registered mark becomes the common descriptive name of an article or substance on which the patent has expired, or has been abandoned or its registration was obtained fraudulently or contrary to the provisions of section 4 or of subsections (*a*), (*b*), or (*c*) of section 2 of this act for a registration hereunder, or contrary to similar prohibitory provisions of said prior acts for a registration thereunder, or if the registered mark has been assigned and is being used by, or with the permission of, the assignee so as to misrepresent the source of the goods or services in connection with which the mark is used, or if the mark was registered under the act of March 3, 1881, or the act of February 20, 1905, and has not been published under the provisions of subsection (*c*) of section 12 of this act; or

(*d*) At any time in the case of a certification mark on the ground that the registrant (1) does not control, or is not able legitimately to exercise control over, the use of such mark, or (2) engages in the production of marketing of any goods or services to which the mark is applied, or (3) permits the use of such mark for other purposes than as a certification mark, or (4) discriminately refuses to certify or to continue to certify the goods or services of any person who maintains the standards or conditions which such mark certifies.

Provided, That the Federal Trade Commission may apply to cancel on the grounds specified in subsections (*c*) and (*d*) of this section any mark registered on the principal register established by this act, and the prescribed fee shall not be required.

Sec. 15. Except on a ground for which application to cancel may be filed at any time under subsections (*c*) and (*d*) of section 14 of this act, and except to the extent, if any, to which the use of a mark registered on the principal register infringes a valid right acquired under the law of any State or Territory by use of a mark or trade name continuing from a date prior to the date of the publication under this act of such registered mark, the right of the registrant to use such registered mark in commerce for the goods or services on or in connection with which such registered mark has been in continuous use for 5 consecutive years subsequent to the date of such registration and is still in use in commerce, shall be incontestable: *Provided,* That—

(1) There has been no final decision adverse to registrant's claim of ownership of such mark for such goods or services, or to registrant's right to register the same or to keep the same on the register; and

(2) There is no proceeding involving said rights pending in the Patent Office or in a court and not finally disposed of; and

(3) An affidavit is filed with the Commissioner within 1 year after the expiration of any such 5-year period setting forth those goods or services stated in the registration on or in connection with which such mark has been in continuous use for such 5 consecutive years and is still in use in commerce, and the other matters specified in subsections (1) and (2) hereof; and

(4) No incontestable right shall be acquired in a mark or trade name which is the common descriptive name of any article or substance, patented or otherwise.

Subject to the conditions above specified in this section, the incontestable right with reference to a mark registered under this act shall apply to a mark registered under the act of March 3, 1881, or the act of February 20, 1905, upon the filing of the required affidavit with the Commissioner within 1 year after the expiration of any period of 5 consecutive years after the date of publication of a mark under the provisions of subsection (*c*) of section 12 of this act.

The Commissioner shall notify any registrant who files the above-prescribed affidavit of the filing thereof.

Interference

SEC. 16. Whenever application is made for the registration of a mark which so resembles a mark previously registered by another, or for the registration of which another has previously made application, as to be likely when applied to the goods or when used in connection with the services of the applicant to cause confusion or mistake or to deceive purchasers, the Commissioner may declare that an interference exists. No interference shall be declared between an application and the registration of a mark the right to the use of which has become incontestable.

SEC. 17. In every case of interference, opposition to registration, application to register as a lawful concurrent user, or application to cancel the registration of a mark, the Commissioner shall give notice to all parties and shall direct the Examiner in charge of interferences to determine and decide the respective rights of registration.

Sec. 18. In such proceedings the Commissioner may refuse to register the opposed mark, may cancel or restrict the registration of a registered mark, or may refuse to register any or all of several interfering marks, or may register the mark or marks for the person or persons entitled thereto; as the rights of the parties hereunder may be established in the proceedings: *Provided,* That in the case of the registration of any mark based on concurrent use, the Commissioner shall determine and fix the conditions and limitations provided for in subsection (*d*) of section 2 of this act.

Sec. 19. In all inter partes proceedings equitable principles of laches, estoppel, and acquiescence, where applicable may be considered and applied. The provisions of this section shall also govern proceedings heretofore begun in the Patent Office and not finally determined.

Sec. 20. An appeal may be taken to the Commissioner in person from any final decision of the Examiner in charge of interferences or of the registration of marks upon the payment of the prescribed fees.

Sec. 21. Any applicant for registration of a mark, party to an interference proceeding, party to an opposition proceeding, party to an application to register as a lawful concurrent user, party to a cancellation proceeding, or any registrant who has filed an affidavit as provided in section 8, who is dissatisfied with the decision of the Commissioner may appeal to the United States Court of Customs and Patent Appeals or may proceed under section 4915, Revised Statutes, as in the case of applicants for patents, under the same conditions, rules, and procedure as are prescribed in the case of patent appeals or proceedings so far as they are applicable: *Provided,* That any party who is satisfied with the decision of the Commissioner shall, upon the filing of an appeal to the Court of Customs and Patent Appeals by any dissatisfied party, have the right to elect to have all further proceedings under Revised Statutes 4915, by election as provided in Revised Statutes 4911. The Commissioner of Patents shall not be a necessary party to an inter partes proceeding under Revised Statutes 4915, but he shall be notified of the filing of the bill by the Clerk of the Court in which it is filed and the Commissioner shall have the right to intervene in the action.

Registration is Notice

SEC. 22. Registration of a mark on the principal register provided by this act or under the act of March 3, 1881, or the act of February 20, 1905, shall be constructive notice of the registrant's claim of ownership thereof.

TITLE II—THE SUPPLEMENTAL REGISTER

SEC. 23. In addition to the principal register, the Commissioner shall keep a continuation of the register provided in paragraph (*b*) of section 1 of the act of March 19, 1920, entitled "An act to give effect to certain provisions of the convention for the protection of trade-marks and commercial names, made and signed in the city of Buenos Aires, in the Argentine Republic, August 20, 1910, and for other purposes," to be called the supplement register. All marks capable of distinguishing applicant's goods or services and not registrable on the principal register herein provided, except those declared to be unregistrable under paragraphs (*a*), (*b*), (*c*), and (*d*) of section 2 of this act, which have been in lawful use in commerce by the proprietor thereof, upon or in connection with any goods or services for the year preceding the filing of the application may be registered on the supplemental register upon the payment of the prescribed fee and compliance with the provisions of section 1 so far as they are applicable.

Upon the filing of an application for registration on the supplemental register and payment of the fee herein provided the Commissioner shall refer the application of the Examiner in charge of the registration of marks, who shall cause an examination to be made and if on such examination it shall appear that the applicant is entitled to registration, the registration shall be granted. If the applicant is found not entitled to registration the provisions of subsection (*b*) of section 12 of this act shall apply.

For the purposes of registration on the supplemental register, a mark may consist of any trade-mark, symbol, label, package, configuration of goods, name, word, slogan, phrase, surname, geographical name, numeral, or device or any combination of any of the foregoing, but such mark must be capable of distinguishing the applicant's goods or services.

Upon a proper showing by the applicant that he has begun the lawful use of his mark in foreign commerce and that he requires domestic registration as a basis for foreign protection of his mark, the Commissioner may waive the requirement of a full year's use and may grant registration forthwith.

Cancellation

SEC. 24. Marks for the supplemental register shall not be published for or be subject to opposition, but shall be published on registration in the *Official Gazette* of the Patent Office. Whenever any person believes that he is or will be damaged by the registration of a mark on this register he may at any time apply to the Commissioner to cancel such registration. The Commissioner shall refer such application to the Examiner in charge of interferences, who shall give notice thereof to the registrant. If it is found after a hearing before the Examiner that the registrant was not entitled to register the mark at the time of his application for registration thereof, or that the mark is not used by the regisrant or has been abandoned, the registration shall be canceled by the Commissioner.

SEC. 25. The certificates of registration for marks registered on the supplemental register shall be conspicuously different from certificates issued for marks registered on the principal register.

General Provisions

SEC. 26. The provisions of this act shall govern so far as applicable applications for registration and registrations on the supplemental register as well as those on the principal register, but applications for and registrations on the supplemental register shall not be subject to or receive the advantages of sections 2 (*e*), 2 (*f*), 7 (*b*), 12 (*a*), 13 to 18, inclusive, 22, 33, and 42 of this act.

SEC. 27. Registration of a mark on the supplemental register, or under the act of March 19, 1920, shall not preclude registration by the registrant on the principal register established by this act.

SEC. 28. Registration on the supplemental register or under the act of March 19, 1920, shall not be filed in the Department of the Treasury or be used to stop importations.

TITLE III—NOTICE OF REGISTRATION

SEC. 29. Notwithstanding the provisions of section 22 hereof, a registrant of a mark registered under the act of March 3, 1881, or the act of February 20, 1905, or on the principal register established by this act, shall give notice that his mark is registered by displaying with the mark as used the words "Registered in U. S. Patent Office" or "Reg. U. S. Pat. Off." or the letter R enclosed within a circle, thus ®; and in any suit for infringement under this act by such a registrant failing so to mark goods bearing the registered mark, or by a registrant under the act of March 19, 1920, or by the registrant of a mark on the supplemental register provided by this act no profits and no damages shall be recovered under the provisions of this act unless the defendant had actual notice of the registration.

TITLE IV—CLASSIFICATION

SEC. 30. The Commissioner shall establish a classification of goods and services, for convenience of Patent Office administration, but not to limit or extend the applicant's rights. The applicant may register his mark in one application for any or all of the goods or services included in one class, upon or in connection with which he is actually using the mark. The Commissioner may issue a single certificate for one mark registered in a plurality of classes upon payment of a fee equaling the sum of the fees for each registration in each class.

TITLE V—FEES AND CHARGES

SEC. 31. The following fees shall be paid to the Patent Office under this act:

On filing each original application for registration of a mark in each class on either the principal or the supplemental register, $25; on filing each application for renewal in each class, $25; and on filing each application for renewal in each class after expiration of the registration, an additional fee of $5; on filing notice of claim of benefits of this act for a mark to be published under section 12 (*c*) hereof, $10; on filing notice of opposition of application for cancellation, $25; on appeal from an Examiner in charge of the registration of marks to the Commissioner, $25; on appeal from an Examiner in charge of interferences to the Commissioner, $25; for issuance of a new certificate of registration following change of ownership of a mark or correction of a registrant's mistake, $10; for certificate of correction of registrant's mistake, $10; for manuscript copies, for every one hundred words or fraction thereof, 10 cents; for comparing other copies, 5 cents for every one hundred words or fraction thereof; for certifying in any case, additional, $1; for each additional registration or application which may be included under a single certificate, 50 cents additional; for filing disclaimer, amendment, surrender, or cancellation after registration, $10.

For abstracts of title: For the search, 1 hour or less, and certificate, $3; each additional hour or fraction thereof, $1.50; for each brief from the digest of assignments of two hundred words or less, $1.

For certificate that trade-mark has not been registered—search and certificate (for deposit in foreign countries only), $3.

For title reports required for office use, $1.

For a single printed copy of statement and drawing, 10 cents; if certified, for the grant, additional, $1; for the certificate, $1; if renewed, for copy of certificate of renewal, additional, $1.

For photographic copies of records and drawings, the reasonable cost of making them.

For recording every assignment or other paper not exceeding six pages, $3; for each additional two pages or less, $1; for each additional registration or application included, or involved in one writing where more than one is so included or involved, additional, 50 cents.

The Commissioner shall refund fees paid by mistake or in excess.

TITLE VI—REMEDIES

SEC. 32. (1) Any person who shall, in commerce, (*a*) use, without the consent of the registrant, any reproduction, counterfeit, copy, or colorable imitation of any registered mark in connection with the sale, offering for sale, or advertising of any goods or services on or in connection with which such use is likely to cause confusion or mistake or to deceive purchasers as to the source of origin of such goods or services; or (*b*) reproduce, counterfeit, copy, or colorably imitate any such mark and apply such reproduction, counterfeit, copy, or colorable imitation to labels, signs, prints, packages, wrappers, receptacles, or advertisements intended to be used upon or in connection with the sale in commerce of such goods or services, shall be liable to a civil action by the registrant for any or all of the remedies hereinafter provided, except that under subsection (*b*) hereof the registrant shall not be entitled to recover profits or damages unless the acts have been committed with knowledge that such mark is intended to be used to cause confusion or mistake or to deceive purchasers.

(2) Notwithstanding any other provision of this act, the remedies given to the owner of the right infringed shall be limited as follows: (*a*) Where an infringer is engaged solely in the business of printing the mark for others and establishes that he was an innocent infringer the owner of the right infringed shall be entitled as against such infringer only to an injunction against future printing; (*b*) where the infringement complained of is contained in or is part of paid advertising matter in a newspaper, magazine, or other similar periodical the remedies of the owner of the right infringed as against the publisher or distributor of such newspaper,

magazine, or other similar periodical shall be confined to an injunction against the presentation of such advertising matter in future issues of such newspapers, magazines, or other similar periodical: *Provided,* That these limitations shall apply only to innocent infringers; (*c*) injunction relief shall not be available to the owner of the right infringed in respect of an issue of a newspaper, magazine, or other similar periodical containing infringing matter when restraining the dissemination of such infringing matter in any particular issue of such periodical would delay the delivery of such issue after the regular time therefor, and such delay would be due to the method by which publication and distribution of such periodical is customarily conducted in accordance with sound business practice, and not to any method or device adopted for the evasion of this section or to prevent or delay the issuance of an injunction or restraining order with respect to such infringing matter.

SEC. 33. (*a*) Any certificate of registration issued under the act of March 3, 1881, or the act of February 20, 1905, or of a mark registered on the principal register provided by this act and owned by a party to an action shall be admissible in evidence and shall be prima facie evidence of registrant's exclusive right to use the registered mark in commerce on the goods or services specified in the certificate subject to any conditions or limitations stated therein, but shall not preclude an opposing party from proving any legal or equitable defense or defect which might have been asserted if such mark had not been registered.

(*b*) If the right to use the registered mark has become incontestable under section 15 hereof, the certificate shall be conclusive evidence of the registrant's exclusive right to use the registered mark in commerce on or in connection with the goods or services specified in the certificate subject to any conditions or limitations stated therein except when one of the following defenses or defects is established:

(1) That the registration or the incontestable right to use the mark was obtained fraudulently; or

(2) That the mark has been abandoned by the registrant; or

(3) That the registered mark has been assigned and is being used, by or with the permission of the assignee, so as to misrepresent the source of the goods or services in connection with which the mark is used; or

(4) That the use of the name, term, or device charged to be an infringement is a use, otherwise than as a trade or service mark, of the party's individual name in his own business, or of the individual name of anyone in privity with such party, or of a term or device which is descriptive of and used fairly and in good faith only to describe to users the goods or services of such party, or their geographic origin; or

(5) That the mark whose use by a party is charged as an infringement was adopted without knowledge of the registrant's prior use and has been continuously used by such party or those in privity with him from a date prior to the publication of the registered mark under subsection (*a*) or (*c*) of section 12 of this act: *Provided, however,* That this defense or defect shall apply only for the area in which such continuous prior use is proved.

(6) That the mark whose use is charged as an infringement was registered and used prior to the publication under subsection (*a*) or (*c*) of section 12 of this act of the registered mark of the registrant, and not abandoned: *Provided, however,* That this defense or defect shall apply only where the said mark has been published pursuant to subsection (*c*) of section 12 and shall apply only for the area in which the mark was used prior to the date of publication of the registrant's mark under subsection (*a*) or (*c*) of section 12 of this act.

(7) That the mark has been or is being used to violate the antitrust laws of the United States.

SEC. 34. The several courts vested with jurisdiction of civil actions arising under this act shall have power to grant injunctions, according to the principles of equity and upon such terms as the court may deem reasonable, to prevent the violation of any right of the registrant of a mark registered in the Patent Office. Any such injunction may include a provision directing the defendant to file with the court and serve on the plaintiff within 30 days after the service on the defendant of such injunction, or such extended period as the court may direct, a report in writing under oath setting forth in detail the manner and form in which the defendant has complied with the injunction. Any such injunction granted upon hearing, after notice to the defendant, by any district court of the United States, may be served on the parties against whom such injunction is granted anywhere in the United States where they may be found, and shall be operative and may be enforced by proceedings to punish for contempt, or otherwise, by the court by which such injunction was granted, or by any other United States district court in whose jurisdiction the defendant may be found.

The said courts shall have jurisdiction to enforce said injunction, as herein provided, as fully as if the injunction had been granted by the district court in which it is sought to be enforced. The Clerk of the Court or judge granting the injunction shall, when required to do so by the court before which application to enforce said injunction is made, transfer without delay to said court a certified copy of all papers on file in his office upon which said injunction was granted.

It shall be the duty of the clerks of such courts within 1 month after the filing of any action, suit, or proceeding arising under the provisions of this act to give notice thereof in writing to the Commissioner setting forth in order so far as known the names and addresses of the litigants and the designating number or numbers of the registration or registrations upon which the action, suit, or proceeding has been brought, and in the event any other registration be subsequently included in the action, suit, or proceeding by amendment, answer, or other pleading, the clerk shall give like notice thereof to the Commissioner, and within 1 month after the decision is rendered, appeal taken or a decree issued the Clerk of the Court shall give notice thereof to the Commissioner, and it shall be the duty of the Commissioner on receipt of such notice forthwith to endorse the same upon the file wrapper of the said registration or registrations and to incorporate the same as a part of the contents of said file wrapper.

Sec. 35. When a violation of any right of the registrant of a mark registered in the Patent Office shall have been established in any civil action arising under this act, the plaintiff shall be entitled, subject to the provisions of sections 29 and 31 (1) (*b*), and subject to the principles of equity, to recover (1) defendant's profits, (2) any damages sustained by the plaintiff, and (3) the costs of the action. The court shall assess such profits and damages or cause the same to be assessed under its direction. In assessing profits the plaintiff shall be required to prove defendant's sales only; defendant must prove all elements of cost or deduction claimed. In assessing damages the court may enter judgment, according to the circumstances of the case, for any sum above the amount found as actual damages, not exceeding three times such amount. If the court shall find that the amount of the recovery based on profits is either inadequate or excessive the court may in its discretion enter judgment for such sum as the court shall find to be just, according to the circumstances of the case. Such sum in either of the above circumstances shall constitute compensation and not a penalty.

Sec. 36. In any action arising under this act, in which a violation of any right of the registrant of a mark registered in the Patent Office shall have been established, the court may order that all labels, signs, prints, packages, wrappers, receptacles, and advertisements in the possession of the defendant, bearing the registered mark or any reproduction, counterfeit, copy, or colorable imitation thereof, and all plates, molds, matrices, and other means of making the same, shall be delivered up and destroyed.

Sec. 37. In any action involving a registered mark the court may determine the right to registration, order the cancellation of registrations, in whole or in part, restore canceled registrations, and otherwise rectify the register with respect to the registrations of any party to the action. Decrees and orders shall be certified by the court to the Commissioner, who shall make appropriate entry upon the records of the Patent Office, and shall be controlled thereby.

Sec. 38. Any person who shall procure registration in the

Patent Office of a mark by a false or fraudulent declaration or representation, oral or in writing, or by any false means, shall be liable in a civil action by any person injured thereby for any damages sustained in consequence thereof.

SEC. 39. The district and territorial courts of the United States shall have original jurisdiction, the circuit courts of appeal of the United States and the United States Court of Appeals for the District of Columbia shall have appellate jurisdiction, of all actions arising under this act, without regard to the amount in controversy or to diversity or lack of diversity of the citizenship of the parties.

SEC. 40. Writs of certiorari may be granted by the Supreme Court of the United States for the review of cases arising under this act in the same manner as provided for in cases under the patent laws.

SEC. 41. The Commissioner shall make rules and regulations, not inconsistent with law, for the conduct of proceedings in the Patent Office under this act.

TITLE VII—IMPORTATION FORBIDDEN OF GOODS BEARING INFRINGING MARKS OR NAMES

SEC. 42. That no article of imported merchandise which shall copy or simulate the name of any domestic manufacture, or manufacturer, or trader, or of any manufacturer or trader located in any foreign country which, by treaty, convention, or law affords similar privileges to citizens of the United States, or which shall copy or simulate a trade-mark registered in accordance with the provisions of this act or shall bear a name or mark calculated to induce the public to believe that the article is manufactured in the United States, or that it is manufactured in any foreign country or locality other than the country or locality in which it is in fact manufactured, shall be admitted to entry at any customhouse of the United States; and, in order to aid the officers of the customs in enforcing this prohibition, any domestic manufacturer or trader, and any foreign manufacturer or trader, who is entitled under the provisions of a treaty, convention, declaration, or agreement between the United States and any foreign country to the advantages afforded by law to citizens of the United States in respect to trade-marks and commercial names, may require his name and residence, and the name of the locality in which his goods are manufactured, and a copy of the certificate of registration of his trade-mark, issued in accordance with the provisions of this act, to be recorded in books which shall be kept for this purpose in the Department of the Treasury, under such regulations as the Secretary of the Treasury shall prescribe, and may furnish to the Department facsimiles of his name, the name of the locality in which his goods are manufactured, or of his registered trade-mark, and thereupon the Secretary of the Treasury shall cause one or more copies of the same to be transmitted to each collector or other proper officer of customs.

TITLE VIII—FALSE DESIGNATIONS OF ORIGIN AND FALSE DESCRIPTIONS FORBIDDEN

SEC. 43. (*a*) Any person who shall affix, apply, or annex, or use in connection with any goods or services, or any container or containers for goods, a false designation of origin, or any false description or representation, including words or other symbols tending falsely to describe or represent the same, and shall cause such goods or services to enter into commerce, and any person who shall with knowledge of the falsity of such designation of origin or description or representation cause or procure the same to be transported or used in commerce or deliver the same to any carrier to be transported or used, shall be liable to a civil action by any person doing business in the locality falsely indicated as that of origin or in the region in which said locality is situated, or by any person who believes that he is or is likely to be damaged by the use of any such false description or representation.

(*b*) Any goods marked or labeled in contravention of the provisions of this section shall not be imported into the United States or admitted to entry at any customhouse of the United States. The owner, importer, or consignee of goods refused entry at any customhouse under this section may have any recourse by protest or appeal that is given under the customs revenue laws or may have the remedy given by this act in cases involving goods refused entry or seized.

TITLE IX—INTERNATIONAL CONVENTIONS

SEC. 44. (*a*) The Commissioner shall keep a register of all marks communicated to him by the international bureaus provided for by the conventions for the protection of industrial property, trade-marks, trade and commercial names, and the repression of unfair competition to which the United States is or may become a party, and upon the payment of the fees required by such conventions and the fees herein prescribed may place the marks so communicated upon such register. This register shall show a facsimile of the mark or trade or commercial name; the name, citizenship, and address of the registrant; the number, date, and place of the first registration of the mark, including the dates on which application for such registration was filed and granted and the term of such registration; a list of goods or services to which the mark is applied as shown by the registration in the country of origin, and such other data as may be useful concerning the mark. This register shall be a continuation of the register provided in section 1 (*a*) of the act of March 19, 1920.

(*b*) Persons who are nationals of, domiciled in, or have a bona fide and effective business or commercial establishment in any foreign country, which is a party to (1) the International Convention for the Protection of Industrial Property, signed at Paris on March 20, 1883; or (2) the General Inter-American Convention for Trade-Mark and Commercial Protection signed at Washington on February 20, 1929; or (3) any other convention or treaty relating to trade-marks, trade or commercial names, or the repression of unfair competition to which the United States is a party, shall be entitled to the benefits and subject to the provisions of this act to the extent and under the conditions essential to give effect to any such conventions and treaties so long as the United

States shall continue to be a party thereto, except as provided in the following paragraphs of this section.

(*c*) No registration of a mark in the United States by a person described in paragraph (*b*) of this section shall be granted until such mark has been registered in the country of origin of the applicant, unless the applicant alleges use in commerce.

For the purposes of this section, the country of origin of the applicant is the country in which he has a bona fide and effective industrial or commercial establishment, or if he has not such an establishment the country in which he is domiciled, or if he has not a domicile in any of the countries described in paragraph (*b*) of this section, the country of which he is a national.

(*d*) An application for registration of a mark under sections 1, 2, 3, 4, or 23 of this act filed by a person described in paragraph (*b*) of this section who has previously duly filed an application for registration of the same mark in one of the countries described in paragraph (*b*) shall be accorded the same force and effect as would be accorded to the same application if filed in the United States on the same date on which the application was first filed in such foreign country: *Provided,* That—

(1) The application of the United States is filed within 6 months from the date on which the application was first filed in the foreign country;

(2) The application conforms as nearly as practicable to the requirements of this act, but use in commerce need not be alleged;

(3) The rights acquired by third parties before the date of the filing of the first application in the foreign country shall in no way be affected by a registration obtained on an application filed under this subsection (*d*);

(4) Nothing in this subsection (*d*) shall entitle the owner of a registration granted under this section to sue for acts committed prior to the date on which his mark was registered in this country unless the registration is based on use in commerce.

(*e*) A mark duly registered in the country of origin of the foreign applicant may be registered on the principal register if eligible, otherwise on the supplemental register herein provided.

The application therefor shall be accompanied by a certified copy of the application for or registration in the country of origin of the applicant.

(*f*) The registration of a mark under the provisions of paragraphs (*c*), (*d*), and (*e*) of this section by a person described in paragraph (*b*) shall be independent of the registration in the country of origin and the duration, validity, or transfer in the United States of such registration shall be governed by the provisions of this act.

(*g*) Trade names or commercial names of persons described in paragraph (*b*) of this section shall be protected without the obligation of filing or registration whether or not they form parts of marks.

(*h*) Any person designated in paragraph (*b*) of this section as entitled to the benefits and subject to the provisions of this act shall be entitled to effective protection against unfair competition, and the remedies provided herein for infringement of marks shall be available so far as they may be appropriate in repressing acts of unfair competition.

(*i*) Citizens or residents of the United States shall have the same benefits as are granted by this section to persons described in paragraph (*b*) hereof.

TITLE X—CONSTRUCTION AND DEFINITIONS

SEC. 45. In the construction of this act, unless the contrary is plainly apparent from the context—

The United States includes and embraces all territory which is under its jurisdiction and control.

The word "commerce" means all commerce which may lawfully be regulated by Congress.

The term "principal register" refers to the register provided for by sections 1 through 22 hereof, and the term "supplemental register" refers to the register provided for by sections 23 through 28 hereof.

The term "person" and any other word or term used to designate the applicant or other entitled to a benefit or privilege or rendered liable under the provisions of this act includes a juristic person as well as a natural person. The term "juristic person" includes a firm, corporation, union, association, or other organization capable of suing and being sued in a court of law.

The terms "applicant" and "registrant" embrace the legal representatives and successors and assigns of such applicant or registrant.

The term "Commissioner" means the Commissioner of Patents.

The term "related company" means any person who legitimately controls or is controlled by the registrant or applicant for registration in respect to the nature and quality of the goods or services in connection with which the mark is used.

The terms "trade name" and "commercial name" include individual names and surnames, firm names and trade names used by manufacturers, industrialists, merchants, agriculturists, and others to identify their businesses, vocations, or occupations; the names or titles lawfully adopted and used by persons, firms, associations, corporations, companies, unions, and any manufacturing, industrial, commercial agricultural, or other organizations engaged in trade or commerce and capable of suing and being sued in a court of law.

The term "trade-mark" includes any word, name, symbol, or device or any combination thereof adopted and used by a manufacturer or merchant to identify his goods and distinguish them from those manufactured or sold by others.

The term "service mark" means a mark used in the sale or advertising of services to identify the services of one person and distinguish them from the services of others and includes without limitation the marks, names, symbols, titles, designations, slogans, character names, and distinctive features of radio or other advertising used in commerce.

The term "certification mark" means a mark used upon or in connection with the products or services of one or more persons other than the owner of the mark to certify regional or other origin, material, mode of manufacture, quality, accuracy, or other characteristics of such goods or services or that the work or labor on the goods or services was performed by members of a union or other organization.

The term "collective mark" means a trade-mark or service mark used by the members of a cooperative, an association or other collective group or organization and includes marks used to indicate membership in a union, an association or other organization.

The term "mark" includes any trade-mark, service mark, collective mark, or certification mark entitled to registration under this act whether registered or not.

For the purposes of this act a mark shall be deemed to be used in commerce (*a*) on goods when it is placed in any manner on the goods or their containers or the displays associated therewith or on the tags or labels affixed thereto and the goods are sold or transported in commerce and (*b*) on services when it is used or displayed in the sale or advertising of services and the services are rendered in commerce.

A mark shall be deemed to be "abandoned"—

(*a*) When its use has been discontinued with intent not to resume. Intent not to resume may be inferred from circumstances. Nonuse for 2 consecutive years shall be prima facie abandonment.

(*b*) When any course of conduct of the registrant, including acts of omission as well as commission, causes the mark to lose its significance as an indication of origin.

The term "colorable imitation" includes any mark which so resembles a registered mark as to be likely to cause confusion or mistake or to deceive purchasers.

The term "registered mark" means a mark registered in the United States Patent Office under this act or under the act of March 3, 1881, or the act of February 20, 1905, or the act of March 19, 1920. The phrase "marks registered in the Patent Office" means registered marks.

The term "act of March 3, 1881," "act of February 20, 1905," or "act of March 19, 1920," means the respective act as amended.

A "counterfeit" is a spurious mark which is identical with, or substantially indistinguishable from, a registered mark.

Words used in the singular include the plural and vice versa.

The intent of this act is to regulate commerce within the control of Congress by making actionable the deceptive and misleading use of marks in such commerce; to protect registered marks used in such commerce from interference by State, or territorial legislation; to protect persons engaged in such commerce against unfair competition; to prevent fraud and deception in such commerce by the use of reproductions, copies, counterfeits, or colorable imitations of registered marks; and to provide rights and remedies stipulated by treaties and conventions respecting trade-marks, trade names, and unfair competition entered into between the United States and foreign nations.

TITLE XI—REPEAL OF PREVIOUS ACTS

SEC. 46. (*a*) This act shall be in force and take effect one year from its enactment, but except as otherwise herein specifically provided shall not affect any suit, proceeding, or appeal then pending. All acts and parts of acts inconsistent herewith are hereby repealed effective 1 year from the enactment hereof, including the following acts insofar as they are inconsistent herewith: The act of Congress approved March 3, 1881, entitled "An act to authorize the registration of trade-marks and protect the same"; the act approved August 5, 1882, entitled "An act relating to the registration of trade-marks"; the act of February 20, 1905 (U. S. C., title 15, secs. 81 to 109, inclusive), entitled "An act to authorize the registration of trade-marks used in commerce with foreign nations or among the several States or with Indian tribes, and to protect the same," and the amendments thereto by the acts of May 4, 1906 (U. S. C., title 15, secs. 131 and 132; 34 Stat. 169), March 2, 1907 (34 Stat. 1251, 1252), February 18, 1909 (35 Stat. 627, 628), February 18, 1911 (36 Stat. 918), January 8, 1913 (37 Stat. 649), June 7, 1924 (43 Stat. 647), March 4, 1925 (43 Stat. 1268, 1269), April 11, 1930 (46 Stat. 155), June 10, 1938 (Public, Numbered 586, Seventy-fifth Congress, ch. 332, third session); the act of March 19, 1920 (U. S. C., title 15, secs. 121 to 128, inclusive), entitled "An act to give effect to certain provisions of the convention for the protection of trade-marks and commercial names made and signed in the city of Buenos

Aires, in the Argentine Republic, August 20, 1910, and for other purposes," and the amendments thereto, including the act of June 10, 1938 (Public, Numbered 586, Seventy-fifth Congress, ch. 332, third session): *Provided,* That this repeal shall not affect the validity of registrations granted or applied for under any of said acts prior to the effective date of this act, or rights or remedies thereunder except as provided in sections 8, 12, 14, 15, and 47 of this act; but nothing contained in this act shall be construed as limiting, restricting, modifying, or repealing any statute in force on the effective date of this act which does not relate to trade-marks, or as restricting or increasing the authority of any Federal department or regulatory agency except as may be specifically provided in this act.

(*b*) Registrations now existing under the act of March 3, 1881, or the act of February 20, 1905, shall continue in full force and effect for the unexpired terms thereof and may be renewed under the provisions of section 9 of this act. Such registrations and the renewals thereof shall be subject to and shall be entitled to the benefits of the provisions of this act to the same extent and with the same force and effect as though registered on the principal register established by this act except as limited in sections 8, 12, 14, and 15 of this act. Marks registered under the "10-year proviso" of section 5 of the act of February 20, 1905, as amended, shall be deemed to have become distinctive of the registrant's goods in commerce under paragraph (*f*) of section 2 of this act and may be renewed under section 9 hereof as marks coming within said paragraph.

Registrations now existing under the act of March 19, 1920, shall expire 6 months after the effective date of this act, or 20 years from the dates of their registrations, whichever date is later. Such registrations shall be subject to and entitled to the benefits of the provisions of this act relating to marks registered on the supplemental register established by this act, and may not be renewed unless renewal is required to support foreign registrations. In that event renewal may be effected on the supplemental register under the provisions of section 9 of this act.

Marks registered under previous acts may, if eligible, also be registered under this act.

Sec. 47. (*a*) All applications for registration pending in the Patent Office at the effective date of this act may be amended, if practicable, to bring them under the provisions of this act. The prosecution of such applications so amended and the grant of registrations thereon shall be proceeded with in accordance with the provisions of this act. If such amendments are not made, the prosecution of said applications shall be proceeded with and registrations thereon granted in accordance with the acts under which said applications were filed, and said acts are hereby continued in force to this extent and for this purpose only, notwithstanding the foregoing general repeal thereof.

(*b*) In any case in which an appeal is pending before the United States Court of Customs and Patent Appeals or any United States circuit court of appeals or the United States Court of Appeals for the District of Columbia or the United States Supreme Court at the effective date of this act, the court, if it be of the opinion that the provisions of this act are applicable to the subject matter of the appeal, may apply such provision or may remand the case to the Commissioner or to the district court for the taking of additional evidence or a new trial or for reconsideration of the decision on the record as made, as the appellate court may deem proper.

Sec. 48. Section 4 of the act of January 5, 1905 (U. S. C., title 36, sec. 4), as amended, entitled "An act to incorporate the National Red Cross," and section 7 of the act of June 15, 1916 (U. S. C., title 36, sec. 27), entitled "An act to incorporate the Boy Scouts of America, and for other purposes," and the act of June 20, 1936 (U. S. C., title 22, sec. 248), entitled "An act to prohibit the commercial use of the coat of arms of the Swiss Confederation," are not repealed or affected by this act.

Sec. 49. Nothing herein shall adversely affect the rights or the enforcement of rights in marks acquired in good faith prior to the effective date of this act.

Sec. 50. If any provision of this act or the application of such provision to any person or circumstance is held invalid, the remainder of the act shall not be affected thereby.

Approved July 5, 1946.

Some Decisions of United States Courts *

The danger of registration being disallowed because of conflict with names already registered is a serious one. It is the practice of the authorities to protect prior registrants by giving them the benefit of any doubt, especially if the new article will be distributed through the same trade channels as the old, or if the old product has been nationally and heavily advertised, even if the two articles are technically in different classes on the register.

The following examples will illustrate recent lines of decision on this point. Similarity of sound is frequently a decisive factor in rejection.

(a) NAMES IN CONFLICT WITH ALREADY REGISTERED NAMES

The names listed in the left-hand column were rejected in the same class on account of the previously registered trade-marks listed in the right-hand column.

BROXIE	MOXIE
TIOL	TYDOL and TYCOL
SYNCERA WAX	CERAWAX
SNOW PRINCESS	PRINCESS
NOVITE	OAKITE
SNOW BIRD	SNOW FLYER
SPORTA	SPORTADOR
LES BOURGEONS	BOURJOIS
TAUREX (a laxative)	TOREX (a beef bouillon)
(because both are distributed by drug stores)	
PLASTEX	PLASTINT

* Cousins and Wadsworth, *Trade Names,* Harlequin Press.

EX-OL	REXALL
REX-A-COLD, OINTREX	REXALL, AGAREX, ALCO-REX
BLACK AND TAN	BLACK AND WHITE
FRIGIDIZED FISH	FRIGIDAIRE
CANZOL	PENNZOIL

FLAMETEX, however, was held registrable against CELOTEX in the same class because -TEX occurs in many other trade names and is not, like the -NZOIL in PENNZOIL, a distinctive and original feature.

(b) DESCRIPTIVE NAMES

MURAL (wall radiators)—Name disallowed.

MODEL-B (milling machinery)—Not registrable.

INDIVIDUALLY WRAPPED—Not registrable, being purely informative and descriptive.

D I P (candy)—Held to be registrable because not *merely* descriptive.

(c) GEOGRAPHICAL NAMES

VIGO (water softener)—Merely geographical, being the name of a county in Indiana and other places—therefore not registrable.

EVEREST—Accepted, although a rare surname and a geographical name, because deception unlikely.

CHRYSLER, PLYMOUTH (accompanied by an historical illustration)—Accepted because the name PLYMOUTH has a special historic significance and is therefore not *merely* geographical.

TRADE NAME HELD MISLEADING *

Higher courts consistently hold that all trade-marks are invalid and unlawful which mislead or deceive the buyer.

---

* L. T. Parker, *Drug and Cosmetic Industry,* August 1945.

For example, in Howe versus Federal Trade Commission, 148 Fed. (2d) 561, reported July, 1945, it was shown that a corporation's place of business was in Seattle, Washington. It was engaged in the sale and distribution of cosmetic preparations. For the purpose of inducing the purchase of the cosmetics, the company used the trade-mark "Hollywood" and the legend "Favorite of the Stars."

A suit was filed against the company by the Federal Trade Commission. During the trial testimony was given that the company manufactured and sold some twenty items, but only three of its items were obtained from sources in Hollywood. Also, the testimony showed that the company's preparations were not recognized by the Hollywood actresses as being of superior quality.

In view of this testimony the Commission held that use of the word "Hollywood" was deceptive and misleading, and concluded such deception to constitute unfair practice within the meaning of the Federal Trade Commission Act. The Commission issued an order to cease and desist from using the word "Hollywood" to designate any product which is not in fact manufactured in Hollywood, California, or using the words, "Favorite of the Stars."

RESTRAINT IN USE OF OWN NAME

A court may restrain a person from using *his own name* to prevent confusion of the buying public where there is bad faith.

For illustration, in one of the leading cases, Vick Medicine Company versus Vick Chemical, 5 Cir., 11 F. (2d) 33, it was disclosed that a man named "Vick" established a business and began to manufacture and sell his product in competition to Vick Chemical Company. The testimony indicated that the new user intended to benefit from the publicity and advertising of the latter company on its "Vicks Vapor Rub."

It is important to know that the higher court directed that the new Mr. Vick *stop using his own name* in the manufacture and sale of any and all products similar to "Vicks Vapor Rub."

Difference between Trade-Mark and Trade Name *

. . . . The law applicable to the use of trade names and trade-marks in actions for unfair competition is substantially the same (Howard versus Henriques, 5 N. Y. Super. Ct. 725, 3 Sandf. 725; Glen and Hall Mfg. Co. versus Hall, 61 N. Y. 226, 19 Am. Rep. 278), although there is a distinction in definition according to geographical limitations on use (Ball versus Broadway Bazaar, 194 N. Y., 429, 87 N. E. 674). It is observed in the last-cited case that a trade name relates to a business and its goodwill rather than a vendible commodity, and that the trade-mark represents the goodwill in the market, while the trade name proclaims it to those who pass the shop.

Qualifying a Trade-Mark for Registration under the Lanham Act †

There is no clear rule as to what trade-marks can be registered under the Lanham Act. Section 11 merely says that the mark "must be capable of distinguishing the applicant's goods."

Both the old and the new laws stress situations where trade-marks either cannot be registered at all or qualify only under exceptional conditions. If you avoid these restrictions, chances are your mark will be approved. This is why it is vital to understand fully the limitations on registration, as will be explained in the following.

These restrictive provisions are mainly limited to the Principal Register.

---

* 194 N. Y., 87 N. E. 674, 675.

† This article, part of a 56-page analysis by the Research Institute of America, describes the types of marks that will qualify for the Principal Register. The analysis, "Preparing for the New Trade-Mark Law," was written by Walter J. Derenberg, attorney and authority on trade-mark law, in collaboration with the Institute's Board of Editors, headed by Leo M. Cherne. The excerpt is reprinted by permission of the Research Institute of America, 292 Madison Avenue, New York City.

REGISTERING GEOGRAPHICAL NAMES

The Lanham Act makes it easier to use geographical names for trade-marks. Under the former law, names which are "merely geographical" could not be registered, but section 2(*e*) of the Lanham Act allows registration of such marks if they are not *primarily* geographically descriptive *when applied to the goods that carry them.*

The following paragraphs indicate the types of names which are eligible.

Words of Remote Geographical Significance

A word like "Kem" for playing cards will be registrable even though it is the name of a river in Siberia. This word was not considered eligible for registration under the old law.

Observation: Until quite recently, the Patent Office refused registration only if the name was "reasonably well-known" in its geographical meaning, but lately *the change in the law will halt this recent tendency of the Patent Office to prohibit registration of names with relatively little geographical significance.*

Geographical Words with Other Meanings

A word like "Canada Dry" has nongeographical meaning, but the fact that it also has a geographical meaning has prevented registration under the former law. Under the Lanham Act, it is probable that a word like "Plymouth" for automobiles will be registrable on the Principal Register on the ground that its meaning, as applied to automobiles, is not "primarily" geographical. Similarly, words like "Aurora," "Reliance" or "Lincoln" may be registrable since the *primary* meaning refers to other characteristics or is of greater historical than geographical significance.

The basic point is that the old law categorically forbade registration of names which were "merely geographical," but the new law adds the words "as applied to the goods of the applicant." A word like "Vienna" for bread may have no apparent geographical significance when applied to bread manufactured in the United States.

Observation: However, the new law, section 2 (e), specifically prohibits the use of geographical terms that might *deceive* the public. For instance, "House of France" or "Parisian" may be refused registration on the ground that they indicate that the trade-marked product originated in France. Where there is no question of such deception, a word like "Paris," as used on men's garters, will be registrable on the Principal Register.

Observation: Note that even under the old law names like "Vienna" bread, and "Gibraltar" brushes have been sustained on the ground that the geographical connotation bears no conceivable relationship to the origin and character of the merchandise.

Semi-Geographical Names

Under the Lanham Act, there is likely to be a considerable difference in the treatment of semi-geographical words like "Mid-West" and "Old English." These words were not permitted registration under the old law (even though "Mid-West" had been registered on many previous occasions). Under the new act, words like "Globe" as applied to a machine, or "Orient" on a typewriter, will probably be registrable since they can hardly be considered "primarily geographically descriptive" in connection with such articles.

It is interesting to note that the Supreme Court, taking a more liberal view than the Patent Office, had given full trade-mark protection to the name "American Girl" as applied to shoes. The Lanham Act follows the Supreme Court, rather than the Patent Office view.

Court Protection for Geographical Words with Secondary Meaning

The underlying theory of the ban against names which are "merely geographical" was explained in the following Supreme Court decision: "Could anyone prevent all others from using them, or from selling articles produced in the districts they describe under those applications, it would greatly embarrass trade, and secure exclusive rights to individuals in that which is the common right of many."

Under this rule, words like "Lackawanna" were denied trade-mark protection. But even such geographical names have been judicially recognized and protected despite their unregistrability in cases of secondary meaning.

A mark may have a primarily geographical meaning and still be protected on the ground that it has acquired a "secondary meaning" as a trade-mark. Names like "Waltham" watches, "Elgin" jewelry, "Chartreuse" cordial, "Budweiser" beer, and many others have been protected because their original geographical meaning is now secondary to their trade-mark meaning.

In the "La Touraine" case, the Second Circuit Court of Appeals held that the name as used on coffee, tea and related products was a valid registered trade-mark despite the fact that it also signified a certain geographical area in France. It was indicated that even if the word "La Touraine" once defined an ancient French province, it had no geographical significance "when applied to the goods of the applicant." Consequently, defendant's use of the word "Lorraine" for the same products was held to constitute trade-mark infringement. The majority of the court significantly observed: "Be that as it may, Congress has shown its continued interest in trade-mark protection by the comprehensive new codification of trade-mark law embodied in the Trade-Mark Act of July 5, 1946, which not merely amplified the Act of 1905, but gave to this property right a legislative standing it had not had before."

Observation: Caution: As noted earlier, a name that was originally geographical may be popularized to the point where it loses not only its geographical connotation but its trade-mark significance as well. Thus, "Camembert" and "Gruyere" cheese have become common nouns for certain types of cheese. On the other hand, "Roquefort" is still a valid trade-mark in this country because of the vigilance and well-planned strategy of the French trade-mark owner. But "Vichy," which at one time had protection similar to such names as "Carlsbad" or "Manitou," has been allowed by the French Government gradually to pass into the public domain in this country.

Lanham Act Protection for Geographical Words with Secondary Meaning

Under the old law, words like "Canada Dry" and a map of Canada were denied registration despite the mark's recognized secondary meaning. It allowed such marks only where there was a 10-year period of exclusive use before 1905. A more liberal approach is taken under the new law. Under it, any originally geographical name may become eligible for registration on the Principal Register if the name has become distinctive of the applicant's goods in commerce.

MERELY DESCRIPTIVE MARKS NOT ALLOWED

The former rules governing the registration of descriptive marks will probably continue. The Lanham Act forbids registration of any mark which "when applicable to the goods of the applicant is merely descriptive or deceptively misdescriptive of them." This undoubtedly includes marks that are descriptive of the goods' character or quality, although the new Act, unlike the old, is not specific on this point.

It will probably be harder to register descriptive terms than surnames or geographical names. The latter are rejected only where "primarily" geographical or surnames. But "primarily" descriptive is not the yardstick for rejection. A term will be turned down if it is "merely descriptive." (Efforts in Congress to loosen that criterion by substituting "primarily merely descriptive" were defeated.)

Suggestive versus Descriptive

If you can prove your mark is actually "suggestive" and not "merely descriptive," you will be safe, but the borderline is narrow. One court approved the mark "Mouse Seed" for an insecticide by laying down the following test for suggestiveness:

"Mature thought would probably lead to but one conclusion—that a mouse poison was indicated—but it requires thought to reach this conclusion. The words used together possess an element of incongruity which make them unusual and unique and therefore, in our opinion, a valid trade-mark."

Illustration: Cases where trade-marks have been upheld as "suggestive" include the following:

"One Minute" for washing machines, "Minit-mix" for prepared biscuit dough and "Uneeda" for biscuits. "Chicken of the Sea" for canned tuna fish was passed by the Patent Office, but held invalid as "descriptive" by the courts.

The problem of distinction is shown by some of the following cases where trade-marks were rejected as "descriptive."

"Hi-Octane" for gasoline (descriptive of physical or chemical characteristics); "Slip Away" for toilet seat covers (descriptive of mode of operation); "Leak Proof" for roofing materials (descriptive of intended use or purpose). "Quikmix" for biscuit flour and "Instant Whip" for whipped cream were also rejected as descriptive. Protection was likewise denied the word "Specs" as applied to a mask for fowl; decision held the word was "but a figurative description of the article."

Recommendation: It is almost impossible to draw the line between "descriptive" and "suggestive." Therefore, in selecting a new trade-mark you should avoid any term which may be too close to the borderline. This applies to picture trade-marks as well.

Misspelling Is no Help

Mere misspelling of an otherwise descriptive term does not make it registrable. Marks like "Rubberoid," "Dioxygen," and "Kantleek" have been thrown out.

Foreign Descriptives Barred too

Words which are descriptive in a foreign language or even in Latin or Greek cannot be registered either. The word "Peau-douce," meaning "softskin" in French, was rejected for a skin lotion. "Dermalait" for a milky skin lotion was also refused because "derma" means skin in Greek and "lait" is French for milk. In one instance even the word "Saniga," Esperanto for "sanitary," was rejected. There is no reason to suppose the Lanham Act will change this policy.

Laudatory Words Are Valid

However, general laudatory words like "Excelsior," "Eureka" and "Majestic" are not considered descriptive and may be registered.

Observation: There are hundreds of "Excelsior" or "Gold Medal" and similar marks in use. As a result, the courts will not protect the owner against an unfair competitor as fully as where a unique and arbitrarily coined name (such as "Kodak") is involved.

Use of Grade Marks

Grade names, used only to distinguish one particular class or quality from other goods of the same manufacturer, may not be registered, but registration is available where a grade mark simultaneously and primarily denotes the origin or ownership. Then it is a valid trade-mark. Thus, the Commissioner said when approving the number "5897":

"It does not appear that anyone else has ever used the numeral '5987' as a trade-mark and it seems to me the mark as used by applicant conveys true trade-mark significance to such an extent that should purchasers see this mark on seed corn produced and sold by others than applicant the purchasers would be deceived and misled into believing the seed corn to be applicant's product."

Similarly, the designation "D-11" was registered as a trade-mark for photographic developer. Theory was that the mark denoted the origin as well as style and quality.

Recommendation: If you make many different articles, consider selecting one trade-mark for all of them and, in addition, using certain grade designations for each item. If this is impractical, each article should be so marked as to give its name an independent trade-mark significance which goes beyond merely designating one of many available grades or styles.

Numerals and Letters Registrable

Numbers, initials, letters of the alphabet may be registered when they distinguish particular goods. Some foreign countries prohibit these registrations but they have always been accepted here. As result, "Z.B.T." (talcum powder), "RCA" (radios), "4711" (perfume), and "57" (groceries) are all registrable.

Misdescriptive Not Allowed

No trade-mark which is "misdescriptive" can be registered. Both the courts and the Patent Office have uniformly denied them protection. Thus, in the case of "Holed Tite," misspelling of "hold" and "tight" was held misdescriptive when used on egg flats or similar articles. So was the word "Metalized" for radio tubes which actually contained no metal. The language of the new law excluding "deceptively misdescriptive" marks merely clarifies, but does not modify, this point.

Observation: Note that rules against descriptive marks do not affect the Lanham Act's protection of descriptive terms which have acquired a distinctive, exclusive trade-mark meaning. This is a big change from the former law. Before July 1947, such terms could not be registered unless used exclusively as trade-marks for at least 10 years before 1905. Under the Lanham Act, these terms can be registered upon proof of distinctiveness. This change is discussed in detail under "New Rules on Secondary Meanings."

Special problems raised by "composite" trade-marks, where only part of the mark is descriptive, are treated under "The Use of Disclaimers."

USING PEOPLE'S NAMES

Under the new law, people's names may be registered as trade-marks much more easily than has been the case in the past. Only names which are *primarily* surnames are now excluded.

Under the old law, no surname received approval unless: (a)

It was exclusively used as a trade-mark for 10 years before 1905; or (b) It fulfilled the test of "distinctive display" (the name is printed so distinctively that it is no longer thought of as a surname but is identified only with the product).

Surnames to Have the Benefit of Doubt

Now, benefit of the doubt goes to the applicant. Rejections will not occur except where there is a currently recognized surname. An arbitrarily chosen name is no longer ineligible simply because it happens to appear in some telephone book. Likewise, names of historical or fictitious characters and names with a predominant meaning other than family names continue to be registrable. But if the term is chiefly known as a common surname, it will still be rejected.

Observation: The new act omits any reference to common surnames "distinctively displayed." It is not certain, therefore, whether surnames such as "Jones" can be registered in situations where they would have qualified under the "distinctive display" test; but it seems certain that such usage will not be considered "primarily" a surname use, and the name may therefore be registrable as thus displayed.

Illustration: Note the following cases where registration will probably be allowed under the Lanham Act even though rejected by the old law:

1. An arbitrarily chosen name which by coincidence happens to be somebody's surname, like "Stann."
2. Names with a different predominant meaning, except such names as "Barber" or "Taylor." These would probably always be associated by the public with a family name rather than with their literary meaning.

Recommendation: Do not select any name which also has an important geographical meaning. "Washington," "Madison," or "Cleveland" will probably be called primarily geographical and be disapproved even where the name clause does not forbid their use. But in a case like "Bismarck," the primary significance may be deemed historical rather than geographical.

3. Family names like "Smith" or "Parker" which have come to be so distinctively associated with a product that their "primary" identity as a surname has been lost. Such names thereby assume "secondary" meaning as a trade-mark and become registrable.

Individual Names Require Consent

Under both the old law and the Lanham Act, no portrait or signature of living individuals can be registered without their written consent. This prohibition probably extends to nicknames or assumed names. In the case of a deceased president of the United States, his widow's consent is necessary. Names like "Babe Ruth," "Ephraim Tutt" and "Franklin Roosevelt" all require written consent.

USE OF CORPORATE NAMES

The old law prohibits the registration of any mark which consists merely of the "name of a corporation." There is no similar provision in the Lanham Act. But this does not mean that the field will be wide open for anyone to register a word already being used as the name of a corporation. Section 2 (d) of the new law forbids the registration of any mark which "so resembles . . . a trade name previously used in the United States . . . and not abandoned, as to be likely . . . to cause confusion." Thus, a corporate name on file with the Patent Office (or otherwise known to the Office) will probably be considered a "trade name," so that no one else could register a name that might be confusingly similar.

It is obvious, however, that no corporation will be able to prevent registration of a name simply by making that word its own corporate title. Under the old law, if a corporation's name were "Simplex, Inc.," the corporation could prevent registration of the word "Simplex" for any other merchandise, no matter how unrelated.

Illustration: Esquire, Inc., the publisher of the magazine, prevented registration of the word "Esquire" for a hamburger-molding machine. Similarly, the Radio Corporation of America prevented registration of the letters "R.C.A." for a wholly unrelated article on the theory that the adoption of the letters "R.C.A." amounted to a complete appropriation of its corporate name.

Under the new law, the applicant who wants to use the word "Esquire" for hamburger-molding machines will, in all probability, be granted registration in the absence of possible confusion or deception of purchasers.

Observation: Under the old law, registration is denied to a newcomer even if he can prove that he actually used the mark before the corporate name was filed. (The corporation cannot, of course, stop the newcomer from continued *use* of the mark, but it can successfully prevent *registration.*) Under the Lanham Act, a corporation will no longer be in a position to object to registration of its name in any case where the newcomer's use *ante*dates the formation of the corporation.

Observation: Where an applicant seeks to register a mark which is only a part of a corporate name, the ordinary rules of trade-mark law will continue to govern, under the Lanham Act as well as the old law. This type of situation would arise, for instance, where an applicant wants to register the word "Simplex" for cutlery, despite the fact that the name "Simplex Heating Corporation" is on file with the Patent Office. The applicant would probably be allowed to register the word "Simplex," if only on the ground that cutlery and heating appliances are not in the same general class.

COLOR AND UTILITARIAN FEATURES

Color

Neither the former nor the new law deals specifically with the problem of registering color as a trade-mark. It is, however, well recognized that a color device may be protected and registered even under the Act of 1905 where a party uses a distinctive color symbol, such as a red star or blue cross or a similar device.

Where the coloring of an article does not serve any utilitarian function but is only used as a means of identification for the consuming public, it may be recognized as a trade-mark at least as against use of the identical color device on the same or similar merchandise. Thus, the Supreme Court many years ago afforded trade-mark protection to a red color stripe which had been used as a means of identification and as a trade-mark for wire rope, but the Patent Office Tribunals have been extremely reluctant to permit registration of color alone even if limited to one particular color and even if no apparent utilitarian purpose is served.

Illustration: The color violet for gasoline was denied registration. Likewise registration was refused in case of a silver capsule for milk bottles. Other cases in which registration was denied involved, for instance, different coloring for various fountain pen parts. Where the color device has a utility function, as in the case of differently colored match parts or nail heads, no trade-mark protection is available.

Observation: Even though not registrable as trade-marks, color devices are frequently the basis of unfair competition suits. Thus, there are numerous decisions involving protection of the "Yellow Taxi-cab." More recently, trade-mark protection was sought but denied for the "red seal" label on Victor records, but a red circular plug in the center of a heel was recently upheld as valid. Again, relief was recently denied to a manufacturer of fishing tackle whose trade-mark consisted of a narrow red stripe, on the ground that the device did not distinctively indicate the origin or ownership of the goods.

Under the new law, such color devices, if originally held unregistrable on the Principal Register for one of the above reasons, may still be registered at a later date if it can be shown that they have become distinctive despite their original defect. (See "New Rules on Secondary Meaning.")

Utility Features

There is nothing in the Lanham Act to indicate that mere utility features of design can ever acquire trade-mark distinctiveness. This continues a rule which existed under the old law.

Illustration: A mark consisting of a herringbone design on fish bait was recently rejected on the ground that the design gave the bait a "fishy" appearance and was therefore utilitarian. The classic example of an unregistrable utility feature was Goodyear's use of a rhomboid device on automobile tires. These ridges were held to be utilitarian parts of the tires, increasing their usefulness. Exactly the same rule will in all probability be applied under the new law.

NEW RULES ON SECONDARY MEANING

The Lanham Act, in one of its most important innovations, now provides for registration on the Principal Register of all marks "which have become distinctive of the applicant's goods in commerce." In other words, even a term which is originally ineligible as merely descriptive, or primarily geographical, or primarily a surname, may now be registered *if its primary meaning has become so insignificant that, for all practical purposes, the trade-mark implication of the word has become its predominant characteristic.*

It should be noted that under the new law certain unregistrable marks can *never* acquire distinctiveness. This is particularly true of immoral and scandalous marks, of the flag or coats of arms and of the Red Cross symbol. In addition, the prohibitions against registration of the name or portrait of a living individual without his consent, or of that of a deceased President of the United States without the consent of his widow, are also absolute prohibitions. Therefore, failure to obtain such consent cannot be cured even by many years of use and resulting trade-mark significance.

Apart from these relatively unimportant absolute prohibitions, *the new law makes it possible to acquire the benefits of an incontestable registered trade-mark for thousands of marks which could not be registered under the Act of 1905.*

NEW PROTECTION FOR SERVICE MARKS

Under the Lanham Act service marks will be registrable for the first time. The new law thus gives great protection to a category of names and designations whose trade importance was not recognized under the old law. Once registered, service names will also be entitled to the same amount of protection as are trademarks. A separate register for these marks will be established.

Illustration: Under the new law, words like "Pullman" (for sleeping car service); "Greyhound" (for bus lines), and "McBride's" (for theater ticket agency) can all be registered. Under the old law, even the name "Dow Jones Stock Averages" for a newspaper service was refused registration, although the names of magazines were considered registrable. Likewise, Pan-American could not register the word "Clipper" under the old law. The names of services of taxi-cab companies and educational institutions also suffered under the old law, but will now receive protection.

Observation: Service marks will receive all the benefits of the new act, and particularly the privilege of incontestability. The only specific limitation, added to Section 3 as a precautionary qualification, refers to cases where service marks are *deceptively* used so "as to represent solely that the owner thereof makes or sells the goods on which such mark is used." In such a case, the use of the service mark could not have protection under general principles of law even if this specific restriction were absent.

What Are Service Marks?

The Lanham Act's definition of "service mark" is very broad. Section 45 says it is "a mark used in the sale or advertising of services to identify the services of one person and distinguish them from the services of others and includes without limitation the marks, names, symbols, titles, designations, slogans, character names, and distinctive features of radio or other advertising used in commerce."

Under the new law, service marks include certain advertising and radio programs which otherwise could not be registered. Program titles such as "Take It or Leave It" or "The Lone Ranger" will be registrable by those who originally owned these programs. The Commissioner of Patents will have to determine what names or designations may be registered, as well as who can be protected, under the new broad definition of service marks.

Limits on Use for Advertising

Probably such phrases, titles and designations cannot be registered as trade-marks for the *goods* they advertise. In other words, "Take It or Leave It" cannot be recorded as a service mark for Eversharp Pencils. This is true even if the pencil company should have the exclusive rights to the program for a number of years.

Recommendation: Until the Patent Office issues new regulations regarding registrability of slogans, manufacturers and businessmen generally should use the services of some private organizations which file and publish slogans under a filing date so as to establish a priority record. Printer's Ink and the United States Trade-Mark Association are two such organizations.

In addition, companies should be prepared to show that they have continuously used such advertising slogans from the date which they intend to establish as the priority basis for the registration.

CERTIFICATION MARKS REGISTRABLE

A "certification mark," according to the definition of the Lanham Act, is a mark "used upon or in connection with the products or services of one or more persons other than the owner of the mark to certify regional or other origin, material, mode of manufacture, quality, accuracy or other characteristics of such goods or services or that the work or labor on the goods or services was performed by members of a union or other organization."

Such marks may be registered on a separate register by the person who exercises legitimate control over the use of the mark (Section 4). That person may register the mark even though he does not himself possess an industrial or commercial establishment.

Illustration: "Good Housekeeping" label shows approval by Good Housekeeping, and its registration as a certification mark will be additional protection both to the magazine and to the public with regard to the authenticity of the seal and the legality of its use. Other illustrations of certification marks would probably be names of famous automobiles, such as "Ford" or "Buick," as authorized for repair parts or garage or service station functions. Another example would be the name of a drink as used on glasses and bottles.

Caution on Registering Certification Marks

The Department of Justice expressed fear at the last minute that certification marks might be abused for monopolistic purposes. Although this apprehension apparently concerned the possible abuse of association and collective marks rather than of *certification* marks, a last-minute amendment to the Lanham Act will, in effect, make it practically impossible or at least inadvisable to register such names as "Buick" or "Ford" or "Esso" as certification marks in addition to registering them as trade-marks.

This amendment to Section 14 (d) authorizes cancellation of a certification mark *at any time* in the following four situations: (a) The registrant is not exercising "legitimate control" in using the mark; (b) the registrant himself is engaged in the production or marketing of the goods so certified; (c) the registrant permits the use of the mark for purposes other than certification marks; (d) the registrant discriminately refuses to certify or to continue to certify the goods or services of a person who maintains the standards or conditions which the mark certifies.

The government also insisted upon an amendment authorizing not only any person damaged thereby, but also the Federal Trade Commission to apply for cancellation of certification marks on these grounds.

Observation: This is the first time in the history of trade-mark law that a government agency is authorized to petition the Patent Office for cancellation of a registered trade-mark. It should be specifically noted that the right of the Federal Trade Commission to ask for cancellation of a certification mark may be asserted *at any time* and not only within the first 5 years after the date of registration. In other words, certification marks will not become "incontestable" even after 5 years if they are shown to have been used in violation of one of the rules noted above.

COLLECTIVE MARKS REGISTRABLE

Collective marks are defined by the new act as marks "used by the members of a cooperative, an association or other collective group or organization"—including union labels. Such marks may now be registered as collective marks wherever they are used to indicate that members of the cooperative, association or union have been connected with the manufacture of the merchandise on which the marks are used.

Observation: The above-mentioned Department of Justice amendment regarding abuses of certification marks does *not* apply to collective marks. A typical illustration of a collective mark under the new act would be the designation "Mohawk Valley" for apples produced by members of the Mohawk Valley Apple Growers Association.

Illustration: Only recently, the Commissioner of Patents refused to register the name "Textile Workers Union of America" appearing on the representation of a scroll above which appeared the words "Union Made." The words "Union Made" were disclaimed and registration sought for hosiery.

Likewise, registration of the letters "R.C.I.P.A." standing for "Retail Clerks International Protective Association" was rejected on the ground that the mark indicated only that the merchandise was serviced by the association but was not a trade-mark in and of itself. *Under the Lanham Act this association mark becomes registrable as a collective mark.*

RULES ON CONFLICTING TRADE-MARKS

Can a name like "Rolls-Royce" be registered as a trade-mark for radio tubes? A word like "Dunhill" for shirts? A word like "Kodak" for bicycles? The problem illustrated in these questions has been one of the perplexing areas of trade-mark law.

The old law set up some rather complicated tests to determine when a mark was to be rejected as "conflicting." The Lanham Act provides simply that a trade-mark previously used or registered by one party shall not be registered for another applicant if it is likely to "cause confusion or mistake or to deceive purchasers" when applied to the applicant's merchandise (section 2 (*b*)).

Similarly, section 32 of the Lanham Act provides an infringement remedy in any case where the alleged infringing mark is likely to cause confusion, regardless of whether or not it is used on merchandise of "substantially the same descriptive properties."

To fully understand the important implications of this change, it is necessary to review the way in which conflicting trade-marks have been viewed under the old law.

When Are Marks Conflicting?

Under the old law, a mark was rejected if (a) it was either identical or confusingly similar to another mark, and (b) it was used on identical or confusingly similar goods. Note that registration was denied only if there was confusion with regard to *both* these matters.

Observation: In practice, the Patent Office has been guided by the *joint effect* of these two factors: it has not examined them separately. This emphasis on the total effect will probably be continued in determining whether or not marks are conflicting under the Lanham Act.

Illustration: The word "Lix" as used on an insect powder was held not to be confusingly similar to "Vicks" used on a medicated salve. The court concluded that "considering the difference in the marks *together* with the difference of the goods, confusion would not be likely to occur."

In determining similarity of marks the following rules, *which are not affected by the Lanham Act,* are already well established:

1. In testing the similarity of two marks, similarity in sound will be considered independently of similarity in appearance. This test has become increasingly important because of the

growing custom of advertising trade-marked goods over the radio.

2. In determining similarity of words, the Patent Office and the courts apply the test of "the casual purchaser." In other words, would an ordinary customer who does not give special attention to the product tend to be confused?
3. Surrounding circumstances such as the distinctiveness of the packaging will be taken into account. Another consideration is whether the goods are luxury items; the idea being that customers tend to use more care and discrimination in choosing such goods. If merchandise is of a type ordinarily purchased only after very careful consideration on the part of the customer, that would be a circumstance which might lead the Patent Office to decide there was less likelihood of confusion.
4. As noted, the two marks will never be dissected in order to detect similarities or differences. They will be compared in their entirety.
5. The two marks will be considered in their entirety even if a part of the mark has been "disclaimed."
6. As a general rule, any doubt regarding similarity of two conflicting trade-marks in registration proceedings will be resolved against the newcomer.

New Benefits in Lanham Act

Several important innovations flow from the Lanham Act's view of conflicting trade-marks. Among the major benefits are the following:

1. The new law makes it very clear that the Patent-Office classification will serve "only for convenience of Patent-Office administration." It will not "limit" or extend the applicant's rights. As a result, it has even less bearing in connection with the determination of confusing similarity.

Note, too that it remains possible to file one application for the registration of a mark for any or all the goods included in one class, as long as the applicant is using the mark in connection with such goods. A further improvement in the new law is the fact that a single certificate may be issued for one mark even though it is registered in several classes. Applicants must, however, pay a fee equaling the sum of the cost of registration in each class.

2. The "confusion in trade" clause will now be applicable *whether or not* the goods are of the same descriptive properties. This will enormously strengthen the position of the first user or first registrant in cases where his mark has become nationally known. The Patent Office will be in a position to apply broad principles of unfair trading in determining whether or not the newcomer's trade-mark should be registered. Where it seems that the newcomer is trying to capitalize on the first user's reputation or goodwill, registration may be refused on that ground alone if the public might conceivably associate the newcomer's product with the first user's business.

Illustration: If an effort were made to register the word "Kodak" for razor blades, the Patent Office would be justified in denying the registration *despite the difference in goods* if the Office were convinced that confusion in the public mind might result.

Recommendation: For this reason alone, a new trade-mark should be as unique and distinctive as possible. The Patent Office and the courts will be more prone to find confusion if a unique name such as "Kodak" is sought to be registered by another party for different goods. A common word like "Eureka" or "Excelsior" would be deemed far less likely to create such confusion.

3. The new law benefits not only the first *registrant* on the Principal Register, but also benefits a prior *user* who has widely used a trade-mark or trade name *without* obtaining a federal registration. Such a first user, whether an individual or corporation, could oppose the registration of the mark under section 13 of the new law or bring cancellation proceedings under section 14, if the mark has already been registered. He would have to show (a) that the mark is still in use by him and not abandoned, and (b) that he will

be damaged by the new registration because public confusion is likely to result. The opposition will be sustained or the registration cancelled if likelihood of confusion can be shown, regardless of whether or not the goods have the "same descriptive properties."

4. The test of "same descriptive properties" has also been eliminated in connection with *interference* proceedings. Under section 16, the Commissioner of Patents may declare an interference in any case where an application is made for a previously registered mark if, in his judgment, the second registration would cause confusion. The same test applies if an interference is declared between two pending applications for the same or similar mark. Under the old law, no interference was declared unless the conflicting marks were, in the Commissioner's judgment, used on merchandise of the "same descriptive properties."

British Legal Requirements *

REGISTRABILITY

(1) **The Firm Name.** When a firm name is registered it is, like any other registered mark, protected only for the classes of goods for which it is entered, e.g., "Leyland" Motors could not contest the use of the word Leyland for cotton goods unless they were actually registered for them or had earned common-law rights for the use of the name on cotton.

(2) **The Surname.** A known surname, even when it is the firm name, cannot be registered as a new trade-mark. Registration can only be obtained by furnishing proof of long and extensive use together with details of turnover and publicity expenditure. It is an exception to the general recommendation that trade-mark registration should precede business operations.

Historic surnames, e.g., Raleigh, however, are normally accepted, provided no direct reference to character or quality of the goods is indicated, and should be registered.

---

* Cousins and Wadsworth, *Trade Names,* Harlequin Press.

(3) **The Geographical Name.** A geographical name is subject to the same restrictions as a known surname (2), and to a further one that the goods for which it is registered must be made at that town or place.

Historic place names, if known to be so, are usually admitted if the town or place has no prominence at the present time.

(4) **The Directly Descriptive Word.** A directly descriptive word can only be registered as a trade-mark upon very strong evidence of distinctiveness similar to that required for the surname (2). The weight of evidence and the period of use cannot be defined, as each case is dealt with on its merits. Registration of such words as "excellent" or "magnifique," however, cannot be hoped for under the current statute and practice.

Foreign words which are directly descriptive are given no latitude and are treated in exactly the same manner, e.g., "Pomme-de-terre" could not be registered for potatoes or any preparation thereof.

(5) **The Indirectly Descriptive Word.** The indirectly descriptive word is usually an invented one. Examples are as follows, and provided they are sufficiently distinctive from ordinary descriptive words, they are registrable.

- (i) Distinctive change of ending, e.g., Chedlet (Cheddar).
- (ii) Stems of words plus another word, e.g., Bisc-o-rye, Ry-vita(min), Bemax (Vitamin B maximum).
- (iii) Mixtures of a living and a dead language, e.g., Aquaturn, Dictaphone, Dri-ped.
- (iv) Compounded Latin words, e.g., Aquascutum.
- (v) New combinations of familiar roots, e.g., Multigraph.
- (vi) Overlap of descriptive words, e.g., Gussetoe (gusset toe).

(6) **Invented Nondescriptive Words.** Apart from the possibility of conflict with some name already on the register for a kindred product, the only danger with an invented word is that it may by accident be a surname, a trade name, a place name or an obscure word. To clear these possibilities, searches of a directory of London or any large town, Longman's Gazetteer and Webster's International Dictionary are advised.

(7) **Disclaimed Words.** Normally unregistrable words are allowed to combine with registrable matter, e.g., a device, invented word or signature, provided a disclaimer of exclusive use is given by the applicant. This affords a 50 per cent registration until such time as the mark has had the long and extensive use (see (2)) which will qualify it for full registration.

STATUTORY REQUIREMENTS

A new trade-mark or name, to qualify for registration, must comply with the following conditions:

I. It must be claimed in respect of particular merchandise or classes of merchandise.

II. It must consist of at least one of the following:

(a) The name of a company, individual or firm represented in a special or particular manner. Surnames alone are not registrable except as mentioned in (2) above. Invented firm names are registrable if coming within subsections (c) or (d) below.

(b) The signature of the applicant or a predecessor in the business.

(c) An invented word or words.

(d) A word or words having no direct reference to the character or quality of the goods and not normally signifying a geographical name or surname.

(e) Any device forming a trade-mark, providing it is deemed distinctive. Letters alone are not registrable except in the form of an interwoven monogram, when they qualify as a device.

III. It must not conflict in any way with any mark or name already registered for the same kind of goods or similar goods.

IV. It must not include any matter which by being calculated to deceive or otherwise would be disentitled to protection in a court of justice, or which would be contrary to law or morality, or any scandalous design.

V. A word or words must not be the practicable names or

descriptions of any single chemical element or compound.

VI. It must not consist of or embody any of the following:

(a) The emblem of the Red Cross, or the words Red Cross or Geneva Cross.

(b) The words Patent, Patented, By Royal Letters Patent, Registered, Registered Design, Copyright, Entered at Stationers' Hall, to counterfeit this is forgery, or words to like effect.

(c) Representations of Their Majesties or of any member of the Royal Family.

(d) Representations of the Royal or Imperial arms or crests, armorial bearings, insignia or devices so nearly resembling them as to lead to mistake.

(e) British, Royal or Imperial Crowns.

(f) British, Royal, Imperial or National Flags.

(g) The words Royal, Imperial, Empire, Dominion, Crown, or any other words, letters, or devices calculated to lead persons to think that the applicant has Royal or Imperial patronage or authorization.

(h) The Anchor devices shown on the Admiralty seal and the Admiralty flag, and the Eagle device and the Wings device shown on the Royal Air Force badges, or devices so similar as to lead to mistake.

The following restrictions are enforced where necessary:

(1) In cases where representations of the armorial bearings, insignia, emblems, decorations or flags of any state, or of any city, borough, town, place, society, body corporate or institution appear on a mark, the registrar may require justification for their use.

(2) Where the names or representations of living persons or persons recently deceased appear on a mark, the registrar may require the consent of such living persons or of the legal representatives of such deceased persons.

(3) Where there appears on the face of a trade-mark the name or a description of the goods to which the mark is applied, the

registrar may refuse registration in respect of any goods other than the goods so named or described. If the name or description of any goods appears on a trade-mark, and such name or description varies in use, the applicant should include in this application a statement to this effect.

(4) Ornamental or colored groundwork, such as tartans or checks, cannot be claimed as part of a mark unless such groundwork be included within the mark by some border or lines.

PARTS A AND B OF THE REGISTER

The British register of trade-marks is divided into two sections, Part A and Part B. In Part A, a name or mark which complies fully with the statutory requirements mentioned above may secure a first-class registration at once, with or without actual use in trade.

In Part B, names or marks which fail to comply with Section II of the statutory requirements given above, but which, having been in bona fide use in Great Britain for 2 years, are claimed to be distinctive, may be granted a registration which carries a prima facie protection. In course of time a name in Part B may become sufficiently well established to secure reregistration in Part A, but it would be unwise to count on this in advance without taking expert opinion. For, although some names, e.g., an uncommon surname or obscure town name, may have an excellent chance, others, as in the case of Perfection (soap), a merely laudatory word, or Liverpool (cables), the name of a great industrial center, may be permanently ineligible for full registration.

RECENT DECISIONS OF BRITISH COURTS

"UCOLITE" (a coal product) held not registrable in view of registered mark "COALITE."

"BRICK" (a coal product) held not registrable in view of registered name "BRICO," and held not capable of distinguishing in Part B of the register from "A boiler-water purifier supplied sometimes in brick form and sometimes in powder form."

"NOTEX" held to be registrable, after opposition by a foreign company, on grounds of use of same word abroad with no registration.

"NAVY SPOT" (wireless apparatus) held to infringe "BLUE SPOT" and an injunction granted.

"RADIATION" held not to be incapable of becoming distinctive, after opposition from the trade (gas fires, stoves, etc.).

"ALLIGATOR PATTERN" held to infringe "ALLIGATOR"—injunction granted.

"ERNALDE" (perfumery, etc.) held not to infringe "NILDE."

"LIVERPOOL CABLE" held not to be registrable either in Part A or Part B of the register.

"EPPELS LTD." (a druggist business) held to be calculated to deceive by its resemblance to "HEPPELS LTD.," the well-known druggists.

Registration Procedure

Registration of a trade name should be sought soon after its birth, before a penny has been spent on printing or publicity. The Trade-Marks Acts were designed for the benefit of industry, and it is foolish not to take advantage of them. What fire insurance is for fixed assets, trade-mark registration is for the goodwill of a business, a voluntary safeguard which every sensible firm treats as compulsory. Even the most innocent infringement of a registered name can incur a court order prohibiting all future sales and virtually confiscating stocks on hand.

Although registration by the amateur is theoretically possible, it is usually better, simpler and, to a busy man, cheaper to place the business of registration in the hands of an expert such as a member of the Chartered Institute of Patent Agents (Staple Inn Buildings, London, W.C.1) in Great Britain, or a registered United States patent attorney (a register is kept in the United States Patent Office at Washington) who is accustomed to dealing with any complications which may arise and will obtain the widest form of protection available.

BRITISH REGISTRATION

Applications for registration in Great Britian are made, with few exceptions, to the "Registrar of Trade-Marks, 25, Southampton Buildings, London, W.C.2."

When the application is filed, an official search takes place. If found to be free from infringement and in other respects registrable, the name or mark is advertised in the Trade-Marks Journal for one month to afford an opportunity to the owner of any registered mark (or, if there is a strong case, of an unregistered mark) to contest the application. At the end of this period, if no opposition is lodged, the final fee is paid and registration is complete.

If, however, the official search discloses conflict with other registrations, he must then endeavor to overcome these objections at a personal hearing, which is the better choice, or by correspondence. If a sound argument is advanced, the registrar may direct that the application may proceed, but if the objections are strong he may impose one or more of the following conditions:

1. A slight amendment of the word or words to bring them within Section II.
2. Restriction of the specification of goods to avoid conflicting citations. (This is common practice.)
3. Where such restriction is not considered sufficient to avoid conflict with other registered marks, the applicant may obtain from the owners a written consent to the registration of his mark.
4. Where the objection is too strong for restriction as in 2, but insufficiently strong for consent as in 3, the registrar may allow the application to proceed to advertisement in the Trade-Marks Journal on condition that the applicant notifies the registered proprietors of conflicting marks of his proposed registration, thus giving them an opportunity to oppose. (This and No. 3 are methods of giving registered proprietors a fair chance of protecting themselves if they think fit.)
5. Where an applicant can prove that his mark has been used

concurrently with the conflicting citations, the application may be allowed to proceed under 4 above.

If official objections cannot be overcome, the applicant will be advised of the refusal of his application. If so advised, the applicant has a right of appeal to either the Board of Trade or to the High Court. Appeals of this nature are rare but sometimes successful.

Every endeavor should be made to complete a registration within 12 months, otherwise it is deemed to be cancelled; there are exceptions to this rule in special cases.

A registration is renewable every 14 years.

A dead or false mark or name, or part of one, will be removed from the register by the Registrar or the High Court upon a successful application being made by an aggrieved person.

SEARCH

The official search is made in the particular class in which registration is requested and in any other class in which similar goods are likely to be found. The following are taken into account as possible causes of conflict:

Similarity of sound,
Literal resemblance,
Typography,
General design.

Color, too, more particularly with device marks, comes under consideration, and sometimes conflict can be overcome by undertaking to use only a certain color scheme.

ASSIGNMENT

A registration can be assigned to a new proprietor if proof is given that the name or mark has been transferred together with the goodwill of the business concerned in the goods for which it is registered. If, however, the mark is one of a related series, objections may be raised. Every care should be taken to notify any change of ownership immediately, as failure to do so, if left beyond 6 months, may entail considerable expense.

Registered owners should be certain that they are entered on the register as proprietors and hold either the original certificate, or, if a change of any kind has taken place, a certificate to that effect.

RETAINING PROPRIETORSHIP

A trade name which is allowed to lose its significance as a name for a specific brand of goods made by a particular firm and to become merely a generic term describing the article ceases to be registrable, i.e., once it loses its distinctiveness and becomes the common property of the trade or the public as a merely descriptive word it cannot be reclaimed into private ownership. In the case of the "Magic Chuck," for instance, in the United States, the makers found some years after their patents had expired that the name had become a trade term and that exclusive ownership was lost.

The regular use of "Reg'd." together with "Trade-Mark" and such words or phrases as "Brand," "a-Co. product," "Made only by..........." and the immediate cautioning of all infringers, are the current methods of preventing this loss of proprietorship.

Other precautions to be taken are as follows. The trade-mark should not be used in a descriptive (or generic) fashion, e.g., as an adjective, adverb or common noun in advertising, labels or correspondence.

Whenever a trade-mark appears, it should be in quotation marks, preferably in capital letters. It should also be followed by a general descriptive word or words in small letters, e.g., "KLEERFILM," transparent cellulose sheet.

To avoid common use of a trade-mark, publishers of dictionaries, periodicals, newspapers, etc., must be informed that whenever they mention a trade-mark it should be followed by "a trade-mark for ...., registered (or property of) .... Co." Particular attention must be given to resellers of trade-marked products who have their own labels and advertising.

As soon as possible after a trade name is adopted, at least small-scale national advertising should be started. The purpose is to acquaint those in other states that the trade-mark in question is the property of the advertiser. Otherwise, under court rulings and the new trade-mark act some one in an other state might get the exclusive right to the trade-mark in his own territory. Exclusive national rights thus should be protected by advertising nationally and selling by mail in all states where the trade-mark owner has no dealers.

Protection of Trade-Marks Abroad *

Adapting a trade-mark to foreign markets is highly important inasmuch as trade-marks suitable for use in one country may be undesirable or offensive in another. There are numerous other matters that should be considered in connection with this subject—among them, those relating to various kinds of marks used as trade-marks, color as a distinctive feature, prohibitions as to the use of flags, public insignia, medals and awards, firm names, registration of labels, assignment and transfer, piracy of marks, seizure, and user. These are discussed in the following pages.

The importance of protecting trade-marks used on goods shipped to foreign markets has been given too little attention by the American exporter. The retention or further expansion of markets already established, as well as the development of new markets abroad, imposes the duty of examining into the means by which exclusive rights to trade-marks are acquired.

A program for the establishment of foreign trade is incomplete without appropriate consideration of industrial property rights and how to protect them from unfair acts of competitors. The unwary manufacturer or merchant who proceeds to sell his products in oversea markets, in the belief that the trade-mark rights he has acquired at home are protected abroad, may find that he can be restrained from selling his goods under these trade-marks because someone else has acquired an exclusive property in them.

---

* *Industrial Property Protection Throughout the World,* U. S. Department of Commerce (1936).

The tendency to simulate American trade-marks, trade names, labels, wrappers, and containers, as well as other distinctive signs by which products are identified, has gone on unabated, and the preference of the foreign consumer for American-made products in recent years has prompted the foreign competitor to profit by the goodwill in such distinctive and identifying media by simulating them.

American magazines, which are sent to all parts of the world, contain advertisements of well-known brands and trade-marks. These magazines are scanned not only by foreign manufacturers and traders who deal in similar classes of goods, but also by those who make a practice of acquiring trade-mark rights in order later to demand payment for the use of a mark which originally, at least in the United States, belonged to the American manufacturer or merchant.

American exporters have been shipping goods bearing unprotected trade-marks to some countries. If there is a ready demand for these goods, competitors may single out one or more of these American trade-marks, register them in accordance with the provisions of the national law, and thereby acquire the exclusive right to use them despite the fact that the American exporter was the first to use them within those countries.

From a strictly legal standpoint, it is sometimes incorrect to call "pirate" one who has registered, and thereby obtained the exclusive right to use a trade-mark which has previously been adopted and used by another. The motive which inspires one to register the mark of another is an important factor in determining his culpability. It often happens that foreign representatives, agents, or customers may register the trade-mark of the American exporter with a view to protecting the interests of the latter, being aware that their own interests may be jeopardized if a third party should acquire, by registration, the exclusive right to the use of the mark. In such instances the registered proprietor will willingly assign his rights to the American principal.

Where the registration has been made in bad faith, it will usually be found that there is no desire on the part of the registered proprietor to make an assignment without the payment of a sum far in excess of registration costs or in consideration of an exclusive agency agreement for a long term and over an extended territory.

Often a foreign agent, in order to consolidate his position, will register the trade-marks of his American principal to prevent the principal from marketing his goods directly or through another agent.

Where there exists a contract in which the agent is directed to register the trade-mark in the name of the principal or to assign rights acquired therein to his principal and he fails to do this, then there would be a right of action on the contract. In cases where trade-mark registrations have been obtained by unauthorized persons through fraud, then, of course, a court would order the registration expunged from the record, but, in the absence of some other factor, registration of the mark of another generally will not be considered fraudulent.

MANNER IN WHICH TRADE-MARK RIGHTS ARE ACQUIRED ABROAD

Trade-marks are protected in foreign countries in various ways. With few exceptions, most of the countries of the world have provided means (usually by statutory enactment) by which those who would obtain the exclusive right to the use of trade-marks may enforce these rights against infringers. The concept of this right is not the same throughout the world, and there are various theories as to the manner in which it comes into existence.

Statutes provide the means by which trade-marks may be registered, but registration is not always the sole criterion of ownership. It is true that registration may be a determining factor; but if this alone established ownership, those who adopt and use trade-marks would be confronted with the necessity for their immediate registration in all countries. Fortunately this is not the test in every country, and those who fail to register their marks in some jurisdictions may not lose the right to use them.

In the United States, and in practically all areas where the common law forms the basis of jurisprudence, rights in a trade-mark are acquired by the one who first adopts and uses it in connection with the goods which he manufactures and sells. Registration in these countries is mainly only prima facie evidence of ownership, and it may be set aside by anyone who can prove that he has a better right to the mark.

In practically all those countries where the civil law forms the basis of jurisprudence, the right is acquired by registration and the corresponding certificate, prior adoption and use by another to the contrary notwithstanding.

Right Acquired by First User

The common-law concept of the property right in a trade-mark prevails in the United States, Great Britain (its dominions and colonies), and in several other countries of the world. The theory of the right is, that the manufacturer or merchant has acquired a property in his trade-mark by reason of its adoption and the use by him in connection with the goods which he manufactures or sells; in other words, the right comes into being by reason of such adoption and use and not as the result of the formality of registration.

The exclusive right to the use of a trade-mark is not entirely without limitation. The Government may regulate what constitutes a mark; may prescribe certain limitations therein; may stipulate the manner of its use; and may impose certain formalities (such as registration, marking, etc.), in order that the owner may claim the benefits contained in the law.

In several countries the registered proprietor of a trade-mark will be conclusively presumed to be the owner thereof if the registration has remained on the register for a stated time. During this period, the prior user may assert his rights; if he fails to do so, then the registered proprietorship will be deemed to be conclusive, the theory being that the registered proprietor should not be subject to annoyance by suits for cancellation after he has spent time and money to associate the mark with his goods.

In countries where this concept of the right obtains, a manufacturer or merchant who has adopted and used a mark in connection with his industry and trade enjoys, if for only a limited period, the right to set aside an unauthorized registration by another. It is desirable, however, as a precautionary measure, to register trade-marks in those countries without undue delay, not only for the value of the evidence which registration establishes, but to avoid vexatious suits which may be necessary if another registers and uses an infringing mark.

Right Acquired by Registration

There is a large group of countries, including most of those in Latin America and several in Europe, where the property right in a trade-mark is acquired solely on the basis of registration. In other words, unless there has been some fraud in obtaining registration the registered proprietor will be entitled to the exclusive right to the use of the registered mark, prior adoption and use by another to the contrary notwithstanding.

This method of obtaining the exclusive right to the use of a trade-mark, although it imposes an obligation on the manufacturer, merchant, or agriculturist who would prevent another from using a mark confusingly similar to his, possesses merit in that one who desires to use a trade-mark in connection with his goods will know just what marks he may not use, since he can refer to those already registered by others. The register of marks is in effect notice to all as to the proprietorship of the marks recorded therein. It would seem that the use of marks which have not been registered in these countries is only tolerated, for, in fact, very often they have no legal existence in the absence of their being recorded in the trade-mark register.

While it is not to be assumed that the jurisprudence on the subject is identical in all these countries, the existence of the right is generally recognized. However, certain equities of prior users also are recognized for a given time, and accordingly provision is made for opposition or cancellation proceedings during this period by those who may be injured as the result of a previous registration.

It would seem that the so-called piracy of trade-marks would be more likely to occur in these countries than where the common-law theory exists. This is quite true, but it should be pointed out that the first user of a mark will be deprived of the right to its exclusive use only if he fails to exercise his right to register it before another has done so. There is no obligation to refrain from registering a mark previously adopted and used by another, when the law gives full protection only to the registered proprietor and usually to the first applicant therefor.

American manufacturers and merchants should be on the alert in protecting their marks in the countries of this group. They should seek registration without delay as soon as it is determined that in these countries there is an existing or potential demand for their goods.

UNITED STATES REGISTRATION REQUIRED

Registration of a trade-mark is, in many foreign countries, predicated upon the registration of the identical mark in the applicant's home country. As a usual thing foreign laws do not grant to persons other than nationals the right to obtain registration of their trade-marks unless there is some reciprocal arrangement. The reciprocity granted does not dispense with the requirement of fulfilling all the provisions of law, including the filing of an application for registration.

If a national of one country may obtain registration in another only on the basis of ownership of the trade-mark in his own country, he may be required, when applying for foreign registration, to attach to his application a certified copy of the registration in his home country. This requirement must be fulfilled even though the exclusive right to the use of the trade-mark in the applicant's home country does not impose upon him the necessity of registering it.

If a national of the United States should apply for registration of his trade-mark in Brazil, he must furnish either a certified copy of his registration in the United States Patent Office, or, if the mark has not been registered, a certificate from that office to the effect that the trade-mark has not been registered by him or anyone else.

It may appear from what has just been said that this requirement of home registration would work a hardship on those who seek registration of their trade-marks abroad. While this may be true to some extent, the requirement acts as a safeguard in preventing unauthorized persons in the applicant's home country from applying for registration in a foreign country of a mark to which they have no right. Where foreign registration is provided for as distinct from domestic registration—that is, where the registration is granted only on the basis of registration in a home country—such foreign registration may endure only during the life of the registration in the home country on which it is based. In such case the foreign registration may be nothing more than a revalidation of the registration in the applicant's home country.

ADAPTING A MARK TO FOREIGN TRADE

The chief office of a trade-mark is to distinguish the goods of a manufacturer from those of his competitors. It is not easy to select a mark that will be entirely different from the millions of other marks already in use, but so far as possible the manufacturer should make his mark distinctive, attractive, and so simple that it readily becomes fixed in the mind of the consumer. The selection of a mark for domestic trade sometimes is a perplexing problem requiring much thought and investigation. The selection of a mark for use in foreign trade presents greater complexities, in that language, psychological viewpoints, and the social and economic conditions of foreign peoples must be taken into consideration.

The average American often experiences difficulty in pronouncing some of the coined words used as trade-marks in domestic markets. Fanciful designs are sometimes so intricate and so lacking in distinctive appeal that the consumer rarely fixes them in his mind. Think, then, of the difficulty the foreign buyer would have if these marks were used abroad. Illiterate persons or those of limited education could hardly be expected to become familiar with the trade-marks of this type. Actually most trade-marks in use in the United States could readily be used abroad, but in the selection of a new mark for foreign use all these factors should be given appropriate consideration in order that the most desirable trade-mark shall be chosen.

The average purchaser the world over prefers to call for the product he desires under its trade-mark or name. He dislikes very much to be put to the trouble of describing the appearance or some other distinctive feature in order that the sales person may understand just what he desires. Trade-marks which consist of or which include distinctive words are perhaps the most desirable and often the least expensive to protect. Word combinations or coined words which are readily understandable make very good trade-marks for use in foreign trade.

A trade-mark which readily appeals to the imagination of the consumer may be said to be a good one. A trade-mark should attract attention, distinguish the product of its manufacturer from those of others, and be suggestive of quality or origin, but not descriptive of the goods on which it is used. Identity is an important matter in contributing to the make-up of a good trade-mark. Difficulty in remembering the mark or a tendency to confuse it with others which are similar will go far toward defeating its primary purpose.

A preference for particular colors or certain fanciful designs by the people most likely to use the product is an important factor, and this is true at home as well as abroad. Trade-marks which consist of pictorial illustrations, colors, and fanciful designs may be preferable to word trade-marks in certain countries, but in their selection religious preferences and the social, racial, and cultural conditions of the people must not be offended.

That the selection of any marks which might cause the slightest offense to national sentiments and viewpoint or which may cause an unfavorable reaction on the part of the consumer is to be avoided has been brought out clearly by American Commercial Attaché Julean Arnold, who called attention to a situation of this kind in China as follows:

In adapting the trade-mark to Chinese trade, it was found that the Chinese word for sun could not be used, since it is a part of the word for Japan. The Chinese characters for seedless raisins read "Wu Tsz," which, while they mean "without seeds," also mean "without sons." As every Chinese wishes to have sons, any product advertised as suggesting "without sons" would be distinctly objectionable. Hence, in the trade-mark in question the use of the expressions "without kernels" was suggested. This illustrates the necessity of exercising great care in the manner of advertising a product in China for use in the Chinese market.

A TRADE-MARK FOR UNIVERSAL USE

A mark which would be universally acceptable and which could be protected in all countries of the world would be a most desirable mark for the American exporter to adopt and use in connection with the sale of his goods abroad. Trade-marks which contain all the desirable features necessary to make them acceptable to the people and registrable under the law of all countries occupy an enviable position in industry. Those marks which include distinctive designs and coined words possess this advantage, and, if they are distinguishable from others in use, could be protected.

It would be no easy task to select a mark of this type—not because the choice itself would be hard, but because similar marks may have previously been registered for identical products in one or more countries. Hundreds of thousands of trade-marks are registered annually throughout the world.

Pictorial designs with the words "Star," "Moon," "Diamond," "Sun," "Lion," "Bear," and such words as "Excelsior," "Rex," etc., have been quite generally used for years both here and abroad in connection with many classes of goods. These words and pictorial marks are likely to be used as trade-marks by the people of any country, and if selected for foreign trade they may not be eligible for exclusive use in some areas because of a prior registration of these or confusingly similar marks. A mark, to be adaptable for world use, should possess novelty; distinctiveness is a most important attribute.

ASSOCIATED MARKS AND SERIES OF MARKS

Provision is made under the laws of some countries for the registration of associated trade-marks or series of marks. This is true of the laws in many British areas. Thus, we read in article 29 of the trade-mark law of Australia:

(1) Where application is made for the registration of a trade-mark so nearly resembling a trade-mark of the applicant which is already on the register as to be likely to deceive or cause confusion if used by a person other than the applicant, the registrar may require as a condition of registration that the trade-marks shall be entered on the register as associated trade-marks.

(2) If the proprietor of a trade-mark claims to be entitled to the exclusive use of any part of it separately he may, if the part satisfies all the conditions of a trade-mark, register it as a separate trade-mark.

(3) When a part of a registered trade-mark is registered separately, it and the trade-mark of which it forms a part shall be deemed to be associated trade-marks, and shall be entered on the register as such, and the user of a whole trade-mark shall for the purposes of this act be deemed to be also a user of the part separately registered as a trade-mark.

(4) Except for the purpose of assignment or transmission, and subject to the provisions of this act as to use of associated trade-marks, associated trade-marks shall be deemed to be registered independently.

The Australian law provides in article 31:

When a person claiming to be the proprietor of several trade-marks for the same description of goods which, while resembling each other in the material particulars thereof, yet differ in respect of—

(a) Statements of the goods for which they are respectively used or proposed to be used; or

(b) Statements of number, price, quality, or names of places; or

(c) Other matter of a nondistinctive character which does not substantially affect the identity of the trade-marks; or

(d) Color,

seeks to register such trade-marks, they may be registered as a series in one registration. All the trade-marks in a series of trade-marks so registered shall be deemed to be, and shall be registered as, associated trade-marks.

In registering associated marks or those referred to as series of marks, their owners may be confronted with certain difficulties, especially if the foreign registration of a trade-mark is contingent upon registration of the identical mark in the home country of the applicant. It is probable that if the associated mark, foreign registration of which is desired, does not differ materially from the original mark registered at home, registration will be granted in the foreign country.

MARKS OF TRADE ASSOCIATIONS OR COLLECTIVE GROUPS

In the United States no provision is made for the registration of marks used by trade associations not actually engaged in commerce. In other countries, however, the marks of trade associations are protected, and there are provisions in many foreign trade-mark laws specifically dealing with such marks and their registration.

Excerpts from the laws of the Irish Free State, Great Britain, Denmark, Japan, Poland, and New Zealand are given below, to illustrate the foreign viewpoint in this regard. In the Irish Free State the following articles relate to this subject:

ART. 101. If application be made for the registration in part A of the register of a trade-mark identical with or so closely resembling a trade-mark of the applicant already on that part of the register for the same goods or description of goods as to be calculated to deceive or cause confusion if used by a person other than the applicant, the tribunal hearing the application may require as a condition of registration that such trade-marks shall be entered on the register as associated trade-marks.

ART. 102. If the proprietor of a trade-mark registered in part A of the register claims to be entitled to the exclusive use of any portion of such trade-mark separately, he may apply to register the same in the said part A as separate trade-marks. Each separate trade-mark must satisfy all the conditions and shall have all the incidents of an independent trade-mark except that when registered it and the trade-mark of which it forms a part shall be deemed to be associated trade-marks and shall be entered on the register as such, but the user of the whole trade-mark shall for the purposes of this act be deemed to be also a user of such registered trade-marks belonging to the same proprietor as it contains.

ART. 103. (1) When a person claiming to be the proprietor of several trade-marks for the same description of goods which, while resembling each other in the material particulars thereof, yet differ in respect of—

(a) statements of the goods for which they are respectively used or proposed to be used; or

(b) statements of number, price, quality, or names of places; or

(c) other matter of a non-distinctive character which does not substantially affect the identity of the trade-mark; or

(d) color;

seeks to register such trade-marks, they may be registered as a series in one registration.

(2) All the trade-marks in a series of trade-marks registered under this section shall if registered in part A of the register be deemed to be, and shall be registered as, associated trade-marks.

ART. 123. (1) Where any association or person undertakes to certify the origin, material, mode of manufacture, quality, accuracy, or other characteristic of any goods, by mark used upon or in connection with such goods, the minister, if and so long as he is satisfied that such association or person is competent to certify as aforesaid, may, if he shall judge it to be to the public advantage, permit such association or person to register such mark as a trade-mark in respect of such goods, whether or not such association or person be a trade association or trader or possessed of a goodwill in connection with such certifying. When so registered such trade-mark shall be deemed in all respects to be a registered trade-mark, and such association or person shall be deemed to be the proprietor thereof, save that such trade-mark shall be transmissible or assignable only by permission of the minister.

(2) The proprietor of a mark registered under this section or

of a mark originally registered in the Patent Office in London under section 62 of the Trade-Marks Act, 1905, and subsequently registered under section 89 (which relates to the registration of trade-marks, registered in the Patent Office in London) of this act in the register of trade-marks in the office, may assign such mark to the Minister and the Minister may take an assignment thereof, and on such assignment being made section 121 (which relates to the registration of trade-marks by Minister) of this act shall apply to such marks as fully as if the Minister had procured the registration thereof under the said section 121.

Registration of the trade-marks of associations is provided for in Great Britain in section 62 of the law of 1905, as follows:

SEC. 62. Where any associaiton or person undertakes the examination of any goods in respect of origin, material, mode of manufacture, quality, accuracy, or other characteristic, and certifies the result of such examination by mark used upon or in connection with such goods, the Board of Trade may, if they shall judge it to be to the public advantage, permit such association or person to register such mark as a trade-mark in respect of such goods, whether or not such association or person be a trading association or trader or possessed of a goodwill in connection with such examination and certifying. When so registered such trade-mark shall be deemed in all respects to be a registered trade-mark, and such association or person to be the proprietor thereof, save that such trade-mark shall be transmissible or assignable only by permission of the Board of Trade.

In an amendment, dated April 29, 1913, to the trade-mark law of Denmark, there is in article 1 a provision relative to collective marks, as follows:

ART. 1. National associations the purpose of which is to safeguard the collective industrial interests of their members may, even when they themselves do not carry on any of the industrial or commercial enterprises mentioned in Law No. 52 of the 11th of April 1890, acquire on behalf of their members, by means of registration, the exclusive right of using collective marks, serving to distinguish in commerce the products of their members from those of other persons or to allow of control.

Danish public authorities entrusted with the safeguarding of the collective industrial interests of certain groups of citizens shall also be allowed to acquire such right.

Marks of this nature shall be governed by the provisions contained in the above-mentioned law, Laws No. 170 of the 19th of December 1898, and No. 71 of the 29th of March 1908, and Decree No. 169 of the 7th of December 1908, in such a way that the collective marks may be assimilated in all respects, even as regards the question whether they are registrable or not, with the marks of manufacture mentioned in the aforesaid laws, subject to provisions to the contrary in the following articles.

The Japanese trade-mark law contains provisions relative to association marks in the following articles:

ART. 27. A juridical person organized by persons in the same business, or by businessmen intimately connected, with the object of promoting the common business interests of the members of the body, may have its mark (hyosho) registered as a corporation mark (dantai-hyosho) in order to enable the members of such body to make exclusive use thereof for the merchandise connected with their business.

Except as otherwise provided in this law, corporation marks shall be deemed to be trade-marks and shall be governed by the provisions of this law relating to trade-marks.

ART. 28. A juridical person desiring to obtain registration of a corporation mark in accordance with the provisions of the preceding article shall provide in its articles of association particulars relating to the use of such corporation mark and obtain the approval of the Director of the Patent Office. The same applies when such particulars are changed.

ART. 29. A claim for damages for an infringement of a corporation mark right also includes damages done to the members of the body (organization).

ART. 30. In case a juridical person referred to in article 27 is amalgamated or divided, if the right arising from an application for the registration of a corporation mark, or a corporation mark right, is to be transferred from one juridical person to another the approval of the Director of the Patent Office shall be obtained. In such case the provisions of article 28 apply mutatis mutandis.

ART. 31. In any of the cases referred to in any of the following numbers, the registration of a corporation mark shall be canceled by a trial:

1. If a juridical person has caused or permitted the members to use the corporation mark contrary to the provisions of the articles of association approved by the Director of the Patent Office under the provisions of article 28 or the preceding article (article 30), or connived at such use;

2. If a juridical person has caused or permitted persons other than the members thereof to use the corporation mark, or connived at the use thereof by persons other than the members.

A juridical person, the registration of whose corporation mark has been canceled under the provisions of the preceding paragraph, cannot obtain registration of an identical or similar corporation mark for identical or similar merchandise for a period of 5 years from the day of cancellation. In this case the provisions of article 16 and article 22 apply mutatis mutandis.

ART. 32. A juridical person for which a corporation mark is registered shall, at the time of registration, pay in a single lump sum of 100 yen as a registration fee for each matter.

A juridical person for which a renewal of the period of duration of a corporation mark right is registered shall, at the time of registration, pay in a single lump sum of 150 yen as a registration fee for each matter.

ART. 33. The provisions of the six (6) preceding articles (27–32) apply mutatis mutandis when a public juridical person (ko-hojin) desires to obtain registration of a corporation mark in order to cause it to be exclusively used by the business men within its district for merchandise connected with their business.

In the Polish law provision is made for the registration of trademarks of associations as follows:

ART. 137. Associations of merchants, being legal bodies within the Republic of Poland, may apply for the registration of trade-marks so as to insure to their members the exclusive right of marking goods, originating from their enterprises, with one mark.

ART. 138. The regulations of part III of this law shall be applied to these trade-marks except where otherwise prescribed by section VII.

ART. 139. The association shall be the owner of the trade-marks; the members of the association shall enjoy the right of using the trade-mark so long as they belong to the association. The association may not transfer the rights in the trade-mark to other parties, and these rights shall expire in case of liquidation of the association. The association alone shall be empowered to prosecute for infringement.

ART. 140. When applying for the registration of a trade-mark the association need not mention any names of enterprises, but shall merely submit to the Registration Department a copy of its statutes and give the names of the persons who represent it. All changes in connection with the names of representatives must be notified to the Registration Department.

The trade-marks of associations shall be entered on a special register.

ART. 141. Anyone, as well as the attorney general of the Republic of Poland, acting in the public interest, may lodge a claim with the Claims Department demanding the cancellation of the rights of the association to a trade-mark, if the members of the association commit abuses which lead chiefly to cheating the consumers.

Foreign legal persons may enjoy the right prescribed in the above regulations in connection with trade-marks of associations only if reciprocity is granted to Polish legal persons in the country concerned.

In New Zealand provision is made for the registration of the special trade-marks in article 93, as follows:

ART. 93. Where any association or person undertakes to certify the origin, material, mode of manufacture, quality, accuracy, or other characteristic of any goods by mark used upon or in connection with such goods, the Registrar, if and so long as he is satisfied that such association or person is competent to certify as aforesaid, may, if he shall judge it to be to the public advantage, permit such association or person to register such mark as a trade-mark in respect of such goods, whether or not such association or person be a trading association or trader or possessed of a goodwill in connection with such certifying. When so registered such trade-mark shall be deemed in all respects to be a registered trade-mark, and such association or person to be the proprietor thereof, save that such trade-mark shall be transmissible or assignable only by permission of the registrar.

The general recognition which is given to the right of associations to register their trade-mark is noted in the International Convention for the Protection of Industrial Property, as revised at The Hague on November 6, 1925, articles 7 bis and 10 ter of which are:

Art. 7 bis. The contracting countries undertake to allow the filing of, and to protect trade-marks belonging to, associations the existence of which is not contrary to law of the country of origin, even if such associations do not possess an industrial or commercial establishment.

Nevertheless, each country shall be the sole judge of the particular conditions on which an association may be allowed to obtain protection for its marks.

Art. 10 ter. The contracting countries undertake to assure to the nationals of other countries of the Union appropriate legal remedies to repress effectively all acts set forth in articles 9, 10, and 10 bis.

They undertake, moreover, to provide measures to permit syndicates and associations representing the industry or the trade interested, and of which existence is not contrary to the laws of their country, to take action in justice or before the administrative authorities in view of the repression of the acts set forth in articles 9, 10, and 10 bis so far as the law of the country in which protection is claimed permits it to the syndicates and associations of the country.

The viewpoint in the Western Hemisphere on this subject is to be noted in the General Inter-American Convention for Trade-Mark and Commercial Protection, signed at Washington on February 20, 1929, article 6 of which is as follows:

ART. 6. The contracting States agree to admit to registration or deposit and to protect collective marks and marks of associations, the existence of which is not contrary to the laws of the country of origin, even when such associations do not own a manufacturing, industrial, commercial, or agricultural establishment.

Each country shall determine the particular conditions under which such marks may be protected.

States, Provinces, or municipalities, in their character of corporations, may own, use, register, or deposit marks, and shall in that sense enjoy the benefits of this convention.

American trade associations desiring to register their trade-marks abroad may experience difficulty when the foreign law requires a certified copy of the home registration in order that protection may be obtained. Until our laws are changed to bring them into conformity with the foregoing conventions, which have been ratified by the United States, it would seem that registration can be obtained abroad only when the foreign law does not require registration in the home country.

NATIONAL OR STATE MARKS

Of late there has been a tendency to establish what are known as National or State trade-marks. Such marks are not limited to a national government but may be used by States, municipalities, and other political subdivisions. Their purpose, as a general rule, is to identify the place of production and to indicate that the goods on which they are used have been produced under a particular mode of manufacture or accuracy and are of a certain quality, quantity, etc. The mark may not be used indiscriminately but only in accordance with the provisions set forth in laws and official regulations.

For a number of years there has been agitation in the United

States for the establishment of a national trade-mark to be used on goods made in this country. As yet, no legislation has been passed by the Federal Government in this regard.

In a law assented to on July 5, 1935, which established the Dominion Trade and Industries Commission, Canada provided for a national trade-mark, to be known as "Canada Standard" or the initials "C. S."[1] Any producer, manufacturer, dealer, or merchant in Canada may apply this national trade-mark to any commodity produced, manufactured, or sold by him if such commodity conforms to the requirements of a specification of a commodity standard established under the provisions of law. The application of this national trade-mark to any commodity in violation of the law usually subjects those guilty to a penalty, for each and every offense, not exceeding $5,000 in the case of a corporation and not exceeding $1,000 in the case of individuals; and, in addition, in the case of an individual, to imprisonment for a term not exceeding 6 months.

The Irish Free State provides, in article 121 of the Industrial Property Act of 1927, for the registration of a mark which would seem to be a National or State trade-mark, thus:

121. (1) Any minister may procure the registration in part A of the register of a mark intended to indicate the origin, material, mode of manufacture, quality, accuracy, or other characteristic of goods for which it is applied; and every such mark when so registered shall be deemed to be in all respects, save as is otherwise provided by this section, a registered trade-mark, and the minister by whom its registration was procured shall be and be registered as the proprietor thereof.

(2) An application for the registration of a mark under the foregoing subsection shall be made in the prescribed manner by a minister, and the registration of the mark shall be subject to

[1] The Supreme Court of Canada on June 17, 1936, handed down a judgment to the effect that sections 18–19 of the Dominion Trade and Industries Commission Act (secs. 18–19 relating to "Canada Standard" or the initials "C. S.") are unconstitutional. This judgment was an "advisory opinion" only and it is likely that an appeal may be taken to the Judiciary Committee of the Privy Council in England for final determination of the legal status thereof.

the provisions of this act relating to the registration of a trade-mark in part A of the register save insofar as such provisions are inconsistent with the provisions of this section.

(3) Any minister may procure the registration in any register maintained in any place outside Saorstat Eireann [the Irish Free State] of a mark (whether registered or not registered under the foregoing provisions of this section) intended to indicate the origin, material, mode of manufacture, quality, accuracy, or other characteristic of goods if and so far as and subject to such conditions as such registration is permitted by the law regulating such register, and in any such case may procure himself to be entered in such register as the proprietor of such mark.

(4) A minister who is the registered proprietor of any such mark as is mentioned in the foregoing subsections of this section may grant to any person a license to use such mark and to apply the same to all or any of the goods or classes of goods in respect of which such mark is registered, but in the case of a mark registered in a register maintained in a place out of Saorstat Eireann only if and so far as the granting of such license is permitted by the law regulating such register.

(5) Every license granted by a minister under the foregoing subsection shall have effect according to the terms thereof and shall contain provisions for insuring that the mark to which the license relates shall be applied by the licensee only to goods grown, manufactured, or produced in Saorstat Eireann, and any such license may also contain such terms and provisions as the minister granting the same shall think proper and in particular provisions for insuring that the mark to which the license relates shall only be applied to goods of a specified quality or description.

(6) A Minister who is the registered proprietor of any such mark as aforesaid may require the controller to enter on or remove from the register in respect of such mark the words "licenses not registrable," and, whenever and so long as such words are so entered in the register, licenses made by the Minister under this section in respect of such marks shall not (notwithstanding the provisions of section 127 (which relate to registration of assign-

ments, etc.) of this act) be or be capable of being entered in the register or be refused admission in evidence in any court merely on account of such nonentry in the register.

(7) A Minister who is the registered proprietor of any such mark as aforesaid may at any time take such lawful steps, whether by action, prosecution at law, or otherwise, as he shall think proper to prevent, restrain, or punish infringements of or otherwise to protect such mark and may take such steps in Saorstat Eireann or any other country in which he is registered as such proprietor.

(8) A mark registered under this section shall be deemed to be a trade-mark within the meaning of any enactment heretofore passed by the Oireachtas relating to the registration of trade-marks by Ministers.

(9) In this section the word "Minister" means a Minister head of a Department of State under the Ministers and Secretaries Act, 1924 (No. 16 of 1924).

International conventions for the protection of industrial property, particularly the convention signed at The Hague on November 6, 1925, and the General Inter-American Convention for Trade and Commercial Protection, signed at Washington on February 20, 1929, contain provisions relative to the registration of national, provincial, municipal, and official control and guaranty marks. Thus by article 6 of the latter convention the contracting States agree to admit to registration or deposit marks of States, Provinces, or municipalities, and all the benefits of the conventions are applicable to those marks.

MULTIPLE TRADE-MARKS

In some business enterprises their owners use but a single trade-mark on their products, whether or not such enterprises produce or sell one or several products. In other enterprises their owners find it desirable to use different marks for each product or one general mark with certain variations or additional combinations to distinguish their various products. The desirability, from a marketing standpoint, of using one or several trade-marks is a question that each individual enterprise must decide for itself.

However, the fact that the use of many trade-marks on different products may be expensive because of the possible necessity for registering each mark should not be overlooked.

This does not mean that where one mark is used on several different kinds of products a single registration will protect it for all of them. In some foreign countries separate applications must be filed for the registration of trade-marks used on goods which are included in different official classifications of merchandise. In only a few countries may a single registration be made for all products. Multiple registration abroad, although expensive, may be necessary and should be considered when protection is sought abroad.

COLOR AS A DISTINCTIVE FEATURE OF TRADE-MARKS

The distinctiveness of a trade-mark is not always confined to the design or configuration; color is often a distinguishing feature. Color as a component part of a trade-mark is readily observed by persons who might otherwise fail to notice a particular or unusual design. It is especially useful when the purchaser is illiterate.

The exporter whose trade-mark consists of color or a combination of colors must be sure that he claims this as a distinctive feature if the foreign law permits. In some countries where a foreign trade-mark can be registered only if it has been registered in the home country of the applicant, the trade-mark will be registered in the identical form in which it had been registered at home. If the color was not protected in the home registration, then it probably cannot be claimed in the registration sought abroad.

In the Irish State a trade-mark may be limited in whole or in part to one or more specified colors, and in such cases color will be considered in determining distinctive characteristics of such marks. If a trade-mark is registered without limitation of color, it will be deemed to be registered for all colors. A like provision appears in the laws of other countries, and care should be taken when applying for registration abroad to indicate the colors desired to be protected and to furnish, when required, copies of the labels or trade-marks with the color clearly indicated.

Attention was called not long ago to the case of a well-known confection, which is extensively marketed in the United States in 5-cent packages the labels of which have various colors, each separate color being used on a different flavor. The candy was not permitted to be sold in a certain country of South America under these labels. Although the American corporation applied for and obtained registration of its trade-mark, no claim was made of exclusive property in the labels and the colors. When the marketing of its goods was peremptorily stopped, the corporation on investigation found that a competitor was selling a similar product under almost identical labels (minus the trade-mark) in the colors used by the American manufacturer. Through its attorneys it applied for registration of all of its labels, claiming the several colors used therein as a distinctive feature. The trade-mark authorities denied the registration on the ground that the competitor had previously registered his labels. There was no alternative but for the American firm to adopt new labels with the different color combinations or to enter into some agreement whereby the competitor would no longer use the labels and would transfer his rights therein to the American corporation.

FLAGS, PUBLIC INSIGNIA, MEDALS, AND AWARDS

Where a product has been the subject of an award at a national or international exhibition, the manufacturer often wants his label to advertise the fact. The use on trade-marks of medals and other badges of distinction has long been in vogue. Going a step further, labels are often so made up as to simulate flags, coats of arms, crests, and other public insignia, appealing in this way to a preference of some consumers for goods which appear to have royal sanction or approval of the State or public authority.

Limitations in Law in New Zealand

In the trade-mark laws of some countries there are specific provisions designed to prohibit or at least to limit the extent to which such distinctive badges may be used. Thus, in New Zealand, the registrar may refuse to accept any application for the registration of a trade-mark upon which the following appear:

Representations of Their Majesties or any member of the royal family.

Representations of the royal or imperial arms or royal crests, or arms or crests so nearly resembling them as to lead to mistake, or of the British royal or imperial crowns, or of the British national flags, or the word "royal" or "imperial," or any other words, letters, or devices calculated to lead persons to think that the applicant has royal patronage or authorization.

Where representations of the armorial bearings, insignia, decoration, or flags of any State, city, borough, town, place, society, body corporate, or institution appear on a mark, the applicant shall, if so required, furnish the registrar with a consent from such official as the registrar may consider entitled to give consent to the use of such emblems.

Provisions in the Japanese Law

Japan prohibits the registration not only of trade-marks which are identical with the public insignia and national flags, but also of those which contain or are similar to a certificate of merit, award, or testimonial. The following trade-marks are nonregistrable:

Those which contain a device identical with, or similar to, the imperial chrysanthemum crest.

Those which are identical with, or similar to, the national flag, the military or naval flags, a decoration (order) a medal of merit, a badge, and those identical with, or similar to, a foreign national flag.

Those which have a device identical with, or similar to, a medal, certificate of merit, or testimonial awarded by an exhibition held by the Government or the administration of a Do, Fu, or Ken, or an equivalent thereto, or with the permission of the Government or by an exhibition held in a foreign country either by or with the permission of the authorities; but this does not apply when a recipient of such a medal, certificate of merit, or testimonial desires to use the device thereof as a part of his trade-mark.

The trade-mark law of Japan was amended to include those identical with or similar to the crests, badges, or flags of a country which is a member of the International Convention for the Protection of Industrial Property and which have been specified by the competent minister.

International Regime on the Subject

The international regime envisages a definite understanding that national flags and public insignia are not subject to appropriation and use in connection with industrial property rights. The International Convention for the Protection of Industrial Property provides:

The contracting countries undertake to refuse or invalidate registration, and to prohibit by appropriate means the use, failing authorization from the competent authority, whether as trade-mark or as components of such, of all coats of arms, flags, and other State emblems of contracting countries, official control and guaranty signs, and stamps adopted by them, and all imitation from an heraldic point of view.

The prohibition of official control and guaranty signs and stamps shall apply only in cases where marks which comprise them are intended to be used on merchandise of the same or a similar nature.

Nationals of each country, who are authorized to make use of State emblems and signs and stamps of their country, may use them even if there be a similarity with those of another country.

The contracting countries undertake to prohibit the unauthorized use in trade of State coats of arms of other countries when such use would be liable to cause confusion as to the origin of the product.

In the Inter-American Convention for Trade-Mark and Commercial Protection, signed at Washington on February 20, 1929, the registration and use without authorization of national flags and public insignia is forbidden:

The contracting States agree to refuse to register or to cancel the registration and to prohibit the use, without authorization by competent authority, of marks which include National and State flags and coats of arms, National or State seals, designs on public coins and postage stamps, official labels, certificates or guarantees, or any national or State official insignia or simulations of any of the foregoing.

The user of such distinctive signs takes the risk of running counter to the law. Further, practically all trade-mark laws, as well as the international conventions referred to above and other agreements between nations, prohibit the use of the Red Cross (Geneva Cross) without authorization.

COMMERCIAL NAMES

The question is often raised whether or not registration of individual, firm, or corporate names under which a business is conducted is obligatory in order to protect the right to their use. As a general rule, protection of such names is afforded without any requirement of registration, but in some countries they may be recorded in registers provided therefor. If a person's name is similar to that already in use by another in the same industry, he must adopt some suitable modification or notation in his name in order to avoid confusion.

In Canada, a trade name under which any business is carried on, whether it be the name of a corporation, a partnership, or an individual, is protected without any formality of registration. However, the protection afforded will not affect the right of any individual or group of individuals to adopt for use and use his or their own personal names or surnames as a trade name for a business commenced and carried on for his or their own direct benefit in good faith and without any intention to deceive.

Foreign laws on this subject are not uniform, but the Argentine law (No. 3975 of November 25, 1900) is illustrative of the legal provisions in some countries:

ART. 42. The name of an agriculturist, merchant, or manufacturer, and that of the firm, that of the sign or the designation of a house or establishment that deals in determined articles or products, shall constitute a property for the effects of this law.

Art. 43. Whoever shall desire to carry on an industry, line of trade, or branch of agriculture, already under exploitation by another person, with the same name or with the same conventional designation, shall adopt a modification that will visibly distinguish that name or that designation from the one that the preexisting house or establishment uses.

Art. 44. If the party injured by the use of a name of manufacture, of commerce, or branch of agriculture, does not lodge claim within the term of 1 year from the day on which it commenced to be used by another, his right shall become outlawed.

Art. 45. Joint stock companies shall have the right to the name that they bear, the same as any individual, and they shall be subject to the same limitations.

Art. 46. The right to the exclusive use of a name as property shall cease when the commercial establishment or the branch of industry or agriculture that bears it has been discontinued.

Art. 47. There shall not be necessary the registration of the name for exercising the rights accorded by this law, except in case it forms part of a mark.

In the international regime on the subject, universal recognition is given to the exclusive right of those who use, in connection with their business, certain trade or commercial names without the requirement of complying with any formalities in the law. An illustration of this may be found in the International Convention for the Protection of Industrial Property, signed at The Hague on November 6, 1925, where we read in article 8:

Art. 8. A trade name shall be protected in all the countries of the Union without the obligation of filing or registration, whether it form part or not of a trade-mark.

In the Inter-American Convention for Trade-Mark and Commercial Protection, signed at Washington on February 20, 1929, an entire chapter is devoted to the protection of commercial names.

REGISTRATION OF LABEL INCLUDING TRADE-MARK

It often is desirable to register an entire label, wrapper, or container which includes in its make-up the trade-mark of the American manufacturer, in those countries where registration may be effected.

An action for infringement of a label cannot always be brought against an infringer if the plaintiff is not the registered proprietor of the label. While there may be a remedy for unfair competition against those who simulate the general appearance of a label or container, proof of the fraud which is the basis of such an action is not always feasible.

Some time ago an American exporter who enjoyed a good market for his products in Chile applied for registration of his trade-mark, which consisted of a word mark superimposed on a fanciful design. He sold various products in Chile and used his trade-mark on all of them. The exporter learned, after a time, that a competitor in that country was marketing similar goods under labels identical with his save that the labels contained a different trade-mark. Inasmuch as the color scheme used on the labels was more apt to attract the attention of the purchaser than the trade-mark, the American manufacturer tried to prevent the competitor from using labels identical with his. Investigation showed, however, that the competitor had obtained registration of the labels and the only course open to the American exporter was to adopt a new label. Mere registration of the trade-mark alone does not always afford the desired protection, and in those countries where the law permits, it may be desirable to register the entire label.

WHAT MAY BE REGISTERED AS TRADE-MARKS

It is difficult to give a definition of what may be registered as trade-marks in view of the fact that the laws of some countries do not indicate what may constitute a registrable mark. By inference, it may be assumed that those marks which are not expressly prohibited from registration would be admissible for registration. It does not always happen, however, that a mark which would be registrable under foreign law is one that would be desirable for use in a particular country.

Illustrative of what may be registered as a trade-mark is the provision relative thereto in the trade-mark law of Colombia, article 30 of which is as follows:

Art. 30. There may be utilized as marks of manufacture, commerce, and agriculture the denominations of objects and the names of persons in a distinctive form, emblems, initials and monograms, coats of arms, engravings, stamps, prints, lithographs, designs, vignettes, signs, labels, seals, borders, bands, figures, invented words, numbers, letters, symbols, phrases having a special design, wrappers, packages, containers, and any other novel sign, by means of which the products of a factory, business, or an agricultural or extractive industry may be distinguished.

The trade-mark law of Italy contains in article 1 the following provision:

Art. 1. Whoever shall adopt a mark or other sign for distinguishing the products of his industry, the merchandise of his commerce, and the animals of a breed belonging to him, shall have the exclusive use thereof provided that he effect the deposit prescribed in this law.

The mark or distinctive sign must be different from those already legally used by other persons, and it must indicate the place of origin, the factory, and the line of business, in such way as to evidence the name of the person, the style of the society, and the denomination of the establishment from which emanate the products or goods; when it is a question of animals and small objects there shall be proposed and approved a special abbreviation or other equivalent sign.

The characteristic signature of the producer, merchant, or proprietor, engraved on products, or reproduced by means of a stamp or any other durable means, or even written by hand, may constitute a mark or distinctive sign.

When the owner of a mark is uncertain as to its registrability abroad, he should refer to the specific provisions of the law on the subject before filing an application for registration and thus save time and filing fees.

NONREGISTRABLE MARKS

Every trade-mark which is in use in the business world is not necessarily one that could be protected under the laws of all countries. There are many trade-marks the use of which would probably be considered illegal in some countries for the reason that they come within the purview of the restrictions contained in the law. Registration of marks of this kind will be prohibited, and no rights in them may be acquired.

Trade-marks which are contrary to good morals or public order and those which are identical with or are confusingly similar to marks previously registered by another for goods of the same class may not generally be registered abroad. Many laws contain provisions prohibiting the registration of marks depicting flags, public insignia, and the like, unless authorization for their use has been obtained. The name or portrait of an individual other than the applicant may not generally be used as a trade-mark, and unless consent for their use has been obtained they would be denied registration.

There is no rule which would be universally applicable by which to determine the marks included in this class. Reference must be made to the laws of each country on the subject.

ASSIGNMENT AND TRANSFER

Title to valuable rights in registered trade-marks has often been acquired by assignment. The mere contract of assignment, while operative as between the parties thereto, will not, under the laws of many countries, be effective against third parties unless due record of the assignment is made in the trade-mark register and, in some instances, by publication in the appropriate journal or other periodical.

The question often arises as to whether or not the transferee has actually obtained the property rights in the mark intended to be transferred—a situation most likely to occur in countries where the law provides that assignment of trade-mark rights can be made only in connection with the goodwill of the business in which the marks are used. In those countries any contract purporting to pass ownership in a trade-mark which did not include the goodwill in the business would give the assignee no exclusive property in the right to the use of the trade-mark.

In Brazil, the trade-mark law contains the following provisions with regard to assignment of registered trade-marks:

ART. 97. A trade-mark is assignable by any of the means of assignment or transfer admitted in law.

ART. 98. A trade-mark may only be assigned with the kind of industry or trade for which it has been adopted, the assignment being recorded on the registration certificate upon examination of the authentic documents.

ART. 99. The transfer or assignment of a trade-mark will not produce effect while it is not registered at the Directorate General of Industrial Property.

ART. 100. Upon presentation of the authentic acts of transfer or assignment, they shall be recorded in the general registry and, after noting the registry on the certificate of the trade-mark, the latter will be returned to the applicant, the documents remaining on file.

In France, no transfer of property, assignment, or concession of a registered trade-mark can be conferred as against third parties, except when due record of the transfer together with the name and address of the assignee is made in the special Register of Marks of Manufacture and Commerce kept in the National Office of Industrial Property.

The trade-mark law of Hungary of January 6, 1890, as amended, contains the following provisions relative to the assignment of trade-mark rights:

ART. 9. The right to a mark shall go with the business for which the mark is intended, shall expire with the same, and shall be transferred to the new proprietor in case of transfer of ownership.

The new owner, however, if he does not continue to conduct

his business under an unchanged name, shall effect the assignment of the mark. Until this assignment has been executed in the Register of the Chamber of Commerce and Industry, he cannot make valid the right to the mark, and all official communications relating to the mark may be forwarded, to his disadvantage, to the registered owner of the mark or to his representative of record.

ART. 20. In order to transfer the right to a mark, within the meaning of art. 9, the assignee must produce proof of his having acquired the business to which it relates.

It is essential that the law on the subject in each country wherein it is intended to assign property rights in a trade-mark be thoroughly understood before any agreement or contract of assignment is formulated. A very important thing to keep in mind is that of making appropriate notation in the trade-mark office of all changes in title.

INHERITANCE OF TRADE-MARK RIGHTS

In some countries trade-mark rights are the subject of inheritance and may be disposed of by last will and testament. In Germany, for example, the law is quite explicit in this regard, article 7 of the trade-mark law of May 12, 1894, as amended, reading:

SEC. 7. Rights resulting from the declaration or registry of a merchandise mark shall pass by inheritance, and may be transmitted to other persons by testamentary disposition. They cannot, however, pass to others except along with the business to which the mark appertains. The transfer shall be entered in the Roll of Marks at the instance of the successor, provided the assent of the original owner is satisfactorily established. If the original owner is deceased, the successor must establish his title.

The new owner cannot benefit by the rights accruing from registration until the transfer has been recorded in the Roll of Marks.

Decisions and judgments of the Patent Office that require to be notified to the proprietor of a mark must be addressed to the proprietor of record. If he is deceased, the Patent Office may, at its discretion, consider the notice as given, or cause search to be made for the heirs, in order to notify them.

The heir or legatee to the right of ownership in a trade-mark should exercise due diligence in making the appropriate change of title in the trade-mark register. If this is not done promptly, action for infringement may be barred.

PIRACY OF TRADE-MARKS

The consumer is aware of the value of trade-marks, labels, and other identifying media, for he sees in them a protection for himself. He is less apt to be convinced that other products "just as good" will answer his purpose, and today more than ever he insists on obtaining the product under its trade-mark or symbol. How can he know that he is receiving the genuine product if similar, although sometimes inferior, products bear the trade-mark so familiar to him?

The usurpation of trade-marks in whole or in part, whether it amounts to an out-and-out piracy or to infringement of a part of the trade-mark by unauthorized persons, has been the cause of considerable annoyance to manufacturers throughout the world. Among the assets of a bankrupt concern put up for sale at public auction in Argentina some years ago were the exclusive rights to the use of well-known American marks which the bankrupt had registered in that country. Thousands of dollars were paid for these rights—which could have been saved if the American manufacturers had taken the precaution of registering the brands.

International conventions and bilateral agreements between countries have done much to strike at unfair trade practices of this kind by giving prior users rights of priority during specified periods. Through these provisions a prior user who has registered his mark in his home country may assert, during such periods of priority, a better right against the acts of another who has applied for registration in the meantime.

The most effective way to combat these unfair practices is to have one's trade-marks registered abroad. It will often be found that the expenditure of as little as $100 in registering a trade-mark on the inception of a marketing program in a particular country will save the expenditure of thousands of dollars later in trying to purchase rights which have been unfairly, although legally, acquired by another.

It would seem that, after all the warnings and admonitions sent out to the public during the past several years by Government agencies, trade associations newspapers, and others, no further discussion of this matter would be required. Nevertheless, thousands of American trade-marks are continually being infringed upon and pirated abroad by unauthorized persons. Export sales managers should realize the necessity of protecting markets established after considerable effort and expense. The law will not countenance laches.

SEIZURE AND SEQUESTRATION

Penalties are sometimes imposed upon those who infringe the trade-mark rights of others. These penalties may be a fine or imprisonment or both. In addition to any action taken by the public authorities, the individual who has been damaged as the result of the infringement may bring an action for indemnity.

As a general rule the laws of all countries afford ample remedies for acts violative of the trade-mark rights of others. The trade-mark law of Peru will serve to illustrate this. It provides in the following terms the penalties which must be paid by those who injure others by usurpation and infringement of their trade-marks:

Usurpation of the right of ownership of a mark of manufacture shall be punished by fines of from 25 to 500 soles, or with imprisonment of from 40 days to 6 months. There shall be liable to this penalty:

(1) Those who falsify or change in any way a mark of commerce or of manufacture;

(2) Those who place upon their own products or articles of commerce a mark that belongs to another person;

(3) Those who knowingly sell, offer for sale, or agree that there be sold to them, or consent to sell or circulate, articles that bear counterfeit or fraudulently affixed marks;

(4) Those who knowingly sell, offer for sale, or agree that there be sold to them, counterfeit marks, or even authentic marks, without the consent of their legitimate owners;

(5) Those who, with intent to defraud, mark or have marked articles with false labels or designations, whether with respect to the nature, quality, quantity, number, weight, or measure, or of the country of origin or manufacture;

(6) Those who knowingly sell, offer for sale, or agree that there be sold to them, articles with the false indications to which the preceding paragraph refers.

In cases of repetition the penalty shall be doubled.

In order that there be infraction or usurpation of the right, it shall suffice that the counterfeit mark shall have been affixed to a single article.

Those who have sold or shall have for sale any article with a counterfeit mark, infringing or usurping legitimate rights, shall be obliged to inform in writing the proprietor of the mark with reference to the name and address of the persons from whom they have made the purchase, or from whom they have received the offer, and the dates on which negotiations commenced. Whoever shall refuse to supply this information may be compelled judicially, under pain of being held as an accomplice in or concealer of the fraud.

Articles with a counterfeit mark that are found in the possession of the counterfeiter or his agents shall be confiscated and sold, the proceeds of the sale being applied to the payment of the costs and indemnification established by law, and the excess to the schools of the provinces in which the sequestration was made.

False marks that are found in the possession of the transgressor, and the instruments and tools employed in the falsification, shall be destroyed.

The right of making criminal accusation against transgressors shall lie exclusively in the one injured; however, the proceedings once begun, the State's Attorney shall take part. The plaintiff may, nevertheless, at any time before the delivery of judgment, withdraw from the accusation and terminate the case.

Persons injured may institute civil action for damages and injuries against the authors of the fraud and their accomplices. The sentence shall be published at the cost of the guilty party. The action shall become outlawed in 3 years from the commission of the infraction, and 1 year after the owner shall have had knowledge thereof.

The Hague revision of the International Convention for the Protection of Industrial Property contains a stipulation whereby goods bearing illegally a trade-mark or trade name will be seized in the country where the mark or name was illegally applied or in the country to which the article bearing it has been imported.

In many countries goods bearing infringing trade-marks will be prohibited entry or, if allowed to enter the customhouse, will be detained there pending adjudication by a court. In some countries they will be confiscated for the benefit of the infringing party or the State.

CUSTOMS PROVISIONS

The owner who has obtained protection for his trade-mark by registering it under foreign laws may have an additional remedy for infringement of his rights under customs and tariff regulations.

The importation into a country of goods bearing fraudulent marks, or which infringe the rights of registered proprietors of similar marks, may be prohibited.

In the United States the following provisions of section 526 of the Tariff Act of 1930 apply in instances of this kind:

SEC. 526. (a) That it shall be unlawful to import into the United States any merchandise of foreign manufacture if such merchandise, or the label, sign, print, package, wrapper, or receptacle, bears a trade-mark owned by a citizen of, or by a corporation or association created or organized within, the United States, and registered in the Patent Office by a person domiciled in the United States, under the provisions of an act entitled "An act to authorize the registration of trade-marks used in commerce with foreign nations or among the several States or with Indian tribes, and to protect the same," approved February 20, 1905, as amended, if a copy of the certificate of registration of such trade-mark is filed with the Secretary of the Treasury, in the manner provided in section 27 of such act, unless written consent of the owner of such trade-mark is produced at the time of making entry.

(b) Any such merchandise imported into the United States in violation of the provisions of this section shall be subject to seizure and forfeiture for violation of the customs laws.

(c) Any person dealing in such merchandise may be enjoined from dealing therein within the United States or may be required to export or destroy such merchandise or to remove or obliterate such trade-mark and shall be liable for the same damages and profits provided for wrongful use of a trade-mark, under the provisions of such act of February 20, 1905, as amended.

Trade-marks registered under the act of March 19, 1930, are entitled to the protection afforded by section 27 of the Trade-Mark Act of February 20, 1905, but are not entitled to the additional protection afforded by section 526, Tariff Act of 1930.

Section 27 of the Trade-Mark Act of February 20, 1905, prescribes:

That no article of imported merchandise which shall copy or simulate the name of any domestic manufacture, or manufacturer, or trader, or of any manufacturer or trader located in any foreign country which, by treaty, convention, or law affords similar privileges to citizens of the United States, or which shall copy or simulate a trade-mark registered in accordance with the provisions of this act or shall bear a name or mark calculated to induce the public to believe that the article is manufactured in the United States, or that it is manufactured in any foreign country or locality other than the country or locality in which it is in fact manufactured, shall be admitted to entry at any customhouse of the United States; and in order to aid the officers of the customs in enforcing this prohibition, any domestic manufacturer or trader, or any foreign manufacturer or trader who is entitled under the provisions of a treaty, convention, declaration, or agreement between the United States and any foreign country to the advantages afforded by law to citizens of the United States in respect to trade-marks and commercial names, may require his name and residence, and the name of the locality in which his goods are manufactured, and a copy of the certificate of registration of his trade-mark, issued in accordance with the provisions of this act, to be recorded in books which shall be kept for this purpose in the Department of the Treasury, under such regulations as the Secretary of the Treasury shall prescribe, and may furnish to the Department facsimiles of his name, the name of the locality in which his goods are manufactured, or of his registered trade-mark; and thereupon the Secretary of the Treasury shall cause one or more copies of the same to be transmitted to each collector or other proper officer of customs.

The United States Tariff Act contains, in section 337, provisions relative to the exclusion from entry of articles the importation of which would have the effect or tendency to destroy or substantially injure an industry or would amount to an unfair method of competition:

SEC. 337. (a) *Unfair Methods of Competition Declared Unlawful.* Unfair methods of competition and unfair acts in the importation of articles into the United States, or in their sale by the owner, importer, consignee, or agent of either, the effect or tendency of which is to destroy or substantially injure an industry, efficiently and economically operated in the United States, or to prevent the establishment of such an industry, or to restrain or monopolize trade and commerce in the United States, are hereby declared unlawful, and when found by the President to exist shall be dealt with, in addition to any other provisions of law, as hereinafter provided. . . . * * *

(e) *Exclusion of articles from entry.* Whenever the existence of any such unfair method or act shall be established to the satisfaction of the President he shall direct that the articles concerned in such unfair methods or acts, imported by any person violating the provisions of this act, shall be excluded from entry into the United States, and upon information of such action by the President, the Secretary shall, through the proper officers, refuse such entry. The decision of the President shall be conclusive.

The Canadian Customs Tariff in item 1209, schedule C, prohibits the importation of any goods manufactured in any foreign state or country which bear any name or trade-mark which is or purports to be the name or trade-mark of any manufacturer, dealer, or trader in the United Kingdom or in Canada, or in any other British country, unless such name or trade-mark is accompanied by a definite indication of the foreign state or country in which the goods were made or produced.

Under the trade-mark law of Bulgaria, goods bearing imitated marks or false commercial inscriptions will be forbidden entry into that country, article 52 providing:

ART. 52. The Customs Administration shall forbid the importation of goods bearing original or imitated marks of Bulgarian merchants or manufacturers or false commercial inscriptions.

Goods marked with the marks of merchants of this country may be admitted if they are intended for the owners of these marks, and if the place, the town, or the country where the goods have been bought or manufactured is clearly and legibly indicated in an indelible manner. The Customs Administration shall confiscate and deliver to the judicial authorities, together with the written testimony required, the marks imported by third persons.

The Customs Administration shall act as organ of the Ministry of Commerce and Agriculture, and it shall come to agreement directly with the latter in all matters affecting the present law.

In Finland the importation of goods bearing a Finnish mark registered in Finland is prohibited unless the consent of the owner of the mark has been obtained. If, however, an importation of this kind has been effected, the offender will be penalized and the goods confiscated. Goods introduced on which a foreign mark registered in Finland has been improperly applied and not being goods in transit will be confiscated.

The unfairness of importing goods illegally bearing a trademark or name, or of circulating them in trade after they have been admitted into a country, has been recognized in a number of international conventions on industrial property. Thus, in article 9 of the International Convention for Protection of Industrial Property, signed at The Hague on November 6, 1925, we read:

ART. 9. All goods illegally bearing a trade-mark or trade name shall be seized on importation into those countries of the Union where this mark or name has a right to legal protection.

Seizure shall be effected equally in the country where the mark or name was illegally applied, or in the country to which the article bearing it has been imported.

The seizure shall take place either at the request of the proper government department or of any other competent authority, or of any interested party or actual or legal person, in conformity with the domestic law of each country.

The authorities are not bound to effect the seizure in transit.

If the law of a country does not admit of seizure on importation, such seizure shall be replaced by prohibition of importation or seizure within such country.

If the law of any country does not admit either of seizure upon importation or of prohibition of importation or of seizure within the country, and until such time as this legislation shall be accordingly modified, these measures will be replaced by the remedies assured in such cases to nationals by the law of such country.

In the General Inter-American Convention for Trade-Mark and Commercial Protection, signed at Washington on February 20, 1929, the signatory countries agree that the manufacture, exportation, importation, distribution, or sale of those articles or products which directly or indirectly infringe any of the provisions of that convention with respect to trade-marks, commercial names, repression of unfair competition, or false indications of geographical origin of source will be forbidden.

Where the law requires that certified copies of trade-mark registration be filed with the customs officials in order to prevent the importation of goods bearing infringing marks, the registered proprietor should see to it without delay that this requirement is fulfilled.

ALTERATIONS OR CHANGES IN TRADE-MARKS

When a trade-mark has been registered for a particular class of goods, it may happen that its owner may desire to make slight alterations in the mark or to use it in its original or changed form with other goods. The question then arises as to the effect of these changes on the title to the registered mark. Much depends upon circumstances. It is possible that the use of a trade-mark in a manner quite different from that in which it was registered would not be considered a use of the registered mark. However, unless the law specifically states that alteration or change in a mark from the manner in which it has been registered will vitiate the right in the mark, it is altogether probable that slight changes which do not materially affect the general appearance of the mark could be made. Reference to the law of the particular country would be necessary in each individual case.

In a suit recently instituted in China, the defendant used a mark identical with that of the registered proprietor and was thereby causing confusion in the mind of the consumer and resulting in injury to the plaintiff. The marks used by both parties were identical, the only difference being that the defendant's mark was very much smaller in size than the plaintiff's.

The court ruled that this was not an infringement; that registration of a trade-mark granted an exclusive right only to that mark in the form and "size" in which it was registered, and use by another in a different size would not be an infringement. This, of course, is an unusual example. It is mentioned here in order that the reader may understand that changes in trade-marks, if made at all, should be made only when the title to a registered trade-mark will not be jeopardized thereby.

While most trade-mark laws are silent with regard to alterations and changes in trade-marks and their use in a manner different from that in which they have been registered, there are provisions in some laws which deal specifically with this subject. In New Zealand the proprietor of a registered trade-mark may apply to the registrar for leave to add to or alter a registered mark in a manner which does not substantially affect its identity. In the Union of South Africa, the trade-mark law contains a provision relative to additions and alterations of registered trade-marks, in article 134, as follows:

ART. 134. The registered proprietor of a trade-mark may in the prescribed manner apply to the registrar for leave to add to or alter the trade-mark in any manner not substantially affecting its identity, and the registrar may refuse or grant the leave on such terms as he thinks fit, but his refusal or the terms on which he grants the leave shall be subject to appeal to the court. If leave be granted, the registrar shall cause the register to be altered and shall in the prescribed manner advertise the trade-mark as altered.

The widespread acceptance of the principle that minor changes shall not impair the protection of the trade-mark may be noted in the General Inter-American Convention for Trade-Mark and Commercial Protection, signed at Washington on February 20, 1929:

ART. 13. The use of a trade-mark by its owner in a form different in minor or nonsubstantial elements from the form in which the mark has been registered in any of the contracting states shall not entail forfeiture of the registration or impair the protection of the mark.

In case the form or distinctive elements of the mark are substantially changed, or the list of goods to which it is to be applied is modified or increased, the proprietor of the mark may be required to apply for a new registration, without prejudice to the protection of the original mark or in respect to the original list of goods.

The requirements of the laws of the contracting states with respect to the legend which indicates the authority for the use of trade-marks shall be deemed fulfilled in respect to goods of foreign origin if such marks carry the words or indications legally used or required to be used in the country of origin of the goods.

Where the changes in registered trade-marks are deemed necessary, appropriate change should be made in the register.

CONCURRENT USE

Without any intent to infringe or defraud, a manufacturer or merchant will sometimes use a mark that is identical with or at least quite similar to one previously adopted and used by another. When a situation of this kind occurs, the question arises as to what are the rights of the respective parties. In those countries where the exclusive right to the use of a trade-mark is acquired solely on the basis of registration and the corresponding certificate, the registrant can restrain the use of the mark by another. He could also bring appropriate action for any damage resulting from an unauthorized use. Registration is notice to all the world of the exclusive rights of the recorded proprietor in the trade-mark.

Under the laws of some countries, where there has been an innocent use of similar trade-marks by two or more persons and their products have become well recognized under those marks, the parties may obtain the right to their continued use. However, the newcomer may be required to make a suitable modification of his mark to avoid confusing the consumer.

An illustration of this may be seen in article 9 of the Japanese trade-mark law, which is as follows:

ART. 9. Any person who has, in respect to identical or similar merchandise, used in good faith from before the application for the registration of a registered trade-mark of another person a mark identical with, or similar to, the same, and which is widely known among dealers and consumers, may continue the use thereof, notwithstanding the registration of the trade-mark of the other person. The same applies to a person who has succeeded to the use of the mark together with the business or pursuit.

In the case contemplated in the foregoing paragraph, the person entitled to the trade-mark right may require the user of the mark to add a suitable indication (hyoji) for preventing a confusion of merchandise.

In the trade-mark law of the Union of South Africa, provision is made that in the case of honest concurrent user or of special circumstances the court may, in its discretion, permit the registration of the same trade-mark or of nearly identical trade-marks for the same goods or description of goods by more than one proprietor, subject to such conditions and limitations (if any) as to mode or place of use or otherwise as it may think fit to impose.

A similar provision is included in the trade-mark law of Australia:

ART. 28. In case of honest concurrent user or of special circumstances, the registrar, law officer, or the court may, in his or its discretion, permit the registration of the same trade-mark or of nearly identical trade-marks for the same goods or description of goods by more than one proprietor, subject to such conditions and limitations as to mode or place of user or otherwise as he or it thinks fit to impose.

There are other countries which have similar provisions in their laws permitting concurrent use of identical or similar trade-marks by two or more persons, even though one is a newcomer, if his subsequent use of the mark was honest. If, however, it can be proved that a subsequent user had knowledge of the prior adoption and use by another, then of course the latter would prevail.

STATUS OF UNREGISTERED TRADE-MARKS

Registration is not the sole criterion by which ownership of a trade-mark is recognized. It may be prima-facie evidence of ownership in some countries, but could be set aside by one showing a better right, such as where the prior user of a mark is entitled to registration and its exclusive use.

In those countries where, in the absence of fraud, registration is conclusive proof of ownership of a mark, a mark which has not been registered will not be protected and can be said to have no legal status. The trade-mark may exist in fact but not in law. If, for example, the statutes decree that a trade-mark which has not been registered may not enjoy the benefits of the law, a court would not be able to afford remedies (such as in infringement proceedings) to those who have not registered their trade-marks as required.

With regard to the right to bring infringement suits on unregistered trade-marks, the trade-mark law of the Gold Coast Colony contains in article 48 the following:

No person shall be entitled to institute any proceedings to prevent, or to recover damages for, the infringement of an unregistered trade-mark unless such trade-mark has been in use for not less than 3 years prior to the commencement of such proceedings, and has been refused registration under this ordinance. The registrar may, on request, grant a certificate that such registration has been refused.

This matter should be clear in the minds of the American owners of trade-marks which they use or intend to use in foreign markets. A knowledge of it should be helpful in overcoming many of the difficulties encountered when competitors try to pass off their goods by using thereon trade-marks identical with or very similar to the trade-marks of another.

ABANDONMENT OF TRADE-MARKS

The purpose of trade-marks is to distinguish goods of manufacture and commerce. Their usage in trade may be an indication of their legal existence. When they cease to be used the right to their ownership may be questioned.

Trade-marks are sometimes abandoned intentionally or otherwise by their owners, and it matters little whether they have been registered. Abandonment may arise from various causes, such as failure to renew an expired registration, but usually an involuntary abandonment occurs through failure to use the mark during a certain length of time. Thus, in Venezuela, a trade-mark which has not been used during two consecutive years will be deemed to have been forfeited and will cease to have the protection of the law. One year after publication of such forfeiture any person may solicit the registration of the mark.

Loss of valuable trade-mark rights has occurred through technical questions of abandonment. Let us suppose that an American manufacturer, who is the owner of a trade-mark which he has used on goods shipped to Great Britain, finds it necessary to discontinue shipment of the manufactured product during a number of years, but, instead, will ship only raw materials without using the trade-mark on them. The raw materials will be fabricated into the finished product in England. He has entered into an agreement whereby he grants a license to the fabricator to use the mark on the finished product during that period. It may be asked what, if any, right the manufacturer or the licensee has in the trade-mark at the end of those years.

Trade-mark rights are acquired in Great Britain on the common-law basis of user. During the years that the American manufacturer ceased using the mark in Great Britain, both consuming public and the trade have associated the mark with the licensee and not with the American manufacturer. It would be a difficult task to prove a right of ownership in a trade-mark that was thus apparently abandoned by its former owner. It is therefore incumbent upon trade-mark owners to maintain their rights in their marks.

Where, owing to a diminution of trade in a particular country, it is not feasible to continue to ship one's trade-marked goods there, it may be desirable to insert from time to time, in local newspapers or other periodicals, an appropriate advertisement or notice of ownership in the mark. Such advertisement or notice may have some evidentiary value in any action arising from a question of abandonment of the trade-mark.

PROCEDURE IN COUNTRIES HAVING TRADE-MARK LAWS

In those countries where specific statutes provide for the protection of trade-marks, the applicant who desires to register his trade-mark must comply with the requirements of the law and the regulations thereunder. These requirements vary with the country, and no uniform rule can be set down which would be equally applicable everywhere.

The Application

When the regulations governing the registration of trade-marks abroad require that an applicant desiring registration of his trade-mark shall solicit such registration on a prescribed form, care should be taken to comply with this stipulation. Where, however, the regulations do not prescribe a specific form, one appropriate for the purpose may be used. Diligence should be exercised in drawing up an application in order that the necessary information be included therein. It should be correct as to legal form, containing the signature of the person claiming ownership of the mark, and in the event the applicant is a corporation it must be signed by the proper official with appropriate authentication.

There should be included in the application all information necessary to indicate what is desired to be registered by the applicant and to enable the officials of the trade-mark office to make appropriate record. For example, if color or a combination of colors forms a distinctive feature of the mark, a statement to that effect must be made. Any other claims should be specifically mentioned, such as the duration of the use of the mark. If the trade-mark (or label) contains matter in which the applicant may have no exclusive right, appropriate disclaimer should be made in order to avoid delay or refusal of registration which may result from the inclusion of such unregistrable matter.

Class of Goods Covered by Trade-Mark

Practically all countries of the world have provisions in their trade-mark laws requiring the applicant to specify the goods on which the mark is to be used. In many areas an official classification has been established, and the applicant must indicate in which class of goods his mark is used or is about to be used.

If the goods fall in more than one class, this should be noted. It may happen that separate applications will have to be filed or that an extra charge for registration will be made for goods included in more than one class.

Although there has been considerable discussion in international circles interested in the subject of industrial property regarding a uniform classification for all countries, thus far no definite understanding has been arrived at in the matter.

Language—Authentication—Facsimiles

In the preparation of applications and other documents care should be taken to see that they are made out in the correct language. If the regulations call for translation into the foreign idiom, this should be made by a competent translator, as the loss of valuable rights may result from failure to state properly the pertinent facts.

Where there is a requirement that the applicant shall first have obtained registration in his home country, proof thereof must be made by filing a certified copy of the home registration, properly authenticated, with the foreign application. For example, in the case of a certificate of registration in the United States Patent Office of a trade-mark for use abroad, it must be duly signed and sealed in that office, then be authenticated in the office of the Secretary of Commerce and the office of the Secretary of State, and finally by the consul or other public official of the particular foreign country located in the United States. Other documents also may need to be legalized before such consul or other official, such as powers of attorney and documentary proof of incorporation.

An additional requirement may be that a certain number of facsimiles of the trade-mark in the manner in which they are used or are intended to be used accompany the application. Where publication of the notice of the application is made for registration abroad, an electrotype (cliché) must be forwarded as well. This electrotype must be of exact dimensions stated in the law in view of the fact that the printing presses of foreign publications are of such dimensions that only electrotypes of the specified size can be used.

Examination or Search

Registration of trade-marks without any formalities or examination on the part of the administrative officials is possible in some areas; in others, an examination is made of documents to see that they meet the requirements of the law.

When the law provides that a trade-mark may not be registered if it is similar to one already on the register, examination or search will be made of existing registrations to ascertain if there is conflict with marks previously recorded. This examination or search acts not only as a protection for proprietors of marks already on the register, but may be an assurance of proprietorship to the applicant.

Publication

While an individual may himself make an appropriate publication giving notice of ownership of a mark, the trade-mark office or other administrative agency of many foreign countries also publishes either in the journal of the trade-mark office or in some other official publication a notice of the application for the registration of a mark. This publication, which usually contains the application number, a reprint of the mark, the name and address of the applicant, and the goods on which it is used, is made once or several times in order that interested parties may have an opportunity to file a protest against the registration.

In some countries, after registration of the trade-mark has been effected, notice thereof is published, as well as additional information such as renewals and changes in title.

Opposition

Where the law affords an opportunity for interested persons to file an opposition to the registration of a trade-mark, a stipulated period of time is granted therefor. This period varies, but as a rule it is 30 days or more, counting from the date of publication.

In protesting against the registration of a trade-mark, prompt action is necessary. The notice of opposition should be properly drawn in accordance with the prescribed requirements. Care should be taken to set forth the grounds on which the opposition is based and such additional data as may be required. If the party filing the notice of opposition relies upon a previous registration, the number, date, and other pertinent facts of such registration should be indicated. The opposition should be properly signed and accompanied by a power of attorney and any other necessary documents such as certified copies of registrations and facsimiles of the mark. An appeal usually lies from a decision granting or refusing an opposition to the registration of trade-marks.

Cancellation

When a trade-mark has been registered abroad, it does not necessarily follow that the person in whose name it is registered has the exclusive right to the use of such mark unless the law contains provision to that effect.

In some countries registration may be only prima facie evidence of ownership, which can be contested by one who shows a better right. This is so in those countries where rights to a trade-mark are acquired on the common-law basis of prior adoption and use.

In other countries the exclusive right to the use of a registered mark may be acquired only after the registration has stood without contest during a stated period—usually 5 years or more.

If the registration is not conclusive proof of ownership and the law provides a means whereby those injured can contest the registration or seek its annulment, such persons may bring appropriate action for cancellation of the offending trade-mark either before the competent administrative authority or the court having jurisdiction in matters of this kind. Here, again, vigilance is necessary, in order that effective action may be taken, to cancel a record of registration. As in the case of opposition, due care should be taken to comply with all the requirements of the law and regulations, seeing to it that the appropriate documents are presented in due form before the competent authority.

As in opposition proceedings, appeal will lie, provided it is exercised, within the statutory limitations.

PROCEDURE IN ABSENCE OF SPECIFIC LAWS

While most countries of the world have statutes which deal specifically with trade-marks and provide for their registration, a few countries have no laws on the subject.

There the usual procedure is to give notice of ownership by

advertisement in some publication in the principal cities of the country in which the protection is desired. Such notice is not conclusive proof of ownership but may be used as evidence in trade-mark infringement proceedings.

This procedure may be followed in India by publication of notice of ownership at suitable intervals in the Gazette or some other paper issued in Calcutta. Advertisements to cover the Straits Settlements may be made in Singapore. In the Federated Malay States of Selangor, Perak, Pahang, and Negri Sembilan a single advertisement in one of the States will suffice for all.

A similar procedure may be followed in the Unfederated Malay States of Johore, Kedah, Kelantan, Trengganu, and Perlis by advertising in a local newspaper in Johore.

HOLDING TRADE-MARK RIGHTS ABROAD

Registration of a trade-mark in accordance with the provisions of foreign statutes in respect thereto is not in itself an assurance that the protection afforded thereby will be enjoyed without any further act on the part of the registered proprietor. Certain other factors must be given appropriate attention.

The question of retaining rights in trade-marks abroad is not confined to those countries where title is obtained by registration; it applies equally where ownership is enjoyed regardless of registration. If such valuable rights are not to be lost, it is essential that their validity be protected by fully complying with all the legal requirements.

Use of a Trade-Mark

The exclusive right to the use of a mark, by which its owner can prevent its infringement by another, is in many cases predicated upon use in connection with the goods which the mark is intended to distinguish. If there has been no user of a mark and title thereto can be obtained only as the result of use, one cannot assert any right therein.

In some countries, when a mark has been registered, failure to use it will not necessarily result in the loss of the rights conferred by the registration. In others, although the title may still remain in the registered proprietor, failure to use the mark within the prescribed period (usually 1 to 3 years) may debar him from bringing an action for infringement.

The point is, use of the mark within the meaning of the law depends largely upon the practice and jurisprudence on the subject in the particular country wherein the question arises. In at least one country an advertisement in a foreign magazine which enjoys wide circulation there, was considered a sufficient use of the mark to sustain a claim of title.

Use of a trade-mark by any other person may not constitute use by the owner. For example, where the foreign subsidiary has been using the mark of the parent corporation the title to which was registered in the name of the parent corporation, the latter may not be entitled to sue for infringement; the court might hold that the subsidiary was fixed in the mind of the consumer as being the owner of the mark. It is wise, therefore, when use of a mark is to be made on goods that are packed and sold by an agent or other foreign representative, to have the name of the owner of the mark appear thereon.

Not long ago attention was called to a case in which it was held that where a party registered a trade-mark without having used it and without any intention of ever using it, the registration was null and void and therefore the registered proprietor was not entitled to the rights derived from registration.

Notice of Registration

The owner of a registered trade-mark may desire to give notice of his proprietorship therein by placing on it a suitable indication to the effect that the mark has been registered. Apart from any voluntary action of this kind, there is a compulsory requirement in a few countries that a trade-mark which has been registered must bear an appropriate notice to that effect. In Guatemala, for example, the trade-mark law decrees:

ART. 18. Registered trade-marks shall bear a visible sign indicating the corresponding number in the register and the class to which the mark belongs, i. e., "Industrial mark registered under No. ......"; "Commercial mark registered under No. ......"; or "Agricultural mark registered under No. ...." These inscriptions may be abbreviated.

Art. 19. Articles protected by a registered trade-mark shall in every case bear the name and address of the person in whose favor the corresponding registration is effected.

Inclusion of a notice of registration on a trade-mark may be very desirable evidence in suits for infringement, even though this notice is not required by law.

Particular care should be taken to see that goods bearing a notice of registration do not enter a country where the notice will be construed to mean registration within that country. In the Irish Free State, trade-marks may not bear an indication that they have been registered unless they are registered in that country.

In those countries where notice is optional, the owner of the trade-mark may use any suitable indication. Thus, in Argentina, Bolivia, Brazil, Colombia, Costa Rica, Ecuador, Honduras, Nicaragua, Panama, Paraguay, El Salvador, Spain, Uruguay, and Venezuela, the words "Marca Registrada" may be used; in Chile, the Dominican Republic, Peru, Portugal, and the Portuguese colonies, the words "Marca Registrada" or the abbreviations "M. R."

In Great Britain and its dominions and colonies, including Australia, Canada, New Zealand, and the Union of South Africa, and in the Irish Free State, the words "Registered Trade Mark" may be used; while in Belgium, Congo Free State, France, Haiti, Luxembourg, Morocco (French Zone), Switzerland, Syria and Lebanon, Tunis, and Turkey, the words "Marque Deposée" would be a suitable indication.

In China, Japan, Poland, Persia, Rumania, and Yugoslavia, the words "Registered Trade-Mark" in the language of the respective country would suffice. The indications which may be used in certain other countries are: Austria, "Schutzmarke"; Bulgaria, "Marque Enregistrée" or abbreviation "M. E."; Czechoslovakia, "Ges. Gesch"; Denmark, "Indregistreret Varemaerke"; and Sweden, "Varumarke" or "Registreradt Varumarke"; Hungary,

"Vedejegy"; Italy, "Marca Depositata"; and Norway, "Registreret Veremarke."

If an article which bears a trade-mark is too small, or if it is not feasible to place on the trade-mark or label a notice that it has been registered, an appropriate indication may be made on the container in which the article is packed.

Taxes and Fees

Applications for the registration of trade-marks must, in most instances, be accompanied by filing fees or taxes. A few countries permit the payment of these fees after the filing of the application, but in any event the certificate of registration will not as a rule be issued until payment has been made.

Practically all countries publish in their patent office gazette or other official journal a notice, often in detail, of the application for the registration of a trade-mark, in order that interested parties may be informed and that protests may be filed by those who believe that they will be injured if the mark is registered. Not a few countries require that the applicant defray the expenses incident to such advertisement or notice by the payment of a specified fee.

The payment of the filing and publication fees is not the only expense involved in registering trade-marks abroad. There are charges which are made for searches of records, stamp taxes, legalization fees, translations, etc. The laws and regulations on the subject abroad are far from uniform.

Renewal of Registration

The registration of a trade-mark is usually granted for a definite time, on the expiration of which the rights may lapse or be extended for an additional period. Where there is a provision for renewal this may be obtained by complying with the requirements of the laws relative thereto. If an application for renewal is not filed within the specified period after the expiration of a previous term, the right to apply for renewal may be lost or the delinquent required to pay an additional fee. When a registration has lapsed because of expiration of the term, and there has been no application for renewal, the mark may be registered by anyone, although in some countries it may not thereafter be appropriated exclusively. But opposition and cancellation proceedings may not ordinarily be instituted against a renewal application filed in proper season.

Change in Ownership of Title

Where there has been an assignment, transfer, or inheritance of a right and title in a trade-mark which has been registered, or any part thereof, care should be taken to duly record such change on the trade-mark register.

Failure to make a proper record of such change in ownership may result in the loss of rights to third parties during the time that the change of title has remained unregistered.

It is imperative, therefore, that those who obtain the rights to the use of a trade-mark either by inheritance or by assignment from another take timely action to record such change in ownership and, where required, make due publication thereof.

SERVICES OF ATTORNEY DESIRABLE

There are many technical and legal problems involved in trade-mark and other industrial-property protection in foreign countries that can best, and in the long run most economically, be handled by an attorney. American attorneys usually have associates abroad through whom they are enabled to protect the rights of their clients in accordance with the foreign laws and regulations and to see that all the requirements of the law are fulfilled.

The services of an attorney are indispensable in infringement matters, inasmuch as court action may be called for to stop the infringement or piracy of a trade-mark. A thorough investigation of all the legal problems involved is necessary if adequate protection is to be obtained.

COINING OF TRADE-MARKS

Types of Trade-Marks

There are four general types of trade-marks:

A. A firm name or its modification, e.g., Goodrich, Stanco, I.C.I.

B. A synthetic or coined word or words which is indirectly descriptive, e.g., Arrid, Duriron, Fiberglas.

C. An ordinary word or words which are not descriptive, e.g., Lucky Strike, North Star, Quaker.

D. A synthetic word that is not descriptive, e.g., Drene, Lux, Pep.

Of course, there are many variations of these four types, e.g., Alcoa is a synthetic word, but is really a contraction of Aluminum Co. of America. However, these four divisions form a good base for the development of this subject.

The Firm Name

A surname used as a trade-mark lends a degree of stability or character. It is distinctive and shows pride of ownership and gives the assurance that the firm will strive to give the best in quality and service. The following surname trade-marks will serve as examples: Coty, Firestone, Ford, Heinz, Jantzen.

Surnames stand the passing of years very well. If anything, they improve with age. However, a long, or clumsy surname should not be used for it may be difficult to pronounce, or remember or it may have undesirable associations.

Modification or contraction of a firm name often results in an ugly or meaningless word that has none of the virtues of a good surname. Many company names are changed to ......co. Perhaps the original contraction of this type was unique and outstanding, but now the many trade names, e.g., ending in.......co are merely brash contractions without any distinction.

Compound names typified by Smijohn (derived from Smith-Johnson) are also undesirable. They are clumsy and graceless. Either Smith or Johnson has character and the other virtues of a good surname, but the split and spliced Smijohn has nothing to commend it, but puerile smartness. While there are exceptions, in general, cut-up and joined names should be avoided.

Letter trade-marks, e.g., B.V.D., I.G., are often used, but are not recommended unless they are rhythmic, musical or imply some desired association. Usually they are not equal to a good name, unless the words the letters represent are well-known and the letter combination sounds well. Examples of well-chosen trade-marks are B. and O. (Baltimore and Ohio), I.C.I. (Imperial Chemical Industries).

Sometimes it is not deemed wise to use a firm name as a trade-mark, e.g.,

A. When a product differing in quality, price, use, etc., is introduced

B. When a product, foreign to the regular line, is to be marketed

C. When a trial is to be made of a product whose good reception is doubtful

D. When the product will be marketed only for a restricted period of time.

Synthetic Indirectly Descriptive Words

A good, indirectly descriptive, synthetic (coined) word is easy to remember and ties up with the use, effect or properties of the product. Thus Dri-Brite, used for a self-polishing (bright-drying) floor polish, reminds one of the result desired with the product—a very useful connotation. Other examples of this type are: Ditto (duplicating machine), Frigidaire (refrigerator), Pliofilm (packaging sheeting), Quink (writing ink).

Other words based on foreign-language roots, prefixes or suffixes or less frequently used English words are not so effective because most people are not familiar with the meaning of such words and to them no descriptive or familiarizing connection is evident. Thus Bovril, derived from bovinus (bovine) and virilus (virile), has no descriptive significance for most people. Similarly Dentyne (dentine), Lucite (lucid) and like words must be remembered by many who do not know their basic meanings.

Nondescriptive Regular Words

Examples of regular, nondescriptive words registered as trademarks are: Swan (soap), Lucky Strike (cigarette), Three Feathers (whiskey), General (tire), International (farm machinery), Arrow (shirts).

In this class the words are usually combined with a visual representation to form a trade-mark comprising a name and a drawing or picture (called *device*) which is described by the name. Thus, the trade-mark "Swan" consists of the name and a picture of a swan. The combination is far more attractive and more easily remembered than the name alone. For natives who cannot read and for export to non-English speaking countries the name alone has no value. The pictorial representation makes the product recognizable to all.

Certain names in this class, although nondescriptive, imply or arouse associations of happiness, well-being, assurance, dignity, security, purity, safety, etc., which have definite secondary values, e.g., Good Humor (ice cream) is a pleasant association, Old Judge (whiskey) implies that it is the favorite brand of a judge of men and liquor. Even though some associations may be tenuous, they have their values.

Care must be taken that none of such associations strikes a discordant or unpleasant note. The associations should not be too unctuous or pretentious, they should be rather subtle than blatant. In no case should they be misleading.

Nondescriptive Coined Words

One of the best examples in this class is Kodak (camera). It is nondescriptive and neutral in character. It is short, complete and perfectly balanced. Time has proved it. Kodak today is almost a synonym for camera in many English and foreign-language speaking countries.

Names in this class have no actual meanings, but must be selected with care so as to be dignified and suitable. Mum (deodorant), Iodent (tooth-paste), and Saran (plastic) are good examples.

Of course, names of this class that have no meaning and, for some time, no associations, are not remembered well. Continuous advertising will gradually impress the name on the memory.

In addition to the before-mentioned types of trade names, there are names using another language, e.g., Lux (soap), or fictional characters, e.g., Lady Baltimore (candy), or Ivanhoe (tobacco).

The Perfect Trade-Mark

Thousands of trade-marks have been registered, but only a very small number is outstanding and of these, a still smaller number has been accepted by consumers to such an extent that they developed into class names, such as Kodak instead of a camera or the Englishman's term, Bass, for a glass of ale. It may be surprising that such common words as linoleum, radiogram and menthol were once trade-marks of individual firms. This general adoption is likely to occur when the product is good, the trade-mark very appropriate, the distribution thorough and the advertising efficient and continued for a long period of time.

In introducing a distinctly new type of product which has not previously been offered, the choice of a suitable trade-mark is simpler than in the case of a product that is already on the market. Thus, when Cellophane * (packaging film sheet) was introduced, it was a distinctly new type of product. Any name would have soon become synonomous with the product. Such is not the case when a new name is given to an old type of product.

In coining a name, survey should first be made of those trade-marks that are already being used for similar products. The use of a similar name should not be attempted because its registration may be refused or an action may be brought even after the registration. A trade-mark registered for a product which belongs

---

* This is no longer a trade-mark, but has become a generic name and is written with a small "c."

to a particular class may, however, be used and registered for a product which belongs to a distinctly different class. For example, Acme may be used for paint, beer and paper by three different firms without any interference. However, its use by a firm other than the trade-mark owner for wine when it is registered for beer would not be allowed as both belong to the same class of products, i.e., beverages.

Selecting A Trade-Mark

It is far simpler for the buyer to remember a trade-mark such as DUZ, REM, etc., than to describe the product or its package. A good trade-mark, therefore, is a great help in merchandising.

A trade-mark should not be adopted just because it appeals to its originator, his family or his friends. A symbol or a short coined word is the most suitable for this purpose. A good trade-mark should *subtly* give an association with the product or its use. A good trade-mark has to conform with the following requirements:

1. It should not be descriptive
2. It should decidedly differ from similar trade-marks
3. It should be simple in form
4. It should be attractive to the eye
5. It should be pleasant sounding
6. It should not arouse dislike, mistrust or doubt
7. It should be easily read and pronounced
8. It should be easily remembered
9. It should create a desire to possess or use it

Surveying the Field *

A most important step in arriving at a trade-mark is to set out exactly the different classes of people by whom the trade-mark will be used and under what circumstances. In the case of a new biscuit, for example, we should have (a) the firm's salesmen, (b) retailers, (c) retail purchasers, mostly women, (d)

* Cousins and Wadsworth, *Trade Names,* Harlequin Press.

consumers other than purchasers, say, children and guests. Next we should estimate roughly the relative importance of these by a percentage, which for a particular biscuit might be as follows:

Salesmen	..
Retailers	10
Retail Buyers (Women)	60
Children	15
Guests	15

We should now consider the social status and average intelligence of the people to whom the article will appeal, perhaps in this case the upper and lower middle classes. We are now in a position to formulate our first conclusions, thus:

1. The name must primarily appeal to upper and lower middle-class women of high and medium intelligence.
2. A secondary appeal might be directed to children, or to use on social occasions.

Care in this first operation will be well repaid. In the case mentioned, for instance, if we consider only children we might choose "Nursery," if we think only of guests we might choose "Parisienne," but each would be unsuited to the other and perhaps a compromise, e.g., "French Doll," ought to be sought which would be acceptable to both.

The relative importance of the various groups of people will vary widely with different commodities. In some cases the retailer's recommendation may be very valuable, and a name which he will be able to use readily should be aimed at. A name to be used by the medical profession should usually be one which would appeal to both nurses and doctors. In general, the upper social limit and the lower limit of intelligence should, if possible, be catered to.

The next point to consider is how the name will be used. If the article is to be named in a mail-order circular, pronounceability is necessary. If it is intended to become a household word, e.g., a new breakfast food or a popular disinfectant, it should be very easy to pronounce indeed. If it is to be used on a small article or package or is likely to be advertised in single-column spaces, it is a great advantage to have few letters so that large type may be used. Note that some words sound short but are fairly long when written and vice versa.

Finally, we turn to the product. Having decided by whom it will be used, we next select those characteristics of the article which we might wish if possible to be reflected in our trade name. Unless we are christening a new rat poison we may take it for granted that the name must not be unpleasant. But beyond that we must decide whether our article needs a name which will stress function and utility or one which stresses beauty; also whether novelty should be emphasized, or reliability, craftsmanship and quality.

As far as one can judge from successes in various fields one might say broadly that if the product will be used by women the name should stress beauty and luxury, if by men, utility, strength, honesty and distinction. If the article possesses novelty this should be shown in the case of women by a neat invented name, or for men by a short indirectly descriptive name or subtitle. If the firm name is long, plain or harsh, it should not be used for women, while for men it may well be used unless it is a very common one, or difficult to remember, or the product has a luxury appeal with which the name is somewhat out of keeping. For children, the name must be simple, and either indirectly descriptive, concrete or very short.

As a result of our survey we should be able to set out briefly:

1. What particular classes should be appealed to
2. How far easy pronunciation is essential
3. Whether the word should be one of few letters
4. The rough characteristics of the name desired, with particular reference to beauty, strength, novelty or fine quality.

This information will serve as simple terms of reference to enable us to judge words rapidly and easily during our search.

The Making of Words *

Every year the discovery of new trade-marks becomes more difficult. Dictionaries have been ransacked, unusual letters like X, K and the terminal -O have been used so extensively that novelty and distinction in some classes seem to be almost unattainable. Nevertheless, the problem is not insoluble. It is largely a question of method, of replacing mere guesswork and analogy, in which the mind invariably wanders along familiar grooves, by a more fruitful process of experimental synthesis. The main key to the problem lies in the properties of the individual letters. Just as, for instance, one can play on the black keys of the piano for an hour without striking a harsh dischord, so one can mix the consonants S, L, V and N almost indiscriminately with vowels without making an ugly sounding word, while the letters K, Q, G and B can hardly make a pleasant one.

Roughly speaking, we may arrange the consonants in order thus:

Soft, Weak and Liquid	Soft and Rich	Sharp	Hard and Strong
L S V N	Y Z R M J	P F H T D C X	W B Q G K

It will be noted that sound does not control the matter, and that appearance counts for a great deal. The words ULIC and ULIK sound the same, but the second is stronger than the first.

The consonants on the extreme left give very smooth words, but only very few good names have been made from them, e.g., Vinolia. Combining with the next four, we have Osram, Marmon, Velma, Anzora, which are richer but still very smooth.

In the third group we find sharp, clear sounds which give crisp words like Fox, Pep, Cutex, Decca, Texaco. When these are combined with the first group we secure Lux, Flit, Tecla, Hovis, St. Ivel and Duplex, which are of the first rank. Combined with the second, we have Mazda, Atora, Murex, Moxie,

* Cousins and Wadsworth, *Trade Names,* Harlequin Press.

Cuticura, which seem duller in comparison. Notice the effect of the letter T in ovaltine, a word which, without it, would be very dull.

Finally, we have the hard, strong sounds B, Q, G and K, which, though they seem to have produced no good names by themselves, have superb mixing qualities. Sanka, Turog, Tek, Probak, Kensitas, Klaxon, Zog, Glaxo, all owe their strength to the presence of these letters.

Vowels are somewhat more subtle. They rank roughly in the order E, I, O, U, A at the beginning of the table, i.e., they are usually weaker than the consonants, but when they have a syllable to themselves, as in IONA, they become more important, and owing to their varying sounds it is better to work for consonants. The addition of vowels to a word softens it considerably.

It will be evident that this table takes us some distance toward solving this problem.

THE ESSENTIAL QUALITY

There is one quality above all others which a trade-mark must possess, viz., that it should be easily remembered. If the name is forgotten, the article cannot be asked for in a shop, recommended to a friend, or discussed in any way except by description of the article, in which case it is the article which is recalled and not the name, and the goods might just as well be branded in Chinese or not branded at all. It is, in fact, the most vital test for nearly all trade-marks, and one which determines their cash value throughout their entire life. If the name is difficult to recall, it will require more advertising to fix it in the public mind in the first year, and more to keep it there in every year that follows. Not merely the initial cost, but the cost of maintenance is increased.

An analysis of some of the factors which seem to be involved is given below. It will be observed that all good names qualify under several headings, and that some factors are more important than others.

SYMMETRY, BALANCE AND DISTINCTIVE OUTLINE

Some words when written in script have a distinctive outline, e.g., C O T Y; others must be shown always in block letters to appear balanced, e.g., **LUX**. Legibility is probably the first consideration, but artistic presentation is hardly less important.

FAVORABLE RECEPTION

A name which makes a favorable impression will be remembered better than one which, by reason of trite form, misspelling or obvious artificiality of the wrong kind, arouses mental criticism.

Beautiful Names *

The effect of beauty in a trade-mark may be secured either by the peculiar construction of an invented word, e.g., Vinolia, or by the use of a word or part of a word which describes a beautiful object, e.g., Carnation. Many words, of course, combine these features. Velma, for instance, probably suggests velvet and a girl's name as well as being a beautiful sounding word, while Palmolive has intrinsic beauty apart from its meaning. The word Zola, on the other hand, though beautiful in itself, is impaired for those who see it as the name of an ultra-realistic novelist.

The outstanding characteristic of these words until recently has been the use of feminine and diminutive endings taken from the romance languages, French, Italian and Spanish. The conventional type can readily be constructed by selecting simple root words containing one or two of the softer letters and perhaps one of the sharper letters C, T, P, F, D, and adding a suitable ending, e.g.:

Root Word			Ending			
Pan-,	Dev-,	Du-,	-elle,	-ie,	-ette,	-a,
Sor-,	Cit-,	Tir-,	-oa,	-ora,	-ore,	-isse,

* Cousins and Wadsworth, *Trade Names,* Harlequin Press.

Az-,	Col-,	Del-,	-esse,	-ia,	-etta,	-sel,
V-,	Cor-,	Mar-,	-ice,	-enne,	-ille,	-elma,
Is-,	Mat-,	Ros-,	-otte,	-sie,	-aire,	-aise,
C-,	Tril-,		-ay,	-isha,	-usha,	-usa,
			-elsa,	-zel,	-ina,	-inka,
			-otta,	-uska,	-usca.	

Other suffixes which may be used, many of them very well worn, however, are -aro, -ande, -ana, -ane, -aine, -alina, -alia, -anda, -beau, -epa, -ene, -een, elda, -ella, -illa, -iere, -ine, -ida, -irma, -ista, -ola, -osa, -ose, -oria, -ona, -onte, -obel, -urna, -une, -yl, -syl.

Another method is to examine words in a dictionary or gazeteer to see whether they have suitable names concealed in them. The removal of an initial consonant or syllable frequently leaves a pleasant sounding word which is quite unlike the original—the word rayon, for instance, might have been thus derived from crayon. The following, chosen at random in about 10 minutes, show the possibilities, and the endings can, of course, be varied:

B	Aronet		L	Apil	y
Bib	Lioma	nia	M	Ariola	try
Cl	Airvoy	ant	N	Obilia	ry
Dete	Riora	te	P	Luto	nomy
D	Irel	y	Qua	Torza	in
D	Ragoma	n	R	Ascal	
F	Lorida		Sa	Veloy	
G	Lorio	us	Si	Milar	
H	Elian		Te	Nuto	
J	Anito	r	V	Otar	y
Jer	Usal	em	W	Astrel	
Ker	Seymere		Z	Ebra	

This may seem to be a somewhat amateurish process, and it is, of course, limited in its scope. Its chief advantage lies in the fact that the letters of existing words are already in pronounceable order.

Turning to our second type, the actual names of beautiful objects, we must of necessity go farther afield. We can frequently find good names in unlikely places, and any of the following are worth trying: Names of vessels in Lloyds' register; catalogs of roses, plants, etc.; names of racehorses, past and present; the names both in the index and in the text of a good book on systematic botany, such as C. A. John's "Flowers of the Field," which gives both English and Latin names; a classical dictionary; a concise biographical or historical dictionary, such as is contained in Pears' Annual, which will contain such words as Raleigh, Cressy, Mozart, which, though surnames or place names, have a special historic or cultural significance, which will permit them to be registered.

It will be noticed that of the word endings given above, 53 out of 62 end in the vowels e or a. The result of this uniformity is that this type of word has become unpleasantly common and has lost much of its distinction. Recently, there has been a tendency to rebel against the tradition that all things esthetic must come from Paris or the Orient. Among current advertised names connected with feminine toilet, we find Modess and Camay have English endings. Dew and Seventeen are English words, while Elizabeth Arden and Dorothy Gray have not the slightest trace of foreignness about them.

Short Names

In certain cases, the short, handy word is invaluable. When space is limited, as on a vertical tube; when the object is small; where the single column advertisement is likely to be used; where the product is comparatively unimportant and a pretentious name would be out of place; or where the object is to appeal to all classes, including the barely literate, words of from three to five letters should be sought. Even where these conditions do not apply, the economy in outlay and maintenance of illuminated signs, the additional space left for illustration and descriptive matter on small posters, the free advertising and immediate stimulus given by a packaged product with large letters which will catch the eye of a customer making other purchases, may be factors worth considering.

The three-letter word, though slightly lacking in dignity, unless as in the case of Jay's and Sak's, it is a personal name, has usually a neat appearance. The total number of practicable names is probably under 1,000 and, on one of the following pages, there is given a table of about 800 English and invented words, which covers perhaps 90 per cent of the combinations that are likely to be serviceable.

Note that alliteration and assonance, e.g., Tec Shirts or Koy Oysters, may help to make a name appropriate and be a guide in selection.

Four-letter combinations run into thousands and are too numerous to give here. They can be easily constructed from the three-letter table by (1) prefixing O, A or U, e.g., Amik, Omol; (2) affixing A, O, U or E, e.g., Kaza, Nubo; (3) inserting R after B, C, D, F, G, K, P and T, e.g., Drek, Trix; (4) inserting L after B, C, F, G, K and P, e.g., Ploy; (5) doubling O or E in the middle of a word, e.g., Roon, or doubling B, D, F, G, L, N, R, S, T or Z at the end, e.g., Tuff.

Another method is to use the dictionary. The following words, for instance, taken from the letter A, seem fairly versatile: Acre, Adar, Adit, Aeon, Agio, Ahoy, Aide, Alga, Alia, Ally, Alto, Amic, Amir, Amyl, Anna, Annon, Ante, Apex, Apse, Aqua, Arab, Arch, Argo, Aria, Aril, Army, Arum, Axis, Axil, Ayah. It will be noticed that several of them, e.g., Adit, Amic, Axil, are sufficiently unfamiliar to pass as invented words, while others, such as Adar, are not unlike surnames.

Five-letters words are more difficult to construct. The most common pattern has three consonants and two vowels balanced, as in Kodak and Lysol, but other patterns, as in Sanka, Buick, Kraft, Roneo, Flora, may be very effective, and are worth experiment.

The ending of the word is important. It may, for instance, suggest foreign origin, e.g., -ti (Italian), solid or liquid structure, e.g., -ite, -ol, or it may be so well worn, e.g., -xo, -co, that it will bore its readers and give an impression that the product is commonplace.

Novelty covers a multitude of sins. The really unusual word excites curiosity and makes a strong impression on the memory. Probably nine people out of ten would have turned down good names like Nujol, Ronuk and Turog for more familiar-looking words. If the product has genuine and unique qualities, the public will generally welcome a striking name and the name in turn will assist in giving it uniqueness.

There are only two rules for the five-letter word which seem worth mentioning. The first is that the stronger sounds should occupy either the ends or the center of the word, e.g., Coker is unbalanced and Corek is better, while Sanka is better than Kasan, and Kasan is better than Kanas or Kasna. The second is that the word should be a united whole, each letter being related to those adjoining it so that the word does not readily fall into two pieces. The weakness of such words as Brillo, Repco and Coldak is that the last syllable does not belong to the word and gives it an artificial appearance. Words like Decca, Sanka, Kodak, have unity and no line of fissure shows itself.

A method of arriving at invented words which may be found useful is to take plain English words at random and modify one or two weak sounds according to the type of word that is required, e.g.:

Can	(Strong)	Kann, Kand
	(Light)	Cania
Table	(Strong)	Tablex, Kablex, Kalex
	(Light)	Tarle
Window	(Strong)	Windog, Quintog
	(Light)	Winosa
Card	(Strong)	Kard
	(Light)	Varda, Verda
Pen	(Strong)	Pex, Pegg
	(Light)	Aspen, Pensa

Indirectly Descriptive Words

The indirectly descriptive name is more popular in the United States than in England, where the tendency is toward words based on Latin or Greek roots, purely invented words, or mere brand names. There is much to be said on both sides. The lack of subtlety in such names as Super Suds, Drano, Enna-Jettick Shoes, Ken-L-Ration, Hurculaces, Odorono and Nonspi, probably defeats its own object and is not considered the best practice. But the unquestionable appropriateness of such names as Zipper, Tintex, Frigidaire, Palmolive, Ry-Vita, makes a strong case for the indirectly descriptive word. Each product has its own problem. The approach to each should be systematic. Every word suggestive of the product—its composition, function, appearance and principal selling points and, in fact, every possible related word, cumbersome or otherwise, should be tabulated as a basis for experiment and the distinctive portion of each word should be underlined. Even if a nondescriptive name is finally chosen, these data will be useful for subtitles, and the possible use of auxiliary words, as in Woodbury's Facial Soap, Valet Auto-Strop Razor, should be noted.

If difficulty in finding allied words or synonyms is experienced, Roget's Thesaurus may prove useful.

It will be noticed that the addition of a hard consonant will strengthen a weak word, e.g., Oval could give Ovalak; while the addition of vowels and weak consonants has a softening effect, e.g., Ovale, Frigidaire. But merely ornamental syllables should be avoided. The -aire in Frigidaire, however, is not an ornament, but acts as a noun, ending similar to -er in Freezer.

The Series of Trade Names

Series of names for different products made by the same firm are often useful. The most common method is the use of the firm name, e.g., Dunlop Tires, Golf Balls, etc., or the use of a common brand name, e.g., Rexall Boric Acid, Lotion, etc. However, other methods are sometimes preferable, and the following may be noted: (1) The use of distinctive syllables, e.g., the -ia ending of Cunarders, -ic of White Star, -castle of Union-Castle line, etc. Also Sanato*gen*, *Gen*atosan, *Gen*aspirin.

(2) The use of the name of the already established product, e.g., "Lux" Toilet Soap; "Ivory" Snow. (Note the advantage of the short, nondescriptive word in this case.)

(3) The use of words with related meanings, e.g., Eagle, Heron, Hawk; President, Senator, Ambassador; Red Label, White Label; Diamond, Ruby.

(4) The use of merely auxiliary words suggesting difference of size, quality, etc., e.g., Morris *Minor, Baby* or *Bantam* Austin, ———— de Luxe, Special, Grade A, etc.; these, however, are not registrable.

The best source for related words of this kind is a thesaurus.

Textile Names—Names for new textile fabrics frequently present difficulties as they are usually wanted in a hurry. For this purpose, a unique stem which cannot be used by another firm is an advantage, e.g., in the textile series Tootal, Tootisha, Tootaline, the stem is the monopoly of a single firm and a wide range of endings can be applied. Syltex, Sylcrepe, Sylsura, however, are owned by different firms, and the syl stem can be used by anyone who cares to add an original ending. These names are not very distinctive and as more variants are registered, they become less so and perhaps actually confusing. If all the names are in good hands, no serious harm may be done. Goodrich and Goodyear have probably profited by their common syllable. But there is a danger that unscrupulous producers of inferior products by registering similar names will debase the whole series, as their goods will be sold at lower prices and in poorer shops.

The safest plan, if a series of this type is required, is to secure a stem which is registrable alone, e.g., Dura, Melba, Wemco; these expand to form Durocrat, Melbad'or, Wemcosyl. If the stem is a part of a well-known firm name, e.g., Courtine (Courtaulds), it may carry additional prestige and be easily remembered. Many name stems, however, do not lend themselves to the formation of delicate or otherwise appropriate words, and they should be used warily.

The series Ilota, Mirilota, Norilota is interesting and unusual. The stem is used as the suffix. Ilota is a good name of unusual delicacy, and the series has beauty even if the stem tends to lose its identity in the longer words. This tendency can be counteracted, if necessary, by such devices as Rose-ilota, Torilota, PENilota.

Although unique suffixes with the delicacy of ilota are not too easy to find, the principle of using a constant suffix—even of a slightly stronger character—seems to be worth experiment, and such series evolve as: Muda, Diamuda, Riomuda, Lamuda, Toymuda; Laird, Twillaird, Karlaird.

The series of names, has, of course, the defect of its qualities. One cannot expect to find a set of words which are individually distinctive, mutually suggestive, and equal in verbal merit. First-class names like Kiddie Cloth or Bo-Peep, for children's prints, can find no worthy peers in a series. Yet in a crowded market, names of such concrete distinctiveness are eminently desirable. In such cases, one of the best solutions is to use a phrase such as "Tommy Tucker—a Munda Product" in order to associate it with the parent name.

Use of the Name Finders

The construction of really useful name finders is harder than it seems. A single device consisting of, say, five concentric discs, each containing a full alphabet and a blank space, would clearly furnish every possible word up to five letters in groups of twenty-seven for each setting. But at two hundred and forty settings an hour for 12 hours a day, it would take 6 months to run through it and would probably only yield about four names a minute which were even barely pronounceable! The explanation is, of course, that consonants would outnumber vowels by over four to one, and most combinations would, therefore, contain clusters of hopelessly unpronounceable letters.

The method which has been adopted aims at producing combinations which are nearly all pronounceable by confining each disc to either vowel or consonant sounds and partial elimination of unsuitable letters.

No. 1 name finder,* for instance, will give words of the "Kodak" pattern in which consonants (c) and vowels (v) alternate c.v.c.v.c.

No. 2 has the "Sanka" pattern c.v.c.c.v.

No. 3 gives a fairly full range of words of one syllable containing three to six letters. Many of these are unusual and, containing several consonants, produce words of the "Kraft" type, which are strong and distinctive.

No. 4 is self-explanatory, and provides alternatively strong or beautiful endings for a variety of three-letter stems.

It has not been thought necessary to give name finders with more than five discs, since good names of six or more letters usually contain a descriptive root, e.g., "Frigid"-aire, and can be more easily discovered by experiment based upon the characteristics of the product itself, as suggested earlier in the consideration of the indirectly descriptive word.

Three-Letter Names—The following table contains practically all the pronounceable three-letter combinations which are sufficiently euphonious to serve as trade names.

These words also serve as useful stems for the formation of four-letter words by the addition of a vowel or consonant.

Aga	Aka	Ama	Ana	Apa	Ara	Asa	Ata
Ava	Aya	Aza	Abe	Ace	Ade	Afe	Age
Age	Ame	Ane	Ape	Are	Ase	Ate	Ave
Axe	Ali	Ami	Avi	Axi	Abo	Ago	Ako
Amo	Avo	Axo	Azo	Alb	Arb	Alc	Arc
Add	Ald	Ard	Arl	Arm	Arn	Ang	Ash
Ack	Alk	Auk	Ark	Ask	Anp	Asp	Ass
Ads	Ans	Ats	Act	Aft	Alt	Ant	Art
Apt	Amy	Any	Atz				
Edd	Eld	Erd	Egg	Eff	Elf	Elk	Erk
Erl	Elm	Ern	Eli	Elt	Eks	Ems	Ens
Ess	Eft	Est	Ept	Eba	Eda	Ema	Ena
Era	Eja	Eza	Ebo	Eco	Ego	Elo	Exo
Ezo	Evo						

* Name finder discs will be found in the flap on the inside back cover of this book.

Ind Iff Ilk Isk Irm Imp Iss Ida
Ina Ira Isa Iza Ice Ide Ike Ize
Ici Izi Ido Iro Ivo Iso Ixo Izo
Ivy

Oda Oma Ona Ora Ota Osa Ova Oza
Oxa Ode Oke Ope Ore Oze Oko Omo
Ono Oso Oto Ovo Ozo Oku Orb Odd
Off Ohm Orm Orn Oss Oft Oxy Opt

Uba Uca Una Ura Uke Uno Uro Urb
Usk Urn Ult

Bee Bab Bob Bid Bud Bok Bal Bem
Bim Ben Bos Bus Bat Biz Boz Buz
Boy Bay Bly

Caw Coy Cue Cub Cof Col Cam Con
Com Cup Cat Cot Cox Cog Cly Cry

Daw Dee Dew Dia Doo Doy Dry Deb
Dib Dub Doc Duc Dog Dag Dak Dek
Dik Dok Duk Dam Dim Dum Dan Den
Din Dan Dun Dap Dip Dop Dup Daq
Dot Dax Dex Dix Dox Dux Daz Diz

Fac Fad Fog Fik Fan Fen Fin Fon
Fip Fop Fir Fax Fex Fox Foy Faz
Fez Fly Fro Flo

Gag Gun Gap Gos Gan Goy Goz Gay
Guy Glo Gro Gee

Haw Hal Hex Hix Hob Hod Hok Hoy
Hub Hum Hut Hux

Jay Joy Jak Jan Jav Jax Jaz Jef
Jen Jif Jig Jik Jix Job Joc Jot
Jon Jol Jut Jux Juz Jag

Kaa Kaw Key Kia Koy Kue Kob Kio
Kub Kid Kud Kog Kim Ken Kin Kap
Kip Kar Kos Kat Kit Kot Kut Kax
Kex Kix Kox Kux Kaz Kuz Kry Kem

Loo Loy Lob Lac Luc Lay Lad Lud
Log Lug Lak Lik Lek Lok Luk Lin
Lap Lip Lop Lit Lot Liv Law Lax
Lex Lox Lix Lux Laz Luz

Mae Mia Mio Moi Moy Mab Mob Mac
Moc Mad Mid Mag Meg Mog Mak Mek
Mik Mal Mel Mul Mol Mum Mem Mam
Mim Min Mop Map Mar Mer Mat Met
Mit Mot Maw Max Mex Mix Mox Maz

Noy Nab Nib Nob Nub Noc Nuc Nod
Ned Nip Nid Nog Nok Nak Nik Nuk
Nul Nil Nem Nom Nan Nun Nap Nat
Net Nut Nox Nax Nix Nux

Pew Poy Pac Pie Pod Pex Pig Pug
Pak Pek Pik Pok Puk Pal Pol Pam
Pim Pom Pan Pen Pin Pon Pun Pep
Pip Pop Pup Par Pas Pat Pet Pit
Pot Pax Pex Pix Paz Poz Pyx Pey
Pry Pro

Quo

Raa Rae Ray Raw Ree Reo Rio Roi
Roy Rue Ruo Rab Roe Rob Rec Roc
Rue Rad Red Rid Rod Rud Reg Rig
Rog Rah Raj Rak Rek Rik Rok Ruk
Rim Rem Ram Rom Ren Run Rep Rip
Rap Ros Rus Rat Rit Rev Riv Rax
Rux Rox Rix Rez Rho

Sea See Soo Soy Sue Sac Sic Sec
Soc Sud Sof Sog Sek Sak Sil Sel
Sol Sul Sam Syl She Shy Sky Ski
Sly Spy Sty Sum Sun San Sap Set
Son Sax Sox Suz

Taf Tif Tuf Tag Teg Tig Tog Tug
Tak Tek Tik Tok Tuk Tel Til Tal
Tol Tul Tri Try Tao Taw Tea Tee
Teo Toi Toy Tua Tuo Tab Tub Tib
Tec Tic Tac Toc Tuc Ted Tod Tid
Tam Tem Tum Tom Tim Tan Tun Tep
Tip Top Tap Tup Tor Tar Ted Tod
Tid Tes Tos Tus Tat Tit Tot Tut
Taw Tax Tex Tix Tox Tux Taz Tez
Tiz Toz Tuz

Veo Via Vie Vio Voy Vow Vue Vib
Vac Vic Vec Voc Vod Vag Vig Vog
Vak Vek Vik Vok Val Vel Vil Vol
Vul Vam Vem Vim Ven Vin Von Vap
Vep Vip Ver Vor Vis Vos Vat Vet
Vit Viv Vov Vex Vix Vox Vax Vaz
Viz

Way Wee Wad Wag Wak War Wat Wax
Wid Wig Wik Win Wit Wix Wiz Wog
Wow Why Who Wry

Yew Yeo Yak Yel Yol Yam Yon Yap
Yet Yax Yox

Trade-Marks Derived from Foreign Languages

The designation "foreign trade-marks" is used in this book to cover those which have been derived fully or partially from words of a foreign language. They may or may not have a meaning. They may designate a property of the product they protect or have no relationship whatsoever to it.

Foreign words or syllables may be combined with one another or foreign prefixes or suffixes may be combined with English terms. For example, the Latin roots *rub*—(referring to red) and *mal*—(referring to apple) may be combined to give *Rubmal* (to cover red apple). The Greek prefix *bio*—(referring to life) may be combined with the English term *salt* to give *Biosalt.*

Of course, a foreign word alone may also be used as a trade name or trade-mark, e.g., the Spanish word for always, *Siempre,* may be selected.

The combination of foreign prefixes or suffixes with English words permits an almost infinite variation of words from which proper trade names can be selected. However, great care must be taken to avoid foreign words in bad taste and a dictionary or a linguist should be consulted as a precaution.

In the following list, some suitable Latin and Greek roots, prefixes and suffixes are given. This and a short five-language dictionary of carefully selected words will be helpful in giving ideas for new trade-name combinations.

LATIN AND GREEK WORDS AND WORD ROOTS

Meaning	*Latin or Greek words or word roots which can be used as a prefix or suffix*	*Meaning*	*Latin or Greek words or word roots which can be used as a prefix or suffix*
above	super-	blood	hemo-
alter	metabol-	brain	cerebro-
beneath	infra-	(to) carry	fer-
beyond	ultra-		phor-
bile	chol-	cause	aetio-
bite, eat into	mord-	change	muta-
black	melan-	circle	cyclo-

Meaning	*Latin or Greek words or word roots which can be used as a prefix or suffix*	*Meaning*	*Latin or Greek words or word roots which can be used as a prefix or suffix*
cloud	nephelo-	heat, warmth	thalp-
coal	carbo-	heavenly	celest-
color	chrom-	hidden	crypto-
decompose	-lytic		krypton-
	-lysis	honey	mell-
dense	pycno-	horse	hippo-
different, other	allo-	hundred	centi-
	ampho-	(to) increase	auxo-
digestion	peps-	indicates privation	des-
dissolved	solut-	iron	ferro-
dissolving	solv-	large	macro-
draw towards	adsorp-	leaf	-phyll
driven together	coagulat-	left	levo-
eight	octa-	life	bio-
eleven	undec-	light	lumin-
equal	iso-		phos-
excess, more	per-		photo-
false	pseudo-	(to) love	-phile
fat	adip-	many, more	pleo-
	lipo-	middle	meso-
fear	-phobe	milk	lac-
fire	pyro-	moving	kinet-
five	pent-	ninth	nona-
(of) flesh	sarco-	oil	ole-
form	morph-	one	uni-
four	tetra-	one and a half	sesqui-
four times	quatern-	one, single	mono-
France	Galli-	opposite, against	anti-
furrow	striat-	other, different	hetero-
glass	vitr-	outside, out of	exo-
goat	capr-	place, arrangement	topo-
gold	auro-	plant	phyto-
golden yellow	chryso-	plate	lamell-
half	semi-	power, force	dynam-
(a) half	hemi-	(to) produce, make	gen-
hammer	malle-	(to) put together	synthet-
hard	sclero-	ray	actin-
heat	calor-	red	erythro-
	thermo-	right	dextro-

Meaning	*Latin or Greek words or word roots which can be used as a prefix or suffix*	*Meaning*	*Latin or Greek words or word roots which can be used as a prefix or suffix*
rock	petr-	turn, change	trop-
same	homo-; iso	twelve	dodec-
self	auto-	twice	bi-
seven	hepta-		di-
shell-like	conchoid-	under, lower than	hypo-
silver	argent-	(to be) visible	phanero-
similar	iso-	water	aqua-
six	hexa-		hydro-
small	micro-	well, easily	eu-
starch	amyl-	wet, moist	hygro-
sugar	sucr-	white	alb-
sulfur	thio-		leuco-
sun	helio-	with, on same side	syn-
sweet	dulci-	within, inside	en-, endo-
	glu(y)co-	without	a-
ten	deca-	wood	lign-
thread	fili-	world	cosmo-
three	tri-	yellow	flavo-
three times	ter-		xantho-
tissue	histo-		

FIVE-LANGUAGE DICTIONARY

English	*French*	*German*	*Italian*	*Spanish*
afternoon	après-midi	Nachmittag	pomeriggio	tarde
apple	pomme	Apfel	mela	manzana
apron	tablier	Schürze	grembiule	delantal
autumn	automne	Herbst	autunno	otoño
bad	mauvais	schlecht	male	malo
beautiful	beau	schön	bello	bello
bed	lit	Bett	letto	cama
belt	ceinture	Gürtel	cintura	cinturón
bird	oiseau	Vogel	uccello	ave
black	noir	schwarz	nero	negro
blue	bleu	blau	azzurro	azul
book	livre	Buch	libro	libro
boy	garçon	Knabe	ragazzo	niño
bread	pain	Brot	pane	pan
cake	gâteau	Kuchen	torta	pasteles
carpet	tapis	Teppich	tappeto	alfombra
castle	château	Schloss	castello	castillo
cheese	fromage	Käse	fromaggio	queso
chicken	poule	Huhn	pollo	gallina

English	*French*	*German*	*Italian*	*Spanish*
clock	montre	Uhr	orlogio	reloj
cloud	nuage	Wolke	nuvola	nube
coat	manteau	Mantel	soprabito	abrigo
cold	froid	kalt	freddo	frio
comb	peigne	Kamm	pettine	peine
cotton	coton	Baumwolle	cotone	algodón
cow	vache	Kuh	vacca	vaca
curtain	rideau	Vorhang	tendina	cortina
dark	foncé, sombre	dunkel	oscuro	oscuro
day	jour	Tag	giorno	día
death	mort	Tod	morte	muerte
door	porte	Türe	porta	puerta
dress	robe	Kleid	vestito	vestido
ear	oreille	Ohr	orcchio	oreja
egg	oeuf	Ei	uovo	huevo
face	visage	Gesicht	faccia	cara
finger	doigt	Finger	dito	dedo
fire	feu	Feuer	fuoco	fuego
fish	poisson	Fisch	pesce	pez
five	cinq	fünf	cinque	cinco
flour	farine	Mehl	farina	harina
flower	fleur	Blume	flore	flor
foot	pied	Fuss	piede	pié
four	quatre	vier	quattro	cuatro
free	libre	frei	libero	libre
garden	jardin	Garten	giardino	jardin
girl	fille	Mädchen	ragazza	niña
glue	colle	Klebstoff	colla	aglutinante
good	bon	gut	buono	bueno
gravy	sauce	Tunke	salsa	salsa
green	vert	grün	verde	verde
hair	cheveux	Haar	capelli	cabello, pelo
hand	main	Hand	mano	mano
hat	chapeau	Hut	cappello	sombrero
head	tête	Kopf	testa	cabeza
heart	coeur	Herz	cuore	corazón
horse	cheval	Pferd	cavallo	caballo
hour	heure	Stunde	ora	hora
house	maison	Haus	casa	casa
hundred	cent	hundert	cento	cien
ice cream	glace	Eis	gelato	helado
iron	fer	Eisen	ferro	hierro
key	clef	Schlüssel	chiave	llave
knife	couteau	Messer	coltello	cuchillo
large	grand	gross	grande	grande
lead	plomb	Blei	piombo	plomo
leg	jambe	Bein	gamba	pierna
lemon	citron	Zitrone	limone	limón
light	clair	hell	chiaro	claro
light	lumière	Licht	luce	luz
lips	lèvres	Lippen	labbra	labios

English	*French*	*German*	*Italian*	*Spanish*
long	long	lang	lungo	largo
man	homme	Mensch, Mann	uomo	hombre
material	étoffe	Stoff	stoffe	tela
meal	repas	Mahlzeit	pasto	comida
meat	viande	Fleisch	carne	carne
milk	lait	Milch	latte	leche
money	argent	Geld	denaro	dinero
moon	lune	Mond	luna	luna
morning	matin	Morgen	mattina	mañana
mountain	montagne	Berg	monte	monte
mouth	bouche	Mund	bocca	boca
needle	aiguille	Nadel	ago	aguja
night	nuit	Nacht	notte	noche
no	non	nein	no	no
noon	midi	Mittag	mezzogiorno	mediodía
nose	nez	Nase	naso	nariz
one	un	eins	uno	uno
pain	douleur	Schmerz	dolore	dolor
pencil	crayon	Bleistift	matita	lápiz
plate	assiette	Teller	piatto	plato
poultry	volaille	Geflügel	volatili	carne de pluma
railway	chemin de fer	Eisenbahn	ferrovia	ferrocarril
rain	pluie	Regen	pioggia	lluvia
red	rouge	rot	rosso	rojo
ring	anneau	Ring	anello	sortija
river	fleuve	Fluss	fiume	rio
road	route	Strasse	strada	calle
rope	corde	Seil	corda	soga
salt	sel	Salz	sale	sal
shirt	chemise	Hemd	camicia	camisa
shoe	chaussures	Schuh	scarpe	zapatos
short	court	kurz	corto	corto
silk	soie	Seide	seta	seda
small	petit	klein	piccolo	pequeño
snow	neige	Schnee	neve	nieve
spectacles	lunettes	Brille	occhiali	anteojos
spoon	cuiller	Löffel	cucchiaio	cuchara
spring	printemps	Frühling	primavera	primavera
star	étoile	Stern	stelle	estrella
steel	acier	Stahl	acciaio	acero
stone	pierre	Stein	pietra	piedra
summer	été	Sommer	estate	verano
sun	soleil	Sonne	sole	sol
sweet	doux	süss	dolce	dulce
teeth	dent	Zahn	denti	dientes
ten	dix	zehn	dieci	diez
thanks	merci	danke	grazie	gracias
thick	épais	dick	grosso	grueso
thin	mince	dünn	sottile	delgado
thread	fil	Faden	filo	hilo
three	trois	drei	tre	tres

English	*French*	*German*	*Italian*	*Spanish*
time	temps	Zeit	tempo	tiempo
today	aujourd'hui	heute	oggi	hoy
town	ville	Stadt	città	ciudad
tree	arbre	Baum	albero	árbol
trousers	pantalon	Hose	calzoni	pantalones
two	deux	zwei	due	dos
tire	pneu	Reifen	copertone	neumático
ugly	laid	hässlich	brutto	feo
valley	vallée	Tal	valle	valle
vegetable	légume	Gemüse	verdura	legumbres
warm	chaud	warm	caldo	cálido, caliente
water	eau	Wasser	acqua	agua
way	chemin	Weg	pia	camino
week	semaine	Woche	settimana	semana
wheat	blé	Korn	frumento	trigo
white	blanc	weiss	bianco	blanco
window	fenêtre	Fenster	finestra	ventana
winter	hiver	Winter	inverno	invierno
woman	femme	Frau	donna	mujer
wood	forêt	Wald	bosco	hosque
wool	laine	Wolle	lana	lana
year	année	Jahr	anno	año
yellow	jaune	gelb	giallo	amarillo
yes	oui	ja	si	sí
zero	zéro	null	zero	cero

International Trade-Marks *

ENGLISH-SPEAKING COUNTRIES

Most trade-marks will have a uniform reception in English-speaking countries. Local variations, however, are sometimes found, e.g., Prince Albert (tobacco), popular in the United States would probably have a mixed reception in England. Thus, if overseas use is contemplated, words which may have a special significance or involve a difference in spelling should be closely scrutinized and the opinion of a native of the overseas territory obtained, either directly or through one's patent lawyer.

FOREIGN-LANGUAGE COUNTRIES

Where a name is to be used in foreign countries which are familiar with our Roman alphabet it is usually mistaken caution

* Cousins and Wadsworth, *Trade Names,* Harlequin Press.

to pick a name which, by having a French or Spanish appearance, seems specially adapted to use by foreigners. The prestige of British and American manufacturers is very high (it may be compared, for instance, with that of French perfumes in the United States or England), and a name lacking in "Englishness" may well lose a valuable distinction. It is better, in fact, to err in the other direction. Just as Le Lion is distinctively French, so The Lion is unmistakably English. The apostrophe S in Pond's, the adjective placed before instead of after the noun, short English words likely to be familiar to foreigners, e.g., Tom Jones, Red Lily, achieve the same result.

Care should be taken to see that the name will be rememberable in the more important languages. It should not, therefore, be too long—though it may be made of short or hyphenated words. If it is of a descriptive nature or has meaning of any kind it should preferably retain this quality by being composed of roots recognizable by foreigners, or it may be assisted conceivably by a bracketed translation beneath, or, especially in backward non-European countries, by a suitable illustration.

A complication which occasionally arises is that a name may have a freak meaning in a foreign language. This is not usually important, however, unless the association is very derogatory and obvious, and unless it is obscene or ridiculous. An accidental meaning may, in fact, be definitely helpful by making the name easy to remember; observe such well-accepted names as Bass, Squibb, Hellmann, Pears, Fry, Younger. A surname, however, has more tolerance in this respect than an invented word, which lacks the dignity of a personal connection.

Since freak meanings may arise through a slang or phonetic association which a dictionary will not reveal, it may be advisable to consult a fluent speaker, preferably a native, or ask one's patent lawyer to check this through his foreign agent.

Finally, the name ought to be pronounceable in the countries concerned. This may be achieved in four different ways:

1. The name chosen may be naturally foolproof, e.g., Kodak, Lux, Tobralco, Coty. This is probably the best method.

2. It may be directed by the use of accent or modification marks—é, ö, ç, etc., or the use of a hyphen, as in Ven-usa.
3. The correct English pronunciation, if not too difficult, may be indicated below in parenthesis. This is usually only advisable when the article is of popular appeal and such instruction not likely to be resented.
4. It may be allowed to take its course, e.g., Michelin has become Anglicized, Chevrolet has not, and Pathé is half way. The fact that the new pronunciation given to the word by the foreigner sounds difficult or barbarous in such cases need not concern us.

The following arrangements of letters will usually produce foolproof names in other languages:

1. Consonants and vowels alternated, e.g., LYSOL, ANITA (Q, W and H, however, are irregular).
2. Double consonants used as in English, e.g., DECCA.
3. Consonants L, R, S, N, Z, M, in inside positions pair well with other consonants, e.g., FROSTINT.
4. Names taken from the two five-letter word finders will almost invariably have good polyglot characteristics.

TRADE-MARK DICTIONARIES

Trade-Marks Classified According to Meaning (Type)

The following classification is by type. Most of the headings are chosen according to the basic idea suggested by the name. Some of the trade-marks could be listed under several headings. The interpretation is to some extent arbitrary and may differ occasionally from the meaning which the trade-mark owner intended.

Some of the following trade names are registered and others are not. No difference between those registered and those not registered has been made. It will be greatly appreciated if errors are brought to the compiler's attention.

TRADE-MARKS CLASSIFIED BY TYPE

Trade-Marks Referring to	*Name*	*Registered for*
Adhesion	**Klutch**	Denture adhesive
	Stictuit	Rubber cement
	Stikfast	Label paster
	Tanglefoot	Fly-paper
	Grip-Tight	Adhesive
	Grip Top	Nonskid belting
Age	**Ancient Age**	Liquor
	Grandma's	Molasses
	Grandpa's	Soap
	Old Abbey	Ale
	Old Angus	Scotch whisky
	Old Grand Dad	Whisky
	Old Mission	Wine
	Old Monastery	Wine
Animals	**Airedale**	Whisky
	Alligator	Rainwear
	Antelope	Bags
	Badger	Hairpins

Trade-Marks Referring to	*Name*	*Registered for*
	Badger	Paper bags
	Bobcat	Twine
	Bug-A-Boo	Insecticide
	Camel	Tire patches
	Cat's Paw	Rubber heels
	Chinchilla	Textiles
	Colt	Boots
	Cub	Water heater
	Dromedary	Dates
	Dry Fly	Sherry
	Elk	Bags
	Great Dane	Coats
	Grizzly	Brake lining
	Kangaroo	Plywood articles
	Lion	Beer
	Lizard	Bags
	Mink	Perfume
	Moose	Bags
	Mustang	Motorcycles
	Otter	Leather
	Panther	Lubricant
	Salamander	Crucibles
	Sea Horse	Outboard motor
	Prime	Cleaner
	Stag	Shaving cream
	Steer	Cottonseed meal
	Tiger	Bedsprings
	Turtles	Candy
	Whale	Tools
	Whippet	Automobiles
	White Rabbit	Egg colors
	White Stag	Ski togs
	Wolverine	Gloves
Appearance or Structure	**Add-A-Pearl**	Necklace
	Bubaloon	Bubble fluid
	Crispie	Potato chips
	Crystaline	Salt
	Egg Shell	China
	Fiberglas	Glass fiber
	Filigree	Toiletries
	Fine Line	Pencils
	Fluffo	Shortening
	Gauzets	Sanitary napkins
	Golden Crust	Bread
	Interwoven	Hosiery

Trade-Marks Referring to	*Name*	*Registered for*
	Keglined	Beer cans
	Krinkles	Noodles
	Krunchy	Fresh vegetables
	Soyflake	Soybean flour
	Webbies	Knitted or woven clothing
Architecture	**Doric**	Dry colors
	Gargoyle	Lubricants
	Gothic	Artists' colors
	Gothic	Watches
	Keystone	Cameras
Artists	**Goya**	Artists' brushes
	Van Dyck	Cigars
	Van Gogh	Artists' brushes
Astronomy or Meteorology	**Aurora**	Brick
	Cloudrift	Yarn
	Comet	Aluminum goods
	Comet	Tobacco
	Constellation	Airplanes
	Corona	Insecticide
	Dew Kist	Wine
	Eclipse	Lawn mower
	Equator	Candy
	Equinox	Piece-goods
	Evening Star	Bread
	Half Moon	Tapes
	Meridian	Piece-goods
	Meteor	Dog food
	Milky Way	Curtains
	Moon	Razor blades
	Northern Lights	Perfume
	North Star	Blankets
	Orbit	Chewing gum
	Rainbow	Wafers
	Red Comet	Tennis rackets
	Satellite	Jewelry
	Sirius	Bronze powder
	Snow Flake	Biscuits
	Star	Razors
	Stratosphere	Toiletries
	Sunbeam	Shoes
	Sunlight	Soap
	Sunrise	Gum
	Sunset	Soap dyes
	Sunshine	Pimentos
	Zenith	Radios

Trade-Marks Referring to	*Name*	*Registered for*
Babies	**Babykin**	Baby bedding
	Babyskin	Soap
	Better Baby	Nursing bottles
	Lullabye	Infants' furniture
	Ween	Puppy food
Beauty	**American Beauty**	Electric iron
	Beauty	Women's wear
	Beauty Rest	Mattresses
	Charm	Shampoo
	Cover Girl	Feminine products
	Crowning Glory	Hair preparations
	Dixie Belle	Sanitary pads
	Fair Skin	Complexion soap
	Lovely Lady	Cosmetics
Birds	**Bird of Paradise**	Candy
	Blue Bird	Cedar chest
	Blue Bird	Flour
	Blue-Jay	Corn remedy
	Bob White	Bed linens
	Cardinal	Kitchenware
	Carrier Pigeon	Airplanes
	Condor	Airplanes
	Dove	Washing powder
	Eagle	Pencil
	Falcon	Camera
	Hawk	Airplanes
	Ibis	Textiles
	Kingfisher	Fishing lines
	Lark	Orange concentrate
	Nightingale	Hosiery
	Old Crow	Whisky
	Oriole	Canned foods
	Parrot	Cocoa
	Peacock	Gin
	Pelican	Seeds
	Sea Gull	Sardines
	Skylark	Luggage
	Snow Goose	Flour
	Swallow	Kitchen machinery
	White Owl	Cigars
	White Swan	Gin
Brightness or Light	**Barreled Sunlight**	White paint
	Bright Star	Flashlight
	Briten	Dental cream
	Britesun	Sun lamp

Trade-Marks Referring to	*Name*	*Registered for*
	Cleanshine	Leather polish
	Double Brite	Polish
	Flik	Cigarette lighters
	Floorgloh	Floor polish
	Glare-Pruf	Goggles
	Glazo	Nail polish
	Gleem	Paint
	Glitter	Cleansing pads
	Glitterine	Lacquer
	Glo-Brite	Floor wax
	Glo-Co	Hair dressing
	Glo-Coat	Polish
	Glo-Hooks	Luminous fish hooks
	Glolite	Cigarette lighter
	Hair Sheen	Shampoo
	Hysheen	Floor wax
	Lustre	Shampoo
	Lustron	Hair lightener
	Miraglo	Artificial leather
	Miraglo	Nail polish
	Mirro	Aluminum kitchenware
	Ray-Bar	Sun visors
	Sea-Flash	Swim suits
	Shinex	Window cleaner
	Shur-Brite	Polish
	Slick Shine	Polish
	Sunbeam	Electrical devices
	Sunbrite	Cleanser
	Sunbrite	Sateen
	Sunsheen	Paints
	Sunshine	Cleaner
Chemicals	**Acetamine**	Chemical
	Acidol	Chemical
	Aminoprod	Medicament
	Carboloy	Hard-cutting metal
	Castoria	Laxative
	Chromanthrene	Dye
	Ergoapiol	Drug
	Ferrisul	Chemical
	Glycidol	Chemical
	Hi-Octane	Gasoline
	Irgamine	Textile chemical
Chinese Words	**Chen Yu**	Nail enamel
	Cumshaw (gift)	Gifts
	Ding How (good wishes)	Textiles

Trade-Marks Referring to	*Name*	*Registered for*
	Yenshu	Cosmetics
Cleanliness	**Daintee**	Bathroom accessories
	Desoil	Laundry detergent
	Dri-Kleen	Cleaning compound
	Immac	Deodorant
	Immaculate	Carbon paper
	Innerclean	Laxative
	Kleenette	Washable leather
	Kleenex	Cleaning tissue
	Kleen Heet	Oil burners
	Kum Kleen	Labels
	Neet	Depilatory
	Prim	Deodorant
	Renuzit	Dry cleaner
	Soil-Off	Paint cleaner
	Spic	Cleaner
	Spic and Span	Cleaner
	Spotless Town	Cleaner
Clubs or Organization	**Club**	Cocktails
	Country Club	Beverages
	Havana Club	Rum
Coined Words	**Alemite**	Lubricant
	Aywon	Shirt
	Biz	Cleanser
	Dic-A-Doo	Paint cleaner
	Dreft	Detergent
	Drene	Shampoo
	Fab	Soap flakes
	Flit	Insecticide
	Fudgicle	Ice-cream stick
	Gaytees	Overshoes
	Haps	Underwear
	Hep	Drug
	Ipana	Tooth paste
	Karo	Corn syrup
	Keds	Sneakers
	Kix	Cereal
	Klek	Soap flakes
	Krene	Plastic products
	Nair	Deodorant
	Nerg	Deodorant
	Prell	Shampoo
	Rad	Cleaner
	Rel	Medicine
	Rem	Medicine

Trade-Marks Referring to	*Name*	*Registered for*
	Rit	Dyes
	Sib	Bleach
	Spam	Meat
	Swerl	Detergent
	Tad	Cuticle remover
	Teba	Shampoo
	Teel	Liquid dentifrice
	Teem	Beverages
	Tek	Tooth brush
	Trol	Hairdressing
	Twink	Soap dyes
	Vel	Washing compound
	Vream	Shortening
	Wix	Personal hygiene products
	Zoop	Soap
Colleges or Schools	**Campus**	Men's clothing
	Collegiate	Garters
	Harvard	Beer
	Princeton	Paint
	University	Loud speakers
	Yale	Brushes
Colors	**Black and White**	Canned foods
	Black and White	Whisky
	Blu-White	Soap flakes
	Ebony	Coal
	Fleecy White	Laundry bleach
	Golden Brown	Potato chips
	Ivory	Soap
	Lily White	Flour
	Scarlet	Tooth paste
	Snow White	Yarn
	White	Trucks
	Yellow	Coaches
Comfort or Fit	**Comfortized**	Shoes
	Comfy	Slippers
	Fitzwel	Girdles
	Foot-Kind	Shoes
	Foot Rest	Shoes
	Footsavers	Shoes
	Formfit	Corsets
	Glove-Grip	Shoes
	Posturbilt	Chairs
	Proper Posture	Girdles
	Skintees	Panties
	Snuggie	Pajamas

Trade-Marks Referring to	*Name*	*Registered for*
	Step Rite	Arch supports
	Sun Rest	Sun glasses
	Trimfit	Hosiery
	X-Act-Fit	Shirt
Comics	**Buster Brown**	Hosiery
	Dinty Moore	Canned meats
	Donald Duck	Orange juice
	Skippy	Peanut butter
Common * Usage	**Bakelite**	Plastics
	Bass	Ale
	Camembert	Cheese
	Cellophane	Transparent sheeting
	Dry Ice	Solidified carbon dioxide
	Gruyère	Cheese
	Keds	Sneakers
	Nylon	Synthetic textile
	Quonset	Portable prefabricated buildings
	Technicolor	Colored movies
	Vichy	Mineral water
Companions or Friends	**Buddy**	Calsomine
	Chum	Razor blades
	Friend	Furniture polish
	Pal	Razor blades
	Shipmate	Marine ranges
Compound Words	**Addressograph**	Addressing machine
	Airkem	Air freshener
	Airtopia	Air conditioning unit
	Airways	Motor oil
	Aquagard	Water-repellent finish
	Aquarome	Water-soluble perfumes
	Aquastop	Waterproof packaging
	Aridifier	Air drier
	Aristo-Tex	Suiting
	Artform	Girdle
	Art-O-Leum	Linoleum
	Artone	Radio set
	Bake-Rite	Shortening
	Band-Aid	Adhesive bandage
	Bathasweet	Soap
	Beutalure	Hair coloring
	Bugamist	Insecticide

* Trade-marks which lost their trade-mark character and became a common designation for the article.

Trade-Marks Referring to	*Name*	*Registered for*
	Covermark	Blemish covering
	Deodorome	Deodorant bases
	Dictaphone	Dictating device
	Exercycle	Exercising device
	Fasteeth	Denture powder
	Frenchef	Food colors
	Mule-Hide	Roofing
	Multigraph	Duplicating machine
	Nevablaze	Flameproofed canvas
	Off-N-On	Skid chains
	Realsilk	Hosiery
	Savaspace	Folding tables
	Shuglovs	Ladies' rubbers
	U-All-No	Mints
	Vise-Grip	Wrenches
	Voicewriter	Dictating device
	Whalehide	Wrapping paper
	Wingfoot	Rubber heels
Contractions or Abbreviations	**Alcoa**	Aluminum
	Alnico	Alloy
	Al-Ox	Aluminum oxide
	B[1] Well	Medicine
	Calafig	Laxative
	Calavo	Avocado
	Califorange	Citrus-fruit juice
	Chipso	Soap flakes
	Churkey	Canned chicken & turkey
	Colotato	Potato
	Comfo	Snow suits
	Conoco	Gasoline
	Dis	Disinfectant
	Duco	Lacquer
	Duxbak	Belting
	Duxkin	Baby pants
	Eatmor	Cranberries
	Elbo-Roni	Macaroni
	Fel-Moc	Felt moccasin
	Flakso	Soap chips
	Flavorite	Flavor
	Flexaust	Flexible exhaust hose
	Flex-Let	Flexible bracelet
	Floralife	Cut-flower preserver
	Fritatoes	Potato chips
	Glink	Ink for glass
	Gre-Solvent	Hand cleaner

Trade-Marks Referring to	*Name*	*Registered for*
	Havanap	Paper napkins
	Hol-Ry	Toast
	Horshu	Shoes
	Ibath	Eye lotion
	Iernoz	Medicine
	Lacq	Lacquer
	Lopor	Lubricating oil
	Lykit	Dog food
	Mapacuba	Cigars
	Mini-Mag	Miniature magnifier
	Nabisco	Crackers
	Nichrome	Nickel-chromium alloy
	Nu-Matic	Shoes
	Nu-Way	Shaving cream
	Nylongerie	Nylon lingerie
	Onandoff	Dress shields
	Produc-Trol	Production control system
	Protex	Toilet tissue
	Quink	Ink
	Sankerchiefs	Mentholated tissue
	Sil-Carb	Silicon carbide
	Stokol	Coal stoker
	T-Mates	Shirts
	Uneeda	Biscuits
	U. No	Candy bar
	Vess	Beverages
	Wa-So	Water softener
	YB Stout	Corsets
	Zestang	Canned foods
Convenience	**Hand-ee**	Grinder
	Handies	Facial tissue
	Handirol	Gummed tape
	Handi-tape	Adhesive bandage
	Rub-No-More	Soaps
Dance	**Ballet**	Piece-goods
	Bolero	Rum
	Fandango	Gloves
	Fandango	Textiles
	Jitterbug	Insect repellent
	Minuet	Crackers
	Polonaíse	Cosmetics
	Prom	Shoe polish
	Terpsichore	Lipstick
	Virginia Reel	Hosiery
Destroying,	**Ab-Scent**	Toilet preparation

Trade-Marks Referring to	*Name*	*Registered for*
Repelling, Eliminating or Preventing	**Ant-B-Gon**	Ant killer
	Antchek	Ant killer
	Ant Doom	Insecticide
	Ant-Foil	Ant killer
	Ant Go	Ant killer
	Antrol	Ant killer
	Ant-X	Ant poison
	Banox	Rustproofing process
	Bansect	Insecticide
	Barweed	Weed killer
	Bif	Fly spray
	Bug Blitzer	Insecticide dispenser
	Bug Bomb	Insecticide
	Bugded	Insecticide
	Bug Doom	Insecticide
	Bug-Geta	Insecticide
	Bugine	Insecticide
	Bug Shoo	Insecticide
	Carboff	Carbon remover
	Chaser	Breath sweetener
	Chex	Wall sealer
	Corn-Off	Corn remedy
	Ded-Lee	Insecticide
	Dogzoff	Dog repellent
	Doom	Roach powder
	d-Ter	Insect repellent
	Dustbane	Sweeping compound
	Dust-Stop	Air filters
	End-O-Pest	Insecticide
	Ends-All	Insecticide
	Ens-Zem	Insecticide
	Expello	Mothicide
	Flyded	Fly spray
	Fly Kil	Insecticide
	Fly-Tox	Fly spray
	Germ-X	Disinfectant
	Gopher Death	Exterminator
	Insect-O-Blitz	Insecticide
	Karbout	Carbon remover
	Killice	Insecticide
	Kill-Pest	Insecticide
	Kil-Mor	Insecticide
	Knox Out	Insecticide
	Kurb	Pain alleviator
	Moth Doom	Insecticide

Trade-Marks Referring to	*Name*	*Registered for*
	No-Pest	Insecticide
	No Sect	Insecticide
	Nox-Odor	Odor absorbent
	Out-Sect	Insecticide
	Perstop	Deodorant
	Pest-B-Gon	Insecticide
	Pestrid	Insecticide
	Pestroy	Insecticide
	Pussy Scat	Cat repellent
	Pyra-No	Flameproof paint
	Ridsmel	Paint deodorant
	Ridz	Insecticide
	Rough On Rats	Rat poison
	Rust Ban	Rust preventive
	Rust Go	Rust remover
	Rust Kill	Rust remover
	Rustop	Rust preventer
	Rust-Rid	Rust remover
	Scarat	Rat repellent
	Scram	Dog repellent
	Skip-Flea	Flea powder
	Slay	Insecticide
	Slug-Em	Snail poison
	Snail-Foil	Snail destroyer
	Snogo	Snow plow
	Stop	Insect barrier
	Sunaway	Venetian blinds
	Sunfoe	Skin lotion
	Sure Death	Insecticide
	Taboo	Deodorant
	Toes-Up	Insecticide
	Vanish	Cleaner
	Weedoom	Weed killer
Diminutives	**Dab**	Paint
	Dwarfies	Cereal
	Little Trojan	Paints
	Micronex	Carbon black
	Nibs	Licorice pieces
	Peewee's	Diapers
	Scarfies	Neckwear
	Seasonettes	Seasoning
	Snacks	Confections
	Soyettes	Soybean products
	Tublets	Bath preparation
Durability,	**Duraglas**	Glass

Trade-Marks Referring to	*Name*	*Registered for*
Permanence	**Endura**	Fountain pen
	Enduro	Rust-resisting steel
	Fast-White	Shoe cleaner
	Hardiweave	Suits
	Holeproof	Hosiery
	Kant-Fade	Textiles
	Kissproof	Lipstick
	Lifetime	Aluminum goods
	Neva-Split	Fur coats
	Neverbreak	Trunks
	On-to-Sta	Gummed fabrics
	Permanite	Corrosionproof material
	Permanized	Paper
	Stacomb	Hair dressing
	Staigreen	Lawn seed
	Staiset	Hair lacquer
	Staze	Denture powder
	Tattoo	Lipstick
	Wearever	Fountain pen
Ease	**Easy Monday**	Laundry starch
	Ezy Edge	Hones
	Ezy-Mix	Salad dressing
	Ez-2	Polish
	No-Rub	Floor polish
	Rediform	Business forms
	Slax	Sport shoes
	Styl-Eez	Shoes
	Treadeasy	Shoes
	Wheel-Ezy	Hand truck
Effect	**Coverall**	Paints
	Do More	Posture chair
	Easyon	Tire chains
	Elasti-Glass	Belts
	Glider	Shaving cream
	Ground Gripper	Shoes
	Mileage	Gasoline
	Skidproof	Floor finish
	Snapout	Manifold forms
	Space Saver	Clothes racks
	Spred	Paints
Emotion or Effect	**Breathless**	Perfume
	Crying	Handkerchiefs
	Deception	Perfumes
	Devastating	Perfume
	Exhilaration	Shampoo

Trade-Marks Referring to	*Name*	*Registered for*
	Heart Break	Perfume
	Intoxication	Perfume
	Irresistible	Perfume
	Libido	Perfume
	Remember	Perfume
	Revelation	Tooth powder
	Shocking	Perfume
Equipment	**Brick Oven**	Baked beans
	Grillator	Food grill
	Kombinators	Homogenizers
	Laundromat	Washing machine
	Liquidometer	Liquid-measuring device
	Motorola	Auto radio
Exclamations	**By Gosh**	Fresh fruits
	Golly	Detergent
	Ha-Ha	Piece-goods
	Hush	Deodorant
	Oh Oh	Deodorant
	Shoo	Cleanser
	Wow	Tobacco
Exhibitions, Pageants	**Big Parade**	Candy
	Cavalcade	Refrigerators
	County Fair	Paints
	Mardi Gras	Malt syrup
	World's Fair	Paints
Expressions	**Ashes of Roses**	Toiletries
	As You Like It	Vanity cases
	Bowl of Roses	Tobacco
	Evening in Paris	Perfume
	File With A Smile	Filing cabinets
	Fit to be Tied	Neckties
	Forget-Me-Not	Bracelets
	Good and Plenty	Licorice candy
	Hide-It	Blemish cream
	It's A Peach	Gloves
	Kiss and Tell	Cosmetics
	Knick and Pull	Paper pencils
	Sweet n' Lovely	Toiletries
Fashion, Style or Distinction	**Beau Brummell**	Tie
	Beau-T-Form	Foundation garment
	Fashion Park	Men's clothing
	Fashion Plate	Shoes
	Figurfit	Swim suits
	Foot Fashion	Shoes
	Glamour	Plastic garment hangers

Trade-Marks Referring to	*Name*	*Registered for*
	Longerlyne	Corsets
	Maiden Form	Brassieres
	Mayfair	Luggage
	Pall Mall	Cigarettes
	Park Lane	Handbags
	Regal	Shoes
	Sophistocract	Shoes
	Style King	Belts
	Stylemaster	Linens
	Stylish Stout	Garment foundations
Feminine or Maternal	**La Senorita**	Corsets
	Lassies	Textiles
	Leading Lady	Cosmetics
	Mama's	Pancake flour
	Milady	Coffee
	Mother's	Oats
	Mother's Friend	Ointment
	Mrs. Filbert's	Margarine
	Mrs. Henry's	Jams
	Mrs. Morrison's	Puddings
	Mrs. Tucker's	Shortening
	Mrs. Wagner's	Pies
	Mrs. Winslow's	Soothing syrup
Fire or Fireproofing	**Campfire**	Marshmallows
	Fire Chief	Canvas
	Fire Chief	Gasoline
	Firemaster	Fire extinguisher
	Flame Thrower	Cigarette lighters
	Flare	Lighters
	Fyr-Fyter	Fire extinguishers
Firm Names	**A. and P.**	Grocery products
	A and S	Dry goods
	Akom	Exercise shirt
	Alseco	Caps and seals
	ASR	Surgeon's blades
	B. and W.	Boilers
	Benson and Hedges	Tobacco
	Black and Decker	Tools
	Crosse and Blackwell	Foods
	Elmanco	Manganese
	Erla	Radio sets
	Firestone	Tires
	Ford	Automobiles
	Gulflube	Motor oil
	Gulfpride	Lubricant

Trade-Marks Referring to	*Name*	*Registered for*
	Nopco	Cod-liver oils
	Sovac	Insecticide
	Supre-Macy	Golf balls
Fishes	**Bass**	Shoes
	Electric Eel	Drain cleaner
	Goldfish	Marmalade
	Marlin	Razor blades
Flexibility	**Flexees**	Girdles
	Flexwood	Plywood
	Hy-Flex	Rubber heels
	Resilio	Neckties
Fluidity	**Evenflo**	Nursing nipples
	Fluid Light	Enamels
	Fulflo	Filters
French Words	**Bien Jolie**	Corset
	Bon Ami	Cleanser
	Chateau	Cheese
	Chic	Lingerie
	Chichi	Perfume
	Coquette	Costume jewelry
	Encore	Beer
	Gillette	Shaving cream
	La France	Fabrics
	Largesse	Writing paper
	Le Roi	Cheese
	Mais-Oui	Face powder
	Mignon	Corsets
	Noblesse	Corsets
	Pique	Flavoring
	Risque	Cosmetics
	Vogue	Perfume
Freshness	**Fresh**	Deodorant cream
	Fresh Nut	Peanut butter
	Garden Fresh	Frozen foods
	Sta-Fresh	Bread
Gallantry	**Don Juan**	Shirts
	Knight-Errant	Jewelry
Games or Game Terms	**Ace**	Armature
	Domino	Cigarettes
	Four Aces	Whisky
	Four Queens	House coats
	Grand Slam	Piece-goods
	Jack of Diamonds	Plug tobacco
	Jack of Hearts	Soap
	Jack Pot	Scouring pads

Trade-Marks Referring to	*Name*	*Registered for*
	Royal Flush	Toiletries
	Skat	Insect repellent
	Top Score	Piece-goods
	Tournament	Checker game
	Trump	Supporter
	Winners	Cigarettes
Geographical Terms	**Acapulco**	Sport shirts
	Albany	Lubricant
	Allegheny	Piece-goods
	Amazon	Rubber belting
	American	Furniture
	Ansonia	Clocks
	Bagdad	Smoking pipe
	Baltic	Flour
	Belfast	Carbonated beverages
	Bengal	Cotton goods
	Berkshire	Meat
	Bermuda	Cosmetics
	Boston	Brown bread
	Bostonian	Shoes
	Buckingham	Cigarettes
	Canada Dry	Beverage
	Canterbury	Clocks
	Cape Cod	Thread
	Capri	Macaroni
	Caracas	Chocolate
	Catalina	Knit goods
	Celtic	Linens
	Chelsea	Clocks
	Chicago	Belting
	Chun King	Chinese-type vegetables
	Copenhagen	Snuff
	Delaware	Punch
	Demerara	Rum
	Detroit	Belt lacing
	Dixie	Beer
	Donnybrook	Coats
	Duquesne	Rum
	Elgin	Margarine
	Genesee	Beer
	Golden Gate	Cement
	Gotham	Champagne
	Granada	Brandy
	Grand Canyon	Stains
	Guiana	Textiles

Trade-Marks Referring to	*Name*	*Registered for*
	Himalaya	Razor blades
	Holland	Gin
	Hollywood	Candy
	Hoosier	Food products
	Iceland	Frozen foods
	Idaho	Gin
	India	Tea
	Iowa	Cream separator
	Isle of Capri	Toiletries
	Italian Swiss Colony	Wines
	Ithaca	Shotguns
	Jah-Va	Coffee
	Java	Cosmetics
	Kantung	Oriental-type perfume base
	Kentucky	Whisky
	Klondike	Oil
	Lancaster	Paper
	Land O'Lakes	Dairy products
	Lexington	Piece-goods
	London	Shoes
	Londonderry	Ale
	London Dew	Topcoats
	Louisville	Golf clubs
	Manhattan	Coffee
	Massachusetts	Piece-goods
	Mecca	Cigarettes
	Miami	Face pack
	Michigan	Apples
	Milwaukee	Milling machinery
	Monte Carlo	Piece-goods
	Monterey	Beer
	Monticello	Whisky
	Morocco	Clothing
	Mountain Valley	Spring water
	Mount Vernon	Whisky
	Mt. Ida	Olives
	Naples	Italian-type foods
	New England	Pancake syrup
	New Haven	Clocks
	Norfolk	Ham
	Normandie	Beauty supplies
	Norway	Antifreeze
	Occident	Flour
	Ohio	Anesthetic gas
	Old English	Cheese

Trade-Marks Referring to	*Name*	*Registered for*
	Old Munich	Malt syrup
	Old St. Croix	Rum
	Old Virginia	Ham
	Old Waukesha	Ale
	Olympia	Beer
	Ontario	Shoes
	Oregon	Preserves
	Oriental	Stucco
	Oshkosh	Horse shoes
	Palm Beach	Neckties
	Paris	Belts
	Parisian	Shoe dressing
	Pennsylvania	Oil
	Philadelphia	Cream cheese
	Philippine	Mahogany
	Picadilly	Men's wear
	Piedmont	Cigarettes
	Pilsener	Beer
	Pinehurst	Tobacco
	Plymouth	Automobile
	Prairie	Wire fence
	Rainier	Beer
	Richmond	Union suits
	Riviera	Bed linens
	Rochester	Thermometers
	Rocky Mountain	Tea
	Roma	Wine
	Rue De La Paix	Piece-goods
	Sacramento	Canned fruits
	Salem	Disinfectant
	Santa Fe	Cigars
	Saratoga	Vegetables
	Sorrento	Perfumery
	South Bend	Lathes
	Stone Mountain	Beverages
	Sun Valley	Sport shirts
	Swissfort	Cheese
	Swiss Knight	Cheese
	Syracuse	China
	Texas	Citrus fruits
	Thousand Islands	Salad dressing
	Tioga	Coal
	Toronto	Mints
	Utica	Clothing
	Valencia	Piece-goods

Trade-Marks Referring to	*Name*	*Registered for*
	Versailles	Shoes
	Wabash Valley	Whisky
	Waukesha	Peas
	Wembley	Ties
	Westfield	Bicycles
	Westminster	Toilet paper
	Westphalia	Pumpernickel
	White Mountain	Refrigerator
	Wilkes-Barre	Curtains
	Wilmington	Vulcanized fiber
	Windsor	Foods
	Wisconsin	Butter
	Worcester	Salt
	Yosemite	Roofing
	Youngstown	Steel sinks
	Yucatan	Chewing gum
German Words	**Arabische Nächte**	Cosmetics
	Bürgermeister	Beer
	Edelweiss	Beer
	Rheingold	Beer
Government or Officials	**Ambassador**	Wine
	Congress	Playing cards
	Diplomat	Whisky
	House of Lords	Coffee
	Parliament	Cigarettes
Greek Words	**Eureka**	Vacuum cleaner
	Omega	Flour
Greetings or Toasts	**Cheerio**	Ale
	Hi Dad!	Toiletries
	Hi-Ho	Crackers
	Skol	Suntan lotion
	Welcome	Soap
Growth	**Gro Pup**	Dog food
	Growmore	Seeds
	Hy-Gro	Plant food
Happy Occasions	**Banquet**	Ale
	Birthday	Children's clothing
	Blessed Event	Maternity dresses
	Festival	Hosiery
	Fiesta	Dinnerware
	Golden Wedding	Whisky
	Happy Days	Liquors
	Jubilee	Shower curtains
	Silver Wedding	Silver-plated ware
Health	**Arch Preserver**	Shoe

Trade-Marks Referring to	*Name*	*Registered for*
	Healene	Ointment
	Health Builder	Feeds
	Healthi	Panty
	Health Sox	Hosiery
	Here's Health	Vegetable juice
	Hospital	Blades
	Hygeia	Nursing bottles
	Nature's Remedy	Medicine
	New Life	Malt tonic
	Physical Culture	Shoes
	Red Cross	Plasters
	Red Cross	Towels
	Spa	Brushes
Height	**Acme**	Animal feed
	Acme	Beer
	Apex	Moth killer
	Elevators	Height-increasing shoes
	Hi-Lift	Well pumps
	Lo-Hed	Electric hoist
Historical Allusions	**Alamo**	Firebrick
	Bunker Hill	Beans
	Liberty	Fruits
	Liberty Bell	Foods
	Mayflower	Doughnuts
	Minute Man	Fire extinguisher
	Valley Forge	Lubricant
Home	**Fireside**	Stoves
	Home	Toothpicks
	Hostess	Cake
	House Beautiful	Drapes
	Kitchen Jewel	Pot cleaner
Honesty or Honor	**Fidelity**	Drug specialties
	Honest	Dog food
	Honor-Bilt	Albums
	Sincerity	Clothing
Hotels	**Hotel Astor**	Coffee
	Savoy	Food products
	Waldorf	Toilet paper
	Waldorf-Astoria	Gin
Indian-American Words	**Blackhawk**	Beer
	Chippewa	Outdoor boots
	Geronimo	Moccasins
	Indian	Fire pumps
	Kickapoo	Medicine
	Manitou	Beverages

Trade-Marks Referring to	*Name*	*Registered for*
	Mohawk	Bed linens
	Mohawk	Sprayers
	Onondaga	Silk
	Pequot	Bedding
	Pontiac	Automobile
	Powhatan	Canned foods
	Sachem	Paper bags
	Sioux	Tools
	Skookum	Apples
	Tepee	Paper bags
	Tillamook	Cheese
	Wyandotte	Piece-goods
Ingredients	**Agarol**	Laxative
	Aspergum	Chewing gum
	Carbonex	Rubber-compounding product
	Derrisol	Insecticide
	Kashmirduna	Woolen goods
	Leadite	Lead paints
	Titanox	Pigment
	TRice	Rice
Insects	**Caterpillar**	Tractors
	Cocoon	Plastic, protective coating
	Firefly	Fluorescent lighting
	Honey Bee	Flour
	June Bug	Cigarette lighters
	Locust	Watches
	Wasp	Aeronautical engines
Italian Words	**Bolognesi**	Wine
	Cara Nome	Cosmetics
	Famiglia	Grapes
Jewels or Jewelry	**Cameo**	Cleanser
	Cameo	Hosiery
	Diadem	Hairpins
	Diamond	Dyes
	Diamond	Walnuts
	Emerald	Wall board
	Gem	Dog food
	Jewel	Shortening
	Pearl	Beer
	Ruby	Abrasive paper
	Sapphire	Pins
	Solitaire	Groceries
	Star Sapphire	Hosiery
	Topaz	Lubricant

Trade-Marks Referring to	*Name*	*Registered for*
Latin Words	**Et cetera**	Toiletries
	Luna	Pencils
	Lux	Marking brush
	Lux	Soap
	Magnavox	Radios
	Sol-Lux	Electric-light fixtures
	Trans-Lux	Projection screens
	Vice Versa	Toiletries
Lengthened Words	**Linene**	Collars and cuffs
	Resine	Resin
Letters	**A.B.C.**	Book cover
	B.C.	Headache medicament
	D.O.M.	Benedictine
	E.Z.	Corn popper
	H-O	Oats
	S.O.S.	Cleaner
	X	Antifreeze
	XYZ	Ointment
Letters and Numbers	**A-1**	Beer
	V-8	Vegetable juice
Letters and Words	**Abdox**	Corset
	B-Dri	Waterproofing
	U-Mak-A	Index tab
Letters—Changed	**Kanana**	Banana flakes
Letters or Numbers Spelled Out	**Bee Dee**	Veterinary products
	Effanbee	Dolls
	Essenay	Fire extinguisher
	Esso	Petroleum products
	Tufordee	2-4D, weed-killer
Literature	**Aladdin**	Lamps
	Annie Laurie	Hosiery
	Balzac	Cordial
	Ben Hur	Coffee and tea
	Chocolate Soldier	Fishing flies
	Don Juan	Lipstick
	du Maurier	Cigarettes
	Emerson	Cigars
	Excelsior	Shoes
	Falstaff	Beer
	Faust	Macaroni
	Gulliver	Canned fish
	Hiawatha	Knitting wool
	Ivanhoe	Lamps
	Jezebel	Piece-goods
	Little Women	Hosiery

Trade-Marks Referring to	*Name*	*Registered for*
	Mark Twain	Shirts
	Monte Cristo	Wines
	Paul Bunyan	Boat propellers
	Penrod	Boys' stockings
	Peter Pan	Canned foods
	Pickwick	Ale
	Plato	Denture cleaner
	Polyanna	Shoes
	Priscilla	Houseware
	Robert Burns	Cigars
	Robin Hood	Flour
	Rob Roy	Gloves
	Sinbad	Toiletries
	Tam O'Shanter	Scotch
	Tam O'Shanter	Short bread
	Tom Sawyer	Boys' clothing
	Trilby	Soap
	Vanity Fair	Underwear
	Victor Hugo	Brandy
	Voltaire	Brandy
	Wabash	Refrigerators
	Walter Scott	Cigars
	Wm. Tell	Lubricant
	3 Musketeers	Candy
Liveliness	**Brisk**	Shaving cream
	Friskies	Dog food
	Pep	Bran flakes
	Perk	Cocktail juice
	Spring Step	Rubber heels
	Spry	Shortening
	Vim	Food products
Love or Romance	**Courtship**	Textiles
	I Love You	Rings
	Lovable	Brassieres
	Lovalon	Hair rinse
	Lovelight	Diamond rings
	Night of Love	Perfume
	Sweetheart	Soap
Masculine	**Cossack**	Men's toiletries
	Gents	Men's toiletries
	His	Men's toiletries
	Hot-N-Tot	Sauce
	Jolly Scot	Ale
	Modern Knight	Men's toiletries
	Norsemen	Snuff

Trade-Marks Referring to	*Name*	*Registered for*
	Paddy	Irish whisky
	Sir	Luggage
	Sportsman	Toiletries
	Squire	Shaving soap
	Tom Burns	Whisky
Master (Boss, Chief, King)	**Air Master**	Dust collector
	Boss	Oven
	Cheeze-Master	Cheese cabinets
	Chessmaster	Chess games
	Coalmaster	Drilling tools
	Cough Master	Cough syrup
	Denmaster	Ash trays
	Farm Master	Dairy equipment
	Fire Chief	Gasoline
	Flow-Master	Pumps
	Gluemaster	Gluing machine
	Gravy Master	Seasoning
	Kennel King	Dog food
	King O'Nuts	Pecans
	Leak Master	Radiator stop-leak
	Master	Motors
	Masterform	Metal-working tools
	Melody King	Harmonicas
	Mistmaster	Spraying devices
Men, Famous	**Ben Franklin**	Whisky
	Daniel Webster	Flour
	Escoffier	Sauces
	Franklin	Engine
	Hamilton	Airplanes
	Henry George	Cigars
	Lafayette	Cordials
	La Salle	Washing machine
	Lister(ine)	Antiseptic
	Longfellow	Cigarettes
	Marshal Ney	Tobacco
	Mercator	Flashlights
	Monroe	Calculating machines
	Orloff	Sachets
	Paul Jones	Middy blouses
	Raleigh	Cigarettes
	Richelieu	Pearls
	Rockefeller	Cigars
	Roosevelt	Electrical devices
	Steuben	Art glassware
	Stillson	Wrenches

Trade-Marks Referring to	*Name*	*Registered for*
	Stonewall Jackson	Flour
	Tweed	Tobacco
	Webster	Cigars
	Wellington	Pipes
	Wm. Penn	Cigars
Military or Naval Terms	**Army and Navy**	Hosiery
	Army and Navy	Playing cards
	Bombardier	Textiles
	Brigadier	Tires
	Cannon	Electrical plugs
	Cannon	Shoes
	Colonel	Dog food
	Commander	Bicycles
	Commander	Men's supporters
	Commodore	Stoves
	Drum Major	Whisky
	General	Paints
	Major	Cement
	Man O'War	Varnish
	Navy	Ropes
Mineralogical Terms	**Coral**	Oleomargarine
	Granite	Roofing
	Lava	Soap
	Onyx	Hosiery
	Silver	Ale
	Soapstone	Textiles
Miscellaneous Languages	**Aloha**	Perfume
	Carioca	Rum
	Kismet	Wine
	Koh-I-Noor	Snap fasteners
	Reb Yussel	Cooking oil
	Vadna	Liquor
Misspelling	**Ayds**	Medicine
	Biltrite	Rubber heel
	Bo-Kay	Cosmetics
	Bran-Nu	Athlete's foot remedy
	Car-Nu	Auto polish
	Chooz	Chewing gum
	Daizee	Dry-cleaning compound
	Dia-Pli	Hair-dye applier
	Doo-Tee	Nursery seat
	Drednaut	Safety goggles
	Dubl-Thik	Fiber tile
	Enna Jettick	Shoes
	Evr-Klean	Seat covers

Trade-Marks Referring to	*Name*	*Registered for*
	Jell-A-Teen	Desserts
	Kala-Fornia	Medicine
	Pick-Ka-Nik	Outing jugs
	Reign-Beau	Perfume base
	Ridgid	Pipe tool
	Rid-Jid	Ironing table
	Su-Purb	Soap
	Trezur	Hosiery
Music or Opera	**Aria**	Piece-goods
	Band Concert	Lipstick
	Blue Danube	Candy
	Carillon	Textiles
	Castanet	Textiles
	Concertina	Skirts
	Evensong	Piece-goods
	Fanfare	Textiles
	Fidelitone	Phonograph needles
	Folksong	Piece-goods
	Harmony	Gin
	Jenny Lind	Fishing lines
	Lakme	Piece-goods
	Lohengrin	Wedding rings
	Lullaby	Knitting yarns
	Madame Butterfly	Textiles
	Manon Lescaut	Face Powder
	Mary Garden	Toiletries
	Mozart	Cigars
	Opera	Cigars
	Sing	Cleaner
	Stradavari	Perfume
	Student Prince	Cigars
	Tambourine	Plastic film
	Trombone	Sprayers
	Woody Herman	Clarinets
	Yankee Doodle	Citrous fruits
Mythology	**Ajax**	Comb
	Ajax	Pigments
	Ambrosia	Cosmetic
	Aphrodite	Piece-goods
	Apollo	Candy
	Argus	Cameras
	Calypso	Millinery braids
	Golden Fleece	Insulation
	Medusa	Cement
	Nestor	Cigarettes

Trade-Marks Referring to	*Name*	*Registered for*
	Olympian	Drugs
	Phoenix	Beer
	Thor	Pneumatic tools
	Venus	Corsets
	Wotan	Pencils
	Zeus	Cigarette holders
Negative	**Nay**	Deodorant
	Nil	Deodorant
	No-Sects	Insecticide
	Noxal	Disinfectant
	Noxem	Pest poison
	Veto	Deodorant
Numbers	**1-2-3**	Flavor
	7-20-4	Cigars
	44	Cigars
	1776	Soap powder
	4711	Eau de Cologne
	18-K	Foods
Numbers plus Words	**2-In-One**	Shoe polish
	3-In-1	Lubricant
	57 Varieties	Food products
	No. 27	Perfume
Nursery Rhymes or Fairy Tales	**Blue Boy**	Canned foods
	Bo-Peep	Children's jewelry
	Brownie	Shoes
	Cinderella	Dresses
	Cinderella	Garbage pails
	Fairy	Shoes
	Fairyland	Dolls
	Goldie Locks	Crib mattresses
	Humpty Dumpty	Toys
	Jack and Jill	Desserts
	Jack 'N Jill	Juvenile furniture
	Jack Spratt	Food products
	Little Boy Blue	Bluing
	Mother Hubbard	Flour
	Old King Cole	Tobacco
	Pied-Piper	Insecticide
	Puss'n Boots	Cat food
	Rock-A-Bye	Nursery accessories
	Snow White	Hair preparation
	Tommy Tucker	Piece-goods
Nuts	**Beech-Nut**	Coffee
	Butternut	Bread
	Grape-Nuts	Breakfast food

Trade-Marks Referring to	*Name*	*Registered for*
	Walnut	Tobacco
Odor	**Aromatex**	Baking flavor
	Kitchen Bouquet	Cooking flavor
	Odorono	Deodorant
	Pet-Scent	Dog deodorizer
	Sweet-Aire	Household deodorant
Painless	**Nodolor**	Medicament
	Num	Medicament
	Painkiller	Medicament
Plants	**Amaryllis**	Cosmetics
	Apple Blossom	Perfume
	Bergamot	Men's toiletries
	Buckeye	Beer
	Cherry	Toiletries
	Clover	Abrasives
	Conifer	Hat braids
	Cotton Blossom	Toiletries
	Daisy	Rifle
	Fruitana	Crackers
	Fruit of the Loom	Cloth
	Holly Berry	Perfume
	Iris	Foods
	Laurel	Razor blades
	Lettuce Leaf	Salad oil
	Lily	Rubber goods
	Lotus	Playing cards
	Magnolia	Alloys
	Milkweed	Face cream
	Morning Glory	Oats
	Old Sycamore	Whisky
	Orange Blossom	Wedding ring
	Palmetto	Industrial packing
	Pansy	Cane syrup
	Passion Flower	Toiletries
	Poppy	Linens
	Rosebud	Toiletries
	Spearmint	Chewing gum
	Spruce	Detergent
	Sunflower	Coal
	Thistle	Leather
	Tree	Tea
	Yucca	Textiles
Pleasure	**Chuckles**	Candy
	Foot Joy	Shoes
	Fro-Joy	Ice cream

Trade-Marks Referring to	*Name*	*Registered for*
	Gladiron	Ironer
	Glad Rag	Polishing cloth
	Good Humor	Ice cream
	Happy	Dog food
	Jests	Digestion tablets
	Joy	Dress shields
	Morning Joy	Coffee
	Plee-Zing	Foods
	Smiles	Cigarettes
	Thrill	Corsets
	Zest	Food products
	Zest	Men's toiletries
Process of Manufacture	**Sprayco**	Powdered milk
	Stone Ground	Flour
Profession or Occupation	**Bankers**	Writing paper
	Chef Paulins	Soups
	Doctor	Shoes
	Dr. Hand's	Teething lotion
	Dr. Thomas	Ointment
	Italian Cook	Salad oil
	Master Painter	Paints
	Professional	Blades
Protection	**Bonded**	Citrus fruits
	Cashgard	Valuables chests
	Dreadnaught	Heavy chain
	Flavor Sealed	Meat products
	Gold Bond	Beer
	Kant-Leak	Waterproofing agent
	Kant-Rust	Razor blades
	Kant-Slam	Door check
	Lockfast	Snaps
	Neva-Clog	Stapling device
	No Risk	Flour
	Old Reliable	Coffee
	Paksure	Food packages
	Pla-Safe	Flour
	Protecto	Garment bags
	Protek-Kote	Floor coating
	Prudence	Canned meat
	Reliance	Motors
	Safe	Locks
	Safedge	Glasses
	Safe-Line	Wire-rope clamp
	Safe-Stor	Garment bags
	Safe-T	Ice-cream cones

Trade-Marks Referring to	*Name*	*Registered for*
	Safety Light	Road lamps
	Saf-Kil	Rat bait
	Saf-T-Wax	Floor wax
	Seald Sweet	Oranges
	Sealed Beam	Headlights
	Sealed Power	Pistons
	Seal-Kap	Bottle caps
	Sealpackerchief	Packaged handkerchief
	Sealright	Liquid containers
	Sealtest	Dairy products
	Security	Dog food
	Shuron	Eyeglasses
	Sure	Breath deodorant
	Sure Shine	Polish
	Sur-Lay	Hair dressing
	Tite Seal	Gasket compound
	Togards	Toe protectors
	Trubl Pruf	Flour
Purity	**Purepac**	Drugs
	Puretest	Drugs
	Puritas	Sanitary napkins
	Purity	Cheese
	Purolator	Oil filters
	Simon Pure	Beer
Quality	**Bilt-Well**	Woodwork
	Creami-Rich	Milk
	Faultless	Pajamas
	Justrite	Bird seed
	Made-Rite	Brief cases
	My-T-Fine	Desserts
	Precision	Scientific equipment
	Richmade	Margarine
	Toastwell	Toasters
	Travelwell	Luggage
	Trubore	Glass tubing
	Veryfine	Vinegar
Quantity	**Double Bubble**	Gum
	Mor-Juice	Oranges
	Mor-Sweet	Malt-sugar syrup
Relatives	**Aunt Jemima**	Pancake flour
	Aunt Phoebe's	Laundry supplies
	Aunt Polly's	Dehydrated soup
	Aunt Stella's	Spaghetti
	Grandma's	Medicines
	Grandson	Clocks

Trade-Marks Referring to	*Name*	*Registered for*
Religious Allusions	**Cherub**	Ship logs
	Father John's Medicine	Medicine
	Huguenot	Brandy
	Madonna	Lockets
	Padre	Wine
	Pilgrim	Rum
	Puritan	Brake fluid
	Quaker	Corn meal
	Rock of Ages	Granite memorials
	St. Bernard	Pills
	St. James	Whisky
	St. Joseph	Aspirin
	Zion	Food products
Repeated Words	**Cen-Cen**	Headache tablets
	Ha-Ha	Piece-goods
	Hubba-Hubba	Ladies' wear
	Rite-Rite	Pencils
	Sen-Sen	Breath deodorant
	Shoo Shoo	Textiles
Reversals	**Dykon**	Contraceptive
	Helmar	Cigarettes
	Herlock Sholmes	Greeting cards
	Klim	Powdered milk
	Nemow	Medicine
	Serutan	Laxative
	Tarpyn	Pine tar
Rhymes	**Eager Beaver**	Steel wool
	Gaba-Daba	Piece-goods
	Jive-Five	Junior clothing
	Killer Diller	Insecticide
	Led-Hed	Roofing nails
	Sho-Blo	Electrical fuses
	Tuff Stuff	Insecticides
Richness	**Dairy-Rich**	Ice cream
	De Luxe	Bed springs
	Luxury	Macaroni
	Splendor	Sheets
Rivers, Lakes, Oceans, etc.	**Atlantic**	Beer
	Concord River	Piece-goods
	Geyser	Mineral water
	Green River	Whisky
	Gulfstream	Water heater
	High Tide	Canned shrimps
	High Tide	Pajamas
	Hood River	Apples

Trade-Marks Referring to	*Name*	*Registered for*
	Hot Spring	Water heater
	Hudson	Hosiery
	Hudson's Bay	Blankets
	Indian River	Citrus fruits
	Mississippi	Cordial
	Niagara	Furnaces
	Nile	Dyes
	Pacific	Boilers
	Rio Grande	Gasoline
	Rogue River	Canned fruits
	Rubicon	Whisky
	Tide	Laundry detergent
	Whirlpool	Washing machines
Royalty or Nobility	**Barbarossa**	Beer
	Baronet	Gloves
	Caliph	Toiletries
	Coronet	Auto chemicals
	Crown	Flush valves
	Dauphin	Optical frames
	Duchess	Jewelry
	Emir	Soap
	Empress	Cosmetics
	King	Leathers
	King Arthur	Yarns
	King Edward	Cigars
	King George IV	Whisky
	King Henry VIII	Food products
	King William IV	Whisky
	Lord Calvert	Whisky
	Louis XIV	Stationery
	Mahatma	Rice
	Majestic	Sun glasses
	Marquis	Shoes
	Marquise	Textiles
	Maximilian	Furs
	Mikado	Pencils
	Mogul	Cigarettes
	Monarch	Beer
	Nobility	Gin
	Prince Albert	Tobacco
	Prince Matchabelli	Perfume
	Princess	Aluminum ware
	Queen	Ant control
	Rajah	Soles
	Rajah	Spark plugs

Trade-Marks Referring to	*Name*	*Registered for*
	Rameses	Cigarettes
	Regent	Cheese
	Rex	Water heater
	Sheik	Prophylactic
	Sir Alfred	Tobacco products
	Tycoon	Eyeglass frames
	Viceroy	Gin
Rustic or Rural	**Farm**	Paint
	Log Cabin	Beer
	Silo	Tile
Sanitary	**Hygienol**	Powder puff
	Sanettes	Face tissues
	Sani	Tissues
Saving	**Ekonomee**	Bottle stoppers
	Econom-Icer	Refrigerator
	Savabrush	Brush cleaner
	Savamaid	Washing machine
	Sav-A-Wave	Bathing cap
	Thrifty	Stocking protectors
Seasons	**Fall**	Textiles
	Indian Summer	Toiletries
	Spring	Dresses
	Spring Air	Mattresses
	Winter	Antifreeze
Selection or Special	**Blue Ribbon**	Beer
	Blue Ribbon	Books
	Champion	Pet foods
	Exclusive	Citrus fruits
	Expert	Playing cards
	Favorite	Cigarettes
	My Favorite	Whisky
	Showpiece	Textiles
Series	**Advagum**	Lighting signal
	Advan	
	Advaresin	
	Advasol	
	Advawet	
	Dowanone	
	Dowax	
	Dowclene	
	Dowco	
	Dowell	
	Dowflake	
	Dowfume	
	Dowicide	

Trade-Marks Referring to	*Name*	*Registered for*
	Dowmetal	
	Dowtherm	
	Santamine	Chemical
	Santicizer	Chemical
	Santobane	Insecticide
Shape	**Arrow**	Poultry feed
	Globe	Needles
	Helix	Clothespins
	Nushape	Soap
	Octagon	Canned fruits
	Oval	Eyeglasses
	Polkadot	Oranges
	Pyramid	Shoes
	Quadrangle	Stationery
	Streamlined	Shoes
	Triangle	Cultivators
	Zig-Zag	
Similar Names (Different Fields)	**Admiration**	Cigar
	Admiration	Hosiery
	Admiration	Coffee
	Airway	Coffee
	Air-Way	Sanitary system
	Airway	Tie
	Birds Eye	Frosted food
	Birdseye	Electric bulb
	Black Hawk	Ham
	Blackhawk	Tools
	Butter-Nut	Coffee
	Butter-Nut	Candy
	Climax	Engines
	Climax	Tobacco
Size	**Compacto**	Folding syringe
	Expando	Wrist-watch straps
	Expanso	Expanding belt
	Gigantic	Watches
	Jumbo	Peanut butter
	Kompakt	Padding
	Leviathan	Tennis rackets
	Mammoth	Wall board
	So-Big	Candies
	X-Pando	Pipe-joint compound
Slang or Colloquialisms	**Bottoms Up**	Whisky
	Cheez-It	Crackers
	Cracker Jack	Confection
	Giddyap	Game

Trade-Marks Referring to	*Name*	*Registered for*
	Green Thumb	Seed beds
	Gunk	Cleaner
	Humdinger	Feed grinder
	Humdinger	Needle polisher
	Jim Dandy	Animal feed
	Nix	Deodorant
	Oomphies	Slippers
	Pay Off	Fruits
	Pdq	Soap
	Say When	Liquid dispensers
	Scram	Pesticide
	Set-Up	Preshaving lotion
	Sharp	Toiletries
	Snafu	Candy
	So-Boss	Cow hobbles
	Spiffy	Collar stay
	Spud	Cigarettes
	Tater	Pancake mix
	Things and Stuff	Scrap books
	Twenty Grand	Cigarettes
	Upsy-Dazy	Automobile jacks
	Yum	Headache medicament
Sleep or Rest	Dreamer	Mattresses
	Dreamflower	Face powder
	Dreamland	Nightwear
	Dreams	Candy
	Luxurest	Mattresses
	Rest Assured	Beds
	Siesta	Tobacco
	Sleep Aids	Sedative
	Sleep Easy	Cribs
	Slumbersoft	Mattresses
	Slumberon	Mattresses
Social Classification or Titles	Aristocrat	Brandy
	Aristocrat	Ice cream
	Director	Watches
	Esquire	Flavors
	Executive	Cigarette lighter
	Patrician	Hardware
	Society Brand	Clothes
	Swank	Men's jewelry
Sound	Acousticon	Hearing aid
	Acoustone	Sound-deadening tile
	Bell	Bread
	Echo	Harmonica

Trade-Marks Referring to	*Name*	*Registered for*
	Hush-A-Phone	Telephone device
	Mission Bell	Radio sets
	Noiseless	Clocks
	Quiet May	Oil burner
	Silentbloc	Vibration mounting
	Westminster Chime	Clocks
	Whistle	Beverages
	Zoom	Cereal
Sovereignties	**Empire**	Bolts
	Federal	Ball bearings
	Imperial	Electrical supplies
	International	Cigars
	National	Ale
	Republic	Lubricant
Spanish Words	**Admiracion**	Shampoo
	Avena	Oat cereal
	Bohio	Rum
	Buena	Skin lotion
	Carta Blanca	Beer
	Casa	Tableware
	Cinco	Cigars
	Coronado	Suits
	Cresta Blanca	Liquor
	Cruz Blanca	Vegetables
	Del Norte	Brandy
	El Dorado	Cigars
	El Maestra	Honey
	El Padre	Rum
	El Producto	Cigars
	Ensenada	Slack suits
	Flor de Habana	Cigars
	Globo	Vermouth
	Hermosa	Tile
	Laguna	Pearls
	La Yerba	Cigars
	Mariposa	Blankets
Speed	**Bisquick**	Flour
	Flash	Ice skates
	Haste	Watches
	Hi-Speed	Gasoline
	Jiffies	Powder puffs
	Kwic-Kleen	Dry cleaner
	Kwik	Ointment
	Presto	Cake flour
	Pronto	Drain cleaner

Trade-Marks Referring to	*Name*	*Registered for*
	Quick	Starch
	Quickies	Facial cleansing pads
	Quick-Way	Excavation equipment
	Quicool	Prickly-heat powder
	Quik-Blend	Shortening
	Quix	Breakfast food
	Rollfast	Skates
	Setfast	Paint
	Speed Demon	Sleds
	Speedways	Conveyors
	Swish	Wall finish
	Whiz	Soap
	Zip	Soap
	Zip-Shave	Shaving cream
Sport	**All American**	Cigarette
	Challenger	Roller skates
	Champ	Hats
	Champion	Pancake syrup
	Coach	Athletic shorts
	Daily Double	Bait
	Foursome	Smoking pipes
	Home Run	Baseball bats
	Kentucky Derby	Whisky
	Kingpin	Tobacco
	Marksman	Rifle cartridges
	Olympic	Radio
	Par	Beverages
	Rugby	Athletic supporter
	Slalom	Ski wear
	Sportsters	Sport shoes
	Spur	Ties
	Tally-Ho	Playing cards
	Walter Hagen	Golf goods
Streets	**Bond Street**	Perfume
	Bond Street	Tobacco
	Fifth Avenue	Candy
	Main Street	Shoes
Strength or Power	**Atlas**	Lathe
	Atomic	Insecticide
	Avalanche	Insecticide
	Dash	Seasoning
	Force	Breakfast food
	Hale and Hearty	Plants
	Huskies	Cereal
	Husky	Plywood

Trade-Marks Referring to	*Name*	*Registered for*
	Hypower	Chili powder
	Ironclad	Draperies
	Mighty Midgett	Cigarette lighter
	Rocket	Bicycles
	Samson	Card tables
	Samsonite	Luggage
	Tenacity	Loose-leaf binders
Success or Award	**Academy Award**	Fountain pens
	Bonus	Chocolate syrup
	Gold Medal	Beer
	Gold Medal	Flour
	Success	Desk calendars
Suffix plus Additions	**Aceloid**	Plastic
	Acryloid	Plastic
	Agitor	Agitating machine
	Alkestane	Chemicals
	Allocide	Chemicals
	Auditone	Textiles
	Colura	Accoustic tiles
	Cordura	Rayon
	Coughlet	Medicated chewing gum
	Decorettes	Chocolate
	Digestoids	Stomach pills
	Dryette	Racks
	Dynola	Radios
	Equinase	Medicament
	Fabrikoid	Imitation leather
	Fiberloid	Plastic
	Flemex	Cold remedy
	Foamite	Fire extinguisher
	Hesperal	Medicament
	Hexoline	Medicament
	Jell-O	Desserts
	Larvex	Insecticide
	Licuron	Medicament
	Lipobin	Medicament
	Listerine	Antiseptic
	Marbeloid	Tile
	Naylon	Nail polish
	Oculine	Eye drops
	Oralator	Inhaler
	Oraline	Tooth paste
	Othinol	Medicament
	Oxo	Soup cube
	Pedicide	Athlete's foot remedy

Trade-Marks Referring to	*Name*	*Registered for*
	Sailtone	Textiles
	Sardinettes	Canned fish
	Sealdite	Capacitor
	Shinola	Shoe polish
	Thermolier	Heaters
	Tintex	Dyes
	Tonene	Medicament
	Tonette	Musical instrument
	Trimo	Shears
	Unguentine	Burn ointment
	Vacuette	Vacuum cleaners
	Vaculator	Coffee maker
	Valvoline	Lubricant
	Vertolan	Medicament
	Vinylite	Plastic
	Vyloid	Vinyl-plastic coated cloth
	Wheatena	Cereal food
	Zonite	Disinfectant
Superlatives	**Bar-Nun**	Rotary sifter
	Beats All	Pencils
	Best-Ever	Macaroni
	Best Foods	Food
	Best Test	Rubber cement
	Dominant	Canned foods
	Everbest	Preserves
	Excello	Towels
	Exquisite	Brassieres
	Fabulous	Perfume
	Famous	Beer
	Farbest	Margarine
	First Prize	Meat products
	Gilt Edge	Beer
	Grand Prize	Beer
	Hy-Test	Shoes
	Ideal	Dog food
	Invincible	Rubber belting
	Marvel	Bread
	Marvelous	Face powder
	Masterpiece	Phonograph records
	Medalist	Cameras
	None Such	Mincemeat
	Nonpareil	Paints
	Out of this World	Chinaware
	Paragon	Hair dye
	Paramount	Motion pictures

Trade-Marks Referring to	*Name*	*Registered for*
	Peerless	Check writers
	Perfection	Hoods
	Premier	Foods
	Premium	Shredded coconut
	Prize	Razor blades
	Snow Leader	Snow wear
	Super	Motor oils
	Superflour	Flour
	Superior	Circulator
	Super Service	Cables
	Super Suds	Soap powder
	Supreme	Steel wool
	Tip Top	Bread
	Topmost	Foods
	Top Notch	Rubber footwear
	Tops	Tobacco
	Triumph	Beer
	Universal	Pajamas
	Veribest	Meat
	Verifine	Evaporated milk
	Victor	Welding equipment
	Wonder	Bread
Superstition or Magic	**Black Cat**	Stove polish
	Good Luck	Desserts
	Hex	Mothproofing agent
	Horse Shoe	Chewing tobacco
	Lady Luck	Bridge cookies
	Lucky Cup	Coffee
	Lucky Forever	Engagement rings
	Magic	Shampoo
	Magic Chef	Cooking range
	Magic Dip	Prepared breading
	Magic Touch	Onion sauce
	Magic Wand	Easter-egg dyes
	Miracle	Adhesive
	Red Devil	Insecticide
	Wishbone	Incubators
	Wizard	Skates
Taste	**Bit-O-Honey**	Candy
	Delicious	Macaroni
	Juicidrink	Beverages
	Juicy Fruit	Chewing gum
	Limey	Beverages
	Savory	Roasters
	Snappy	Cheese

Trade-Marks Referring to	*Name*	*Registered for*
	Sunsweet	Prune juice
	Tang	Processed meat
	Taystee	Bread
	Tendersweet	Food products
Temperature	**Airtemp**	Air-condition equipment
	Arctic	Ice box
	Cimcool	Cutting oil
	Coolair	Exhaust fan
	Coolstream	Water cooler
	Eskimo	Electric fans
	Freezo	Jelly dessert
	Frigidaire	Refrigerator
	Frostair	Refrigerator
	Frost-Chek	Antifreeze
	Frostilla	Skin lotion
	Froz-N-Gold	Frozen food
	Glacier	Coating for ice-cream sticks
	Heatrola	Ranges
	Hot Blast	Blow torches
	Hot Point	Electric appliances
	Hot Spot	Stoves
	Icy-Hot	Thermos bottle
	Jack Frost	Cold ointment
	Keep-Kool	Summer suits
	Kold-Hold	Refrigerating plate
	Kool	Cigarette
	Koolshade	Sun screens
	Northcool	Tropical suit
	Polar	Kitchenware
	Redi-Heat	Heating block
	Snowed In	Frozen foods
	Solar Glow	Electric heaters
	Sunrayed	Tomato juice
	Thermo	Lubricant
	Toridheet	Oil burners
	Tropic	Boilers
	Warm Morning	Heaters
	Zerone	Antifreeze
Texture or Feel	**Doeskin**	Hats
	Downyflake	Baking mix
	Sea Velvet	Sponges
	Shag	Rugs
	Smoothie	Neckties
	Sofskin	Skin cream

Trade-Marks Referring to	*Name*	*Registered for*
	Softasilk	Flour
	Softee	Cleaner
	Softex	Baby pants
	Sof-Tred	Rugs
	Swans Down	Flour
	Veldown	Sanitary napkins
	Velvatissue	Toilet papers
	Velveeta	Cheese
	Velvet	Pencils
	Velvetta	Suede
Theater, Motion Picture	**Follies Begère**	Toilet water
	Judy Garland	Slips
	Marie Dressler	Dresses
	Punchinello	Dolls' clothes
	Pygmalion	Leather
	Ziegfeld Follies	Toilet water
Time	**A.M.**	Shaving cream
	Century	Asbestos board
	Dawn	Cruisers
	Dawn to Dusk	Stationery
	Day and Night	Spectacles
	Day Nite	Distress signals
	Early Morn	Pancake syrup
	Eight O'Clock	Coffee
	Lifetime	Tree stand
	Minit Kote	Metal cleaner
	Minit-Rub	Liniment
	Now	House organ
	One-A-Day	Vitamins
	Slumbertime	Mattresses
	Time Tested	Paints
	Time Will Tell	Watches
	3-Minute	Oat flakes
	5 P.M.	Textiles
	6 O'clock	Muffin mix
	7-Minit	Pie crust
	18th Century	Powder make-up
	20th Century	Gas producer
Use or Result	**Abrasite**	Abrasive
	Absorbit	Floor compound
	Bubble Up	Carbonated beverage
	Coin-Tainer	Purses
	Dancin	Girdles
	Dim-A-Lite	Electric-light control
	Dipin	Cracker meal

Trade-Marks Referring to	*Name*	*Registered for*
	Dippo	Silver cleaner
	Doall	Machine tool
	Double Bubble	Soap
	Double Bubble	Chewing gum
	Dubbleware	Work clothing
	Dryback	Work clothing
	Dyanshine	Shoe polish
	Even-Heat	Stoves
	Ever Ready	Desk pads
	Eversharp	Razor blades
	Gets-It	Corn remedy
	Gripper	Fasteners
	Grips	Sneakers
	Hair Groom	Hair dressing
	Help	Cleaner
	Hold-Bob	Bobby pins
	Hold Heat	Soldering iron
	Holdrite	Belts
	Ironrite	Ironers
	Jell-Well	Gelatin dessert
	Kant-Kom-Off	Covers
	Keen Kutter	Cutlery
	Lashtint	Mascara
	Mop-It-On	Varnish
	Muscle-Rub	Liniment
	No Doz	Sleep preventer
	No-Drip	Cork coating
	No-Freeze	Antifreeze
	Non-Skid	Flooring
	No Streak	Wall cleaner
	No-Tip	Utility chests
	Nox-Rust	Rustproofing agent
	Nu Edge	Razor hone
	Oil-Dri	Oil absorbent
	Patch-It	Patching plaster
	Peel	Wallpaper remover
	Pin-In	Dress shields
	Press-On	Mending tape
	Rollpruf	Surgical gloves
	Rustless	Stainless steel
	Shave-Well	Shaving cream
	Shedfast	Textiles
	Sippers	Drinking straws
	Size-It	Wall sizer
	Slipit	Drawer lubricant

Trade-Marks Referring to	*Name*	*Registered for*
	Snap-On	Screen patches
	Stanzoil	Oilproof gloves
	Sta-Tite	Compression rings
	Staturaid	Elevating shoes
	Stayform	Foundation garments
	Steelbinder	Steel strap tightener
	Tilt Out	Tray
	Turn-A-Page	Copy holders
	Up-N-Off	Bottle-cap remover
	Wall-Wipe	Wall cleaner
	Wear-Right	Gloves
	Wipe-On	Varnish
	Zip-In	Snow suits
Value	**Mor-Val**	Condiment
	Standard	Telescopes
	Sterling	Salt
	Xtra-Value	Paints
Vision	**C-Far**	Field glasses
	Clearsite	Clear, plastic containers
	Ful-Site	Eyeglasses
	Illusion	Shower curtains
	Klear-Vu	Safety goggles
Water or Rain	**Aquaduk**	Waterproof textiles
	Aquasec	Waterproofing process
	Aquastop	Waterproof coating
	Dritex	Waterproof textiles
	Kant-Wet	Crib mattress
	Mermaid	Rubber goods
	Raincraft	Rainwear
	Rain-Repel	Waterproof textiles
	Splash	After-bath lotion
	Sta-Dri	Tarpaulins
	Wat-A-Tite	Water-repellent finish
	Waterfoil	Waterproof building coating
	Wet Pruf	Adhesive tape
Weather or Wind	**Blizzard**	Oil lanterns
	Scotch Mist	Overcoat
	Sirôcco	Perfume
	Snowdrift	Shortening
	Stormtight	Roofing
	Tempest	Rubber shoes
	Tidal Wave	Flour
	Tornado	Cigar lighters
	Weathermaster	Outside paints

Trade-Marks Referring to	*Name*	*Registered for*
	Whirlwind	Draperies
	Whirlwind	Engines
	Wind Boss	Cigarette lighters
	Windbreaker	Outdoor clothing
	Zephyr	Electric shavers
Weight	**Exact Weight**	Scales
	Feathertouch	Fountain pen
	Tish-U-Weight	Hats
Women, Famous	**Betsy Ross**	Venetian blinds
	Cleopatra	Canned fish
	Dolly Madison	Bed spreads
	Du Barry	Cosmetics
	Florence Nightingale	Nurses' uniforms
	Lilly Dache	Hair nets
	Marie Antoinette	Cigars
	Queen Bess	Flour
	Recamier	Perfumes
	Virginia Dare	Flavors
Youth	**Debs**	Ladies' cigarettes
	Debutante	Costume jewelry
	Debutot	Infants' wear
	Flaming Youth	Girdles
	Junior Miss	Dresses
	Little Folks	Cough syrup
	Tots	Dessert
	Youth	Corsets

Old Trade-Marks *

Year of Origin	*Brand Name*	*Product*
1751	ROYAL WORCESTER	*Porcelains*
1759	WEDGWOOD	*China*
1770	SPODE	*China*
1817	MALLORY	*Headwear*
1821	COPENHAGEN	*Snuff*
1823	WILSON	*Whisky*
1827	DIXON'S	*Graphites*
1832	CORTICELLI	*Threads*
1835	DeVOE	*Snuff*
1835	OLD CROW	*Whisky*
1836	FERRIS	*Ham*

* Brand Names Foundation Inc., New York City.

Year of Origin	*Brand Name*	*Product*
1837	LIEBMANN RHEINGOLD	*Beer*
1838	KNOX	*Headwear*
1839	CHAMPION	*Crackers*
1840	BALLANTINE'S	*Ale and Beer*
1840	WILLIAMS	*Soap*
1841	McKESSON & ROBBINS	*Pharmaceuticals*
1842	HAVILAND	*China*
1842	SCHAEFER	*Beer*
1843	HECKERS' SUPERLATIVE	*Flour*
1844	MILLER	*Lighting Equipment*
1845	COX'S	*Gelatin*
1845	ALEXANDER SMITH	*Rugs*
1845	WADSWORTH-HOWLAND	*Paint*
1846	HECKERS' CREAM FARINA	*Cereal*
1847	1847 ROGERS BROS.	*Silver-Plated Ware*
1847	HENDERSON'S TESTED SEEDS	*Seeds*
1847	PIERCE PAINT	*Paint*
1848	DEVOE & RAYNOLDS	*Paint*
1848	DILL'S BEST	*Tobacco*
1848	HUNTER	*Whisky*
1848	SKINNER'S	*Silks*
1850	CAMARGO	*Shade Cloth*
1850	THATCHER	*Heating Equipment*
1851	BLATZ	*Beer*
1852	OTIS ELEVATORS	*Building Material*
1853	STEINWAY & SONS	*Pianos*
1853	WOOLSEY	*Paint*
1854	RITTER	*Food Products*
1855	BABBITT'S	*Lye*
1856	BRUCKMANN'S	*Beer*
1856	DEVOE	*Paint*
1856	EAGLE	*Pencils*
1857	GAIL BORDEN'S EAGLE BRAND CONDENSED MILK	*Milk*
1857	ROBT. BURNS	*Cigars*
1857	MOUNT VERNON	*Whisky*
1857	SEAGRAM'S	*Whisky*
1857	WATERBURY	*Clocks*
1858	CROFUT & KNAPP	*Headwear*
1858	EAU DE QUININE	*Hair Tonic*
1858	KRUEGER	*Beer*

Year of Origin	*Brand Name*	*Product*
1858	SQUIBB	*Pharmaceuticals*
1860	HENSLER	*Beer*
1863	BELDING	*Thread*
1864	BERG	*Headwear*
1864	CHASE & SANBORN	*Coffee*
1865	DUNLAP	*Headwear*
1865	PAUL JONES	*Whisky*
1866	CASHMERE BOUQUET	*Soap*
1866	LONGINES	*Watches*
1866	DR. LYON'S	*Tooth Powder*
1866	OTIS	*Underwear*
1866	WILLIAM ROGERS & SON	*Silver-Plated Ware*
1866	ROYAL	*Baking Powder*
1866	VALVOLINE	*Lubricants*
1866	WITTNAUER	*Watches*
1867	BEAR BRAND	*Knitting Yarns*
1867	FLEISHER	*Knitting Yarns*
1867	PEASLEE-GAULBERT	*Paint*
1867	PEE GEE	*Paint*
1869	BIXBY'S JET OIL	*Shoe Polish*
1869	GALENA	*Lubricants*
1869	GOLDEN WEDDING	*Whisky*
1869	MANHATTAN	*Shirts*
1869	SAPOLIO	*Soap*
1870	ACME	*Jams*
1870	CALVERT	*Whisky*
1870	FLEISCHMANN'S	*Yeast*
1870	H-O OATS	*Cereal*
1870	JOHNSON'S	*Soap*
1870	McCALL PRINTED PATTERNS	*Dress Patterns*
1870	SCOTT'S EMULSION	*Medicine*
1870	STROOCK	*Woolens*
1870	VANTINES	*Incense*
1870	VASELINE	*Pharmaceuticals*
1870	Y & S	*Licorice*
1871	DIAMOND	*Dyes*
1871	SIMMONS	*Bedding*
1872	BURTON'S	*Flavoring Extracts*
1872	I. W. HARPER	*Whisky*
1872	CHAS. H. PHILLIPS'	*Milk of Magnesia*
1873	ARM & HAMMER BRAND	*Baking Soda*

Year of Origin	*Brand Name*	*Product*
1873	COLGATE DENTIFRICES	*Dental Cream*
1873	REMINGTON	*Typewriters*
1874	WARNER'S	*Corsets*
1875	HOLLAND RUSK	*Rusk*
1875	STAR	*Safety Razors*
1876	B.V.D.	*Underwear*
1876	COW BRAND	*Baking Soda*
1876	HINDS HONEY AND ALMOND FRAGRANCE CREAM	*Lotions*
1876	C. C. PARSONS'	*Household Ammonia*
1876	PREMIUM	*Crackers*
1876	600-W	*Lubricating Oil*
1876	SPALDING	*Sporting Goods*
1876	SWANS DOWN	*Flour*
1878	BATES	*Bedspreads*
1878	CHAS. H. FLETCHER (Castoria)	*Laxative*
1878	LION BRAND	*Knitting Yarns*
1879	DAVIS	*Baking Powder*
1879	H & E	*Sugar*
1879	VAPO CRESOLENE	*Medicine*
1879	WHEATENA	*Cereal*
1880	BRUTON SCOTCH SNUFF	*Snuff*
1880	D & P	*Rock Candy*
1880	DOXSEE'S	*Clam Products*
1880	HIGGINS	*Drawing Inks*
1880	HUDSON	*Lye*
1880	KAYSER	*Gloves*
1880	PAAS	*Egg Dyes*
1881	A. NO. 1	*Confectionery*
1881	CHAMPION	*Lye*
1881	HALL'S STAR	*Lye*
1882	MINETTO	*Shade Cloth*
1882	OLD GRAND-DAD	*Whisky*
1882	RE UMBERTO	*Olive Oil*
1882	SMITH BROTHERS	*Cough Drops*
1883	BANNER	*Lye*
1883	RED SEAL	*Lye*
1883	VITALIS	*Hair Tonic*
1884	ADAMS BLACK JACK	*Chewing Gum*
1884	McCALLUM	*Hosiery*
1884	SNIDER'S	*Food Products*

Year of Origin	*Brand Name*	*Product*
1884	WATERMAN'S	*Fountain Pens*
1885	ARROW	*Shirts*
1885	BIGELOW HARTFORD SAXONY	*Carpets*
1885	DAISY	*Lye*
1885	DOMINO	*Sugar*
1885	McQUADE	*Paint*
1885	NONE SUCH	*Mince Meat*
1885	PENN METAL	*Steel Building Materials*
1886	BON AMI	*Household Cleanser*
1886	CRESTA BLANCA	*Wine*
1886	FIVE O'CLOCK TEA	*Biscuit*
1886	MASLAND	*Rugs*
1886	NAZARETH	*Underwear*
1886	VACUOLINE	*Lubricating Oil*
1887	HOLMES & EDWARDS	*Silver Plate*
1887	LOG CABIN	*Syrups*
1887	MONOTYPE	*Typesetting Machines*
1887	OCTAGON	*Soap*
1887	OLD TAYLOR	*Whisky*
1887	RARUS	*Lubricating Oil*
1888	COLGATE	*Shaving Sticks*
1888	FOUR ROSES	*Whisky*
1888	MERRY WAR	*Lye*
1888	MUM	*Deodorant*
1888	OLD OVERHOLT	*Whisky*
1888	DR. POSNER SCIENTIFIC SHOES	*Footwear*
1888	REIS	*Textiles*
1889	BLACK FLAG	*Insecticides*
1889	LILAC VEGETAL	*Toiletries*
1889	NEW JERSEY COPPER PAINT	*Paint*
1889	SOCIAL TEA	*Biscuits*
1889	U. S. SEAL	*Tires*
1890	ALBOLENE	*Mineral Oil*
1890	BATES	*Numbering Machines*
1890	BEEMAN'S PEPSIN	*Chewing Gum*
1890	BLACK CROWS	*Gum Drops*
1890	EXCELSIOR	*Pumps*
1890	LYSOL	*Disinfectant*

Year of Origin	*Brand Name*	*Product*
1890	STANDARD BALL	*Lye*
1890	VELOCITE	*Lubricating Oil*
1891	AMERICAN EXPRESS	*Travelers Cheques*
1891	BOTANY	*Woolen Fabrics*
1891	CERESOTA FLOUR	*Flour*
1891	INGRAM'S	*Toiletries*
1891	MERCK	*Chemicals*
1891	OLD SUNNY BROOK	*Whisky*
1892	ETNA	*Lubricating Oil*
1892	FIG NEWTONS	*Cookies*
1892	HAMILTON	*Watches*
1892	RHEINGOLD	*Beer*
1892	RUBEROID	*Roofing*
1892	VISCOLITE	*Lubricating Oil*
1893	BECKWITH-CHANDLER	*Lacquers*
1893	CALOX	*Tooth Powder*
1893	GIANT	*Lye*
1893	INGERSOLL	*Watches*
1894	ABBOTTS DE LUXE "A" MILK	*Milk*
1894	J. B. L. CASCADE	*Colon Irrigator*
1894	CRYSTAL WHITE	*Soap*
1894	ELECTRIC	*Lye*
1894	3-IN-ONE	*Oil*
1894	VICKS	*Medicaments*
1895	BAKER'S	*Coconut*
1895	BIG BONANZA	*Lye*
1895	E-Z	*Underwear*
1895	FRANKLIN	*Lye*
1895	RICHARD HUDNUT	*Cosmetics*
1895	SANFORD	*Rugs*
1895	UNDERWOOD	*Typewriters*
1896	COLUMBIA	*Window Shades*
1896	MOUSE SEED	*Mouse Exterminator*
1896	OLD ENGLISH	*Wax*
1896	ROYAL SCARLET	*Packaged Foods*
1896	TOOTSIE ROLL	*Candy*

Trade-Marks Classified According to Industry

When choosing a trade-mark, it is important to know which marks are already registered in the special field of industry. In the following, two lists for special trade-marks are included. List A is arranged according to industries or products; list B gives the books, directories, catalogs and periodicals referring to the special trade-marks on the industries and products of list A.

LIST A

Industry or Product	*Number* *
Abrasives	7, 97, 105
Accelerators, Rubber	See Chemicals
Accident-Prevention Devices	137
Acidproofing Chemicals	97, 105
Adhesives	97, 105
Agricultural Equipment	139
Agricultural Sprays	See Insecticides
Air Conditioning	2, 46, 47, 70, 97, 131
Alcoholic Beverages	55
Alkalies	See Chemicals
Alloys	See Metals
Animal Dips	33
Animal Oil	33
Antifreezes	33, 97
Antioxidants	See Chemicals
Antiseptics	See Drugs
Asphalt Emulsions	97, 105
Automotive Equipment	13, 14, 57, 97, 145
Aviation	1, 14, 15, 145
Bedding	16
Belt Dressings	33, 97
Beverages	22, 55, 59, 145
Bicycles	145
Bleaches	See Chemicals
Boat Supplies	95, 97, 135, 145
Boiler Compounds	See Chemicals
Boilers	60, 97, 112
Bookbinding	126
Brewery Equipment and Supplies	22
Brick	23, 97
Bronze Powders	105
Brushes, Paint	97, 105
Building Materials, Construction	23, 25, 26, 70, 97, 145, 150
Burner Oil (See also Petroleum Products)	109
Calcimine	105
Cameras	8
Canned Goods	See Food Products
Carbon, Activated	See Chemicals
Carbon Black	See Chemicals
Carpets	30, 69, 136, 145
Caulking	See Putty
Cement (See also Stone)	105
Cement, Adhesive	See Putty
Ceramics	31, 38, 97
Cereals	107, 145

* The numbers refer to the numbers given in list B.

Industry or Product	*Number* *
Chemical Equipment	32, 33, 110
Chemicals	3, 18, 20, 32, 33, 34, 61, 65, 74, 84, 97, 98, 110, 141, 152, 161, 170
Cigarettes	See Tobacco
Cigars	See Tobacco
Clay	23, 97, 105
Clay Products	23, 97, 130
Cleaners	3, 41, 105, 145, 161
Clothing	See Wearing Apparel
Coal	82, 94, 97
Coatings	See Paints
Colors, Dry	See Paints
Colors	See Dyes
Concrete	See Cement
Cooking Utensils	79, 103
Corsets	36
Cosmetics	See Toilet Goods
Crockery	38
Cutting Oil (See also Chemicals)	97
Dairy Equipment and Supplies	39
Dental Preparations	See Drugs and Toilet Goods
Depilatories	See Toilet Goods
Detergents (See also Cleaners)	19, 97 169
Diesel Engines	14, 97
Disinfectants	See Drugs
Driers	See Paints
Drugs	4, 18, 33, 34, 48, 67, 98, 106, 110, 145, 170
Dyes	3, 35, 66, 74, 84, 170
Electrical Appliances and Equipment	49, 50, 51, 52, 97, 145
Electronics	51, 53, 78, 128
Emulsifiers	18, 19, 33, 105, 161, 170
Enamel, Paint	See Paints
Enamel, Vitreous	33
Enzyme Products	33
Explosives	18, 33, 97

Industry or Product	*Number* *
Fabrics	See Textiles
Fans (See also Electric Equipment)	11
Farm Equipment	77, 97
Feed, Animal	124, 145
Fertilizers	33, 145
Fibers	33
Fillers (See also Chemicals)	105
Finishes	See Paints
Fireproofing	37, 97, 105
Fire Protection	137
Fish Oil	33
Fish Products	138
Flameproofing	See Fireproofing
Flavors	See Food Products
Floor Coverings	See Carpets
Flotation Agents	See Chemicals
Flour	107
Fly Sprays	See Insecticides
Food Products	58, 59, 66, 107, 138, 145, 165
Foundry Compounds	See Chemicals
Fuel, Liquefied Gas	6, 145
Fuels	See Coal
Fungicides	See Insecticides
Furniture	28
Gas Equipment and Supplies	6, 97
Gasoline	See Petroleum Products
Germicides	See Antiseptics
Gifts	63, 108
Glass	31, 38, 130
Gloves (See also Wearing Apparel)	64
Glue	See Adhesives
Graphite	97, 105
Gravel	See Stones
Grease	See Petroleum Products
Gums, Vegetable	32, 33, 34
Hair Preparations	See Toilet Goods
Hardware	57, 72, 97, 145

Industry or Product	*Number **
Heating	See Air Conditioning
Heating Appliances	6
Hormones, Plant	5
Herbicides	5
Hospital Equipment	75, 79, 97
Household Goods	12, 28, 76, 103
Household Furnishings	28, 69, 76, 145
Hygiene, Industrial	137
Industrial Equipment and Supplies (See also Machinery)	57, 97, 100, 118
Industrial Hygiene	137
Ink	9, 105
Insecticides	5, 68, 105, 139, 161
Instruments, Measuring and Controlling	80, 97
Insulation	97
Ion Exchangers	See Chemicals
Iron	See Metals
Jewelry	143, 145, 148
Knit Goods (See also Wearing Apparel)	83
Laboratory Equipment	97, 153
Laquers	See Paints
Latex	See Rubber
Laundry Equipment and Supplies	85, 86
Leather Chemicals (See also Chemicals)	33, 34, 73, 87
Leather Goods	73, 87, 91, 140
Lighting Equipment	See Electrical Equipment
Limestone	See Stones
Linoleum	See Carpets
Liquefied Gas Fuel	6, 145

Industry or Product	*Number **
Liquor	See Beverages
Locomotives (See also Railroad Equipment)	90
Lubricants	See Petroleum Products
Luggage	See Leather Goods
Machinery (See also Industrial Equipment)	9, 11, 32, 44, 57, 90, 92, 93, 97, 99, 100, 105, 145, 153
Marble	88
Marine Supplies	168
Mattresses	16
Measuring and Controlling Instruments	80, 97
Meat Products	66
Mechanical Products	See Machinery
Medicines	See Drugs
Metals	18, 32, 56, 57, 84, 92, 97, 99, 104, 142, 147, 157
Mildewproofing	37, 105
Mill Equipment and Supplies	See Industrial Equipment
Mineral Oil	See Petroleum Products
Molding Powder	See Plastics
Moth Sprays	See Insecticides
Motors	See Electrical Equipment
Naval Stores	See Chemicals
Notions	108
Novelties	108
Office Equipment and Supplies	97, 145, 160
Oil, Animal	33
Oil, Burner (See also Petroleum Products)	109
Oil, Fish	33
Oil, Mineral	See Petroleum Products
Oil, Vegetable	33, 66, 105
Oils	See Paints

Industry or Product	*Number**
Optical Goods	**97**
Paints	**33, 62, 70, 97, 105, 145**
Paper	**9, 43, 45, 89, 97, 113, 114, 146**
Paving Materials	See Stones
Perfume Ingredients	See Chemicals
Perfumes	See Toilet Goods
Petroleum Products	**97, 116, 145**
Pharmaceuticals	See Drugs
Photographic Materials and Equipment	**8**
Pigments	See Paints
Plant Hormones	**5**
Plasticizers	See Paints
Plastics and Plastics Equipment	**24, 54, 92, 97, 101, 102, 120, 121**
Plating Materials	**97**
Plumbing Supplies	**47, 70, 97, 145**
Polishes	**97, 105**
Poultry Equipment and Supplies	**124**
Preservatives	See Chemicals
Printing	**9, 146**
Provisions	See Meat Products
Putty	**97, 105**
Radio Equipment	**12, 51, 78, 128, 145**
Railroad Equipment	**29, 90, 97**
Rayon	See Textiles
Refractories	**31, 97, 130**
Refrigeration	**47, 131, 145**
Refrigerators	**12**
Resins (See also Chemicals)	**54, 62, 105**
Rubber Accelerators	See Chemicals
Rubber Goods	**97**
Rubber Ingredients	See Chemicals
Rubber, Synthetic (See also Chemicals)	**105**
Rugs	See Carpets
Rustproofing; Rust Remover (See also Chemicals)	**105**
Safety Equipment	**137**
Seeds	**139, 145**
Shellac	**33, 105**
Shoes (See also Wearing Apparel)	**73, 140**
Silverware	See Jewelry
Soap	**4, 97, 145, 156**
Soldering Flux	**97**
Solvents (See also Chemicals and Paints)	**81, 105**
Sporting Goods	**144, 145**
Stain Remover	See Cleaners
Stains	See Paints
Starch	See Chemicals; Food Products
Stationery	See Office Equipment and Supplies
Steel	See Metals
Stones	**88, 97, 117, 125**
Stoneware	See Ceramics
Surface-Active Agents	See Wetting Agents
Synthetic Rubber (See also Chemicals)	**105**
Tanning Materials	See Chemicals
Telephone Equipment (See also Electrical Equipment)	**27**
Television	See Radio Equipment
Textile Chemicals	See Chemicals
Textile Finishes	**37**
Textiles	**37, 42, 96, 97, 129, 153**
Thinners	See Solvents

Industry or Product	*Number**	*Industry or Product*	*Number**
Tiles	See Ceramics	Waterproofing	See Chemicals; Paints
Tobacco Equipment and Supplies	66, 154	Water Purifiers	See Chemicals
Toilet Goods	153, 156, 159	Water Softener	See Chemicals
Tools	72, 97, 118	Wax (See also Chemicals)	17, 37, 105
Toys	122, 145, 155	Wearing Apparel	36, 64, 71, 73, 83, 140, 145
Traction Equipment	51, 97	Weed Killers	See Chemicals
Twine	97	Welding Flux	97
Upholstery (See also Furniture)	69	Wetting Agents (See also Chemicals)	3, 105, 169
Varnish	See Paints	Wine	See Beverages
Varnish Remover	See Paints	Wire (See also Metals)	97, 167
Vegetable Gums	32, 33, 34	Wireless	See Radio Equipment
Vegetable Oil	33, 66, 105	Wood Preservatives	See Chemicals
Ventilating	See Air Conditioning		
Vitamins	See Drugs		
Vitreous Enamel	33		

LIST B

Number	*Books and Trade Journals Listing Trade-Marks*
1	*Aero Digest,* Aeronautical Publishing Corp., New York City
2	*Air Conditioning Blue Book,* Domestic Engineering Co., Chicago, Ill.
3	American Association of Textile Chemists and Colorists, *Annual Directory,* Lowell, Mass.
4	*American Druggist Blue Book,* New York City.
5	*American Fruit Grower, Directory Issue,* Cleveland, O.
6	American Gas Association, *Classified Directory,* New York City
7	*American Machinist,* **81**, 642 (1937), New York City
8	*American Photography,* **33**, 851 (1939), Boston, Mass.
9	*American Printer Buying Guide,* New York City
10	American Society for Testing Materials, *Proceedings,* Philadelphia, Pa.
11	American Society of Mechanical Engineers, *Mechanical Catalog,* New York City
12	*Appliance Specifications and Directory,* McGraw-Hill, New York City

Number	*Books and Trade Journals Listing Trade-Marks*
13	*Automobile Facts and Figures,* Automobile Manufacturers Association, New York City
14	*Automotive and Aviation Industries,* Philadelphia, Pa.
15	*Aviation Equipment Red Book,* Haire Publishing Co., New York City
16	*Bedding Buyers' Guide,* Bedding, Chicago, Ill.
17	Bennett, *Commercial Waxes,* Chemical Publishing Co., Brooklyn, N. Y.
18	Bennett, *Concise Chemical and Technical Dictionary,* Chemical Publishing Co., Brooklyn, N. Y.
19	Bennett, *Practical Emulsions,* Chemical Publishing Co., Brooklyn, N. Y.
20	Bennett, *The Chemical Formulary,* Chemical Publishing Co., Brooklyn, N. Y.
21	Brady, *Materials Handbook,* McGraw-Hill, New York City
22	*Brewery Directory and Supplies,* Atlas Publishing Co., New York City
23	*Brick and Clay Record,* Industrial Publications Inc., Chicago, Ill.
24	*British Plastics Year Book,* Iliffe and Sons Ltd., London, England
25	*Building and Building Management,* Chicago, Ill.
26	*Building Trades Directory,* Kelly's Directories Ltd., London, England
27	*Buyers' Guide,* Telephone Engineer Publishing Co., Chicago, Ill.
28	*Cabinet, Furnishing and Upholstery Trades Directory,* Kelly's Directories Ltd., London, England
29	*Car Builders Cyclopedia,* Simmons-Boardman Publishing Co., New York City
30	*Carpet Annual,* British-Continental Press, London, England
31	*Ceramics Data Book,* Industrial Publications Inc., Chicago, Ill.
32	*Chemical Engineering Catalog,* Reinhold Publishing Co., New York City
33	*Chemical Industries, Buyers Guide Book,* New York City
34	*Chemical Industries Directory,* Kelly's Directories Ltd., London, England

Number	*Books and Trade Journals Listing Trade-Marks*
35	*Colour Index,* Society of Dyers and Colourists, London, England
36	*Corset Trade Directory,* Haire Publishing Co., New York City
37	Cotton Textile Institute Inc., *List of Finishes,* New York City
38	*Crockery and Glass Journal,* Haire Publishing Co., New York City
39	*Dairy Industries Catalog,* Olsen Publishing Co., Milwaukee, Wis.
40	Davis, *Chemistry and Technology of Rubber,* Reinhold Publishing Co., New York City
41	Denny, *Complete Spotting Guide,* Cleaning and Dyeing Publications, New York City
42	Denny, *Fabrics and How to Know Them,* Lippincott and Co., Philadelphia, Pa.
43	*Dictionary of Paper,* American Pulp and Paper Association, New York City
44	*Directory of Engineering Aids,* Allis-Chalmers Co., Milwaukee, Wis.
45	*Directory of Paper and Allied Trades,* Lockwood Trade Journal Co., New York City
46	*Domestic Engineering, Blue Book,* Chicago, Ill.
47	*Domestic Engineering Catalog,* Domestic Engineering Co., Chicago, Ill.
48	*Druggist Circular Red Book,* New York City
49	*Electrical Appliance Directory,* McGraw-Hill, New York City
50	*Electrical Buyers Reference Book,* McGraw-Hill, New York City
51	*Electrical Industry, Wireless and Allied Trades Directory,* Kelly's Directories Ltd., London, England
52	*Electrical World, Buyers Reference Issue,* McGraw-Hill, New York City
53	*Electronics, Buyers' Guide,* New York City
54	Ellis, *Chemistry of Synthetic Resins,* Reinhold Publishing Co., New York City
55	*Encyclopedic Directory of Alcoholic Beverage Industries, Red Book,* Liquor Publications Inc., New York City
56	*Engineering Alloys,* American Society for Metals, Cleveland, O.

Number	*Books and Trade Journals Listing Trade-Marks*
57	*Engineering, Hardware, Metal and Motor Trades Directory,* Kelly's Directories Ltd., London, England
58	*Food Industries Catalog,* Food Industries, New York City
59	*Food Products Directory,* W. J. McComman, San Francisco, Cal.
60	*Fuel Oil Journal, Boiler Trade Names,* New York City
61	Gardner, *Chemical Synonyms and Trade Names,* Technical Press Ltd., London, England
62	Gardner, *Physical and Chemical Examination of Paints, etc.,* Institute of Paints and Varnish Research, Washington, D. C.
63	*Gift Directory,* Andrew Geyer Inc., New York City
64	*Gloves Directory,* Gloves, Gloversville, N. Y.
65	Gregory, *Condensed Chemical Dictionary,* Reinhold Publishing Co., New York City
66	*Grocery, Provision, Oil, Colour and Tobacco Trades Directory,* Kelly's Directories Ltd., London, England
67	Gutman, *Modern Drug Encyclopedia,* Paul B. Hoeber, New York City
68	Hamilton, *Entoma,* Department of Entomology, N. J. Agric. Exp. Station, New Brunswick, N. J.
69	*Handbook of Interior Decorative Trades,* Clifford and Lawton Inc., New York City
70	*Hardware Age Merchandise Directory,* Chilton Publishing Co., New York City
71	*Hat Life, Yearbook,* New York City
72	*Heating, Piping and Air Conditioning Directory,* Keeney Publishing Co., Chicago, Ill.
73	*Hide and Leather and Shoes, Blue Book,* Chicago, Ill.
74	Hodgman, *Handbook of Chemistry and Physics,* Chemical Rubber Publishing Co., Cleveland, O.
75	*Hospital Purchasing File,* Modern Hospital Purchasing Co., Chicago, Ill.
76	*House Furnishings Directory,* Haire Publishing Co., New York City
77	*Implement and Tractor, Implement Directory,* Kansas City, Mo.
78	Institute of Radio Engineers, *Yearbook,* New York City
79	*Institutions Catalog Directory,* Domestic Engineering Co., Chicago, Ill.

Number	*Books and Trade Journals Listing Trade-Marks*
80	*Instruments,* Instruments Publishing Co., Pittsburgh, Pa.
81	*Jordan, Technology of Solvents,* Chemical Publishing Co., Brooklyn, N. Y.
82	*Keystone Coal Buyers' Manual,* McGraw-Hill, New York City
83	*Knit Goods Trade Directory,* Davison Publishing Co., New York City
84	Lange, *Handbook of Chemistry,* Handbook Publishers, Sandusky, O.
85	*Laundry Age,* Laundry Age Publishing Co., New York City
86	*Laundry and Allied Trades Directory,* Kelly's Directories Ltd., London, England
87	*Leather Trades Directory,* Kelly's Directories Ltd., London, England
88	Lent, *Trade Names of Marbles, Stones, etc.,* Stone Publishing Co., New York City
89	*Lockwood's Directory of Paper and Allied Trades,* Lockwood Trade Journal Co., New York City
90	*Locomotive Encyclopedia,* Association of American Railroads, Washington, D. C.
91	*Luggage and Leather Goods Buyer,* Haire Publishing Co., New York City
92	*Machine Design, Annual Supplement,* Penton Publishing Co., Cleveland, O.
93	*Machinery,* Industrial Press, New York City
94	*Mac's Coal Directory,* Coal Information Bureau, Pittsburgh, Pa.
95	*Marine Catalog,* Simmons-Boardman Publishing Corp., New York City
96	Mauersberger, *Rayon and Staple Fiber Handbook,* Rayon Publishing Co., New York City
97	*McRae's Blue Book,* New York City
98	*Merck Index,* Merck and Co., Rahway, N. J.
99	*Metal Industries Catalog,* Reinhold Publishing Co., New York City
100	*Mill Supplies, Directory Issue,* New York City
101	*Modern Plastics Catalog,* Modern Plastics, New York City
102	*Modern Plastics, Directory Issue,* New York City

Number	Books and Trade Journals Listing Trade-Marks
103	*National Housewares Directory,* Associated Pot and Kettle Clubs of America, San Francisco, Cal.
104	*National Metals Handbook,* American Society for Steel Treating, Cleveland, O.
105	National Paint, Varnish and Lacquer Association, *Trade-Mark Directory,* Washington, D. C.
106	*New and Non-Official Remedies,* American Medical Association, Chicago, Ill.
107	*Northwestern Miller, Annual Directory,* Miller Publishing Co., Minneapolis, Minn.
108	*Notion and Novelty Review, Directory of Notions,* New York City
109	*Oilburner Manufacturers,* Fuel Oil Journal, New York City
110	*Oil, Paint and Drug Reporter, Green Book,* New York City
111	*Palmer, Tool Steel Simplified,* Carpenter Steel Co., Reading, Pa.
112	Pape, *Boiler Reference Book,* John S. Swift and Co., New York City
113	*Paper and Pulp Mill Catalog,* Fritz Publications, Chicago, Ill.
114	*Paper Catalog,* Walden Sons and Mott Inc., New York City
115	*Pattern Index, Flatware,* Jeweler's Circular Keystone, New York City
116	*Petroleum Register,* New York City
117	*Pit and Quarry Handbook,* Complete Service Publishing Co., Chicago, Ill.
118	*Plant (Industrial) Purchasing Directory,* Plant Purchasing Directory, Chicago, Ill.
119	*Plastic Annual Directory,* Ziff-Davis Inc., Chicago, Ill.
120	*Plastics Buyer,* Cleworth Publishing Co., New York City
121	*Plastics Year Book,* Plastics Press Ltd., London, England
122	*Playthings Directory,* McCready Publishing Co., New York City
123	*Plumbing and Heating Catalog,* Domestic Engineering Co., Chicago, Ill.
124	*Poultry Supply Dealer, Directory and Buyers' Guide,* Chicago, Ill.

Number	*Books and Trade Journals Listing Trade-Marks*
125	*Power's Road Catalog,* Gillette Publishing Co., Chicago, Ill.
126	*Production Year Book,* Colton Press, New York City
127	*Radiator Reference Book,* Fuel Oil Journal, New York City
128	*Radio's Master,* United Catalog Publishers Inc., New York City
129	*Rayon and Silk Standard Guide,* Davison Publishing Co., New York City
130	*Refractories Industry Directory,* American Refractories Institute, Pittsburgh, Pa.
131	*Refrigeration and Air Conditioning Directory,* Business News Publishing Co., Detroit, Mich.
132	*Register of Perfumes, Cosmetics, etc.,* Toilet Requisites Co., New York City
133	*Rubber Index,* Rubber Age, London, England
134	*Rubber Red Book,* Rubber Age, New York City
135	*Rudder Buyers' Guide,* Rudder Publishing Co., New York City
136	*Rug Profits Floor Covering Directory,* Bill Bros. Publishing Co., New York City
137	*Safety Directory and Catalog,* Alfred M. Best Co., New York City
138	*Salmon Packers' Register,* Consolidated Publishing Co., Seattle, Wash.
139	*Seed World, Buyers Guide,* Chicago, Ill.
140	*Shoe and Leather Reporter, Annual Directory,* Boston, Mass.
141	Snell, *Chemicals of Commerce,* D. Van Nostrand Co., New York City
142	Sobel, *Metal and Alloys Dictionary,* Chemical Publishing Co., Brooklyn, N. Y.
143	*Speed Book,* National Jeweler Inc., Chicago, Ill.
144	*Sporting Goods Dealer, Annual Directory,* St. Louis, Mo.
145	*Standard Advertising Register,* National Register Publishing Corp., New York City
146	*Stationers, Printers, Publishers, Booksellers and Paper Makers Directory,* Kelly's Directories Ltd., London, England
147	*Steel Yearbook,* Penton Publishing Co., Cleveland, O.

Number	Books and Trade Journals Listing Trade-Marks
148	*Sterling Silver Flatware Pattern Index,* Jewelers Circular Keystone, New York City
149	Stewart, *National Paint Directory,* Stewart Research Laboratory, Alexandria, Va.
150	*Sweet's Catalog File,* Sweet's Catalog Service, New York City
151	*Synthetic Resins and Their Raw Materials,* U. S. Tariff Commission, Washington, D. C.
152	*Textile Chemical Specialty Guide,* Rayon Publishing Co., New York City
153	*Thomas Register,* Thomas Publishing Co., New York City
154	*Tobacco Directory,* Costa's Directories Co., New York City
155	*Toys and Bicycle Guide,* Toys and Bicycle Publishing Co., Chicago, Ill.
156	*Trade Mark Record,* Drug and Cosmetic Industry, New York City
157	*Trade Names of Stainless Steels,* Rustless Iron and Steel Corp., Baltimore, Md.
158	*Trouble Shooter's Manual,* John F. Rider Inc., New York City
159	*T. R. Register,* Pope Publishing Co., New York City
160	*Tube Complement Book,* Sylvania-Hygrade Corp., Emporium, Pa.
161	U. S. Department of Agriculture, Bureau of Entomology and Plant Quarantine, *Bulletins,* Washington, D. C.
162	U. S. Department of Commerce, Bureau of Foreign and Domestic Commerce, *Bulletins* (Medicinal Products), Washington, D. C.
163	U. S. Department of Commerce, Bureau of Standards, *Bulletins,* Washington, D. C.
164	*Vanderbilt Handbook,* R. T. Vanderbilt Co., New York City
165	*Wholesale Grocery and Kindred Trades Register,* Thomas Publishing Co., New York City
166	*Who Makes It and Where?* Andrew Geyer Inc., New York City
167	*Wire Buyers' Guide,* Quinn Brown Publishing Corp., Stamford, Conn.

Number	*Books and Trade Journals Listing Trade-Marks*
168	*World Ports Annual Directory,* World Ports, Chicago, Ill.
169	Young and Coons, *Surface Active Agents,* Chemical Publishing Co., Brooklyn, N. Y.
170	Zimmerman and Lavine, *Handbook of Material Trade Names,* Industrial Research Service Publications, Dover, N. H.

Trade-Marks Referring to Chemicals and Allied Products

TRADE-MARK OWNERS

LIST C

Trade-Mark	*Number**	*Trade-Mark*	*Number**
Abalyn	309	Acto	611
Abopon	280	Actoflux	113
Abrac	97	Actusol	213
Abril Wax	370	Adbac	480
Absorbit	226	Adheso Wax	280
Acasol	269	Adipol-BCA	474
Accelator	343	Adlube	4
Accozine	152	Admolene	62
Aceko	118	Advagum	4
Acele	217	Advan	4
Aceloid	29	Advaresin	4
Acetamine	217	Advasol	4
Acetine J	270	Advawet	4
Acidoin	58	Aerocarb	35
Acidol	480	Aerocase	35
Acidolate	716	Aerocat	35
Acidole	720	Aeroclear	35
Acidolene	411	Aerofloat	35
Aciterge-Ol	167	Aerogel	433
Acrawax	280	Aerolube	35
Acrin	217	Aeroseal	35
Acrol	224	Aeroset	35
Acrosyl	433	Aerosize	35
Acryloid	549	Aerosol	35
Acrylon	35	Aerotex	35
Acrysol	549	Afton	666
Actalyte	30	Agagel	215
Activex	329	Agchem	5
Activite	89	Agdite	670
Activol	109	Age Rite	681

* The numbers in the right-hand column refer to list D including the names of the trade-mark owners.

Trade-Mark	*Number**
Agfanol	6
Agicide	7
Agilite	708
Agramon	217
Agrinite	22
Agripol	546
Agr Syl	336
Ahcol	67
Ahcomerse	67
Ahcopan	67
Ahcopel	67
Ahcostrip	67
Ahcovel	67
Ahcovat	67
Ahcowet	67
Aidtex	305
Airex	590
Akal	24
Akaustan	270
Akbar	217
Akcocene	35
Akoil	35
Akrelac	99
Akroflex	217
Akro Gel	8
Aksel	426
Aktivin	9
Akusaka Wax	174
Alacet	59
Alase	637
Albacar	709
Albacer	280
Albalith	455
Albaoil	411
Albasan	451
Albasol	464
Albatan	411
Albatex	152
Alberene	10
Albertol	563
Albinol	684
Albone	217
Alborit	286
Albusol	401
Alcal	42
Alcobutate	612
Alco Dexatol	17
Alcolan	562
Alcolium	58
Alcolloid	490
Alconox	620
Alcophate	727
Alcotone	166
Aldarco	343
Aldo	280
Aldophene	491
Alert	482
Alfenthal	433
Alframine	425
Alfrax	125
Alfronin	425
Algaloid	215
Algepon	65
Algol	270
Algosol	270
Algrain	167
Alizarol	441
Alkalate	621
Alkamerce	305
Alkamine	20
Alkanol	217
Alkapen	109
Alkaterge-O	167
Alkathene	334
Alkazene	207
Alkolene	411
Alkon	401
Alkor	73
Alkylate	354
Alkymol	707
Allcast	447
Allymer	164
Alodine	30
Alorco	19
Alox	16
Aloxite	125
Alperox	390
Alpha Protein	279
Alphasol	35
Alphazurine	441
Alphite	217
Alpolene	58
Alrochlor	17
Alrohydrine	17
Alromine	17
Alronol	17
Alropel	17
Alrophil	17
Alropon	17
Alroresin	17
Alrosene	17
Alrosept	17

Trade-Mark	*Number**
Alrosol	17
Alroterge	17
Alrowet	17
Alrozone	17
Alsec	19
Alsifer	680
Alsilox	222
Alsite	276
Altax	681
Alubra	354
Alumbrite	53
Aluminide	553
Alunaze	480
Alundum	467
Alvar	583
Alwax	35
Amacel	132
Amacid	25
Amaform	25
Amaldehyde	118
Amalg	244
Amalgol	118
Amalthion	118
Amandol	217
Amanil	25
Amanol	25
Amano S	25
Amanthrene	25
Amasize	625
Amberex	610
Amberlac	549
Amberlite	549
Amberol	549
Ambertex	449
Ambrac	27
Ambrene	217
Ambriol	269
Ambrox	653
Amchem	30
Amcomid	21
Amcosul	21
Amerchol	32
Amerigum	23
Ameripol	283
Amerite	26, 52
Amerse	686
Amicrol	9
Amidazo	118
Amidex	305
Amidine	118
Amijel	176

Trade-Mark	*Number**
Amilig	693
Aminac	404
Aminox	451
Amioca	44
Ammate	217
Ammonyx	480
Ammo-Phos	35
Amodor	412
Amodyn	74
Amoil	224
Amo-phos	35
Amora	451
Amotate	86
Amo Wax	537
Amphenol	48
Amsco Solvent	45
Amuno	420
Amuskal	269
Amyliq	693
Amyloform	501
Amyloid	51
Amylon	449
Anasol	168
Anchorset	67
Anex	343
Anglamol	389
Anhydrol	122
Anhydrone	80
Anhydrox	83
Ankord	60
Anodex	393
Anol	55
Anoxyl	563
Ansbor	57
Ansol	670
Anthomine	65
Anthramine	65
Anthrapole	65
Anticide	466
Antifoam	217
Antilac	58
Antimol	580
Antimonex	58
Antimot	472
Antimucine	573
Antisol	297
Antox	217
Antranox	679
Antronox M	679
Antu	520
A. N. W. Solution	84

Trade-Mark	*Number**
Apasol	118
Apco	56
Apcolene	56
Apexinol	58
Apexscour	58
Apimela	120
Applicet	59, 67
Appramine	695
Appretan	270
Appretole	695
Aquadag	3
Aquadam	352
Aquadye	64
Aquagel	83
Aquakal	356
Aqualube	280
Aquamag	253
Aquanel	58
Aquanol	86
Aquanon	522
Aquapel	309
Aquaplex	549
Aqua Proof	720
Aquaresin	280
Aquarex	217
Aquarol	65, 259
Aquarome	245
Aqua-sec	60
Aquasit	528
Aquasol	35
Aquaspray	481
Aquatain	292
Aquatex	699
Aquatone	58
Aquazinc	86
Aquoid	664
Aradite	71
Araflex	61
Arafoam	71
Aramite	71
Aranox	451
Arapol	71
Arasan	217
Araskleen	433
Areskap	433
Aresket	433
Aratac	71
Aratein	71
Arathene	71
Aratite	61
Aratone	71
Arazate	451
Arazin	71
Arazym	563
Arbicole	58
Arboneeld	217
Arcloride	66
Arctic Syntex	159
Ardol	62
Arflex	52
Argam	641
Argasole	58
Aridase	693
Aridex	217
Aridize	669
Aridye	64
Aripel	65
Aristoloy	175
Aristowax	506
Arkanum	65
Arkogel	65
Arkol	65
Arkotan	65
Arlacel	74
Arlamec	74
Arlex	74
Armac	66
Armasol	391
Armeen	66
Armid	66
Armoflote	66
Armol	391
Armone	66
Armowax	66
Arneel	66
Arnil	66
Arochem	670
Arochlor	433
Arodure	670
Arofene	670
Arolene	295
Aromine	109
Aromol	109
Aroplaz	670
Arosol	47, 269, 627
Arostit	573
Arquad	66
Arseco	560
Arsenol	587
Artexol	24
Artisil	573
Artwax	600

Trade-Mark	*Number* *	*Trade-Mark*	*Number* *
Aruba	711	Babosil	304
Arylene	305	Bakelast	79
Arylpen	354	Bakelite	77
Asbestine	348	Barak	217
Asbestocel	352	Barbak	35
Asbestol	714	Bardex	84
Asbestol Filler	387	Bardol	84
Ascarite	649	Baride	142
Aseptisil	499	Barisol	198
Aseptoform	259	Baroco	83
Askarel	271	Barofine	142
Asplit	499	Baroid	445
Astracel	270	Barolith	142
Astrolith	142	Barretan	84
Astrotone	217	Barroco	445
Astrulan	35	Bartyl	278
Atcopon	69	Barvac	441
Atcosoft	69	Basicol	260
Atcosyn	69	Basofor	429
Atcotal	69	Bayol	618
Atcowet	69	Beaconal	86
Athenon	224	Beatsol	330
Atlacide	138	Beckacite	546
Atlanite	70	Beckamine	546
Atlox	74	Beckolin	546
Atomal	6	Beckophen	546
Atomite	650	Beckopol	546
Atrapol	480	Beckosol	546
Attaclay	75	Becktone	217
Atvar	583	Bedafin	334
Aubepine	217	Bedesol	334
Auric Brown	217	Belro	309
Aurinol	480	Bemul	86
Aurosal	78	Benoclor	158
Auxanine	270	Benol	601
Auxinine	270	Bensopol	716
Avenex	536	Benzoline	94
Aversol	304	Benzo-Sol	586
Avirol	217	Beramine	92
Avitex	217	Be Square Wax	82
Avitone	217	Bestowax	67
Avonac	441	Beta-chlor	244
Azanol	18	Beta Chlora	692
Azoanthrene	18	Betanol	86
Azo Citrox	54	Betanox	451
Azogum	449	Betasol	35
Azolan	109	Bethadur	91
Azolith	54	Bethalon	91
Azosol	270	Beufa	433
Azurwite	665	Beutene	451
		Bexin	273

Trade-Mark	*Number**
Bickanol	92
Bim	369
Bindarene	345
Bindex	137
Bindtex	327
Biobate	693
Bionol	270
Bituvia	547
Bixamine	92
B-J-F	451
Black Leaf	655
Blacosolv	96
Blancal	714
Blancol	221
Blancote	336
Blandite	161
Blandol	601
Blankit	270
B-L-E	451
Blendene	280
Boerite	464
Bonderite	492
Bondite	86
Bondogen	681
Boon	210
Boontex	210
Borascu	487
Borcote	253
Bordow	207
Borno	329
Borol	214
Borolon	2
Borosoap	487
Bortam	653
Bozetol	305
B. R. C.	84
Breadlac	99
Bresin	309
Breton Oil	100
Brex	524
Brisgo	309
Britex	58
Bromofume	237
Bronoco	106
Brovira	6
B. R. T.	84
Brunzol	472
B. R. V.	84
Brymul	618
Brytex	107, 433
Brytexol	107

Trade-Mark	*Number**
Bubbilfil	217
Bubene	453
Buca	435
Buna	249, 284, 618
Bunac	710
Bunarex	497
Bunnatol	86
Buramine	582
Burkol	109
Burmol	270
Buromin	110
Butac	329
Butacite	217
Butanol	167
Butaprene	249
Butasan	433
Butazate	451
Butesso	618
Butex	474
Butoben	420
Butone	611
Butrax	284
Butvar	583
Butyl Eight	681
Butyl rubber	618
Butyl Zimate	681
Buxine	278
B W H	451
B-X-A	451
B. Z. Wax	280
Cadaloy	217
Cadalyte	217
Cadmolith	142
Cal-Add	688
Calade	114
Calafene	58
Calcene	162
Calcide	22
Calciferol	713
Calcodur	112
Calcosol	112
Calcotex	112
Calcyanide	35
Calex	699
Calfast	268
Calfix	108
Calglo	114
Calgolac	114
Calgon	114
Calgran	253

Trade-Mark	*Number* *
Calgreen	148
Calite	117
Calo-Clor	401
Calodorant	482
Calogreen	401
Calopone	669
Caloride	599
Calsimag	253
Caltox	116
Calum	114
Calumite	39
Camacyl	118
Camalt	118
Camasol	118
Cameko	118
Camelite	118
Captax	681
Carabond	127
Caragum	176
Caramide	127
Caramine	127
Caraplex	127
Carapol	127
Carbalose	58
Carbic	386
Carbic Anhydride	122
Carbitol	122
Carbium	199
Carbo	125
Carbocell	442
Carbocera	177
Carbodite	86
Carbofene	483
Carbofilm	51
Carbofrax	125
Carbo-Korez	73
Carbolac	111
Carbolene	720
Carbolineum	124
Carbolite	386
Carbo Moytol	615
Carbonex	84
Carbonite	265
Carbonox	38
Carbon Twelve	111
Carbortam	653
Carborundum	125
Carboseal	122
Carbosota	84
Carbowax	122
Carboxide	122
Carboxymethocel A	207
Carburite	442
Cardamide	350
Cardanol	350
Cardinole	58
Cardis	695
Cardolac	350
Cardolite	350
Cardoxide	428
Carex	471
Carilloy	128
Caro Gant	305
Caroxite	250
Carpenol	699
Carragar	374
Carrene	217
Carsene	58
Cascamite	130
Cascophen	130
Casco Resin	130
Cascorez	130
Casize	601
Castorwax	79
Castrolite	567
Castung	79
Catabond	131
Catalin	131
Catalite	217
Catalpo	435
Catavar	131
Catex	343
Catylon	305
Causplit	499
Cecolene	217
Cedrol	217
Ceepryn	421
Ceglin	631
Celascour	25
Celaton	222
Celax	67, 309
Celcon	132
Celeron	173
Celesterol	596
Celfon	631
Celite	352
Cellate	106
Celliton	270
Cellofas	334
Cellolyn	309
Cellosize	122
Cellosolve	122

Trade-Mark	*Number* *
Celludye	198
Celluflex	132
Cellufloc	530
Celluloid	132
Cellulube	132
Celomite	151
Celoron	173
Celox	309
Celutate	724
Celvacene	202
Centrol	133
Centrosene	598
Ceraflux	280
Ceral	573
Ceraloid	161
Ceramitalc	346
Ceranine	573
Cerasnow	339
Cerasynt	679
Cerate	457
Cerax	177
Cercon Wax	384
Cerelose	176
Ceremul	598
Ceresan	217
Cerese Wax	598
Ceresinol	480
Cerex	433
Cerfak	327
Cerfax	327
Cerol	161, 573
Cerophyl	134
Cerrobase	135
Cerrobend	135
Cerrolow	135
Cetab	553
Cetal	562
Cetamium	80
Cetasize	625
Cethane	86
Cetosol	625
Chamosheen	480
Char	139
Charlab	140
Charlite	140
Charon	111
Chemcot	602
Chemicarl	140
Chemigum	284
Chemlin	707
Chemoil	707

Trade-Mark	*Number* *
Chemosol	145
Chemros	707
Chenol	109
Cheriol	269
Chiffonol	601
Chitosan	217
Chlorantine	152
Chlorasol	122
Chlorax	698
Chlorazol	334
Chlorcosane	433
Chloresco	179
Chlorex	122
Chlorextol	15
Chlorimet	219
Chlor-Isopol	662
Chloron	302
Chlorosol	122
Chlorowax	199
Chlorpropane Wax	319
Chovis	231
Chromacid	118
Chromanthrene	18
Chromazine	118
Chromel	325
Chromitron	35
Chromol	411
Chromotex	413
Chromotone	413
Churnolac	371
Cibanite	152
Cicoil	102
Circosol	627
Citrella	68
Citrene	278
Citrex	28
Citrolene	451
Clarase	637
Clarene	153
Clarex	336
Clarion	458
Clarite	453
Clarofin	413
Clarogen	153
Clarol	153
Clarsol	153
Clavanol	198
Clavodene	198
Clearate	154
Clearcarb	35
Clenesco	179

Trade-Mark	*Number**
Cliderite	95
Cliffchar	155
Clintose	157
Clix	184
Clor	499
Clorafin	309
Cloroben	158
Coblax	236
Cocate	159
Cocoon	318
Cocosol	625
Codban	35
Colas	586
Colene	58
Colesco	179
Colite	86
Collatone	382
Collocarb	329
Collocel	207
Colloidine	86
Colloidol	472
Colloresin	270
Collupulin	693
Colodorant	616
Coloidex	94
Coloidol BT	42
Colorex	624
Colox	83
Comacid	168
Comal	500
Comcotex	168
Cominol	168
Compar	550
Compregnite	130
Comprodull	166
Compromine	166
Compropaste	166
Comprozyme	166
Concamine	171
Concental	67
Conconex	171
Concoset	172
Condensite	77
Conductex	94
Conduline	424
Conjulin	715
Conjusoy	715
Continex	714
Convertit	693
Copacite	169
Copapel	270
Copar	268
Copene	453
Coprantine	152
Coprein	176
Coragum	176
Coramine	152
Corasil	210
Coray	236
Cordex	469
Cordura	217
Cordurol	601
Corekal	270
Coresin Oil	685
Corial	270
Corilene	334
Coronol	271
Corpolin	9
Corumba wax	174
Cosma	181
Cosmetol	231
Cosmol	596
Cosmoline	327
Cosol	453
Coveral	270
Coverene	280
Covinylblak	94
C-P-B	451
Creamsol	109
Crecote	548
Cremba	181
Creosolv	129
Creosotan	563
Crepitine	358
Cresolite	17
Cresopen	556
Cresophan	259
Cresopine	556
Crestex	17
Crill	181
Croflex	664
Cromodine	30
Croplast	482
Crown Wax	507
Crylene	451
Cryptone	455
Crysalba	433
Crystalite	343
Crystamet	341
Crystarose	217
Crystex	624
Crystol	65

Trade-Mark	*Number**
Crystolene	302
Crystolon	467
Crystox	586
Cubor	148
Culicide	598
Cullite	185
Culofix	65
Cumar	84
Cumate	681
Cuminone	269
Cumol	675
Cuprax	681
Cuprinol	186
Cuprocide	563
Cuprodine	30
Cuprotek	30
Cuprotela	11
Curbay B-G	670
Curbay Binder	670
Curodex	433
Curosalt	182
Cutrax	681
Cutrilin	35
Cyanegg	217
Cyanine	724
Cyanobrite	217
Cyanogas	35
Cyanogran	217
Cyclamal	269
Cycline	433
Cyclocel	519
Cyclocell	75
Cyclodone	632
Cyclonol	217
Cyclopon	270
Cyclotene	207
Cyko	6
Cymanol	336
Cyrene	453
Cytox	35
Dacolyte	217
Dactin	217
Dag	3
Daigen	217
Daintex	309
Dairyco	35
Dapol	277
Darco	189
Darex	197
Darpo Stripper	409
Darsil	217
Darvan	197
Dastar	181
Dat	116
Daxad	197
D-B-A	451
DC Antifoam A	208
Decal	696
Decalin	217
Decalso	503
Deceresol	35
Decerinol	65
Decholin	558
Decolorex A	223
Decroline	270
Deenate	217
Deenax	611
Deenol	217
Defloc	179
Defoama	716
Degalol	558
Degomma	563
Degumozene	58
Degumtex	305
Dehydranone	122
Dehydrite	649
Dehydrol	587
Dehydrol O	217
Dekol	270
Dektol	224
Delac	451
Delsterol	217
Deltyl	278
Delustrene	601
Delustrol	65
Delvoil	502
Demal	231
Demerol	713
Deminrolit	503
Dendrol	617
Denol	217
Densol	522
Deo-base	601
Deodol	231
Deoxidine	30
Deoxo	80
Deoxylyte	30
Deoxyvat	398
Dependip	56
Depilin	35
Derex	670

Trade-Mark	*Number**
Dergon	65
Dermabate	37
Dermasol	660
Dermolate	464
Derox	22
Derramine	699
Desicchlora	80
Desiccite	246
Desoil	179
Desol	579
Detanol	168
Detergetex	528
Detergo	240
Detergol	660
Detersol	17
Dethdiet	495
Developene	356
Dewaxit	480
Dexene	198
Dexolene	198
Dextrol	198
Diadmerol	62
Diafilt	336
Diafoam	563
Diagen	217
Dialite	301
Dialyte	553
Diamond Gum	67
Dianil	270
Dianol	535
Diapene	535
Diaperm	535
Diarmeen	66
Diasmol	451
Diastafor	613
Diastazyme	716
Diastine	168
Diatex	528
Diatol	670
Diax	403
Diazamine	573
Diazine	441
Diazopon	270
Diazyme	716
Dicalite	200
Dicarbo	553
Dichloricide	420
Dielex	297
Diesterex	451
Diflex	203
Digestase	403
Dilectene	173
Dilecto	173
Dilex	322
Diluex	252
Dimalone	670
Dinopol	474
Diol	236
Diolamine	86
Diolin	217
Dioxorb	401
Dipex	236
Dipolymer	309
Dipyrazo	509
Discolite	567
Dispersaid	94
Dispersal	161
Dispersex	681
Dispersite	201
Dispersol	334, 586
Disperzout	696
Distal	596
Distoline	715
Dithane	563
Dixiedensed	664
DN-111	207
DOP	405
Dorscopol	206
Doucil	510
Dowanone	207
Dowax	207
Dowclene	207
Dowco	207
Dowell	207
Dowflake	207
Dowfume	207
Dowicide	207
Dowmetal	207
Dowtherm	207
Drakeol	498
Dralyte	553
Drapolein	209
Drax	109
Dreft	524
Drench	67
Drene	524
Dresinate	309
Dresinol	309
Drierite	299
Drigel	161
Dri-Knit	535
Driocel	75

Trade-Mark	*Number**
Driox	386
Drisize	161
Drisoy	606
Dryall	141
Dry-Ice	532
Drymet	341
Dryolene	56
Dryorth	341
Dryseq	341
Drytex	567
Dry-Tex	437
D-Scour	109
Duclean	217
Duco	217
Ducolite	214
Ducosolve	214
Ducozone	214
Dulac	392
Dullatone	480
Dullit	270
Dullite	660
Dulrite	292
Dulstan	615
Dultex	600
Dunnflex	216
Dunngel	216
Dunnglue	216
Dunntex	216
Dunntite	216
Duofol	305
Duolite	144
Duolith	217
Duosolve	354
Duozinc	217
Duphax	610
Duponol	217
Duracite	674
Duralon	674
Duralum	697
Duraplex	549
Duratex	159
Duraval	217
Durawax	177
Durepel	638
Durez	274
Durichlor	219
Duridine	30
Durimet	219
Duriron	219
Durite	681
Dur-Lana	695
Durobrite	217
Durocer	280
Durol	441
Duron	55
Dustrol	598
Dutox	217
Dutrex	586
Dyal	587
Dybryte	112
Dyclene	393
Dyesolve	556
Dyetex	556
Dykan	625
Dymal	587
Dynax	217
Dynesol	20
Dynol	217
Dypenol	198
Dyphene	587
Dyphenite	587
Dyset	58
Dytin	459
Eastone	643
Ebcomulsion	95
Ebonol	234
Ebrok	555
Ecconol	225
Econo-Plast	710
Edamin	584
Edwal	227
Ela	217
Elaine	230
Elastine	625
Elastoflex	438
Elastoil	338
Elastolac	280
Elastolin	438
Elcarb	229
Elconite	229
Electrolon	2
Electromet	228
Elemite	716
Elgetol	217
Elkol	587
Elon	224
El-Sixty	217
Emargol	231
Emcol	231
Emulcene	600
Emulgor A	280

Trade-Mark	*Number* *
Falkovar	241
Falkyd	241
Falo	499
Fanal	270
Farbamine	240
Fastogene	25
Fastolux	57
Fastona	57
Fatosan	58
Feltoscour	270
Feltron	270
Fen	20
Fermate	217
Ferri-floc	642
Ferrisol	492
Ferrisul	433
Ferrocarbo	125
Ferrox	624
Fibacon	109
Fibaweld	480
Fiberglas	484
Fiberite	699
Fiberjel	449
Fiberlac	433
Fiberloid	433
Fiberlon	433
Fibertex	449
Fibestos	433
Fibretex	352
Fibron	350
Fibrotex	83
Fijiolene	321
Filabond	161
Filac	323
Filaseal	20
Filcote	681
Filfloc	540
Filtchar	336
Filter-Cel	352
Filtrablend	505
Filtranauba	505
Filtrasol	505
Filtrawax	505
Filtrol	246
Filtrona	505
Filtros	247
Finol	617
Firmatex	305
Firmtex	567
Firzite	672
Fixacol	152
Fixalt	433
Fixapret	270
Fixateur	269
Fixatone	269
Fixodor	204
Fixol	678
Fixoresin	574
Fixtan	217
Flacol	309
Flamenol	271
Flavite	279
Flectol	433
Flexal	305
Flexalyn	309
Flexamine	305
Flexglass	672
Flexin	9
Flexol	122
Flexole	381
Flexoresin	280
Flexowax	280
Flex-synol	23
Flexwood	672
Flo	499
Floex	309
Flomine	678
Florafal	269
Floragard	217
Floraid	252
Floranol	269
Flordine	68
Florex	252
Floridin	252
Florigel	252
Florisil	252
Florite	252
Floto	309
Flotol	231
Flotox	116
Flozene	601
Fluf	599
Fluorex	39
Fluoroleum	217
Fluxit	217
Fluxol	254
Fluxrite	188
Foamex	280
Foamicide	721
Foamite	40
Foliafume	495
Folianol	269

Trade-Mark	*Number**
Folin	503
Folione	278
Folotex	309
Fomon	194
Fonap	257
Fonate	86
Fonoline	601
Forasite	546
Foremul	716
Formacide	300
Formanil	25
Formaset	695
Formetic Acid	720
Formica	255
Formocinic Acid	58
Formopon	563
Formosul	104
Formrite	337
Formvar	583
Fortisan	132
Fosforizer	433
Fosklor	694
Fosol	257
Fosolene	257
Fractol	611
Freezene	601
Freon	367
Freoxid	253
Frianite	115
Frigol	588
Fruitone	30
Fulgayne	109
Fullitin	95
Fumex #3	58
Fumol	583
Fungiseal	433
Fungizyme	716
Fungol	161
Furetone	350
Furnex	163
Fuzon	623
Fybrol	601
Fyrex	687
Galex	446
Gallopont	217
Gamal	250
Gambade	640
Gammacide	116
Gammexane	334
Ganol	699
Gardanthrol	207
Gardinol	217
Gartex	263
Gastex	267
Gatex	267
Gelaglaze	168
Gelamite	309
Gelatine Gum	67
Gelex	176, 217
Gelloid	716
Gelowax	280
Gelva	583
Gem Wax	507
Genasco Primer	81
Generon	268
Genetron	268
Genidust	268
Genitol	268
Genitox	268
Gensol	459
Geon	283
Germ-I-Tol	248
Gesarol	264
Girbotol	277
Glassheen	280
Glaurin	280
Globak	94
Glosso	168
Gluantine	601
Glucarine	280
Glucosate	293
Glufil	7
Glutol	61
Glutoline	4
Glutrin	561
GLV	433
Glycaid	280
Glycerowax	601
Glycidol	269
Glycinol	377
Glycolube	280
Glycopon	280
Glycosine	259
Glycosterin	280
Glyco Wax	280
Glycox	280
Glycyl	258
Glydag	3
Glyecine	270
Glypex	377
Glyptal	271

Trade-Mark	*Number**
Glysorbine	695
Glyzone	211
Goldstik	58
Goodrite	282
Goulac	561
Gradol	277
Grainal	680
Gramix	668
Granophos	30
Graphicol	508
Graphidox	680
Graysol	285
GR-M	217
Groco	290
GR-P	648
GR-S	283, 284
Guantal	433
Gui-a-phene	160
Gulfwax	291
Guminol	615
Gumolite	567
Gunk	187
Guntex	251
GVL	433
GY-4	262
Gyco	264
Gycolan	264
Gycotan	264
Gycuero	264
Hafoil	438
Hagan Phosphate	294
Halazone	433
Halloid	372
Halo	159
Halopont	217
Halowax	296
Hamico	292
Hamp Wax	714
Hansa	270
Harchemex	302
Harcol	302
Harflex	302
Hartal	305
Hartex	305
Hartolan	181
Hartolein	305
Hartopene	305
Harvel	350
Hastelloy	308
Haveg	307

Trade-Mark	*Number**
Haystellite	308
HB-40	433
Helio	270
Heliogen	270
Helioline	715
Heliophan	259
Heliozone	217
Hept	433
Hepteen	451
Herco-HT	311
Hercolyn	309
Herco-Plas	311
Hercose	309
Hercosett	309
Hercosol	309
Herco-Wax	311
Herculite	309
Herculoid	309
Heresite	310
Herkolite	271
Hevealac	280
Heveatex	312
Hexalin	217
Hexatol	563
Hexcide	369
Hexogen	4
Hexsote	369
Hexsulate	369
Heydenol	314
Hibitite	433
Hifoam	231
Hiperco	714
Hippuran	401
Hopcalite	428
Hormodin	420
Hormosan	420
Hornkem	322
Houdrane	327
H-Scale	132
HTH	413
Humidogene	472
Hyalin	679
Hyamine	587
Hycar	331
Hycol	420
Hydel Acid	36
Hydralase	716
Hydraldehyde	699
Hydralo	80
Hydraphthal	217
Hydratex	329

Trade-Mark	*Number**
Hydrene	86
Hydrex	303
Hydrholac	563
Hydrine	17
Hydrite	276
Hydrocal	669
Hydrocide	563
Hydrocop	380
Hydrodarco	189
Hydrofol	596
Hydroform	493
Hydrogel	191
Hydrogum	546
Hydrol	604
Hydrolac	101
Hydrolal	278
Hydrolase	716
Hydrolic	699
Hydroliquid	716
Hydrolite	65
Hydrolux	695
Hydrolyn	309
Hydromalin	280
Hydromite	669
Hydron	270
Hydrone	217
Hydronol	217
Hydronyx	480
Hydropel	168
Hydrophil	98
Hydroresin	280
Hydros	104
Hydroscent	520
Hydrosol	380
Hydrosorb	2
Hydrostrip	716
Hydro Sulvat	480
Hydrotan	217
Hydrotex	86
Hydroxamide	302
Hydroxanil	398
Hydroxcene	356
Hydroxene	58
Hydrowax	280
Hydrozin	716
Hyfac	230
Hyferox	35
Hyflex	350
Hyflo	352
Hygell	150
Hygienized	535
Hyglin	631
Hyglo	459
Hygro	210
Hygrola	161
Hygrolit	360
Hylite	598
Hymag	253
Hymolit	305
Hymolon	305
Hymotol	305
Hyodol	596
Hypol	9
Hyrex	273
Hytergen	305
Ichthymall	401
Ichthynat	314
Ichtozyme	235
Igepal	270
Igepon	270
I G Wax	270
Immersol	472
Imol	611
Impedex	217
Impermex	83
Impregnole	695
Inceloid	51
Inconel	344
Indalone	204
Indanthrene	270
Indigolite	716
Indigosol	121
Indoil	617
Indonex	617
Indopol	617
Indopon	563
Indralatum	339
Indulin	336
Indur	548
Indusoil	336
Infrax	125
Infusite	666
Ingresene	58
Inhibitol	65
Inkowax	177
Insecti-Sol	498
Insulac	113
Insurok	555
Intawax	349
Integritol	270
Intracol	634

Trade-Mark	*Number**
Intral	634
Intramine	634
Intrapol	596
Inulose	354
Invadine	152
Inventol	397
Iodeikon	401
Ionac	35
Ionamine	242
Ion-Ose	454
Irga	264
Irgalevone	264
Irgamine	264
Irgatan	264
Iridite	552
Iso Beeswax	35
Isocel	75
Isocreme	181
Iso Gum	535
Isohol	280
Isolac	217
Iso-Lan	281
Isolene	446
Isoline	715
Isomal	278
Isomerpin	217
Isonol	480
Isorome	211
Isothan	480
Janusol	634
Japcere	480
Japsol	280
Japsyn	528
Jasminol	269
Jatene	58
Jetal	17
Jet Wax	507
Jozite	607
Kadox	455
Kal	356
Kalco	35
Kalinex	268
Kalista	111
Kalite	531
Kalpinol	356
Kalva	357
Kalvan	681
Kanatol #1	58
Kandar	673
Kaolloid	650
Kapak	477
Kaplex	356
Kapsol	474
Karbate	442
Karbol	601
Karmex	217
Kasil	510
Kasinol	62
Kastolene	62
Katanol	270
Katazyme	637
Kathro	181
Katigen	270
Katozyme	637
Kaykote	359
Kelapol	660
Kelcoloid	362
Kelgin	362
Kelite	363
Kellin	606
Kellsoy	606
Keloform	259
Keltex	362
Keltone	362
Kel-Vi-Tol	606
Kem	309
Kemidol	669
Kemithal	334
Kemopene	364
Kemopole	364
Kempol	587
Kemsolene	180
Kendex	365
Kenoline	720
Kensol	365
Keralin	35
Kerodor	278
Keroid	664
Kerozone	278
Kessco Wax	366
Ketonone	35
Kierasol	118
Kierex	600
Kierol	556
Kierole	695
Kierolene	502
Kilfoam	55
Kirksite	444
Kiton	152
Kleanrol	217

Trade-Mark	*Number* *
Klearol	601
Kloranol	24
Koda	643
Kodalith	224
Kodaloid	224
Kodalon	224
Kokobace	464
Kolac	673
Kolineum	369
Kollamine	270
Koloc	451
Kolstrip	696
Komel	361
Konag	443
Konate	35
Kontakt	230
Kopan	198
Kopol	546
Koreon	439
Koresin	266
Korez	73
Kornite	24
Korogel	283
Koroseal	283
Kosmink	664
Kosmovar	664
Kotol	451
Kovat	449
KP-23	474
Krafteen	371
Kragel	371
Kralex	371
Kraystay	371
Krebolith	217
Krel	721
Kremol	588
Kremoline	588
Krenite	217
Kriston	283
Kromasperse	375
Kromeflake	304
Kromeko	118
Kromfax	122
Kromide	322
Kromoid	411
Kronisol	474
Kronitex	474
Kruzite	287
Kryocide	499
Kryoflux	499
Kryolith	499

Trade-Mark	*Number* *
Kupramite	428
Kutwell	236
Kyrite	200
Lacet	168
Lacolene	106
Lactanx	561
Lactol Spirits	45
Lactonate	601
Lamepon	526
Lamicoid	424
Laminac	35
Lanaclarin	217
Lanafin	615
Lanalbine	472
Lanaset resin	35
Lanese	132
Lanette Wax	217
Lanitol	65
Lanol	24
Lanole	695
Lanolubric	327
Lanone	170
Laolin	131
Lapidolith	601
Larsynol	58
Larvacide	341
Larvex	378
Latekoll	4
Latol	657
Lauralene	86
Lauramine	380
Laurelin	58
Laureltex	380
Laurelton Oil	58
Laurene	86
Laurex	451
Laurezol	380
Laurine	278
Lauxite	379
Lauxtol	433
Lava	524
Lavekol	270
Lavosal	118
Lawsone	608
Laxol	58
Leadlube	53
Leafox	455
Lecivit	355
Ledate	681
Lef	405

Trade-Mark	*Number* *
Lemenone	280
Lentin	420
Leonil	270
Leophen	270
Leptyne	513
Lesamite	650
Lethane	563
Lethelaire	689
Leucogene	217
Leucosol	217
Leucothol	480
Leucotrope	104, 716
Leukanol	563
Leukopal	4
Levana	573
Levelene	25
Levelol	35
Leveltex	398
Levenol	240, 615
Lewisol	385
Lewtex	305
Lexol	411
Lexone	217
Lignasan	217
Lignocol	314
Lignolite	405
Lignone	345
Lilanal	269
Lilanthal	269
Linazol	70
Lincos	430
Lindol	132
Linogel	62
Linsize	161
Lionite	265
Liovatine	573
Liqro	336
Liquadol	6
Liquafix	6
Liro	483
Lissolamine	334
Literite	387
Lithfix	28
Lithoform	30
Lithos	622
Lithosol	217
Lithotine	592
Lizarol	270
Loabond	131
Loalin	131
Lo-Bax	413
Lobeite	279
Longolin	707
Loomkill	388
Loosol	643
Lopor	236
Lorinol	217
Lorium	280
Loro	217
Lorol	217
Lorridol	86
Lotol	451
Loupene	716
Loupole	716
LP-3	648
Lub-Base	66
Lubocole	58
Lubosan	58
Lubrene	305
Lubrex	329
Lubriknit	360
Lubriseal	649
Lubrisol	601
Lubrol	161
Lucidol	390
Lucite	217
Lucitone	217
Ludigol	270
Lufax	563
Lumarith	132
Lumercine	716
Luminal	713
Luperco	390
Luperox	390
Lupogum	716
Lupomin	716
Luposec	716
Luposol	716
Lusterine	727
Lusteroff	556
Lusterpine	727
Lustron	433
Luxol	217
Luxolene	210
Lykopon	563
Lynol	100
Lyofix	152
Lyrone	305
Lysol	382
Lytonate	601

Trade-Mark	*Number**
Magbond	253
Magicol	305
Magnesol	706
Makalot	399
Manganox	253
Manucol	12
Mapico pigments	94
Mapro Degum	480
Maprofix	480
Mapromin	480
Mapromol	554
Maproset	480
Marabond	405
Marasperse	405
Maratan	405
Marathon Extract	405
Marblette	406
Marbon	407
Marcanol	398
Marcanon	398
Marcaton	398
Marcol	236
Marcomin	398
Mardol	408
Markset	17
Marmix	407
Marvanol	409
Marvantex	409
Marvinol	410
Maskol	679
Mastolyn	309
Mattolin	269
Maxitol	198
Maypon	414
Mazein	176
MBT	217
Meadol	417
Mearlin	418
Medicol	588
Mekon	695
Melantine	152
Meleine	716
Melhi resin	309
Melilotin	259
Melioran	313
Mellol	309
Mellostrine	472
Melmac	35
Melotan	137
Melotex	35
Meloward	371

Trade-Mark	*Number**
Meltopax	653
Mentor	236
Mentor Oil	618
Meon	100
Mercaid	17
Mercepen	601
Mercerade	480
Mercerite	24
Mercerol	573
Merceron	601
Mercetex	615
Mercevine	166
Mercine	354
Merclor	433
Mercol ST	646
Mercopen	556
Merco Softener	356
Merfenel	297
Merj	681
Merko	513
Merlon	443
Merpentine	217
Merphenyl	297
Merpol	217
Mersize	433
Mersol	433
Mersolite	65, 90
Mertanol	433
Mertela	11
Mervar	459
Metachloron	18
Metalate	621
Metalex	393
Metallac	423
Metaphene	727
Metasap	423
Metasil	394
Metasol	109
Metex	393
Methacrol	217
Methasan	433
Methazate	451
Methide	433
Methocel	207
Metholene Acid	58
Methox	474
Methyl Tuad	681
Methyl Zimate	681
Metol	224
Metopryl	475

Trade-Mark	*Number**
Metric	58
Metrosol	380
Metrox	422
Metso	510
Mettap	217
Meufa	433
Mexol	628
Micabond	173
Micalith	142
Micarta	714
Micatex	83
Micatone	232
Michelene	425
Micris	165, 384
Microbex	413
Microdol	224
Micromet	114
Micromul	535
Micronex	163
Micronite	569
Midophate	231
Migasol	152
Migralube	113
Milban	217
Milducide	556, 717
Millical	199
Millimar	681
Milmer	433
Miltex	159
Mimax	513
Mineralite	253
Minerol	100
Minicol	227
Minotint	100
Minovar	344
Minpro	217
Minralex	94
Minvar	344
Mipol	435
Miragum	483
Miranol	432
Mirasol	483
Miscibol	280
Mitin	264
Modicol	464
Modinal	217
Modulex	329
Modx	295
Moistol	615
Moldex	280
Moldine	86

Trade-Mark	*Number**
Moldlube	305
Moldol	508
Moldslip	280
Moly	156
Mondur	433
Monel	344
Monex	451
Monnowax	188
Monoastral	217
Monol	231
Monolanic Acid	665
Monoplex	549
Monopole oil	716
Monostearin	280
Monosulph	464
Monothiurad	433
Monsanto Salt	433
Montar	433
Monten	86
Monty Wax	714
Mor-Bond	437
Morcosize	437
Mordaline	720
Mordantine	58
Morfex	451
Morlex	122
Morpel	437
Morpeloil	437
Morpeltex	437
Morpelwet	437
Morwet	437
Mowilith	4
Mowital	4
Moytol	615
2-MT	217
Muginol	269
Mugol	217
Mulag	508
Mullfrax	125
Mulsag	508
Mulsene	280
Mulsivon	601
Mulsor	634
Multicel	639
Multifen	270
Multiflex	199
Multi-Plast	710
Multiwax	506
Murac	179
Mycoban	217

Trade-Mark	Number*
Nacan	441
Naccolene	441
Nacconol	441
Naccosol	441
Naccotan	441
Nacelan	441
Naftex	710
Naftolen	710
Nalex	449
Namate	681
Naphthanil	217
Naphtholite	45
Naphthone	616
Naphthosol	112
Napoleum Spirits	243
Napso	210
Napterge	398
Naptex	210
Naptol	593
Naugahyde	673
Naugalite	673
Naugatex	451
Naugaton	673
Naybasol	452
Nayben	452
Nayfex	452
Naypar	452
Nayrez	452
N. D. G. A.	465
Neantine	278
Necton	236
Neetol	411
Negamine	634
Nekal	270
Nelgin	280
Nelio	279
Neobon	73
Neocid	264
Neo-Fat	66
Neol	127
Neolan	152
Neolene	502, 582
Neolite	284
Neolith	354
Neolyn	309
Neomerpin	217
Neonaphtol	398
Neopen	217
Neophax	610
Neopone R	578
Neoprene	217
Neosol	585
Neotone	217
Neozone	217
Neozyme	567
Nerium	160
Nervastral	568
Neufume	480
Neutracol	727
Neutraline	214
Neutrol	246
Neutroleum	260
Neutronyx	480
Neutroscent	260
Neutrotone	413
Nevasota	453
Nevillac	453
Nevillite	453
Nevilloid	453
Nevindine	453
Nevinol	453
Nevoll	453
Nevsol	453
Nevtex	453
Niagathal	461
Niaproof	460
Niathal	461
Nibren	4
Nichrome	212
Nicotrol	28
Nilo	573
Nimcol	402
Ninol	462
Niox	217
Nipabenzyl	572
Nipabutyl	572
Nipasept	572
Nipasol	281
Nipocer	280
Ni-Soap	240
Nit-O-Nol	535
Nitramac	404
Nitramon	217
Nitron	433
Nixonoid	463
Noca	114
Nodoroil	56
Nogas	217
Noheev	510
Nojel	161
Nomo	472
Nonisol	17

Trade-Mark	*Number**	*Trade-Mark*	*Number**
Nopalcol	464	Nycolene	457
Nopco	464	Nycolloid	457
Nopcogen	464	Nylonol	535
Nopcosorb	464	Nyltex	556
Nopcov	464	Nynit	380
Norane	695	Nypene	453
Norbide	467	Nytron	599
Norit	46		
Norot	695	Oakite	473
Northide	466	Ocenol	217
Northol	466	Octab	553
Nor-Zone	167	Octa-Klor	332
Novac	297	Octimet	553
Noval ketone	670	Octoate	626
Novelione	451	Odorfix	679
Novex	451	Odorol	679
Novocaine	713	Odrene	278
Novocell	559	OEL	673
Novolak	77	Oilate	469
Novonacco	441	Oildag	3
Novowax	280	Oilex	618
Nox-Fome	436	Oilsolate	549
Nuact	469	Oilzout	696
Nuade	469	Oitioil	102
Nuba	453	Olamine	380
Nuban	673	Olate	524
Nubon	673	Olev-ol	596
Nubro	459	Oiltex	380
Nuchar	336	Olivene	143, 168
Nullapon	270	Olivesco	179
Nulocrystal	468	Ondal	217
Nulomoline	468	Ondulum	280
Nuocide	469	Onesta	524
Nuodex	469	Onyxide	480
Nuodite	469	Onyxol	480
Nuolate	469	Opalon	433
Nuomix	469	Opalwax	217
Nuosperse	469	Opax	653
Nuron	334	Opoil	571
Nuroz	459	Oranap	716
Nuso	236	Orangeol	217
Nusol	103	Oranit	313
Nusope	469	Orapret	313
Nutrosan	472	Oratan	563
Nutx	295	Oratol	716
Nuva	270	Orchidee	632
Nuzan	103	Orchidone	632
Nyacet	472	Orel	217
Nyanzym	472	Oridex	198
Nyasil	727	Orolin	482
Nyasol	472	Oronite	482

Trade-Mark	*Number**
Oroplast	4
Oropon	563
Orotan	563
Orthalate	621
Orthamine	227
Orthazite	227
Ortho Bas	24
Orthocat	24
Orthocen	24
Orthochrom	563
Ortho Chrome	720
Orthodye	24
Ortholeum	217
Orthonyl	24
Orthophen	582
Orthopol	24
Orthosil	499
Orthosilk	24
Orthowet	24
Orthozym	563
Orvus	524
Orzol	601
Ovac	451
Oxawax	594
Oxene	211
Oxidex	260
Oxigel	596
Oximony	429
Oxolac	289
Oxolene	587
Oxone	217
Oxydon	214
Oxyfume	122
Oxylite	713
Oxynone	433
Ozonite	524
Ozoturp	214
Ozowax	280
Paco	529
Palasol	720
Palatinol	4
Palatone	207
Palmalene	86
Palmeto Wax	349
Palmitone	66
Palmol	610
Paludrine	334
Panelyte	489
Pantopaque	224
Paracide	319
Parachol	280
Paracol	309
Paracole	58
Paradene	453
Paradi	319
Parador	278
Paradow	207
Paradura	491
Paradyne	233
Parafilm	419
Paraflow	233
Para-flux	295
Paraforce	435
Paralan	41
Para Lene	295
Paralketone	16
Para Lube	295
Paramet	491
Paramin	233
Paramine	65
Paramul	35
Paranol	491
Paranox	233
Para Oil	716
Parapel	17
Parapen	491
Paraplex	549
Parapoid	233
Parapol	435
Parapon	65
Parapont	217
Para Resin	295
Paraseal	598
Parasept	314
Parasheen	233
Paratac	233
Paratex	65
Paratone	233
Paravar	451
Para zene	491
Parazone	217
Par Clay	681
Parez	35
Parical	268
Pariflux	253
Parisul	268
Parlodion	401
Parlon	309
Parmone	217
Parmosa	217
Parmr	94

Trade-Mark	*Number**
Paroïl	55, 498
Parolite	567
Paroxan	95
Parsenol	58
Pechiney	347
Pectinol	563
Peersol	354
Pelinite	256
Pelletex	267
Peltex	86
Pemeko	118
Penacid	720
Penacol	496
Penacolite	496
Penatrol	86
Penchlor	499
Penequik	601
Penesolve	601
Penetex	528
Penetone	494
Penetox	397
Penetralene	601
Penetrex	309
Penetrol	86, 214, 358, 696
Penetrolin	65
Penetrone	168
Penite	499
Pennex	499
Pennsalt	499
Pennsalum	499
Pennsoline	498
Pennwax	505
Penofen	152
Penolene	665
Penoline	720
Penotex	699
Penozone	499
Penros	459
Pensal	499
Pensol	720
Pent-Acetate	582
Pentacizer	314
Pentaform	314
Pental	464
Pentalarm	582
Pentalene	582
Pentalyn	309
Pentamull	314
Pentaphen	582
Pentaryl A	582
Pentasicon	420
Pentasol	582
Pentawax	314
Pentek	314
Pentex	161, 451
Penthanco	495
Pentocine	354
Pentogen	305
Pentoterge	354
Pentrocene	240
Pentrol	358
Pentronate	601
Pentrosulf	398
Penzone	499
Pepacon	615
Pepton 22	35
Peramel	380
Perbunan	611
Perchloron	499
Perclene	217
Peregal	270
Perfectol	671
Perflectol X	433
Perfumol	161
Perkolene	502
Perliton	327
Perlof	573
Perma Carb	544
Perma Cide	544
Perma Fix	544
Permalene	544
Permalith	587
Permalux	217
Permamul	35
Permanite	217
Permanol	433
Perma Par	544
Permasan	433
Perm-Aseptic	538
Perma Terge	544
Permaton	112
Permatox A	138
Perma Wet	544
Permeko	118
Permel resin	35
Permex	309
Permiset	35
Permolite	65
Permount	250
Permutit	503
Peroline	30
Perone	217

Trade-Mark	*Number* *
Peroxol	356
Perpentol	313
Persol	502
Petrex	309
Petrobenzol	56
Petroblend	601
Petroflux	601
Petrohol	611
Petrolene	56
Petrolyte	601
Petromask	211
Petromix	601
Petronate	601
Petronyx	480
Petropol	533
Petrosene	598
Petrosul	498
Petrowet	217
Pharmanil	509
Pharmasol	121
Pharmol	509
Phenac	35
Phenal	52
Phenester	453
Phenex	295
Phenite	52
Pheno	112
Phenoid	136
Phenolite	450
Phenoxetol	572
Phibrolite	511
Philblack	512
Philplast	512
Phi-O-Sol	480
P. H. O.	453
Phomaide	534
Phosflake	164
Phosilage	433
Phosmul	335
Phosphosol	433
Phosphotex	433
Photol	420
PH-PLUS	413
pHR	217
Phthalocine	546
Phygon	673
Picco	497
Piccocizer	497
Piccolastic	497
Piccolyte	497
Piccoumaron	497
Piccovar	497
Piccovol	497
Pictar	497
Pictol	401
Pigmentar	160
Pinalox	304
Pinealco	321
Pineol	65
Pineotrene	380
Pinetrol	240
Pinola	214
Pipazate	451
Pip-Pip	433
Pipsol	433
Pipsolene	433
Pircine	354
Pittchlor	164
Pixol	25
Plaskon	433
Plaspreg Resin	261
Plastac	4
Plastacele	217
Plastak	396
Plastamine Resin	582
Plastex	94
Plasticell	559
Plasticose	240
Plastoflex	4
Plastogen	681
Plastoil	143
Plastol	4
Plastolein	230
Plastomoll	4
Plastone	306
Plastopal	4
Plexene M	563
Plexiglas	563
Plexigum	563
Plexite	563
Plicote	250
Pliochlor	284
Pliofilm	284
Plioflex	284
Plioform	284
Pliolite	284
Pliowax	284
Plumb-O-Sil	444
Pluramine	360
Plyophen	546
Pocolene	533
Polac	58

Trade-Mark	*Number**
Polar	264
Polectron	266
Polefinal	4
Polidase	576
Pol-Mer-Ik	62
Polon	673
Polvin	433
Polyac	217
Polybond	109
Polybutene	611
Polycet	152
Polychlor C	248
Polycol	336
Polyethylene	350
Polyfibre	207
Polyform	217
Polylube	556
Polymel	113, 516
Polymerin	342
Polypen	109
Polyphenyl	264
Polyphos	718
Polyplastex	518
Polysan	548
Poly-Scour	109
Polysorb	109
Polytex	109
Polythene	122
Poly-Tint	710
Polyzime	637
Pomol	116
Ponol	67
Ponolith	373
Ponsol	217
Ponsolve	217
Pontachrome	217
Pontacyl	217
Pontagen	217
Pontalite	217
Pontamine	217
Pontol	217
Porocel	75
Porofos	268
Powersol	521
Prenol	446
Preservatol	679
Prestabit	270
Preventol	4
Primal	563
Primol	611
Printex	535
Printogen	573
Procase	133
Procite	599
Prodag	3
Proflex	280
Prolaurin	280
Prolein	280
Prolon	525
Promulsin	698
Pro-Nyl	604
Proofit	280
Propasol	122
Prorex	598
Prosotex	535
Protectoid	132
Protectol	122
Protegin	281
Protek-Sorb	191
Protela	11
Protenol	171
Protesal	576
Protex Gel	152
Protexol	527
Protobasol	528
Protoba Wax	528
Protoflex	280
Protol	601
Protolin	563
Protonoc	198
Protopet	601
Protosol	720
Protostase	716
Protovac	130
Protowax	528
Protozyme	716
Puerine	411
Puregel	601
Pureode	716
Purepol	168
Puresinol	533
Purite	413
Purogen	411
Purol	214
Purosol	533
Purotex	533
Purozinc	217
PVA	217
Pynol	459
Pyralin	217
Pyrano	433
Pyrax	681

Trade-Mark	*Number**
Pyrazol	573
Pyrefume	495
Pyrene	534
Pyrenone	204
Pyrepel	535
Pyrexcel	495
Pyridium	420
Pyridose	401
Pyrin	520
Pyriscent	520
Pyrobor	50
Pyrofax	122
Pyrogene	152
Pyrol	687
Pyrolene	615
Pyromine	720
Pyronex	305
Pyropel	354
Pyropruf	638
Pyrotex	615
QED	488
Quadrafos	569
Quartol	480
Quasol	535
Quatronyx	480
Quinopol	58
Quinosin	433
Quix	440
Quixite	440
Quixol	167
Radiactine	573
Radul	152
Ramadux	270
Ramapol	270
Ramasit	270
Ramasol	270
Ramol	716
Ramosel	270
Ramoset	270
Ramplex	538
Rapidase	693
Rapidogen	270
Rapidole	695
Rauxene	670
Rauzene	670
Rayamo	541
Raybar	681
Raycal	681
Raycolite	540
Rayconol	601
Raycote	540
Raygel	161
Raylubric	327
Raymix	540
Rayocine	354
Ray-O-Jell	511
Rayol	528, 604
Rayolene	601
Rayonol	305
Rayonthrene	25
Rayonyx	480
Rayox	681
Raysil	681
Raysize	528
Ray-Size	109
Raythro	601
RBH Resin	542
Recla	188
Redium	681
Redmanol	77
Redolene	303
Redotex	703
Redoxyvat	480
Redsol	35
Reducin	573
Reducite	58
Reductone	699
Redux	549
Reflux	653
Refrax	125
Remosil	706
Removene	453
Renesite	74
Renex	74
Reogen	368
Repcolene	544
Repelite	522
Repel-O-Flame	480
Repelon	305
Repelotex	480
Resicol	483
Resifin	152, 716
Resiloid	161
Resilon	674
Resimene	433
Resinette	17
Resinex	306
Resinox	433
Resipon	65
Resistex	488

Trade-Mark	*Number**
Resisto	522
Resistol	210
Resloom	433
Resolin	573
Resonet	327
Resproof	433
Restex	601
Resyn	449
Resynon	67
Retardex	295
Retardine	615
Retardit	480
Retardsol	45
Retravon	152
Retrol	246
Revatol	573
Reversol	604
Revertex	551
Rewettal	17
Rexan O	198
Rexar	459
Rez	379
Rezistal	183
Rezite	433
Rezoglaz	4
Rezowax	280
Rezyl	35
Rhodione	217
Rhodol	217
Rhonite	563
Rhoplex	563
Rhotex	563
Rhothane	563
Rhozyme	563
Richspin	556
Ridacto	557
Rinfors	573
Rinsynol	17
Rio resin	681
Risor	309
Roccal	713
Rocheltex	393
Rockresin	86
Rodine	495
Rodo	681
Roleic	303
Rongalite	270
Ronopole Oil	58
Rootone	30
Rosalamine	556
Rosanol	269
Rosanthrene	152
Rosesol	397
Rosinol	58
Roskol	556
Rosoap	280
Rosopen	556
Rossaloy	565
Rotalin	217
Rotax	681
Royox	567
RPA	217
RSO	547
Rubber-Glo	295
Rubberlith	714
Rubberol	275
Rubbersol	273
Rubbex	396
Rubinol	259
Rub-Sol	56
Rubtack	714
Rubtar	714
Rudol	601
Rufat	712
Rufite	279
Rumetan	508
Rusticon	510
Rustop	41
Rutgers 612	122
Rycolene	548
Rycosol	548
Ryose	400
Sabacide	415
Safex	451
Saflex	433
Salamac	217
Salitone	58
Salixol	269
SALP	58
Salu Gum	720
Sandocarnit	573
Sandopan	573
Sandozol	573
Sanforol	601
Sanicres	109
Saniprene	283
Sanitose	480
Sansoil	499
Santamine	433
Santicizer	433
Santobane	433

Trade-Mark	*Number* *
Santobrite	433
Santocel	433
Santochlor	433
Santocure	433
Santoflex	433
Santol	140
Santolene	433
Santolite	433
Santolube	433
Santomask	433
Santomerse	433
Santophen	433
Santopoid	433
Santopour	433
Santosite	433
Santotan	433
Santovar	433
Santowax	433
Santowhite	433
Sanyon	625
Sapamine	152
Sapanole	472
Sapapine	479
Sapozole	652
Saran	207
Sarkolin	168
Savaco	312
Savaloid	598
Savit	186
Savonafix	260
Scourclean	556
Scourite	535
Scourol	210, 327
Scourolan	95
Scourtex	305
Sebacol	693
Secal	231
Sec-a-seal	503
Seedine	715
Selazate	451
Selectol	62, 224
Selectol A	210
Selectron	513
Selenac	681
Sellogen	716
Semesan	217
Semicat	556
Seminex	351
Septol	214
Seravon	20
Sericite	708
Seriken	305
Serisoap	161
Serisolve	118
Seristan	217
Seritol	472
Seriwol	718
Serizyme	693
Seronex	354
Seroseal	354
Serotram	354
Serrid	196
Serseal	384
Servex	58
Setit	653
Setoran	313
Setsit	681
Seyco	580
Sheerset	35
Shellacol	167, 305
Sherdye	587
Sherolatum	588
Sheroline	588
Sherosol	588
Sherosope	588
Sherowax	588
Shirlan	217
Shopal	625
Sicaseal	280
Sierra White	590
Silanic	591
Silastic	208
Silcalite	253
Silcaride	697
Silcaz	228
Silene	164
Silester	591
Silex	427
Silfrax	125
Silical	297
Silicone	208, 271
Silimite	15
Silkene	502
Silkonol	601
Sil-o-cel	352
Siltex	703
Siltex Gum	480
Silvatol	152
Silvaz	228
Simol	152
Sintra wax	370
Sinturlite	593

Trade-Mark	Number*	Trade-Mark	Number*
Siolite	401	Sol-Tar	95
Sipalin	217	Sol-Tex	727
Sirrix	573	Soltrol	512
Sirvene	147	Sol-U-Bon	25
Sitol	217	Solucene	600
Sixide	167	Solugel	600
Skellysolve	595	Solupon	600
Slozit	356	Solusize	600
Smentoy	83	Solutol	600
Smite	60	Soluwax	600
Snodotte	596	Solux	217
Snofos	268	Solvadine	152
Snow Flake Crystals	599	Solvamin	167
Snow Floss	352	Solvar	583
Snow White Filler	669	Solvatone	122
Soapalite	179	Solvawax	177
Soapotol	168	Solvenal	168
Sobenate	579	Solvenol	309
Socal	616	Solventol	109
Sodacet	460	Solvesso	618
Sodax	504	Solvex	204
Sodite	116	Solvit	231
Sodosil	268	Solvoil	528, 720
Softenol	109	Solvopen	556
Softex	327	Solvose	214
Softol	198	Solvotex	17
Soiliron	624	Solvsol	651
Sokolene	364	Solwax	58, 547
Solac	58	Sombre	354
Sol-Amidine	118	Sonaquol	601
Solantine	441	Sonofin	601
Solapine	13	Sonojell	601
Solbrol	269	Sonolan	601
Solcastol	35	Sonolene	601
Solcornol	35	Sopanox	433
Soldina	615	Sopet	433
Solene	598	Sorbinol	109
Sol Hex	309	Sorbit	17
Solidina	615	Sorbitan	305
Solidogen	270	Sorbo	74
Soligen	4	Sorolene	480
Solinux	606	Soromine	270
Soliol	478	Sovalent	598
Solite	24	Sovaloid	598
Solivol	356, 548	Sovalsol	395
Solmet	109	Sovasol	598
Solophenyl	264	Soyagel	62
Solox	670	Soyalene	62
Solozone	217	Soyflake	606
Solros	273	Soyol	685
Solstock	556	Sozol	548

Trade-Mark	Number*
Span	74
Speedi-Dri	700
Spensol	605
Spermafol	596
Spheron	111
Spotex	535
Spotsol	556
Spra Kast	715
Spray Cop	268
Sprodamine	604
Sprodco	604
Sprodcopen	604
Sprodcoscour	604
Sprodcosol	604
Sprodex	604
Spry	383
Spunsize	161
SRA	217
S. R. O.	84
Stabalin	698
Stabilene	122
Stabilide	401
Stabilisal	4
Stabilite	83, 295
Stabilon	25
Stabinol	309
Stablex	312
Staclor	55
Stacol	280
Stafast	268
Stakleen	356
Stalite	283
Stamptex	675
Standafin	615
Standapol	615
Stanteosine	615
Stanisol	617
Stannochlor	523
Stannoil	58
Stanolene	617
Stanolind	617
Staneosine	615
Stantex	615
Stan-Tone	306
Starbuck Gum	67
Statex	94, 163
Staybelite	309
Stazrite	535
Stearex	94
Stearinall	35
Stearite	714
Stearol	515
Stearonyx	480
Stearoricinol	280
Stearosol	109
Stellar-R Clay	614
Stellite	308
Stenol	217
Sterilan	39
Sterox	433
Sterozol	693
Sterox	433
Stimtox	520
Stod-Sol	56
Stollamine	58
Stroba Wax	280
Strodex D	198
Stymer	433
Styraloy	207
Styramic	433
Styrofoam	207
Styron	207
Subenon	579
Sublac Resin	517
Sublan	280
Suchar	592A
Sul-Castor	600
Sulchlor	126
Sulfadol	86
Sulfamine	601
Sulfan A, B.	268
Sulfanole	695
Sulfanthrene	217
Sulfasan	433
Sulfatex	601
Sulfax	327
Sulfex	601
Sulfindone	441
Sulfogene	217
Sulfoko	356
Sulfol	327
Sulfoline	598
Sulforon	217
Sulfoxite	217
Sulframin	660
Sul-Olive	600
Sulphon	270
Sulphopet	601
Sulphorol	466
Sulphosal	698
Sulphosoap	86
Sulphosol	86

Trade-Mark	*Number**
Sulprene	52
Sulzoate	581
Sunaromes	245
Sunoco Spirits	627
Sunolith	142
Sunproof	451
Sunsoy	606
Sunwax	627
Super Alkali	599
Super-Cel	352
Superclear	716
Super-Floss	352
Supergel	380
Superloid	362
Supermylite	18
Superoxol	420
Supersol	638
Super-Sol	498
Supersulfate	380
Superteck	498
Supertex	94, 716
Supertine	691
Suprafix	270
Supramine	270
Supranol	270
Supratol	305
Suprex	329
Surfax	327
Surfex	531
Suspendite	280
Suspenso	531
Suspensone	280
Sussex Gum	625
Sweetose	609
Swiss Gum	67
Syan	342
Sylca	360
Sylene oil	58
Sylon	431
Sylvenol	207
Synacol	109
Synaryl	14
Synasol	122
Syncast	597
Syncoat	597
Synco Resins	597
Syndeet	673
Synektan	716
Synkopon	718
Synoca	114
Synosol	528
Synotex	528
Syn-o-tol	210
Synprolac	635
Synprowax	113
Syn-Tac	295
Syntergent K	464
Syntex	159, 251
Synthane	633
Synthecin	600
Synthe-Copal	546
Synthenol	606
Synthetex	604
Synthogel	436
Synthol	275
Synthomenthol	88
Synthrapol	67
Synthravon	67
Syntrag	625
Synvar	636
Synvaren	636
Synvarite	636
Synvarol	636
Syrase	693
Systenyll	58
Syton	433
Syzon	601
Tackol	433
Takalab	637
Talase	637
Tallene	704
Tallex	704
Tallofin	615
Tallosan	270
Tallowene	67
Talp	314
Tam	653
Tamol	563
Tanak	35
Tanarc	92
Tanasol	716
Tanax	35
Tanolin	411
Tanoyl	464
Tantaloy	243
Tantung	243
Tarene	446
Tarlene	720
Tarmul	699
Tarnel	160
Tarol	309

Trade-Mark	*Number**
Tarpyn	459
Tartarone	58
Tartrazole	480
Tec	643
Teca	643
Tecmangam	304
Tec-Quinol	643
Tecsol	643
Tectase	695
Tectyl	677
Teepol	585
Teflon	217
Tegacid	280
Tegin	280
Teglac	35
Tego film	549
Tegosept	280
Tego Stearate	280
Tegul	644
Telkanol	198
Telloy	681
Telura	236
Tellurac	681
Tenacell	559
Tenesol	140
Tenex	273
Tenite	643
Tensol	634
Tepidone	217
Tergamine	240
Tergavon	152
Tergitol	122
Tergolene	195
Tergopon	240
Terposol	309
Terra Tox	719
Tersan	218
Tervan	236
Terylene	334
Tet	315
Tetracarnit	573
Tetrakierol	480
Tetral	217
Tetralin	217
Tetramine	122
Tetranol	65
Tetrapol	270
Tetrasan	480
Tetrasol	17
Tetrolin	615
Tetrone	217
Tetrosan	480
Texamine	168
Texavon	35
Tex-Dul	464
Texel	535
Tex-O-Dor	278
Texogum	528
Texol	109
Texolan	528
Textac	309
Textarid	601
Textase	403
Textee	210
Textile Spirits	180
Textiline	601
Textiloc	398
Textolite	716
Textone	413
Textopet	601
Thalid	433
Thalloid	161
Thanasol	309
Thanite	309
Theop	280
Thermax	681
Thermoflex	217
Thermoil	683
Thermol	535
Thermoplex	549
Thermoprene	283
Thiamate	227
Thiodor	278
Thiofide	433
Thiogen	710
Thiokol	648
Thional	573
Thionex	217
Thionone	317
Thiosan	218
Thiotax	433
Thiovanol	238
Thiurad	433
Thiuram	217
Thor	130
Thyon	512
Ti-Bar	217
Ti-Cal	217
Tidolith	667
Tilite	499
Timber Tox	719
Timonox	645

Trade-Mark	*Number**
Tinofix	264
Tinopal	264
Tinophen	264
Tintinol	100
Tintol	604
Ti-Pure	217
Tiron	376
Ti-Sil	217
Titafin	652
Titalene	652
Titamine	652
Titanalba	253
Titanex	652
Titanite	652
Titanole	652
Titanolith	142
Titanox	654
Titaphene	652
Titapole	652
Titawet	652
Titazole	652
Ti-Tone	217
Tollac	453
Tolu-Sol	585
Tonkene	217
Tonox	451
Tonsil	570
Tornesite	309
Torridex	695
Toxaphene	309
Tracel	304
Tragasol	656
Tragon	656
Tragsub	716
Tragtex	67
Tramolin	309
Tramsize	161
Transote	547
Transphalt	497
Trapineol	480
Trek	442
Trenamine	13
Treopax	653
Tretolite	658
Trex 40	288
Tri-A-Mine	575
Trianol	168
Triapon	198
Triasol	122
Tribase	444
Tricatonate	380
Triclene	217
Tridee	713
Trigamine	280
Trikalin	280
Trilene	334
Trimene	451
Trimol	62
Tri-Ol	601
Triox	116
Trisila	30
TRI-SO	391
Trisolvoil	502
Trisulfon	573
Triton	563
Trolvoil	56
Tromete	706
Tromex	706
Trono	50
Trostol	122
Troxide	700
Trukon	305
Truline Binder	309
Tuads	681
Tuex	451
Tunguran	4
Turgum	329
Turkelene	280
Turpenol	35
Tween	74
Tycol	651
Tygon	674
Tylose	270
Ty-Ply	681
Typowax	177
Tyron	340
Tysonite	681
UAL	217
Ubapol	662
Ubatex	662
Ucon	122
Uformite	549
Ulto	295
Ultracene	660
Ultramine	660
Ultranate	70
Ultrapol	660
Ultrapon	660
Ultrapone DL	578
Ultrasene	70
Ultrasorb	70

Trade-Mark	*Number**
Vinylsol	52
Vinyon	122
Vinysol	52
Violamine	270
Violite	695
Viscanol	119
Viscoform	573
Viscoloid	217
Viscosene	600
Viscosine	100
Viskoplus	4
Viskord	690
Vispronal	4
Vistac	4
Vistanex	4
Vitasol	118
Vitoloil	513
Vitreosil	647
Vitrolan	573
Viv	309
Vixon	674
V-meth-L	689
Vodol	545
Volclay	33
Volite	553
Voltex	664
Vuelite	433
Vuepak	433
Vulcalock	283
Vulcanex	217
Vulcanoil	52
Vulcanol	13
Vulcanosol	270
Vulcoid	173
Vulcone	217
Vulkacit	4
Vulprene	52
Vultac	582
Vultamol	4
Vultex	272
Vultramine	270
Vultrol	283
Vycor	178
Vyram	433
Warco	695
Warcocide	695
Warcofix	695
Warcoplex	695
Warcosan	695
Warcosol	695
Warpot	161
Washine	696
Weavelok	695
Weedone	30
Weetose	400
Weightex	615
Weirite	701
Weirton	701
Weirzin	701
Weldalene	253
Weldwood	672
Wetanol	280
Wetol	153
Wetsit	716
Wettal	231
Wetzout	696
Whitene	707
Whitetex	435
Whitex	707
Wigo	459
Wilcor	710
Wilcorite	710
Wilcorol	710
Wilmac	710
Wilmex	710
Witcarb R	714
Witcogum	714
Witcolac	714
Witresin	714
Wolman Salts	43
Wooline	671
Woolrex	598
Woolube	604
Woolustre	556
Wooncolite	720
Wooncoluse	720
Wooncosol	720
Worstex	535, 598
Wyex	329
Wyobond	722
Wyrol	611
Wytase	589
Xerol	259
Xtafoam	58
Xylex	249
Xynocol	480
Xyonomine	480
Xyno Resin	480
Xynoset	480

Trade-Mark	*Number**
Yarmor	309
Yarnolene	305
Yelkin	566
Yumidol	280
Zafil	73
Zamak	455
Zanolix	58
Zatex	73
Z-B-X	451
Zelan	217
Zenite	217
Zeo-Dur	503
Zeogel	83
Zeo-Karb	503
Zephiran	713
Zerex	217
Zerice	236
Zerlate	217
Zerok	73
Zerolene	616
Zerone	217
Zikol	459
Zilloy	455
Zimate	681
Zinar	459
Zinlac	724
Zinol	459
Zin-O-Lyte	217
Zintox	268
Zipolite	567
Zirconite	653
Zircopax	653
Zircotan	563
Zirex	459
Zirkonalba	253
Zirkosil	253
Zirmet	253
Zirnu	253
Ziropax	653
Zito Chromate	455
Zitro	273
Zolon	674
Zonite	725
Zopaque	142
Zophar	726
Zophite	726
Zurnoil	727
Zyklon	35
Zymezate	613
Zymino	289
Zymol	62

LIST D

Number	*Firm*
1	Abbott Laboratories, Chicago, Ill.
2	Abrasive Co., Philadelphia, Pa.
3	Acheson Colloids Corp., Port Huron, Mich.
4	Advance Solvents and Chem. Corp., New York, N. Y.
5	Agawam Chemicals Inc., West Springfield, Mass.
6	Agfa-Ansco Corp., Binghampton, N. Y.
7	Agicide Labs., Milwaukee, Wis.
8	Akron Chemical Co., Akron, O.
9	Aktivin Corp., New York City, N. Y.
10	Alberene Stone Corp. of Virginia, Schuyler, Va.
11	Albi Chem. Corp., New York City, N. Y.
12	Albright and Wilson Ltd., Oldbury, Birmingham, England
13	Alco Oil and Chem. Corp., Philadelphia, Pa.
14	Alkydol Labs. Inc., Cicero, Ill.
15	Allis-Chalmers Mfg. Co., Milwaukee, Wis.
16	Alox Corp., Niagara Falls, N. Y.
17	Alrose Chemical Co., Cranston, R. I.
18	Althouse Chem. Co., Reading, Pa.
19	Aluminum Co. of America, New York City, N. Y.

Number *Firm*

20 Amalgamated Chem. Corp., Philadelphia, Pa.
21 Amco Chem. Corp., Newark, N. J.
22 Amer. Agricultural Chem. Co., New York City, N. Y.
23 Amer. Alkyd Industries Inc., Carlstadt, N. J.
24 Amer. Aniline and Extract Co., Philadelphia, Pa.
25 Amer. Aniline Products Co., New York City, N. Y.
26 Amer. Anode Co., Akron, O.
27 Amer. Brass Co., Waterbury, Conn.
28 Amer. British Chem. Supplies, New York City, N. Y.
29 Amer. Cellulose Co., Indianapolis, Ind.
30 Amer. Chem. Paint Co., Ambler, Pa.
31 Amer. Chlorophyll Inc., Washington, D. C.
32 Amer. Cholesterol Products Inc., Milltown, N. J.
33 Amer. Colloid Co., Chicago, Ill.
34 Amer. Crayon Co., Sandusky, O.
35 Amer. Cyanamid and Chem. Corp., New York City,, N. Y.
36 Amer. Dyewood Co., New York City, N. Y.
37 Amer. Extract Co., Port Allegany, Pa.
38 Amer. Firstoline Corp., New York City, N. Y.
39 Amer. Fluoride Corp., New York City, N. Y.
40 Amer. LaFrance Foamite Corp., Elmira, N. Y.
41 Amer. Lanolin Corp., Lawrence, Mass.
42 Amer. Lecithin Corp., Elmhurst, N. Y.
43 Amer. Lumber and Treating Co., Chicago, Ill.
44 Amer. Maize Products Co., New York City, N. Y.

Number *Firm*

45 Amer. Mineral Spirit Co., New York City, N. Y.
46 Amer. Norit Co., New York City, N. Y.
47 Amer. Oil and Supply Co., Newark, N. J.
48 Amer. Phenolic Corp., Chicago, Ill.
49 Amer. Plastics Corp., New York City, N. Y.
50 Amer. Potash and Chem. Corp., Trona, Cal.
51 Amer. Products Mfg. Co., New Orleans, La.
52 Amer. Resinous Chemicals Corp., Peabody, Mass.
53 Amer. Smelting and Refin- Co., New York City, N. Y.
54 Amer. Zinc Sales Co., Columbus, O.
55 Ammeco Chemicals Inc., New York City, N. Y.
56 Anderson-Prichard Oil Corp., Chicago, Ill.
57 Ansbacher Siegle Corp., Rosebank, N. Y.
58 Apex Chemical Co. Inc., Elizabeth, N. J.
59 Applied Chemical Corp., New York City, N. Y.
60 Aqua-Sec Corp., New York City, N. Y.
61 Arabol Mfg. Co., New York City, N. Y.
62 Archer-Daniels-Midland Co., Minneapolis, Minn.
63 Arco Co., Cleveland, O.
64 Aridye Corp., Fairlawn, N. J.
65 Arkansas Co., Newark, N. J.
66 Armour and Co., Chicago, Ill.
67 Arnold, Hoffman and Co. Inc., Providence, R. I.
68 Aromatic Products Inc., New York City, N. Y.
69 Atlantic Chem. Co., Centredale, R. I.
70 Atlantic Refining Co., Philadelphia, Pa.
71 Atlantic Research Associates, Newtonville, Mass.

Number	Firm
72	Atlantic Stainpruf Co., Chatham, N. J.
73	Atlas Mineral Prod. Co., Mertztown, Pa.
74	Atlas Powder Co., Wilmington, Del.
75	Attapulgus Clay Co., Philadelphia, Pa.
76	Baird and McGuire, Holbrook, Mass.
77	Bakelite Corp., New York City, N. Y.
78	Baker and Co. Inc., Newark, N. J.
79	Baker Castor Oil Co., New York City, N. Y.
80	Baker Chem. Co., J. T., Phillipsburg, N. J.
81	Barber Asphalt Corp., Barber, N. J.
82	Bareco Oil Co., Tulsa, Okla.
83	Baroid Sales Division, Los Angeles, Cal.
84	Barrett Co., New York City, N. Y.
85	B. B. Chemical Co., Cambridge, Mass.
86	Beacon Co., Boston, Mass.
87	Behr-Manning Corp., Troy, N. Y.
88	Bendix Chemical Corp., New York City, N. Y.
89	Bennett-Clark Co. Inc., Nacogdoches, Tex.
90	Berk and Co., F. W., New York City, N. Y.
91	Bethlehem Steel Co., Bethlehem, Pa.
92	Bick and Co., Reading, Pa.
93	Billings-Chapin Co., Cleveland, O.
94	Binney and Smith Co., New York City, N. Y.
95	Bischoff Co., Ernest, New York City, N. Y.
96	Blakeslee and Co., G. S., Chicago, Ill.
97	Boake, Roberts and Co. Ltd., A., London, England
98	Bopf-Whittam Corp., Linden, N. J.
99	Borden Co., New York City, N. Y.
100	Borne Scrymser Co., Elizabeth, N. J.
101	Bowman and Co., Charles, New York City, N. Y.
102	Brazil Oiticica Inc., New York City, N. Y.
103	Brewers Scientific Labs., Rahway, N. J.
104	Brotherton and Co. Ltd., Leeds, England
105	Brown Co., Berlin, N. H.
106	Brown Co., R. J., St. Louis, Mo.
107	Bryant Chem. Corp., Quincy, Mass.
108	Bugbird Co., H. C., Hoboken, N. J.
109	Burkart-Schier Chem. Co., Chattanooga, Tenn.
110	Buromin Co., Pittsburgh, Pa.
111	Cabot, Godfrey L., Boston, Mass.
112	Calco Chem. Co., Bound Brook, N. J.
113	Caldwell Co., Akron, O.
114	Calgon Inc., Pittsburgh, Pa.
115	Cal. Industrial Minerals Co., Friant, Cal.
116	Cal. Spray Chem. Co., Richmond, Cal.
117	Calorizing Co., Pittsburgh, Pa.
118	Campell and Co., John, New York City, N. Y.
119	Canadian Aniline and Extract Co., Hamilton, Ont., Canada
120	Cantol Wax Co., Bloomington, Ind.
121	Carbic Color and Chem. Co., New York City, N. Y.
122	Carbide and Carbon Chem. Corp., New York City, N. Y.
123	Carbola Chem. Co., Natural Bridge, N. Y.
124	Carbolineum Wood Preserving Co., Milwaukee, Wis.

Number	Firm
125	Carborundum Co., Niagara Falls, N. Y.
126	Carlise Chem. Works, Reading, O.
127	Carlstadt Chem. Co., Carlstadt, N. J.
128	Carnegie-Illinois Steel Corp., Pittsburgh, Pa.
129	Carolina Aniline and Ext. Co., Charlotte, N. C.
130	Casein Co. of America, New York City, N. Y.
131	Catalin Corp., New York City, N. Y.
132	Celanese Corp., New York City, N. Y.
133	Central Soya Co. Inc., Ft. Wayne, Ind.
134	Cerophyl Labs., Kansas City, Mo.
135	Cerro de Pasco Copper Corp., New York City, N. Y.
136	Chalmers Chem. Co., Newark, N. J.
137	Champion Fiber Co., Canton, N. C.
138	Chapman Chemical Co., Chicago, Ill.
139	Char Products Co., Indianapolis, Ind.
140	Charlotte Chemical Labs., Charlotte, N. C.
141	Chase Driers and Chemicals Inc., W. S., Pittsburgh, Pa.
142	Chemical and Pigment Co., Baltimore, Md.
143	Chemical Oil Processing Co., Toronto, Canada
144	Chemical Process Co., San Francisco, Cal.
145	Chemo Puro, Long Island City, N. Y.
146	Chesebrough Mfg. Co., New York City, N. Y.
147	Chicago Rawhide Mfg. Co., Chicago, Ill.
148	Chipman Chem. Co., Bound Brook, N. J.
149	Chiris Co., Antoine, New York City, N. Y.
150	Chittenden Turner Co., Boston, Mass.
151	Chrystal, Chas. B., Co., New York City, N. Y.
152	Ciba Co., New York City, N. Y.
153	Clarion Chemical Corp., Newark, N. J.
154	Cleary Corp., W. A., New Brunswick, N. J.
155	Cliffs-Dow Chem. Co., Marquette, Mich.
156	Climax Molybdenum Co., New York City, N. Y.
157	Clinton Industries Inc., Clinton, Ia.
158	Cloroben Corp., Jersey City, N. J.
159	Colgate-Palmolive-Peet Co., Jersey City, N. J.
160	Colledge Inc., E. W., Cleveland, O.
161	Colloids Inc., Newark, N. J.
162	Columbia Alkali Corp., New York City, N. Y.
163	Columbian Carbon Co., New York City, N. Y.
164	Columbian Chemical Co., Pittsburgh, Pa.
165	Commerce Oil Corp., Warren, Pa.
166	Commercial Products Co., New York City, N. Y.
167	Commercial Solvents Corp., New York City, N. Y.
168	Commonwealth Color and Chem. Co., Brooklyn, N. Y.
169	Consolidated Water Power & Paper Co., Wisconsin Rapids, Wis.
170	Continental Chemical Co., Detroit, Mich.
171	Continental Chemical Co., New York City, N. Y.
172	Continental Chemical Co., Passaic, N. J.
173	Continental Diamond Fibre Co., Newark, Del.

Number	Firm
174	Cooper and Co., T. G., Philadelphia, Pa.
175	Coppenweld Steel Co., Glassport, Pa.
176	Corn Products Refining Co., New York City, N. Y.
177	Cornelius Products Co., New York City, N. Y.
178	Corning Glass Co., Corning, N. Y.
179	Cowles Detergent Co., Cleveland, O.
180	C. P. Chemical Solvents Inc., New York City, N. Y.
181	Croda Ltd., Rawcliffe Bridge, Goole, Yorks, England.
182	Croton Chemical Corp., New York City, N. Y.
183	Crucible Steel Co., New York City
184	Cudahy Packing Co., Chicago, Ill.
185	Culligan Zeolite Co., Northbrook, Ill.
186	Cuprinol Inc., Boston, Mass.
187	Curran Corp., Malden, Mass.
188	Damascus Mfg. Corp., Cleveland, O.
189	Darco Corp., New York City, N. Y.
190	Davies-Young Soap Co., Dayton, O.
191	Davison Chem. Corp., Baltimore, Md.
192	Deep Rock Oil Corp., Chicago, Ill.
193	Defender Photo-Supply Co., Rochester, N. Y.
194	DeLamar and Son, J. H., Chicago, Ill.
195	De Paul Chemical Co., Long Island City, N. Y.
196	Derris Inc., New York City, N. Y.
197	Dewey and Almy Chem. Co., Cambridge, Mass.
198	Dexter Chemical Corp., New York City, N. Y.
199	Diamond Alkali Co., Painesville, O.
200	Dicalite Co., New York City, N. Y.
201	Dispersions Process Inc., New York City, N. Y.
202	Distillation Products Inc., Rochester, N. Y.
203	Diversey Corp., Chicago, Ill.
204	Dodge and Olcott, New York City, N. Y.
205	Dolge Co., C. B., Westport, Conn.
206	Dorward and Sons Co., San Francisco, Cal.
207	Dow Chem. Co., Midland, Mich.
208	Dow Corning Corp., Midland, Mich.
209	Draper Soap Co., Pawtucket, R. I.
210	Drew and Co. Inc., E. F., New York City, N. Y.
211	Dreyer Co., P. R., New York City, N. Y.
212	Driver Co., Wilbur B., Newark, N. J.
213	Du Bois Co., Cincinnati, O.
214	Ducas Co., B. P., New York City, N. Y.
215	Duché and Sons Inc., T. M., New York City, N. Y.
216	Dunn Co., Thomas W., New York City, N. Y.
217	Du Pont Co., Wilmington, Del.
218	Du Pont Semesan Co., Wilmington, Del.
219	Duriron Co. Inc., Dayton, O.
220	Dye and Chemical Co. Ltd., Kingston, Canada
221	Dyestuff and Chemicals Inc., St. Louis, Mo.
222	Eagle-Picher Lead Co., Cincinnati, O.
223	Eastern Chem. Co., Kenilworth, N. J.
224	Eastman Kodak Co., Rochester,, N. Y.
225	Eaton-Clark Co., Detroit, Mich.
226	Economics Lab. Inc., St. Paul, Minn.

Number	Firm
227	Edwal Labs. Inc., Chicago, Ill.
228	Electro Metallurgical Co., New York City, N. Y.
229	Elgin Softener Corp., Elgin, Ill.
230	Emery Industries, Cincinnati, O.
231	Emulsol Corp., Chicago, Ill.
232	English Mica Co., New York City, N. Y.
233	Enjay Co. Inc., New York City, N. Y.
234	Enthone Co., New Haven, Conn.
235	Enzyco Inc., San Francisco, Cal.
236	Esso Marketers, New York City, N. Y.
237	Eston Chemicals Inc., Los Angeles, Cal.
238	Evans Chemetics Inc., New York City, N. Y.
239	Exolon Co., Tonawanda, N. Y.
240	Fabric Chemicals Co., Jersey City, N. J.
241	Falk and Co., Pittsburgh, Pa.
242	Fancourt and Co., W. F., Philadelphia, Pa.
243	Fansteel Metallurgical Corp., Chicago, Ill.
244	Feedwaters Inc., New York City, N. Y.
245	Felton Chem. Co., Brooklyn, N. Y.
246	Filtrol Corp., Los Angeles, Cal.
247	Filtros Inc., Rochester, N. Y.
248	Fine Organics Inc., New York City, N. Y.
249	Firestone Tire and Rubber Co., Akron, O.
250	Fisher Scientific Co., Pittsburgh, Pa.
251	Flintkote Co., New York City, N. Y.
252	Floridin Co., Warren, Pa.
253	Foote Mineral Co., Philadelphia, Pa.
254	Forest Products Chem. Co., Memphis, Tenn.
255	Formica Insulation Co., Cincinnati, O.
256	France, Campbell and Darling Inc., Kenilworth, N. J.
257	Freedom Oil Co., Pittsburgh, Pa.
258	Fries and Fries, Cincinnati, O.
259	Fries Bros., New York City, N. Y.
260	Fritzchie Bros., New York City, N. Y.
261	Furane Plastics and Chem. Co., Los Angeles, Cal.
262	Galey Mfg. Co., Cleveland, O.
263	Garco Products Inc., Butler, Pa.
264	Geigy Co., New York City, N. Y.
265	General Abrasive Co., Niagara Falls, N. Y.
266	General Aniline Corp., New York City, N. Y.
267	General Atlas Carbon Co., New York City, N. Y.
268	General Chem. Co., New York City, N. Y.
269	General Drug Co., New York City, N. Y.
270	General Dyestuffs Corp., New York City, N. Y.
271	General Elec. Co., Schenectady, N. Y.
272	General Latex and Chem. Corp., Cambridge, Mass.
273	General Naval Stores Co., New York City, N. Y.
274	General Plastics Inc., Tonawanda, N. Y.
275	Genseke Bros., Chicago, Ill.
276	Georgia Kaolin Co., Elizabeth, N. J.
277	Girdler Corp., Louisville, Ky.
278	Givaudan-Delawanna, New York City
279	Glidden Co., Cleveland, O.
280	Glyco Products Co., Brooklyn, N. Y.

Number	*Firm*
281	Goldschmidt Chemical Corp., New York City, N. Y.
282	Goodrich Chemical Co., B. F., Cleveland, O.
283	Goodrich Co., B. F., Akron, O.
284	Goodyear Tire and Rubber Co., Akron, O.
285	Gray and Co., Wm. S., New York City, N. Y.
286	Greef and Co., R. W., New York City, N. Y.
287	Green Fire Brick Co., A. P., Mexico, Mo.
288	Griffin Chemical Co., San Francisco, Cal.
289	Griffith Lab., Chicago, Ill.
290	Gross and Co., A., Newark, N. J.
291	Gulf Oil Co., Pittsburgh, Pa.
292	Haas-Miller Corp., Philadelphia, Pa.
293	Haering and Co., D. W., Chicago, Ill.
294	Hagan Corp., Pittsburgh, Pa.
295	Hall Co., C. P., Akron, O.
296	Halowax Corp., New York City, N. Y.
297	Hamilton Laboratories, Hamilton, O.
298	Hamilton Laboratories Inc., New York City, N. Y.
299	Hammond Drierite Co., Yellow Springs, O.
300	Hammond Paint and Chem. Co., Beacon, N. Y.
301	Harbison Walker Refr. Co., Pittsburgh, Pa.
302	Hardesty Chem. Co., New York City, N. Y.
303	Hardesty Co., W. C., New York City, N. Y.
304	Harshaw Chem. Co., Cleveland, O.
305	Hart Products Co., New York City, N. Y.
306	Harwick Standard Chem. Co., Akron, O.
307	Haveg Corp., Newark, Del.

Number	*Firm*
308	Haynes Stellite Co., New York City, N. Y.
309	Hercules Powder Co., Wilmington, Del.
310	Heresite and Chemical Co., Manitowoc, Wis.
311	Herron Bros. and Meyer, New York City, N. Y.
312	Heveatex Corp., Melrose, Mass.
313	Hexoran Co. Ltd., Manchester, England
314	Heyden Chem. Corp., New York City, N. Y.
315	Himark Products Co., Muncie, Ind.
316	Hizone Products, Muncie, Ind.
317	Holliday and Co., L. B., Huddersfield, England
318	Hollingshead Corp., R. M., Camden, N. J.
319	Hooker Electrochemical Co., New York City, N. Y.
320	Hooper Sons, Wm. E., Baltimore, Md.
321	Hopkins and Co., J. L., New York City, N. Y.
322	Horn Co., A. C., Long Island City, N. Y.
323	Horn Jeffreys and Co., Burbank, Cal.
324	Hoskins Mfg. Co., Detroit, Mich.
325	Hoskins Co., W. J., Chicago, Ill.
326	Houdry Process Corp., New York City, N. Y.
327	Houghton and Co., E. F., Philadelphia, Pa.
328	Howarth Stand. Chem. Co., Akron, O.
329	Huber Inc., J. M., New York City, N. Y.
330	Huron Milling Co., New York City, N. Y.
331	Hycar Corp., Akron, O.
332	Hyman, J. and Co., Denver, Colo.
333	Hynson, Westcott and Dunning Inc., Baltimore, Md.

Number	*Firm*
334	Imperial Chem. Industries Ltd., London, England
335	Industrial Chem. Prod. Co., Detroit, Mich.
336	Industrial Chem. Sales Co., New York City, N. Y.
337	Industrial Conversions Inc., New York City, N. Y.
338	Industrial Oil Prod. Corp., Los Angeles, Cal.
339	Industrial Raw Materials Co., New York City, N. Y.
340	Industrial Rayon Corp., Cleveland, O.
341	Innis, Speiden Co., New York City, N. Y.
342	Interchemical Corp., New York City, N. Y.
343	International Filter Co., Chicago, Ill.
344	International Nickel Co., New York City, N. Y.
345	International Paper Co., New York City, N. Y.
346	International Pulp Co., New York City, N. Y.
347	International Selling Corp., New York City, N. Y.
348	International Talc Co., New York City, N. Y.
349	International Wax Ref. Co., Brooklyn, N. Y.
350	Irvington Varnish and Insulator Co., Irvington, N. J.
351	Jefferson Lake Sulphur Co., Houston, Tex.
352	Johns-Manville Corp., New York City, N. Y.
353	Johnston Co., George G., New York City, N. Y.
354	Jordan, Jr., W. H. and F., Philadelphia, Pa.
355	Jungmann and Co., New York City, N. Y.
356	Kali Mfg. Co., Philadelphia, Pa.
357	Kalva Corp., Waukegan, Ill.
358	Kay-Fries Chem. Inc., New York City, N. Y.
359	Kaykote Division, Sparks, Md.
360	Kearny Mfg. Co., Kearny, N. J.
361	Keever Starch Co., Columbus, O.
362	Kelco Co., New York City, N. Y.
363	Kelite Products Inc., Los Angeles, Cal.
364	Kem Products Co., Newark, N. J.
365	Kendall Refining Co., Bradford, Pa.
366	Kessler Chem. Co., Philadelphia, Pa.
367	Kinetic Chemicals Inc., Wilmington, Del.
368	King and Lang Co., Norwalk, Conn.
369	Koppers Co., Pittsburgh, Pa.
370	Koray Ltd., London, England
371	Kraft Foods Co., Chicago, Ill.
372	Kraus Ceramic Products Co., Sparks, Md.
373	Krebs Pigment Co., Wilmington, Del.
374	Krim-Ko Co., Scituate, Mass.
375	Kroma Chem. Corp., Raritan, N. J.
376	La Motte Chem. Prod. Co., Baltimore, Md.
377	Landsberger Chemical Co., New York City, N. Y.
378	Larvex Corp., New York City, N. Y.
379	Laucks Inc., I. F., Seattle, Wash.
380	Laurel Soap Mfg. Co., Philadelphia, Pa.
381	Leatex Chemical Co., Philadelphia, Pa.
382	Lehn and Fink Prod. Corp., Bloomfield, N. J.
383	Lever Bros., Cambridge, Mass.
384	Lewis Co., Harry R., Warren, Pa.

Number	*Firm*
385	Lewis Inc., John D., Providence, R. I.
386	Linde Air Products Co., New York City, N. Y.
387	Litter Co., D. H., New York City, N. Y.
388	Loomis Talc Corp., W. H., Gouverneur, N. Y.
389	Lubrizol Sales Co., Cleveland, O.
390	Lucidol Corp., Buffalo, N. Y.
391	Maas Chemical Co., A. R., South Gate, Cal.
392	Maas and Waldstein, Newark, N. J.
393	MacDermid Inc., Waterbury, Conn.
394	MacKenzie Laboratories, Inc., Chester, Pa.
395	Magnolia Petroleum Co., Amarillo, Tex.
396	Magnus Chem. Co., Garwood, N. J.
397	Magnus, Mabee and Reynard Inc., New York City, N. Y.
398	Maher Color and Chem. Co., Chicago, Ill.
399	Makalot Corp., Boston, Mass.
400	Malex Corp., New York City, N. Y.
401	Mallinckrodt Chem. Works, St. Louis, Mo.
402	Malstrom, N. I. and Co., Brooklyn, N. Y.
403	Malt Diastase Co., Brooklyn, N. Y.
404	Maltine Co., New York City, N. Y.
405	Marathon Corp., Rothschild, Wis.
406	Marblette Corp., Long Island City, N. Y.
407	Marbon Corp., Gary, Ind.
408	Marden-Wild Corp., Somerville, Mass.
409	Marlowe-Van Loan Corp., High Point, N. C.
410	Martin Co., Glenn L., Baltimore, Md.
411	Martin Dennis Co., Newark, N. J.
412	Maschmeijer, Jr., A., Inc., Newark, N. J.
413	Mathieson Alkali Works, New York City, N. Y.
414	Maywood Chemical Works, Maywood, N. J.
415	McConnon and Co., Winona, Minn.
416	McLaughlin, Gormley King Co., Minneapolis, Minn.
417	Mead Corp., Chillicothe, O.
418	Mearl Corp., New York City, N. Y.
419	Menasha Products Co., Menasha, Wis.
420	Merck and Co., Rahway, N. J.
421	Merrell Co., Wm. S., Cincinnati, O.
422	Metals Refining Co., Hammond, Ind.
423	Metasap Chem. Co., Harrison, N. J.
424	Mica Insulator Co., New York City, N. Y.
425	Michel Export Co., New York City, N. Y.
426	Michigan Chemical Co., Essexville, Mich.
427	Michigan Quartz Silica Co., Milwaukee, Wis.
428	Mine Safety Appliance Co., Pittsburgh, Pa.
429	Mineral Pigments Corp., Muirkirk, Md.
430	Minnesota Linseed Oil Paint Co., Minneapolis, Minn.
431	Minnesota Mining and Mfg. Co., St. Paul, Minn.
432	Miranol Chemical Co., Inc., Irvington, N. J.
433	Monsanto Chem. Co., St. Louis, Mo.
434	Monsanto Chemicals Ltd., London, England
435	Moore and Munger, New York City, N. Y.
436	Morningstar, Nicol Inc., New York City, N. Y.

Number	Firm
437	Morton Chemical Co., Greensboro, N. C.
438	Murray Oil Prod. Co., Philadelphia, Pa.
439	Mutual Chem. Co. of America, New York City, N. Y.
440	Naphthole Inc., Boonton, N. J.
441	National Aniline and Chem. Co., New York City, N. Y.
442	National Carbon Co., New York City, N. Y.
443	National Graphite Co., New York City, N. Y.
444	National Lead Co., New York City, N. Y.
445	National Pigments and Chem. Co., St. Louis, Mo.
446	National Rosin Oil and Size Co., New York City, N. Y.
447	National Smelting Co., Cleveland, O.
448	National Southern Prod. Corp., Tuscaloosa, Ala.
449	National Starch Products, New York City, N. Y.
450	National Vulcanized Fibre Co., Wilmington, Del.
451	Naugatuck Chem. Co., New York City, N. Y.
452	Naylee Chemical Co., Philadelphia, Pa.
453	Neville Co., Pittsburgh, Pa.
454	New Haven Syrup Co., New Haven, Conn.
455	New Jersey Zinc Co., New York City, N. Y.
456	New Wrinkle Inc., Dayton, O.
457	New York Color and Chem. Co., New York City, N. Y.
458	New York and Pennsylvania Co., New York City, N. Y.
459	Newport Industries Inc., New York City, N. Y.
460	Niacet Chem. Corp., Niagara Falls, N. Y.
461	Niagara Alkali Co., New York City, N. Y.
462	Ninol Laboratories, Chicago, Ill.

Number	Firm
463	Nixon Nitration Works, Nixon, N. J.
464	Nopco Chemical Co., Harrison, N. J.
465	Nordigard Corp., Chicago, Ill.
466	North Inc., Frank G., Atlanta, Ga.
467	Norton Co., Worcester, Mass.
468	Nulomoline Co., New York City, N. Y.
469	Nuodex Products Corp., Elizabeth, N. J.
470	Nutrition Research Labs., Chicago, Ill.
471	Nutritional Research Assn. Inc., Whitley, Ind.
472	Nyanza Color and Chem. Co., New York City, N. Y.
473	Oakite Products Inc., New York City, N. Y.
474	Ohio-Apex Inc., Nitro, W. Va.
475	Ohio Chemical and Mfg. Co., New York City, N. Y.
476	Ohio Steel Foundry Co., Springfield, O.
477	Ohmlac Paint and Refining Co., Chicago, Ill.
478	Oil States Petroleum Co., New York City, N. Y.
479	Olive Oil Soap Co., Paterson, N. J.
480	Onyx Oil and Chem. Co., Jersey City, N. J.
481	Orbis Prod. Corp., New York City, N. Y.
482	Oronite Chemical Co., San Francisco, Cal.
483	Osborn Co., C. J., New York City, N. Y.
484	Owens-Corning Fiberglas Corp., Toledo, O.
485	Ozokerite Mining Co., Grand Rapids, Mich.
486	Pabst Sales Co., Chicago, Ill.
487	Pacific Coast Borax Co., New York City, N. Y.
488	Painsley Prod. Co., New York City, N. Y.

Number	Firm
489	Panelyte Division, New York City, N. Y.
490	Papermakers Chem. Co., Wilmington, Del.
491	Paramet Chem. Corp., Long Island City, N. Y.
492	Parker Rustproof Co., Detroit, Mich.
493	Peerless Color Co., Plainfield, N. J.
494	Penetone Co., Tenafly, N. J.
495	Penick and Co., S. B., New York City, N. Y.
496	Pennsylvania Coal Prod. Co., Petrolia, Pa.
497	Pennsylvania Industrial Chem. Co., Clairton, Pa.
498	Pennsylvania Refining Co., Butler, Pa.
499	Pennsylvania Salt Mfg. Co., Philadelphia, Pa.
500	Penola Inc., Pittsburgh, Pa.
501	Perkins Glue Co., Lansdale, Pa.
502	Perkins Soap Co., Springfield, Mass.
503	Permutit Co., New York City, N. Y.
504	Perolin Co., New York City, N. Y.
505	Petroleum Specialties Co., St. Louis, Mo.
506	Petroleum Specialties Inc., New York City, N. Y.
507	Petrolite Corp. Ltd., New York City, N. Y.
508	Pfaltz and Bauer, New York City, N. Y.
509	Pharma Chem. Corp., New York City, N. Y.
510	Philadelphia Quartz Co., Philadelphia, Pa.
511	Philipp Bros. Chemicals Inc., New York City, N. Y.
512	Phillips Petroleum Co., Bartlesville, Okla.
513	Pittsburgh Plate Glass Co., Pittsburgh, Pa.
514	Plaskon Co., Toledo, O.

Number	Firm
515	Plymouth Organic Labs., New York City, N. Y.
516	Polymel Corp., Baltimore, Md.
517	Polymel Corp., Middlesex, N. J.
518	Polyplastex Inc., Woodside, N. Y.
519	Porocel Corp., Wilmington, Del.
520	Powell and Co., John, New York City, N. Y.
521	Power Oil Co., Conshohocken, Pa.
522	Price Fire and Waterproofing Co., Poughkeepsie, N. Y.
523	Prior Chemical Corp., New York City, N. Y.
524	Procter and Gamble Co., Cincinnati, O.
525	Prophylactic Brush Co., Florence, Mass.
526	Protean Chemical Corp., New York City, N. Y.
527	Protexol Corp., Kenilworth, N. J.
528	Providence Textile Chem. Co., Providence, R. I.
529	Publicker Com. Alcohol Co., Philadelphia, Pa.
530	Puget Sound Pulp and Timber Co., Bellingham, Wash.
531	Pure Calcium Products Co., Painesville, O.
532	Pure Carbonic Inc., New York City, N. Y.
533	Pure Oil Co., Chicago, Ill.
534	Pyrene Mfg. Co., Newark, N. J.
535	Quaker Chem. Prod. Corp., Conshohocken, Pa.
536	Quaker Oats Co., Chicago, Ill.
537	Quaker State Oil Ref. Corp., Bradford, Pa.
538	Rampel Chemical Co., Mamaroneck, N. Y.
539	Rare Chemicals Inc., Flemington, N. J.

Number	*Firm*
540	Rayon Processing Co. Inc., Central Falls, R. I.
541	Rayonier Inc., New York City, N. Y.
542	R-B-H Dispersions, Bound Brook, N. J.
543	Reardon Co., St. Louis, Mo.
544	Refined Products Co., Lyndhurst, N. J.
545	Refining Unincorporated, Chicago, Ill.
546	Reichhold Chemicals, Detroit, Mich.
547	Reilly Tar and Chem. Co., Indianapolis, Ind.
548	Reilly-Whiteman-Walton Co., Conshohocken, Pa.
549	Resinous Prod. and Chem. Co., Philadelphia, Pa.
550	Resistoflex Corp., Belleville, N. J.
551	Revertex Corp. of Amer., Long Island City, N. Y.
552	Rheem Research Prod. Inc., Baltimore, Md.
553	Rhodes Co., James H., Chicago, Ill.
554	Richards Chem. Works, Jersey City, N. J.
555	Richardson Co., Cincinnati, O.
556	Richmond Oil, Soap and Chem. Co. Inc., Philadelphia, Pa.
557	Ridbo Labs. Inc., Paterson, N. J.
558	Riedel-de Haen Inc., New York City, N. Y.
559	Riordan Sales Corp. Ltd., Montreal, Canada
560	Riverside Chem. Co., Tonawanda, N. Y.
561	Robeson Process Co., New York City, N. Y.
562	Robinson Wagner Co., New York City, N. Y.
563	Rohm and Haas, Philadelphia, Pa.
564	Ross Co. Inc., Frank B., New York City, N. Y.
565	Ross-Gould Co., St. Louis, Mo.
566	Ross-Rowe Inc., New York City, N. Y.
567	Royce Chem. Co., Carlton Hill, N. J.
568	Rubber and Plastics Compound Co., New York City, N. Y.
569	Rumford Chem. Works, Rumford, R. I.
570	Salomon and Bro., L. A., New York City, N. Y.
571	Salt Cake Sales Corp., New York City, N. Y.
572	Samuelson and Co., P., London, England
573	Sandoz Chem. Works, New York City, N. Y.
574	Schimmel and Co., New York City, N. Y.
575	Scholler Chem. Co., Philadelphia, Pa.
576	Schwarz Labs. Inc., New York City, N. Y.
577	Scientific Filter Co., New York City, N. Y.
578	Seaboard Distributors Inc., Newark, N. J.
579	Seydel Chem. Co., Jersey City, N. J.
580	Seydel-Wooley and Co., Atlanta, Ga.
581	Sharp and Dohme, Philadelphia, Pa.
582	Sharples Solvents Corp., Philadelphia, Pa.
583	Shawinigan Chemicals, New York City, N. Y.
584	Sheffield Farms Co., Inc., New York City, N. Y.
585	Shell Chem. Co., San Francisco, Cal.
586	Shell Oil Co., San Francisco, Cal.
587	Sherwin-Williams Co., Cleveland O.
588	Sherwood Petroleum Co., Englewood, N. J.
589	Short Milling Co., J. R., Chicago, Ill.

Number	Firm
590	Sierra Talc Co., Los Angeles, Cal.
591	Silicon (Organic) Developments Ltd., London, England
592	Sinclair and Valentine Co., New York City, N. Y.
592A	Sinclair Process Corp., New York City, N. Y.
593	Sinclair Refining Co., New York City, N. Y.
594	Skal Chemical Co., New York City, N. Y.
595	Skelly Oil Co., Chicago, Ill.
596	Smith Co., Werner G., Cleveland, O.
597	Snyder Chemical Corp., Bethel, Conn.
598	Socony-Vacuum Oil Co., New York City, N. Y.
599	Solvay Sales Corp., New York City, N. Y.
600	Solvol Corp., Providence, R. I.
601	Sonneborn Sons Inc., L., New York City, N. Y.
602	Southern Chem. Cotton Co., Chattanooga, Tenn.
603	Sparhawk Co., Sparkill, N. Y.
604	Specialty Products Co., Jersey City, N. J.
605	Spencer Chemical Co., Kansas City, Mo.
606	Spencer Kellogg and Sons, Buffalo, N. Y.
607	St. Joseph Lead Co., New York City, N. Y.
608	St. Just and Co. Ltd., Theodore, London, England
609	Staley Mfg. Co., A. E., Decatur, Ill.
610	Stamford Rubber Supply Co., Stamford, Conn.
611	Stanco Distributors Inc., New York City, N. Y.
612	Standard Alcohol Co., Wilmington, Del.
613	Standard Brands Inc., New York City, N. Y.
614	Standard Chem. Co., Akron, O.
615	Standard Chem. Products Inc., Hoboken, N. J.
616	Standard Oil Co. (Cal.), San Francisco, Cal.
617	Standard Oil Co. (Ind.), Chicago, Ill.
618	Standard Oil Co. (N. J.), New York City, N. Y.
619	Standard Oil Co. (N. Y.), New York City, N. Y.
620	Standard Scientific Supply Corp., New York City, N. Y.
621	Standard Silicate Co., Pittsburgh, Pa.
622	Standard Ultramarine Co., Huntington, W. Va.
623	Stanley Chem. Co., East Berlin, Conn.
624	Stauffer Chem. Co., New York City, N. Y.
625	Stein, Hall and Co., New York City, N. Y.
626	Stresen-Reuter Inc., Fred'k A., Chicago, Ill.
627	Sun Oil Co., Philadelphia, Pa.
628	Surpass Chemical Co., Albany, N. Y.
629	Swan Finch Oil Corp., New York City, N. Y.
630	Swift and Co., Chicago, Ill.
631	Sylvania Industrial Corp., New York City, N. Y.
632	Synfleur Scientific Labs., Monticello, N. Y.
633	Synthane Corp., Oaks, Pa.
634	Synthetic Chemicals Inc., Paterson, N. J.
635	Synthetic Products Co., Cleveland, O.
636	Synvar Corp., Wilmington, Del.
637	Takamine Lab., Clifton, N. J.
638	Talco Corp., Hoboken, N. J.
639	Tamms Silica Co., Chicago, Ill.
640	Tannade Co., Chicago, Ill.

Number	*Firm*
641	Tannin Prod. Export Corp., New York City, N. Y.
642	Tennessee Corp., Atlanta, Ga.
643	Tennessee Eastman Corp., Kingsport, Tenn.
644	Texas Gulf Sulphur Co., New York City, N. Y.
645	Texas Mining and Smelting Co., Laredo, Tex.
646	Theobald Industries Inc., Kearney, N. J.
647	Thermal Syndicate Ltd., New York City, N. Y.
648	Thiokol Corp., Trenton, N. J.
649	Thomas Co., Arthur H., Philadelphia, Pa.
650	Thompson-Weinman and Co., Cartersville, Ga.
651	Tidewater Assn. Oil Co., Associated, Cal.
652	Titan Chem. Products, Jersey City, N. J.
653	Titanium Alloy Mfg. Co., Niagara Falls, N. Y.
654	Titanium Pigment Co., New York City, N. Y.
655	Tobacco By-Products and Chem. Corp., Louisville, Ky.
656	Tragasol Products Ltd., Hooton, Cheshire, England
657	Trask Co., Arthur C., Chicago, Ill.
658	Tretolite Co., St. Louis, Mo.
659	Turco Products Co., Los Angeles, Cal.
660	Ultra Chem. Works, Paterson, N. J.
661	Union Bag and Paper Corp., New York City, N. Y.
662	Union Bay State Chem. Co., Cambridge, Mass.
663	Union Oil Co., Los Angeles, Cal.
664	United Carbon Co., Charleston, W. Va.
665	United Chem. Prod. Corp., Jersey City, N. J.

Number	*Firm*
666	United Clay Mines Corp., Trenton, N. J.
667	United Color and Pigment Co., Newark, N. J.
668	U. S. Graphite Co., Saginaw, Mich.
669	U. S. Gypsum Co., Chicago, Ill.
670	U. S. Industrial Chemicals, New York City, N. Y.
671	U. S. Oil Co., Providence, R. I.
672	U. S. Plywood Corp., New York City, N. Y.
673	U. S. Rubber, Co., New York City, N. Y.
674	U. S. Stoneware Co., New York City, N. Y.
675	U. S. Testing Co., Hoboken, N. J.
676	Valentine Sugar Co., New Orleans, La.
677	Valvoline Oil Co., Cincinnati, O.
678	Van Ameringen-Haebler Inc., New York City, N. Y.
679	Van Dyk and Co. Inc., Belleville, N. J.
680	Vanadium Corp. of Amer., New York City, N. Y.
681	Vanderbilt Co., R. T., New York City, N. Y.
682	Varcum Chem. Corp., Niagara Falls, N. Y.
683	Vegetable Oil Prod. Co. Inc., Wilmington, Cal.
684	Vellner, Eugene, Philadelphia, Pa.
685	Velsicol Corp., Chicago, Ill.
686	Vestal Laboratories Inc., St. Louis, Mo.
687	Victor Chem. Works, Chicago, Ill.
688	Virginia-Carolina Chem. Co., Richmond, Va.
689	Virginia Smelting Co., West Norfolk, Va.
690	Visking Corp., Chicago, Ill.
691	Vulcan Chemical Co., Birmingham, Ala.

Number	Firm
692	Wallace and Tiernan Co., Newark, N. J.
693	Wallerstein Co., New York City, N. Y.
694	Warner Chem. Co., New York City, N. Y.
695	Warwick Chem. Co., W. Warwick, R. I.
696	Washine - National - Sands, Inc., Long Island City, N. Y.
697	Washington Mills Abrasive Co., Grafton, Mass.
698	Watford Chem. Co., Ltd., London, England.
699	Watson Park Co., Boston, Mass.
700	Waverly Petroleum Prod. Co., Philadelphia, Pa.
701	Weirton Steel Co., Weirton, W. Va.
702	Welch, Holme and Clark Co., New York City, N. Y.
703	Werk Co., M., Cincinnati, O.
704	West Virginia Pulp and Paper Co., New York City, N. Y.
705	Westinghouse Electric Co., Pittsburgh, Pa.
706	Westvaco Chlorine Prod. Corp., New York City, N. Y.
707	Wharry and Co., G. A., New York City, N. Y.
708	Whittaker, Clark and Daniels Inc., New York City, N. Y.
709	Williams Co., C. K., Easton, Pa.
710	Wilmington Chem. Corp., Wilmington, Del.
711	Wilson Carbon Co., New York City, N. Y.
712	Wilson-Martin Co., Philadelphia, Pa.
713	Winthrop Chem. Co., New York City, N. Y.
714	Witco Chem. Inc., New York City, N. Y.
715	Woburn Degreasing Co., Harrison, N. J.
716	Wolf and Co., Jacques, Passaic, N. J.
717	Wolff-Alport Chem. Corp., Brooklyn, N. Y.
718	Woolen Chem. and Supply Co., Paterson, N. J.
719	Wood Treating Chemicals Co., St. Louis, Mo.
720	Woonsocket Color and Chem. Co., Woonsocket, R. I.
721	Wyandotte Chem. Corp., Wyandotte, Mich.
722	Wyodak Chem. Co., Cleveland, O.
723	Xylos Rubber Co., Akron, O.
724	Zinsser and Co., Wm., Hastings-on-Hudson, N. Y.
725	Zonite Products Corp., New York City, N. Y.
726	Zophar Mills, Brooklyn, N. Y.
727	Zurn Co., O. F., Philadelphia, Pa.

COMPOSITION OF TRADE-MARKED PRODUCTS

Chemists, engineers and purchasing agents often need to know at least the approximate composition of trade-marked chemicals and allied products. The composition of these products can be seldom inferred from the trade name, and often the same or similar preparations are marketed under different trade-marks. The following list E referring to the composition of trade-mark products is quite extensive, but is not claimed to be complete.

The data on composition and use are based on published and private communications. Some of the trade-marks listed are registered at the Patent Office and others are not. No differentiation between those registered and those not registered has been made. Errors found may be due to transcription or changes in the product. It will be greatly appreciated if such errors are brought to the compiler's attention.

For contributing to this section grateful acknowledgment is made to:

Aries, Robert S., Polytechnic Institute of Brooklyn
Calkin, John B., Union Bag and Paper Corp.
Farber, Eduard, Consulting Chemist
Goetz, Alvin C., Eagle-Picher Co.
Gwynn, Marion H., Technical Consultant
Hall, Lloyd A., The Griffith Laboratories
Herman, Stanford L., Stanetal Corp.
Kellogg, Jr., H. Dudley, Consultant
Levey, H. A., American Products Mfg. Co.
Lieber, Eugene, Nox-Rust Chemical Corp.
Lincoln, Bert H., Continental Oil Co.
Maglio, M. Martin, Advance Solvents and Chemical Corp.
Rasch, Carl H., Riverside Chemical Co.
Rhodes, R. K., L. Sonneborn Sons, Inc.
Seymour, Raymond B., Industrial Research Institute
Stamm, Alfred J., U. S. Forest Products Laboratory
Smith, Julian F., Institute of Textile Technology
Sweet, H. A., General Dyestuff Corp.

LIST E

Composition of Trade-Marked Products

A-1. Thiocarbanilide; rubber accelerator.

A-10. Condensation product of aniline and formaldehyde; plasticizer for natural rubber.

A-19. Formaldehyde derivative of a condensation product of aniline and acetaldehyde; accelerator for the vulcanization of rubber.

A-32. Reaction product of butyraldehyde and butylidene aniline; rubber accelerator.

A-77. Condensation product of acetaldehyde and aniline; accelerator for hard rubber.

Composition of Trade-Marked Products

A-100. Aldehyde derivative of Schiff's base; hard rubber accelerator.

Aamcolose. Dextrin.

Abadol. Aminothiazole; used in medicine.

Abalyn. Methyl abietate; plasticizer, solvent for resins, rubber, etc.

Abamide. *p*-Aminomethyl benzene sulfonamide hydrochloride; used in medicine.

Abasin. Acetyl diethylbromoacetyl urea; sedative.

Abbcite. Ammonia dynamite containing high percentage of alkali chloride; explosive.

Abelite. Ammonium nitrate and trinitrotoluene; explosive.

Abie. Pine oil.

Abopon. Water-soluble sodium borophosphate; flameproofing agent.

Abracol G.M.S. Glyceryl monostearate.

Abracol P.G.S. Propylene glycol monostearate.

Abracol 203. *p*-Toluene sulfanilide.

Abracol 234. Dicresyl glyceryl ether.

Abracol 777. Monocresyl glyceryl ether diacetate.

Abracol 789. Toluene sulfonamide.

Abracol 888. Dicresyl glyceryl ether acetate.

Abracol 1001. *tert*-Butyl phenol.

Abrasite. Aluminum oxide; abrasive.

Abrodil (Skiodan). Sodium iodomethane sulfonate.

Abron SFN. Mixture of higher fatty alcohols (41.8), higher fatty acids (29.9) and hydrocarbon solvent (28.2); used in fat-liquoring (German).

Absorbit. Activated carbon.

Acardite. N,N-Diphenyl urea.

Accelerator Z-51. Zinc dithiocarbamate; vulcanization accelerator.

Accelerator 2-MT. 2-Mercaptothiazoline; vulcanization accelerator.

Accelerator 8. Formaldehyde-*p*-toluidine; vulcanization accelerator.

Composition of Trade-Marked Products

Accelerator 85. Aqueous solution of potassium 2-mercaptobenzothiazole (50%); used in vulcanization of rubber.

Accelerator 89. Aqueous solution of potassium pentamethylenedithiocarbamate; used in vulcanization of rubber.

Accelerator 122. Aqueous solution of potassium pentamethylenedithiocarbamate (10%) and potassium mercaptobenzothiazole (40%); used in vulcanization of rubber.

Accelerator 531. Mixture of zinc 2-mercaptobenzothiazole, inert hydrocarbon, anhydroformaldehyde *p*-toluidine and di-*o*-tolyl guanidine; vulcanization accelerator.

Accelerator 552. Piperidinium pentamethylene dithiocarbamate; vulcanization accelerator.

Accelerator 808. Condensation product of butyraldehyde and aniline; vulcanization accelerator.

Accelerator 833. Condensation product of butyraldehyde and monobutyl amine; vulcanization accelerator.

Acecoline. Acetylcholine chloride; medicament.

Aceite. Bitumen plastic.

Acele. Cellulose acetate yarn.

Aceloid. Nitrocellulose recovered from washed photographic film scrap.

Acerdol. Calcium permanganate; used for sterilizing water, in textile industry.

Acetamine Developer AD Extra. β-Hydroxynaphthoic acid; dye developer.

Acetannin. Acetyl tannic acid; used in medicine.

Acetarsone. See Stovarsol.

Acetoform. Hexamethylenetetramine and aluminum acetocitrate; medicament.

Composition of Trade-Marked Products

Acetole. Rosin size.

Acetosol. Acetylene tetrachloride.

Acetoveratrone. 3,4-Dimethoxyacetophenone; medicament.

Acetylarsan. Diethyl amine Acetarsone; used in medicine.

Acidogen. Glutamic acid hydrochloride; used in medicine.

Acidol. Bataine hydrochloride; used in medicine.

Acidolate. Mixture of sulfated vegetable oil, mineral oil and water.

Acidolene. Sulfonated oil.

Acidulin. Glutamic acid hydrochloride; used in medicine.

Acimul. Modified glyceryl monostearate; emulsifying agent.

Aciterge. Fatty acid salt of substituted oxazoline; wetting agent and detergent for leather.

Aciterge-ol. Salt of substituted oxazoline; cationic, surface-active agent.

Acraglas. Acrylic plastic.

Acrawax. Synthetic wax.

Acrawax C. Synthetic wax; waterproofing agent.

Acrin. Condensation product of hexamethylene tetramine benzyl chloride and mercaptobenzothiazole; rubber accelerator.

Acrisin. Condensation product of formaldehyde, acrolein and urea; used in shrinkproof textile finishes.

Acrol. 2,4-Diaminophenol dihydrochloride used in photographic developers.

Acronal. Polyacrylic synthetic resin; used in varnish and adhesives.

Acronal V6. Mixed polymer of equal parts of methyl acrylate and vinyl isohexylate.

Acronal V26. Mixed polymer of equal parts of vinyl acetate and vinyl isohexylate.

Acronal 1. Polymer of methacrylic acid.

Acronal 2. Polymer of ethacrylic acid.

Composition of Trade-Marked Products

Acronal 4. Polymer of butacrylic acid.

Acronal 1,2,4. Dispersion of mixed polymers of methyl acrylate, ethyl acrylate and *n*-butyl acrylate.

Acronal 500-D. Copolymer of butyl acrylate, vinyl acetate and a small amount of acrylic acid; used in waterproofing.

Acryloid. Polymerized acrylic acid ester.

Acrylon. Mixture of equal amounts of acrylonitrile and carbon tetrachloride; insect fumigant.

Acrysol. Emulsion of Acryloid.

Acrysol GS. Sodium salt of polyacrylic acid; thickener for latex.

Acrysol C9 and ER. Acrylic-resin dispersion.

Activite. Natural bleaching clay; used in removing green color from oils.

Activol. Sodium salt of dialkyl naphthalene sulfonate; wetting agent.

Actomag. Calcined dolomite; used in fertilizers.

Actusol. Petroleum solvent.

Adalin. See Carbromal.

Adalox. Aluminum oxide; abrasive.

AD-aluminum. Copper-base alloy consisting of approximately 15% zinc, 2% aluminum, and 1% tin.

Adamite. Aluminum oxide; abrasive.

Adamsite. Diphenyl amine chlorarsine.

Adbac. Alkyl dimethyl benzyl ammonium chloride; antiseptic.

Adheron. Hydrocarbon resin; plasticizer.

Adinol. Triethyl citrate.

Adipol-BCA. Dibutoxyethyl adipate; plasticizer.

Aditex LU-1. Soluble terpene oils; used for kier boiling.

Admiralty brass. Copper-base alloy containing approximately 29% zinc and 1% tin.

Admiralty bronze. Copper-base alloy, containing approximately 10% tin and 2% zinc.

Composition of Trade-Marked Products

Admiralty gun metal. Alloy of 88% copper, 10% tin, and 2% zinc.

Admiralty metal. See Admiralty brass.

Adnic. Copper-base alloy containing approximately 29% nickel, and 1% tin.

Adrenalin. Epinephrine; used in medicine.

Adronol. Cyclohexanol.

Adronol acetate. Cyclohexyl acetate (German).

Adsorbin. Paraffin wax emulsion with egg albumen and aluminum acetate; waterproofing agent (German).

Adurol. 2-Chlorohydroquinone or 2-bromohydroquinone.

Advaresin 100. Synthetic resin; used in varnish.

Advawax 2575. Dispersion of polyisobutylene in paraffin wax; used in paper coating.

Advawet 15. Sodium petroleum hydrocarbon sulfonate; wetting agent.

Aeral. Alloy of 91.85% aluminum, 3.5% copper, 1.8% magnesium, 0.6% silicon and 2.25% cadmium.

Aerocarb. Series of salt mixtures; used for case hardening.

Aerocase. Series of case-hardening salt mixtures containing sodium and calcium chlorides and calcium cyanide.

Aerocrete. Porous, light-weight concrete.

Aerodux 14. Phenol-formaldehyde molding powder.

Aerofloat. Sodium dicresyl dithiophosphate; flotation reagent.

Aerolite. Alloy of 91.93% aluminum, 0.12% zinc, 0.45% silicon, 0.97% iron, 1.15% copper, and 0.38% manganese.

Aerolite. Urea-formaldehyde cement.

Aerolube. Dithiophosphate in combination with metallic or organic radicals containing sulfur and phosphorus; lubricant, detergent additive.

Composition of Trade-Marked Products

Aero metal. Aluminum-zinc casting metal containing approximately 67% aluminum, 28% zinc, 4% copper, and fractional percentages of iron and silicon.

Aeron. Alloy of 95% aluminum, 4% copper, 1% silicon.

Aerosol. Freon 85 (20%), pyrethrum solution (2%), DDT (3%), cyclohexanone (5%) and lubricating oil in a pressure container; insecticide.

Aerosol AS. Aqueous solution of diisopropyl naphthalene sodium sulfonate; wetting agent.

Aerosol AY. Diamyl sodium sulfosuccinate; wetting agent.

Aerosol M. Quaternary ammonium compound; germicide.

Aerosol MA. Dihexyl sodium sulfosuccinate; wetting agent, emulsifier, detergent.

Aerosol OS. Isopropyl naphthalene sodium sulfosuccinate; wetting agent.

Aerosol OT 100%. Dioctyl sodium sulfosuccinate; wetting and emulsifying agent.

Aerosol OT Aqueous. Aqueous dispersion of dioctyl sodium sulfosuccinate; wetting agent.

Aerosol OT Clear. Solution of dioctyl sodium sulfosuccinate; wetting agent.

Aerosol 1B. Dibutyl sodium sulfosuccinate; wetting agent.

Aerotex M-3. Melamine-formaldehyde condensate.

Aeterna. Modified yellow brass with about 40% zinc; the modifying elements, present in fractional percentages, are tin, lead, and manganese.

Afenil. Calcium chloride urea; used in medicine.

AFPT. See Accelerator 8.

Agalite. Talc; used to give stiffness and gloss to paper.

Composition of Trade-Marked Products

Agaloid. Irish moss extract; thickener.

Agdite. Denatured alcohol.

AgeRite Alba. Hydroquinone monobenzyl ether; antioxidant.

AgeRite Blend. Hydrocarbon-substituted diaryl amines; rubber antioxidant.

AgeRite Gel. Ditolyl amines and paraffin wax; rubber antioxidant.

AgeRite Hipar. Mixture of phenyl-β-naphthyl amine and diphenyl *p*-phenylene diamine; rubber antioxidant.

AgeRite Powder. Phenyl β-naphthylamine; rubber antioxidant.

AgeRite Resin. $C_{10}H_7N{:}CH.CH_2.$-$CHOH.CH_3$; antioxidant for rubber.

AgeRite Resin D. Polymerized trimethyl dihydroquinoline; antioxidant for rubber.

AgeRite Stalite. Mixed alkylated diaryl amines; antioxidant for rubber.

AgeRite White. Di-β-naphthyl *p*-phenylene diamine; antioxidant for rubber.

Agilite. Talc.

Aglutol 5. Softener made from glucose (German).

Agrifos. Colloidal phosphatic clay; fertilizer.

Agrinite. Organic ammoniate fertilizer.

Agripol. See Norepol.

Agroxone. 4-Chloro-2-methyl phenoxy-acetic acid; weed-seed killer.

Agr Syl. Diatomaceous earth.

Ahcol. Sulfonated castor oil compound; used in textile finishing.

Ahcomerce. Cresylic acid compound; mercerizing assistant.

Ahco Penetrant L. Alkyl aryl sulfonate; textile wetting agent.

Ahcowet SM. Alkyl aryl sulfonate; wetting agent.

Aich's metal. Brass alloy containing copper, zinc and a small proportion of iron or tin.

Composition of Trade-Marked Products

Airoform. Bismuth iodosubgallate; antiseptic.

Airogen. Bismuth iodosubgallate; antiseptic.

Airol. Bismuth iodosubgallate; antiseptic.

Aitch metal. See Aich metal.

Ajax bull. Bearing metal containing approximately 17% antimony, 7% tin, and 76% lead.

Ajax metal. Alloy containing 84.24% copper, 10.98% tin, 7.27% lead, 0.37% arsenic or phosphorus; used in antifriction bearings.

Aji-no-moto. Water-soluble meat flavor consisting essentially of sodium glutamate.

Akardit II. Stabilizer made from diphenyl amine, phosgene and methyl amine (German).

Akbar. See Accelerator 8.

Akcocene. Sulfonated oil and solvent.

Akco resin. Natural resin modified with phenol.

Akoil. Sulfonated oil and solvent.

Akroflex C. Diphenyl *p*-phenylene diamine (35%) and phenyl α-naphthylamine (65%); antioxidant.

Aktiplast. Zinc salts of C_{10} and C_{11} synthetic fatty acids; rubber softener.

Aktivin. Chloramine-T; antiseptic.

Aktivin S. $CH_3C_6H_4SO_2NClNa.$-$3H_2O$; solubilizing agent for sizes and finishes.

A. L. 63. Antilouse powder based on D.D.T.

Alabrase. Aluminum oxide; abrasive.

Alacet. Aluminum acetate.

Aladdinite. Casein plastics.

Alamalt. Flour made by grinding sweet potato crisps.

Albacer. White synthetic wax.

Albalith. White lithopone; used in paints.

Albaoil. Sulfonated oil; used in textile industry.

Composition of Trade-Marked Products

Albasan. β-Naphthol and organic bases; rubber antioxidant.

Albasol. Sulfonated oils or fats; emulsifying agent.

Albata. See Albatra.

Albatex. Mixture of titanium dioxide (20) and talc (80); used in textile finishing.

Albatex BD. Sodium *m*-nitrobenzene sulfonate; textile kier-boiling assistant.

Albatex O. Phenolic condensate; mordant and fixing agent for basic dyestuffs.

Albatex PO. Sulfonate of a complex stearyl alkyl compound; levelling, penetrating or stripping assistant.

Albatex WS. Phenolic condensate; used in dyeing.

Albatra. Copper-base alloy, containing about 20% nickel and 20% zinc.

Alberid. Synthetic tar-acid resin.

Albertalate. Synthetic alkyd resin.

Albertol. Synthetic tar-acid resin; used in oil varnishes.

Albikote. Asphalt emulsion.

Albolene. Liquid, refined petrolatum; used in medicine, cosmetics.

Albone. Hydrogen peroxide (13%).

Albucid. Sulfacetamide.

Albumol. Complex albuminoid; emulsifying agent.

Albusol. Egg albumin solution; used in photo-engraving.

Alcal. Phosphatide-lecithin compound.

Alchlor. Aluminum chloride; catalyst.

Alclad. Duralumin coated with 99.7% pure aluminum.

Alcoa. Aluminum-base alloys.

Alcoflex. Aqueous urea-formaldehyde resin solution; used in textile finishing.

Alcolan. Absorption base containing cholesterol, other sterols, lanolin, alcohols, etc.; used in cosmetic creams.

Composition of Trade-Marked Products

Alconox. Blend of sodium phosphates and sodium hydrocarbon sulfonates; detergent.

Alcopon. Sodium hexametaphosphate; water softener (Swiss).

Alcor. Alumina brick; refractory.

Alcotone-1. Mixture of ethyl alcohol, acetone, esters, hydrocarbons and methyl alcohol; used in paint and lacquer removers.

Alcrosil steel. Low-alloy steels with 4–6% chromium and normally less than 0.15% carbon.

Alcumite. Corrosion-resistant aluminum bronze with about 8% aluminum, 2% iron, and 1% nickel.

Alcunic. Copper-base alloy, with approximately 16–27% zinc, 2% aluminum, 1% nickel, and optionally, 1% tin.

Aldal. Alloy of 94.4% aluminm, 4% copper, 0.5% magnesium, 0.5% manganese, 0.6% silicon.

Aldamine. Aldehyde-ammonia compound.

Aldarco. Activated carbon.

Aldo. Glyceryl monostearate; bread and cake improver.

Aldo 28. Glyceryl monostearate; used in baking.

Aldo 33. Monostearin; used in baking.

Aldoform. Formaldehyde.

Aldrey. Alloy of 98.9% aluminum, 0.5% magnesium, 0.6% silicon.

Alferium. Alloy of 96.1% aluminum, 2.5% copper, 0.6% magnesium, 0.5% manganese, 0.3% silicon.

Alfol. Thin, corrugated aluminum foil; used for thermal insulation.

Alformin. Solution of aluminum subformate (16%); used in medicine.

Alframine DCA. Sulfated glyceryl amide; detergent.

Alframine DGA. Alkyl aminoalcohol sulfate; textile detergent.

Alfrax. Electrically fused alumina; refractory.

Composition of Trade-Marked Products

Alftalat. Glyptal-type resin or its solution (German).

Algagel. See Algaloid.

Algaloid (Algagel). Purified extract of Irish moss; thickening and emulsifying agent.

Algol. Anthraquinone vat dyestuff.

Algol blue K. N-dimethyl indanthrene blue.

Algol red. 1,4-Dibenzoyl aminoanthraquinone; vat dye.

Algol red 5G. Dibenzoyl 1,4-diaminoanthroquinone.

Algosol. Leuco ester of vat dye.

Alipal Cl. Sodium sulfonate of dodecyl phenyl polyglycol ether; detergent.

Alipal Cl. Sodium dodecyl phenyl polyglycol ether sulfonate; detergent (German).

Alipon OAN. Sodium salts of esters of oxy fatty acid chlorides, soap and salt (German).

Alkalate. Soda.

Alkamerse. Cresylic acid compound; mercerizing assistant.

Alkamine. Sulfated higher fatty amide; dyeing assistant.

Alkamine SJ. Fatty amine; textile detergent.

Alkamine W. Sulfonated fatty alkanolamine; textile wetting agent.

Alkanol B. Alkyl naphthalene sodium sulfonate; wetting agent.

Alkanol HG. Sodium alkyl naphthalene sulfonate; wetting agent.

Alkanol PF. Derivative of alkyl naphthalene sodium sulfonate; wetting agent.

Alkanol S. Sodium tetrahydronaphthalene sulfonate; dispersing agent.

Alkanol SA. Alkyl derivative of naphthalene sodium sulfonate; wetting agent.

Alkanol WXN. Sodium hydrocarbon sulfonate; wetting agent.

Alkanol M-48, M-54, M-60. Solutions of organic sodium salts; wetting agent.

Composition of Trade-Marked Products

Alkargen. Dimethyl arsinic acid.

Alkarsin. Bisdimethyl arsenic oxide.

Alkaterge-O. Substituted oxazoline; penetrant for lubricants, corrosion inhibitor.

Alkathene. Polyethylene plastic.

Alkazene 3. Triethyl benzene.

Alkazene 6. Hexaethyl benzene.

Alkazene 8. Diethyl diisopropyl benzene.

Alkazene 9, 10, 17. Chloroethyl benzene.

Alkazene 12. *m*-Diisopropyl benzene.

Alkazene 13. Triisopropyl benzene.

Alkazene 14. Tetraisopropyl benzene.

Alkazene 16. Triisopropyl toluene.

Alkazene 20. *m*-Chloroethyl benzene.

Alkazene 21. Polyisopropyl benzene.

Alkazene 24. 1,2-Dichloroethyl benzene.

Alkazene 25. Dichloroethyl benzene.

Alkazene 28. Chlorodiethyl benzene.

Alkazene 31. Polyisopropyl benzene.

Alkazene 32. Ethyl pentachlorobenzene.

Alkazene 34. Dichlorodiethyl benzene.

Alkazene 36. Chlorotriethyl benzene.

Alkazene 40. Bromoethyl benzene.

Alkazene 42. Dibromoethyl benzene.

Alkazene 45. Bromodiethyl benzene.

Alkazene 47. Bromoisopropyl benzene.

Alkazene 60. Chloroisopropyl benzene.

Alkazid DIK. Potassium dimethyl glycine; absorbent for H_2S (German).

Alkazid M. Potassium N-methyl alanine; absorbent for CO_2 and H_2S (German).

Alketh. Polyethylene plastic (British).

Alketo acid. Complex mixture produced by controlled oxidation of

Composition of Trade-Marked Products

petroleum fractions; corrosion inhibitor.

Alketone. Mixture of ketones, alcohols and other compounds produced by controlled oxidation of petroleum fractions; corrosion inhibitor.

Alkon. Alkanolamine-carbonate polymers.

Alkor. Polyfurane compound with carbon filler; corrosion-resistant cement.

Alkor S. Polyfurane compound with silica filler; acidproof cement.

Alkydal. Synthetic alkyd resin.

Alkydal T. Mixture of glyceryl phthalate (51%) and linseed oil (49%); used in varnishes.

Alkydalöl. See Alkydal UTC.

Alkydal UTC (Alkydalöl). Glyptal-type resin (German).

Alkymol. Alkyd resin; used in paints.

Allan (red) metal. Mechanical mixture (not a true alloy) containing approximately equal parts of copper and lead.

Allegheny metal. Series of corrosion and heat-resistant stainless steels containing 11–30% chromium, up to 21% nickel and small percentages of manganese, molybdenum, columbium and titanium.

Allergosil. Solution of ethylene disulfonate.

Alloprene. Chlorinated rubber.

Allymer. Allyl-resin monomer.

Almag. Alloy of 2.5% copper, 0.7% magnesium, 0.6% silicon and 96.2% aluminum.

Almalec. High-tensile-strength aluminum alloy containing 0.7% magnesium, 0.5% silicon, and 98.8% aluminum.

Almasilium. Alloy of 1% magnesium, 2% silicon and 97% aluminum.

Alnico. Alloy series, containing approximately 20% nickel, 12–20% aluminum, 5–10% cobalt, 0.4% manganese and silicon combined, 62% iron, and not more than 0.15% carbon; used for permanent magnets.

Alnovol. Alcohol-soluble phenolic resin; used in paints.

Alocol. Colloidal aluminum hydroxide; used in medicine.

Alox. Series of complex methyl esters of high-molecular-weight alcohols, acids and lactones; wetting agents in metal lubricating.

Aloxite. Artificial corundum; abrasive.

Alpax. Aluminum alloy containing 8–11% silicon, magnesium, manganese or cobalt and smaller amounts of titanium, copper, etc.

Alperox C. Lauroyl peroxide.

Alphasol OT. Sodium salt of an alkyl ester of sulfosuccinic acid.

Alphazurine. Acid dye.

Alphenal Sodium. Sodium 5-allyl 5-phenyl barbiturate; hypnotic drug.

Alphenate. Rosin-modified phenolic resin; used in paints.

Alphozone. Succinyl peroxide; used in medicine.

Alplate. Aluminum-clad steel.

Alpro. Series of aluminum-base alloys, most commonly with copper and nickel.

Alprokyd. Alkyd resin; used in air-drying finishes.

Alresat. Phenolic resin (German).

Alresate. Oil-soluble maleic resin; used in varnishes.

Alresene. Oil-soluble phenolic resin; used in paints.

Alrogent. Sodium alkyl aryl sulfonate; wetting agent.

Alronol 90. Propylated amines; emulsifying agent.

Alropel G-4. Dihydroxydichlorodiphenyl methane; used in mildewproofing and waterproofing of textiles.

Alropon. See Alrowet.

Composition of Trade-Marked Products

Alroresin UF. Urea-formaldehyde resin; textile stiffener.

Alrosene. See Alrowet.

Alrosept. Quaternary ammonium compound; antiseptic.

Alrowet (Alropon; Alrosene). Modified sodium lauryl sulfate; wetting agent.

Alsec. Partial esters of polyhydric alcohols and higher fatty acids; acid-stabilized emulsifier.

Alsifer. Alloy containing approximately 40% iron, 40% silicon, and 20% aluminum, no carbon; deoxidizer for steel.

Alsilox. Product of fusion of lead oxide and silica; used in ceramic glazing.

Alsol. Aluminum acetotartrate.

Altal. Triphenyl phosphate.

Altax. Benzothiazyl disulfide.

Altenit. Quicklime and magnesium chloride.

Alucol. Colloidal aluminum hydroxide; used in medicine.

Aludur. Age-hardening aluminum alloy, containing approximately 0.7% silicon, 0.5% magnesium, and 0.5% iron.

Alukalin. Alumina gel adsorbed on activated kaolin; used in medicine.

Alumac. Aluminum-base alloys, with 5–13% silicon and, sometimes, up to 4% copper.

Alumalun. Antislip metal with aluminum as matrix.

Alumel. Nickel-base alloy, containing approximately 2.5% manganese, 2% aluminum, and 1% silicon.

Aluminon. Aurin tricarboxylic acid; reagent for detecting aluminum.

Alurate. Allyl isopropyl barbituric acid; used in medicine.

Alusite. Alumina brick; refractory.

Alvar. Vinyl acetate-aldehyde resin.

Alypin hydrochloride. Benzyl 1,3-tetramethyl diamino-2-ethyl isoproponol monohydrochloride; used in medicine.

Composition of Trade-Marked Products

Amacel. Dye for cellulose acetate.

Amagol. Benzaldehyde; used in flavors.

Amaldehyde. Aqueous solution of $Zn(HSO_2.CH_2O)_2$.

Amalgol. Sulfonated higher fatty alcohol; textile detergent.

Amanol AGF. Polyamine acetate; inhibitor.

Amano S. Alkylaminosulfate; boil-off assistant.

Amanthrene. Vat dye.

Amasize. Amioca starch compound; warp size.

Amatol. Mixture of trinitrotoluene and ammonium nitrate; explosive.

Amatoxol. Mixture of trinitroxylene and trinitrotoluene; explosive.

Amber. Neutral tallow soap; detergent.

Amberex. Vulcanized oil; used in rubber compounding.

Amberite. Phenol-formaldehyde thermosetting resin.

Amberlac. Synthetic modified alkyd resin; used in varnish.

Amberol. Synthetic tar-acid resin of the modified phenolic type; used in varnish.

Amberol F-7. Modified phenol-formaldehyde resin.

Amberol K-12-A. Modified, non-esterified phenol-formaldehyde resin.

Amberol M-93. Modified phenol-formaldehyde resin; used in varnish.

Amberol ST-137X. Non-reactive, unmodified phenol-formaldehyde resin; used in varnish.

Amberol 226. Modified phenol-formaldehyde resin.

Amberol 750. Unesterified, fortified rosin-maleic resin.

Amberol 801, 801-P, 806-P, 808. Esterified, rosin-modified maleic resins.

Ambrac A. "Nickel-silver" alloys, containing about 75% copper, 20% nickel, 5% zinc.

Composition of Trade-Marked Products

Ambrene. Selected fraction of distilled and refined labdanum gum; used in perfumes.

Ambresit. Synthetic tar-acid resin.

Ambroin. Plastic made from copal and silicates.

Ambrox. ZrO_2, TiO_2, SiO_2 and Na_2O; used in enamels.

Amcosul. Sodium higher alkyl sulfate; wetting agent.

Americhol S. Oil-soluble cholesterol compound.

Amerchol L-101. Lanolin sterols; emulsifying agent.

Amercut. Simple steels rendered free-cutting by the presence of up to 0.2% sulfur.

American alloy. Aluminum-base alloy containing 3% copper, 1% manganese, 1% magnesium.

American silver. White alloy of 50–60% copper, 20–24% zinc, 15–24% nickel, and optional low percentages of manganese, iron, lead, tin, and aluminum.

Ameripol. Synthetic rubber of the butadiene-copolymer type.

Amerite. Aqueous, synthetic rubber dispersion.

Ameroid. Casein resin.

Amersil. Fused vitreous silica.

AMF. High-nickel steel, with about 48% nickel; used in refrigeration machinery.

Amidine. Direct dye.

Amijel. Dried, gelatinized starch.

Amilin 5. 2-Amido-5-naphthol-7-sulfonic acid (German).

Aminac. Digested protein containing amino acids and peptides.

Aminine S. Fatty acid soap of amino alcohols; emulsifying agent.

Aminostearin. Modified amine ester of stearic acid; emulsifier.

Amiodoxyl benzoate. Ammonium *o*-iodoxy-benzoate; used in medicine.

Amiprote. Protein hydrolysate; used in therapeutic nutrition.

Composition of Trade-Marked Products

Ammate. Ammonium sulfamate; weed killer.

Ammonal. Compound with ammonium nitrate, powdered aluminum and T.N.T.; explosive.

Ammonyx. Higher aliphatic quaternary ammonium halide.

Ammonyx T. Trialkyl benzyl ammonium chloride.

Ammonyx 00. Oleyl dimethylamine oxide; emulsifier.

Ammo-Phos. Compound containing ammonia and phosphoric acid; fertilizer.

Ammoplaste. Synthetic tar-acid resin.

Amoa. Reaction product of caustic potash and casein; emulsifying agent.

Amoa Falco. Sulfated higher fatty alcohol.

Amoia steel. Low-alloy steel containing manganese and molybdenum.

Amolex. Colorless volatile liquid; corrosion inhibitor for steam boilers.

Amotate. Ammonium sulforicinoleate; emulsifier.

Ampcoloy. Copper-base alloy with aluminum or tin up to 10% and low percentages of iron, nickel and lead.

Ampco Metal. Corrosion-resistant aluminum bronze with 82 to 88% copper, 9 to 14% aluminum and 2.5 to 5.5% iron.

Amphenol. Polystyrene plastic.

Amphoseife DN. Reaction product of commercial stearic acid with sulfur trioxide; detergent (German).

Amsco Alloy. Nickel-chromium-iron alloy.

Amsco Solvent. Petroleum hydrocarbons.

Amunite. Silicon carbide; abrasive.

Amylit. Enzyme preparation; used for desizing textiles.

Amyloform. Formaldehyde-carbo-

Composition of Trade-Marked Products

hydrate condensation product; used for reinforcing rubber.

Amyloid. Plasticized starch hydrate; plastic film.

Anaconda. Copper-base alloys of brass and bronze type.

Anazol. Ethyl phthalate.

Anex. Resinous anion exchanger.

Anglamol 35, 77-x. See Cresol Z-2.

Anhydrex AA-LL. Deproteinized rubber product; insulating material for cables.

Anhydrex AA-60. Deproteinized rubber product; substitute for gutta-percha in submarine cables.

Anhydrone. Magnesium perchlorate; drying agent.

Anka steel. Stainless steel with about 15.5% chromium and 10% nickel.

Ankord. Alkali-soluble cellulose ether.

Anol. Cyclohexanol.

Anon. Cyclohexanone.

Ansandum. Aluminum oxide; abrasive.

Ansol. Anhydrous ethyl alcohol and ethyl acetate; solvent.

Ansolox. Aluminum oxide; abrasive.

Antergan. Dimethyl aminoethyl benzyl aniline hydrochloride.

Anthralan. Acid dyestuff.

Anthralin. 1,8-Dihydroxyanthranol; used in medicine.

Anthrapole. Sulfonated oil and solvent; surface-active agent.

Anticide. Cresylic acid emulsion; antiseptic.

Anticorodel. Corrosion-resistant aluminum-base alloy with low percentages of magnesium, silicon, manganese and iron.

Antifoam HF. *n*-Decanol.

Antifoam LF. Mixture of lower fatty alcohols.

Antiformin. Aqueous solution of caustic soda and sodium hypochlorite; disinfectant.

Antikarol. Water solution of sodium silicate; used to prevent pipe corrosion (German).

Composition of Trade-Marked Products

Antilusterole WA. Sulfated vegetable oil and pigments; delustering and dulling agent for rayon.

Antimol. Sodium benzoate compound; preservative.

Antipyr. Formaldehyde solution.

Antiscorch T. Preventive for premature rubber curing.

Antox. Butyraldehyde-aniline condensation product; antioxidant.

Antu. α-Naphthyl thiourea; rodenticide.

Apasol. Sulfonated oil; used in textile finishing.

Apco 18. Petroleum solvent.

Apco 125. Petroleum solvent.

Apco thinner. Petroleum solvent.

Aperitol. Compound containing phenolphthalein and isovaleric acid; laxative.

Apexscour. Mixture of cresylic acid, tall oil and red oil soap; used in textile finishing.

Apex zinc alloy. Zinc-base alloy with about 4% aluminum, up to 3% copper and fractional percentages of magnesium.

Aphrosol. Foam stabilizer.

Aphtiria. Hexachlorocyclohexane; insecticide.

Apiezon. Petroleum-hydrocarbon mixtures; lubricant.

Apimela. Beeswax compound; electrotype wax.

Apoloy. Copper-bearing steel with about 0.08% carbon and 0.25% copper.

Apothesine hydrochloride. Diethyl aminopropyl cinnamate hydrochloride; used in medicine.

Applicet. Aluminum acetate powder; used in waterproofing.

Appramine. Substituted higher fatty amide; textile softener.

Appretan. Polymerized vinyl acetate.

Appretan A. Aqueous emulsion con-

Composition of Trade-Marked Products

taining Acronal 1 (25%); used in textile finishing.

Appretan B. Aqueous emulsion containing Acronal 2 (25%); used in textile finishing.

Appretan H. Mixture of polyvinyl acetate (95%) and croton aldehyde (5%) dissolved in alcohol with a small amount of ammonia to facilitate emulsification in water; felt stiffener.

Appretan G1. Emulsion containing water (50%) and of a mixture (50%) of equal parts of butyl acrylate and vinyl acetate; used in textile finishing.

Appretole. Glyceryl sulforicinoleate; dying assistant.

Appretole 3–0. Sulfated polyhydric fatty acid ester; used in textile printing.

Aqua-day. Colloidal solution of Acheson graphite in water; lubricant.

Aquagel. Colloidal bentonite; drilling-mud ingredient.

Aqualene-Z. Sodium soaps of hydrocarbon sulfonic acids; used in cutting oils.

Aqualoid. Lecithin and alcohol; emulsifying agent.

Aquamag. Magnesium hydrate.

Aquamel. Brown wax; emulsifying agent for polishes.

Aquanel. Mixture of Calgon, Aerosol OT and water; water softener.

Aquanol-SO. Wetting agent.

Aquapel. Paraffin wax emulsion; waterproofing agent.

Aquaphil. Oxycholesterin; absorption base.

Aquaplex. Synthetic alkyd resin dispersed in an aqueous medium.

Aquaresin GB. Modified glyceryl borate; lubricant, plasticizer.

Aquarex D. Sodium lauryl and myristyl sulfates; wetting agent.

Aquarex F. Sodium isopropyl naphthalene sulfonic acid; used for stabilizing rubber latex.

Composition of Trade-Marked Products

Aquarex SMO. Aqueous solution of monosodium sulfated methyl oleate; compounding agent in rubber.

Aquasec. See Aquatec.

Aquasol. Highly sulfonated castor oil.

Aquatec (Aquasec; Proofit). Paraffin wax emulsion with or without aluminum acetate; used for waterproofing textiles.

Aquatergent. Sulfated boro fatty acid amide; detergent for textiles.

Aquatone. Mixture of Calgon and Santomerse; water softener.

Aqua Xerol. Glyceryl monosterate; used in cosmetics.

Aquazinc. Dispersion of zinc stearate in water; used in rubber-latex compounding.

Aquoid. Colloidal, carbon black dispersion in water.

Aracite. Mixture of sodium sulfite and sodium bisulfite.

Aralac. Casein synthetic fiber.

Aralen. 7-Chloro-4-(4-diethyl amino-1-methyl butyl amino) quinoline diphosphate; used in medicine.

Aramite. Diatomite; pigment.

Aranox. *p*-(*p*-Tolyl sulfonyl amido)-diphenyl amine; rubber antioxidant.

Arasan (Thiosan). Compound with tetramethyl thiuram disulfide; seed fungicide.

Arasan SF. Compound containing 75% tetramethyl thiuramdisulfide; fungicide.

Aratein. Soybean casein.

Arathene. Tall-oil resin.

Aratone-270. Finely ground mica; pigment.

Arbicole. Mixture of sugar, urea and sodium alginate; used in weighting textiles.

Arboneeld. Dimethylol urea; used in mfg. thermosetting resins.

Arborite. Commercial lignin; used in plastics.

Composition of Trade-Marked Products

Acrolite. Phenol-formaldehyde plastic.

Arctic Syntex A. $CH_3(CH_2)_7CH$:$CH(CH_2)_7COOC_2H_4SO_3Na$; wetting and emulsifying agent.

Arctic Syntex M. $CH_3(CH_2)_{10}COOCH_2CHOHCH_2OSO_3Na$; wetting, dispersing, emulsifying agent.

Arctic Syntex M Liquid. Coconut oil fatty acid glyceryl ammonium sulfonate; wetting agent, detergent.

Arctic Syntex T. Sodium salt of sulfonated ethyl methyl oleyl amide; wetting agent, detergent, emulsifier.

Ardal. Alloy with 2% copper, 1.7% iron, 0.6% nickel and 95.7% aluminum.

Ardil. Synthetic textile fiber made from peanut protein.

Areskap. Monobutyl phenyl phenol sodium sulfonate; used in embalming, in fruit washing, penetrant for textiles.

Aresket. Monobutyl diphenyl sodium monosulfonate; wetting and spreading agent in insecticides.

Aresklene. Dibutyl phenyl phenol sodium disulfonate; emulsifier, mold lubricant, penetrant.

Aretan. Mixture of methoxyethyl mercuric chloride and soda ash with a dye; seed disinfectant.

Argasole. Aqueous solution of sugar and gum arabic plus preservative; ribbon softener.

Argosite. Bentonite.

Argyrol. Colloidal protein with 20–30% silver, probably as silver oxide; medicament.

Arheol. Santalol; used in medicine.

Aridex. Paraffin wax emulsion with aluminum acetate or formate; used for waterproofing textiles.

Aridize. Gypsum; molding powder.

Aridye. Insoluble pigment.

Ariginal. Methyl formate compound; insecticide.

Composition of Trade-Marked Products

Aristogen. Hydroquinone solution; photographic developer.

Aristol. Thymol iodide; used in medicine.

Aristoloy. Stainless steel.

Aristowax. Refined paraffin wax.

Arlacel. Anhydrohexitol partial oleate; emulsifier.

Arlacel A. Mannide monooleate; emulsifier.

Arlacel B. Mannitan monooleate; emulsifier.

Arlacel C. Sorbitan monooleate; emulsifier.

Arlex. Commercial sorbitol syrup.

Arlitan. 1,4-Monoanhydride of sorbitol.

Armac C. Coconut oil amine acetate.

Armac HT. Hydrogenated tallow amine acetate.

Armac O. Octadecenyl amine acetate.

Armac S. Soybean oil amine acetate.

Armac T. Tallow amine acetate.

Armac 8. Octyl amine acetate.

Armac 10. Decyl amine acetate.

Armac 12. Dodecyl amine acetate.

Armac 14. Tetradecyl amine acetate.

Armac 16. Hexadecyl amine acetate.

Armac 18. Octadecyl amine acetate.

Armasol. Mixture of sodium phosphates; detergent.

Armeen. Aliphatic long-chain amine.

Armeen HT. Hydrogenated tallow amine.

Armeen O. Octadecenyl amine.

Armeen S. Soybean oil amine.

Armeen T. Tallow amine.

Armeen 8. Octyl amine.

Armeen 10. Decyl amine.

Armeen 12. Dodecyl amine.

Armeen 14. Tetradecyl amine.

Armeen 16. Hexadecyl amine.

Armeen 18. Octadecyl amine.

Armelene. Trisodium phosphate.

Armid. Aliphatic long-chain amine.

Armid C. Coconut oil amide.

Armid HT. Hydrogenated tallow amide.

Armid O. Octadecen amide.

Composition of Trade-Marked Products

Armid S. Soybean oil amide.
Armid T. Tallow amide.
Armid TO. Tall oil amide.
Armid 8. Octan amide.
Armid 10. Decan amide.
Armid 12. Dodecan amide.
Armid 14. Tetradecan amide.
Armid 16. Hexadecan amide.
Armid 18. Octadecan amide.
Armite. Crude anhydrous trisodium phosphate; water softener.
Armol. Monomethyl *p*-amidophenol sulfate; photographic developer.
Armowax. Long-chain fatty acid amide; synthetic wax.
Arneel. Long-chain aliphatic nitrile.
Arneel C. Coconut oil nitrile.
Arneel HT. Hydrogenated tallow nitrile.
Arneel O. Octadecane nitrile.
Arneel S. Soybean oil nitrile.
Arneel T. Tallow nitrile.
Arneel 8. Octane nitrile.
Arneel 10. Decane nitrile.
Arneel 12. Dodecane nitrile.
Arneel 14. Tetradecane nitrile.
Arneel 16. Hexadecane nitrile.
Arneel 18. Octadecane nitrile.
Aromatex. Glyptal-type resin (German).
Arochem. Modified phenolic resin; used in lacquers.
Arochlor. Chlorinated diphenyl resin; plasticizer.
Arofene. Phenolic resins; used in varnishes.
Aromine. Solution of an alkyl aryl sulfonate; wetting agent, detergent.
Aromol. Alkyl aryl sulfonate; dyeing assistant.
Aroplaz. Alkyd resin; used in lacquers.
Arostit Zet. Sodium hydrosulfite; dye-discharging agent.
Arox. Colloidal silver oxide.
Arquad O. Octadecenyl trimethyl ammonium chloride.
Arquad 8. Octyl trimethyl ammonium chloride.

Composition of Trade-Marked Products

Arquad 10. Decyl trimethyl ammonium chloride.
Arquad 12. Dodecyl trimethyl ammonium chloride.
Arquad 14. Tetradecyl trimethyl ammonium chloride.
Arquad 16. Hexadecyl trimethyl ammonium chloride.
Arquad 18. Octadecyl trimethyl ammonium chloride.
Arseco. Solution of calcium abietate in a petroleum solvent.
Arterenal. 3-4-Dihydroxyphenyl ethyl methyl amine; medicament.
Artic. Methyl chloride; used for refrigeration.
Artifex. Synthetic tar-acid resin.
Artilana. Wool-like fiber (German).
Arubren. Mixture of heptachlorterphenyl, Pergut and crude tetrachloronaphthalene; fire extinguisher (German).
Arylene. Sulfonated isopropyl naphthalene; textile wetting agent.
Arylpen. Sodium alkyl aryl sulfonate; textile penetrant.
ASA. *n*-Butyraldoxime; antiskinning agent in paint.
Asarcoloy. Cadmium-base bearing alloy; contains about 1.3% nickel.
Asbestine. Fibrous variety of talc; used in paints.
Asbestol. Fibrous talc.
Asbeston. Asbestos yarn; used for asbestos fabrics.
Ascabiol. Benzyl benzoate; miticide.
Ascarite. Sodium hydroxide and asbestos; absorbent for carbon dioxide.
Ascoloy. Chromium steel with or without substantial amounts of nickel.
Asco Wax 55. Emulsifiable vegetable wax; substitute for carnauba wax.
Aseptisil (Pensal). Sodium subsilicate; detergent.
Aseptoform. Alkyl ester of *p*-hydroxybenzoic acid; antiseptic.

Composition of Trade-Marked Products

Ashalite. Sal soda; detergent.

Asidbar. Plastic-impregnated wood; resistant to acids.

Asmit. Synthetic ion-exchange resin; used in purifying industrial water.

Aspigran. Special form of acetyl salicylic acid U.S.P.; used for tablet making.

Aspirin. Acetyl salicylic acid; medicament.

Asplit. Cement of phenol-formaldehyde resin containing carbon or an other acid resisting powder.

Asplit E1. Copolymer of vinylchloride and maleic anhydride, phenol-formaldehyde resin and *p*-toluene sulfone chloride with mineral filler; acidproof cement (German).

Astralit. Ammonium nitrate, containing nitroglycerin; explosive.

Astralon. Copolymer of methyl acrylate (20%) and polyvinyl chloride (80%); used in plastic sheeting.

Astrole. Acid dye.

Astrolith. Special lithopone; pigment.

Astrotone. Synthetic musk; used in perfumery.

Atabrine dihydrochloride. Quinacrine hydrochloride; used in medicine.

Atco Resin 150. Urea-formaldehyde resin; used in textile finishing.

Atcosol 66. "Soluble" pine oil; boil-off assistant.

Atcosyn. Alkyl aryl amide sulfonate; wetting agent.

Atcowet. Alkyl aryl sulfonate; wetting agent.

Athenon. *p*-Hydroxyphenyl amino-acetic acid; photographic developer.

Atlacide. Calcium chlorate; weed killer.

Atlas. Copper-base alloys with aluminum, iron or lead.

Atlas A. Aqueous solution of sodium arsenite; weed killer.

Composition of Trade-Marked Products

Atlascide. Calcium chlorate; weed killer.

Atlas G-630. Mannitan laurate; emulsifier.

Atlas G-650. Sorbitan triricinoleate; emulsifier.

Atlas G-759. Sorbitan monolaurate; emulsifying and penetrating agent.

Atlas G-904. Mannitan monolaurate; emulsifier.

Atlas G-905. Mannitan monopalmitate; emulsifier.

Atlas G-908. Mannitan monostearate; emulsifier.

Atlas G-909. Sorbitan monostearate; bodying agent for cosmetics and drugs.

Atlas G-954. Mannitan monooleate; emulsifier.

Atlas G-2000. Mixed polyether of mannitan monopalmitate; emulsifier.

Atlas G-2800. Mannitol oleate; emulsifier.

Atlas K-100. Triisopropylidene mannitol; antioxidant.

Atlas K-101. Trimethylene mannitol; plasticizer.

Atlas K-103. Triethylidene mannitol; plasticizer.

Atlas K-110. Triisopropylidene sorbitol; plasticizer.

Atlas K-111. Trimethylene sorbitol; hardener.

Atlas K-113. Triethylidene sorbitol; plasticizer.

Atlasoil. Sulfonated oil.

Atlox G-1243-I. Mixed tall oil ester of polyalkylene sorbitol containing a small amount of isopropyl alcohol; emulsifier.

Atlox 1045-A. Mixed oleic-lauric acid ester of polyoxalkylene sorbitol; emulsifier.

Atomite. Calcium carbonate; filler in rubber.

Atophan. 2-Phenyl quinoline 4-carboxylic acid; medicament.

Atophan. Cinchophen; used in medicine.

Composition of Trade-Marked Products

Atrapol. Sulfated olive oil blend; used in textile finishing.

Attaclay. Finely divided fullers' earth; insecticide carrier or diluent.

Aubepine. Anisic aldehyde; used in perfumery.

Auric brown. Hydrated ferric oxide of very fine particle size; pigment.

Aurinol. Sulfated oleyl alcohol; wetting agent and detergent.

Aurol. See Neutralin.

Aurosal. Gold oxide.

Australole. Pine oil.

Autan. Mixture of paraformaldehyde and barium (or strontium) dioxide; disinfectant.

Auxanine BA. Phospho-tungstate compound; dyeing assistant.

Aveeno. Corn-germ oil; antioxidant in vegetable oils.

Avenex. Powdered oat flour; antioxidant.

Aversol. Heavy metal naphthenate; paint drier.

Avertin. 1,1,1-Tribromo ethanol-2; basal anesthetic.

Avialite. Aluminum bronze containing approximately 9% aluminum and small percentages of tin, nickel, and iron.

Avional. Alloy containing 4.75% copper, 0.5% magnesium, 1% manganese, 1.4% silicon and 92.71% aluminum.

Avirol AH. Sodium butyl ricinoleate; wetting agent.

Avirol CS. Mineral oil with sodium lauryl sulfate and sulfonated oil; textile lubricant (German).

Avirol OS. Sulfated fatty alcohol; emulsifying agent.

Avirol WS. Sulfated fatty alcohol; emulsifying agent.

Avirol-80. Sodium octyl sulfate; emulsifying agent.

Avisco. Viscose yarn.

Avitex. Sulfated higher fatty alcohols; textile finishing and softening agent.

Composition of Trade-Marked Products

Avitex AD. Fatty alcohol sulfate; surface-active agent.

Avitone A. Sodium hydrocarbon sulfonate; emulsifying agent.

Avivage K. Aqueous paraffin wax emulsion; textile softener (German).

Avolin. Dimethyl phthalate.

Avonac. Sodium salt of sulfated aliphatic ester; wetting agent.

Axel. Ketone-amine reaction product; rubber accelerator.

A.X.F. Synthetic rubber of the polyphenylene-ethylene type.

Azamin. Melamine.

Azanol. Acid dye.

Azo Citric. Zinc oxide; used in agricultural sprays.

Azoguard. Product used as an addition to printing paste to increase color fastness.

Azolith. Lithopone; pigment.

Azosol Fast. Light-fast azo dye; used in lacquers.

Azurwite. Sodium perborate compound; bleach.

Backdura. Synthetic tar-acid resin.

Bacterol. Cresol soap; disinfectant.

Badex. Dextrin.

Bakelaque. Synthetic oil-soluble tar-acid resin.

Bakelast. Solid polymerized and oxidized vegetable oils.

Bakelite. Trade name that covers a large group of thermosetting (phenolics and ureas) and thermoplastic (polystyrenes, and cellulose plastics) resins, plastics and coating materials.

Bakelite P. Polystyrene plastic.

Bakelite BR-4036. *p-tert*-Butyl phenol-formaldehyde resin; used in varnish.

Baker P-8. Glyceryl triacetoricinoleate; plasticizer.

BAL. 2,3-Dimercaptopropanol; antiarsenical used in treatment of Lewisite casualties.

Composition of Trade-Marked Products

Barak. Dibutyl ammonium oleate; rubber accelerator.

Barbak-C. Mercuric phenyl cyanamide and cadmium oxide; corn-seed disinfectant.

Bardional. Sulfathiourea (German).

Bardol. Viscous, liquid coal-tar hydrocarbon; rubber softener.

Barkite. Methyl cyclohexyl oxalate; lacquer plasticizer.

Baroco. Barytes.

Barofine. Bleached ground baryte.

Baroid. Non-corrosive material manufactured from barytes; used in oil-well drilling.

Barolith. Barium sulfate-lithopone pigment.

Barutin. Theobromine barium sodium salicylate; medicament.

Bascosol. Mycrocrystalline petroleum wax; used in rubber compounding.

Basifrit. Quick-setting magnesite; refractory.

Basilite. Mixture of sodium fluoride and dinitrophenol aniline; wood preservative.

Basofor. Precipitated barium sulfate; pigment.

Bayko yarn. Cotton or silk thread coated with cellulose acetate.

Bayol. Colorless and odorless mineral oil.

Bayol-D. Colorless mineral oil; solvent.

Bayol 50,85. Technical, white mineral oil; used on textile finishing.

Beaconol A. Monoethyl phenyl phenol sodium sulfonate; dispersing and wetting agent.

Beaconol M. Monoethyl phenyl phenol potassium sulfonate; dispersing and wetting agent.

Beaconol S. Monoethyl phenyl phenol aminosulfonate; detergent and wetting agent.

Beaconol T. Monoethyl phenyl phenol guanidine sulfonate; dispersing and wetting agent.

Beacon red. Fine-particle red pigment lake having an aluminum hydrate base.

Bearite. Series of lead-base bearing metals containing about 17% antimony and fractional percentages of copper and bismuth.

Bearium. High-lead bronze with 18 to 26% lead.

Beckacite. Synthetic phenol-formaldehyde or alkyd resin.

Beckamine. Synthetic urea resin.

Beckol. Synthetic alkyd resin.

Beckolin. Drying oil; used in enamels.

Beckophen. Thermosetting phenolic plastic.

Beckopol. Synthetic phenolated copal resin; used in varnish.

Beckosol. Pure or modified alkyd resin or its solution; used in paints.

Becktone. Lithopone pigment.

Bedafin-CM. Thermoplastic synthetic resin; finish for textiles.

Bedafin-H. Water-soluble synthetic resin; finishing agent.

Bedafin-20. Resin, oxidizing in air; used for transparent finishes.

Bedesol. Synthetic resin; used in paints, lacquers, etc.

Beetle. Urea-formaldehyde, thermoplastic resin.

Bellaton. Nitrobenzimidazole; used in photographic developing.

Bellit. Mineral oil emulsified with soap, sulfonated oil and water (German).

Bellite. Ammonium nitrate and dinitrobenzene; explosive.

Belloid F-2. Triethanol amine soap; wetting agent.

Belro resin. Hard, brittle, dark, non-crystalline rosin by-product; used in asphalt compositions.

Bemberg. Cuprammonium rayon.

Bemul. Commercial glyceryl monostearate; emulsifying agent.

Benalite. Mixture of cellulose, lignin and a small amount of resin (German).

Composition of Trade-Marked Products

Benadryl. β-Dimethylaminoethyl benzhydryl ether hydrochloride; used in medicine.

Benclor-3. Chlorinated benzene; weed-killer.

Benedict metal. Copper-nickel alloy, with 14 to 16% nickel; used for mfg. tubing.

Benowax. Microcrystalline petroleum wax.

Bensapol. Combination of sulfonated oils and a solvent; wetting agent.

Bensulfen. Dibenzoyl disulfide.

Benthal. Technical benzoic acid; dispersing agent in grinding pigments.

Benvar. Polyvinyl benzal; synthetic resin.

Benzedrine. Desoxy-norephedrine; used in medicine.

Benzestrol. 1,3-Bis-(*p*-hydroxyphenyl) 1,2-diethyl 3-methyl propane; synthetic sex hormone.

Benzo-Sol. Aromatic petroleum solvent.

Bepanthen. Pharmaceutical based on pantothenol.

Beraloy. Copper-base alloys with up to 2.5% beryllium.

Berylco alloy. Alloys consisting of beryllium and copper.

Be Square Wax. Microcrystalline petroleum wax.

Betabion. Vitamin B.

Beta Sol. Quaternary ammonium salt; dispersing and wetting agent.

Betasol OT-A. Sulfonated esters of a dicarboxylic acid; wetting agent.

Betaxin. Synthetic vitamin B_1.

Bethadur. Stainless steel containing up to 21% chromium and 11% nickel.

Bethalon. Free-machining stainless steel, containing fractional percentages of sulfur for greater machinability.

Beth-cu-loy. Copper-bearing alloy; used for construction purposes.

Composition of Trade-Marked Products

Bethanized. Iron- or steel-electroplated zinc.

Betitol. Inositol.

Beufa. Butyl esters of unsaturated C_{18} fatty acid; plasticizer.

Beutene. Tributylidene aniline.

Betramine. Sulfonated condensation product of aliphatic aldehydes of high molecular weight.

Bexin. Resin; antioxidant, plasticizer.

Bexoid. Cellulose acetate plastic.

Bexone. Polyvinyl-resin molding powder.

Bexone F. Polyvinyl acetal; thermoplastic sheeting.

Biancal. Oleyl naphthalene persulfonate.

Biancol. White mineral oil.

Bidery metal. Zinc-base alloy containing about 6% copper, 6% lead, and, optionally, 1% tin.

Biliposol. Bismuth compound of α-carboxyethyl β-methyl nonoic acid; used in medicine.

Biliselectan. β-(4-Hydroxy-3, 5-diiodophenyl) α-phenyl propionic acid.

Biloptin. Diiodoatophan.

Bindarene. See Clarion.

Bindex. Sulfite liquor containing lignin, glucose, tannates and resinates; binder and filler.

Bionol A. Quaternary ammonium salt; antiseptic.

Bismal. Bismuth methylene digallate.

Bismarsen. Sulpharsphenamine bismuth.

Bismo-cymol. Basic bismuth camphocarboxylate.

Bismon. Colloidal bismuth hydroxide.

Bismosol. Aqueous solution of glucose containing potassium-sodium bismuthotartrate and piperazine.

Bismutose. Bismuth-albumin compound.

Bister T (Dampfgrün S). Bisulfite

Composition of Trade-Marked Products

of nitroso-β-naphthol; used in dyeing (French).

Blackbird. Black clay.

Black Leak-40. Nicotine sulfate.

Black Leaf-155. Nicotine and bentonite.

Bladan. Hexaethyl tetraphosphate; insecticide (German).

Blancote. Precipitated chalk.

Blandol. U.S.P. white mineral oil.

Blankit. Sodium hydrosulfite.

Blastine. Explosive consisting of TNT, ammonium perchlorate, sodium nitrate and paraffin wax; used in mining.

Blendene. "Soluble" pine oil.

Blendoyl. Mixture of rapeseed and castor oils.

B Liquor. Aqueous solution of NH_3 (30% by weight).

Blowing Agent #15. Finely ground mixture of biuret and urea; used in making sponge rubber.

Blue-Flo. Green liquid consisting of denatured ethyl alcohol and a rust inhibitor; antifreeze.

3 B Mercaptan. *tert*-Dodecyl mercaptan; polymerization controller.

Bodygum. Powdered sterilized carob bean gum.

Boerite. Sulfated oleic acid; emulsifier.

Bondite. Cellulose flock or flour; filler for plastics.

Bonoform. 1,1,2,2-Tetrachloroethane.

Boontex. See Spry.

Bordow. Copper containing fungicide.

Boriresin. Synthetic borophosphate resin.

Bornyval. Bornyl isovalerate.

Boro-Klor. Boron trichloride; used in aluminum alloys.

Borolon. Alumina.

Borosoap. Sodium metaborate.

Borsalyl. Sodium borosalicylate.

Bortam. Boron-containing master alloy with 16 to 18% titanium, 13 to 15% aluminum, 22 to 24% manganese, 20 to 25% silicon, and 1.5 to 2.0% boron, with carbon not exceeding 1%.

Bourbonal. 3-Ethoxy-4-hydroxybenzaldehyde.

Bozetol. Sulfonated derivative of castor oil; wetting agent in textile industry.

Braconyl. Mixture of glycerides and sulfides of polychlorcyclane; insecticide.

Brassicol. Mixture with pentachloronitrobenzene (20%) and talc (20%); soil disinfectant (German).

Brassisan. Mixture with 1,2,4-trichloro-3,5-dinitrobenzene (20%), talc (77%) and machine oil (3%); fungicide for plants (German).

Braylite. Phenol-formaldehyde plastic.

Breadlac. Non-fat dry milk solids; used in baking.

Brentamine. Amino base or stabilized diazotized amino base.

Brenthol. Phenolic and naphtholic compounds; used in the coloring of fibers.

Brex. Soap and alkali; detergent.

Brino. Magnesium benzoate; preservative.

Britex. Composition of beeswax, sulfated oil and potash soap; used in softening paper.

Bromalbacid. Albumin bromate.

Bromalin. Hexamethylene tetramine bromethylate.

Brometone. Tribromo-*tert*-butyl alcohol.

Brominol. See Bromipin.

Bromipin. Bromine addition product of a vegetable oil.

Bromisoval. See Bromural.

Bromotan. Bromotannin methylene urea.

Bromofume. Mixture of ethylene dichloride, carbon tetrachloride and methyl bromide.

Brom-Tetragnost. Tetrabromophenolphthalein sodium.

Composition of Trade-Marked Products

Bromural. α-Monobromoisovaleryl urea.

Brovalol. Bornyl bromoisovalerate.

B.R.T. Refined coal tar.

Brutal. Mixture of equal parts of carbon tetrachloride, tetralin and ethylene dichloride; seed fumigant (German).

B.R.V. Coal-tar oil.

Brymul A. "Soluble" Stoddard solvent; kier-boiling aid.

Bubene. *sec*-Butyl benzene.

Buna N (Perbunan). Butadiene copolymer with acrylonitrile.

Buna S. Copolymer of butadiene and styrene.

Buna SS. Butadiene copolymer with styrene.

Buna 32. Viscous, low-molecular-weight sodium butadiene polymer.

Buna 85. Butadiene polymer.

Buna 115. Butadiene polymer.

Bunte salts. Sodium alkyl thiosulfates.

Buramine. Crude N-mono-*n*-butyl urea.

Buranil LL. Aqueous dispersion of sodium fatty alcohol sulfate with hydrocarbon solvent (about 10%); textile assistant (German).

Burloy steel. Corrosion-resistant high-chromium and stainless steels.

Burmol. See Blankit.

Burnus. Mixture of tryptase and soda ash; used in fat splitting (German).

Burofume. Calcium cyanide.

Buromin. Sodium hexametaphosphate glass.

Butac. Modified, refined pine gum.

Butacite. Polyvinyl-acetal resin.

Butagas. Compressed butane.

Butalyde. *n*-Butyraldehyde.

Butaprene N. Modified copolymers of butadiene and acrylonitrile.

Butasan. Zinc salt of dibutyl dithiocarbamic acid.

Butazote. GR-S rubber.

Composition of Trade-Marked Products

Butesin. Butyl *p*-aminobenzoate; used in medicine.

Butex. Pentadiene-styrene latex.

Butoben. *n*-Butyl *p*-hydroxybenzoate.

Butone. Mixture of butyl alcohol and higher homologs and esters; solvent (German).

Butoxyl. Methyl 1,2-butylene glycol acetate.

Butvar. Polyvinyl butylal.

Butyl. Dibutyl aminopropyl *p*-aminobenzoate sulfate.

Butylac. Similar to Nekal; wetting agent (German).

Butyl Zimate. Zinc dibutyl dithiocarbamate.

Buxine. Amyl cinnamic aldehyde; used in soap perfume.

Byketol S. Cymol; solvent (German).

Cadaloy. Cadmium-mercury-zinc alloy.

Cafasol. See Caparol.

Cal-Add. Calcium phosphate; additive for enriched flour.

Calafene H. Water-dispersed pigment and binder; filler and binder in leather finishing.

Calamine. Zinc oxide with ferric oxide (about 0.5%); used for treatment of skin diseases.

Calbroben. Calcium dibromobehenate.

Calcene. Special calcium carbonate.

Calcid. Calcium cyanide; plant fumigant.

Calciferol. Pure crystalline vitamin D_2.

Calcinite. Silicon carbide; abrasive.

Calcinol. Calcium lactate.

Calcocid. Series of acid dyes.

Calcodur. Series of light-fast direct colors; used in dyeing rayon, cotton.

Calcogene. Series of sulfur colors; used in dyeing vegetable fibers.

Calcoloid. Series of colloidal vat dye

Composition of Trade-Marked Products

pastes; used in dyeing and printing rayon, cotton.

Calcomine. Series of direct dyes; used for dyeing cotton, rayon, paper.

Calconese. Direct dye for cellulose acetate.

Calcosol. Series of vat dyes; used in dyeing and printing cotton, rayon.

Calcozine. Series of basic colors; used in dyeing cotton, leather, paper.

Caledon. Series of vat dyes made from anthraquinone; used in dyeing, printing rayon, cotton.

Calex Crystals. Agglomerated Calgon.

Calfast. Calcium arsenate with adhesive; insecticide.

Calfix. Calcium carbonate.

Calflax 270. Resin.

Calgolac. Mixture of sodium hexametaphosphate (30%) and alkalies (70%); used in cleaners.

Calgon (Kornite). Sodium hexametaphosphate; water softener.

Calgonite. Mixture based on Calgon; detergent.

Calgran. Calcium carbonate granules; used in welding flux.

Calgreen. Mixture of copper metarsenite and calcium arsenate; insecticide.

Califlake. Calcium chloride.

Calite. Heat- and oxidation-resistant iron-nickel-chromium alloys with 8 to 64% nickel, 5 to 20% chromium, and low percentages of aluminum, manganese, silicon.

Callogen. Aqueous emulsion of oil, fatty acids and potassium soap; textile assistant (German).

Calmicro. Calcium carbonate.

Calmonal. Urethan calcium bromide.

Calo-clor. Mixture of mercurous and mercuric chlorides.

Calodorant. Mixture of hydrocarbons and organic sulfur compounds.

Composition of Trade-Marked Products

Calomelol. Mixture of Hg_2Cl_2 with proteids.

Calopone. Anhydrous calcium sulfate.

Caloride. Cubes of calcium chloride.

Calphos. Phosphate rock; fertilizer.

Calsolene Oil HS. Sulfonated oil.

Calsprate. Calcium acetyl salicylate.

Calurea. Calcium urea nitrate.

Cal-Zinc. Calcium arsenate-zinc sulfate preparation.

Camasel. Sulfonated castor oil.

Cameko. Solution of sodium pyrosulfite; dye-stripping agent.

Camelite. $Zn(OH)(HSO_2CH_2O)$; dye-stripping agent.

Camphrosal. *p*-Toluene sulfamide.

Canfornia. Turpentine (Spanish).

Cantan. Synthetic vitamin C.

Capa. Calcium pantothenate.

Capain. Hydrolysate of casein made by digesting it with papain; blood plasma substitute.

Capalan. Polyethacrylate (German).

Caparol (Cafasol). Aqueous emulsions of polymethacrylate resin with egg albumen and ammonia (German).

Caprokol. 4-Hexyl resorcinol.

Captax. Mercaptobenzothiazole.

Caramide. Sodium higher fatty acid amide sulfate; detergent.

Caranol. Aqueous dispersion of sodium fatty alcohol sulfate; used in textile finishing (German).

Carapin. Sodium fatty alcohol sulfate (6.5%), balance inorganic salts and small amounts of water; textile assistant (Polish).

Carasol. Sulfonated oil.

Carbagel. Calcium chloride absorbed on activated charcoal.

Carbalose. Aqueous solution of calcium chloride and starch; textile weighter.

Carbamite. Symmetrical diphenyl diethyl urea.

Carbic. Calcium carbide briquettes.

Carbic. Resin made from cyclopen-

Composition of Trade-Marked Products

tadiene, maleic anhydride, glycerol and linoleic acid.

Carbitol. Diethylene glycol monoethyl ether.

Carbocell. Porous carbon, bonded.

Carbofilm. Plasticized carbohydrate sheeting.

Carbofrax. Silicon carbide.

Carbo-Korez. A-stage phenolic resin with carbon filler; corrosion-resistant cement.

Carbolac. Specially prepared gas black; used in lacquers.

Carbolan. Acid dye; used for printing on wool and silk.

Carbolite. Calcium carbide.

Carbolite. Phenol-formaldehyde resin with sulfonated hydrocarbons.

Carbomang. Low-alloy tool steel containing approximately 1% carbon, 1% manganese, 0.5% chromium and 0.5% tungsten.

Carbonex. Solid coal-tar hydrocarbon with high, free-carbon content.

Carbonex S. Solid coal-tar hydrocarbon with a small amount of fatty acid; reinforcing softener for rubber.

Carbon Met. Chlorinated coal-tar distillate fraction.

Carbon Twelve. Finely divided carbon, about 99% pure; used in electrodes.

Carboraffin. Decolorizing carbon black.

Carbosterol. Carbitol stearate.

Carbowax. Polyethylene glycols.

Carbowax-1500. Polymerized glycol; soft wax; softener, size, lubricant for textiles.

Carbowax-4000. Polymerized glycol; translucent solid; binder for pigments, lubricant in sizing.

Carboxide. Liquefied mixture of ethylene oxide and carbon dioxide.

Carboxymethocel A. Carboxymethyl cellulose aluminum salt.

Carboxymethocel S. Sodium cellulose glycollate.

Composition of Trade-Marked Products

Carbromal (Adalin). Bromodiethyl acetyl urea.

Carbrosolite. Silicon carbide.

Carbrox. Decolorizing carbon.

Carcholin. Carbamyl choline chloride.

Cardamide. *tert*-Alkyl urea.

Cardiazol. See Metrazol.

Cardice. Solidified carbon dioxide.

Cardis. Microcrystalline petroleum wax.

Cardolite. Synthetic resin made made from high-molecular-weight unsaturated phenolics extracted from cashew-nut shells.

Cardox. Solidified carbon dioxide; fire extinguisher.

Carenol. Vitamin A.

Carex. Carrot oil dissolved in an edible oil.

Cargan. Casein textile fiber (Belgium).

Cargentos. Colloidal silver compound of casein.

Carnofil. Textile fiber made from animal muscle tissues (German).

Carosal A. Aqueous dispersion of higher fatty acids with lecithin; textile assistant (German).

Carosel. Diaminoazobenzene.

Carovit. Chlorophyll-β-carotene complex (British).

Carragar. Carragheen extract; thickener for foods.

Carrene-1. Methylene chloride; refrigerant.

Carrene-2. Trichloromonofluoromethane; refrigerant.

Cascorez. Casein-resin emulsion; extender for latex in shoe adhesives.

Castoloy. High-carbon, high-chromium die steel with about 1.5% carbon, 13% chromium and fractional percentages of manganese and molybdenum.

Castrix. Acetic ester, urea, chlorine reaction product; rodenticide (German).

Carsene. Mixture of carbon tetra-

Composition of Trade-Marked Products

chloride and naphtha; leather cleaner.

Carstulat. Zinc stearate (German).

Cartox. Mixture of ethylene oxide (1%) and carbon dioxide (9%).

Cascamite. Urea-formaldehyde plastic.

Cascophen. Resorcinol-formaldehyde resin; adhesive.

Casco resin. Urea-formaldehyde resin; adhesive.

Casein PV-7631. Ammonium caseinate.

Caseite. Hydrated aluminum silicate.

Castorday. Graphite dispersed in vegetable oil; lubricant.

Castorwax. Hydrogenated castor oil.

Castrolite. Sulfonated castor oil.

Castung. Dehydrated castor oil.

Catabond B. B-stage phenol-formaldehyde resin.

Catalin. Phenol-formaldehyde thermosetting resin.

Catalite. Anthraquinone paste; catalyst in dye discharge.

Catalpo. Aluminum silicate; rubber filler.

Catapak. Phenol-formaldehyde plastic molding compound.

Catavar. Melamine-urea-formaldehyde resin; used in laminating.

Catavar 100–117. Phenol-formaldehyde resin; used in laminating.

Catex. Artificial zeolite.

Cationic Agent C. Lauryl amidoethyl phosphoric acid; surface-active agent.

Cationic Agent D. Stearyl amidoethyl phosphoric acid; cationic surface-active agent.

Cationic Amine 220. 1-Hydroxyethyl 2-heptadecyn glyoxalidine.

Catmul. Aqueous phenol-formaldehyde rosin emulsion; bonding agent.

Catol. Alkyl triethyl ammonium chloride.

Catol 607. Lauryl pyridinium chloride compound; cation-active soap.

Catylon D. Formate of a condensation product of stearic acid and hydroxyethylene diamine, mixed with fatty acid amide.

Cebione. Ascorbic acid.

Cecolene 1. Trichlorethylene.

Cecolene 2. Perchlorethylene.

Ceepryn. Cetyl pyridinium chloride; germicide.

Celanese. Artificial silk made from cellulose acetate.

Celanthrene. Anthraquinone dye.

Celastine. Black, molded sheets of cellulose acetate.

Celastoid. Cellulose acetate sheeting.

Celaton. Diatomaceous silica; filter aid.

Celax. "Soluble" mineral oil; used in textile finishing.

Celcon. Ethyl cellulose plastic.

Celcont. Ethyl cellulose.

Celeen. Cellulose wadding.

Celescot. Cellulose acetate plastic.

Celesterol. Unsaturated portions of sardine oil.

Celestol. Polyhydric alcohol-polybasic acid resin.

Celfil. Cellulose fiber.

Celfon. Solution of cellulose in caustic soda, metallic oxide and water.

Celite. Hydrated amorphous silica.

Celite 391. Amorphous diatomaceous silica.

Cellkapret. Methyl cellulose.

Cellastine. Cellulose acetate.

Cellcosan. Water-soluble cellulose derivative; textile sizing (Swedish).

Cellemold. Cellulose acetate molding powder.

Cellit. Cellulose acetate.

Cellit B. Cellulose acetobutyrate.

Celliton. Fast dye; used for printing and dyeing acetate rayon.

Cellofas. Solution of sodium alginate with or without other water-soluble organic additives.

Composition of Trade-Marked Products

Cellomold. Cellulose acetate molding powder.
Cellon. 1,1,2,2-Tetrachloroethane.
Cellophane. Transparent flexible sheeting consisting of regenerated cellulose plus plasticizers with or without a moistureproofing coating.
Celloprit. Carboxymethyl cellulose.
Cellorit. Cellulose laurate; laminating plastic (German).
Cellosan. See Cellosize.
Cellosize. Aqueous solution of hydroxyethyl cellulose (10%); used in textile sizing.
Cellosize WS. Aqueous solution of hydroxyethyl cellulose (10%).
Cellosolve. 2-Ethoxyethanol.
Celluflex. Aryl alkyl phosphate.
Cellugel. Sodium cellulose glycollate.
Celludine. Celloidin.
Celluloid. Cellulose nitrate and camphor plastic.
Cellulon. Fiber made from wood pulp.
Cellulube. Aryl phosphate.
Cellusol. *p*-Toluene sulfamide.
Celnax. Benzyl cellulose.
Celomite. Diatomaceous earth.
Celon. Cellulose acetate plastic.
Celospar. Feldspar.
Celotex. Artificial building board made from bagasse.
Cenex. Rubber latex.
Centralite I. Diphenyl diethyl urea.
Centralite II. Diphenyl dimethyl urea.
Centrol. Commercial mixture of about equal parts of lecithin, cephalin, and soybean oil.
Centrosene. Petroleum wax.
Ceraflux. Refined paraffin.
Ceraloid 235A. Mixture of higher fatty alcohols and hydrogenated oils; used in textile finishing.
Ceral TGl. Emulsion of dihydroxydichlorodiphenyl methane; used in waterproofing and rotproofing textiles.

Composition of Trade-Marked Products

Ceralumin. Alloy of 92.8% aluminum, 2.5% copper, 1.5% nickel, 1.2% silicon, 1.2% iron, 0.8% magnesium.
Ceramitalc. Talc; used in ceramics.
Ceramite. Solution of fluosilicate.
Cerasnow. Powdered, microcrystalline petroleum wax.
Cerasynt. Glyceryl monostearate.
Cereclor. Chlorinated paraffin; used in rubber compounding.
Cerelose. Commercial glucose
Ceremul C. Emulsion with paraffin wax (about 45%).
Ceremul M. Emulsion with microcrystalline petroleum wax (40%).
Ceresan. Ethoxyethyl mercuric phosphate compound; insecticide (German).
Cerese Wax. Microcrystalline paraffin wax.
Cerex. Polystyrene plastic.
Cerfak. Alkylated, aromatic hydrocarbon sulfonate.
Cerol K. Aqueous emulsion of paraffin wax with egg albumen and alum; waterproofing agent (Swiss).
Cerol FS. Paraffin wax emulsion; textile waterproofing agent.
Cerol TGI. Paraffin wax emulsion containing dihydroxydichlordiphenyl methane; mildewproofing agent.
Cerrobase. Alloy with 58% bismuth.
Cerrobend. Bismuth alloy with 27% lead, 13% tin, 10% cadmium.
Cerol S. Paraffin wax emulsion; used in textile waterproofing.
Cerromatrix. Bismuth alloy with 15% tin, 29% lead, and 9% antimony.
Cerrosafe. Alloy of 40% bismuth, 40% lead, 11% tin, and 9% cadmium.
Cerrotru. Eutectic alloy of bismuth and tin.
Cetamium. Cetyl trimethyl ammonium bromide; germicide.

Composition of Trade-Marked Products

Cetamoll MB. Dimethyl glycol phosphate (German).

Cetamoll Q. Tri-(β-chloroethyl) phosphate (German).

Cetavlon (CTAB). Trimethyl cetyl ammonium bromide; bactericide.

Cetosten. Cetyl alcohol.

Chamosheen. Sulfated olive oil; used in textile finishing.

Charcalite. Granular charcoal impregnated with calcium chloride; drying agent.

Chardonize. Viscose yarn.

Charlton white. Lithopone.

Chaulmestrol. Ethyl chaulmoograte; used in medicine.

Chemaco EC. Ethyl cellulose.

Chemick. Solution of calcium hypochlorite.

Chemigum. Synthetic rubber of Buna N type.

Chemisan. Aqueous solution of calcium or magnesium chlorides with or without propyl alcohol; antifreeze (German).

Chenal. Mixture of a highly sulfonated naphthalene derivative (4%), inorganic salts and moisture; textile assistant (German).

Chiniofon. 7-Iodo-8-hydroxyquinoline 5-sulfonic acid.

Chloramine-B. Sodium benzene sulfonchloramine.

Chloramine-T (Chlorazene). Sodium *p*-toluene sulfon chloramine.

Chlorasol. Mixture of carbon tetrachloride and ethylene dichloride.

Chlorax. Chlorinated hydrocarbon wax; used in polishes.

Chlorazene. Chloramine -T.

Chlorcosane. Chlorinated paraffin.

Chloresco. Calcium hypochlorite.

Chlorex. Bis-β-chloroethyl ether.

Chlor-Isopol. Chlorinated synthetic-rubber powder.

Chlorocosane. Chlorinated paraffin.

Chloroil. Technical oleyl chloride.

Chloron. Monochlorinated kerosene fraction; used in detergents.

Composition of Trade-Marked Products

Chlorovene. Polyvinyl chloride copolymer.

Chlorovene. Polyvinyl acetal plastic.

Chlorowax. Chlorinated paraffin wax.

Chlorpropane Wax 130. Chlorinated paraffin wax; used in dielectric coatings.

Choleval. Colloidal silver-sodium cholate.

Chromax. High-temperature and abrasion-resistant alloy cast irons containing 20 to 35% nickel, 15 to 20% chromium; used for furnace parts, chains subjected to heat.

Chromel. Nickel-chromium alloys with nickel predominant and iron optional; used for heating elements.

Chromoform. Methyl hexamethylene tetramine dichromate.

Chromosan mordant. Mixture of soluble alkali bichromate and ammonium phosphate.

Chromoxane. Light-fast mordant dye; used for dyeing wool.

Chroninol oil. Water-soluble stain-remover; used in textile industry.

Chrystolon. Silicon carbide.

Churnolac. Mixture of buttermilk, whey and wheat flour; used in baking.

Cialit. 2-Ethyl mercury mercaptobenzoxazol 5-carboxylic acid sodium salt; fungicide.

Ciba. Light- and wash-fast vat dye; used for printing and dyeing cotton, silk and rayon.

Ciba Blue B. Tribromo indigo; used in dyeing.

Ciba Blue 2B. Tetrabromo indigo; used in dyeing.

Ciba Blue G (Indigo MLB 5B). Mixture of tetra- and pentabromo indigo; used in dyeing.

Cibanaphthol. Series of β-hydroxynaphthoic acid derivatives; dye developers.

Composition of Trade-Marked Products

Cibanit. Aniline-formaldehyde condensation product; plastic molding powder.

Cibanoid. Urea-formaldehyde plastic.

Cibanone. Light-, bleach-and wash-fast anthraquinone derivative; used for dyeing and printing silk, cotton and rayon.

Ciba salt. Stabilized diazotized amine; paint intermediates.

Cibasol. Light-fast organic pigment; used for coloring paper.

Cicoil. Oiticica oil.

Cidan-l. Mixture of methyl, ethyl and isopropyl cresols.

Cinemoid. Cellulose acetate sheeting; light filters for movie projectors.

Cinnabex. Cellulose acetate sheeting.

Cirine wax. Ceresin.

Citratus. Dicalcium phosphate.

Citriteg. Citric acid-tetraethylene glycol resin; stopcock lubricant.

Citronin A. 2,4-Dinitro-l-naphthol 7-sulfonic acid sodium or potassium salt; dye for silk, food.

Citrophen. *p*-Phenetidin citrate.

Clairfoil. Cellulose acetate foil.

Clar-Apel. Viscose sheeting.

Clarase. Mixture of maltase, lipase, trypsin, erepsin and hemolysin; used in clarifying beverages.

Clarex. Activated clay.

Clarifoil. Cellulose acetate foil.

Clarion extract (Bindarene). Modified waste sulfite liquor concentrated to 50% solids.

Clarogent RA. See Clarsol A.

Clarsil. Activated clay.

Clarsol A (Clarogent RA). Higher fatty acid amide; boil-off assistant.

Clayton yellow. $C_{28}H_{19}O_6N_5S_4Na_2$; used in dyeing cotton.

Clearate. Phosphatide from soybeans containing lecithin and cephalin phosphatides.

Clenesco. Anhydrous sodium metasilicate.

Composition of Trade-Marked Products

Cliderite. Plastic composition based on ethyl cellulose flakes.

Cliffchar. Activated wood charcoal; used in deodorizing water.

Climeline. Trisodium phosphate.

Clintose. Refined corn sugar.

Clix. Hydrogenated lard; used in baking.

Clophen. Chlorinated diphenyls; plasticizer.

Clophen A60. Slightly chlorinated diphenyl.

Clor. Sodium hypochlorite solution.

Clorafin. Chlorinated paraffin.

Cloroben. Compound containing *o*-dichlorobenzene and an emulsifier; bactericide.

Clorox. Aqueous hypochlorite solution; bleaching agent.

Coagulen. Extract from bovine blood; used in medicine.

Coblac. Carbon-pigment lacquer base consisting of cellulose nitrate, dibutyl phthalate, carbon black.

Cocate. Methyl ester of coconut-oil fatty acids; plasticizer.

Cocoon. Modified vinyl-resin solution in volatile solvents.

Codban. Liquid consisting of β-naphthol (40%) and mineral oil (60%).

Codeonal. Codeine and sodium diethyl barbiturate; medicament.

Codimer. Mixture of polymerized butylenes.

Codur. Synthetic baking enamel with an alkyd-and urea-formaldehyde-resin base.

Cohaerit. Condensation product of trimethylol propane, hexantriol and adipinic acid; adhesive.

Cohesan. Preparation based on a nitrocellulose solution; adhesive.

Cohrlastic. Woven glass-fiber tape coated with silicone rubber; electric insulating tape.

Colalin. A mixture of oxidized ox-bile acids, with magnesium carbonate; used in medicine.

Colasta. Synthetic tar-acid resin.

Composition of Trade-Marked Products

Colene. Casein, gelatin, glycerin and ammonia water; binder in paper mfg.

Colas. Asphalt emulsion.

Colistatin. Succinyl sulfathiazole.

Collactivit. Product made by treating carbonaceous material with strong sulfuric acid, washing with water, drying and grinding; used in decolorizing sugar.

Collanoll. Dehydrated castor oil.

Collargol. Colloidal silver, colloidal silver oxide and egg albumin; antiseptic.

Collatone. Alkali compound of *p*-chloro-*m*-cresol.

Collocel. Sodium carboxymethyl cellulose.

Collocel A. Aluminum cellulose glycollate; used in greaseproofing paper.

Collocide. *o*-(*n*-Butyl)-phenyl sulforicinate; antiseptic.

Colloresin. Methyl cellulose.

Colloresin DK. Methyl cellulose; adhesive.

Colloresin V. Carboxymethyl cellulose; used in adhesives.

Colmenthol. Menthyl ethyl glycocolate.

Coloido BT. Refined soybean lecithin.

Coloidol BT. Soya lecithin.

Colox. Red iron oxide; used in oil-well drilling mud.

Colstone (Coltrock). Phenol-formaldehyde plastic.

Coltrock. See Colstone.

Comet metal. Iron-base alloy containing 30% nickel and up to 5% chromium.

Cominol. Derivative of a higher sulfonated alcohol; wetting agent, detergent in textile industry.

Compar. Compounded polyvinyl alcohol resin.

Compreg. Hardwood impregnated with phenolformaldehyde resin.

Compregnated Wood. See Pregwood.

Composition of Trade-Marked Products

Compregnite. Phenol-formaldehyde resin solution; used for impregnation.

Compromine D. See Compropaste H.

Compromine N. Sodium alkyl naphthalene sulfonate; dyeing assistant.

Compropaste H (Compromine D, DR). Sulfated alkyl amine; boil-off assistant.

Concental. Sulfated tallow.

Concentrolac A. Latex concentrate.

Concoset. Modified urea-formaldehyde resin.

Condensite. Phenol-formaldehyde resin.

Conductex. Electrical-conductive channel carbon black.

Congo red. Sodium diphenyl diazo-bis-α-naphthyl amine sulfonate.

Conite. Vulcanized fiber.

Conjulinol. Dehydrated linseed oil.

Conjusoy. Dehydrated soybean oil.

Conolite. Fiberglass or synthetic fabric impregnated with a thermosetting resin.

Consolwold. High-strength, laminated paper-base plastic.

Constantan. Copper-nickel alloy containing 10 to 55% nickel having constant electrical resistivity irrespective of temperature; used for electrical resistance thermocouples.

Contro. Rounded latex or cut rubber threads; used in elastic fabrics.

Convertit. Enzyme preparation; used in mfg. syrups and confectionery.

Coomassie. Mill- and wash-fast acid dye.

Copacite. Powdered sulfite lignin; used in foundry-core binders.

Copapel. Cuprammonium carbonate; mildew preventive.

Coposil. Copper ammonium silicate.

Coppatone. Copper sulfate dust; fungicide.

Composition of Trade-Marked Products

Coppercarb. Copper carbonate; seed disinfectant.

Copper Komel. 2-Monocopper glucosan; mildewproofing agent.

Coprein. Modified corn protein.

Coptal N. Sodium alkyl naphthalene sulfonate; wetting agent.

Coralac. Yarn made of combed cotton, viscose rayon and casein fibers.

Coramine. Pyridine β-carboxylic acid diethyl amide; medicament.

Corbasil. *o*-Dihydroxyphenyl propanol amine hydrochloride.

Cordex. Copper naphthenate solution; fungicide.

Cordfil. Chopped cotton cord; used as plastics filler.

Cordol. Tribromophenyl salicylate.

Corekal A. Sodium alkyl naphthalene sulfonate.

Coresinblak. Mixture of carbon black (18%), resin (32%), and solvent (50%); used in resin finishes.

Co-Ro-Lite. Rope-fiber plastic.

Corporin. See Progesterone.

Corrosiron. Cast iron with about 14% silicon; used for chemical equipment.

Cor-ten steel. Corrosion resistant steels with chromium 0.50 to 1.50% and optional fractional percentages of copper and silicon, carbon not exceeding 0.10%.

Corubin. Aluminum oxide.

Corvic. Polyvinyl chloride polymers; plastic.

Coryfin. Menthyl ethyl glycolate.

Cosal. Coal-tar solvent.

Cosal. Isobutyl polyvinyl ether.

Cosal D12. Polyvinyl isobutyl ether (41.3), casein (8), ammonia (0.34) and water (51); adhesive (German).

Cosaprin. Sodium acetyl sulfanilate.

Cosavult. Compound based on natural rubber latex; adhesive.

Cosma. Mixed wool wax alcohols.

Composition of Trade-Marked Products

Cosmetol N. Alkanol amine salt of a sulfoacetamide derivative.

Cosmin. Salicyl α-methyl phenyl hydrazine.

Cosmol. Hydrogenated sperm oil.

Cosmoline 850. Sodium petroleum sulfonate; wetting agent.

Coswiga. Barium chloride (69), barium carbonate (15.1), barium hydroxide (4.7) (German).

Cotilanol D. Sodium fatty alcohol sulfate (23%), large amounts of inorganic salts and water (6%); textile assistant (Italian).

Courlana. Casein textile fiber (England).

Covinylblak. Mixture of carbon black, vinyl resin and plasticizer; coloring agent.

Creamsol. Stabilized stearic acid emulsion; used in textile finishing.

Cremba. See Isocreme.

Cremnitz white. Lead carbonate and hydrated lead oxide.

Creolin (Cresoline). Solution of creosote and rosin soap; disinfectant.

Cresalol. Cresyl salicylate.

Cresatin. *m*-Cresol acetate; used in medicine.

Crescour. Mixture of soap, sulfonated oil and solvent; textile wetting agent.

Cresol Z-2 (Anglamol 35, 77-x). Sulfurized, chlorinated aliphatic hydrocarbons; used in cutting oils.

Cresol Z-4. Chlorinated, sulfurized naphthenic soap; used in cutting oils.

Cresophan. Alkyl *m*-cresol.

Cresopine. Cresol-sulfated oil composition; textile penetrant.

Crestanol resins. Modified phenol-formaldehyde and maleic anhydride resins; used in lacquers, printing inks, etc.

Crestin resin. Phenolic resin; used in chemically resistant varnishes.

Crill. Higher fatty acid ester; emulsifier.

Composition of Trade-Marked Products

Crioplasto E. Triethyl citrate; plasticizer (Italian).

Crisal 42. Aqueous solution of sodium lactate and methanol; antifreeze (German).

Crisalbine. Gold sodium thiosulfate.

Cristite. High-alloy iron with about 17% tungsten, 11% chromium, 3% carbon, optional low percentages of molybdenum and titanium.

Crocar. Iron-base alloy containing about 12% chromium, 2% carbon, 0.3% silicon, 0.75% vanadium and 0.75% cobalt; used where heat and abrasion resistance is required.

Cromoco. High-carbon die steel containing about 12% chromium, 1% cobalt, 1% molybdenum and 1.6% carbon.

Cro-Sil. Series of corrosion-resistent high-chromium alloys containing 10 to 14% chromium.

Crotvar. Polyvinyl crotonal.

Crovolit. Crotonic acid esters.

Crown wax. Microcrystalline petroleum wax.

Crown wax 1035. American ozokerite-type wax.

Cryptone. White pigment containing varying amounts of titanium dioxide, lithopone, etc.

Crystalite. Methyl methacrylate; thermoplastic molding powder.

Crystallose. Sodium benzosulfimide.

Crystalon (Crystolon). Silicon carbide product; used for refractory and abrasive purposes.

Crystamet. Sodium metasilicate pentahydrate.

Crystarose. Trichloromethyl phenyl carbinol acetate; used in perfumes.

Crystex. Amorphous sulfur; used in rubber compounding.

Crystolex. Colorless acrylic resin mix; used in dentistry.

Crystol-K. Treated fish oil; used in mfg. varnishes, paints, enamels, etc.

Crystol-K. Treated fish oil.

Composition of Trade-Marked Products

Crystox. Unsaturated C_{18} ketol; insecticide.

Crystur. Urea-formaldehyde plastic.

Cubor. Rotenone on a powdered carrier; insecticide.

Culicide oil B. Mixture of methyl and polymethyl naphthalenes.

Cullite. Zeolite; used in water conditioning.

Cumar. Coumarone-indene resin.

Cumate. Cupric diethyl dithiocarbamate.

Cunico. Alloy of copper, nickel and cobalt; used for permanent magnets.

Cunife. Alloy of copper, nickel and iron; used for permanent magnets.

Cupa. Mixture of Cumar (35), bitumen (35), Naftolen (30).

Cuprama. Cuprammonium staple fiber.

Cuprax. Cupric mercaptobenzothiazole.

Cuprex. Mixture of hydrocarbons containing a copper salt of a fatty acid.

Cuprinol. Metallic naphthenate.

Cuprocide. Red copper oxide.

Cuprocide Yellow. Yellow copper oxide.

Cuprodine. Copper sulfate, sodium chloride and a pickling inhibitor; lubricant for metal wire drawing.

Cupro-K. Copper oxychloride.

Cuprol. Copper nucleinate.

Cupron. β-Benzoinoxime.

Cuprotela. Cuprammonium carbonate; mildewproofing agent.

Cuprotrol 6. Talc containing powdered copper (6%); agricultural insecticide.

Curacit. Mixture of cholic acid, triethanol amine and water; glycerin substitute.

Curbay binder. Evaporated fermented molasses residue; core binding material in foundry practice, in road construction.

Curbay B-G. Riboflavin concentrate; poultry-feed additive.

Composition of Trade-Marked Products

Curgon drier. Metallic naphthenate; drier for paints, emulsifying agent, etc.

Cyanegg. Sodium cyanide.

Cyangran. Sodium cyanide.

Cyanobrite. Sodium cyanide; used in electroplating.

Cyanogas. Calcium cyanide.

Cyclanon OA. Sodium salt of sulfated oleyl alcohol; used in textile finishing.

Cyclite. Benzyl bromide.

Cyclocel. Calcined bauxite.

Cyclon. Hydrogen cyanide adsorbed on kieselguhr; fumigant.

Cyclonite. *sym*-Trimethylene trinitramine.

Cyclonol. Methyl cyclohexanone glyceryl acetate.

Cyclonol N. Cyclohexanone glyceryl acetal.

Cyclopal. Cyclopentene allyl barbituric acid; analgesic.

Cyclopon. Condensation product of fatty and sulfonic acids.

Cyclopon A. Fatty acid amide alkyl sulfonate.

Cyclopren T. Natural rubber (German).

Cyclops 17 metal. Alloy of iron, nickel, chromium, manganese and carbon; resistant to sulfuric acid, sea water, etc.

Cyclops steel. Rust and heat-resistant high-alloy steel containing 4 to 8% chromium, nickel, tungsten, vanadium, cobalt, molybdenum; used for tools, high-temperature tubing.

Cycloran M. Mixture of soap and methyl hexalin.

Cyclosul. Morpholine sulfite.

Cymag. Mixture of sodium cyanide and magnesium sulfate.

Cymanol. Methyl isopropyl benzene.

Cyomyl. 3,4-Dicyandiphenyl (German).

Cyprian vitriol. $CuSO_4 3ZnSO_4 \cdot 28H_2O$.

Composition of Trade-Marked Products

Cystogan. $(CH_3)_2NCSSNH_2(CH_3)_2$; insecticide (German).

Cythrene. Perhydrocyclopentanophenanthrene.

Cytoflav. Phosphorylated riboflavin.

Cyw steel. Low-alloy hot-die steel containing about 3.5% chromium and 1% carbon.

Dagenan. Sulfapyridine; medicament.

Dagenite. Acid- and base-resistant asbestos filler composition; used for accumulator cases.

Daintex. Liquid pine-oil soap; wetting agent and penetrant in the laundry industry.

Daisite. Thermit containing sulfur.

Damarda. Synthetic oil-soluble tar-acid resin.

Dambonitol. Dimethyl ether of inositol.

Damol. Tetramethyl didecyl β-hydroxypropylene diammonium bromide.

Dampfgrün S. See Bister T (German).

Danitra. Sodium nitrate.

Darco. Decolorizing carbon.

Darex AEA. Triethanol amine salt of a sulfonated hydrocarbon.

Dartex. Chlorinated rubber.

Darvan 1. Alkyl naphthalene sulfonic acid sodium salt; pigment-dispersing agent, accelerator in rubber industry.

Dastar. Wool-wax alcohols containing about 50% cholesterol; used in cosmetics.

Daxad 11. See Darvan 1.

Daxad 21. Monocalcium salt of polymerized aryl alkyl sulfonic acids.

Daxad 27. Mixture of monosodium salts of polymerized aryl alkyl sulfonic acids and an inorganic suspending agent.

DD. Mixture of 1,3-dichloropropylene and 1,2-dichloropropane; nematode poison.

Composition of Trade-Marked Products

DDD. Dihydroxydichlorodiphenyl methane; insecticide.

DDNP. Diazodinitrophenol.

DDT. Dichlorodiphenyl trichloroethane; insecticide.

De-Acidite. Aliphatic amine resin; ion-exchanger in water treatment.

Decal. Similar to Calgon; water softener.

Decalin. Decahydronaphthalene.

Decalso. Synthetic zeolite; water softener.

Decanol. Alkyl aryl sodium sulfonate.

Deceresol AN (Deceresol TA; Dexolene). Sodium salt of alkyl naphthalene sulfonate; wetting agent.

Deceresol AY. Sodium salt of diamyl sulfosuccinate.

Deceresol MA. Sodium salt of dimethylamyl sulfosuccinate.

Deceresol OS. Sodium salt of diisopropyl naphthalene sulfonic acid.

Deceresol OT. Dioctyl sodium sulfosuccinate.

Deceresol SE. Quaternary ammonium compound; used in textile finishing.

Deceresol TA. See Deceresol AN.

Deceresol C-61. Alkyl guanidine-amine complex; dispersing agent.

Decholin. Sodium dehydrocholate; medicament.

Decorite. Casein plastic.

Decroline Soluble. $Zn(HSO_2CH_2O)_2$; dye-reducing agent.

Decroline X4. $Zn(OH)(HSO_2CH_2O)$; dye-reducing agent.

Deenate. DDT containing compound; agricultural insecticide.

Deenol 10-A. Dusting powder with DDT (10%).

Deenol 25-C. Oil concentrate with DDT (25%).

Deenol 25-EM. Emulsifiable oil with DDT (25%).

Deenol 50-F. Wettable powder with DDT (50%).

Deenol 5-H. Oil spray with DDT (5%); insecticide.

Composition of Trade-Marked Products

Defiheat Rustless Iron. High-chromium steel with 25 to 30% chromium, about 0.3% carbon and the usual quantities of manganese and silicon.

Defirust Rustless Iron. Series of chromium steels highly resistant to corrosion containing 12 to 18% and below 0.12% carbon with manganese and silicon in the usual fractional percentages.

Defistain Rustless Iron. Stainless steel with 17 to 19% chromium, 7 to 9% nickel, 0.5% manganese, 0.5% silicon and $< 0.2\%$ carbon.

Defluorite. Tricalcium phosphate.

Defluorophos. Defluorinated calcium phosphate.

Defoama. Sulfonated fats and solvent; antifoaming agent.

Degalol. Compound of dioxycholanic acid and menthol; medicament.

Degomma DL. Pancreatic gland extract.

Dehydranone. Dehydroaceteic acid.

Dehydrite. Anhydrous, granular magnesium perchlorate.

Dehydrol. Dehydrated castor oil; used in varnish.

Dekalin. Decahydronaphthalene.

Dekol N. Sulfite-cellulose waste liquor.

Dekorit. Synthetic tar-acid resin.

Dekrolin. Zinc sulfoxalate-formaldehyde.

Delac A. Diphenyl guanidine salt.

Delac J. Diphenyl nitrosoamine; vulcanization activator.

Delac P. Diphenyl guanidine phthalate; vulcanization activator.

Dellatol. Methyl butyl benzene sulfonamide; plasticizer.

Delsterol. Irradiated animal sterol rich in vitamin D; used in poultry feed.

Deltaform. Bismuth dithiosalicylate.

Deltamine. 1,8-Diamino naphtalene; dye intermediate.

Deltyl. Isopropyl palmitate.

Composition of Trade-Marked Products

Deltyl Extra. Isopropyl ester of fatty acids derived from spermaceti.

Delvinal. Ethyl methyl butenyl barbituric acid.

Demal 14. Polyhydric alcohol ester of higher fatty acid.

Demerol. 1-Methyl 4-phenyl piperidine 4-carboxylic acid ethyl ester hydrochloride.

Deminrolit B. Synthetic resin; used in water purification.

Densodrin. Low-molecular-weight polymer of vinyl isobutyl ether; waterproofing agent (German).

Densodrin NH (I. G. Wax NH). Polyvinyl ether (German).

Densodrin V (I. G. Wax V). Wax-alcohol vinyl ether (German).

Denzox. Product containing zinc oxide; used in the ceramic industry.

Deo-Base. Deodorized kerosene.

Deodol. Acid-stabilized, higher fatty acid ester.

Deodorit. Deodorizing carbon.

Deracil. 2-Thiouracil; used in medicine.

Deramin. Glycoether amine; emulsifying agent.

Deravet. Thiouracil preparation; used in veterinary medicine.

Derex. Solution of derris extractives in butyl mesityl oxide oxalate; insecticide.

Derinatrol. Basic bismuth gallate; used in medicine.

Dermacrine. 5-Aminoacridine monohydrochloridedihydrate; bacteriostatic.

Dermatol. Bismuth subgallate; used in medicine.

Dermol. Bismuth chrysophenate; used in medicine.

Desavin. Diphenoxyethyl formal; plasticizer.

Desencin. Mixture of benzyl *p*-iodethoxybenzoate and *pseudo*-sulfamidobenzamide; used in medicine.

Deseptyl. Sulfanilamide.

Composition of Trade-Marked Products

Desichthyol (Desichtol). Deodorized ichthyol.

Desichtol. See Desichthyol.

Desmidure. Chlorinated Buna S (German).

Desmodur. Polyurethane plastic.

Desmodur H. Hexamethylene diisocyanate (German).

Desmodur R. Triisocyanate of triamine triphenyl methane.

Desmodur T. Toluene diisocyanate (German).

Desmophen 0–0. Polyester of oxalic acid and hexanetriol (German).

Desmophen 100. Condensation product of adipinic acid, 1,4-butylene glycol and hexanetriol (German).

Desmophen 900. Condensation product of adipic acid and trimethylol propane; used in adhesives (German).

Desmophen 1100. Polyester of adipic acid and 1,4-butylene glycol and trimethylol propane (German).

Desmophen 1200. Polyester of adipic acid, 1,4-butanediol and trimethylol propane (German).

Desmophen 800S. Polyester of trimethylol propane with adipinic and phthalic acids (German).

Desmosite C. 1-Chlorophenylene 2,4-diisocyanate; used in tanning (German).

Desmosite H. Hexamethylene diisocyanate; used in adhesives (German).

Desmosite O. Polyhexamethylene diisocyanate; used in adhesives (German).

Desmosite T. Tolylene diisocyanate; used in adhesives (German).

Desogen. Quaternary ammonium compound; disinfectant.

Dessichlora. Anhydrous barium perchlorate; dessicant.

Dessicite. Dehydrated bentonite; drying agent.

Detanol. Salt of a sulfonated amide; textile wetting agent, detergent.

Composition of Trade-Marked Products

Detel. Chlorinated rubber; used in mfg. chemically resistant paints.

Detergo. Compound containing sodium hydrocarbon sulfonates; degumming agent.

Detersol. See Turpenol.

Deward steel. Non-deforming steel with approximately 1.6% manganese, 0.3% silicon, and 1.0% carbon.

Dewaxit. Super-fatted soap solution in organic solvent; emulsifier.

Dexatol. Sulfated fatty amide; wetting agent.

Dexene. Water solution of low-viscosity vegetable gums; used in textile finishing.

Dexo. See Spry.

Dexolene. See Deceresol AN.

Di-48. Liquid consisting of low- and high-boiling isomers of dichlorethylene.

Diafilt. Diatomaceous earth; filtering aid.

Diafoam. Octyl alcohol; antifoaming agent.

Diafor. Urea acetyl salicylate; used in medicine.

Diagen. Stabilized azoic dye.

Diakon. Thermoplastic acrylate resin; plastic.

Dial. 5,5-Diallyl barbituric acid; used in medicine.

Dialyte. Water-ground pumice; abrasive.

Diamantine. Mordant acid dye.

Diaminogen. Direct or developed dye.

Diamond dry cleaner. Liquid consisting of carbon tetrachloride and chlorinated hydrocarbons; used in dry cleaning.

Diamond Gum. See Gelatin Gum.

Diamondite. Tungsten carbide.

Diane. Dihydroxydiphenyl propane; varnish resin.

Dianol RX. Sodium higher-alcohol sulfate; wetting agent.

Diapene AE-P. Melamine-resin dispersion; textile sizing.

Composition of Trade-Marked Products

Diapene GP-50. Emulsion of an alkyd resin; textile sizing.

Diapene OA-50. Acrylic resin.

Diaperm H. Cation active amide; emulsifier.

Diarmeen O. *sec*-Octadecenyl amine.

Diarmeen 8. *sec*-Octyl amine.

Diarmeen 10. *sec*-Decyl amine.

Diarmeen 12. *sec*-Dodecyl amine.

Diarmeen 14. *sec*-Tetradecyl amine.

Diarmeen 16. *sec*-Hexadecyl amine.

Diarmeen 18. *sec*-Octadecyl amine.

Diastafor. Standardized mixture containing amylolytic and proteolytic enzymes; desizing agent.

Diastersol NOS. Sodium salt of dinaphthyl methane disulfonate.

Diastyzme. Standardized mixture of amylolytic and proteolytic enzymes; desizing agent.

Diatex. Diastatic enzyme; desizing agent.

Diatol. Diethyl carbonate (90%) and alcohol (about 10%).

Diax. Malt diastase.

Diazil. *p*-Aminobenzene sulfonamido dimethyl pyrimidine.

Diazine. Direct and developed dye.

Diazo. Series of direct colors; used for dyeing cotton and rayon.

Diazophenyl. Series of dyes; used for dyeing cotton and rayon.

Diazopon. Water solution containing a condensation product of fatty alcohol with ethylene oxide (33%); leveling agent.

Diazopon AN. Polyether; dyeing assistant.

Dibenal. Sulfapyrimidine; used in medicine.

Dicodid. Dihydrocodeinone; used in medicine.

Dicy. Dicyan diamide.

Dielene. Dichlorethylene.

Dielex. Plasticized gilsonite; used in rubber compounding.

Difoline. Powder obtained from digitalis leaves; used in medicine.

Dienol. Dehydrated castor oil; used in varnish.

Composition of Trade-Marked Products

Digestase. Liquid malt containing diastase; used in mfg. adhesives and sizings.

Digestin. Commercial diastase.

Digidox. Digitoxin.

Digifolin. Powdered extract of the active principles of the digitalis leaf; used in medicine.

Digipoten. Mixture of glucosides from digitalis and milk sugar; used in medicine.

Digipuratum. See Digitan.

Digitalon. Alcohol-free solution of the principles of digitalis; used in medicine.

Digitan. Digitalis extract; used in medicine.

Dihydrolin. Hydrogenated rotenone and rotenoids; insecticide.

Diindiol. Reaction product of diacetylene and acetone or another ketone.

Diiodyl. See Periodyl.

Dilaudid. Dihydromorphinone hydrochloride; narcotic.

Dilecto. Synthetic phenol-formaldehyde resin.

Dilex. Highly purified sulfolignin; dispersing agent in latex industry.

Dillantin. Sodium diphenyl hydantoinate; used in epilepsy treatment.

Diliturate. Nitrobarbiturate.

Dileux. Floridin-type powder; diluent in insecticides.

Dilur. Formaldehyde.

Dilver. Alloy of iron with 42 to 50% nickel; glass to metal seal.

Dimelone. Dimethyl ester of "carbic" anhydride; insect repellent.

Dimethophol, 1-1′-Dihydroxy-4,4′-dimethoxy-2,2′-binaphthyl; dye intermediate (German).

Dimondite. Cemented tungsten carbide, with cobalt (5 to 13%).

Dinitrol. Dinitro-*o*-cresol; insecticide.

Dinol. Diazodinitrophenol; used in blasting caps.

Composition of Trade-Marked Products

Dinopol. Di-*n*-octyl phthalate; plasticizer.

Diodoquin. 5,7-Diiodo-8-hydroxyquinoline.

Diodrast. Diethanol amine 3,5-diiodo-4-pyridone N-acetate.

Dioform. 1,2-Dichloroethylene.

Diogenal. Dibromopropyl diethyl barbituric acid; used in medicine.

Di-Oil. Commercial grade dinitrotoluene; used in explosives.

Diol 55. High-boiling, aliphatic petroleum fraction.

Diolin. Octadecanediol; plasticizer.

Diolin A. Octadecanediol diacetate; plasticizer.

Dionin. Ethyl morphine hydrochloride, used in medicine.

Diophane. Regenerated cellulose film.

Dioprol. Diisopropyl carbinol; used in lacquer solvents.

Dipex M. Oil-soluble refined sodium sulfonates of petroleum (50–55%), mineral oil (5–10%) and water (40%); emulsifying agent.

Dipex Sp-702. Water dispersion of sodium sulfonates; wetting agent.

Dipolymer. Polymerized Solvenol.

Dipropäsin. $CO(NHC_6H_4COOC_3H_7)_2$; hypnotic.

Diproxid. Diisopropyl xanthogen disulfide; polymerization regulator (German).

Discolite. $NaHSO_2.CH_2O.2H_2O$; textile-printing reducing agent.

Dismulgan. Mixture of sulfonated amine soaps or amides of fatty oils; defoaming agent.

Dismulgan III. Dodecyl phenol polyglycol ether; used for breaking emulsions (German).

Dismulgan IV. Sodium salt of sulfated oleyl ethyl anilide; demulsifying agent for crude petroleum (German).

Disparine. Lead arsenate; insecticide.

Dispergine CB. Sulfonated formo-

Composition of Trade-Marked Products

napthalene sodium salt; dispersing agent.

Dispersite. Water dispersed rubber and resins; used for coating and bonding fibrous materials.

Dispersol. Insoluble azo dye.

Dispersol L. Sodium naphthalene sulfonate; wetting agent.

Dissolving Salt BA New. Sodium benzyl sulfanilate; used in textile printing.

Distoline. Commercial oleic acid, derived from vegetable oils.

Distrene. Polystyrene plastic.

Disulphine. Acid dye.

Dithane. Disodium ethylene bisdithiocarbamate hexahydrate; insecticide.

Dithion. Sodium dithiosalicylate; used in medicine.

Diuresine. Condensation product of di- and poly-urethans with formaldehyde; plastic.

Diuretin. Theobromine sodium salicylate; used in medicine.

Dixantogen. Bisethyl xanthogen solution in oil; fungicide.

Dixie Clay. Kaolin powder; rubber filler.

Dixonac. Finely divided graphite in paste form, dispersible in water.

Dizan. N-(phenyl diazo)-piperidine (2.5%) and talc (97.5%); insecticide.

DMU. Dimethylol urea.

DN-111. Diclohexylamine salt of dinitro-*o*-cyclohexyl phenol; fungicide.

Doboline Oil. Dehydrated castor oil.

Dolantin. Chlorhydrate of 1-methyl 4-phenyl piperidine 4-carbonic acid ethyl ester; morphine substitute.

Dolantine. Ethyl 1-methyl 4-phenyl 4-piperidine carboxylate; used in medicine.

Dolesco. Dolomite.

Dopploy. Chemically resistant high-alloy cast iron with 17 to 20% nickel, approximately 2% chromium and 2% silicon.

Composition of Trade-Marked Products

Dormiol. Solution of amylene chloral (50%); sedative.

Doron. Glass-fiber fabric and synthetic-resin laminate.

Doryl. Carbamyl choline chloride; medicament.

Dosol. Dark wood rosin; used in printing ink.

Doucil. Aluminum silicate; water-softening agent.

Dow 9-B. Zinc trichlorophenate; seed protectant.

Dowanol-1. 2-Phenoxyethanol.

Dowanol-2. 1-Phenoxy-2-propanol.

Dowanol-3. *sec*-Butyl phenoxyethanol.

Dowanol-4. *tert*-Butyl phenoxyethanol.

Dowanone. Vat dye.

Dowax. Paraffin wax-bentonite emulsion; used in horticulture.

Dowco. Mixture of metallic copper and lead arsenate in powder form; insecticide, fungicide.

Dowex-30. Condensation product of *o*- and *p*-phenol sulfonic acid with formaldehyde; ion-exchange resin.

Dowflake. Calcium chloride in flake form.

Dowfume. Mixture of ethylene dichloride and carbon tetrachloride; fumigant.

Dowfume BR-10. Methyl bromide mixed with chlorinated hydrocarbons; fumigant.

Dowfume-75. Mixture of ethylene dichloride and carbon tetrachloride; fumigant.

Dowicide A. Sodium *o*-phenyl phenate.

Dowicide B. Sodium 2-4-5-trichlorophenate; germicide.

Dowicide C. Sodium chloro-*o*-phenyl phenate; antiseptic.

Dowicide D. 2-Chloro-4-phenyl phenol sodium; germicide.

Dowicide E. 2-Bromo-4-phenyl phenol sodium; fungicide.

Dowicide F. Sodium tetrachlorophenate; germicide.

Composition of Trade-Marked Products

Dowicide G. Sodium pentachlorophenate.

Dowicide H. Sodium tetrachlorophenoxide; industrial antiseptic.

Dowicide 1. *o*-Phenyl phenol; germicide.

Dowicide 3. Chloro-*o*-phenyl phenol; germicide.

Dowicide 4. 2-Chloro-4-phenyl phenol; high-efficiency germicide.

Dowicide 5. Bromo-*p*-phenyl phenol; germicide.

Dowicide 6. Tetrachlorophenol; germicide.

Dowicide 7. Pentachlorophenols; oil-soluble antiseptic.

Dowmetal. Series of alloys containing about 90% magnesium, the balance being aluminum, copper, cadmium, manganese and zinc.

Dow Plasticizer 2. *tert*-Butyl phenyl monophenyl phosphate.

Dow Plasticizer 5. Diphenyl mono-(*o*-xenyl) phosphate.

Dow Plasticizer 6. Di-*o*-xenyl monophenyl phosphate.

Dow Plasticizer 7. Tri-*p*-*tert*-butyl phenyl phosphate.

Dow Plasticizer 11. Di-5-*tert*-butyl 2-xenyl mono-*p*-*tert*-butyl phenyl phosphate.

Dow Plasticizer 12. Di-5-*tert*-butyl 2-xenyl mono-*p*-*tert*-butyl phenyl phosphate.

Dowspray 66. Dinitro butyl phenol in oil solution; plant growth retardant.

Dowspray Dormant. Solution of 2,4-dinitro-6-cyclohexyl phenol in petroleum oil; dormant spray.

Dowtherm-A. Mixture of diphenyl and diphenyl oxide; heat-transfer medium.

D.P.G. Diphenyl guanidine; used as rubber accelerator.

Drackett Azlon. Soybean fiber.

Drakeol. U.S.P. refined mineral oil.

Dralyte. Water-ground pumice; abrasive.

Composition of Trade-Marked Products

Drapolein. Soap; used in textile scouring.

Drawinella. Wool-type cellulose acetate staple (German).

Drax. Emulsion of waxes and aluminum salts; waterproofing agent.

Dreft. Sodium lauryl sulfate; household detergent.

Drene. Fatty alcohol sulfate; surface-active agent, shampoo.

Dresinate. Dry, powdered sodium resinate.

Dresinate 731. Rosin soap; emulsifier.

Dresinol. Emulsion containing 40–45% solids of sodium and ammonium soap dispersions of modified rosins and special resin acids.

Drierite. Anhydrous calcium sulfate; dessicant.

Dri Frost. Solid carbon dioxide; refrigerant.

Drigel 90. Technical gelatin; used in textile finishing.

Dri Kold. See Dry Ice.

Driocel. Activated bauxite; dehydrating agent.

Driox. Nitrogen.

Drisize 120. Technical gelatin with softeners; used in textile finishing.

Drisoy. Drying oil made from soybean oil.

Dryall. Metallic linoleate resinate; paint drier.

Dry Arasklene-400. Sodium salt of an alkylated aryl compound; wetting agent.

Dry Ice (Dri Frost; Dri Kold; Dry-Kold). Solidified carbon dioxide.

Dry-Kold. See Dry Ice.

Drymet. Anhydrous sodium metasilicate; detergent.

Dryorth. Anhydrous sodium orthosilicate; detergent.

Dryseq. Technically anhydrous sodium sesquisilicate.

Drytex. Paraffin wax emulsion; waterproofing agent.

Duatol. Guiacol acetate.

Composition of Trade-Marked Products

Dubay 1451-D. Ethyl mercury *p*-toluene sulfonanalide; used in seed treatment.

DuBay 1452-C. Ethyl mercury *p*-toluene sulfonanilide; seed fungicide.

Duclean-1. Concentrated (60° Bé.) sulfuric acid containing an inhibitor; rust remover.

Duclean-2. Concentrated hydrochloric acid containing an inhibitor; used for removing hard-water scale and rust.

Ducosolve. Triethanolamine soap and trichloroethylene.

Ducozone. Sodium peroxide.

Dulac. Cellulose ester-base lacquer.

Dulux resin. Alkyd resin; used in lacquers.

Dumold (Dummold). Cellulose nitrate plastic.

Dunnflex. Plasticized gelatin; used in adhesives.

Dunngel. Animal gelatin; used in adhesives.

Dunnglue. Animal glue; used in adhesives.

Dunnite. Ammonium picrate.

Dunntex. Plasticized gelatin; used in rayon sizing.

Dunntite. Blend of resins and gelatin; used in adhesives.

Duolith. Titanated lithopone; pigment.

Duosol. Liquid propane and cresol solvent; used in refining petroleum.

Duosolve. Sodium hexametaphosphate; boil-off agent.

Duozinc. Zinc-mercury alloy anodes; used in zinc plating.

Duponol ES. Technical sodium oleyl sulfate; wetting agent.

Duponol ME. Technical sodium lauryl sulfate; wetting agent.

Duponol WA. Flake or powder consisting of sodium lauryl sulfate; sodium sulfate and sodium chloride; wetting agent.

Duponol WS. Oil-soluble higher fatty alcohol sulfate; emulsifying agent.

Composition of Trade-Marked Products

Duponol L-142. Sodium cetyl sulfate; emulsifier.

Duponol 80. Sodium octyl sulfate; used as wetting agent.

Du Pont accelerated salt. Fused cyanide mixture; used for treatment of steel with heat.

Du Pont carburizing salt. Fused cyanide mixture; used for case-hardening steel.

Du Pont FD-3. Liquid containing phenyl mercury oleate; used to preserve certain non-edible oils.

Du Pont LE-5 fungicide. Oily liquid containing ethyl mercury oleate; used to prevent mildew in textile fibers.

Du Pont LE-6 fungicide. Mixture of ethyl and phenyl mercury oleates; used to prevent formation of sap stain in lumber.

Du Pont Metal Deactivator. Solution of N,N′-disalicylidene 1,2-diaminopropane xylene (80%).

Du Pont plant spray No. 2. Oil containing ethyl mercury oleate; insecticide in horticulture.

Du Pont Retarder LA. Stearyl trimethyl ammonium bromide; used in textile printing.

Duprene. See Neoprene.

Dura. Synthetic phenolic resin.

Duracite. Furan resin; used in acid-proof cement.

Durafil. See Fortisan.

Dural. See Duralumin.

Duralon. Liquid, synthetic furan resin.

Duraloy. Series of high-chromium steels, with up to 30% chromium, optionally up to 15% nickel.

Duralum. Aluminum oxide; abrasive.

Duralumin (Dural). Aluminum alloy with approximately 4% copper, fractional percentages of magnesium and manganese and small amounts of iron and silicon.

Composition of Trade-Marked Products

Duranols. Aminoanthraquinone compounds; acetate-silk dyes.

Duraplex E-71. Pure alkyd resin; used in inks.

Duraplex resin. Alkyd resin; used in lacquers.

Durapulp. Cellulose fibers or pulp.

Duratex. Aluminum phosphate.

Duratone. Stearin.

Duraval. Vat dye.

Durax. Synthetic tar-acid resin.

Durazol. Light-fast dye.

Durbar bronze. High-lead bronze with 20 to 24% lead and 4 to 10% tin; used for bearings.

Durco. Heat-resistant and corrosion-resistant high-chromium steels with 12 to 30% chromium, up to 15% nickel, approximately 1% silicon, optional additions of 2 to 4% molybdenum.

Durex. Zeolite; used in water treatment.

Durez. Thermosetting phenol-formaldehyde resin.

Durez 202 resin. Oil-soluble, heat-hardening phenol-formaldehyde resin.

Durheat. Heat-resistant cellulose lacquer; used on metals.

Durichlor. Cast iron with approximately 14% silicon and 3% molybdenum.

Durimet. Series of nickel-chromium steels resistant to heat and corrosion.

Durindone. Light-fast, wash-fast indigoid vat dye.

Duiron. Ferrous alloy containing 14.5% silicon, 0.35% manganese, and 0.85% carbon.

Durite. Phenol-furfural or phenol-formaldehyde thermosetting resin.

Durodi steel. Steel with 1.5% nickel and fractional percentages of molybdenum, chromium, manganese and carbon.

Duro Gloss. Low-carbon steels with 12 to 29% chromium.

Composition of Trade-Marked Products

Duron. Ligno-cellulose plastic molding compound.

Duronze. Series of corrosion-resistant bronzes with approximately 2% tin and 1% silicon.

Durophen. Synthetic tar-acid resin.

Dutox. Powder containing barium fluosilicate, sodium fluoaluminate and inert ingredients; non-arsenical insecticide.

Dutrex. See Naftolen.

Duxalid. Alkyd resin.

Duxol. Alkyd resin.

Dyal. Alkyd resin.

Dybryte. Basic dye.

Dykan. Sodium diacetate.

Dymal. Maleic resin; used in varnish.

Dynagen. Polyisobutylene.

Dynesol. Sodium alkyl naphthalene sulfonate; wetting agent.

Dynesol D50. Salt of naphthalene sulfonic acid; textile wetting agent..

Dypenol B, HT, SE. Polyhydric alcohol with cresylic acid; mercerizing assistant.

Dyphene. Phenol-formaldehyde resin.

Dyphenite. Modified phenol-formaldehyde resin.

Dytin. Technical dipentene; solvent in paints.

Easy-Flo. Alloy consisting of silver, copper, zinc, and cadmium.

Economo steel. Machine steel containing approximately 0.2% molybdenum.

Edamin. Enzymatic processed milk protein; used in medicine.

Edinol. Mixture of aminosaligenine, acetone, sulfite, potassium hydroxide and potassium bromide; photographic developer.

Effusan 3436. 1-Hydroxy-2, 4-dinitrotoluene; insecticide.

Egalisal. Hydrolyzed protein.

Eganol P. Aqueous solution of a

Composition of Trade-Marked Products

polyglycol alkyl ether; textile assistant (German).

Eikonogen. 1-Amino-2-naphthol sodium 6-sulfonate; used in photographic developing.

Elaol. Glycol ester of synthetic fatty acids (C_5—C_9); plasticizer.

Elaol I. Triester of hexanetriol and synthetic fatty acids (C_5—C_9); plasticizer (German).

Elaol II. Triester of hexanetriol and synthetic fatty acids (C_7—C_9); plasticizer.

Elaol III. Triester of pentaerythritol and synthetic fatty acids (C_5—C_7); plasticizer.

Elaol IV. Triester of pentaerythritol and synthetic fatty acids (C_7—C_9); plasticizer.

Elarson. Strontium chloroarsenobehenate; used in medicine.

Elastoil. Sulfur chloride-treated linseed and sardine oil; used in paint.

Elastoil R. Alkali-refined sardine oil; used in paint.

Elastol. Ethyl amide of *p*-toluene sulfonic acid containing also *m*- and *p*-toluene sulfamide.

Elastolac. Esterified shellac dispersion; used in hair lacquer.

Elastolith. Synthetic tar-acid resin.

Elateron. Mineral rubber.

Elbon. Cinnamoyl *p*-hydroxyphenyl urea; medicament.

Elcomet. Corrosion-resistant nickel-chromium steel of high-silicon content.

Elconite. Zeolite.

Eldrol. Petroleum sulfonate; emulsifier.

Electrocide. Calcium arsenate dust; agricultural insecticide.

Electrocollargol. Colloidal silver; used in medicine.

Electrolon. Silicon carbide; used in abrasives.

Electromartiol. Colloidal iron; used in the treatment of cancer.

Electromercural. Colloidal suspension of metallic mercury (0.1%) in dilute sodium arabate; used in medicine.

Composition of Trade-Marked Products

Electromet. Iron-base alloy.

Electron alloys. Light alloys of about 95% magnesium, 4.5% copper, 0.5% zinc.

Electron metals. Magnesium alloys.

Electrophos. Compound containing about 48% available phosphoric acid; fertilizer.

Electrum. Gold-base alloy with 15 to 45% silver; also nickel-silver alloy, containing approximately 25% nickel and 25% zinc.

Elmet metal. Compound of tungsten or molybdenum and copper or silver; used in mfg. circuit breakers.

Elemite. Mixture of sulfonated oils and solvents; wetting agent.

Eleudron. Sulfathiazole.

Elf black. Powdered carbon black; used in inks.

Elgetol. Sodium dinitro-*o*-cresylate; insecticide.

Elinvar. Nickel-chromium steel with approximately 36% nickel, 12% chromium, optional percentages of manganese and tungsten.

Elite Fast. Acid color; used for dyeing loose wools.

Elkson. 6-Sulfanilamido-2,4-dimethyl pyrimidine; used in medicine.

Elmet metal. Compound of tungsten or molybdenum and copper or silver; used in circuit breakers.

Elo. Synthetic phenol-formaldehyde resin.

Elon. *p*-Methyl aminophenol sulfate.

El Sixty. Dibenzothiazyl dimethylthiol urea; rubber accelerator.

Elvacet. Polyvinyl acetate.

Elvanol. Polyvinyl alcohol.

Elverite. Wear-resistant chilled cast iron.

Emargol. Mixture of mono- and diglycerides and their sulfoacetates; emulsion stabilizer.

Composition of Trade-Marked Products

Em briquets. Briquets of ferro alloys of silicon, chromium or manganese.

Emcol CA. Blend of mono-and diglycerides of higher fatty acids plus soap; emulsifier.

Emcol CAD. Diethylene glycol monoester of higher fatty acid; emulsifier.

Emcol CD. C_{16} and C_{18} fatty acid esters of a polyglycol; emulsifier.

Emcol CE. Glycol ester of fatty acids; emulsifier.

Emcol DS. Polyhydroxyether stearate; detergent.

Emcol ES. Glycol monostearate; used in cosmetic emulsions.

Emcol IL. Isopropyl laurate.

Emcol IP. Isopropyl palmitate.

Emcol L. Blend of mono- and diglycerides of higher fatty acids; emulsifier.

Emcol MS. Blend of mono- and diglycerides of higher fatty acids.

Emcol O. Blends of mono- and diglycerides of higher fatty acids; emulsifier.

Emcol PS. Polyhydroxymonostearate; emulsifier.

Emcol RE. Glyceride of hydrogenated fatty acids; used in emulsions.

Emcol DL50. Monodiethylene glycol fatty acid esters; emulsifier.

Emcol EL50. Monoethylene glycol fatty acid esters; emulsifier.

Emcol PI50. Monopropylene glycol fatty acid esters; wetting agent.

Emcol PO50. Monopropylene glycol fatty acid esters; emulsifier.

Emcol 12. Fatty acid ester of a polyhydroxyalcohol; wetting agent.

Emcol 14. Fatty acid ester of a polyhydroxyalcohol; emulsifier.

Emcol 18. Palmitic-stearic ester of a polyhydric alcohol; emulsifier.

Empire alloy. Ferrous-base casting low-alloys and high-alloys with chromium as chief alloying agent.

Empirin. Compound containing aspirin, caffeine and phenacetin; medicament.

Composition of Trade-Marked Products

Emulgor A. Higher glycol ester of fatty acids; used in emulsions.

Emulphor A extra (Remolgan A). Di-(isohexyl isoheptyl) phenyl polyglycol ether; emulsifying agent (German).

Emulphor AG (Emulphor ELA). Ethylene oxide condensate with fatty acids; emulsifier.

Emulphor E.L. Condensation product of ethylene oxide and castor oil; emulsifying agent (German).

Emulphor ELA. See Emulphor AG.

Emulphor O. Reaction product of octadecyl alcohol and ethylene oxide; emulsifier.

Emulphor ON. Polyethylene oxide condensation product with oleyl alcohol; emulsifying agent.

Emulphor STX. Potassium salt of dodecyl xylene sulfonic acid mixed with mineral oil; emulsifying agent (German).

Emulsamin. Menthol diurethane; emulsifying agent.

Emulsept. Solution of N-(acyl colamino formyl-methyl) pyridinium chloride (10%); germicide.

Emulsept 607 M. Quaternary ammonium compound; germicide.

Emulsifier W-763-A. Sodium naphthenic sulfonate.

Emulsital. Tallow emulsion; used in textile finishing.

Emulsoblak. Aqueous dispersion of carbon black.

Emulsol X-1. Ammonium salt of diethylene glycol sulfate.

Emulsol 607L. Lauryl α-alanine hydrochloride; surface-active agent.

Emulsol 488B. Sodium salt of butyl Carbitol sulfate.

Emulsol 660B. Lauryl pyridinium iodide.

Emulsol 607. Myristyl colamine

Composition of Trade-Marked Products

formyl methyl pyridinium chloride; germicide.

Emulsol 1031. Sodium octyl sulfoacetate.

Emulsone B. Activated carbohydrate gum; emulsifying agent.

Encoloid. Soybean lecithin.

Endochin. 3-Alkyl quinoline; antimalarial drug.

Endoiodin. Hexamethyl diaminoisopropanol diiodide; used in medicine.

Endrop. Oil solution of α-naphthalene acetic acid; used in fruit preharvest spray.

Enesol. Mercuric salicyl arsenate.

Englo. Dull viscose rayon.

Eosote. Creosote valerate.

EPC. Channel carbon black; used in rubber compounding.

Epenone. *p*-Methoxyacetophenone.

Epersol-Y. Hydrolyzed protein; wetting agent.

Ephetonal. *p*-Aminophenyl 1-hydroxy-2-methyl propane hydrochloride; used in medicine.

Ephetonin. Synthetic racemic ephedrine hydrochloride; used in medicine.

Epicarin. β-Hydroxynaphthyl *o*-hydroxy *m*-toluic acid; used in medicine.

Epiphasol. Sulfonated mineral oil.

Epok. Synthetic oil-soluble phenolformaldehyde resin; used for impregnation.

Eponit. Activated carbon; decolorizing and deodorizing agent.

Erasol. Formaldehyde sulfoxylate product; used for discharge printing.

Eraydo. Zinc-base alloy of higher strength than commercial rolled zinc, with 1 to 3% copper, up to 0.17% silver.

Ereton. Natural vitamin E.

Erganol. Dibenzyl ether.

Ergol. Mixture of Optol, tetrahydrofuran, furfuryl alcohol and aniline; rocket fuel.

Composition of Trade-Marked Products

Ergotrate. Ergonovine maleate; used in medicine.

Erinite. Alkyd-resin coating.

Erinofort. Cellulose acetate plastic.

Erinoid. A synthetic resin made from casein and formaldehyde; used for plastics.

Erinol. Alcoholic solution of phenolformaldehyde resin; used for waterproofing.

Erinoplex A. Polyvinyl-acetal plastic.

Erio. Acid color; used for dyeing wool.

Erkalin. Alkyl aryl sulfate salt; surface-active agent.

Ermal. High-test cast iron with approximately 2.3% carbon, 1% silicon, and 0.8% manganese.

Ermalite. High-test cast iron with approximately 2.5% carbon, 2% silicon, 0.4% nickel.

Ermite. Synthetic oil-soluble phenolformaldehyde resin.

Ertron. Activated ergosterol; used in medicine.

Erustocide. Alkali metal acid fluoride; used in laundries as germicide and brightener.

Ervol. U.S.P. light mineral oil.

Escalol 106. Glyceryl mono-*p*-aminobenzoate; sun-screen agent.

Escapon. Hard synthetic rubber (Russian).

Eshalit. Tar resin (German).

Es-Min-El. Essential fertilizer minerals including copper, iron and manganese sulfates and boron in small quantities.

Esmodil. Trimethyl methoxypropenyl ammonium bromide; used in medicine.

Essex Black. Furnace black; used in rubber.

Esskol. Treated linseed oil; used in place of chinawood and dehydrated castor oil.

Essowax. Paraffin wax.

Esteramin. $R.CO.O.(CH_2)_2.N(CH_3)_2$ where R is a fatty acid

Composition of Trade-Marked Products

radical; emulsifying agent (German).

Esterex. Dinitrophenyl benzothiazyl sulfide; vulcanization accelerator.

Esteril. Higher esters of *p*-hydroxybenzoic acid.

Esterine. Commercial glyceryl monostearate; used in baking.

Esterol. Emulsifiable blend of alkyl derivatives of higher fatty acids and highly refined mineral oil.

Estersel. Sulfated polyhydric alcohol fatty acid ester; boil-off aid.

Ethasan. Zinc diethyl dithiocarbamate; used in rubber compounding.

Ethide. 1,1-Dichloro-1-nitroethane; insecticide.

Ethobrom. 2,2,2-Tribromoethanol.

Ethocain. Procaine hydrochloride.

Ethocel. Ethyl cellulose; used in plastic molding.

Ethofoil. Ethyl cellulose film; used in electrical insulating.

Ethovan. 3-Ethoxy-4-hydroxybenzaldehyde.

Ethox. Reaction product of Cellosolve and phthalic anhydride; plasticizer.

Ethulose. Mixture of water-dispersible cellulose ethers.

Ethycol. Dispersed pigments in ethyl cellulose and plasticizer; used in protective coatings.

Ethyl Cetab. Cetyl dimethyl ethyl ammonium bromide; antiseptic.

Ethyl Decab. Octadecenyl dimethyl ethyl ammonium bromide; antiseptic.

Ethyl Silicate 40. Polymer of tetaethyl orthosilicate; used in stone preservatives.

Ethyl Zimate. Zinc diethyl dithiocarbamate.

Etrol. Ethyl acetate.

Eubaryt. Purified barium sulfate; used in X-ray work.

Eucodal. See Eukodal.

Eucodin. Codeine methyl bromide.

Composition of Trade-Marked Products

Eucupin. Isoamyl hydrocupreine; used in medicine.

Eudermol. Nicotine salicylate.

Eukodal (Eucodal). Dihydrohydroxycodeinone hydrochloride; sedative.

Eulan AL. 3,4-Dichlorophenyl N-methyl sulfonamide; moth-repellent.

Eulan CN. Cyclic, sulfonic acid derivative; used in mothproofing.

Eulan NK. Triphenyl 3,4-dichlorophenyl phosphonium chloride; moth-repellent.

Eulysine A. Organic amine; textile crabbing assistant.

Eumydrin. Atropine methyl nitrate.

Eunarcon. Solution of sodium isopropyl bromoallylmethyl barbiturate (10%); narcotic.

Eunatrol. Sodium oleate.

Euonymit. Dulcitol.

Euporphin. Apomorphine methyl bromide.

Eupyrine. Carbethoxyvanillylidene *p*-phentidine.

Euresol. Resorcin monacetate.

Eurhodine. Aminophenazine.

Eurhodol. Hydroxyphenazine.

Europhen. Diisobutyl *o*-cresol iodide.

Eusol. See Perchloron.

Eusolvan. Ethyl lactate.

Eustenin. Mixture of sodium iodide and theobromine sodium; used in medicine.

Eutex. Glass-fiber yarn.

Eutinol. Mixture of sodium alkyl aryl sulfonate and a cationic detergent; textile printing aid.

Euvernil. N-Sulfanil carbamide.

Evansteel. Low-alloy steel with approximately 2% nickel, 1% chromium.

Everbrite. Copper-base alloys of approximately 30% nickel, with optional low percentages of iron, silicon and chromium; used for corrosion resistant equipment.

Composition of Trade-Marked Products

Everdur. Alloy consisting of copper, silicon and manganese.

Evipal. N-methyl cyclohexenyl methyl barbituric acid; used in medicine.

Evipan. *n*-Methyl cyclohexenyl methyl malonyl urea; used in medicine.

Exaltone. Cyclopentadecanone.

Exanol. Synthetic resin made by polymerization of unsaturated hydrocarbons.

Excelsior Oil A. Sulfated fatty acids; used in textile finishing.

Exelon. Abrasive similar to alundum.

Exolon. Fused aluminum oxide; abrasive.

Expyrol Z (Intravan NK). Ammonium sulfate compound; flameproofing agent (German).

Exsize. Standardized solution of amylolytic and proteolytic en-

Extol. A sulfated compound with solvents; detergent in the textile industry.

Exton bristle. Nylon bristle; used in tooth and toilet brushes.

Extralin. Liver-stomach concentrate; used in medicine.

Ez stainless steel. Corrosion-resistant steel containing 13% chromium, 0.3 to 0.4% carbon and approximately 0.25% sulfur.

F-14. Carbon tetrafluoride; refrigerant.

F-23 (Freon-23). Trifluoromethane; refrigerant.

Fabcano. Sodium salts of alkylated hydrocarbon sulfonates; detergent.

Fabcolene. Sodium hydrocarbon sulfonate; wetting agent.

Fabrifil. Chopped rag fiber; rubber filler.

Fabrisop. Saponified low-titer fatty acid; detergent.

Fabritex. Indian-gum paste; thickener for textile printing.

Composition of Trade-Marked Products

Fabroil. Synthetic tar-acid resin.

Fabrol. Blend of sulfonated oils; textile softener.

Fabrolite. Synthetic tar-acid resin.

Facoil. Refined tall oil.

Factolac. Mixture of vegetable gums; emulsifying agent.

Fael. Coloring matter extracted from leaf chlorophyll; pigment for food products.

Fagine. Choline.

Fahlun metal. Alloy of about 60% tin and 40% lead; used for ornamental purposes.

Fahralloy. Nickel, chromium and iron, heat and corrosion-resistant alloys of diverse composition.

Fahrite. Iron alloy containing 19 to 40% nickel, 18 to 32% chromium, optional low percentages of silicon and manganese.

Falls alloy. Master alloys, most commonly of copper and aluminum base; used in foundry and related operations.

Fanal. Light-fast phosphotungstic lake; used for printing inks.

Fantan. Phenyl cinchonoyl urethane.

Farnico. Low-expansion, iron-base alloy containing about 28% nickel and 18% cobalt; used for sealing metal wire into hard glass.

Faspos. Crystalline solid containing monoammonium phosphate; fungicide, accelerator, textile-fireproofing agent.

Fastell alloy. Silver-tungsten, silver-molybdenum, and copper-tungsten composites; used for heavy-duty electrical contacts.

Fastogene. Quaternary ammonium salt; used in textile finishing.

Faturan. Synthetic tar-acid resin.

Fecraloy. Iron-base alloy containing about 15% chromium and 4% aluminum.

Feculose. Starch substance obtained by treating dry starch with glacial

Composition of Trade-Marked Products

acetic acid; substitute for gelatin and gums.

Federated solder. Lead-base solders containing 6 to 30% tin, 1.75% silver, 0.5 to 5.0% bismuth, 0.5% antimony.

Fedrin. Ephedrine.

Feltoscour AS. Sulfonated fatty acid amide derivative; textile detergent.

Fen. Paraffin wax emulsion containing aluminum salt; waterproofing agent.

Fenton's metal. Anti-friction alloy containing 80% zinc, 14.5% tin, 5.5% copper.

Feran. Aluminum-clad sheet iron.

Fermasol F. Amylotytic enzyme; desizing agent (Swiss).

Fermate. Ferric dimethyl dithiocarbamate; fungicide.

Fermine. Methyl phthalate.

Fernichrome. Low-expansion iron-base alloy containing about 30% nickel, 25% cobalt, 8% chromium; used for sealing metal wire into glass.

Fernite. Cast nickel-chromium iron alloys with chromium content up to 28% and nickel up to 65%.

Ferratin. Sodium iron albuminate; used in medicine.

Ferratose. Flavored Ferratin solution; used in medicine.

Ferrichlor. Iron chloride; used in sewage and water treatments.

Ferri-Floc. Iron sulfate.

Ferrigan P. Oxidized iron salt of sulfonated phthalic anhydride; used in leather tanning.

Ferrinol. Iron nucleinate; used in medicine.

Ferisul. Anhydrous ferric sulfate; used in water treatment.

Ferrocarbo. Granular silicon carbide; deoxidizer and graphitizer in steel.

Ferrox. Hydrated iron oxide; pigment.

Ferrozell. Synthetic tar-acid resin.

Composition of Trade-Marked Products

Ferry metal. Lead-base bearing metal containing about 2% barium, 1% calcium, and fractional percentages of mercury.

Fiberglas. Glass fibers.

Fiberlac. Cellulose nitrate plastic.

Fiberloid. Cellulose nitrate plastic.

Fiberlon. Phenol-formaldehyde thermosetting resin.

Fiberoid. Vulcanized fiber.

Fibestos. Cellulose acetate thermoplastic.

Fibrene. Fibrous California talc.

Fibro. Viscose staple.

Fibroc. Synthetic tar-acid resin.

Fibrolysin. Aqueous solution of thiosin amine and sodium salicylate; used in medicine.

Fibron. Extruded polyethylene plastic.

Filac. Washed nitrocellulose photographic film scrap.

Filax oil. Mixture of aromatic hydrocarbons and esters with long side chains; linseed oil substitute.

Filcote. Clay for paper coating.

Filmaron. $C_{47}H_{54}O_{16}$; used in medicine.

Filt-Char. Bone charcoal; decolorizing, deodorizing and filtering medium.

Filter-Cel. Natural, milled diatomaceous powder of very fine particle size; used in clarifying liquids.

Filtra Blend. Purified petroleum sulfonates; emulsifying agent.

Filtragol. See Filtral.

Filtral (Filtragol). Pepsin-splitting enzyme.

Filtrasol. Water-dispersible sulfonated mineral oil compound containing varying amounts of mineral oil; used in making soluble oils.

Filtrawax. Tacky non-crystalline petroleum wax.

Filtrol. Acid-activated bleaching earth; adsorbent.

Filtrona. Product containing sul-

Composition of Trade-Marked Products

fonated mineral oil (62%) and mineral oil (35%); used in making soluble oils.

Filtros. Porous acid-proof substance, essentially silica; filtering, diffusing, aerating medium.

Finish BG. Oleyl diethyl aminoethyl amide; textile-softening agent.

Fire-frax. Refractory cement made from kaolin.

Firthaloy. Cemented tungsten carbide; used for wire drawing.

Firthite. Cemented tungsten carbide with cobalt as the cementing matrix; used for tools.

Fixacol. Quaternary ammonium derivative.

Fixanol. Cetyl pyridinium chloride; dye fixative.

Fixanol C. Aqueous solution of cetyl pyridinium bromide; antiseptic.

Fixapret BNA. Stabilized urea-formaldehyde resin; textile-finishing agent.

Fixol. Hydroxycitronellal; perfume fixative.

Flamenol. Plasticized, polymerized vinyl resin; used in electrical insulation.

Flavazole. Compound of sulfathiazole and proflavine base; bacteriostatic.

Flavite (Lobeite; Rufite). Limed rosin; used in varnish.

Flectol A. Ketone amine; antioxidant.

Flectol B. Ketone amine; rubber antioxidant.

Flectol H. Condensation product of acetone and aniline; rubber antioxidant.

Flectol White. Aryl oxyketone; rubber antioxidant.

Flexalyn. Diethylene glycol ester of rosin; used in coatings.

Flexalyn C. Ethylene glycol ester of rosin; plasticizer.

Flexbond. Emulsified polyvinyl acetate adhesive.

Composition of Trade-Marked Products

Flexol Plasticizer DOP. Di-2-ethyl hexyl phthalate; resin plasticizer.

Flexol Plasticizer TOF. Trioctyl phosphate; plasticizer.

Flexol Plasticizer 4GO. Polyethylene glycol di-2-ethyl hexoate; plasticizer.

Flexon. Copolymer of butene and diolefin.

Flexoresin. Terpene resin; used in paints.

Flexo steel. Silicon-manganese steel, containing approximately 2% silicon, 0.8% manganese, and 0.60% carbon; used for the manufacture of springs.

Flexo Wax C. Long-chain hydrocarbon, amorphous wax; used for coatings.

Flextol-H. Polymerized trimethyl di-hydroquinoline; antioxidant for rubber.

Flo-Brite. Clarifying agent from Florida fuller's earth; used in purification of petroleum.

Flocgel. Converted potato starch.

Floex. Condensation product of higher fatty alcohol; wetting agent in paints and lubricants.

Flomine. Amyl cinnamic aldehyde; used in perfume.

Floramid. Urea derivative; fertilizer.

Florex. Very absorptive Florida fuller's earth; used for decolorizing mineral oils, waxes.

Floridin. Florida fuller's earth; used in decolorization and clarification of oils.

Florigel. Colloidal clay; filler, fungicide carrier, emulsifying agent.

Florite. Heat-treated bauxite; decolorizing agent.

Flotol A. Crude sulfate-process turpentine.

Flotox. Sulfur dust; agricultural insecticide.

Fluf. Extra light soda ash (58%).

Flugrol. Rosin oil.

Flumerin. Disodium-2-hydroxymercurifluorescein; used in treatment of syphilis.

Fluo-Hard. Mixture of magnesium and zinc fluosilicates; used for setting cement, concrete.

Fluorex. Mixture of sodium bifluoride and sodium silicofluoride; hide disinfectant.

Fluorex T. Fluorine compound; insecticide for leather and hides.

Fluorogesarol (Gix). 1,1-Di-(*p*-fluorophenyl) - 2,2,2 - trichloroethane; insecticide.

Fluo-Sour. Mixture of acid fluorides and fluosilicates; neutralizing agent in textile processing.

Fluxol. Hardwood tar pitch; rubber softener.

Flystone. Cobalt-ore powder suspended in aqueous sugar solution; fly poison.

Foam A. Barium sulfate; used in glass, ceramics.

Foamex. Mixture of aliphatic esters; defoamer.

Foamite (Firefoam). Licorice extract; used in fire extinguishers to produce a foam.

Folione. Methyl heptine carbonate; used in violet perfume.

Folotex. Soluble pine oil.

Fomon. Hydrolyzed soybean protein; foaming agent.

Fonate. Triethanol amine salt of sulfated coconut-oil fatty acids; dispersing agent.

Fonoline. Petrolatum, U.S.P.

Fontamide. *p*-Aminobenzene sulfonyl thiourea; used in medicine.

Formadine. Direct dye.

Formalplex. Synthetic, oil-soluble tar-acid resin.

Formaset 10, 20. Modified urea formaldehyde; finish for textiles.

Formaset 60. Alkyd resin compound; used in textile finishing.

Formex. Polyvinyl methylal; synthetic resin.

Formidine. Methylene diiodosalicylic acid; used in medicine.

Formocinic Acid. Mixture of lactic and formic acid; dye assistant.

Formolite. Wood pulp.

Formopon. See Discolite.

Formopyrine. Methylene diantipyrine; antiseptic.

Formosol. Ethyl formate.

Formosul. See Hydralite.

Formvar. Polyvinyl acetate-methylal resin; used in lacquers.

Forticel. Cellulose propionate plastic.

Fortisan (Durafil). Strong, fine, regenerated cellulose fiber.

Fortoin. $CH_2(C_{14}H_{11}O_4)_2$; used in medicine.

Fosforizer. Ferrophosphorus; used in iron casting.

Fosfo rosin. Mixture of wood rosin and lime; used in making matches, printing ink.

Fosklor. Chlorinated trisodium phosphate.

Fossilite. Kieselguhr.

Fractol. Petroleum ether.

Fractol A. Refined mineral oil.

Frebol. Compound containing zinc resinate (9.6%); used in paint.

Freon-11. Trichloromonofluoromethane; refrigerant.

Freon-12. Dichlorodifluoromethane; refrigerant.

Freon-13. Chlorotrifluoromethane; refrigerant.

Freon-21. Dichloromonofluoromethane; refrigerant.

Freon-22. Difluoromonochloromethane.

Freon-23. See F-23.

Freon-31. Monochloromonofluoromethane; used in insecticide aerosols.

Freon-113. Trichlorotrifluoroethane; refrigerant.

Freon-114. Dichlorotetrafluoroethane; refrigerant.

Freon-115. Monochloropentafluoroethane.

Freon-142. Chlorodifluoromethyl methane.

Composition of Trade-Marked Products

Freoxid. Manganese dioxide.

Frianite. Powdered California pumice; insecticide carrier.

Frigen. Dichlorodifluoromethane; refrigerant.

Frigol. White mineral oil; used in air conditioning machines.

Frigor. Mixture of calcium chloride, magnesium chloride and water; refrigerating brine.

Friotin. Ethylene glycol with triethanolamine phosphate (0.8%); antifreeze (German).

Frontier alloy. Copper-base alloys of the brass and bronze types.

Fruitone (Stop-Drop). Naphthyl acetamide and naphthalene acetic acid; used in fruit sprays.

Frulite. Thiocarbamide; used to maintain original color and flavor of canned, sliced fruit.

Frutol. Refined mineral oil.

Fullogel. Fuller's earth.

Fulsoy. Defatted soyflour blended with refined soybean oil; used in food products.

Fumerane. 2-Hydroxymercurifuran; germicide.

Fumex #3. Compound of triethanolamine, formic acid and ethylene glycol; used to prevent gas fading of dyed acetate textiles.

Fumol. Aldehyde condensation product; frothing agent.

Fumonex. Gas carbon black.

Fungizyme. Proteolytic enzyme; used in tanning.

Furac No. 2. Zinc dithiofuroate; used in rubber vulcanization.

Furac No. 3. Lead dithiofuroate.

Furacin. 5-Nitro-2-furfuraldehyde semicarbazone; antiseptic.

Furnex. Carbon black.

Fybrene Wax. Amorphous paraffin wax; used in ointments.

Fyrex. Crystals of ammonium phosphate; used in mfg. fireproof paper.

G-4-S sealing agent. Viscous aqueous solution of sodium silicate; used for sealing containers.

Gabian oil. Naphtha.

Gadex. Alcoholic extract of cod-liver oil.

Gadol. Isomer of vitamin A isolated from shark-liver oil.

Galagum C. Refined vegetable carbohydrate; emulsifying agent.

Galalith. Plastic molding substance made from casein and formaldehyde.

Galex. Catalytically treated rosin consisting chiefly of dehydro-, dihydro- and tetrahydroabietic acid; rubber softener.

Galex W-100. Mixture of dehydro-, dihydro-, and tetrahydroabietic acid.

Gallal. Aluminum subgallate; used in medicine.

Galvanite. Steel coated with zinc.

Gamal. Alumina; used in metallographic polishing.

Gammexane (666). 1,2,3,4,5,6-Hexachlorocyclohexane; insecticide.

Gamone. Sex hormone.

Garantose. Saccharin.

Gardenal. Phenobarbital.

Gardinol (Duponol). Sulfated lauryl alcohol sodium salt; wetting agent.

Gardinol CA. Sodium stearyl sulfate.

Gardinol K. Sodium salt of sulfated cetyl alcohol; used in textile treatment.

Gardinol KD. Sodium sulfonate of oleyl alcohol.

Gardinol LS. Sodium salt of oleyl sulfate; emulsifier, wetting agent, detergent.

Gardinol WA. Sodium salt of lauryl sulfate; wetting agent, emulsifier, detergent.

Gardlite. Synthetic resin formed by condensation of toluol sulfonamides and formaldehyde.

Gasoline Antioxidant #5. N-butyl *p*-aminophenol.

Composition of Trade-Marked Products

Gasoline Antioxidant #6. Isobutyl *p*-aminophenol.

Gasoline Antioxidant #22. N,N'-dibutyl *p*-phenylene diamine.

Gastex. Carbon black; used to reinforce rubber.

Gavicide K. Sodium fluoaluminate compound with or without sulfur; insecticide.

Geaphthal. Synthetic alkyd resin.

Gédopal. Phenolic resin; used in varnish.

Gelaglaze. Solubilized starch; used in textile finishing.

Galamite. Semi-gelatin nitroglycerin; explosive.

Gelatin Gum (Diamond Gum; Swiss Gum). Dextrin compound; used in textile finishing.

Geletrol. Aluminum oleate; gelling agent for gasoline (Australian).

Gelex. Wet-milled corn starch; used in baking.

Gelfoam. Surgical sponge made of partially denatured protein.

Gelignite. Nitroglycerin, ammonium nitrate and nitrocotton; explosive.

Gelowax. Modified paraffinic hydrocarbon wax.

Gelva. Series of polymerized vinyl acetate resins; used for lacquers, adhesives.

Gem Wax. Microcrystalline petroleum wax.

Genalloy. Corrosion- and heat-resistant iron-nickel-chromium alloys, with 31 to 40% nickel, 12 to 21% chromium, and up to about 0.50% carbon.

Genapol. Reaction product of ethylene oxide and stearyl alcohol; sold as 30% aqueous solution; detergent.

Genelite. Graphited bearing metal with a matrix of bronze, approximately 13% tin, 10% lead, and the metallic balance, copper.

Genesee steel. Heat- and corrosion-resistant steels with up to 25% chromium, and up to 65% nickel.

Composition of Trade-Marked Products

Genetron. Aliphatic, organic fluorine compound; refrigerant.

Genetron 100. CH_3CHF_2; aerosol dispersant.

Genetron 101. $CH_3.CClF_2$; refrigerant.

Genicide. Xanthone; insecticide.

Genidust. See Genitox.

Genitol. See Genitox.

Genitox (Genitol; Genidust). DDT-base insecticide.

Genmag. Magnesia.

Gensol. Turpentine.

Geon. Vinyl- or vinylidene chloride polymer resins.

Geon 100. Polymers of vinyl chloride; thermoplastic resin.

Geon 200. Copolymer of vinyl chloride and vinylidene chloride; thermoplastic resin.

Geon Polyblend. Blend of polyvinyl resins and nitrile rubber polymers; extruding plastic.

Geosote. Guaiacol valeriate.

Gerlon I. Reaction product of an oxalic ester and ethylene imine.

Gerlon II. Reaction product of tolylene diisocyanate and ethylene imine.

Gesarol. 2,2-Bis-(*p*-Chloro-phenyl)-1,1,1-trichloroethane; insecticide.

Gix. Difluorodiphenyl trichlorethane; insecticide.

GKS-5. Mixture of complex aromatic sulfonic acids and aromatic acids with aliphatic side chains; emulsifying agent.

GL-4C. Protein-amino acid compound; wetting agent for cosmetics.

Glaurin. Diethylene glycol monolaurate; plasticizer.

Gliddol. Crude soybean lecithin containing lecithin (about 30%), cephalin (40%) and soybean oil (30%).

Gliddol-R. Commercial soybean lecithin.

Globar. Silicon carbide.

Globlak. Carbon black-lacquer base

Composition of Trade-Marked Products

consisting of nitrocellulose (55%), plasticizer (20%), carbon black (25%).

Globucid. *p*-Aminobenzene sulfonamide ethyl thiodiazole; used in medicine.

Glosso L. Paste of calcium linoleate; used in paint.

Glucarine B. Glycol carbohydrate; substitute for glycerin.

Glueglis. Mixture of glue and glyerol; used in mfg. printers' rollers.

Glufil. Walnut-shell flour; filler for plastic adhesives.

Glutoline. Methyl cellulose.

Glyakol. Diglyceryl ether tetraacetate.

Glycaid. Non-ionic, polyhydric alcohol higher fatty acid ester; used in textile dyeing.

Glycene. Alkyd resin.

Glycerogen. Glycerin, hexitols, dihydric alcohols and water; glycerin substitute.

Glyco. Lead-base alloys containing up to 22% antimony and up to 8% tin.

Glyco-ester. Glycol acetate.

Glyco metal. See Glyco.

Glycophène N.F. Phenolic resin.

Glycopon. Compounds which may be polyalkyl glycols, ethers or their condensation products with organic acids; emulsifiers.

Glycosine (Sucrol). *p*-Phenetol carbamide; sweetening agent.

Glycotauro. Concentrated ox bile containing sodium glycocholate and sodium taurocholate; used in medicine.

Glyco Wax-A. Polyhydric alcohol fatty acid ester; synthetic wax.

Glycox 1300. Lauroyl octaethoxy ethanol; emulsifier for DDT, etc.

Glydag. Graphite-glycerin lubricant.

Glyp. See Glyptal.

Glyptal (Glyp). Synthetic resin made by heating phthalic anhydride and glycerin together with or without higher fatty acids; used in paints, varnishes, lacquers.

Glyptanite. Glycerol-phthalic anhydride resin with a powdered mica filling; used for making molded insulators.

Glysal. Glycol salicylate.

Glysantin. Ethylene glycol containing minor amounts of diethylene glycol and propylene glycol and small percentages of potassium fluoride and potassium dichromate; antifreeze.

Glysogath. Dextrose (24.5) with invert sugar (38.7); glycerin substitute (German).

Glysorbine. Sodium hydroxy aliphatic carboxylate; plasticizer and humectant.

Goldstik. Compound containing shellac, casein, sulfonated oil, alcohol and ammonia water; goldleaf adhesive.

Gomagel. Modified vegetable protein; emulsifying agent.

Gonacrin. Acriflavine.

Goulac. Concentrated waste of the sulfite-pulp process; binder.

GR-A. Buna N.

Grac. Lead-base antifriction alloy hardened with about 10% tin, and small quantities of graphite, copper, antimony, arsenic and either nickel or cadmium.

Grainal. Alloys containing 15 to 20% titanium, 10 to 20% aluminum and either 13 to 25% vanadium or 6% zirconium.

Gramix. Graphited bearing metal with a copper-tin matrix.

Graney bronze. Antifriction alloy containing 75.8% copper, 9.2% tin, and 15% lead.

Graphalloy. Graphite impregnated at high pressure with a metal, such as copper, lead, silver, or cadmium; used for bearings and similar purposes.

Graphicell. Bonded, porous graph-

Composition of Trade-Marked Products

ite; used in mfg. non-corrosive tubes, plates, etc.

Graphidox #4. Alloy containing 45 to 50% silicon, 9 to 11% titanium and 5 to 8% calcium; used in graphitization of iron.

Grasselerator 552. Piperidinium pentamethylene dithiocarbamate; used in vulcanization.

Grasseli In-181 wetting agent. Flakes containing sodium lauryl sulfate; used in agricultural sprays.

Grasseli In-438 wetting agent. Liquid containing sodium oleyl sulfate; ingredient of agricultural sprays.

Grasseli In-930. Isobutyl undecylenamide; insecticide.

Grasseli spreader-sticker. Sodium oleyl sulfate and synthetic resinous sticker; used in insecticides.

Grenite. Nitrostarch, gum arabic, petroleum and some moisture; explosive.

Grief Faturan. Synthetic tar-acid resin.

Griffith's White. Lithopone.

Grinrod sulfur. Wettable sulfur of very fine particle size ($<$ 5 microns in diameter); fungicide.

GR-P (Thiokol N). Synthetic rubber of the polysulfide class.

GR-S-AC. Copolymer of butadiene and styrene.

GR-S:10. GR-S synthetic rubber made with rosin soap.

G-4-S sealing agent. Viscous aqueous solution of sodium silicate; used for sealing containers.

Guacamphol (Guaiacamphol). Guaiacol camphorate; used in medicine.

Guaiacamphol. See Guacamphol.

Guaiamar. Guaiacol glyceryl ether.

Guaiasanol. Diethyl glycocoll guaiacol hydrochloride.

Guantal. Diphenyl guanidine phthalate; activator for Ureka C.

Composition of Trade-Marked Products

Gujasanol. Diethyl glycocoll guaiacol hydrochloride.

Gulf solvent. Petroleum solvent.

Gulfwax. Paraffin wax.

Gumolite. Refined Indian gum; used in textile sizing.

Gunite. Cast iron with about 3% carbon and 2% silicon.

Guntex. Bituminous emulsion.

Gyco. Dye.

Gynergen. Egotamine tartrate.

Gynesin. Trigonelline.

Gynestrol. Mixture of estrogenic substances from urine of pregnant mares.

Gynoval. Isobornyl valerate.

Hafoil B. Partially esterified and blown sardine-oil fatty acids; used in paint.

Hagan phosphate. Sodium phosphate glass containing about 66% P_2O_5; used in boilers to prevent scale formation.

Halazone. *p*-Sulfone dichloramidobenzoic acid; sterilizing agent for water supplies.

Halenol. 2,2-Dihydroxy-5,5-dichlorodiphenyl methane; skin fungicide in ointments, powders, or solutions.

Halloid. Colloidal aluminum silicate; used in rubber compounding.

Halo. Sulfate of mixed fatty acid monoglycerides; used in shampoo.

Halopont. Paper dye.

Halowax. Chlorinated naphthalene; used in electrical insulation.

Hamico 169. Sulfonated ester; surface-active agent.

Hampden steel. High-carbon chrome tool steel with approximately 12% chromium, 2.1% carbon and fractional percentages of nickel and manganese.

Hamp wax. Hard, amorphous petroleum wax; used in moistureproofing.

Hansa. Lake dye.

Hansa oil. Polymerized marine-

Composition of Trade-Marked Products

animal oil; used in soap making.

Hapamine. Histamine-protein compound.

Harchemex. Long-chain secondary fatty alcohol.

Harcol. Aryl benzene; intermediate for detergents.

Harcose. Brewers' syrup.

Hardite. Nickel-chromium-iron heat-resistant alloys with nickel varying from as little as 6% to as high as 93%, with 12 to 25% chromium, 2 to 5% silicon, and normally about 2% manganese.

Hardtem steel. Low-alloy, oil-hardening die steel, with fractional percentages of chromium, nickel, vanadium, and molybdenum.

Hares L. Synthetic urea resin.

Hargus steel. Non-deforming steel with approximately 1.0% manganese, 0.3% chromium, and 1.0% carbon.

Harrington bronze. Antifriction alloy of 55.73% copper, 42.67% zinc, 0.97% tin.

Hartal H-152. Sulfated tallow compound; used in textile finishing.

Hartex Oil D-65. Sulfonated castor oil and pine oil; used in textile finishing.

Hartex Oil K-40. Sulfated oils and solvents; surface-active agent.

Hartex Oil L-33. Glycol soaps and alkali; surface-active agent.

Hartolan. Solid alcohols and sterols from wool grease; emulsifying agent.

Hartolein K-122. Pine-oil soap and alkali; surface-active agent.

Hartopene. Pine-oil gel; surface-active agent.

Hartosol. Isopropyl alcohol.

Harvel 612-C. Condensation product of formaldehyde and the phenols from cashew nut shells; varnish.

Hascrome. High-chromium iron alloy containing approximately 4% manganese; primarily used for hard-facing welding rods.

Hastelloy. Nickel-base alloys with varying amounts of molybdenum, chromium, manganese, copper, silicon and iron; used for purposes requiring resistance to high temperature, hydrochloric acid, wet chlorine, and other chemicals.

Haveg. Phenol-formaldehyde compound with asbestos.

Haynes metal. Cobalt-chromium-iron and cobalt-tungsten-chromium alloys.

Haystellite. Tungsten carbide; used for cutting tools.

HC mixture. Screening smoke consisting of zinc dust, ammonium perchlorate, hexachloroethane, ammonium chloride and calcium carbonate.

Heat Treating Salt No. 3A. Chloride-carbonate mixture containing borax (2%); used for steel hardening.

Heat Treating Salt No. 6. Mixture of alkali and alkaline earth chlorides; used in treating steel.

Hegonon. Silver nitrate ammonia albumose; used in medicine.

Helcosol. Basic bismuth pyrogallate.

Helicon. Aspirin.

Helindon. Vat dye; used for dyeing wool.

Helindon yellow C.M. Di-(*p*-chloranilo)-quinone; dye.

Heliogen. Light-fast phthalocyanine dye; used in lacquers, printing inks, etc.

Helioline-D. Refined fraction of cottonseed oil fatty acid; used in place of sunflower oil fatty acid.

Heliophan. Menthyl salicylate; sun-screening agent in cosmetics.

Heliozone. Mixture of paraffin and vegetable waxes; used in rubber to prevent sun-checking.

Helix rosin. Wood rosin containing lime (about 5.6%); used in mfg. printing ink.

Composition of Trade-Marked Products

Helmitol. Methenamine anhydromethylene citrate; antiseptic.

Hemodal. Synthetic vitamin K.

Hemogenit W. Sodium salt of lauryl phosphate.

Hennig Purifier. Soda ash briquette; used to remove oxides and nonmetallic inclusions in steel mfg.

Hept. Hexaethyl tetraphosphate; insecticide.

Hepteen. Mixture of 20% heptaldehyde aniline and 80% light mineral oil; accelerator.

Hepteen Base. Heptaldehyde aniline; rubber vulcanization accelerator.

Hercoal F. High explosive.

Hercogel. High explosive.

Hercolyn. Dihydromethyl abietate; plasticizer.

Hercomite. High-count ammonia-type dynamite.

Hercose AP. Cellulose acetate propionate; used for waterproof lacquers.

Hercose C. Cellulose acetate butyrate.

Hercosett. Ethyl cellulose; used on textiles to give durable finishes.

Hercosol 80. Mixture of terpene hydrocarbons and terpene ketones; solvent.

Herco-Wax. Plasticized petroleum wax; used in rubber compounding.

Hercules CMC. Sodium carboxymethyl cellulose.

Hercules metal. Alloy of 67% copper, 31% zinc, and 2% aluminum.

Herculite. Phenol-formaldehyde resin.

Herculoy. Corrosion-resistant silicon bronze, of approximately 3.3% silicon and about 0.5% tin.

Herkolite. Phenol-formaldehyde plastic.

Herolith. Phenol-formaldehyde resin.

Hertolan. β-Naphthol benzoate.

Hetocresol. *m*-Cresol cinnamate; used in medicine.

Hetralin. Hexamethylene tetramine resorcinol; used in medicine.

Heusler alloy. Non-ferrous magnetic alloy of copper, manganese and aluminum.

Hevealac. Plasticized-resin solution; used for coating rubber products.

Heveatex. Rubber latex.

Hexal. See Hexalet.

Hexalet (Hexal). Methenamine sulfosalicylate; used in medicine.

Hexogen (Cyclonite). Trimethylene trinitramine.

Hexogen. Calcium, cobalt, lead, manganese or zinc salt of an 8 carbon, saturated organic acid; paint drier.

Hexone. 4-Methyl 2-pentanone.

Hexone T-4. Trimethylene trinitramine.

Hexonit. Mixture of trimethylene trinitramine, nitroglycerin and Penthrite; powerful explosive.

Hexophan. Hydroxyphenyl quinoline dicarboxylic acid; used in medicine.

Hexsote. Creosote wood preservative.

Hexyl. Hexanitrodiphenyl amine; explosive for military use.

Hiblak. Aqueous colloidal dispersion of carbon black; used for coloring concrete.

Hi-Cyan. Sodium cyanide; used in electroplating.

Hiden. Compressed thermosetting resin-impregnated wood.

Hi-Flash naphtha. High-flash point petroleum product.

Hi-florite. Bauxite impregnated with manganous chloride (12–14%); dehydrating agent.

High Foam. Pure crystalline sulfoacetamide derivative; foaming agent.

Hi-gloss. Stainless steel of 18% chromium, 8% nickel; or of 12% chromium, 12% nickel.

Hiperco. Alloy of iron, cobalt and chromium.

Composition of Trade-Marked Products

Hipernick. Alloy of equal parts of nickel and iron.

Hipersil. Silicon-iron alloy; used in transformers.

Hi-Speed tinning flux. Aqueous solution of $ZnCl_2$ and NH_4Cl; fluxing solution in mfg. metallic equipment.

Hi-steel. Low-carbon, high-strength steel, with carbon usually below 0.12%, containing approximately 1% copper, 0.5% nickel, 0.6% manganese, and not over 0.3% silicon.

Hi-White clay. Hydrous aluminum silicate; filler.

Hocoloid. Bentonite.

Holite. Synthetic tar-acid resin; used for molding and laminating.

Holocaine hydrochloride. *p*-Diethoxyethenyl diphenyl amidine hydrochloride.

Holoplast. Special Kraft paper impregnated with a phenolic resin, coiled and laminated and then cured by heat and pressure.

Hooker Solvent T. Mixture of di-, tri- and tetrachlorobenzenes; wood preservative.

Hormodin. Indole butyric acid; plant-root stimulant.

Hormonal. Peristaltic hormone; used in medicine.

Hormono. Powdered weed killer containing the sodium salt of 2,4-D (16%).

Hornkem 1 (Marathon Agent 340–2). Lignin sulfonic acid salts; dispersing agent.

Hornkem 3. Sulfite liquor with a wetting agent; dispersing and wetting agent.

Hornkem 12. Glucoside extract; dispersing agent.

Hornkem 31. Sulfite liquor; surface-active agent.

Hornkem 101. Sulfolignin; dispersing agent.

Hornolith. Synthetic tar-acid resin.

Hoskins alloy. Nickel-base alloy, with low percentage of alloying elements, such as manganese and silicon, or high percentages of nickel, up to 35% and iron.

Hostalon OB. Polyvinyl alcohols mixed with cyclohexanone and acetaldehyde.

Hostaphen. Mixture of Mepasin sulfonic acid and sulfuric acid; used in cutting oils.

H-scale. Lacquer or solvent in which small plate-like crystals of mercurous chloride are suspended; used in pearly coatings.

HTH. Calcium hypochlorite powder containing 70% chlorine; used for bleaching and sterilizing.

HTH-15. Sodium hypochlorite setting free about 15% chlorine; germicide, stain remover.

HT Phosphate. Monocalcium phosphate; used in mfg. baking powder.

HTS. Mixture of sodium nitrite and nitrate and potassium nitrate; heat-transfer medium.

Hubbelite. Magnesium oxychloride cement in which metallic copper powder has been dispersed to achieve greater strength and germicidal action.

Humectol. Sodium salt of a sulfonated aromatic amide.

Humectol C.A. Sulfated oleic amide sodium salt; wetting agent.

Huron aluminum alloy. Aluminum-base alloys, with fractional or low percentages of copper, manganese, magnesium, nickel, cobalt, chromium or cadmium.

Huron steel. High-carbon chrome steel with approximately 12% chromium, 1% vanadium, fractional percentages of manganese and silicon, and 2.1% carbon.

Husmann's alloy or metal. Tin-base bearing metal, with approximately 11% lead, 11% antimony and 4% copper.

Composition of Trade-Marked Products

Hyacylene. Dimethyl acetal phenyl acetaldehyde; perfuming agent.

Hyamine. Quaternary ammonium salt; germicide.

Hyamine A. *tert*-Aryl dialkyl amine.

Hyamine 1622. Diisobutyl phenoxyethoxyethyl dimethyl-benzyl ammonium chloride; used in disinfectant cleaners.

Hyamine 3258. Quaternary ammonium pentachlorophenate; fungicide.

Hyblum. Aluminum-base alloy, with approximately 1% chromium and 1% nickel.

Hybnickel. Nickel-chromium-iron alloy of excellent heat and corrosion resistance, containing 5 to 35% nickel and 18 to 35% chromium.

Hycar. Synthetic rubber of Buna N type.

Hycar OR-15. Modified butadiene-acrylonitrile copolymer; rubber substitute.

Hycar OS-20. Modified butadiene-styrene copolymer; rubber substitute.

Hycc steel. High-chromium, approximately 12%, high-carbon, approximately 2.2%, abrasion-resistant steel with fractional percentages of vanadium.

Hy-Chlor. Calcium hypochlorite; disinfectant.

Hyclorite. Chlorinated soda solution; surgical antiseptic.

Hycol. Dark liquor containing high-boiling cresols and coal-tar oils; deodorant and disinfectant.

Hycoloid. Cellulose nitrate-plastic tubes.

Hydralime. Slaked lime.

Hydralin. Cyclohexanol.

Hydralo. Activated alumina.

Hydralite. Formaldehyde sodium sulfoxylate; used in textile printing.

Hydrargol. Mercury imidosuccinate; used in medicine.

Composition of Trade-Marked Products

Hydratex. Iron oxide; pigment.

Hydratex clay. Hydrous aluminum silicate; filler.

Hydratex-R. Refined clay for rubber compounding.

Hydratite. Ammonium stearate paste; used in waterproofing cement.

Hydrholac. Aqueous nitrocellulose-lacquer emulsion; used in leather finishing.

Hydro. Hydrazodiethyl dicarbonate.

Hydrocal. High-strength, low-consistency calcium sulfate base cement.

Hydrocerin (Boerocerin). Absorption base containing oxycholesterols; used in ointments and cosmetic creams.

Hydrocide. Alkyl hydroxybenzyl dimethyl ammonium phosphate.

Hydro-Cy. Hydrocyanic acid; used for fumigation.

Hydrodarco. Activated carbon; decolorizing agent.

Hydrofol acids. Technical stearic acid.

Hydrogel. Colloidal silica.

Hydrogum. Ester gum made with hydrogenated rosin; used in varnishes.

Hydrol. Corn-sugar molasses; foundry binder.

Hydrolac. Protein hydrolysate; food flavor and nutrient.

Hydrolal. Hydroxycitronellal; perfume fixative.

Hydro liquid. Aqueous solution of sodium formaldehyde sulfoxylate.

Hydrolux D. Polyalkyl sulfate; textile printing aid.

Hydrolyn. Ester of hydroabietyl alcohol; used in protective coatings.

Hydromalin. Carnauba wax with emulsifier; emulsifier in rubless floor polishes.

Hydromehl. Soluble starch; thickener (German).

Hydromel. Fermented honey.

Composition of Trade-Marked Products

Hydromite. Gypsum-synthetic resin molding compound.

Hydron. Vat dye.

Hydrone. Sodium-lead alloy; used for producing pure hydrogen.

Hydropalat B. Dibutyl hexahydrophthalic ester; plasticizer.

Hydropel. Paraffin wax emulsion containing aluminum salts; used in textile waterproofing.

Hydrophil. Absorption base containing sterols and alcohols from lanolin; used in cosmetics.

Hydrosulfite A. W. See Discolite.

Hydrosulfite A.W.C. Sodium formaldehyde sulfoxylate; used in printing textiles.

Hydroresin. Amino-abietic acid resin; binder.

Hydroterpin. Hydrogenated wood turpentine; varnish thinner.

Hydrotex. Concentrated paraffin wax emulsion; waterproofing agent.

Hydrowax N. Emulsion of carnauba wax; used in rubless floor polishes.

Hydroxal. Water dispersion of aluminum hydroxide (6–7%); used in medicine.

Hydroxamide. Monoethanol amide of stearic acid; wetting agent.

Hydroxylin. Lignin plastic containing cellulose filler.

Hyfac acids. Higher-molecular-weight fatty acids produced by hydrogenation of fish oils.

Hyferox. Yellow iron oxide; pigment.

Hyflo. Diatomaceous silica; filter aid.

Hygell. Carob-bean flour.

Hyglin. Water-soluble cellulose ether; emulsifying agent.

Hy-glo steel. Steel of approximately 18% chromium, 0.65% carbon; used for cutlery.

Hylastic steel. Manganese steel with approximately 1.6% manganese and 0.10% vanadium.

Hylite. Petroleum solvent.

Composition of Trade-Marked Products

Hymag. Short-fiber asbestos.

Hymotol R-31. Polyglycol monoester of a higher fatty acid; dyeing assistant.

Hyodol. Synthetic drying oil.

Hypernik. Alloy of 50% nickel and 50% iron.

Hyperol. Urea hydrogen peroxide; used in medicine.

Hypnal. Antipyrine chloralhydrate; used in medicine.

Hypnone. Acetophenone.

Hypol 35, 158. Calcium hypochlorite; disinfectant.

Hypophysin. Posterior-pituitary extract.

Hyporice. Rice-sized crystals of sodium thiosulfate.

Hypotonin. Ethylene diamine isovalerate; used in medicine.

Hyrex. Rosin; used in rubber adhesives.

Hyros. Wood rosin; used in varnish.

Hysiz. Dextrose mother liquor; glycerin substitute.

Hytemco. Nickel-base alloy, with approximately 30% iron.

Hytensl bronze. Alloy consisting of copper, zinc, aluminum, iron and manganese.

Hytergen. Sulfated fatty acid amide; detergent in textile industry.

Iatrol. $NHC_6H_5O_2C_2H_5OI_2$; used in medicine.

Ichtalbin. Albuminated ichthyol; used in medicine.

Ichtozyme. Proteolytic enzyme.

Ichtyol. Sulfonated distillate of bituminous shales; used in medicine.

Icorol. *m*-Hydroxy-N-ethyl N-diethyl aminoethyl aminobenzol solution; used in medicine.

Icyl. Dye for viscose rayon.

Idonit (Kondensite; Resinit). Phenol-formaldehyde resin (German).

Idrapid. Octahydroanthracene sulfonic acid; used in splitting of fat.

Igamid. Polymerization product of 1,6-hexane diisocyanate and 1,4-

Composition of Trade-Marked Products

butylene glycol or other diols; artificial fiber.

Igamid A. Superpolyamide similar to nylon.

Igamid B. Nylon-type material made with aminocaproic acid (German).

Igamid BS. Igamid B of lower degree of polymerization.

Igamid CA. Copolymer of Igamid A and B.

Igamid Q. Plastic made from 1,6-hexamethylene diisocyanate and 1,4-butanediol.

Igamid U. Solution of polyurethane of 1,6-hexamethylene diisocyanate and 1,4-butendiol in monochlorobenzene (German).

Igamid 5A. See Lupamid 5A.

Igamid 6A. See Lupamid 6A.

Iganil. Aniline-formaldehyde resin (German).

Igelit. Polyvinyl chloride plastic.

Igelit DC. Copolymer of vinyl chloride and ethylene glycol dicrotonate (German).

Igelit MP. Polymer consisting of vinyl chloride (80), dimethyl maleate (10) and diethyl maleate (10) (German).

Igelit MP-A. Copolymer consisting of vinyl chloride (80) and dimethyl maleate (20), stabilized with sodium carbonate (German).

Igelit MP-K. Copolymer of vinyl chloride and methyl acrylate; cable insulation (German).

Igelit MP-S. Copolymer consisting of vinyl chloride (60) and vinyl acetate (40) (German).

Igelit MP-400. Copolymer of vinyl chloride and vinyl isobutyl ether (German).

Igelit PC (Vinoflex). Chlorinated polyvinyl chloride containing 65% chlorine (German).

Igelit PCU. Finely powdered polyvinyl chloride.

Igelit VB10. Mixed polymer containing vinyl chloride (86) and butyl acrylate (14) (German).

Composition of Trade-Marked Products

Igelit VV. Copolymer of vinyl chloride and vinyl acetate; adhesive (German).

Igelit V2. Copolymer of vinyl acetate and vinyl chloride (German).

Igelit V6. Copolymer of vinyl chloride and isohexylic acid vinyl ester (German).

Igenal. Dye; used for coloring chrome-tanned leather.

Igepal B. Di-(isohexyl isoheptyl)-phenyl polyglycol ether sodium sulfonate (50%); detergent.

Igepal C. Dodecyl phenyl polyglycol ether; detergent.

Igepal CA. Condensation product of ethylene oxide and alkylated cresol; wetting agent.

Igepal CE. Polymerized ethylene oxide; emulsifying agent.

Igepal CTA. Condensation product of ethylene oxide and alkylated cresol; wetting agent.

Igepal F. Isooctyl phenyl polyglycol ether; detergent.

Igepal N. See Igepal C.

Igepon A. $CH_3(CH_2)_7CH{=}CH(CH_2)_7COOC_2H_4SO_3Na$; surface-active agent.

Igepon AP. Sodium sulfonate of an aliphatic oleic ester.

Igepon AP extra. Sodium salt of sulfonated ethyl oleate; wetting agent.

Igetex. Aqueous Buna S dispersion (30%) (German).

Igetex NN. Latex containing 45% solids.

Igetex S. Latex.

Igetex SS. Latex of high-styrene Buna SS containing 45% total solids.

Igevin. Polyvinyl ethers; plasticizer.

Igevin A. Polyvinyl ethyl ether (German).

Igevin DJ. Copolymer of vinyl isobutyl and decalol vinyl ethers (German).

Igevin I. Polyvinyl isobutyl ether (German).

Igevin J. Polyvinyl isobutyl ether (German).

Igevin M. Polyvinyl methyl ether (German).

I-Gummi. Long-chain polyester of adipic acid and diisocyanate; oil-resistant thermoplastic.

I. G. Wax NH. See Densodrin NH.

I. G. Wax V. Reaction product of acetylene and octadecyl alcohol.

Ikarol. Pigmented nitrocellulose lacquer (German).

Iletin. Insulin; used in medicine.

Illium. Alloy containing 63% nickel, 21% chromium, 6.5% copper, 5% molybdenum, 2% tungsten, 1% iron, 1% manganese, 1% aluminum, traces of silicon; used in regulating and control equipment.

Immersol TX Powder. Alkyl naphthalene sulfonate; wetting agent.

Immetal. Isobutyl diiodoerucate.

Imol. White refined mineral oil.

Impedex. Ammonium ferrous phosphate.

Impermex. Starch powder.

Implenal. Sodium phthalate; used to exhaust tanning liquor.

Impletol. Compound of Novocaine and caffeine; used in medicine.

Imprägnol. See Impregnole.

Impreg. Synthetic resin-treated laminated wood.

Impregnole (Imprägnol). Aqueous dispersion of waxes and aluminum salts; waterproofing agent.

Imprimal. Phenol-formaldehyde resin; used in plywood laminating.

In-181-P. Sodium alkyl sulfates, principally lauryl sulfate; wetting agent.

In-181. Sodium alkyl sulfates, principally lauryl sulfate; wetting agent.

In-438. Sodium oleyl sulfate; wetting agent.

In-930. Isobutyl undecylene amide; insecticide.

In-3622. Hydrocarbon sodium sulfonate; wetting agent for insecticides.

Composition of Trade-Marked Products

Inalium. Alloy of 96.6% aluminum, 1.7% cadmium, 1.2% magnesium, 0.5% silicon.

Inceloid. Plasticized cellulose acetate sheeting.

Inconel. Nickel-base, heat- and oxidation-resistant alloys with approximately 13% chromium, 6% iron, small amounts of manganese, silicon, copper; used in food industry equipment.

Indalone. α,α-Dimethyl α'-carbobutoxydihydro-γ-pyrone; used in insecticides.

Indanthrene navy blue RB. Tetrachloro violanthrone; dye.

Indanthrene colors. Vat dyes derived from anthraquinone.

Indanthrene golden yellow G.K. Chloro derivative of dibenzpyrene quinone; dye.

Inderon. Plastic faced resin-bonded plywood.

Indigisol. Water-soluble light-fast vat dye.

Indigisol O. Sodium salt of Indigisol.

Indigolite. Sodium formaldehyde sulfoxylate with Leucotrope W; dye discharge.

Indopol. Polybutenes of molecular weights 330–940; used with elastomers.

Indralatum. See Velatrum.

Indulin. Lignin from pine wood.

Induline Blue 6B. $(C_6H_5NH)_4(C_6H_2)_2NN(C_6H_5)Cl$; used for coloring varnishes.

Indur. Synthetic tar-acid resin.

Indurite. Smokeless powder consisting of guncotton and nitrobenzene.

Indusoil. Refined tall-oil fatty acids; used for cutting oils.

Inertol BX. Sodium salts of sulfated higher fatty alcohols and a sulfonated naphthalene derivative with sodium sulfate and water; textile assistant (Polish).

Inferol NFK. Cyclohexylamine lauryl sulfate (about 50%) with water; textile assistant (German).

Infundin. Pituitary-gland extract; used in medicine.

Infusite. Powdered fire clay; refractory.

Ingersoll DBL high-speed steel. High-speed steel, containing tungsten, molybdenum, and vanadium; used for hack-saw blades.

Ingolin. Concentrated hydrogen peroxide; used in rocket fuels.

Insecti-Sol (Super-Sol). Odorless petroleum distillate; solvent for DDT.

Insecti-sol. Deodorized kerosene; used in insect sprays.

Insect Repellent 6–12. 2-Ethyl 1,3-hexanediol.

Insidline. Amosite and diatomaceous earth mixture; used for heat insulation.

Insulac W. Treated gilsonite; used in rubber compounding.

Insuluminum. Steel impregnated with aluminum on its surface.

Insurok. Synthetic tar-acid resin.

Integritol 65. Sulfonated alkylated benzene; wetting and penetrating agent for textiles, leather, etc.

Integrol. Mixed sulfonated oils, esters, alcohols; surface-active agent.

Intracaine. *p*-Ethoxybenzoyl diethyl aminoethanol hydrochloride; used in medicine.

Intracol. Long-chain fatty acid amide containing multiple amino groups; cationic surface-active agent.

Intraderm. Xylene, a wetting agent and propylene glycol.

Intral 222. Saturated long-chain fatty acid ester containing multiple ether linkages; wetting agent.

Intral 224. Saturated fatty acid ester

Composition of Trade-Marked Products

with multiple ether linkages; surface-active agent.

Intral 231. Unsaturated, long-chain fatty acid ester containing multiple ether linkages; wetting agent.

Intramine PC. Sodium salt of sulfated butyl or myristal collamide; surface-active agent.

Intrasolvan E. Mixture of isobutyl alcohol (85%) and higher-boiling alcohols (up to 140°C) (15%); lacquer solvent.

Intravan. Saturated solution of zinc hydroxide in concentrated ammoniacal diammonium phosphate; used in flameproofing.

Intravan NK. See Expyrol Z.

Invadine B. Sodium alkyl phenylene sulfonate; wetting agent.

Invadine C. Alkyl naphthalene sulfonic acid; wetting agent.

Invadine N. Sodium alkyl naphthalene sulfonate; wetting agent.

Invar. Alloy containing 63.8% iron, 36% nickel, 0.2% carbon; used in thermostats.

Invaro steel. Non-deforming steel, with approximately 1.1% manganese, 0.5% tungsten, 0.5% chromium, 0.3% vanadium and approximately 0.90% carbon.

Inventol. Blend of American nut oils; used in pharmaceutical and cosmetic products.

Iocamfen. Product containing iodine, phenol, and camphor; antiseptic.

Iodalbin. Blood albumin and iodine; used in medicine.

Iodaline LL. Oleyl disulfonate.

Iodeikon. Tetraiodophthalein sodium; used for X-ray examination of the gall bladder.

Iodistol. Thymol iodide; antiseptic.

Iodival. Iodisovaleryl urea; used in medicine.

Iodobismitol. Sodium bismuth iodide dissolved in glycol containing acetic acid (about 0.1%); used in medicine.

Composition of Trade-Marked Products

Iodocrol. Carvacrol iodide; used in medicine.

Iodoformal. Iodoformin ethyl iodide; used in medicine.

Iodoformin. Iodoformohexamethylene tetramine; antiseptic.

Iodoglidin. Iodized glidin containing 10% iodine; used in medicine.

Iodohemol. Hemol with iodine; used in medicine.

Iodoline. Quinoline chloromethylate iodochloride; used in medicine.

Iodomenin. Bismuth-casein compound containing iodine (10%); used in medicine.

Iodostarin. Diiodotariric acid; used in medicine.

Iothion. 1,3-Diodoisopropyl alcohol; used in medicine.

Iodotriferrin. Iodized iron nucleate; used in medicine.

Iodoxyl. See Uropac.

Iodyloform. Gelatin containing iodine (10%); used in medicine.

Ioflow. Potassium iodide preparation; used in cattle feed.

Iomag. Mixture of potassium iodide and magnesium carbonate; used in cattle feed.

Ionac A-293. Anion-exchange resin; used in water softening.

Ionamines. Formaldehyde-bisulfite compounds of primary or secondary amines; acetate-silk dyes.

Ionex. Synthetic resin; used in water treatment.

Ion-Ose. Maltose syrup, purified by the ion-exchange process.

Iopax. Sodium 2-oxo-5-iodopyridine N-acetate; used in medicine.

Iosol. Dyestuff for coloring gasoline.

Iporka. Urea-formaldehyde resin; used in refrigerator insulation.

Ipral. Ethyl isopropyl barbituric acid; medicament.

Iralia. Ionone; used in perfumes.

Irgafen. *n*-Dimethyl benzoyl sulfanilamide.

Composition of Trade-Marked Products

Irgamide. *n*-Dimethyl acroyl sulfanilamide.

Irgatan. Synthetic tanning agent; used for chrome leather.

Irium. Sodium lauryl sulfate; detergent.

Ironac. Steel with 14% silicon.

Irox. Ferrous gluconate; used in medicine.

Isacen. Di-(acetyl oxyphenyl) isatin.

Isatophan. 8-Methoxy-2-phenyl quinoline 4-carboxylic acid; used in medicine.

Iso-Beeswax. Mixture of beeswax, emulsifying and stabilizing agents; used in cosmetic creams.

Isobrom. Bromisovaleryl urea.

Isocel. Activated bauxite, impregnated with anhydrous aluminum chloride; isomerization catalyst.

Isocreme (Cremba). Mixture of certain wool wax alcohols and wool wax esters; absorption base.

Isolac. Thermoplastic, hard, dark-brown, resinous crude rubber derivative; used for shoe soles, waterproofing, etc.

Isolene. Polyisobutylene.

Isoline. Synthetic drying oil containing triglycerides of isomeric linoleic acids.

Isonol CL1. Higher quaternary ammonium halide; wetting agent.

Isonol DL1. Dilauryl dimethyl ammonium bromide; bactericide.

Isopral. 1,1,1-Trichloroisopropyl alcohol.

Isothan. Lauryl isoquinolinium bromide; used in plant fungicides.

Isothan DL1. Dimethyl dilauryl ammonium chloride; fungicide.

Isothan Q4. Lauryl pyridinium bromide; fungicide.

Isothan (215, Q15). Lauryl isoquinolinium bromide; fungicide.

Istizine. Synthetic dihydroxyanthaquinone; used in medicine.

Itrol. Silver citrate; used in medicine.

Ivaleur. Cellulose nitrate plastic.

Composition of Trade-Marked Products

Ivorax. Synthetic tar-acid resin.

Iwnal. Phenolic resin; used in wood impregnating.

Jalcase steel. Low-alloy steels with up to 1 to 1.65% manganese.

Jal-ten steel. Low-alloy, high-strength steel, with not over 0.35% carbon, 1.25 to 1.75% manganese, and not over 0.40% copper.

Janusol. Mixture of lauryl and myristyl esters containing amino and sulfated groups; dispersing agent.

Japsol. Water-dispersible Japan wax; used in textile finishing.

Jasminolene. Hexyl cinnamic aldehyde; used in jasmin perfume.

Jatene. Mahogany sulfonates, Japan wax and sulfated oil; dye assistant.

Jewell alloy. Heat- and corrosion-resistant, low-alloy cast iron, with low percentages of silicon, manganese, nickel and chromium.

Jicwood. Compreg.

Joanite. Synthetic tar-acid resin.

Jozite. Mixture of zinc oxide and iron oxide; accelerator activator.

Jutlac. Jute-shellac laminate; used for boxes and drums (Indian).

Kakol. Mixture of coal tar and rosin; rubber softener.

Kalco. Calcium caseinate; insecticide spreader.

Kal-Fos. Calcium phosphate; used in breeding domestic animals.

Kalinex. Mixture of powdered sulfur and calcium arsenate; agricultural insecticide.

Kalite No. 1. Calcium carbonate powder containing stearic acid (1%); filler for rubber.

Kalite No. 3. Calcium carbonate powder containing stearic acid (3%).

Kallite. Infusorial earth.

Composition of Trade-Marked Products

Kallith. Lepidolite; used in ceramics.

Kallodent (Stellon, Lumacryl, Portex, Thermolite). Acrylic resin; used in dentures.

Kalmopyrin. Calcium acetyl salicylate.

Kalotex. Composition of sodium fluoride, dinitrophenol and disodium arsenate; insecticide.

Kalox zinc oxide. Colloidal zinc oxide; used for hardening slow-drying paints.

Kalsetal. Calcium acetyl salicylate.

Kalva. Extract of iridophycus (seaweed); used in dairy products.

Kalvan. Calcium carbonate powder; filler in rubber.

KA-L-MO Steel. Stainless steel with 18% chromium, 8% nickel, low-carbon range, and approximately 3% molybdenum.

Kanatol #1. Sulfated castor oil and Tergitol #7; dye assistant.

Kandar. Aqueous dispersion of a thermoplastic resin; used in textile sizing.

Kapak. Refined elaterite.

Kapsol. Methyl Cellosolve oleate; plasticizer.

Kaptol. Mercaptobenzothiazole.

Karbate #10. Petroleum-coke-base carbon, made impervious by impregnation with a synthetic resin.

Karbate #20. Petroleum-coke-base carbon, graphitized in an electric furnace before resin impregnation to render it impervious.

Karmex. Ammonium 2,4-dichlorophenoxyacetate (88) and inert material (12); weed killer.

Kasil. Concentrated solution of potassium silicate; binder in welding rods.

Kastolene. Dehydrated castor oil; used in varnish.

Katanol-ON. Reaction product of phenol, sulfur and soda ash (German).

Katanol O Sol. Solubilized, sulfur-

Composition of Trade-Marked Products

ized phenol condensate; dyeing assistant.

Katanol WL. Condensation product of trichlorobenzyl chloride and sulfonated phenol.

Katapol CNS. Cationic hydrosulfate salt of a polyethylene glycol derivative of a fatty amine; textile detergent.

Kathro. Wool wax alcohols containing cholesterol (>70%); used in cosmetics.

Katigen. Sulfur dye.

Katozyme. Mixture of diastatic and proteolytic enzymes; desizing agent for textile fabrics.

Kaurit AF-1. Tetramethylol acetylene diurea; used in textile waterproofing.

Kaurit AK-2. Condensation product of melamine, formaldehyde and triethanol amine; used in waterproofing textiles (German).

Kaurit F-1. Aqueous solution of dimethylol formamide; used in textile waterproofing.

Kaurit KF. Dimethylol urea.

Kaurit MKF. Tetramethylol melamine.

Kautschol. Brown coal tar.

Kaydol. U.S.P. heavy white mineral oil.

Kaykote. Alkali aluminum silicate with hydrocarbons; used in protective coatings.

Kaylorite. Infusorial earth; rubber filler.

Ka-Z steel. Stainless steel with 18% chromium, 8% nickel, of low-carbon range.

KD Oil. Sorbitan esters of dehydrated castor-oil fatty acids; synthetic drying oil.

Keebush. Synthetic oil-soluble tar-acid resin.

Keene's cement. Dead-burnt gypsum or partially calcined gypsum mixed with alum which catalyzes rehydration; used in making imitation marble.

Composition of Trade-Marked Products

Kelcoloid. Water-dispersible algin compound; emulsifier and thickener in food products.

Kelene. Ethyl chloride; used in medicine.

Kelgin. Sodium aglinate; emulsifying agent.

Kellite. Synthetic tar-acid resin.

Kellsoy. Soybean oil; used in varnish.

Kelo-Form. Ethyl amino benzoate.

Keltex. Sodium salt of alginic acid; emulsifying agent.

Keltone. Sodium salt of alginic acid; emulsifying agent.

Kelvitol. Treated linseed oil of low-acid value that polymerizes spontaneously; varnish oil.

Kemidol. Agricultural lime.

Kemikal. Lime.

Kemilime. Lime.

Kemithal. 5-Cyclohexanyl 5-allyl 2-thiobarbituric acid; anesthetic (British).

Kempol (Sulprene; Witcogum). Polymerization and condensation product of triglycerides in the presence of resinous or non-elastic substances; rubber substitute.

Kempruf. Carbon brick or tile.

Kemsolene. Petroleum naphtha.

Kemvite. Sulfaguanidine-niacin compound; used in medicine.

Kendex. Thermoplastic black hydrocarbon resin; used in laminating.

Kennametal. Tungsten-titanium carbide; used for high-speed cutting tools.

Kensol. Petroleum-hydrocarbon solvents.

Keokuk alloy iron. Pig iron containing about 20% silicon; deoxidizer.

Kephrine. Methyl aminoacetocatechol.

Ker. Butadiene polymer; synthetic rubber.

Keralin F. Compound containing a proteolytic enzyme; used in bating hides.

Kerazon. Plastic-coated fabric.

Composition of Trade-Marked Products

Kerocain. Procaine hydrochloride; drug (British).

Keroid. Dispersed carbon black.

Kerrysol. Methyl acetate.

Keryl. Chlorinated kerosene.

Keryl benzene. Chlorinated benzene.

Keryl chloride. Chlorinated (13.85% Cl) kerosene fraction (12–14 C atoms).

Kesscocide. α-Naphthyl isothiocyanate.

Ketacine. Thermosetting resins made by reacting organic amines and keto-acids.

Ketenone M.O. Methyl ethyl benzoyl benzoate.

Ketol. Mixture of ketones, chiefly dipropyl ketone.

Ketonone B. Butyl benzoyl benzoate.

Ketonone E. Ethyl *o*-benzoyl benzoate.

Ketonone M. Methyl *o*-benzoyl benzoate.

KEX. Potassium ethyl xanthate.

Keystone filler. Mineral black.

Kierasol 670. "Soluble" pine oil; boil-off assistant.

Kierole. "Soluble" pine oil; bleaching assistant.

Kilfoam. Octyl alcohol; antifoaming agent.

Kimpreg. Phenolic-resin impregnated paper.

Kineurine. Quinine glycerophosphate.

Kingston's metal. Antifriction alloy of 88% tin, 6% copper, 6% mercury.

Kinite. Steel with approximately 14% chromium, 1.1% molybdenum, 1.5% carbon, fractional percentages of cobalt, nickel, manganese and silicon; used in dies.

Kirksite A. Zinc-base alloy; used for tools.

Kiski steel. Non-deforming steel with approximately 1.5% manganese, 0.60% tungsten, 0.50% chromium and 0.20% vanadium.

Kiton Fast. Acid dye.

Klason lignin. Product isolated from wood meal.

Kleanrol. Mixture of zinc chloride and ammonium chloride; soldering flux.

Klearol. Colorless mineral oil.

Klop. Chloropicrin.

Kloranol BA. Sodium lauryl sulfate; dyeing assistant.

K Monel. Age-hardening modified Monel metal containing approximately 3% aluminum.

Koda. Continuous-filament acetate rayon.

Kodalin. Trihydroxymethylene.

Kodaloid. Transparent nitrocellulose sheets.

Kodapak. Thin transparent cellulose acetate sheets.

Kodelon. *p*-Aminophenol hydrochloride; used in photographic developing.

Kogasin. Mixture of aliphatic hydrocarbons chlorinated to 52% chlorine content; used in insecticides.

Kogasin II. Hydrocarbons of distillation range of 220–330°C.

K-Oil. Sorbitan esters of linseed fatty acids; synthetic drying oil.

Kokobase. Coconut-oil soap; used in shampoos.

Kolineum. Refined coal-tar creosote.

Kollag. Suspension of graphite in oil.

Kollidon. Polyvinyl pyrrolidone.

Kolloxoline. Pyroxylin and alcohol.

Kolodust (Kolofog). Mixture of powdered bentonite and sulfur; agricultural fungicide.

Kolofog. See Kolodust.

Koltreat. Calcium chloride with an inhibitor; used for dust- and freezeproofing of coal.

Komel. Monosodium glucosan.

Konel. Nickel-base alloy, with about 17% cobalt, 9% titanium, and frac-

Composition of Trade-Marked Products

tional percentages of other metals; used in radio-tube work.

Konik steel. High-strength steel with 0.10 to 0.20% carbon, 0.10 to 0.30% copper, 0.30 to 0.50% nickel, up to 0.30% chromium.

Kontack A-10. Aluminum sulfate; catalyst.

Kontakt 9823. Manganese dioxide (35) and aluminum oxide (65); catalyst.

Kopan. Cellulose in aqueous solution of caustic soda and zinc oxide; textile sizing.

Kopol. Processed fossil gum; used in varnish.

Koraton. Synthetic tar-acid resin.

Korelen. Mixture of Koresin (1) and Naftolen (2) (German).

Koreon. Basic chromium sulfate; used in tanning.

Koresin. *tert*-Butyl phenol acetylene condensation product; rubber tackifier.

Korez. A- stage phenolic resin with silica filler; corrosion-resistant cement.

Korogel. Highly plasticized polyvinyl chloride.

Kormin. Mixture of Koresin (1) and mineral oil (2); used in rubber compounding.

Kornite. See Calgon.

Korolac. Solution of Koroseal; used for protective coatings.

Koron. Polyvinyl chloride.

Koron 101. Koroseal molding powder containing organic phosphate plasticizer.

Koroseal. Plasticized highly polymerized vinyl chloride.

Kosmobile. Granules of dustless carbon black; reinforcing agent in rubber products.

Kosmolak. Carbon black.

Kosmos. Compressed carbon black; reinforcing agent in rubber products.

Kovar. Low-expansion, iron-base alloy with 28 to 30% nickel, 15 to 18% cobalt, fractional percentages of manganese; used for sealing metal wire into hard glass.

KP-23. Butoxyethyl stearate; plasticizer.

KPO oil. Vegetable drying oil polymerized under carbon dioxide.

Krafelt. Wood fiber.

Krafteen. Milk fat; used in foods.

Kralex. Non-fat dry-milk solids; used in foods.

Kraystay. Extract of Irish moss; thickener and emulsifier.

Krebolith. Powder consisting of ZnS (50%) and $BaSO_4$ (50%); used in paints.

Krel. Alkyl aryl sulfonate or salt; wetting agent.

Kremoline. White mineral jelly; lubricant.

Krenite. Aqueous solution of sodium dinitroorthocresylate; agricultural insecticide.

Kreosal. Creosote tannate.

Kresamin. Ethylene diamine tricresol; disinfectant.

Kresival. Calcium salts of cresol sulfonic acids.

Kresosolvin. See Creolin.

Krist-O-Kleer. Mixture of equal parts of dextrose and levulose with water; used in candy.

Kromeflake. Chromic acid.

Kromekube. Chromium salt containing 25 to 30% Cr_2O_3; used in coloring ceramics.

Kromfax. Thiodiethylene glycol; dye solvent.

Kronisol. Reaction product of phthalic anhydride and butyl Cellosolve; plasticizer.

Kronitex AA. Product consisting of phenolic phosphates; plasticizer.

Kryocide. Cryolite.

Kryocide C. Mixture of powdered cryolite and a copper salt; agricultural insecticide.

Kryocide 50. Mixture of equal parts of talc and cryolite; agricultural insecticide.

Composition of Trade-Marked Products

Kryptol. Mixture of graphite, silicon carbide and clay.

Krysid. α-Naphthyl thiourea; insecticide (Russian).

K.U. #1. Glucosan monocarbamate; thickening agent.

Kunstharz 26Z. Synthetic tar-acid resin (German).

Kurrol salts. Sodium or potassium hexametaphosphate; used in water treatments.

K. W. Steel. Low-alloy steel containing 3.5% tungsten and approximately 1.3% carbon; used for dies, small tools.

Kybol. Alkyl benzols; additive for high-octane fuels.

Kyrite. Diatomaceous earth covered with a synthetic ion-exchange resin; used in purifying sugar.

Kys-Ite. Molding compound consisting of fast-curing phenolic resin and strong-fibered wood pulp.

La Bour alloy. Complex nickel-chromium alloys with 8 to 63% nickel, approximately 25% chromium, 6% copper, 2 to 4% molybdenum and 1 to 54% iron.

Lacalac. Defatted dry-milk solids; used in baking.

Lacanite. Shellac plastic.

Lacarnol. Extract of striated muscle tissue; medicament.

Laccain. Synthetic tar-acid resin.

Lacet Resin. Melamine-formaldehyde resin with or without other resins, pigments, etc.; used in textile finishing.

Lacimoid. Synthetic, plastic-resinoid product; used as building material for walls, ceilings and cabinets.

Lacolene. Petroleum-hydrocarbon solvent; used in lacquers.

Lacrtex. Pyroxylin-coated fabric.

Lactacolle. Aqueous solution of acrylic resins.

LacTan-X. Vegetable tannin.

Composition of Trade-Marked Products

Lactofil. Casein textile fiber (Dutch).

Lactoid. Highly polishable, casein-formaldehyde; plastic composition resembling natural horn.

Lactol. 2-Naphthyl lactate.

Lactonate. Petroleum sulfonate.

Lactoprene. Acrylic ester copolymers having vulcanizable unsaturated groups, e.g., methyl acrylate and butadiene.

Lactoprene EV. Elastomer of ethyl acrylate (95%) and chloroethyl vinyl ether copolymer (5%).

Lake red C amine. 2 -Amino-5-chloro-*p*-toluene sulfonic acid.

Laksol. Distillate from pine wood.

Lamepon A (Lamepon 4C; Lamepon 10-N). Protein-fatty acid condensate; surface-active agent.

Lamicoid. Laminated plastic-impregnated paper or fabric sheets.

Laminac. See Textolite.

Lampwax. Paraffin wax.

Lanaclarin LM. Gardinol and methyl hexalin; dyeing and wetting assistant.

Lanara (Prolon; Aralac). Protein textile fiber.

Lanaset. Melamine resin; used in shrinkproofing textiles.

Lanette wax. Mixture of normal, primary fatty alcohols, mainly C-18 alcohol.

Lanette wax SX. Mixture of partially sulfated or phosphated hexadecyl and octadecyl alcohols; emulsifier.

Lanichol. Anhydrous lanolin.

Lanicol. Starch derivative; sizing agent for textile fibers.

Laniol. Anhydrous lanolin.

Lanital. Casein synthetic fibers.

Lanitol P. Sodium alkyl aryl sulfonate; surface-active agent.

Lanitol S. Sodium alkyl aryl sulfonate and alkali; surface-active agent.

Lanole B. Sodium oleate and solvents; surface-active agent.

Composition of Trade-Marked Products

Lanone. Water-in-oil emulsifier consisting of sterols, sterol esters, higher alcohols and their esters, fatty acid ether esters and hydrocarbons.

Laolin. Polystyrene injection-molding compound.

Largin. Silver protalbin; used in medicine.

Larocaine. 1-Aminobenzoyl 2-dimethyl 3-diethyl aminopropanol hydrochloride; local anesthetic.

Larosan. Casein containing calcium oxide (2.5%); used in medicine.

Larostidin. Aqueous solution of *l*-histidine hydrochloride; used in medicine.

Larvacide. Chloropicrin; fumigant.

Lastex. Latex thread wrapped with textile thread.

Lasto. Ethylene polysulfide rubber.

Latac. Hexamethylene ammonium hexamethylene dithiocarbamate.

Latekoll. Ammonium polyacrylate; latex thickener (German).

Latekoll A. Aqueous solution of ammonium polyacrylate (10%) adhesive.

Latekoll N. Aqueous solution of sodium polyacrylate (25%); adhesive.

Latexin. Sodium lauryl sulfate (about 82%) with sodium sulfate, sodium chloride and water; textile assistant (German).

Latex Telloy. Finely powdered tellurium; secondary vulcanizing agent.

Lauralene. Fatty acids of coconut oil.

Laurex. Zinc salt of lauric acid; used in compounding rubber.

Laurical. Technical lauric acid.

Laurine. Hydroxycitronellal; used in perfumery.

Lauth's violet. Thionine.

Lauxite 101. Urea-formaldehyde resin; adhesive.

Lavendine. Naphthalene, scented with lavender; insecticide.

Composition of Trade-Marked Products

Laventin HW. Igepon T and a solvent.

Lawsone. 2-Hydroxy-1,4-naphthaquinone; used in hair dyeing.

Leadlube. Alloy containing 70% copper, 25% lead and 5% tin; bearing metal.

Leadtex. Sheet copper coated with lead.

Leafox. Lead-free zinc oxide; used in agricultural sprays.

Leatherlubric. Sulfonated oil compound; used for fat liquoring.

Leatheroid. Vulcanized fiber.

Ledate. Lead dimethyl dithiocarbamate; vulcanization accelerator.

Ledrite brass. Free-cutting, yellow brass with approximately 3% lead.

Lef. Lignin-enriched cellulose; filler for rubber.

Lemenone. Terpene aldehyde; odorant.

Lemonal. Citral; used in flavors.

Lenigallol. Pyrogallol triacetate.

Lenokal AL. Highly sulfonated oil with solvent.

Lenorol ROH. Mixture of a monoacid with dipropyl dichlorobenzene (German).

Lentin. Carbamyl choline chloride; used in medicine.

Leonil FFO Ex. Condensation product of ethylene oxide and naphthol; textile detergent.

Leonil O. High-molecular polyether alcohol.

Leonil SA. Alkyl naphthalene sodium sulfonate; wetting agent.

Leophen KD. Cresylic acid derivative; mercerizing assistant.

Leophen M. Sodium salt of incompletely sulfated hexyl alcohol; wetting agent.

Lesamite. Water-ground natural calcium carbonate; filler in rubber compounding.

Lethalaire. Aerosol containing Freon-12, pyrethrum extract, DDT, petroleum derivatives and xylol; insecticide.

Composition of Trade-Marked Products

Lethane A-70. Dithiocyanodiethyl ether; insecticide.

Lethane 60. Solution of thiocyanoethyl esters of C_{10}-C_{18} fatty acids; used in insecticides.

Lethane 384. Solution of β-butoxy-β′-thiocyanodiethyl ether; used in insecticides.

Lethane 384 Special. Mixture of *n*-butyl carbitol thiocyanate, β-thiocyanoethyl laurate and paraffin oil; used in insecticides.

Leucosol. Vat color; used for textile printing.

Leucothol. Titanous sulfate solution.

Leucotrope O. Dimethyl phenyl benzyl ammonium chloride; used in textile finishing.

Leucotrope WX. Calcium salt of disulfonated dimethyl phenyl benzyl ammonium chloride; used in textile printing.

Leukanol. Sulfonic acid compound; bleaching agent for leather.

Leukon. Acrylate resin.

Leukonin (Leuconine). Sodium metaantimonate (98%); substitute for tin oxide in enameling.

Leukopal O. Oil-soluble resin; used in varnishes.

Leukorit. Synthetic tar-acid resin.

Leukotrope O. Dimethyl phenyl benzyl ammonium chloride; used in dyeing textiles.

Leukotrope OW. Dimethyl benzyl ammonium chloride.

Leukotrope W. Calcium salt of disulfonated dimethyl phenyl benzyl ammonium chloride; used in dyeing textiles.

Leuna gas. Compressed propane; fuel.

Leunaphos G. Nitrogen fertilizer.

Leunasalpeter BASF. Nitrogen fertilizer.

Leunophoska. Mixture of diammonium phosphate, potassium chloride, and ammonium sulfate; fertilizer.

Composition of Trade-Marked Products

Levelene. Quaternary ammonium salt; used in textile finishing.

Levelol. Sulfated castor oil; used in textile finishing.

Levenol. Sulfated oil; dye assistant.

Levenol G. Modified, sulfonated hydrocarbon sodium salt; dyeing assistant.

Levulcan. Buna SS.

Lewisol 2L. Maleic, alkyd-modified rosin ester.

Lewisol maleic resin. Maleic-rosin-glycerol resin; used in lacquers, varnishes, etc.

Lewisol phenolic resin. Rosin-glycerol ester-modified phenol-formaldehyde resin; used in varnishes and enamels.

Lexin. Vegetable lecithin.

Lexinol. Lecithin and associated phosphatides; emulsifying agent.

Lexone. See Sixide.

Lignasan. Ethyl mercury phosphate; fungicide.

Lignasan fungicide. Ethyl mercury chloride; used to prevent fungus growth on raw lumber.

Lignin KSC. Sodium salt of crude lignin; used in drilling mud and adhesives.

Lignolite. Laminated cellulose-lignin sheets; used in mfg. pattern plates.

Lignone. Crude calcium lignosulfonate (60%) and water (40%); dispersing agent.

Lim-Cal. Calcium carbonate.

Limolith. Whiting.

Lincos. Crude lecithin; paint emulsifier.

Lincrusta. Paper or cloth coated with linoxyn, resins and fillers; wall covering.

Lindol. Technical tricresyl phosphate; plasticizer, lubricating agent, fire-retarding agent.

Lindol EP. Tricresyl phosphate, lubricating grade; lubricating agent, plasticizer.

Composition of Trade-Marked Products

Lindol MP. Non-toxic, chemically pure tricresyl phosphate.

Lin-O-Gel. Gelled linseed oil; used in paint.

Lipiodol. Iodinated poppy oil; used in medicine.

Lipobromol. Poppy seed oil containing bromine (33%); sedative.

Lipoiodine. Ethyl diiodobrassidate; used in medicine.

Lipone. Sulfonated vegetable oil; used as antifoam.

Liqro. Mixture of crude tall-oil acids; used in asphalt emulsions and cheap soaps.

Liro. Limed rosin; used in paint.

Lissamine. Acid dye; used for dyeing wool.

Lissolamine. Octadecyl pyridinium bromide; used in textile finishing.

Lissolamine V. Hexadecyl trimethyl ammonium bromide.

Lithocorn. Synthetic tar-acid resin.

Litholite. Fused alumina; abrasive.

Litholite A. Lithium stearate.

Lithotine. Petroleum solvent.

Lithowax. Paraffin wax, modified with lithium stearate.

Lithoxin. Lithopone.

Litmopyrine. Lithium acetyl salicylate.

Lizarol D, DC. Sulfonated oil; used in textile finishing.

Loalin. Polystyrene molding compound.

Lo-Bax. Product containing chlorine (50%); used for sterilization.

Lobeite. See Flavite.

Lo-cro. Low-alloy steel with 4–6% chromium, and up to 1.25% tungsten or molybdenum.

Locron. Synthetic urea resin.

Lodal. 6,7-Dimethoxy-2-methyl 3,4-dihydroisoquinoline chloride; used in medicine.

Lo-ex. Low-expansion aluminum alloy containing approximately 13% silicon, 2% nickel, 1% copper, and 1% magnesium.

London Purple. Mixture of tricalcium arsenate and arsenite, calcium arsenate and color; insecticide.

Lonester M. Phenyl malonic acid dimethyl ester.

Loomfibre. Talc.

Loomite. Talc.

Loomkill. Talc powder; insecticide-dust diluent.

Loosite. Petroleum solvent.

Lorium. Lauryl pyridinium chloride; germicide and surface-active agent.

Lorival. Synthetic tar-acid resin; used for molding and laminating.

Loro. Oil containing lorol thiocyanate; agricultural insecticide.

Lorol amine. Technical lauryl amine; cationic surface-active agent.

Lorol Chloride. Mixture of lauryl chloride (55%), myristyl chloride (20%) and alkyl chlorides with more than 14 carbon atoms.

Lorol Fatty Alcohol. Mixture of normal fatty alcohols, chiefly lauryl alcohol; used in plasticizers, insecticides, etc.

Lorolin. Preparation of alkyl dimethyl benzyl ammonium chloride; germicide.

Lorol Insecticide. Oily liquid containing Lorol rhodanates; insecticide.

Lotol. Processed and compounded latex.

Loupene. Mixture of sulfonated oils and solvents; surface-active agent.

Loupole. Sulfated oils with chlorinated hydrocarbons; dry cleaner.

Loupole W-950. Mixture of solvents with sulfonated oils; detergent.

LP-3. Disulfide of bis-(2-chloroethyl) formal; rubber softener.

Lub-Base. Stabilized, higher, natural fatty acids; used in lubricating grease.

Lubrico. High-lead bronze with approximately 21% lead; used for bearings, etc.

Composition of Trade-Marked Products

Lubriseal. Petroleum-base grease; lubricant for glass surfaces.

Lucex. Ethyl chlorobenzene; chlorinated at the side chain; insecticide.

Lucidol. Benzoyl peroxide.

Lucite (Pontalite). Thermoplastic methyl methacrylate resin.

Lucitone. Acrylic plastic; used in dentures.

Lucosil. 2-Sulfanilamido-5-methyl 1,3,4-thiodiazole.

Lucronal JFM. Copolymer of isobutylene or vinyl chloride with dimethyl fumarate (German).

Lucrylan 1 (Acronal 1). Polyacrylic acid methyl ester (German).

Lucrylan IV (Acronal IV). Polyacrylic acid butyl esters.

Ludigol. Sodium *m*-nitrobenzene sulfonate; used in textile finishing.

Ludlite. Stainless-steel sheet integrally bonded to a fireproof, heat-insulating backing.

Lufax. Zirconium oxide; opacifier for porcelain enamels.

Lukens steel. Low-alloy steels containing low percentages of nickel, chromium, or manganese.

Lumacryl. See Kallodent.

Lumarith. Cellulose acetate plastic.

Lumen alloy. Series of copper-base alloys, brasses and bronzes.

Lumen bronze. Zinc-base bearing alloys, with approximately 10% copper and 4% aluminum.

Lumen metal. Tin-base bearing alloys, with 4 to 10% copper, and 5 to 8% aluminum.

Lumercine. Mixture of Vinylite compounds and higher polyalcohols; mercerizing assistant.

Luminal. Sodium phenobarbital; used in medicine.

Lumite. Fabric woven from extruded filaments of Saran; used in automobile seat covers.

Lumogen. Dye which luminesces under ultraviolet light; used in luminescent paint.

Composition of Trade-Marked Products

Lumogen L Blue. 2,5-Dioxyterephthalic diethylester; dye.

Lumogen L- Brilliant Green. Combination product of 1 mol terephthal aldehyde and 3 mols of cyanethyl acetate; dye.

Lumogen L-Brilliant Yellow. Dioxynaphthaldazin; dye.

Lumogen L Red. Rhodamine B extra (1.1%) mixed with Igelit MP-K; pigment.

Lumogen L Red Orange. 2-Anilido-4(2′-5′-dichlorobenzoyl amino)-1-9-anthrapyrimidine; dye.

Lumogen L-Yellow. 9,10-Dianilidoanthraquinone; dye.

Lumogen L Yellow Orange. Salicyl aldazin; dye.

Lunosol. Mixture of sucrose and silver chloride; used in medicine.

Lupamid 5A (Igamid 5A). Condensation product of hexamethylene adipinate and caprol lactam (German).

Lupamid 6A (Igamid 6A). Condensation product of hexamethylene, adipinic acid and aminocapronic acid lactam (German).

Lupamid 85B, 70B (Igamid 85B, 70B). Copolymer of aminocaprolactam and ketopimelic acid hexamethyl diamine (German).

Luperco AC. Aromatic acyl peroxide and an organic filler; polymerization catalyst.

Luperco ATP. Benzoyl peroxide-aryl phosphate compound; catalyst.

Luperox. Paste of benzoyl peroxide and castor oil; catalyst for polymerizations.

Luperox 2. Benzoyl peroxide-castor oil paste; catalyst.

Luphen L. Phenol-formaldehyde resin, dissolved in butyl alcohol; used in varnish.

Lupogum. Refined locust-bean gum; thickener for printing textiles.

Lupolen. Polyethylene plastic.

Composition of Trade-Marked Products

Lupolen N. Polyethylene of relatively low molecular weight.

Lupomin. Aminoamide; finish for textiles.

Lupomin Q. Quaternary fatty acid amide; used in textile finishing.

Luposec. Emulsion containing paraffin wax and aluminum salt; waterproofing agent for textiles.

Luposol. Water solution of locust-bean gum; textile sizing.

Luposol S. Purified locust-bean gum.

Luprenal (Pastopal). Mixed condensation product of adipinic acid, trimethylol propane and ureaformaldehyde resin (German).

Luran N. 6-Aminocaproic acid lactam.

Lurex. Yarn made from an aluminum foil between two plies of plastic foil; used in textiles.

Lurgi metal. Lead-base bearing metal containing approximately 3% barium and fractional percentages of calcium and sodium.

Lurisin F PT. Condensate of ammonium sulfate, formaldehyde and acetaldehyde.

Lustron. Polystyrene molding compound.

Lustrone. Aniline dye.

Luton LW. Copolymer of vinyl methyl ether and wax alcohol vinyl ether.

Lutonal. Polyvinyl ethyl ether; synthetic resin, resembling soft rubber or hard wax.

Lutonal 13. Polyvinyl isobutyl ether (German).

Luvican. Polyvinyl carbazole; synthetic resin.

Luvimal B1. Copolymer of vinyl chloride and isobutyl maleate (German).

Luvimal B2. Copolymer of vinyl chloride and benzyl maleate.

Luvimal FM20. Copolymer of vinyl chloride and methyl fumarate (German).

Luvimal JP18. Copolymer of vinyl chloride and diisopropyl maleate (German).

Luvimal FB. Copolymer of vinyl chloride and butyl fumarate (German).

Luvimal FJB. Copolymer of vinyl chloride and isobutyl fumarate (German).

Luvimal FMG. Copolymer of vinyl chloride and methyl glycol fumarate (German).

Luvimal MG. Copolymer of vinyl chloride and methyl glycol maleate (German).

Luvinit. Copolymer of methyl acrylate and vinyl isohexylate; used in paints.

Luvitherm. Polyvinyl chloride sheet.

Luxmasse. Natural iron oxide; catalyst.

LX-283. Partly hydrogenated indene dimer.

Lyafol. Polyamide of nylon type.

Lykopon (Vatrolite). Concentrated sodium hydrosulfide; reducing agent in dyeing textiles.

Lynite. Aluminum-base alloy with 9 to 13.5% copper and optional additions of manganese, magnesium, and silicon; used as piston alloy.

Lyocyte. Dried, human blood-cell preparation; used in medicine.

Lyofix. Mixture of $C_{12}H_{31}$ and $C_{17}H_{35}$ quaternary ammonium salts; leveling agent in dyeing.

Lyofix DE. Quarternary ammonium salt mixture; leveling agent for basic dyes.

Lysol. Alkaline salts of phenol and (or) cresols with oils and rosin soaps and water; disinfectant.

Lythene. Petroleum spirits.

MacHempite. Iron-base alloys, with up to 4% nickel, up to 40% man-

Composition of Trade-Marked Products

ganese, up to 1.25% chromium and 0.4 to 3.0% carbon.

Mach's alloy. See Magnalium.

Macite. Cellulose acetate plastic.

Maddrell salt. Sodium metaphosphate; used in water treatment.

Magecol. Lamp black; used in rubber compounding.

Magisal. Magnesium acetyl salicylate; used in medicine.

Mag-li-flux. Magnesium quicklime; flux in glass, steel.

Mag-li-kote. Synthetic dolomite consisting of magnesium, limestone and clay; used for coating hot metal ingot molds.

Magnalite. Aluminum-base casting alloy, with about 2.5% copper, 1.5% nickel, 1.5% magnesium and 0.5% zinc.

Magnalium. Series of aluminum-base alloys, with 5 to 30% magnesium, and, optionally, small quantities of copper, nickel, tin, and lead; used for casting purposes.

Magnesol. Magnesium silicate; deodorizing and decolorizing agent.

Magnespirin. Magnesium acetyl salicylate.

Magno. Nickel-base electric-resistance alloy containing 4 to 5% manganese.

Magnocid. Mixture of magnesium hydroxide and magnesium hypochlorite; deodorant, germicide.

Magnolia metal. Lead-base bearing metal, with approximately 15% antimony, tin and other elements being optional.

Maizena. Cornstarch.

Majamin. Sodium salt of tetrahydronaphthalene sulfonate.

Makalot. Synthetic phenolic or alkyd resin.

Malakin. Salicylidene *p*-phenetidine.

Malarin. Acetophenone *p*-phenetidine.

Mallophen. Phenyl azodiaminopyridine hydrochloride; used in medicine.

Maltine. Extract of malt.

M. and B. 693. Sulfapyridine; used in medicine.

Mandelamine. Methenamine mandelate; used in medicine.

Manganin. Copper-base alloy, containing approximately 12% manganese and 4% nickel; used in electrical instruments.

Mangano steel. Non-deforming steel with approximately 1.6% manganese, 0.2% chromium, 1.0% carbon.

Manganox. Brown manganese oxide.

Mangin white. Lithopone.

Manhattan spirit. Purified methyl alcohol.

Mannheim gold. Copper-base alloy containing 7 to 20% zinc, and up to approximately 9% tin; used for cheap jewelry.

Mannol. Ethyl acetanilide; plasticizer (German).

Manol. White mineral oil; used in cosmetics.

Man-ten steel. High-strength manganese steel with 1.25 to 1.75% manganese, approximately 0.20% copper, 0.20% silicon, and 0.30% carbon.

Manucol V. Sodium alginate; emulsifying agent (British).

Mapasin. Phenol-formaldehyde resin (German).

Mapharsen. 3-Amino-4-hydroxyphenyl arsine oxide hydrochloride; drug.

Mapico black. Magnetic iron oxide; rust inhibitor in paints.

Mapico brown. Finely ground iron oxide; used in paints.

Mapico red. Iron oxide powder; used in rubber, varnishes, etc.

Mapico yellow. Iron oxide (ic) powder; used in enamels, lacquers, cement, etc.

Maprenal A. Benzoguanidine-for-

Composition of Trade-Marked Products

maldehyde condensation product in isobutylene (German).

Maprenal MJB. Condensation product of melamine and formaldehyde in butanol; used in lacquers.

Mapro Degum. Sulfated cetyl alcohol; detergent for textiles.

Maprofix. Sodium borosulfate of technical cetyl to octadecenyl alcohol; emulsifying agent.

Mapromin. Sulfated fatty alcohol; surface-active agent.

Mapromol. Sodium borosulfate of technical octadecenyl alcohol; surface-active agent.

Maproset. Sulfated octadecenyl alcohol compound.

Marabond. Crude lignin sulfonate salt; used in foundry-core binders.

Maraspere. Lignin sulfonic acid compound; dispersing agent.

Marathon Agent 340–2. See Hornkem 1.

Marathon Extract. Commercial lignin sulfonate.

Marblette. Cast phenolic plastic.

Marbolith. Synthetic tar-acid resin.

Marbon. Rubber hydrochloride.

Marbon B. Rubber resin.

Marcol. White refined mineral oil; used in cosmetics.

Marcol JX. U.S.P. light, white mineral oil.

Marcomin. Alkylaminosulfate; detergent.

Marena. Textile fiber made from waste hide and leather (German).

Marfanil. See Sulfamylon.

Margo. Soya lecithin.

Marinol. Homogenized cod-liver oil, sea water and seaweed.

Marmix. Water dispersion of Marbon S resin; used in synthetic rubber latices.

Marprontil. 4-Aminomethyl benzene sulfonamide; bactericide.

Marter White. Ground aluminum silicate; pigment in rubber.

Martonite. Mixture of monobromoacetone and monochloroacetone; tear gas.

Marvinol. Plasticized vinyl elastomer.

Marv rosin. Wood rosin containing lime (about 1.5%); used in varnishes.

Mascolite. Bonded vermiculite; used in heat insulation.

Masslinn. Non-woven resin bonded cotton fabric.

Mathesius metal. Lead-base bearing alloy with approximately 3% calcium and up to 2% strontium or barium.

Max-el steel. Machine steel containing approximately 1% manganese and 0.2% molybdenum.

Maxim powder. Double-base powder consisting of soluble and insoluble nitrocellulose, nitroglycerin and castor oil.

Maxite. Tool steel with approximately 18% tungsten, 4% cobalt, 4% chromium, and 2% vanadium.

Maxitol No. 10. Highly sulfated oil; wetting agent.

Maxoclor. Product consisting essentially of calcium hypochlorite with 70% available chlorine; bleaching agent.

Maxwhite. Dispersion of titanium dioxide in casein solution, sulfonated castor oil, and mineral oil; used for finishing white leather.

Maypon. Protein-fatty acid condensation product; wetting agent.

Maypon K, 4C. Formerly Lamepon.

Mazein fiber. Synthetic fiber made from zein.

Mazlo. Series of magnesium-base alloys.

Mazola. Refined edible corn oil.

MBT. Mercaptobenzothiazole; rubber accelerator.

MBTS. Benzothiazyl disulfide; rubber accelerator.

McAdams alloy. Aluminum-base alloys with up to 55% copper, up to 43% chromium, up to 23% zinc,

Composition of Trade-Marked Products

up to 8% cadmium, up to 8% tin, up to 5% antimony, and up to 1% silver.

McGill metal. Aluminum bronze containing approximately 2% iron and 9% aluminum.

McNamee Clay. White kaolin powder; rubber filler.

MDN. Picric acid and dinitronaphthalene; explosive.

Meadol. Water-soluble alkaline hard-wood lignin.

Mearlin. Hydrolyzed fish protein; foam and emulsion stabilizer.

Mecholin. *o*-Acetyl β-methyl choline chloride; medicament.

Mecholyl. *o*-Acetyl β-methyl choline chloride; medicament.

Medialan A. Reaction product of oleyl chloride and sodium salt of sarcosine; surface-active agent.

Medicol. Refined mineral oil; used in cosmetics.

Meehanite metal. Special cast iron of high resistance to heat and corrosion.

Megilp. Mixture of linseed oil and mastic varnish; used in oil paints.

Mekon. Black microcrystalline paraffin wax.

Melantine FN. Water-soluble melamine-formaldehyde resin; used in creaseproofing textiles.

Melilotin. Dihydrobenzopyrone; antioxidant for vitamin A.

Mellol. Sulfonated oil; used in textile finishing.

Mellose. Invert sugar syrup.

Melmac. Thermosetting melamine resin in an organic solvent.

Melocol. Polyamide-formaldehyde plastic.

Melopas. Melamine-formaldehyde resin or its solution in butanol; used in coatings.

Meloward. Non-fat dry-milk solids; used in sausages.

Meltopax. White powder consisting of sodium zirconium silicate and zircon; opacifier in enamels.

Composition of Trade-Marked Products

Melubrin. Sodium 1-phenyl 2,3-dimethyl 5-pyrazolone 4-aminomethane sulfonate.

Melurac. Melamine-urea-formaldehyde resin with a filler; adhesive.

Membranit. Alkyd-resin emulsion (German).

Menaphthone. Synthetic vitamin K analog; used in medicine.

Menthospirine. Menthyl acetyl salicylate.

Mepacrine. Atabrine.

Mepal. Melamine-formaldehyde resin and filler; used in plastic molding.

Mepasin. Aliphatic hydrocarbons (German).

Mepasinphenol. Condensation product of Mepasin and phenol (German).

Mepranol. Melamine-formaldehyde condensate (German).

Merasin. $C_9H_5N(C_6H_5)CONHC_6H_4COOH$.

Merbak. 2-Acetoxymercuri-4-diisobutyl phenol; antiseptic.

Merbaphen. See Novasurol.

Merbromin. Sodium dibromhydroxymercurifluorescein; antiseptic.

Mercerol. Mixture of xylenols.

Merchlor D. Sodium hypochlorite solution with 12% available chlorine by volume; disinfectant.

Mercoloy. Copper-base alloy, with approximately 25% nickel, 10% zinc, 2% iron, 2% lead, and 1% tin; used for valves.

Mercresin. *o*-Chloro-mercuriphenol and *sec*-amyl tricresol; antiseptic.

Mercuriol. Mercury amalgam with aluminum; used in medicine.

Mercurol. Mercury nucleate; used in medicine.

Mercurophen. Sodium hydroxymercuri-*o*-nitrophenolate; antiseptic.

Mercurosal. Disodium hydroxymercurisalicyloxyacetate; antisyphilitic.

Composition of Trade-Marked Products

Merfene. Phenyl mercuric borate.

Merfenel. Phenyl mercuric acetate; fungicide.

Merj. Sorbitan stearate; used in baking.

Mer-Lin. Colloidal mercury linoleate.

Merlon. Aqueous dispersion of polystyrene; textile coating.

Merpentine. Sodium alkyl naphthalene sulfonate and pine oil; dyeing assistant.

Merphenyl. Phenyl mercuric salts; bactericide, fungicide.

Merphenyl Acetate (Mersolite-8). Phenyl mercuric acetate; fungicide.

Merpol. Long-chain fatty alcohol sulfate; wetting agent.

Merpsol. Neatsfoot oil.

Merrillite. High-purity zinc dust.

Mersize. Alkaline water solution of a resin containing three active carboxyl groups; used with rosin in paper sizing.

Mersolat. Sulfonated, hydrogenated Fischer-Tropsch hydrocarbons (C_{12}-C_{20}) (German).

Mersol H. Sulfochlorinated Mepasin (German).

Mersolite 1. Phenyl mercuric hydroxide; fungicide.

Mersolite 2. Phenyl mercuric chloride; fungicide.

Mersolite 3. Phenyl mercuric stearate; fungicide.

Mersolite 6. Phenyl mercuric *o*-benzoicsulfimide; fungicide.

Mersolite 8. Phenyl mercuric acetate.

Mersolite 19. Phenyl mercuric salicylate.

Mersolite 90. Phenyl mercuric borate; fungicide.

Mertanol. Naphthalene-sulfonic acid condensation product; tanning agent.

Mertela. Phenyl mercuric derivative; mildewproofing agent.

Composition of Trade-Marked Products

Mertela SS. Solution of Mertela; mildewproofing agent.

Merthiolate. Sodium ethyl mercurithiosalicylate; germicide.

Merusol. White refined mineral oil.

Mervar. Mixture of polymerized terpenes; drying oil substitute.

Mesamoll. Sulfophenolates of C_{12}–C_{18} hydrocarbons; plasticizer (German).

Mesotan. Methoxymethyl salicylate; used in medicine.

Mesudin. Sulfabenzamine.

Mesurol. Basic bismuth methoxyhydroxybenzoate; used in medicine.

Metachloridine. 2-Metanilamido-5-chloropyrimidine; antimalarial drug.

Metachrome mordant. Mixture of soluble alkali bichromate and ammonium sulfate; dyeing mordant.

Metakalin. Synthetic tar-acid resin.

Metallac. Zinc stearate; used in flat varnish.

Metalline. Alloy of 30% copper, 25% aluminum, 10% iron, 35% cobalt.

Metandren. Methyl testosterone.

Metaphen. 4-Nitro-5-hydroxymercuri-*o*-cresol anhydride; germicide.

Metasil. Sodium metasilicate pentahydrate; detergent.

Metasol. Sodium hexametaphosphate.

Metastyrol. Synthetic polystyrene resin.

Methacrol BE. Methacrylate resin, dispersed in water; used in textile finishing.

Methal NP. Mixture of magnesium chloride (21.4), invert sugar (17.5) and water (60.6); glycerin substitute (German).

Methargyl. Methylene blue and silver nitrate; antiseptic.

Methasan. Zinc salt of dimethyl dithiocarbamic acid; used in latex and cements.

Composition of Trade-Marked Products

Methazate. See Methasan.

Methide. Wax containing free stearic acid (90%); used for impregnating paper, textiles, wood.

Methiodal. Sodium iodomethane sulfonate.

Methocel. Methyl cellulose.

Metholene Acid. Glauber's salt, sugar and dilute sulfuric acid; dye assistant.

Methophal. 4-Methoxy-1-naphthol; dye intermediate (German).

Methox. Methoxyethyl phthalate; plasticizer.

Methoxone. 2,4-Dichlorophenoxyacetic acid; weed-killer.

Methylanol. Methyl cyclohexanol.

Methylanon. Methyl hexanone and methyl cyclohexanone; plasticizer.

Methyl Tuads. Tetramethyl thiuram disulfide; vulcanization accelerator.

Methyl Zimate. Zinc dimethyl dithiocarbamate; vulcanization accelerator.

Metol. *p*-Methyl aminophenol sulfate; photographic developer.

Metopryl. *n*-Propyl methyl ether.

Metrazol. Pentamethylene tetrazol; used in medicine.

Metric. Metholene acid containing acetic acid (about 5%); dye assistant.

Metso 22. Sodium metasilicate compound; general cleaning agent.

Metso 99. Sodium sesquisilicate hydrate; detergent.

Metso Granular. Sodium metasilicate pentahydrate; laundry detergent.

Metycaine. Benzoyl (2-methyl) piperidinopropanol hydrochloride; local anesthetic.

Meufa. Synthetic varnish oil consisting of the methyl esters of C_{18} unsaturated fatty acids.

Micalith-G. Muscovite mica containtaining naturally combined graphite flakes (about 0.5%) within individual mica crystals; paint pigment.

Micanite. Synthetic alkyd resin.

Micarok. Sheet mica; used for electrical insulation.

Micarta. Synthetic tar-acid resin.

Micatex. Finely powdered mica; used in oil-well drilling fluids.

Micatone. Fine micaceous matter; inert filler.

Michelene W. Sodium alkyl naphthalene sulfonate; dyeing assistant.

Michiana alloy. Heat- and corrosion-resistant ferrous-base alloys, with up to 28% chromium and up to 20% nickel.

Micris 3717. Microcrystalline petroleum wax.

Microcarb. Carbon black; pigment.

Micromul. Aqueous emulsion of microcrystalline petroleum wax; used in waterproofing textiles.

Micronex. Carbon black.

Micronil. Aqueous emulsion of metallic naphthenate; used for rotproofing.

Micro Nu-Cop. Neutral copper sulfate containing 53% powdered metallic copper; insecticide.

Midvale ATV-1. Alloy consisting of iron, nickel, chromium, manganese and carbon.

Midvale ATV-3. Alloy consisting of iron, nickel, chromium, tungsten, manganese and carbon.

Migasol PC. Paraffin wax emulsion; softening agent.

Migasol PJ. Paraffin wax and aluminum salt emulsion; softening agent.

Mikrobin. Sodium *p*-chlorobenzoate.

Millical. Calcium carbonate; pigment.

Milmer. Copper quinolinolate; textile preservative.

Milorganite. See Nitrorganic.

Milowite. Silica pigment.

Milwaloy. Corrosion-resistant, high-

Composition of Trade-Marked Products

alloy steels with up to 30% chromium and up to 15% nickel.

Milwaukee steel. See Milwaloy.

Mineralex. Carbon black.

Mineralite. Natural potassium aluminum silicate; filler.

Mineralite. Powdered mica; filler in rubber compounding.

Minol. TNT, ammonium nitrate and aluminum powder; explosive.

Minoline. Mixture of sulfonated castor, mineral and fatty oils; softening agent in dyeing cotton and wool.

Minovar. Nickel-alloyed cast iron.

Minpro. Feldspar.

Minvar. Ferrous alloys with 28 to 38% nickel and 1 to 3% chromium.

Mipolam. Polyvinyl chloride plastic.

Mipol M-20. Rubber-like polymer with microcrystalline wax in ratio 20:80.

Miracil. 1-Diethyl aminoethyl amino-4-methyl thioxanthone; used in medicine.

Miralite. Alloy of 96% aluminum, 4% nickel.

Mirametal. Acid-resisting alloy with 74.75% copper, 16.35% lead, 6.78% antimony, 0.9% tin, 0.61% zinc, 0.43% iron, 0.24% nickel, 0.24% cobalt.

Miranol. Sulfated fatty acid amide and dry diluents; detergent.

Mirapon. Sulfated fatty acid amide derivatives and diluents; detergent.

Mirapon RK. Sulfonated long-chain fatty acid amide; detergent.

Mirasol resin. Alkyd-base resin; used in lacquers.

Mirol. N-methyl *p*-amidophenol sulfonate; film developer.

Miscibol. Water-dispersible potassium oleo-abietate; emulsifying base.

Misco. Series of steels of varied composition, especially high-nickel, high-chromium steels of good chemical- and heat-resistance.

Misco C. Alloy consisting of iron, 28 to 30% chromium, 8 to 10% nickel, 1.5% silicon, 0.4 to 0.5% manganese, and 0.5 to 0.7% carbon.

Miscrome. Iron alloys with 16 to 30% chromium and approximately 0.25% carbon.

Mitigal. Dimethyl thianthrene.

Mixacoid. Mixture of sorbitol monostearate, milk solids (defatted) and egg yolk; emulsifier in food products.

ML steel. High-carbon alloy steel with about 18% tungsten, 4% chromium, 2% vanadium, 1% molybdenum, and approximately 0.8% carbon; used in mfg. tools.

Mobilane. Liquified petroleum gases; fuel.

Modinal D. Sodium salt of lauryl and oleyl sulfates; wetting agent.

Modinal T. Long-chain alcohol sulfate; wetting agent.

Modotiol. Thiokol-type elastomer (Swedish).

Modulex. High-modulus furnace (carbon) black.

Mohawk steel. High-alloy steel of approximately 14% tungsten, 3.5% chromium, 0.60% vanadium, and about 0.50% carbon.

Moldarta. Synthetic tar-acid resin.

Moldex. Carbinyl *p*-oxybenzoate; preservative.

Moldine. *p*-Hydroxybenzoic acid alkyl ester; preservative.

Moldol. Mixture of sodium benzoate and benzoic acid; preservative.

Mollit. Synthetic polystyrene resin.

Mollit B. Glyceryl tribenzoate.

Mollit GH. Trimethylol propane trichloroacetate; plasticizer.

Mollit L. Diethyl diphenyl urea.

Molochite. Calcined kaolin.

Mo-max. High-speed steel with 7.75 to 9.25% molybdenum, 3.50 to 4.00% chromium, 1.25 to 2.00%

Composition of Trade-Marked Products

tungsten, 0.90 to 1.50% vanadium, 0.60 to 0.85% carbon; used for cutting tools.

Monacrin. 5-Aminoacridine hydrochloride; antiseptic.

Monastral colors. Copper phthalocyanine or its derivatives.

Mona wax. Irish peat wax.

Mond gas. Combustible carbon monoxide, hydrogen and nitrogen mixture.

Mond metal. Nickel-base alloy with approximately 26% copper and 4% manganese.

Monel. Alloy containing 60 to 70% nickel, 25 to 35% copper, 1 to 3% iron, 0.25 to 2% manganese, 0.02 to 1.5% silicon, 0.3 to 0.5% carbon; used for acidproof apparatus.

Monex. See Thionex.

Monobel. Ammonium nitrate containing nitroglycerin; explosive.

Monocaine. Monoisobutyl aminoethyl *p*-aminobenzoate hydrochloride; used in medicine.

Monochloramine B. Sodium benzene sulfonchloramide; germicide.

Monococate. Coconut oil fatty acid monoester of glycerin or propylene glycol.

Monofrax. Refractory of alumina and other oxides.

Monogas. Nitrogen-rich gas; protective atmosphere in annealing of metals.

Monol. Partial higher fatty acid esters of glycerol; viscosity reducer for emulsions.

Monolite. Insoluble lake color; used in paints.

Monoplex DBS. Dibutyl sebacate; plasticizer.

Monoplex DCP. Dicapryl phthalate; plasticizer.

Monoplex DOS. Dioctyl sebacate; plasticizer.

Monoplex 5. Dibenzyl sebacate; plasticizer.

Monoplex 7. Dibutoxy ethyl sebacate; plasticizer.

Composition of Trade-Marked Products

Monopole oil. Sulfonated castor oil; surface-active agent.

Mono-Sil. Lead silicate; pigment.

Monostearin. Glyceryl monostearate; edible emulsifier.

Monosulph. Sulfonated castor oil; wetting agent.

Mono Thiurad. Tetramethyl thiuram monosulfide; used in curing rubber.

Monotrean. Mixture of papverine and quinine; used in medicine.

Monsanto salt. *o*-Chloro-*p*-toluene sodium sulfonate; dye intermediate.

Montanilla Wax. Bleached montan wax; used in polishes.

Montegal. Alloy of aluminum with 0.95% magnesium and 0.8% silicon.

Monylen. Vinyl chloride (German).

Mordex. Invert sugar solution.

Morfex. Thiuram-thiazole compound; accelerator in rubber vulcanization.

Morkit. Mixture of anthraquinone and fillers.

Morpeltex D, DP, KD, SD (Morwet B). Sodium alkyl naphthalene sulfonate; wetting agent.

Morpholon. Dimorpholine diphenyl.

Morphosan. Morphine methyl bromide; used in medicine.

Mortar black-1. Carbon black; used for coloring cement.

Morwet B. See Morpeltex D.

Moskene. Artificial musk; used in perfumery.

MO steel. Molybdenum steels with up to 1% molybdenum, fractional percentages of chromium and manganese.

Motaline. Antiknock compound based on iron carbonyl.

Mo-tung. High-carbon alloy tool steel with approximately 8% molybdenum, 4% chromium, 1.5% tungsten, 1% vanadium and 0.80% carbon.

Mouldrite. Synthetic tar-acid resin

Composition of Trade-Marked Products

for molding and laminating; synthetic urea resin.

Mowilite. Polyvinyl chloride.

Mowilith. Vinyl chloroacetate and acetate polymer; substitute for gum copal (German).

Mowilith AB. Polymer of polyvinyl acetate and polyvinyl benzoate; waterproofing agent (German).

Mowilith ABC. Copolymer of polyvinyl acetate, polyvinyl benzoate and crotonic acid (German).

Mowilith D32. Polyvinyl acetate with phthalate plasticizers.

Mowilith D300. Copolymer of vinyl acetate and vinyl chloride in aqueous emulsion (German).

Mowilith 20, 30, 50, 70, 90. Copolymers of vinyl acetate and propionaldehyde (German).

Mowital. Polyvinyl acetal (German).

MP-189. Hydrocarbon sodium sulfonate; wetting agent, emulsifier, detergent.

MP-189-S. Aqueous solution of hydrocarbon sodium sulfonate; wetting agent, emulsifier, detergent.

MP-646-S Paste. Petroleum hydrocarbon sodium sulfonate; surface-active agent.

MPC black. Channel carbon black.

MPD-189. Sulfonated chlorinated hydrocarbons; emulsifying agent.

2-MT. 2-Mercaptothiazoline; vulcanization accelerator.

Mucilose. Purified hemicellulose; used in medicine.

Mugol. Dimethyl acetal hydroxycitronellal; used in perfumery.

Mulsor. Long-chain fatty acid ester containing multiple ether linkages; emulsifier.

Mulsoya. Water-soluble isolated soybean-protein derivatives; used for textile and other sizes.

Multicel. Diatomaceous earth.

Multifex. Colloidal calcium carbonate; pigment and filler.

Composition of Trade-Marked Products

Multopren. Polyurethane-plastic foam.

Mu Metal. Nickel-steel alloy containing 17 to 20% iron, about 5% copper and low percentages of manganese or chromium.

Muntz metal. Brass containing 59 to 62% copper and the remainder zinc.

Murac. Strong mineral acid with inhibitor; metal descaler.

Mustone. Neoprene (Japanese).

Mycalex. Dielectric made of mica and glass.

Mycoban. Calcium propionate mold inhibitor; used in bread making.

Myconyx. Dihydroxydichlorodiphenyl methane; fungicide.

Mykroy. Mica-glass fusion product; used in electric insulation.

Myochrysine. Sodium aurothiomalate; used in medicine.

Myorgal (Lacarnol; Nucladen). Muscular tissue extract of warm-blooded animals containing a standardized amount of active nucleosides; used in medicine.

Myrol. Methyl nitrate; used in rocket propellants.

Myrtan. Redunca-wood extract; used in tanning.

Mytan. Myrobalan extract; tanning agent.

Nacan. Sodium *m*-nitrobenzene sulfonate; textile assistant.

Nacara. Cellulose nitrate plastic.

Naccolene F. Modified alkyl aryl sulfonate; surface-active agent.

Nacconols: E; EP; N; NR; NRNO; NRSE. Sodium alkyl aryl sulfonate; surface-active agent.

Naccosol A. Sodium alkyl naphthalene sulfonate; surface-active agent.

Naccotan A. Sodium alkyl aryl sulfonate; used in retanning chrome-tanned leather.

Nacelan. Dye for cellulose acetate.

Naco. Mixture of rosin (25) and

Composition of Trade-Marked Products

Naftolen (75); used in rubber compounding.

Nacoll. Sodium salt of aminodimethyl glycine.

Naco steel. Low-alloy casting steel containing about 1.5% manganese and about 0.35% carbon.

Nada NT alloy. Casting bronze containing about 3.75% nickel, 3.75% tin, and 0.75% lead.

Naftex. Combination of carbon black and sulfur; plasticizer for rubber.

Naftolen. Unsaturated hydrocarbons from acid petroleum sludge; plasticizer for rubber.

Nalcite A. Organic zeolite-type exchange substance.

Nalco 21. Sodium pentachlorophenate; disinfectant.

Nalco 23. Mixture of Dowicide C. and G.

Nalcoag. Colloidal silica.

Nalcolite. Zeolite; water-purifying aid.

Namate. Sodium diethyl dithiocarbamate; vulcanization accelerator.

Naphthin. Naphthoquinoline.

Naphthole T, TK (Naptex). Soap powder; used in textile scouring.

Naphtholite. Mineral spirits; solvent.

Naphthosol. Azo dye.

Napoleum Spirits. Petroleum distillate solvent.

Nargol. Silver nucleinate containing 10% silver; used in medicine.

Narphin. Morphine-narcotine meconate; sedative.

NA steel. Corrosion-resistant iron-nickel-chromium alloys, with chromium between 15 and 30%, and nickel up to 70%.

Nationalloy. High-nickel, high-chromium steels; used for chemically resistant products.

Nayfex. Chlorinated paraffin wax containing 55 to 60% chlorine.

Naypar. Chlorinated paraffin wax containing 41 to 43% chlorine.

Composition of Trade-Marked Products

Nayrez. Chlorinated paraffin wax containing 68 to 72% chlorine.

Neantine. Diethyl phthalate.

Neazote. Synthetic rubber compound.

Neetol. Emulsifiable neatsfoot oil; used in fat liquors.

Negamine. Cation-active amino ester of long-chain fatty acids; dispersing agent.

Nekal A. Sodium alkyl naphthalene sulfonate; wetting agent.

Nekal AEM. Alkyl naphthalene sulfonate with addition of glue; emulsifying agent.

Nekal BX. Sodium alkyl naphthalene sulfonate; dye assistant.

Nelgin. Activated colloidal silicate; used in emulsions.

Neilo resin. Natural purified wood rosin.

Neloy. Low-alloy casting steel with about 1.2% manganese and about 0.35% carbon.

Nembutal. Sodium pentobarbital; used in medicine.

Neobon. Neoprene-base compound; used to replace rubber tank linings.

Neocid. Powder containing DDT (50%); insecticide.

Neocinchophen. Ethyl phenyl cinchoninate.

Neodorm. α-Isopropyl α-bromobutyramide; hypnotic.

Neo-Fat. Refined fatty acids.

Neo-Fat No. 3R. Linoleic acid (59%) and oleic acid (39.5%).

Neo-Fat No. 1–56. Palmitic acid (90%), oleic acid (4%) and stearic acid (6%).

Neo-Fat No. 1–65. Stearic acid (90%), palmitic acid (6%) and oleic acid (3%).

Neo-Fat No. 7. Caprylic acid (90%), capric acid (7%) and caproic acid (3%).

Neo-Fat No. 11. Lauric acid (90%), myristic acid (9%) and unsaturated acids (1%).

Composition of Trade-Marked Products

Neo-Fat No. 13. Myristic acid (90%), lauric acid (4%), palmitic acid (4%) and unsaturated acids (2%).

Neo-Fat No. 15. Capric acid (90%), lauric acid (7%) and caprylic acid (3%).

Neo-Fat No. 17. Mixture of polymerized glycerides and fatty acids.

Neo-Fat No. 19. Unsaturated C_{20} acids.

Neo-Fat No. 23. Soybean acids.

Neo-Fat No. 170. Synthetic drying oil.

Neo-Fat No. 190. Synthetic drying oil.

Neo-Fat No. 290. Bodied synthetic drying oil.

Neogen. Alloy of 58% copper, 27% zinc, 12% nickel, 2% tin, and fractional percentages of aluminum and bismuth.

Neohombreol. Testosterone propionate.

Neo-iopax. Disodium N-methyl 3,5-diiodo-4-pyridoxyl 2,6-dicarboxylate; used in medicine.

Neo-Kontakt. Twitchell reagent; used in commercial fat-splitting.

Neolan. Light-fast azo dye.

Neolan Salt II. Quaternary salt of an organic base of $C_{12}H_{26}$ or higher; assistant for dyeing.

Neolene. Nonyl naphthalene.

Neolyn resin. Alkyd-type resin made with rosin.

Neolyn 40. Soft rosin alkyd; used in coatings.

Neolyn 41. Modified alkyd resin.

Neomerpin. Alkyd naphthalene sodium sulfonate; wetting assistant.

Neomerpin N. Alkyl naphthalene sulfonic acid; surface-active agent.

Neomerpin VD. Sodium alkyl naphthalene sulfonate; surface-active agent.

Neonal. *n*-Butyl ethyl barbituric acid; sedative.

Neonalium. Alloy containing aluminum with 6% copper.

Composition of Trade-Marked Products

Neopen SS. Sodium abietene sulfonate; wetting agent.

Neophax. Vulcanized vegetable oil; rubber extender.

Neopol T. See Igepon T.

Neoprene. Long-chain polymerized chlorophene; rubber substitute.

Neoprontosil. Azosulfamide; used in medicine.

Neoquinophan. Ethyl phenyl cinchoninate.

Neor. Abrasion-resistant alloy steel with about 13% chromium and fractional percentages of nickel, silicon and manganese.

Neoresit. Synthetic tar-acid resin.

Neosol-1. Mixture of *sec*-butyl acetate and diacetone; lacquer solvent.

Neosyl. Amorphous silica (British).

Neosyl MH. Precipitated silica containing magnesium oxide (about 7%); used in reinforcing rubber.

Neotron. Laminated cellulose or other fibers and plastic sheeting.

Neozone A. Phenyl α-naphthyl amine; antioxidant.

Neozone B. Metatoluylene diamine; antioxidant.

Neozone C. Mixture of phenyl α-naphthyl amine and *m*-toluylene diamine; antioxidant.

Neozone D. Phenyl β-naphthyl amine; antioxidant.

Neozyme. Amolytic and proteolytic enzyme; desizing agent.

Neradol. Condensation product of formaldehyde with phenol or naphthalene sulfonic acid; tanning agent.

Nerail P.A.S. Sulfonated rosin.

Nerolin I. β-Naphthyl methyl ether.

Nerolin II. Ethyl naphthyl ether.

Nestorite. Synthetic tar-acid resin; used for molding and laminating.

Nettolin. Humus fertilizer.

Neuronal. Diethyl bromoacetamide.

Neutralin (Aurol; Subsidol). Hydrogen peroxide (German).

Neutrol. Activated bleaching clay.

Composition of Trade-Marked Products

Neutronyx. Non-ionic fatty acid condensate; dispersing agent.

Neutronyx 228. Polyglycol fatty acid ester.

Nevasota. Refined creosote oil; used in wood preserving.

Nevillac. Phenol-indene-coumarone resin; used in paints.

Nevillac OA. Alkylated phenol; plasticizer.

Nevillite. Cycloparaffin or naphthene polymer resin; used in varnishes.

Nevillite Oil. Hydrogenated indene dimer.

Nevilloid. Cumarone-indene resin emulsion.

Nevilloid C-55. Water-dispersible cumarone-indene emulsion.

Nevindene. Similar to Nevillac.

Nevinol. Indene dimer.

Nevtex resins. Specially processed cumarone-indene polymers; used in textileproofing.

N-Glo-5. Solution of limed rosin in mineral spirit; used in varnishes.

Niag. Nickel silver containing approximately 47% copper, 41% zinc, 9% nickel and 3% lead with optional fractional percentages of other metals.

Niagathal. Tetrachlorophthalic anhydride.

Niaproof. Aluminum acetate.

Niathal. Tetrachlorophthalicanhydride.

Niazo. 2′,6′-Diamino-2-butyl oxy 5,5′-azopyridine; used in medicine.

Nico-Tone. 40% nicotine sulfate; plant insecticide.

Nicral. Aluminum-base alloys with fractional percentages of chromium, magnesium, copper; high-chromium and high-chromium-nickel steels.

Nicrosilal. Austenitic alloy cast iron containing 18.65% nickel, 6.42% silicon, 2.02% chromium, and 72.61% cast iron.

Ni-Hard. Abrasion-resistant alloy cast iron containing about 4.5% nickel, 0.5% silicon, and 1.5% chromium.

Nile blue. Oxazine dyestuff.

Nilex. Alloy consisting of iron with 36% nickel characterized by low expansion.

Nilvar. Iron alloy with about 36% nickel, showing extremely low coefficient of temperature expansion.

Ninol. Condensation product of diethanol amine and a fatty acid.

Ninol X. Condensation product of diethanol amine and stearic acid.

Ninol 737. Mixed fatty acid (C_{10}–C_{16})-alkylol amine condensate; detergent and wetting agent for textiles, fur, etc.

Niox. Ammonium nitrate U.S.P. with a special inhibitor; used for generating nitrous oxide.

Nipa 49. Propyl gallate; antioxidant for oils.

Nipabenzyl. Benzyl *p*-hydroxybenzoate; preservative (British).

Nipabutyl. Butyl *p*-hydroxybenzoate; preservative (British).

Nipacombin-A. Propyl and ethyl *p*-hydroxybenzoate sodium salt.

Nipa ester. Ester of *p*-hydroxybenzoic acid; preservative.

Nipagin. Methyl *p*-hydroxybenzoate.

Nipagin M. Methyl ester of *p*-oxybenzoic acid; preservative.

Nipasept. Mixture of *p*-hydroxybenzoic esters; preservative (British).

Nipasol. Propyl ester of *p*-oxybenzoic acid; preservative.

Nipasol-Sodium. Sodium salt of the propyl ester of *p*-oxybenzoic acid; preservative.

Nip-Nip. Combination of Nipasol and Nipagin; preservative.

Nipocer. Modified fatty acid ester; emulsifier.

Ni-Resist. Austenitic alloy cast iron containing 6% copper, 2% chromium and 14% nickel.

Nirex. Nickel-base alloy with ap-

Composition of Trade-Marked Products

proximately 14% chromium and 6% iron.

Nirosan. Compound with 1,3,6,8-tetranitrocarbazole; insecticide.

Nirosta. Stainless steel with 18% chromium and 8% nickel.

Nirvanin. Diethyl glycocoll *p*-amino-*o*-oxybenzoic methyl ester hydrochloride.

Nirvanol. 5-Ethyl 5-phenyl hydantoin; drug.

Nitracyl. 4-Nitro *p*-acetodiphenyl (German).

Nitralloy. Alloy with iron, chromium, molybdenum and aluminum which lends itself effectively to nitriding.

Nitramac. Protein hydrolysate.

Nitraprill. Ammonium nitrate with small amounts of dusting agent to prevent caking.

Nitrard. High-alloy nitriding steel containing approximately 2% chromium, 1% molybdenum, 1% vanadium, and 1.5% carbon.

Nitril AHZ. *m*-Amidocinnamic acid nitrile (German).

Nitril MGU. Copolymer of acrylonitrile and methyl glycol vinyl ether (German).

Nitril NHZ. *m*-Nitro-α-chlorhydrocinnamic acid nitrile (German).

Nitril V6. Copolymer of acrylonitrile and isohexylic acid vinyl ester (German).

Nitrocol. Pigment dispersed in nitrocellulose and a plasticizer; used in lacquers.

Nitropenta. Pentaerythritol tetranitrate; explosive.

Nitrophoskas IG. Ammonium nitrate, diammonium phosphate and potassium chloride; fertilizer.

Nitrorganic (Milorganite). Dried activated sewage-sludge fertilizer.

Nixon E.C. Ethyl cellulose.

Nizin. Zinc sulfanilate; antiseptic.

NNO. Mannitan monolaurate; wetting agent.

Noca. Detergent based on Calgon.

Composition of Trade-Marked Products

Nodoroil. Deodorized naphtha; spray-insecticide vehicle.

Nogroth metal. Cast iron with about 1.9% carbon, 1.5% nickel, 0.3% chromium, 0.3% manganese.

Noheet. Antifriction alloy of lead with 1.3% sodium, 0.11% antimony, 0.08% tin.

Noheev. Sodium silicate powder; used in oil-well drilling mud.

Nomag. Non-magnetic cast iron containing 10 to 12% nickel and 5 to 6% manganese.

Nomesan. Tetramethyl thiuram disulfide; seed disinfectant.

Noncorrodite. Corrosion-resistant steel with about 22% chromium, low percentages of silicon and manganese, fractional percentages of nickel and copper.

Nongro. Alloy containing iron with 36% nickel.

Nonox NS. Phenol-aldehyde-amine condensation product; rubber antioxidant.

Nonpareil Flakes. Neutral soap.

No-Odorol. Sulfated vegetable oil; used in textile finishing.

Nopalcol. Non-ionic ethylene oxide and/or polyhydric-alcohol higher-fatty acid derivatives; surface-active agent.

Nopalcol 4L. Tetraethylene glycol monolaurate; surface-active agent.

Nopalcol 6L. Hexaethylene glycol monolaurate; surface-active agent.

Nopco 1010. Sebacic acid.

Nopco 1067. Long-chain alkyl aromatic sulfonate; textile detergent.

Nopco 1285. Sulfated butyl oleate (65%); surface-active agent.

Nopco 1440. Pine oil; used in disinfectants.

Nopco 1471. Sulfated vegetable oil; surface-active agent.

Nopco 1935. Sulfonated vegetable oil, surface-active agent.

Nopco 1967. Sulfonated alkyl hydrocarbon; surface-active agent.

Composition of Trade-Marked Products

Nopco 2031. Sulfated hydroxystearic acid; textile-dye assistant.

Nopco 2067. Butyl palmitate; lubricant for textiles.

Nopco 1060-C. Methyl ricinoleate; pigment in inks.

Nopco 2179-B. Oleyl amide.

Nopco 1073-B. Oleic amine ester; emulsifying agent.

Nopco 1086-B. Short-chain aliphatic ester sulfonate; wetting agent.

Nopco 1179-C. Dihydroxyethyl lauramide; emulsifier.

Nopco 1179-R. Dihydroxyethyl lauramide (30%); surface-active agent.

Nopco 1807-C. Short-chain alkyl aromatic sulfonate; wetting agent.

Nopco 1920-X. Sulfated butyl oleate; dyeing assistant.

Nopco 2265-L. Coconut-oil fatty acid amine acetate (45%); surface-active agent.

Nopcob. Sulfated vegetable oil; surface-active agent.

Nopcocastor. Special sulfated castor oil.

Nopco CVT. Oleic amine; wetting agent.

Nopco DID. Sulfonated oleic amine; penetrating agent.

Nopco ESI. Aqueous dispersion of calcium stearate (40%); used in paper coating.

Nopcogen. Fatty amine or amide; surface-active agent.

Nopco QCL. Lauryl dimethyl benzyl ammonium chloride; used in disinfectant cleaners.

Nopco SHCO. Sulfonated hydrogenated castor oil; emulsifying agent.

Nopcov. Highly sulfated oleoglyceride.

Nopoline. Polyvinyl chloride plastic.

Norane. Long-chain pyridinium compound; used in textile waterproofing.

Norelac. Alcohol-soluble polyamide resin made from soybean or linseed oils.

Norelite. Mixture of soybean meal, corn gluten and water-soluble phenolic resin; plywood adhesive.

Norepol. Polyesters of dimerized and sulfurized drying-oil acids from soya bean; rubber substitute.

Norit. Amorphous vegetable carbon; decolorizing agent.

Norit A. Activated charcoal.

Norot CF. Copper ammonium fluoride; textile mildewproofing agent.

Nostal. Isopropyl bromoprophenyl barbituric acid; sedative.

Novac. Selenium dibutyl dithiocarbamate; ultra-accelerator for rubber.

Novac A-13. Mixture of selenium dibutyl dithiocarbamate (1) and benzothiazyl disulfide (3).

Novacetyl. Magnesium acetyl salicylate.

Novadelox. Mixture of benzoyl peroxide and calcium phosphate; used in bleaching flour.

Noval ketone. 5-Diethyl amino-2-pentanone.

Novargan. Silver proteinate containing 10% silver; used in medicine.

Novatone. Anisic ketone; used in soaps.

Novatophan. Ethyl phenyl cinchoninate.

Novatropine. Homatropine methyl bromide.

Novellon. Clear cellulose acetate sheeting.

Novemol. Sulfonated terpene alcohols; wetting agent.

Novex. Benzal bis-(dimethyl dithiocarbamate).

Novit. Mixture of TNT and Hexyl; explosive.

Novocaine. Procaine hydrochloride.

Novocell. Wood cellulose; used in rayon.

Novo-Fermasol F. Proleolytic enzyme desizing agent (Swiss).

Composition of Trade-Marked Products

Novoldiamine. 1-Diethyl amino-4-aminopentane.

Novonacco. Modified sodium alkyl naphthalene sulfonate; wetting agent in textile industry.

Novonacco NN. Modified alkyl naphthalene sulfonic acid; surface-active agent.

Novonal. Diethyl allyl acetamide; sedative.

Novoplas A. Thioplast.

Novotext. Synthetic tar-acid resin.

Novoviol. Ionone.

Novowax. Polymerized hydrocarbon wax; used in molding.

Nox-Rust #202. Solution of metallic and mahogany soaps in petroleum solvent; rust preventive.

Nuade. Heavy-metal naphthenate with organic polymers; dispersing and wetting agent (non-aqueous media).

Nuba. Cumarone-indene resin.

Nubon. Styrene-butadiene copolymer; synthetic rubber.

Nubun. Electrical insulation made from modified Buna S emulsion.

Nuchar. Activated carbon; used in decolorizing and deodorizing.

Nujol. Heavy refined paraffin oil; used in medicine.

Nullapon. Salt of aminocarboxylic acid; used in textile finishing.

Nullapon A. Sodium salt of a complex organic acid; water-softening agent.

Nullapon B. Salt of aminocarboxylic acid; used in textile finishing.

Nulocrystal. Partially inverted sugar syrup consisting of sucrose, dextrose, levulose and moisture; used in baking.

Nulomoline. Invert sugar consisting of dextrose, levulose and moisture; used in baking.

Numal. Isopropyl allyl barbituric acid; used in medicine.

Nuocide 321. Solution of phenyl mercury naphthenate; fungicide.

Composition of Trade-Marked Products

Nuodex. Metallic naphthenate; paint drier.

Nuodex Copper. Copper naphthenate.

Nuodite Copper. Copper hydroxynaphthenate.

Nupercaine. Butyl oxycinchoninic acid diethyl ethylene diamide hydrochloride; local anesthetic.

Nusite. High-speed steel containing about 13% cobalt.

Nusoil. Ammonium sulfate; used in fertilizer.

Nusope. Naphthenic soap.

Nusope P50. Alkali soap of naphthenic acids; surface-active agent.

Nusope 33A. Alkali soap of naphthenic acids; surface-active agent.

Nutricod. Blend of cod and mineral oils; used for fat-liquoring.

Nutrose. Sodium caseinate.

Nuva B. Sulfonated fatty amide complex; used in textile finishing.

Nuzan. Concentrate of hydrolyzed soluble proteins and aminoacids; foam stabilizer.

Nyafat. Hydrogenated coconut oil; shortening.

Nycolene. Sodium alkyl aryl sulfonate; wetting agent.

Nypene. Terpene-polymer resin; used in varnishes.

Nysol. Mixture of nitroxylenes and nitronaphthalenes; used for lowering the freezing point of dynamite.

N-Z amine. Tryptic digest of casein containing amino acids and peptides.

Ocenol. Technical oleyl alcohol; emulsifying agent.

Octab. Octadecyl dimethyl benzyl ammonium chloride; surface-active agent.

Octa-Klor. Chlordan ($C_{10}H_6Cl_8$); insecticide.

Octalin. Octahydronaphthalene.

Octimet. Octadecyl dimethyl ethyl ammonimum bromide; antiseptic.

Composition of Trade-Marked Products

Octin. 6-Methyl amino-2-methyl heptene; used in medicine.

Oil-Dag. Colloidal suspension of graphite in oil; lubricant.

Oildie steel. Low-alloy steel with approximately 1.6% chromium, 0.8% carbon, and 0.5% tungsten.

Oilite. Graphited bearing metal with a matrix containing approximately 10% tin, copper being the metallic base.

Oilsolate. Heavy metal soap; drier in paint.

Oitioil. Oiticica oil; used in paint.

OKC Resin. Oxycresyl camphone; rubber antioxidant.

OKO Oil. Drying oil polymerized under vacuum; used in varnish.

Okronitril. 1-Methyl 2-cyan-4-chloro-5-nitrobenzol.

Oktaton. Sodium salt of octahydroanthracene sulfonate.

Olate. Low-titer neutral soap flakes; textile detergent.

Oldsmoloy. Nickel-silver with approximately 39% zinc, 14% nickel, and 2% tin; used principally in cast form.

Oleo Glyceryl Sulfate C. Sodium salt of a sulfated ricinoleic acid ester; dispersing agent.

Oleonat. Mixture of olein (1) and sulfuric acid (1); used in textile processing.

Olev-ol. Glyceride obtained from olive oil.

Olive Elaine. Light-colored commercial oleic acid.

Olivene. Sulfonated vegetable oil.

Olivene L. Saturated non-drying glycerides obtained by solvent extraction of linseed oil; used in soap.

Oltapone. Sulfated fatty alcohol; detergent (Swiss).

Olympic bronze. High-strength silicon bronze, with approximately 1% zinc and 2.75 to 4.25% silicon and optionally up to 0.5% lead.

Omega brand alloy. Copper-base alloys, of the phosphor-bronze and nickel-silver types.

Omnipon. Mixture of sodium salts of sulfated fatty alcohols and highly sulfonated aromatic compounds, sodium sulfate and water; textile assistant (German).

Onalkali. Sodium lauryl sulfate; emulsifier (German).

Onazote. Ebonite.

Ondal A. Sodium lauryl sulfate with an oxidizing agent; oxidant.

Ondol. Sulfated higher fatty alcohol of the gardinol type.

Ondulum. Modified vegetable carbohydrate; used in hair-waving lotions.

Onesta. Hydrogenated peanut oil; used in bakers' shortening.

Ontario steel. Non-deforming steel with approximately 11% chromium, 1.50% carbon, 0.80% molybdenum, 0.30% manganese, and 0.30% silicon.

Onyx BTC. Alkyl dimethyl benzyl ammonium chloride.

Onyxol 66. Oil ester sulfate; wetting agent.

Onyxsan. Alkyl amidoalkyl imidazoline; wetting agent.

Opacol. See Iodeikon.

Opalwax. Hydrogenated castor oil; used in place of natural waxes.

Opax. ZrO_2,SiO_2,Na_2O and Al_2O_3; opacifier for glass.

Oppanol. Mixture of Oppanol B (90%) and polystyrene (10%); used in plastic sheeting.

Oppanol B. Polyisobutylene copolymerized with a small amount of diisobutylene; plastic.

Oppanol C. Polymerized vinyl isobutyl ether; thermoplastic resin.

Oppanol K. Polypropylene plastic.

Oppanol V. Copolymer of isobutylene and isoprene or butadiene (German).

Oppanol BU1. Polyisobutylene cross-linked with *p*-divinyl benzene.

Composition of Trade-Marked Products

Optochin. Ethyl hydrocupreine; used in medicine.

Optol. Hydrogenated lignite-tar fraction; rocket fuel.

Oranap. Sodium alkyl naphthalene sulfonate; wetting agent.

Orasthin. Oxytocic portion of posterior-pituitary extract; used in medicine.

Oratol. Sulfonated amide; wetting agent.

Oratol N. Sodium salt of a hydrocarbon sulfonate; detergent.

Oratol L-48. Sulfonated aliphatic amide; penetrant.

Orchidee. Amyl salicylate; used in perfumery.

Orchidone. Isobutyl salicylate; used in perfumery.

Orcinol. Mixture of crude C_8–C_{16} alcohols; emulsifying agent (German).

Ordoyal. Synthetic tanning agent similar to Neradol.

Oreson. Guaiacol glyceryl ether.

Orestanol 524. Abietomaleic glycerol ester.

Oreton. Testosterone propionate; used in medicine.

Oreton-M. Methyl testosterone.

Organocide R4OL2. Talc containing rotenone 0.4% and Lethane (2%); agricultural insecticide.

Organolite. Synthetic resin; used in water treatment.

Oridex D. Blend of potassium salts of sulfated amides of C_{10}–C_{18} straight-chain fatty acids; used in scouring textiles.

Oridine. Preparation of calcium salts of iodinated cottonseed-oil fatty acids; used in medicine.

Ornalith. Synthetic tar-acid resin.

Oronap. Sodium alkyl naphthalene sulfonate; wetting agent.

Oronite. Sodium petroleum-hydrocarbon sulfonate; detergent.

Oroplast. Neutral unsaturated cyclic hydrocarbons from petroleum; rubber plasticizer.

Composition of Trade-Marked Products

Oropon. Mixture of ammonium chloride, wood fiber and dry pancreas; leather bate.

Orphal. Bismuth β-naphtholate.

Orr's white. Lithopone; pigment.

Ortal. Ethyl hexyl barbituric acid; used in medicine.

Ortal sodium. Sodium *n*-hexyl ethyl barbiturate; used in medicine.

Orthazite. Benztriazole; photographic restrainer.

Orthene. 1,2-Dichlorobenzene; solvent.

Ortho Bas. Sodium lauryl sulfate compound; used in textile finishing.

Orthocaine. Methyl *m*-amino-*p*-hydroxybenzoate; used in medicine.

Orthocen. Sulfonated phenol; wetting agent.

Orthochrom. Pigmented lacquer.

Orthocoll. Potassium guaiacol sulfonate; used in medicine.

Ortholate. Mixture of orthosilicate of soda and complex phosphates; used in laundries as detergent.

Ortholeum 162. Phosphate of long-chain alcohols; used in special lubricants.

Ortholeum 200. Sulfurized terpene; used in cutting oils.

Ortholeum 202. Sulfurized terpene; lubricant, corrosion preventive.

Ortholeum 410. Tributyl phosphite (20) with tricresyl phosphate (80); antioxidant for lubricants.

Orthophen. *o*-Amyl phenol; antioxidant.

Orthosil. Sodium orthosilicate.

Orthowet. Alkyl aryl sulfonate; wetting agent.

Orthoxenol. *o*-Phenyl phenol.

Orthozym. Proteolytic enzyme.

Ortol. Hydroquinone and methyl *o*-aminophenol; photographic developer.

Orvus WA. Sodium lauryl sulfate; wetting agent.

Oryzyme. Commercial diastase.

Orzol. U.S.P. heavy mineral oil.

Composition of Trade-Marked Products

Oscodal. Preparation containing the non-saponifiable fraction of cod-liver oil; used in medicine.

Osmo-Kaolin. Purified, colloidal aluminum silicate; used in cosmetics.

Otiscoloy steel. Low-alloy steel with 1.0 to 1.35% manganese, not over 0.5% copper, not over 0.12% carbon, and not over 0.1% each nickel and chromium.

Otisel steel. Steels with 12 to 30% chromium, optionally 12 to 20% nickel, and low percentages of tungsten or molybdenum.

Otonol. Solution of benzyl cinnamate (3.2%) in peanut oil; used in medicine.

Ovaclene. Carbon tetrachloride with ethylene dichloride; spot remover.

Oxenes. Mixture of essential oils and aromatic chemicals; used in insecticides.

Oxilac. Mixture of cattle blood and milk.

Oximony. Red iron oxide.

Oxol. Thiodiglycol.

Oxolac. Protein complex-phospho protein hemin histone; dietary protein.

Oxone. Sodium peroxide.

Oxydrene. *dl*-Desoxyephedrine hydrochloride; used in medicine.

Oxyfume. Solution of ethylene oxide (20%) in ethylene dichloride; fumigant.

Oxymel. Mixture of honey and vinegar; used in medicine.

Oxynone. 2,4-Diaminodiphenyl amine; rubber antioxidant.

Ozoturp. "Soluble" pine oil; wool-scouring agent.

Ozowax. Synthetic brown wax; substitute for ozokerite.

Paalsgaard oil. Schou oil.

Padutin. Hormone obtained from the pancreas; used in medicine.

Palamoll. Copolymer of diethyl fumarate and butadiene; used in paints.

Composition of Trade-Marked Products

Palatinol. Ethyl phthalate.

Palatinol A. Diethyl phthalate; lacquer plasticizer.

Palatinol AH. Diethyl hexyl phthalate.

Palatinol BB. Butyl benzyl phthalate; plasticizer.

Palatinol C. Dibutyl phthalate.

Palatinol DP. Dilauryl phthalate.

Palatinol E. Diethyl glycol phthalate.

Palatinol HS. Phthalic ester of aliphatic alcohols.

Palatinol JC. Diisobutyl phthalate.

Palatinol K. Dibutoxyethyl phthalate.

Palatinol L. Phthalic acid ester of aliphatic alcohols.

Palatinol M. Methyl or dimethyl phthalate.

Palatinol O. Dimethyl glycol phthalate.

Palatinol P. Diphenyl phthalate.

Palgum. Carob-seed gum; thickener in food products.

Palladol. Liquid containing palladium and gold; used in ceramic glazing.

Palmalene. Fatty acid mixture similar to palm fatty acids.

Palmitone. 16-Hentriacontanone.

Palmolate. Ester of palm-oil fatty acids.

Palmoleostearate. Ester of tallow fatty acids.

Pamaquine. See Plasmochin.

Pancal. Calcium *d*-pantothenate; dietary supplement.

Pandura. Synthetic tar-acid resin.

Panelyte. Synthetic tar-acid resin.

Panilax. Aniline-formaldehyde impregnated board; used in electrical insulation.

Panitrin. Papaverine nitrite.

Pankreon. Mixture of ferments of the pancreas and tannin; used in medicine.

Pantex. Vinyl-plastic film.

Composition of Trade-Marked Products

Panthesin. $C_{18}H_{32}N_2O_5S$; anesthetic.
Pantholin. See Pancal.
Pantocain. *p*-Butyl aminobenzoyl dimethyl aminoethanol hydrochloride; local anesthetic.
Pantopaque. Ethyl iodophenyl undecoate; X-ray contrast substance.
Pantopon. Mixture of opium alkaloid hydrochlorides; used in medicine.
Pantothaxin. See Pancal.
Papreg. Resin-treated, compressed laminated paper.
Para. *p*-dichlorobenzene.
Paracide. *p*-Dichlorobenzol; insecticide.
Paracol. Emulsion of wax or wax-resin; used in paper finishing.
Paracole. Mixture of glycerin, Santomerse and Tergitol Penetrant 7; textile softener.
Paracon. High-molecular-weight condensation product of hydroxy acids or of dibasic acids with glycols; has rubber-like properties.
Paradol. Condensation product of methylene and cresol sulfonic acid; used in tanning.
Paradone. Vat dye; used for dyeing cotton.
Paradow. *p*-Dichlorobenzene.
Paradura. Phenolic synthetic resin; mineral rubber.
Paradyne Inhibitor A. 2,6-Di-*tert*-butyl 4-methyl phenol; gasoline antioxidant.
Paraffion. Paraffin wax emulsion containing aluminum sulfate; used in waterproofing textiles.
Parafilm. Paraffin wax modified with an elastomer to give a flexible, thermoplastic sheet or film.
Paraflow. Carbocyclic aromatic compound and chlorinated petroleum wax; oil pour-point depressant.
Paraflow P.D. Hydrocarbon wax—naphthalene condensation product; pour-point depressant.
Paragerm. Methyl propyl diphenol *p*-oxybenzoate.

Composition of Trade-Marked Products

Paragon clay. Hydrous aluminum silicate; rubber filler.
Paragon steel. Steel with about 1.7% manganese, 1.00% carbon, 0.60% chromium, 0.25% vanadium.
Paragutta. Deproteinized rubber, gutta-percha hydrocarbon and wax; used for submarine cables.
Paralac. Alkyd resin; used in varnish.
Paralaudin. Diacetyl dihydromorphine; used in medicine.
Para Lene. Mixture of high-boiling petroleum hydrocarbons; used in rubber compounding.
Paraleukanilin. Triamidotriphenyl methane.
Paramul 115. Emulsion of wax and aluminum salts; water repellent.
Paranaph. Mixture of soft soap, naphthalene and kerosene; insecticide.
Paranol. Modified phenolic and maleic resins.
Paranox 447-X. Combination of Paranox 105 and 441; lubricant, antioxidant.
Paranox 12. Sulfurized olefin; lubricant, corrosion inhibitor.
Paranox 105. Barium salt of an organic compound with phosphorus- and sulfur-containing groups; lubricant, corrosion inhibitor, detergent.
Paranox 441. Diisobutyl phenol; antioxidant.
Paranox 492. High-molecular-weight amine compound; lubricant, color stabilizer, and metal deactivator.
Para Oil. Saponified oils; surface-active agent.
Parapen. Pentaerythritol resin; used in varnish.
Paraplex. Alkyd resin; used in varnish.
Paraplex RG-2. Glyceryl trisebacate.
Parapoid 10-C. Hydrocarbon compound with sulfur, chlorine and a

Composition of Trade-Marked Products

rust inhibitor; extreme-pressure lubricant.

Parapol B-25. Rubber-like polymer and paraffin wax mixture.

Parapont. *p*-Dichlorobenzene; used in insecticides.

Paraprene. Polymerized divinyl containing a mineral filler.

Para resin. Polymerized hydrocarbon resin; used in rubber.

Paraseal. Paraffin wax; used in sealing preserve jars.

Parasept. *p*-Hydroxybenzoic ester; preservative.

Paratac. High-molecular-weight isobutylene polymer; tackifier.

Paratex. Paraffin wax emulsion; used for waterproofing.

Paratone. Linear isobutylene polymer of controlled molecluar weight; used to increase the viscosity of lubricants.

Paravar. Chlorinated rubber.

Parazone. *p*-Phenyl phenol.

Parchfoil. Aluminum foil laminated between parchment paper sheets; used in food packaging.

Parclay. Kaolin; rubber filler.

Paredrine. *p*-Hydroxy-α-methyl phenethyl amine hydrobromide; used in medicine.

Parenamine. Acid-hydrolyzed casein with tryptophan added; used in medicine.

Par-Exc steel. Steel with 2% tungsten, 1.5% chromium, 0.3% vanadium, and 0.50% carbon; hot-die steel.

Parez. Synthetic resin; used in paper manufacture.

Parez 607. Melamine-formaldehyde resin; paper impregnant.

Parian cement. Anhydrous calcium sulfate; used in construction.

Parical. Paris green and calcium arsenate powder; agricultural insecticide.

Pariflux. Calcium fluoride powder; used in welding.

Composition of Trade-Marked Products

Paris metal. Copper-base alloy with 6 to 16% nickel, up to 5% iron, up to 5% zinc, about 2% tin, and 1% cobalt.

Paris Top. White clay.

Parisul. Mixture of Paris green and sulfur; agricultural insecticide.

Parlodion. Collodion; used for embedding microscopic specimens.

Parlon. Chlorinated rubber; used in adhesives.

Parmentine. Mixture of gelatin, dextrin, glycerol, zinc sulfate and sodium sulfite; used for sizing and finishing cotton, wool and silk.

Parmo. Petroleum jelly; used in cosmetics.

Paroidin. Active principle of the parathyroid gland of cattle in aqueous solution; used in medicine.

Paroil. Series of chlorinated paraffins; plasticizers.

Parolite. $Zn(HSO_2.CH_2O)_2$; reducing and decoloring agent.

Parowax. Paraffin wax.

Paroxyl. Acetarsone.

Parsenol. Sulfated castor oil, octyl alcohol and sodium soap; textile softener.

Parson's alloy. Copper-base alloy with about 41% zinc, 1% iron, fractional percentages of tin, aluminum and manganese.

Parson's white brass. Tin-base bearing metals with up to 35% zinc, 14% lead, 11% antimony, 5% copper.

Pasilco. Epsom salt.

Patapar. Vegetable parchment.

Patax. Heavy waxed paper.

Pavatrine. β-Diethyl aminoethyl fluorene 9-carboxylate hydrochloride; antispasmodic.

Paxolin. Phenol-formaldehyde compound; used for electrical insulation.

Pearl oil. Isoamyl acetate.

Composition of Trade-Marked Products

Pe-Ce-Fibre. Synthetic fiber based on polyvinyl chloride (German).

Pechiney. Trichlorethylene; dry cleaning solvent.

Pectinate H-69. Acid demethylated pectin.

Pectinol A. Enzyme preparation containing pectinase; used for clarifying apple juice.

Pectinol enzymes. Pectinase-enzyme complex; clarifier for liquids containing suspended matter.

Peerless clay. Domestic China clay; rubber filler.

Peerless steel. Steel with 9 to 15% tungsten, 2 to 3% chromium, and fractional percentages of vanadium.

Pekaglas. Polymerized vinyl compound.

Pelletex. Carbon black in pellet form; used in rubber goods.

Pellidol. Dimazon; used in medicine.

Peltex. Paraffin wax-aluminum acetate water emulsion; waterproofing agent.

Pelviren acid. 3,5-Diiodo-4-oxo-1(4)-pyridine acetic acid.

Pemeko. Sulfated alcohol; surface-active agent.

Penacolite. Resorcinol-formaldehyde adhesive.

Penacolite G. Resorcinol-formaldehyde plastic.

Penequik. Sulfonated ester; penetrating agent.

Penetrant M-7X. Alkyl aryl sulfonate; wetting agent.

Penetrex. Sulfonated oil in a solvent; used in textile finishing.

Penetrol 60. Sodium and potassium salts of sulfonated esters of dicarboxylic acids; penetrating agent.

Penetrol 65. Sodium and potassium salts of sulforicinoleic acids; penetrating agent.

Penetrolin AC. Sodium salt of alkylated naphthalene sulfonic acid; wetting agent.

Composition of Trade-Marked Products

Pennane. Heptamethyl nonane.

Pennsalt FA-42. Aqueous solution containing fluoboric acid (42%) and a small quantity of boric acid; used in electroplating baths.

Pennsalum. Sodium aluminum sulfate.

Pennsoline. U.S.P. petrolatum.

Pennwax. Petrolatum wax.

Penofen. Alkyl aryl sulfonate and a mildew inhibitor; mildewproofing agent.

Penozone. Hydrogen peroxide solution with stabilizer and wetting agent; used in bleaching.

Penros (Rexar). Polymerized rosin; used in varnish.

Pensal. See Aseptisil.

Pentacat L. Aqueous dispersion of lithium naphthenate (50%); catalyst.

Pent-Acetate. Amyl acetate-amyl alcohol solvent; used in lacquers.

Pentacizer 131. Acetate of pentaerythritol; plasticizer.

Pentacizer 152. Triacetate and tripropionate of dipentaerythritol; liquid plasticizer.

Pentacizer 176. Acetate and propionate of pentaerythritol; plasticizer.

Pentacizer 180. Mixed esters of polypentaerythritol.

Pentacizer 185. Reaction product of ethylene oxide and pentaerythritol.

Pentacizer 188. Reaction product of ethylene oxide and dipentaerythritol.

Pentacizer 203. Monoester of pentaerythritol and a fatty acid; emulsifier.

Pentacizer 226. Propionate of pentaerythritol; plasticizer.

Pentacizer 317. Pentaerythritol triacetate monostearate; lubricant in molding compositions.

Pentaform. Pentaerythritol acetals.

Pentalarm. Product containing amyl mercaptan; used for imparting

Composition of Trade-Marked Products

warning odor to odorless fuel gases.

Pentalene. Amyl naphthalene.

Pentalene 92. Polyamyl naphthalene; plasticizer.

Pentalene 95. Crude, mixed amyl naphthalenes.

Pentalene 103. Monoamyl naphthalene; solvent.

Pentalene 195. Mixed amyl naphthalenes.

Pentalyn A. Pentaerythritol ester of rosin.

Pentalyn G. Heat-stable pentaerythritol ester of resin; used in varnishes.

Pentalyn M. Phenol-modified pentaerythritol resin; used in varnishes.

Pentamidine. Diamidinodiphenoxypentane.

Pentamul. Pentaerythritol monoesters of commercial fatty acids.

Pentamul 6. Pentaerythritol monostearate; emulsifying agent.

Pentamul 87. Pentaerythritol soybean fatty acid monoester; emulsifying agent.

Pentamul 126. Pentaerythritol monooleate; surface-active agent.

Pentamul 147. Pentaerythritol monolaurate; surface-active agent.

Pentamul 149. Pentaerythritol monocaprate; surface-active agent.

Pentaöl. See Lucex.

Pentaphen. *p-tert*-Amyl phenol.

Penta Preservative. Pentachlorophenol (5%) in a petroleum solvent; termite and soil poison.

Pentaryl A. Monoamyl biphenyl.

Pentaryl B. Diamyl biphenyl.

Pentasol. Mixture of isomeric amyl alcohols; used in pyroxylin lacquers.

Pentawax. Microcrystalline petroleum wax.

Pentawax 177. Pentaerythritol stearate.

Pentawax 217. Modified pentaerythritol stearate.

Composition of Trade-Marked Products

Pentawax 242. Dipentaerythritol hexastearate.

Pentazicon T. Sulfonated product of vegetable oils, fats and hydrocarbons; penetrating agent.

Pentek. Mixture of pentaerythritol and dipentaerythritol; intermediate in mfg. drying oils.

Pentex. Dithiocarbamate; accelerator.

Penthrinite. Mixture of pentaerythritol tetranitrate and nitroglycerin; powerful explosive.

Penthrite. Pentaerythritol tetranitrate; explosive.

Penticide. Pentachlorodiphenyl ethane; insecticide.

Pentothal sodium. Sodium salt of ethyl (1-methyl butyl)-thiobarbituric acid; used in medicine.

Pentrinit. See Penthrinite.

Pentrit. Pentaerythritol tetranitrate; spasmolytic drug (Swiss).

Pentritol. Mixture of pentaerythritol tetranitrate and trinitrotoluene; explosive.

Pentrocene. "Soluble" cresylic acid; boil-off assistant.

Pentronate. Purified petroleum sulfonate; wetting agent.

Pentrosulf. Alkyl naphthalene sulfonate; used in textile dyeing.

Pentryl. Trinitrophenyl nitramine ethyl nitrate.

Pepticase. Mixed amino acids obtained from enzymatic hydrolysis of milk proteins.

Perabrodil. 3,5-Diiodo-4-pyridone acetic acid; X-ray contrast substance.

Peralga. Aminopyrine diethyl barbiturate; sedative.

Perandren. Testosterone propionate; used in medicine.

Perbromol. Tetrabromoketodihydrobenzene; neutralizing agent for mustard gas.

Perbunan. Copolymer of butadiene and acrylonitrile; synthetic rubber.

Percachinon. Condensation product

Composition of Trade-Marked Products

of perhydrocarbazole and 1-chloroanthraquinone; fluorescent dye (German).

Percaine. See Nupercaine.

Perchloron. Calcium hypochlorite; bleaching agent.

Per-Clene. Perchloroethylene; used in degreasing.

Percorten. Desoxycorticosterone acetate; used in medicine.

Perduran. See Perduren.

Perduren. Organic polysulfide rubber.

Perduren G. Synthetic rubber made from dichlorethyl ether and sodium polysulfide.

Perduren H. Product made from dichloroethyl, formaldehyde, acetal and sodium polysulfide.

Perduren L. Mixture of Perbunan and Perduren.

Perduren L Special. Mixture of Perbunan and Perduren.

Perduren SP. Aqueous suspension of Perduren H.

Peregal O. Condensation product of a higher fatty acid with 20 mols ethylene oxide, sold as 20% aqueous solution; leveling agent in dyeing.

Perfectol. Mixture of sodium and potassium soaps.

Perflectol X. N,N′-Diphenyl *p*-phenylene diamine; antioxidant.

Pergamyn. Greaseproof, imitation parchment paper, made from sulfite pulp by beating until gelatinous.

Pergut. Chlorinated rubber; used in anticorrosion paints.

Perhydrit. See Hyperol.

Perhydrol. Hydrogen peroxide.

Perhydrol-urea. See Hyperol.

Periodyl. Diiodoricin stearolic acid; used in medicine.

Peristaltin. Glucoside from Cascara sagrada; used in medicine.

Periston. Solution containing polyvinyl pyrrolidone (2.5%); human-blood substitute.

Composition of Trade-Marked Products

Perka-glycerin. Concentrated aqueous solution of calcium and sodium lactates.

Perlon. Synthetic fiber similar to nylon.

Perlon L. Polymer of ω-aminocaprolactam; synthetic fiber.

Perluxe. Perchlorethylene.

Perma Carb (Rinsynol 5OL). Concentrated aqueous solution of alkyl aryl sulfonic acid; wetting agent.

Perm-A-Chlor. Degreasing solvent with a trichlorethylene base.

Perma-Cide. Organomercuric salt; antiseptic.

Perm-A-Kleen. Perchlorethylene-base compound; used in dry cleaning.

Permalene WS. Blend of sodium alkyl aryl sulfonate and sodium phosphates; textile assistant.

Permalite. Perlite and diatomaceous silica; filler.

Permalloy. Alloy of iron with about 40 to 80% nickel; used for applications requiring high magnetic permeability and resistivity.

Permalux. Di-*o*-tolyl guanidine salt of dicatechol borate; used in rubber to improve aging.

Permanite. Steel with 17% cobalt; used in magnets.

Permansa Orange. Dinitraniline orange.

Permansa Red. *o*-Chloroparanitraniline; red pigment.

Permaplastic. Synthetic tar-acid resin; used for molding and laminating.

Permasan. Pentachlorophenol in an organic solvent; used to preserve wood.

Permatol A. Solution of chlorophenol (5%); used to preserve dry lumber.

Permaton. Lake dye.

Permatox A. Solution of pentachlorphenol (5%) in petroleum solvents.

Composition of Trade-Marked Products

Perma Wet. Alkyl aryl sodium sulfonate; wetting agent.

Permeko. Sodium alkyl naphthalene sulfonate; wetting agent.

Permex. Dehydrogenated rosin.

Permigel. Gelatinous permissible explosive; used in mining.

Perminal N. Mixture of sulfonated alkyl naphthalenes; wetting agent.

Perminvar. Nickel-base alloy containing about 22.5% iron and 7.5% cobalt, having a constant magnetic permeability for variable magnetic fields of low intensity.

Permite. Aluminum-base alloys, with optional small percentages of silicon, magnesium, iron, nickel.

Permolith. Lithopone; pigment.

Permount. Solution of a naphthalene polymer in toluol; cement.

Permutit. $Na_2O.Al_2O_3.2SiO_2.6H_2O$, synthetic zeolite; used in softening water.

Pernax. Compounded raw rubber; used for electrical insulation.

Pernoston. Butyl β-bromoallyl barbituric acid; used in medicine.

Perone. Hydrogen peroxide; used in food industry.

Perox. Mixture of litharge and red lead; used in making pastes for positive battery plates.

Persil. Mixture of sodium perborate (10 parts), soap (35 parts), soda ash (25 parts) and sodium silicate (5 parts); detergent.

Persistol. Paraffin wax emulsion containing zirconium oxychloride; used in textile waterproofing.

Persistol VS. Aqueous emulsion of *n*-octadecyl ethylene urea; used in waterproofing textiles.

Perspex. Methyl methacrylate polymer plastic.

Perspirit. Isopropyl alcohol.

Pertunol. Phenolic resin; adhesive (German).

Pervinan. Copolymer of vinyl chloride with vinyl acetate or maleic ester.

Composition of Trade-Marked Products

Petralol. Liquid petrolatum.

Petrex 5. Glycol ester of terpene-maleic anhydride; synthetic resin used in varnish.

Petrex acid. Reaction product of maleic anhydride and a monocyclic terpene; used in making varnish resins.

Petrex resins. Alkyd resins produced from Petrex acid.

Petro. Liquid petrolatum.

Petroacid. Mixture of fatty acids from oxidation of petroleum fractions.

Petrobenzol. Petroleum solvent.

Petroflux. Petroleum sulfonate-soluble oil base.

Petrohol. Isopropyl alcohol.

Petrolene. Petroleum solvent.

Petrolyte. Sodium salt of petroleum sulfonates.

Petronate. Sodium salt of sulfated naphthenates; emulsifying agent.

Petronite. See Petrosul.

Petropol 2138. Mixture of polymerized olefinic hydrocarbons from petroleum.

Petropon. Synthetic petroleum resin.

Petrosene. Microcrystalline wax.

Petrosol C-50. Petroleum sulfonate; wetting agent.

Petrosul (Petronite). Petroleum sulfonate; emulsifier.

Petrowet R. Sodium salts of saturated hydrocarbon sulfonates; wetting agent.

Petrowet WN. Fatty alcohol sulfate; used in acidizing oil wells.

Phanodorm. Cyclohexenyl ethyl barbituric acid; used in medicine.

Phanodure. Phenolic resin (German).

Pharmagel. Refined gelatin; emulsifying agent.

Pharmagel B. Purified gelatin.

Pharmasol. Insoluble azo dye.

Phemeride. *p*-Octyl phenyl dimethyl ammonium chloride; antiseptic, detergent.

Phemerol. *p-tert*-Octyl phenoxy-

Composition of Trade-Marked Products

ethoxyethyl dimethyl benzyl ammonium chloride; germicide.

Phenacetin. *p*-Acetophenetide.

Phenac resins. Series of modified phenol-formaldehyde resins; used in paint.

Phenal. Liquid phenol-formaldehyde resin; used in varnish.

Phenalin. Thermosetting phenol-formaldehyde cast resin.

Phenamine. Phenocoll hydrochloride.

Phenegol. Mercury potassium *p*-nitrophenol sulfonate; used in medicine.

Phenester. Cumarone-indene resin containing a large amount of uncondensed phenolics; used in varnishes.

Phenester M. Phenyl acetic acid ethyl ester.

Phenetelle. Phenyl acetaldehyde; used in perfume.

Phenex. Salts of the aldehyde-amine type; vulcanization accelerator.

Pheniodol. α-Phenyl β-4-hydroxy-3,5-diiodophenyl propionic acid; contrast medium in cholecystography.

Phenite. Water-dispersible phenol-formaldehyde resin; laminating adhesive.

Phenoform. Series of dyes; used for coloring synthetic resins.

Phenoglaze. Phenol-formaldehyde plastic solution; used for protective coatings.

Phenolite. Plastic made by treatment of cloth, paper, etc., with phenol-formaldehyde resins.

Phenolplaste. Synthetic tar-acid resin.

Phenoxetol. β-Phenoxyethyl alcohol; antiseptic (British).

Phenyform. $[C_6H_4(OH)CH_2OH]_x$-CH_2O; used in medicine.

Phenysol. Isobutyl phenyl acetate.

Philgas. Liquefied natural gas; fuel.

Phi-O-Sol. Sodium salt of an alkyl ester of an aliphatic fatty acid sulfate; wetting agent.

Phi-O-Sol W.A. Carboxylic acid ester sulfate; wetting agent.

P.H.O. Phenolic heavy oil; plasticizer.

Phono bronze. Copper-base alloy, with about 1.25% tin; used for electrical conductor wires.

Phosflake. Mixed sodium hydroxide and trisodium phosphate in flakes; detergent.

Phosilage. Phosphoric acid (75%); used for ensilaging fodder crops.

Phosote. Creosote phosphate.

Phosphazote. Essentially a mixture of urea and an acid phosphate; fertilizer.

Phosphen 1. Diphenyl mono-[*p-tert*-butyl phenyl] phosphate.

Phosphen 2. Di-[*p-tert*-butyl phenyl]-monophenyl phosphate; plasticizer.

Phosphen 3. Diphenyl mono-[*o*-chlorophenyl] phosphate.

Phosphen 4. Di-[*p*-chlorophenyl]-monophenyl phosphate.

Phosphen 5. Diphenyl mono-*o*-xenyl phosphate; plasticizer.

Phosphen 6. Di-*o*-xenyl monophenyl phosphate.

Phosphen 7. Tri-[*p-tert*-butyl phenyl] phosphate.

Phosphen 8. Tri-*o*-chlorophenyl phosphate.

Phosphen 9. Tri-*o*-xenyl phosphate.

Phosphosol. Tetrapotassium pyrophosphate; detergent.

Phosphostritan. Triphenyl methyl phosphonium chloride (German).

Phosphotex. Tetrasodium pyrophosphate; detergent.

Photol. *p*-Methyl aminophenol sulfate; photographic developer.

Photophor. Calcium phosphide.

Phygon. 2,3-Dichloro-1,4-naphthoquinone; insecticide.

Phyllicin. Theophylline calcium salicylate.

Piccocizer. High-boiling polymer-

Composition of Trade-Marked Products

ized aromatic oil; synthetic-rubber plasticizer.

Piccolastic. Elastic thermoplastic resin composed of polymers of styrene, substituted styrene and its homologs.

Piccolyte. Thermoplastic hydrocarbon-terpene resin.

Piccoumaron. Coumarone-indene resin.

Piccovar. High-indene resin; plasticizer.

Piccovol. Coal-tar bitumen mixture; rubber softener.

Picrargol. Silver picrate; used in medicine.

Picratol. Silver picrate.

Pictol. *p*-Methyl aminophenol sulfate; photographic developer.

Pigmentar. Pine tar; used in rubber compounding.

Pigmentar Oil. Pine-tar oil.

Pinalox. Activated aluminum oxide; catalyst.

Pinaperol. Isobutyl furyl propionate; synthetic pineapple aroma.

Pineol. Sulfonated oil and terpenes; surface-active agent.

Pinesol. Pine-oil solvent.

Pinetrol. "Soluble" pine oil; boil-off assistant.

Pioloform. Polyvinyl acetate plastic.

Pioneer alloy. Alloys with 20 to 65% nickel, about 25% chromium, and up to 5% molybdenum, remainder being iron.

Pipazate. Zinc pentamethylenedithiocarbamate; ultra-accelerator.

Piphen. Phenol-formaldehyde resin; used in varnish.

Pip-pip. Piperidine pentamethylene dithiocarbamate.

Pipsolene. Reaction product of carbon bisulfide and methylene dipiperidine.

Pircine. Sulfonated oil-cresylic acid emulsion; dyeing assistant.

Pictocin. Aqueous solution of α-hypophamine; used in medicine.

Pitressin. Aqueous solution of β-hypophamine; used in medicine.

Composition of Trade-Marked Products

Pittchlor. Commercial calcium hypochlorite.

Pixalbol. Purified coal tar; used in medicine.

Planadalin. See Carbromal.

Plaskon. Urea-formaldehyde molding resin.

Plasmochin. Diethyl aminoisopentyl 8-amino-6-methoxyquinoline; used in medicine.

Plasmon. Mixture of casein and sodium carbonate.

Plaspreg. Plaster cast or structure impregnated with low-viscosity furane resin.

Plassitil. Glycol or glyceryl monolactate triacetate; plasticizer.

Plastabrac AA. Glyceryl diacetoabietate.

Plastacele. Cellulose acetate plastic.

Plastamine resin. Urea resin; plasticizer.

Plastazote. Polyvinyl-formal plastic.

Plastic "A." Glyceryl tribenzoate.

Plasticizer "SC." Triethylene glycol ester of low-boiling acids of coconut oil.

Plasticizer 3GH. $(C_5H_{11}COO)_2$:-$[C_2H_4(C_2H_4O)_2]$.

Plasticose. Copolymer of modified vinyl acetate; used in textile finishing.

Plast-Iron. Very pure electrolytically produced iron powder; used in powder metallurgy.

Plastoflex. Tributyl phosphate; plasticizer.

Plastoform I. Benzyl alcohol.

Plastogen. Mixture of mineral oil (98), sulfonated petroleum (1.6) and *n*-butyl alcohol (0.4); rubber plasticizer.

Plastoil. Air blown Olivene; plasticizer.

Plastol C II. Mixture of *p*-toluene sulfonamide (65–70%) and *o*-toluene sulfonamide (30–35%); plasticizer.

Composition of Trade-Marked Products

Plastolein X-55. Diethylene glycol dipelargonate; plasticizer.

Plastolin I. Benzyl acetate.

Plastol M. Mixture of toluene sulfonamide (18.5%), ethyl *p*-toluene sulfonamide (73%) and diethyl-*p*-toluene sulfonamide (8.5%).

Plastol MBM. Monobutyl benzene sulfonamide.

Plastomoll BMB. Butyl benzene sulfonamide.

Plastomoll KF. Triethylene glycol ester of C_7–C_9 synthetic fatty acids.

Plastomoll TAH. Thiodibutyric diester of ethyl hexyl alcohol.

Plastomoll TB. Thiodibutyric diester of butylene glycol; plasticizer.

Plastomoll SW. Vinyl methyl ether (German).

Plastomoll TF. Tetrahydrofurfuryl alcohol ester of C_7–C_9 synthetic fatty acids.

Plastomoll TV. Thiodibutyric diester of C_5–C_7 alcohols.

Plastopal W. Urea-formaldehyde resin.

Plastopol. Urea-formaldehyde resin (50%) dissolved in butyl alcohol (50%); lacquer.

Plasto-Resin. Alkyd resin.

Plastozote. Foamed polyvinylformal plastic.

Plastron. Plastic polyvinyl chloride film; waterproof fabric.

Plast-Sponge. Iron Powder made by reduction of iron oxide; used in powder metallurgy.

Plastybcol. Blown (oxidized) linseed oil; used in paint.

Plat-chrome. Mixture of chlorides of several rare-earth metals and palladium, chromium and molybdenum.

Platino. Alloy of 80% gold and 20% lead.

Platinol. Liquid mixture containing platinum and gold; used in ceramics.

Composition of Trade-Marked Products

Platinor. Alloys of platinum with silver, copper, nickel and zinc.

Platnam. Alloy of 54% nickel, 33% copper and 13% tin.

Plexene M. Modified polystyrene thermoplastic injection-molding powder.

Plexiglass. Acrylate resin.

Plexiglass M 33. Methyl methacrylate with dibutyl phthalate (3%).

Plexigum. Polymerized methacrylate resin in ethylene dichloride having rubber-like properties; laminating layer in safety glass.

Plexilene. Aqueous dispersion (10%) of polyacrylonitrile; used in creaseproofing textiles (German).

Plexipole. Montan wax.

Plexon. Fibers coated with very thin plastic or resin solution; used for textiles.

Plextol. Aqueous dispersion of ethyl acrylates; used in textile finishing.

Plimber. Construction material made from cellulosic waste materials chemically treated and bonded with synthetic resins.

Pliochlor (Pliolite S-1). Chlorinated polyisoprene.

Plioflex. Vinyl vinylidene chloride and compounding ingredients; rubber substitute.

Pliofilm. Rubber hydrochloride.

Pliofoam. Low-density foamed urea-formaldehyde plastic.

Plioform. Plastic derived from rubber.

Pliolite. Cyclicized rubber derivative; used in moistureproof coatings.

Pliolite S-1. See Pliochlor.

Pliolite S-3. Resinous copolymer of styrene (85%) with butadiene (15%); used in rubber compounding.

Plumb-O-Sil. Lead orthosilicate and silica gel; stabilizer for vinyl plastics.

Composition of Trade-Marked Products

Pluswood. See Pregwood.
Pluviusin. Synthetic urea resin.
Plyamine. Water-resistant urea-formaldehyde resin; plywood adhesive.
Plymetyl. Laminated metal and plywood; used in construction.
Plyophen. Phenol-formaldehyde resin; used in laminating.
Polana. Casein fiber.
Primal. Aqueous dispersion of syn-
Polane. Chloromethyl stearate; used in lubricants.
Polaroid. Two sheets of ordinary glass with an interposed layer of cellulose acetate fiber; used in special lenses.
Polava. Casein fiber.
Polectron. Synthetic mica substitute; used in electrical condensers.
Polidase. Mixture of amyolytic, proteolytic and phosphorolytic enzymes; used for digestion of proteins and carbohydrates.
Polidase-C. Refined mold.
Polinlite. Plastic made from coffee-bean extractive, furfural and acids.
Polital. Alloy of aluminum with 1.1% silicon, 0.75% magnesium, 0.4% manganese, 0.15% nickel.
Pollantin. Serum from horses treated with pollen toxin; used in the treatment of hay fever.
Pollapas. Urea-formaldehyde plastic.
Pol-Mer-Ik. Polymerized vegetable oil; used in paint.
Polmin. Aqueous solution of a polyethylene amine.
Polvin. Polyvinyl chloride plastic.
Polyamide Resin DET. Reaction product of dimerized and trimerized linoleic and linolenic acids of soybean oil with diethylene triamine; used in coatings.
Polyamide Resin ED. Reaction product of dimerized and trimerized linoleic and linolenic acids of soybean oil with ethylene diamine; used in coatings.
Polycel. Pulverized wood pulp.

Composition of Trade-Marked Products

Polycol. Cellulose fibers.
Polydon. Methacrylate resin; used in making artificial teeth.
Polyfiber. Fine plastic fiber based on polystyrene; used in low-temperature insulation.
Polyflex. Polystyrene plastic.
Polyglas. Plastic composed of poly-2,5-dichlorostyrene-silicon resin or other suitable thermoplastic and powdered or fiber glass; used in electrical insulation.
Polynol A. Linolic acid esters of starch (German).
Polypentek. Technical tripentaerythritol.
Polyplastex. Modified Laminac; used in sealing porous castings.
Polysolvan A. Isoamyl alcohol (German).
Polysolvan AO. Chloracetic acid and Polysolvan A; solvent (German).
Polysolvan J. Crude isobutyl alcohol; solvent (German).
Polysolvan O. Crude isobutyl glycolate; used in lacquer solvents.
Polystyrol EH. Styrol, acrylonitrile and vinyl carbazole (German).
Polystyrol EN. Styrol and acrylonitrile (German).
Polystyrol 30B. Styrene and butyl acrylate copolymer (German).
Poly-Tint. Aqueous dispersion of pigments; used in coloring latices.
Polyvinyl Chloride C. Chlorinated polyvinyl chloride (German).
Polyviol. Polyvinyl alcohol.
Polyweld. Liquid polystyrene; adhesive.
Polyxile oil. Decarboxylated rosin acids; plasticizer.
Polyxile resin. Reaction product of cellulose and rosin acids; plastic.
Polyzime. See Talase.
Polyzime P. Amylolytic enzyme prepared from Aspergillus oryzae.
Ponolith. Lithopone pigment.
Pontalite. See Lucite.

Composition of Trade-Marked Products

Pontamine Developer MPD. *m*-Phenylene diamine.

Pontamine Developer TN. *m*-Toluylene diamine; dye developer.

Pontamine Developer ZN. 1-Phenyl 3-methyl 5-pyrazolone; dye developer.

Pontar. Refined coal tar.

Porocel. Activated bauxite; desiccant.

Porofor DB. Diazoaminobenzene.

Porofor N. Azoisobutyric acid dinitrile.

Porofor 505A. Azodicarbonamide.

Porofor 476. Diethylazodicarbonate; used in Buna rubber.

Porophor. Foamed polyvinyl chloride plastic.

Postonal. Water-soluble polyethylene oxide; cocoa butter substitute in suppositories (German).

Pourex. Alkylated naphthalene; lubricant, pour-point depressant.

Povimal. Copolymer of maleic and vinyl esters.

Povimal C. Copolymer of vinyl chloride and maleic anhydride.

Povimal EE. Copolymer of maleic-anhydride and vinyl acetate (German).

Povimal St. Copolymer of maleic-anhydride and styrene (German).

P.P.D. Piperidine pentamethylene dithiocarbonate; vulcanization accelerator.

Pragmoline. Acetyl choline bromide; used in medicine.

Pranone. Anhydrohydroxyprogesterone; used in medicine.

Prästabitol. Sulfonated castor oil; used in textile processing.

Pregwood (Hiden; Pluswood; Compregnated Wood; Compreg.). Compressed wood treated with phenolic resin.

Pressal. Melamine resin; adhesive (German).

Pressurdie steel. Alloy tool and die steels with about 5% chromium, optionally 5% tungsten, and fractional percentages of vanadium, molybdenum, cobalt, silicon.

Prestabit Oil. Sodium fatty acid sulfonate; dyeing assistant.

Prestolite. Solution of acetylene, under pressure, in acetone; used for illumination.

Prestone. Ethylene glycol containing additives to prevent corrosion and foaming; antifreeze.

Presto steel. Low-alloy steel with about 1.5% chromium, 1% carbon; used for antifriction bearings.

Preventol. Phenol.

Preventol GD. 2,2′-Dihydroxy-5,5′-dichlorodiphenyl methane; mildewproofing agent.

Preventol GDC. Alkaline solution of Preventol GD; antiseptic.

Preventol KB. Preservative based on monobenzyl phenol and *p*-chloro-*m*-cresol.

Primal. Aqueous dispersion of synthetic acryloid resin; used in finishing leathers.

Primol D. Medicinal mineral oil.

Primoxid. Manganese dioxide.

Printset PW. Compound based on sodium fatty alcohol sulfate; used in textile printing.

Priodax. β-(4-Hydroxy-3,5-diiodophenyl) α-phenyl propionic acid; gall-bladder contrast medium in roentgenology.

Priscol. 2-Benzyl 4,5-imidazoline hydrochloride; gastric secretion stimulant.

Privine. α-Naphthyl 2-methyl imidazoline; used in medicine.

Privine hydrochloride. Naphthyl methyl imidazoline hydrochloride; used in medicine.

Procase. Soybean protein; used in place of casein.

Procholon. Dehydrocholic acid; used in medicine as choleretic.

Prodag C. Semi-colloidal dispersion of graphite in water.

Product 300. Rubber substitute of the Thiokol type.

Composition of Trade-Marked Products

Product QB. Lauryl trimethyl ammonium bromide; cationic surface-active agent.

Product Q Paste. Stearyl trimethyl ammonium bromide; cationic surface-active agent.

Profenil. Bis-γ-phenyl propyl ethylamine; used in medicine.

Proferrin. Iron nucleoproteid; used in medicine.

Proganol. Silver-protein compound containing 8% silver; used in medicine.

Progesterone. Corpus luteum hormone.

Progestoral. Pranone; used in medicine.

Progynon-B. Estradiol benzoate.

Progynon-DP. α-Estradiol dipropionate; used in medicine.

Prolaurin. Propylene glycol monolaurate; emulsifier.

Prolein. Propylene glycol monooleate; emulsifier.

Prolon. Textile fiber made from casein or zein.

Proluton. Progesterone; used in medicine.

Promal. Malleable cast iron with about 0.4% combined carbon, 1.4% tempered carbon.

Prominal. Phenyl ethyl methyl barbituric acid; used in medicine.

Promizole. 4,2′-Diaminophenyl 5′-triazole sulfone.

Promoloid. Fertilizer (Japanese).

Prontosil. See Prontosil red.

Prontosil album. Sulfanilamide.

Prontosil red. $C_{12}H_{13}O_2N_5.HCL$; used in medicine.

Prontyl chloride. Acetanilid sulfone chloride.

Prontylin. Sulfanilamide.

Proofit. See Aquatec.

Propadrine hydrochloride. α-hydroxy-β-aminopropyl benzene hydrochloride; used in medicine.

Propaesin. Propyl aminobenzoate.

Propamidine. Diamidinophenoxypropane.

Composition of Trade-Marked Products

Proponal. 5,5-Dipropyl barbituric acid.

Proposote. Creosote phenyl propionate; used in medicine.

Propytal. 5,5-Dipropyl barbituric acid; used in medicine.

Prosein. Mechanically refined soybean protein; adhesive.

Prosoy G. Special soybean protein; filler for molding resins.

Prostearin. Propylene glycol monostearate; emulsifier.

Prostigmine bromide. Dimethyl carbamic acid ester of 3-hydroxyphenyl trimethyl ammonium bromide; used in medicine.

Prostigmine methyl sulfate. Dimethyl carbamic acid ester of 3-hydroxyphenyl trimethyl ammonium methyl sulfate; used in medicine.

Protalene L. Salts of hydrolyzed protein-fatty acid condensates; emulsifying agent.

Protan. Tannin nucleoproteid; used in medicine.

Protargentum. Protein silver with about 8% silver content; antiseptic.

Protargin. Protein silver.

Protargol. Protein silver containing about 8% silver; antiseptic.

Protectoid. Cellulose acetate plastic; used for transparent wrappings.

Protectol. See Dekol N.

Protectol III. Sulfite-cellulose waste liquor; dyeing assistant.

Protegin X. Chiefly petrolatum and oxycholesterin; absorption base.

Protek-Sorb. Silica gel; used for absorbing moisture.

Protela SB. Cuprammonium fluoride; mildewproofing agent.

Proteol. Casein-formaldehyde compound.

Protex Gel. Aliphatic lauryl amide sulfonated alkyl benzimidazol; dispersing and emulsifying agent.

Protinol. Hydrolyzed leather proteins; wetting agent.

Composition of Trade-Marked Products

Protoflex. Aqueous dispersion of protein; used for coating leather.

Protol. Decolorized mineral oil.

Protolac. Calcium caseinate.

Protolin. Zinc sulfoxylate formaldehyde; used in textile printing.

Protolin W. Zinc hydrosulfite.

Protostase. Amylolytic and proteolytic enzymes; stabilizer of beer.

Protovac. Casein compound; used in adhesives.

Protowax. Refined petrolatum from which liquid and semi-liquid hydrocarbons have been removed; used in cosmetics and pharmaceuticals.

Protozyme. Amylolytic and proteolytic enzymes; used for liquefaction of gelatin.

Protozyme PX. Mixture of proteolytic and amylolytic enzymes.

Provimal AA. Copolymer of maleic-anhydride and vinyl ethyl ether (German).

Provimal AE. Copolymer of maleic-anhydride and vinyl formate (German).

Provimal C. Copolymer of maleic-anhydride and vinyl chloride (German).

Provimal EE. Copolymer of maleic-anhydride and vinyl acetate (German).

Provimal MA. Copolymer of maleic-anhydride and vinyl methyl ether (German).

Provimal St. Copolymer of maleic-anhydride and styrene (German).

Prystal. Synthetic tar-acid resin.

Psicaine. *d*-Pseudococaine bitartrate; local anesthetic.

Puerine (Purogen). Mixture of enzymes, ammonium chloride and ammonium sulfate; tanning bate.

Puralox. Active aluminum oxide in tablet form; desiccant, catalyst.

Puratized LN. Phenyl mercury organic acid compound; mildew preventive.

Puratized N5D (Puraturf). Phenyl mercuric triethanol ammonium lactate; fungicide.

Puraturf. See Puratized N5D.

Pure-Tan. Quebracho crystals; used in tanning.

Purit. Vegetable decolorizing carbon.

Puritan Filler. White gypsum; filler.

Purite. Fused soda ash; used for desulfurizing and refining iron, steel, etc.

Purol C. Sulfonated castor oil and solvents; emulsifier.

Purogen. See Puerine.

Puro resin. Petroleum hydrocarbon still-residue resin.

Pyagra. Benzol extract of pyrethrum; insecticide.

Pyelosil. See Diodrast.

Pylakrome. Light-fast dye or stain.

Pylumbrin. See Diodrast.

Pynol. Refined pine oil.

Pyralin. Cellulose nitrate plastic.

Pyramidon. Aminopyrine; used in medicine.

Pyrano. Neutral ammonium phosphate; used in flameproofing.

Pyranton A. Diacetone alcohol.

Pyrasteel. Nickel-chromium iron alloys with 4 to 35% nickel, 25% chromium, and low percentages of silicon.

Pyrax. Ground aluminum silicate; filler in paints.

Pyrefume. Standardized concentrated pyrethrum extract; insecticide.

Pyrene. Carbon tetrachloride; fire extinguisher.

Pyrexcel 20. Pyrethrum concentrate; insecticide.

Pyrex glass. Heat-resistant glass composed of silica (80%), boron oxide (12%), sodium oxide and alumina.

Pyridose. Pyridyl mercuric acetate; germicide.

Pyrin. Concentrate of the active principle of pyrethrum and iso-

Composition of Trade-Marked Products

butyl undecylen amide; insecticide.

Pyro. Denatured alcohol; antifreeze.

Pyrobor. Dehydrated borax.

Pyrocarb. See Microcarb.

Pyrocide. Pyrethrum extract.

Pyrofax. Compressed propane gas; used for heating.

Pyrogene. Wash-fast sulfur dye; used for dyeing cotton and rayon.

Pyrol. Borophosphate resin; used in fireproofing textiles.

Pyronite. Trinitrophenyl methyl nitramine.

Pyropel. Sodium borophosphate complex; flameproofing agent.

Pyrosal. Antipyrine acetyl salicylate.

Pyrote. Rotenone-pyrethrum mixture; insecticide.

Q alloy. Steels with 12 to 30% chromium, optional additions up to 23% nickel.

Q. B. Oiticica Oil. Polymerized oiticica oil; used in paint.

Quadrafos. Sodium tetraphosphate; detergent.

Quaker 3-X. Sulfonated pine oil; surface-active agent.

Quaker 700-X. Sulfonated cresylic compound; surface-active agent.

Quaker Dianol D. Sulfonated higher alcohol and aldehyde condensate; wetting agent.

Quaker Pro-So-Tex 55. Aromatic sodium sulfonate; wetting agent for textiles.

Quaker Pro-So-Tex 58. Sulfonated petroleum derivative; wetting agent.

Quaker Pro-So-Tex 75. Alkylated aryl sulfonate; detergent.

Quakester. Higher fatty acid ester; used in textile processing.

Quartol. Oleyl dimethyl ethyl ammonium bromide; used in disinfectant cleaners.

Composition of Trade-Marked Products

Quatresine. Tetradecyl γ-picolinium chloride; antiseptic.

Quellin. Water-soluble starch; used in sizing, finishing textiles.

Quinalgen. 5-Benzamido-8-ethoxyquinoline.

Quinaphenine. Quinine carbophenetidide; used in medicine.

Quinisal. Quinine bisalicylosalicylate; used in medicine.

Quinitol. Cyclohexane-1,4-diol.

Quinoform. Quinine formate.

Quinophan. Cinchophen.

Quinosol. 8-Hydroxyquinoline sulfate; used in medicine.

Quix. Sulfated fatty acid; wetting agent.

Quixite. Sulfonated fatty acid; detergent.

Quixol No. 1. Mixture of denatured anhydrous ethyl alcohol, ethyl acetate and a hydrocarbon; solvent.

R-2 Crystals. Reaction product of carbon disulfide with methylene dipiperidine; rubber accelerator.

Radiactine. Solution of alginate and soap in water; used for textile finishing.

Radianite. Stainless steel containing about 17% chromium, 0.75% carbon; used for cutlery.

Radumine. Oxalic acid.

Raldeine. Methyl ionone; used in perfume.

Ramadux. Solid, water-dispersible paraffin wax compound; used in textile waterproofing.

Ramapo blue. Copper phthalocyanine; pigment.

Ramasit. Paraffin wax emulsion containing aluminum salts; used in textile waterproofing.

Ramasit I. Stabilized paraffin wax emulsion; used in waterproofing textiles.

Ramasol. Paraffin wax emulsion containing inorganic salts; used in textile waterproofing.

Composition of Trade-Marked Products

Ramasol NA. Paraffin wax emulsion with aluminum acetate or formate; waterproofing agent.

Ramol 205. Refined mineral oil.

Ramol PW. Aldehyde condensation product of sulfonated naphthalene; dispersing agent.

Raolin. Chlorinated rubber.

Rapidase. Standardized mixture of amylolytic and proteolytic enzymes; desizing agent.

Rapidazol. Stabilized azoic-naphthol compounds; used for textile printing.

Rapidogen. Stabilized azoic-naphthol dyes; used in textile printing.

Rapidole. Solution of sulfated vegetable oils; used in textile finishing.

Rapidole H. Saponified sulfonated vegetable oils and solvents; surface-active agent.

Raschit. Chlorinated naphthalene.

Rauzene. Synthetic alkyd resin; used in varnish.

Ravolen. Petroleum residue containing unsaturated and aromatic hydrocarbons (British).

Rayamo. Wood cellulose; used in mfg. cellophane.

Raybar. Titanium dioxide and barium sulfate; pigment.

Raycal. Titanium dioxide and calcium sulfate; pigment.

Raymet. Untwisted aluminum yarn.

Raymix. Rayon flock.

Rayol 10, 76, 80. Sulfated vegetable oils; fiber lubricant.

Rayonol L-10. "Soluble" mineral oil; fiber lubricant.

Rayophane. Regenerated cellulose film.

Rayox. Titanium dioxide.

Rayprene. Lead-rubber sheeting; used for protection against X-rays.

Raysil. Titanium dioxide and magnesium silicate; pigment.

Rayspun. Twisted aluminum yarn.

Raywhite. Refined sulfite pulp.

Rectidon. Sodium salt of *sec*-amyl-β-bromallyl barbituric acid; sedative.

Composition of Trade-Marked Products

Redmanol. Phenol-formaldehyde resin.

Redolene (Crystolene). Red oil.

Redoxon. Ascorbic acid.

Redoxyvat. Antioxidant.

Red Star Tungsten Steel. Low-alloy steel with about 1.6% tungsten, 0.90% carbon, and fractional percentages of chromium and vanadium; used for tools, dies.

Reducite. Zinc formaldehyde sulfoxalate; printing-discharge agent.

Redux. Phenol-formaldehyde resin; adhesive.

Refinite. Aluminum silicate; used in water softening.

Reflex P. Potassium titanate; welding-rod coating.

Reflux. Compounds containing rutile (76.9–98%) and small amounts of zircon, silica, etc.; used in welding rod coatings.

Refrasil. Fibrous silica in form of bat or cloth; heat insulator.

Refrax. Recrystallized silicon carbide; lining for furnaces.

Reilit. Cellulose triacetate sheet (German).

Remolgan A. See Emulphor A extra.

Remonol. Resorcinol monoacetate; used in hair treatments.

Renacit. Thio-β-naphthol; rubber softener.

Renacit 3. Anthranyl mercaptan; rubber softener.

Renyx. Die-casting alloys of aluminum-base and of zinc-base type.

Reogen. Compound of mineral oil (80), sulfonated petroleum (15), *n*-butyl alcohol (5); rubber plasticizer.

Reomol E. Alkyl glycol phosphate.

Repasolin. Mixture of phenyl *p*-toluene sulfonate and castor oil; plasticizer (German).

Repcolene. Neutral blend of higher fatty acid esters and aromatic sul-

Composition of Trade-Marked Products

fonates; used in textile finishing.

Repellat. Alkyl pyridinium bisulfate.

Resenoplast. Synthetic tar-acid resin.

Resifin. Water emulsion or dispersion of ureaformaldehyde resin (50%); used for textile finishing.

Resiftal B. Glyptal-type resin (German).

Resiloid 998. Urea-formaldehyde resin; used in textile finishing.

Resilon. Hydrocarbon resin.

Resimene. Melamine-formaldehyde resin or molding powder.

Resimene 801K. Melamine laminating resin.

Resimene 803A. Cellulose filled melamine-formaldehyde plastic molding compound.

Resimene 875. Melamine resin; textile-finishing agent.

Resin C. Semi-solid coal-tar derivative; used in rubber.

Resin MS 2. Cyclic ketone resin; used in varnish.

Resin R-7. Cumarone-indene resin.

Resin VMCH. Tripolymer of vinyl chloride, vinyl acetate and a dicarboxylic acid.

Resinex. Polymerized aromatic resin; rubber softener.

Resinit. Synthetic rubber similar to Thiokol (Russian).

Resinol. Phenol-formaldehyde resin, mixture of rosin (45%) and mineral oil (55%); used in rubber mfg.

Resinox 801, 803, 840. Melamine resin; molding compounds.

Resipol DL. Glyceryl dilactate.

Resipol ML. Glyceryl monolactate.

Resipon. Urea-formaldehyde resin; used for finishing textiles.

Resistac. Alloy consisting of copper, aluminum and iron.

Resistal. Modified aluminum bronze containing about 9% aluminum and 1% iron.

Composition of Trade-Marked Products

Resistox. Aldol-aniline compound; antioxidant for rubber.

Resite. C-stage phenol-aldehyde resin.

Resitol. B-stage phenol-aldehyde resin.

Resloom M-75. Methylol-melamine resin; used in textile finishing.

Resloom resin. Modified melamine-formaldehyde resin; used on textiles.

Resochin. 4-Aminoquinoline; used in medicine.

Resoglaz. Polystyrene resin.

Resol. A-stage phenol-aldehyde resin.

Resolin NCP. Aqueous emulsion of Turkey-red oil and chlorobenzol; textile assistant (Swiss).

Resomil. Water solution of copper ammonium fluoride; used in mildewproofing.

Resynon NS. Water-soluble alkylurea resin; for shrinkage control of rayon and cotton.

Retarder LA. Cetyl dimethyl benzyl ammonium chloride.

Retarder W. Mixture of salicylic acid and a dispersing agent; used to prevent after-vulcanization of rubber products.

Retardex. Mixture of benzoic acid and benzoates; vulcanization-accelerator retarder.

Retardit. Sodium *m*-nitrobenzene sulfonate.

Retardox. Aldehyde-amine condensation product.

Retardsol. Petroleum naphtha; industrial solvent.

Retrol. Acid activated montmorillonite; adsorbent.

Revalon. Copper-base alloy containing about 22% zinc and 2% aluminum; used for tubing.

Revatol S. Sodium *m*-nitrobenzene sulfonate; used in textile dyeing.

Revertex. Concentrated natural rubber latex, containing about 75% dry solids.

Composition of Trade-Marked Products

Revultex. Vulcanized or partially vulcanized rubber latex.

Rewettal. Acetylated hydroxy fatty acid amide; wetting agent.

Rexar. See Penros.

Rex-T-Mo tool steel. High-carbon high-speed alloy containing 8% molybdenum, 4% chromium, 2% tungsten, 1% vanadium; used in tools.

Rex tool steel. High-speed alloy steels containing about 18% tungsten, 4% chromium or cobalt, optionally 1% vanadium, fractional percentages of manganese and silicon.

Rextox. Copper with a layer of cuprous oxide, formed by heat, on the surface.

Rezistal. Stainless steel of the general 18% chromium and 8% nickel type.

Rezoglas. Polystyrene plastic.

Rezo Wax A. Synthetic wax; used in mfg. records.

Rezyl. Modified glycerol phthalate resin; used in coatings.

Rheolan. Pyrolized bitumen; waterproofing agent.

Rheotan. Alloy containing 84% copper, 4% zinc, 12% manganese; used for electrical resistances.

Rheumatin. Saloquinine salicylate; used in medicine.

Rhodaphane. Sheeting of cellulose acetate and plasticizer; used for packaging.

Rhodiant. Rhodium salts; used in electroplating.

Rhodoid. Mixture of triphenyl phosphate (29), *p*-toluene sulfonamide (24), dimethyl phthalate (9) and acetin (37); plasticizer.

Rhodoid. Non-inflammable cellulose acetate compound.

Rhoduline. Basic dye; used for dyeing and printing textiles.

Rhoflax. Mixture of alkyl cellulose ethers; water-soluble thickener.

Composition of Trade-Marked Products

Rhonite. Aqueous solution of urea-formaldehyde resin.

Rhoplex. Emulsion of polymerized acrylic acid ester.

Rhotex. Sodium salt of a polymerized resin; thickening agent.

Rhothane. 1,1-Dichloro-2,2-bis-(*p*-chlorophenyl) ethane; insecticide.

Rhothane D3. Dichlorodiphenyl dichloroethane; insecticide.

Rhovinal E. Polyvinyl formal, triacetin, *p*-toluene sulfonamide, silica and a dye; plastic (German).

Rhozyme. Saccharifying enzyme.

Ribosol. Riboflavin derivative.

Ricement. Mixture of rice hulls and cement; building material.

Rid-O. β,β'-Dithiocyanodiethyl ether; miticide.

Rinsynol. Sodium alkyl naphthalene sulfonate; wetting agent.

Rinsynol 5OL. See Perma Carb.

Risol. Pine oil; used in the flotation process.

Risor. Pine oil; used in the flotation process.

Rivanol. 2-Ethoxy-6,9-diaminoacridine lactate; antiseptic.

Rizimal. Castor oil-maleic anhydride compound; adhesive (German).

Roburite. Smokeless and flameless safety explosive consisting of ammonium nitrate and dinitrobenzene or dinitrochloro benzene; used in mines.

Roccal. Aqueous solution of benzyl trialkonium chloride; bactericide and fungicide.

Rockite. Synthetic tar-acid resin; used in molding and laminating.

Rodalon. Solution of alkyl dimethyl benzyl ammonium chloride (90%); antiseptic.

Rodine. Concentrated, red squill-extract solution; rat poison.

Rohagit. Copolymer of methacrylic acid with either methyl methacrylate or methyl acryl amide.

Rohagit S. Alkali-soluble polymer

Composition of Trade-Marked Products

of methacrylic acid (65%) and methyl methacrylate (35%); adhesive.

Rol-Man steel. High-manganese steel with 11 to 14% manganese, and 1% carbon.

Rongalite C. See Discolite.

Rongalite CW. Rongalite CX with white pigment; dye-reducing agent.

Rongalite CX. $NaHSO_2.CH_2O.2H_2O$; dye-reducing agent.

Ronilla. Polystyrene (German).

Ronopole oil. Sulfated castor oil, neutralized with potash with or without some urea; textile softener.

Ronopole soap. Soap of highly oxidized sulfated castor oil; used in textile finishing.

Rosalamine. Buffered sodium fatty alcohol sulfate; degumming agent.

Rosamine. Phenylated pyronine dye.

Rosanthrene. Azo dye, fast to washing; used on cotton, rayon and silk.

Rosite. Inorganic molding plastic composed of microcrystalline calcium aluminosilicate and asbestos fibers.

Roskol. Sulfated oil and sodium lauryl sulfate; textile softener.

Rosoap A. Sodium oleo-abietate; emulsifier.

Rosopen. Sodium lauryl sulfate; textile penetrant.

Rossaloy. Powdered, natural minerals; used in rubber compounding.

Rotax. Purified mercaptobenzothiazole; accelerator.

Roxenol. Solution of chloroxylenol and terpineol in aqueous-alcoholic soap solution; disinfectant.

Royox. Pine oil and soap; surface-active agent.

Rozeen oil. Rosin oil.

Rozolin. Rosin oil.

RPA No. 1E. Mixture of the double salt of phenylhydrazine and zinc chloride and inert hydrocarbons; softening agent in rubber.

RPA No. 2. Mixture of naphthyl β-mercaptan (33.3%) and inert hydrocarbon (66.7%); plasticizer for rubber.

RPA No. 3. Xylyl mercaptan and an inert hydrocarbon; plasticizer for rubber.

RPA No. 4. Mixture of aryl mercaptans; peptizing (softening) agent for rubber.

Rubberlith. Lithopone.

Rubbersol. Mixture of pine terpenes; rubber softener.

Rubbone. Rubber oxidized under catalytic action of cobalt linoleate; used in varnishes.

Rubinol. Sulfonated coconut oil.

Rubinol. *tert*-Butyl pyrogallol; photographic developer.

Rubite. Rosin oil.

Rub-Sol. Petroleum naphtha; rubber solvent.

Rucopol D. Sodium lauryl sulfate-cyclohexanol dispersion in water; textile assistant (German).

Rufat. Fatty acids produced by hydrogenation of fish or other oils.

Ruffex. Cellulose without nutritional value; used in animal-feeding tests.

Rufite. See Flavite.

Rumetan. Zinc phosphide; rodenticide.

Ruselite. Aluminum-base, die-casting alloy with low percentages of copper, chromium, molybdenum, and titanium.

Rusticon. Special sodium silicate; used in laundry.

Rustone. "Soluble" oil; corrosion inhibitor.

Rutenol. Salt formed from nitroacridine (2) and arsenic trioxide (3); used in chemotherapy.

Rutger's 612. 2-Ethyl hexanediol-1,3; insect repellent.

Rycar steel. Simple steel containing approximately 1% manganese and

Composition of Trade-Marked Products

0.15% carbon; used in screw stock.

Rycolene. Sulfated castor or other oils; dyeing assistant.

Sabacide. Sabadilla-seed concentrate; insecticide.

Sabeco metal. High-lead bronze; used for bearings.

Sabromin. Calcium dibromobehenate; used in medicine.

Safalloy. See Cerrosafe.

Safe-n-lead. Zinc hydrate; insecticide.

Safex. Dinitrophenyl dimethyl thiocarbamyl sulfide; accelerator.

Saflex. Polyvinyl-acetal sheet plastic; interlayer in making safety glass.

Saflex M. Modified polyvinyl butyral and solvents; fabric coating.

Sajodin. Calcium iodobehenate; used in medicine.

Salamac. White brick of compressed pure ammonium chloride; used for soldering.

Salamide. Salicyl amide; used in medicine.

Salethyl. Ethyl salicylate.

Saliformin. Hexamethylenamine salicylate; used in medicine.

Salipyrin. Antipyrine salicylate; used in medicine.

Salitone. Sodium sulfate with formaldehyde; used in setting textile dyes.

Salophen. Acetoaminosalol; used in medicine.

Salp. Sodium antimony lactophenate; insecticide.

Salyrgan. Mersalyl.

Salysal. Salicyl salicylic acid.

Samol. Menthyl salicylate.

Samson steel. Low-alloy steels with approximately 1.25% nickel and 0.60% chromium content.

Sandofix B. Polypropanol polyethanol amine; used in textile processing.

Composition of Trade-Marked Products

Sandoptal. Isobutyl allyl barbituric acid; used in medicine.

Sandoz copper. Composition based on copper hydroxide and a wetting agent; used in viniculture sprays.

Sandozol G. Sulfonated aryl alcohol; surface-active agent.

Sangajol. Petroleum distillate; turpentine substitute (German).

Sanilime. Hydrated lime; used in agriculture.

Saniprene. Hard vulcanized rubber.

Sanocrysin. Gold sodium thiosulfate.

Santicizer B-16. Butyl phthalyl butyl glycollate; solvent for nitrocellulose.

Santicizer E-15. Ethyl phthalyl ethyl glycollate; plasticizer.

Santicizer M-17. Methyl phthalyl ethyl glycollate; plasticizer.

Santicizer 1-H. Cyclohexyl *p*-toluene sulfonamide; plasticizer.

Santicizer 3. N-ethyl *p*-toluene sulfonamide; plasticizer.

Santicizer 8. Mixture of *o*- and *p*-N-toluene ethyl sulfonamides; plasticizer.

Santicizer 9. Mixture of *o*- and *p*-toluene sulfonamides; plasticizer.

Santicizer 10. *o*-Cresyl *p*-toluene sulfonate; plasticizer.

Santicizer 131. N-Isopropyl benzene toluene sulfonamide; plasticizer.

Santicizer 140. Phenyl cresyl phosphate; plasticizer.

Santobane. DDT.

Santobrite. Sodium pentachlorophenate; industrial preservative.

Santocel. Silica aerogel; heat-insulating agent.

Santochlor. *p*-Dichlorobenzene; used in deodorizing.

Santocure. N-cyclohexyl 2-benzothiazole sulfenamide.

Santoflex A. Mixture of a ketone amine with diphenyl *p*-phenylene diamine; antioxidant.

Santoflex B. Condensation product

Composition of Trade-Marked Products

of acetone and *p*-aminodiphenyl; rubber antioxidant.

Santoflex BX. Blend of Santoflex B and diphenyl *p*-phenylene diamine; rubber antioxidant.

Santol. Sulfated alkyl alcohol; wetting agent.

Santolite. Synthetic resin formed by condensation of toluol sulfonamides and formaldehyde; plasticizer.

Santolite K. Sulfonamide-aldehyde alkyl resin; plasticizer.

Santolite MHP. Sulfonamide-aldehyde resin; plasticizer.

Santolite MS. Condensation product of formaldehyde and aromatic sulfonamides; plasticizer.

Santol S. Solution of substituted aromatic sulfonic acid; textile wetting agent.

Santol T. Solution of substituted aromatic sulfonic acid; wetting agent.

Santolube 303-A. Wax-phenol compound containing combined baium and sulfur; detergent additive for lubricants.

Santolube 31. High-molecular weight alkyl phenyl phosphate; antioxidant for lubricants.

Santolube 261. Sulfurized tin salt of an alkyl phenol carboxylic acid; additive for crank-case oils.

Santomerse. Salt of substituted aromatic sulfonic acid; wetting agent.

Santomerse D. Decyl benzene sodium sulfonate; wetting agent.

Santomerse S. Aqueous solution of Santomerse D; wetting agent.

Santomerse No. 1. Alkyl aryl sodium sulfonate; wetting agent.

Santomerse No. 2. Inorganic salt of substituted aromatic sulfonic acid; wetting agent.

Santomerse No. 3. Dodecyl benzene sodium sulfonate; wetting agent.

Santomerse 43. Amine salt of dodecyl benzene sulfonic acid; wetting agent.

Composition of Trade-Marked Products

Santomerse 43P. Salt of dodecyl benzene phosphinic acid; emulsifier.

Santophen 7. Benzyl phenol; insecticide.

Santophen 20. Pentachlorophenol; industrial preservative.

Santoresin. Synthetic petroleum resin.

Santosite. Technical anhydrous sodium sulfite; used to remove oxygen from water.

Santotan KR. Product containing $Cr_2(SO_4)_2(OH)_2$ (about 50%); used in tanning.

Santovar A. Alkylated polyhydroxy phenol; varnish-anti-skimming agent.

Santovar-O. Alkylated polyhydroxyphenol; rubber antioxidant.

Santowax M. *m*-Diphenyl benzene; used in waxing citrus fruits.

Santowax MH. Hydrogenated Santowax M; plasticizer.

Santowax OH. Hydrogenated *o*-terphenyl; plasticizer.

Santowhite. Polyalkylated phenol monosulfide; non-discoloring antioxidant for rubber.

Santyl. Santalol salicylate; used in medicine.

Sapamine. Trimethyl β-oleamidoethyl ammonium sulfate; cationic wetting agent.

Sapamine A. Diethyl aminoethyl oleyl amide acetate; leveling agent in textiles.

Sapamine CH. N-diethyl aminoethyl oleyl amide hydrochloride; detergent.

Sapamine FL. Sulfonate of a complex octadecyl-alkyl compound; used in the dye bath.

Sapamine KW. Diethyl aminoethyl stearyl amide hydroacetate; cation-active fixing agent for direct dyes.

Sapapine. "Soluble" pine oil; detergent.

Saphal. Sodium lauryl sulfate, lauryl

Composition of Trade-Marked Products

alcohol (total—30%) with sodium salts and water; textile assistant (German).

Sapidan. Solution of a sulfated fatty alcohol.

Sapolene. Red oil.

Saran. Polyvinylidene chloride plastic.

Saran B. Copolymer of vinylidene chloride and vinyl chloride.

Saratoga steel. Non-deforming steel containing approximately 1.5% manganese, 0.50% chromium, 0.40% tungsten or molybdenum and 0.90% carbon.

Sarelon. Textile fiber made from peanut protein.

Satco metal. Alloy with about 97% lead, remainder primarily tin and the alkali and alkaline-earth metals; used for bearings.

Savelon. Peanut-protein textile fiber.

Saxin. Saccharin.

Scarab. Urea-formaldehyde plastic.

Scarat. Synthetic urea resin.

Sclerolac. Solvent-extracted shellac.

Scleron. Aluminum-base alloy, containing 12% zinc, 3% copper, 0.5% silicon, 0.2% manganese, 0.1% lithium.

SD-5. Carbon black; used in printing inks.

SDO. Polymerized divinyl acetylene in a hydrocarbon solvent; vehicle in paints.

Secal. Partial higher fatty acid esters of glycerol; acid-stabilized emulsifier.

Sec-A-Sil. Silica gel; dehumidifier.

Sedatin. Isovaleryl *p*-phenetidine; used in medicine.

Sedormid. Allyl isopropyl acetyl carbamide; sedative.

Seedine. Mixture of higher fatty acids, with 20% wool fat; used in rubber compounding.

Sekurit P. Composition of Mersolat (19.1), sodium lauryl sulfate (8.8), monosodium phosphate (5.4), sodium sulfate and chloride (39.9 total), water (27.4); textile assistant (German).

Composition of Trade-Marked Products

Selenac. Selenium diethyl dithiocarbamate; vulcanizing agent.

Self-lub. Compacted, powdered iron, impregnated with oil.

Selinon. $C_6H_2CH_3(NO_2)_2.ONa$; insecticide base (German).

Sellogen. Sodium alkyl aryl sulfonate; wetting agent.

Sellogen C. Higher fatty alcohol sulfate; wetting agent.

Selloxine 52. Dichloromelamine.

Selocide. Composition based on potassium ammonium selenosulfide; insecticide.

Semesan. Product consisting of hydroxymercurichlorophenol (30%) and inert filler (70%); seed fungicide.

Semesan Bel. Product consisting of hydroxymercurinitrophenol (12%), hydroxymercurichlorophenol (2%), and inert material (86%); seed fungicide.

Semesan Jr. Ethyl mercury phosphate; corn-seed fungicide.

Semesan Special. Sodium salts of hydroxymercuricresol and hydroxymercuriphenol; turf fungicide.

Seminex. Carbon black.

Seminole steel. Tool steel with approximately 0.5% carbon, 2% tungsten, 1.4% chromium, and 0.2% vanadium.

Septasin. *p*-Benzyl aminobenzene sulfonamide; antioxidant.

Septol. Sodium 2,4,5-trichlorophenate with formaldehyde; antiseptic.

Seraceta. Cellulose acetate yarn.

Seravon. Polyhydric alcohol partial higher fatty acid esters; dyeing assistant.

Serenium. 2,4-Diamino-4′-ethoxyazobenzene hydrochloride.

Serichrome. Chrome dye; used for silk.

Composition of Trade-Marked Products

Sericose LCD extra. Cellulose acetate compound; used in textile printing.

Seriken. Emulsion of higher aliphatic alcohols and their high fatty acid monoesters; scrooping agent.

Serisol. Sulfonated olive oil; textile-finishing agent.

Serisolve. Red-oil soap; silk-degumming agent.

Serizyme. Proteolytic enzyme; used in desizing fabrics containing protein sizing.

Seronex. Glycol monooleate sodium soap; textile detergent.

Seroseal. Emulsion of paraffin wax and aluminum acetate or formate; waterproofing agent.

Serseal. Black petroleum wax compounds.

Serval. Asphalt-impregnated asbestos-fiber felt.

Servital O1. Mixture of Emulphor MW (66.6), mineral oil (33.3) and C_6–C_9 fatty acids (0.5).

Setacyl. Direct dye; used for cellulose acetate.

Setilon 315. Sodium lauryl sulfate-dextrin mixture (German).

Sextol. Methyl cyclohexanol; plasticizer.

Sextol lactate. Methyl cyclohexanol lactate.

Sextone. Cyclohexanone.

Sextone B. Methyl cyclohexanone.

Seymourite. Copper-base alloy containing approximately 18% nickel, 18% zinc.

Shakudo. Copper-base alloy containing approximately 4% gold and 1% silver; used for ornamental purposes.

Sheenol. Emulsion of synthetic resin; used on leather, wood, metal to give a lustrous coating.

Sheerset Resin. See Lacet Resin.

Shellacol. Denatured alcohol.

Shell carbon. Soft carbon black.

Shell solvents. Petroleum solvents.

Composition of Trade-Marked Products

Sher-dye. Pigment or dye colloidally dispersed in a solution of synthetic resin; used in textile printing.

Sheroline. White, mineral-oil jelly; used in creams, ointments.

Sherosine. Ceresine wax; used in creams, polishes.

Sherosope. Sodium sulfonaphthenate; emulsifying agent.

Sherowax. Amorphous petroleum wax; used in creams, polishes.

Shirlan. Salicyl anilide; used for mothproofing and mildewproofing textiles.

Shopal. Modified starch; used in printing gums.

Sicapon. Fermented lignin extract solution; binder in cements.

Siccal S. See Impregnole.

Sicoid. See Celon.

Sicromal. Series of low-sulfur, low-phosphorus iron-base alloys with aluminum and chromium as the alloying elements.

Sicromo steel. Low-alloy steel with approximately 2.5% chromium, 0.5% molybdenum, and up to 0.15% carbon; used for still and condenser tubes.

Sidac. Regenerated cellulose film.

Sideraphite. Acid-resistant, iron-base alloy, containing approximately 23% nickel, 5% aluminum, 5% copper, and 4% tungsten.

Sidonal. Piperazine quinate.

Siemensit. Electro-cast chrome-spinel refractory.

Sigal. Silicon-aluminum compound.

Sigmaform. Bismuth tribromophenate; used in medicine.

Signal bronze. High-copper phosphor bronze containing approximately 1.8% tin.

Silal. Heat-resistant cast iron containing approximately 5% silicon.

Silanca. Silver of at least 92.5% silver content hardened with 4% antimony, 1 to 3% cadmium and up to 2.5% zinc.

Composition of Trade-Marked Products

Silanic. Organic silicon compound (British).

Silastic. Elastic organo-silicon-oxide high polymer.

Silberol. Silver phenol sulfonate.

Silcalite. Calcium metasilicate.

Silcaride. Silicon carbide; abrasive.

Silcaz alloy. Boron-containing master alloy with 35 to 40% silicon, about 10% titanium, 10% calcium, 7% aluminum, 4% zirconium and 0.5% boron; used for increasing the hardenability of steel.

Silcrome. High-chromium steels containing up to 0.20% carbon, up to 28% chromium, approximately 1% silicon, 1% copper, optionally up to 11% nickel and 3% molybdenum.

Silenan. Camphor sulfonic acid salt of sulfanilamide.

Silenc. Precipitated hydrated calcium silicate; pigment.

Silester. Ethyl silicate and other esters (British).

Sil-Fos. Alloy of silver, copper and phosphorus.

Silical. Aluminum silicate; rubber filler.

Silimite. Magnesia lime.

Silkonol. Sulfonated neatsfoot oil; used in textile finishing.

Silkovan. Mixture of animal glue (60%) and partially saponified polyacrylic-nitrile resin (40%); textile sizing (German).

Silmac. Sodium silicate.

Silmalec. Aluminum alloy with 0.6% magnesium, 1% silicon.

Silmanal. Magnetic alloy of silver, manganese, and alumin.

Sil-man steel. Steel with approximately 2% silicon, 0.3% vanadium, 0.3% chromium and 0.60% carbon.

Sil-O-Cel. A heat-insulating material made from diatomaceous earth.

Silox. Silica-silicon carbide; heat insulator.

Composition of Trade-Marked Products

Siloxicon. Silicon carbide; refractory.

Sil-ten steel. Steel containing 0.60 to 0.90% manganese and 0.20 to 0.30% silicon, up to 0.20% copper may be added for corrosion resistance.

Silumin. Aluminum-base alloy containing up to 14% silicon.

Siluminite. Dielectric made from cement and asbestos impregnated with oil or bitumen.

Silvatol. Pine-oil soap solution; detergent for grease and tar.

Silvaz alloy. Alloy with 35 to 40% silicon, about 10% titanium, 10% vanadium, 6% aluminum, 6% zirconium, and 0.5% boron.

Silvol. Protein silver.

Sil-X. Ferrosilicon; used in making special steels.

Simanal. Iron alloy containing 18 to 22% silicon, 16 to 20% manganese and 18 to 22% aluminum; deoxidizer in steel making.

Simmonds steel. Steel containing 15 to 25% chromium and 20 to 35% nickel.

Sinox. Aqueous paste of sodium dinitro-*o*-cresylate; weed killer.

Sinteel G. Compressed, powdered steel infiltrated with molten copper alloy.

Sintol T. 2,6-Dimethyl thianthrene.

Siolite. Silica gel; flatting agent for varnish.

Sipalin AOC. Dicyclohexyl adipate; plasticizer.

Sipalin AOM. Dimethyl cyclohexyl adipate; plasticizer.

Sipalin MOM. Dimethyl cyclohexyl methyl adipate.

Sipilite. Synthetic tar-acid resin.

Sirvene. Composition of synthetic oil-resistant elastomers; used in molded mechanical packings.

Sitapon L30. Sulfated fatty alcohols; used in textile finishing (Swiss).

Sitol. Sodium salt of *m*-nitrobenzene

Composition of Trade-Marked Products

sulfonic acid; mild oxidant for use in dyeing.

Sixide (Lexone). Benzene hexachloride; insecticide.

Skellysolve. Industrial petroleum naphtha solvents.

Skiabaryt. Mixture of barium sulfate (85%) with sugar, tragacanth, cacao and a flavor; used for X-ray diagnosis.

Skiodan. Sodium iodomethane sulfonate.

Slayz-Weed. Compound with 2-4D (70%); weed killer.

Sliwopon. Mixture of sodium lauryl sulfate (27.5), lauryl alcohol (7.3), sodium sulfate (10.2), water (55); textile assistant (Polish).

Smenol. Commercial sodium lauryl sulfate; textile assistant (German).

Smithco steel. Low-alloy machine steels containing 0.80% to 1.35% manganese, 0.50% to 1.20% nickel, 0.40% to 0.75% chromium and up to 0.75% silicon.

S Monel. Monel metal containing approximately 4% silicon as an additional constituent.

SMZ alloy. Alloy consisting of 60 to 78% silicon, 5 to 8% manganese and 5 to 8% zirconium.

Snofibre. Talc.

Sno-Float. Whiting.

Snofos. Monocalcium phosphate; used in baking powder.

Snowcrete. Very light-colored Portland cement.

Snowflake crystals. Sodium sesquicarbonate.

Snowflake soldering salts. Product containing $ZnCl_2$ and NH_4Cl; flux in soldering.

Snow White Filler. Anhydrous calcium sulfate.

Soamin. Sodium arsanilate.

Soapotol. Salt of sulfonated higher fatty amide; wetting agent.

Sobenate. Specially refined sodium benzoate; preservative.

Composition of Trade-Marked Products

Sodatol. Mixture of sodium nitrate and TNT; used in military explosives.

Sodite. Sodium arsenite; insecticide.

Sodium Catex. Carbonaceous and resinous zeolites; ion-exchange resins.

Softenol AA. Sulfated castor oil; used in textile finishing.

Softol AD. Cationic amine salt of a fatty acide amide; used in textile finishing.

Soilime. Lime residue from cyanamide; used in fertilizers.

Soiliron. Iron sulfate; used in fertilizers.

Solaesthin. Methylene chloride.

Solagen. Manganese or cobalt salts of higher fatty acids; paint drier (German).

Solargentum. Compound of silver and gelatin; used in medicine.

Solarson. Ammonium chloroheptene arsonate; used in medicine.

Solar steel. Steel containing approximately 1% silicon, 0.5% molybdenum, and 0.5% carbon; used in tools.

Solbar. Mixture of sulfur and barium sulfide.

Solbrol. Methyl *p*-hydroxybenzoate; preservative.

Solbrol M. Methyl *p*-hydroxybenzoate; preservative.

Solbrol P. Propyl *p*-hydroxybenzoate; preservative.

Solcastol. Sulfated castor oil.

Solcod. Sulfonated cod oil; used in leather stuffing.

Solcornol. Sulfonated corn oil.

Solfosol. Sodium sulfide; used in tanning.

Solganal. Disodium 4-sulfomethyl amino-2-auromercaptobenzene 1-sulfonate.

Solidogen K. Quaternary ammonium salt; used in textile finishing.

Soligen. Metallic naphthenate; paint drier.

Composition of Trade-Marked Products

Solinox. Hydroxylated linseed oil; used in varnish.

Soliol. Refined sodium petroleum sulfonate; detergent.

Solite. Sodium hexametaphosphate.

Solka-Fil. Wood-cellulose pulp; filler.

Solka-Floc. Fibrous purified wood cellulose; used in rubber compounding.

Sol Naphtha. Petroleum solvent.

Solox. Alcohol denatured with aviation gasoline (1) and ethyl acetate (5) per 100 gal. alcohol; solvent.

Solozone. Sodium peroxide powder.

Solpon W. Commercial ammonium lauryl sulfate; textile assistant (German).

Solros. Wood rosin.

Solstock. "Soluble" mineral oil; spinning oil.

Sol-U-Bon. Sodium formate; dyeing assistant.

Solugel. Gelatin compound; textile sizing.

Solux. (*p*-Hydroxyphenyl) morproline; antioxidant.

Solvadine NC. Alkyl aryl sulfonate; textile wetting agent.

Solvadine R. Sodium aryl alkyl ether sulfate; detergent.

Solvamin. Natural riboflavin; used in pharmaceutical and food products.

Solvamyl. Concentrated proteolytic enzyme; substitute for malt diastase.

Solvar. Polyvinyl alcohol.

Solvay Fluf. Light soda ash.

Solvenol. Mixture of monocyclic terpenes.

Solvenon B. 1,3-Butylene glycol formal; used in lacquers.

Solvesso. Petroleum naphtha.

Solvex. Creosote oil.

Solvit. Diacetyl tartaric acid ester of a monoglyceride; surface-active agent.

Solvit A. Fatty acid ester of a polyhydroxycarboxylic acid; emulsifier.

Composition of Trade-Marked Products

Solvoplast. Dimethyl cyclohexyl oxalate; plasticizer.

Solvose. Amylolytic and proteolytic enzymes; degumming agent.

Sonneryl. See Neonal.

Sopanox. Amino compound; antioxidant for soap.

Sopet. Aqueous solution of sodium potassium ethyl phosphate (60%); fiber lubricant.

Sophol. Silver methylene nucleate; antiseptic.

Sopronol. Sodium propionate; fungicide.

Soramin. See Soromin.

Sorban. Aqueous solution containing sorbitol (83%).

Sorbinol SF. Sulfonated oil compound; wetting agent.

Sorbit AC. Sodium alkyl naphthalene sulfonate; wetting agent.

Sorbitol B. Mixture of sorbitol (70%), glucose (10%) and water (20%).

Sorbo. Aqueous solution containing *d*-sorbitol (70%).

Sorbo-Cel. Diatomaceous silica; filter aid.

Sorbotex. Mixture of cholesterol, other higher fatty alcohols and polyhydroxy alcohol-fatty acid esters; absorption base.

Sorbotex 301. Higher fatty alcohols and their long-chain fatty acid esters in a petrolatum base; absorption base.

Soromin. Polyethylene stearate containing sodium soap; used in rayon finishing (German).

Soromin A. Triethanol amine stearate; used in softening finish for rayon hosiery.

Soromin A.F. Diethanol amine monostearate with ethylene oxide; used in textile softening.

Soromin B.S. Stearyl diguanide with Emulphor O; used in textile finishing.

Composition of Trade-Marked Products

Soromin FFB. Polyester of adipinic acid (German).

Soromin S.G. Hexaglycol monostearate; textile softening agent.

Sovasol. Petroleum naphtha; solvent.

Sovprene. Synthetic rubber corresponding to Neoprene (Russian).

Soyalene. Fast-bodying processed soybean oil; used in varnish.

Soya Solinox. Hydroxylated soybean oil; used in varnish.

Soyate. Metallic salts of soybean oil; paint driers.

Soyco. Soybean protein of minimum fat content; albumin substitute.

Soylon. Textile fiber derived from soybean.

SP-315. Sodium petroleum sulfonate; emulsifying agent.

Span. Polyhydric alcohol anhydride partial higher fatty acid ester; emulsifying agent.

Span 20. Sorbitan monolaurate; emulsifying agent.

Span 40. Sorbitan monopalmitate; emulsifying agent.

Span 60. Sorbitan monostearate; emulsifying agent.

Span 80. Sorbitan monooleate; emulsifying agent.

Span 85. Sorbitan trioleate; emulsifying agent.

Speco. Solid sal ammoniac; soldering flux.

Speedi-Dri. Fuller's earth; absorbent.

Spensol. Aqueous solution of ammonium nitrate (55.5–66.8%) and anhydrous ammonia (16.6–26.0%); fertilizer.

Spergon. Tetrachloro-*p*-benzoquinone; seed disinfectant.

Spermafol. Sperm-oil fatty acids derivative.

Spermotol. Hydrogenated fish or vegetable oil.

Spirocid. See Stovarsol.

Spiroform. Phenyl acetyl salicylate.

Spirosal. Glycol salicylate.

Composition of Trade-Marked Products

Spongex. Resilient, spongy, blown rubber.

Spray Cop. Basic copper sulfate; fungicide.

Spred-Rite. Liquid potassium fish-oil soap; insecticide spreader.

Sprodamine. Sulfated higher fatty acid amide; textile-scouring agent.

Sprodcoscour 17. Sulfated higher fatty acid amide; degumming agent.

Sprodcosol WA. Sulfated ricinoleic acid ester; wetting agent.

Sprodex AD, HSB. Cationic amine; textile softener.

Spry (Dexo; Boontex). Partially hydrogenated vegetable oil; shortening.

SRA dye. Water-insoluble dye dispersed in water with sulforicinoleic acid.

SRA No. 1. Mixture of MBT and DPG; rubber accelerator.

SRA No. 2. Chemically activated benzothiazole; vulcanization accelerator.

S.R.O. Tar oil; used in reclaiming rubber.

Stabilide. Potassium iodide stabilized with calcium stearate.

Stabilit. Hard vulcanized rubber.

Stabilite. Diphenyl ethylene diamine; rubber antioxidant.

Stabilite Alba. Ditolyl ethylene diamine; antioxidant.

Stabilite-L. Diphenyl propylene diamine; antioxidant for rubber.

Stabilizer No. 1. Isopropyl cresol.

Stablex A. Naphthalene sulfonate; wetting agent.

Stablex B. Sodium salt of sulfonic acid; dispersing agent.

Stablex C. Naphthalene sulfonic acid; wetting agent.

Stablex G. Sulfonate of petroleum hydrocarbons; wetting agent.

Staclor. Chlorinated paraffin; plasticizer for rubber.

Stacol. Sodium borophosphate com-

Composition of Trade-Marked Products

plex; used in water-soluble coatings.

Stafast. α-Naphthalene acetic acid with a wetting agent and adhesive; agricultural hormone spray.

STA gloss steel. Corrosion-resistant steels containing 12 to 18% chromium, and 0.4 to 0.6% carbon.

Stainex. Corrosion-resistant, 13 to 17% chromium steels, with carbon content from 0.1 to 0.65%.

Stalite. Isoheptene and β-naphthyl amine; antioxidant in rubber.

Stamikol. Polythioplast; used in rubber compounding.

Standard Neozone. Mixture of *m*-toluylene diamine, phenyl α-naphthyl amine and stearic acid; used in rubber.

Stanisol. Petroleum naphtha; solvent.

Stanley steel. Corrosion-resistant high-chromium steels with nickel content optional up to 9%.

Stannochlor. Anhydrous stannous chloride.

Stannoil. Sulfated castor oil with ethylene dichloride; leather penetrant.

Stanodex. Mixture of maltose, soluble dextrins and small amounts of other sugars.

Stanofill. Mixture of soluble dextrins and maltose.

Stanolax. Refined mineral oil; used in medicine.

Stanolene. Purified white petrolatum.

Stanreduce. Alloy of antimony and iron; used in chemical analysis.

Stantol. See Elgetol.

Stanwax. Paraffin wax.

Star-Zenith tool steel. High-carbon tool steel containing approximately 18% tungsten, 4% chromium and 1% vanadium.

Statex. Carbon black; used in rubber.

Staybelite. Resin obtained from the partially and completely hydrogenated acid and non-acid constituents of rosin; used in adhesives.

Staybelite ester No. 1. Ethylene glycol ester of hydrogenated rosin.

Staybelite ester No. 2. Diethylene glycol ester of hydrogenated rosin.

Staybelite ester No. 10. Glycerol ester of hydrogenated rosin.

Staybrite. Series of stainless steels of the chromium-nickel type with 18% chromium, and 8% nickel (British).

Staybwood. Dimensionally stabilized wood.

Staypak. Hardened, toughened and dimensionally stabilized wood made by heating moistened wood and compressing it to twice the normal density.

Stearax (H.O.S. Wax). Hydrogenated stearine.

Stearex. Stearic acid.

Stearinall WS. Mixture of sulfated and saponified fats; used in textile finishing.

Stearite. Technical stearic acid.

Stearol. Natural, refined palmitic-stearic acid mixture; used in cosmetics.

Stearonyx. Copper ammonium fluoride; wetting agent.

Stearonyx 8. Copper ammonium carbonate; fungicide.

Stearosol. Stearic acid and soap; textile softener.

Stearyl Sapamine Base. Diethyl aminoethyl stearyl amide; surface-active agent.

Steenol. Octadecanol.

Stellon. See Kallodent.

Stenol. Mixture of stearyl and cetyl alcohols; emulsifying agent.

Stenolat. Sodium salt of sulfated stearyl alcohol.

Stentor steel. Steel containing approximately 1.5% manganese and 0.9% carbon.

Steri-Chlor. Mixture of sulfon chlor-

Composition of Trade-Marked Products

amide and chloramine-T; disinfectant.

Sterilan. Aluminum fluoride composition; used in mothproofing.

Sterlite. Copper-base alloy containing 25% nickel, 20% zinc and fractional percentages of manganese, iron and silicon.

Sterotex. Waxy hydrogenated vegetable oil.

Sterox. Polyethylene oxide-fatty acid condensation product; detergent.

Stetaroline. Mixture of sulfonated animal and mineral oils; used in lubricating leather.

Stibophen. Sodium antimony bispyrocatechol-3,5-disulfonate; used in medicine.

Stilbamidine. Diaminostilbene.

Stilronate. Diethyl stilbestrol dipropionate.

Stimtox. Activated, fortified pyrethrum powder; insecticide.

Stipolac. Iodeikon.

Stixo. Sodium silicate; adhesive.

Stoodite. Iron alloy with approximately 35% chromium; used for hard-facing welding rods.

Stovarsol (Acetarsone). Acetyl aminohydroxyphenyl arsonic acid; used in medicine.

Stramid. Sulfanilamide.

Streptocide. Sulfanilamide.

Stressite. Compacted powdered copper-base and iron-base alloys.

Strex. Elastic cotton fabric, made by twisting fibers into coiled spring shape.

Stripper Y. Aqueous solution of titanous sulfate, used for removing dyes from textiles.

Stroba Wax. Modified synthetic glyceride wax; used in records.

Strodex D. Aqueous paste of sulfated higher fatty acid amide; wetting agent.

Stymer. Styrene-maleic anhydride copolymer; textile finish.

Stypticin. Cotarnine hydrochloride.

Composition of Trade-Marked Products

Styptol. Cotarnine phthalate.

Styraloy. Rubber-like plastic made from styrene and butadiene.

Styramic. Polystyrene-plastic molding compound.

Styramic HT. Polydichlorostyrene plastic.

Styresin H. Styrene-phenol resin; used in lacquers.

Styroflex. Thin polystyrene film.

Styrofoam. Aerated light-weight multi-cellular polystyrene plastic.

Styron. Polystyrene.

Styronal B. Copolymer of styrene and butyl maleate.

Styronil. Copolymer of styrene and acrylonitrile.

Subenon. Calcium double salt of benzoic acid and succinc acid benzylester; used in medicine.

Subsidol. See Neutralin.

Suchar. Activated carbon; used in decolorizing.

Sucrol. See Glycosine.

Sudan. Azo dye; used for coloring fats, oils, waxes, etc.

Sudan G. See Sudan red III (A).

Sudan red III (A). Tetrazobenzene β-naphthol; used for coloring oils.

Sulchlor. Sulfurized and chlorinated oil; used in cutting oils.

Sulfaethan. Methyl oxyethyl amide of methane sulfonic acid (German).

Sulfamezathine. Sulfadimethyl pyrimidine; used in medicine.

Sulfamine. Sulfated amine; detergent.

Sulfamyd. Sulfacetamide.

Sulfamylon. Sulfabenzamine; used in medicine.

Sulfan A. Partially stabilized sulfur trioxide; used in sulfonating.

Sulfan B. Stabilized sulfur trioxide.

Sulfan C. Unstabilized sulfur trioxide.

Sulfanole. Fatty amide sodium sulfonate; detergent.

Sulfanole K. Sulfated fatty amide

Composition of Trade-Marked Products

and an organic solvent; emulsifier.

Sulfanole PB. Sulfated fatty amide; emulsifier, detergent.

Sulfanthrene. Thioindigoid; vat dye.

Sulfarsenol. Sulfarsphenamine.

Sulfasan. Diethyl xanthogen; rubber vulcanizing agent.

Sulfasuxidine. Succinyl sulfathiazole; used in medicine.

Sulfatate. Sodium salt of sulfonated hydrocarbon; wetting agent.

Sulfathalidine. Phthalyl sulfathiazole; used in medicine.

Sulfex. Fatty acid amide sulfonate.

Sulfindone. Sulfur dye.

Sulfogen. Fused mixture of sulfur (80–90%) and iron oxide (10–20%); on ignition liberates SO_2 for fumigation.

Sulfogene. Sulfur color; used in dyeing cotton.

Sulfolane (Sulfolene). Thiocyclopentane 1-dioxide.

Sulfonated Luxolene. Fatty ester sulfonate; surface-active agent.

Sulfosol. Sodium sulfide.

Sulfo Turk S. Sodium salt of sulfonated hydrocarbons; wetting agent.

Sulfovin. Liquid sulfur dioxide.

Sulfoxite. Sodium sulfoxylate.

Sulfoxite C. Sodium sulfoxylate formaldehyde.

Sulfoxite S Conc. Zinc sulfoxylate formaldehyde.

Sulframin. Alkyl aminosulfate; detergent.

Sulforon. Wettable sulfur; fungicide.

Sulmet. Sulfamethazine preparation; bactericide for poultry.

Sulmor. Plasticized sulfur.

Sulphon. Acid dye; used on wool and silk.

Sulphonamide P. Sulfanilamide.

Sulphopet. Petroleum sulfonate.

Sulpine. Sulfate-process wood turpentine; solvent.

Sulprene. See Kempol.

Composition of Trade-Marked Products

Sulrote. Rotenone-sulfur dust; insecticide.

Sulvinite. Ethyl chlorosulfonate.

Sumet bronze. Copper-lead alloy with up to 30% lead and (optionally) up to 5% tin; used for bearings.

Sunaptic acid. Mixture of oil and naphthenic acid; used in Neoprene latex.

Suncole. Low-temperature coke; used in making gas.

Sundora. Cellulose acetate sheeting.

Sunoco spirits. Petroleum naphtha; solvent.

Sunolith. Lithopone; pigment.

Sunscreen No. 2. Menthyl anthranilate; used in sun-tan preparations.

Sunwax 1290. Microcrystalline petroleum wax; used in moistureproofing.

Super Alkali. Soda ash.

Super-Beckacite. Pure, phenolic synthetic resin.

Superchrome. Mordant acid dye.

Superclear. Refined clarified solution of natural gums; thickener for printing textiles.

Superdex. Starch solution; used for sizing and finishing textiles.

Super-Filtchar. Activated carbon.

Super Filtrol. Activated clay.

Supergel T.B. Soluble terpene sulfonate; surface-active agent.

Superglycerin. Solution of glycerin (21.8), sugar (23.6), sodium lactate (8.4) and water (43); glycerin substitute (German).

Superlan. Light-fast acid color; used for dyeing wool.

Superlith. Zinc sulfide; pigment.

Superloid. Ammonium alginate; surface-active agent.

Superoxol. Hydrogen peroxide (30%).

Super-Sol. See Insecti-Sol.

Super-spruce extract. Refined

Composition of Trade-Marked Products

spruce-lignin extract; used in tanning.

Supersulfate F.S. Powder. Sulfated aryl alcohol; wetting agent.

Supertex gum. Clarified solution of natural gum; thickener in textile printing.

Supertone. Pure gas-black; pigment.

Supralan G.L. Mixture of sodium naphthalene sulfonate (27), trichlorethylene (12) and water (58); wetting agent (German).

Suprarenin. Adrenalin.

Supraresen. Synthetic tar-acid resin.

Supratol. Highly sulfated vegetable oil; used in degumming.

Supremo. Lard oil; lubricant.

Supremus tool steel. Steel with approximately 18% tungsten, 4% chromium, 1.5% vanadium and (optionally) 1% molybdenum.

Suprex clay. Hydrous aluminum silicate; rubber filler.

Suprex white. Precipitated calcium carbonate; rubber filler.

Suprifen. *p*-Oxyephedrine hydrochloride; used in medicine.

Surfax T.R. Solution of sodium alkyl aryl sulfonate; dyeing assistant.

Surfex. Treated calcium carbonate; pigment.

Surgaloy. Heat-treated chromium-nickel alloy steel.

Surpasol. Mixture of sulfonated oils, esters and alcohols; surface-active agent.

Suspendite. Activated colloidal clay.

Suspenso. Precipitated calcium carbonate.

Suspensone. Highly activated colloidal clay; emulsifying agent.

Sweetaloy. High-chrome and nickel-chrome steels of the corrosion-resistant and stainless type.

Sweetose. Enzyme-converted corn syrup; used in food.

Swiss Gum. See Gelatin Gum.

Syan blue. Copper phthalocyanine; pigment.

Composition of Trade-Marked Products

Sycose. Saccharin.

Sylphane. Transparent, regenerated cellulose sheet.

Sylphrap. Cellophane.

Sylplast. Urea-formaldehyde plastic molding compound.

Sympatol. Acetic acid salt of *p*-methyl aminoethanol phenol; used in medicine.

Synasol. Denatured alcohol.

Syncrolite. Cryolite.

Syndolag. Rice-size clinkered dolomite; used in the electric furnace.

Sylene oil. Sulfated castor oil with formaldehyde; dye assistant.

Synolac. Glyptal resin; used in lacquers.

Synourin. Dehydrated castor oil; used in varnish (French).

Syntellac. Synthetic tar-acid resin.

Syntex. Synthetic tar-acid, alkyd or urea resin.

Syntex M. Sodium glyceryl monolaurate sulfate; detergent.

Synthane. Synthetic tar-acid resin.

Synthe-Copal. Ester gum.

Synthenol. Dehydrated castor oil; used in varnish.

Synthetex 500, 560. Soya protein; used in textile sizing.

Synthin. Mixture of hydrocarbons; synthetic petroleum.

Synthol. Motor fuel (German).

Synthracene. Anthraquinone dye.

Synthralizarine. Anthraquinone acid dye.

Synthraquinone. Anthraquinone dye.

Syntropan. $C_6H_5CH(CH_2OH)COOCH_2C(CH_3)_2CH_2N(C_2H_5)_2.H_3PO_4$; used in medicine.

Synvaren. Liquid phenol-formaldehyde resin.

Synvaren PLS. Resorcinol-formaldehyde resin; used in adhesives.

Synvarite. Urea-formaldehyde resin.

Synvar-ol. Liquid urea-formaldehyde resin.

Systogen. Tyramine hydrochloride.

Composition of Trade-Marked Products

Syton. Colloidal dispersion of silica; used in textile finishing.

Syton W20. Highly polymerized silica dispersed in water; used in textile finishing.

Tackol. Blend of resins and oils; used in rubber.

Tagolene. Petroleum hydrocarbon oil.

Taka-diastase. Amylolytic enzyme preparation; digestive agent.

Takalab. Powder of diastatic and proteolytic enzymes; stripping and desizing agent.

Takatol. *p*-Aminophenol.

Talase (Polyzime). Mixture of diastatic and proteolytic enzymes; desizing agent.

Tallene. Tall-oil pitch.

Tallex. Abietic acid from tall oil.

Tallofin. Sulfated tallow; textile softener.

Tallosan RC. Sulfonated tallow; used in textile finishing.

Tallso. Crude tall-oil soap.

Tamasol J. Solvent with isobutyl acetate (85%).

Tamol. Sodium salt of sulfonic acid; dye resistant.

Tamol NNO. Formaldehyde-naphthalene sulfonic acid condensation product; wetting agent.

Tamol R. See Darvan 1.

Tanak MR. Melamine resin; used in tanning.

Tanarc. Titanium zirconium ferrate; used in welding-rod coating.

Tanigan A. Compound of 4,4′-dioxydiphenyl sulfone, waste sulfite liquor and formaldehyde; tanning agent (German).

Tanigan Extra A. Mixture of dioxydiphenyl sulfone and dioxydiphenyl sulfone-formaldehyde resin in sulfite liquor; used in tanning (German).

Tanigan Extra B. Condensate of partially sulfonated 4,4′-dihydroxydiphenyl methane and formaldehyde; tanning agent (German.)

Tannopin. Hexamethylene tetramine tannin.

Tannothymol. Condensation product of formaldehyde, thymol and tannin; used in medicine.

Tanol. Isooctane; used in antiknock motor fuels.

Tanolin. One-bath chrome-tanning compounds of the basic chromium sulfate type; used in mfg. chrome-tanned leathers.

Tanolin-T. Chrome liquor (basic chromic sulfate).

Tanoyl 1170. Blend of phosphorated cod oil, sulfonated cod oil and degras; used in stuffing leather.

Tanoyl 1170X. Mixture of phosphorated and sulfonated coconut oils; used for stuffing light leather.

Tantiron. Iron alloy containing 15% silicon.

Tantung. Wear-resistant alloy of cobalt, chromium, and tungsten containing tantalum carbide and columbium carbide; used for castings.

Targo. Calcium arsenate; insecticide.

Tarol. Pine oil; used in reclaiming rubber.

Tarol-1. Compounded pine oil; used in rubber industry.

Tarola. Coal-tar product; cattle and sheep dip.

Tarpyn. Pine tar; rubber softener.

Tartarone. Nitre cake, Glauber's salt, and corn dextrin; used in textile finishing.

Tatmo tool steel. High-carbon steel with about 8% molybdenum, 4% chromium, 2% tungsten, and 1% vanadium.

Taylor-White steel. Steel with about 8% tungsten, 3% chromium and 1% carbon.

Teca. Acetate staple fiber having a crimpy or wavy form.

Composition of Trade-Marked Products

Tec-Char. Granulated charcoal; deodorant.

Tecmangam. Manganese sulfate; used in fertilizers.

Tec-Quinol. Technical hydroquinone; resin stabilizer.

Tectase. Powder consisting of concentrated amylolytic and proteolytic enzymes; desizing agent.

Tedescan. Pentaerythritol ester of abietic acid and maleic anhydride; used in varnish (German).

Teel. Aqueous, colored solution of sodium lauryl sulfate; dentifrice.

Teepol. Sodium salts of higher alkyl sulfates, derived from petroleum; detergent.

Teflon. Polymerized tetrafluoroethylene; synthetic plastic.

Tegacid. Glyceryl monostearate with wetting agent; emulsifier.

Tegacid P. Propylene glycol monostearate with wetting agent; emulsifier.

Tegin. Glyceryl monostearate; emulsifier.

Tegin P. Propylene glycol monostearate; emulsifier.

Tegin 515. Purified glyceryl monostearate.

Teglac. Synthetic alkyd resin modified with natural resin acids; used in varnish.

Tego. Phenolic resin; used for plywood.

Tegofan. See Alloprene.

Tego glue. Phenol-formaldehyde resin; adhesive.

Tegosept. *p*-Hydroxybenzoic acid ester; preservative.

Tegosept M. Methyl *p*-hydroxybenzoate; preservative.

Tegosept P. Propyl *p*-hydroxybenzoate; preservative.

Tegul. Plasticized sulfur.

Tekaol. Heavy-bodied linseed oil from which soluble and less valuable substances are extracted.

Tekwood. Resin-bonded hardwood core with kraft paper facing; used in mfg. containers.

Telcoseal. Nickel-iron-cobalt alloy; used in metal-to-glass seals.

Telkanol. Ethylene oxide-higher fatty acid condensation product; dyeing assistant.

Telectal. Alloy of aluminum with 1.5% silicon and lithium 0.3%.

Telloy. Finely ground tellurium; vulcanizing agent in rubber.

Tellurac. Tellurium diethyl dithiocarbamate; vulcanization accelerator.

Telnic bronze. Alloy consisting of 97.68% copper, 1.1% nickel, 0.22% phosphorus, 0.5% tellurium and 0.5% zinc; used for bolts, nuts, etc.

Telura 35. Refined low-viscosity mineral oil.

Tenac. Asphalt emulsion.

Tenazit. Synthetic tar-acid resin.

Tenex. Wood rosin.

Tenite. Cellulose acetate plastic.

Tenite I. Cellulose acetate molding compound.

Tenite II. Cellulose acetate butyrate molding compound.

Tensilite. Manganese bronze of about 21 to 29% zinc, 3% manganese, 4% aluminum, up to 2% iron.

Tensol. Sulfonated alkyl naphthalene ether; dispersing agent.

Tensulate. Mineral wool; thermal insulator.

Tepidone. Solution of sodium dibutyl dithiocarbamate (60%) in water.

Terekan 12. Rope-fiber base impregnated with synthetic rubber latex; artificial leather.

Tereson. Sodium lactate (60) and water (40); antifreeze (German).

Tergamine. Polyalkylated hydrocarbon sulfonates; detergent.

Tergitol Penetrant 4T. Amine salt of a higher alkyl sulfate; surface-active agent.

Composition of Trade-Marked Products

Tergitol Penetrant 08. 2-Ethyl hexanol sodium sulfate; wetting agent.

Tergitol Penetrant 4. 7-Ethyl 2-methyl undecanol-4 sodium sulfate; wetting agent.

Tergitol Penetrant 4.7. Sodium salt of a higher alkyl sulfate; surface-active agent.

Tergitol Penetrant 7. 3,9-Diethyl tridecanol-6 sodium sulfate; wetting agent.

Terhyd. Malt-diastase concentrate; used in textile processing.

Ternalloy. Aluminum alloy.

Terpesol 3. Terpenyl methyl ether; solvent.

Terpesol 8. Terpenyl glycol ether; solvent.

Terpidone. Aqueous solution of sodium dibutyl dithiocarbamate; rubber accelerator.

Terpilene dihydrochloride. Eucalyptene hydrochloride; used in medicine.

Terposol. Terpene ether; solvent.

Terra Tox (Timber Tox). Pentachlorophenol solution; wood preservative.

Terylene. Synthetic fiber produced from a polyester of terephthalic acid and ethylene glycol (British).

Tervan. Polybutene and paraffin wax; used for impregnation.

Tetmosol. Tetraethyl thiura ammonium sulfate; miticide.

Tetrakierol. Benzol-soap solution; used in textile finishing.

Tetralin. Tetrahydronaphthalene; solvent.

Tetralin Extra. Mixture of Tetralin (20) and Dekalin (80); solvent.

Tetrolin. See Turpenol.

Tetrone. Tetrahydro-*p*-methyl quinoline.

Tetrone A. Dipentamethylene thiuram tetrasulfide; rubber accelerator.

Tetrosan. Aqueous solution of quaternary ammonium halide; germicide.

Composition of Trade-Marked Products

Texapon. Triethanolamine lauryl sulfate.

Texavon DS. Mixture of sulfonated oils and solvents; boil-off assistant.

Texgum. Pectinous, vegetable gum free from starch and dextrin; used in textile sizing.

Texol. Fatty acid condensate; wetting agent.

Texon. Latex-impregnated fibers; used in shoe linings.

Texscour Neutral, low-titer soap flakes; detergent.

Textase. Liquid malt containing diastase.

Textee. Edible hydrogenated stearin.

Textiline. White mineral oil.

Textolite. Phenol-formaldehyde filled resin.

Textolite bleach. Solution of sodium hypochlorite; used for bleaching textiles.

Texwax. Paraffin wax.

Thalloid 303. Solution of alkyd resin in ammonia water; used in textile finishing.

Thanite. Liquid terpene thiocyanate; insecticide.

Thaumaphos. Sodium pyrophosphate.

Theolactin. Theobromine sodium lactate; drug.

Theonacet. Theobromine sodium acetate.

Theophorin. Theobromine sodium formate.

Theosol. Theobromine calcium salicylate.

Thephorin. Theobromine sodium formate.

Thephyldine. Theophylline ethylene diamine.

Therlo. Copper-base alloy with 10 to 13% manganese and 2 to 6% aluminum.

Thermalloy. Nickel-chromium-iron

alloys with 2 to 65% nickel, 8 to 30% chromium, 1% silicon, 1% manganese, and the balance iron.

Thermax. Carbon; used in rubber compounding.

Thermax S. Dustless powder composed of Thermax (83%) and a plasticizer (17%); used in rubber compounding.

Thermazote. Phenol-formaldehyde plastic.

Thermisilid. High-silicon cast iron containing about 15% silicon; used for chemical equipment.

Thermoflex A. Mixture of di-*p*-methoxydiphenyl amine (25%), diphenyl *p*-phenylene diamine (25%) and phenyl β-naphthyl amine (50%); antioxidant.

Thermoflex C. Mixture of secondary aromatic amines; used in rubber compounding.

Thermoil A. Segregated fish oil; used in paint.

Thermoil L. Drying portion of polymerized linseed oil; used in paint.

Thermolite. See Kallodent.

Thermon. See Freon-21.

Thianol. Mixture of urea and sodium alginate; used in textile finishing.

Thiofide. 2,2′-Dithiodibenzothiazole; vulcanization accelerator.

Thiogen. Naftolen containing 6 to 10% sulfur; rubber plasticizer.

Thiogomme S. Polymer of ethylene tetra sulfide (French).

Thiokol. Organic polysulfide; synthetic rubber.

Thiokol A. Ethylene dichloride and sodium tetrasulfide; synthetic rubber.

Thiokol B. Dichloroethyl ether and sodium tetrasulfide; synthetic rubber.

Thiokol RD. Copolymer of butadiene and acrylonitrile; synthetic rubber.

Composition of Trade-Marked Products

Thiokol SC-10. Dithioglycol; solvent.

Thiomersalate. Sodium ethyl mercurithiosalicylate; antiseptic.

Thionex. Tetramethyl thiuram monosulfide; rubber accelerator.

Thionol. Sulfur dye; used on cotton and rayon.

Thionone. Sulfur color; used for dyeing cotton.

Thiosan. Tetramethyl thiuram disulfide; fungicide.

Thiotax. Mercaptobenzothiazole; vulcanization accelerator.

Thiotax A. Mercaptobenzothiazole; rubber accelerator.

Thiovanol. α-Monothioglycerol.

Thiurad. Tetramethyl thiuram disulfide.

Thiuram E. Tetraethyl thiuram disulfide; accelerator in vulcanization of rubber.

Thiuram M. Tetramethyl thiuram disulfide; rubber accelerator.

Thyloquinone. 2-Methyl 1,4-naphthoquinone; used in medicine.

Thymegol. Mercuric potassium thymol sulfonate; germicide.

Thyon. High-molecular-weight heteropolymeric reaction product of unsaturated hydrocarbons and their derivatives with sulfur dioxide; thermoplastic resin.

Thyrite. Silicon carbide; ceramic used in electric insulation.

Ti-Bar. Pigment consisting of TiO_2 and $BaSO_4$.

Tibatin. Galactoside of *p,p′*-diaminodiphenyl sulfone; germicide.

Ti-Cal. Pigment of TiO_2 and $CaSO_4$.

Tidolith. See Cryptone.

Timang. Steel with 12 to 15% manganese, about 3% nickel and about 0.70% carbon.

Timber Tox. See Terra Tox.

Timken steel. Low-alloy and high-alloy steels, commonly with carbon below 0.20%.

Timonox. Antimony oxide; pigment.

Composition of Trade-Marked Products

Tinapol Oil NE. Sulfonated ester; surface-active agent.

Tiolan (Thiozell). Casein textile fiber (German).

Ti-Pure. Titanium dioxide; pigment.

Tirex. Rubber compound vulcanized with selenium; used in electrical insulation.

Tiron. Disodium 1,2-dihydroxybenzene 3,5-disulfonate; reagent for determining titanium.

Ti-Sil. Pigment consisting of TiO_2 (30%) and $MgSiO_3$ (70%).

Tiska. Stainless steels with up to 22% chromium and 10% nickel.

Titadine TA. Alkyl naphthalene sulfonic acid ester and sulfated alcohols; wetting agent.

Titafin KT. Diethyl aminoethyl oleyl amido hydroxy acetate; surface-active agent.

Titalene. Soluble cresylic acid; fungicide.

Titamine TCP. Sulfonated alcohol derivative; wetting agent.

Titanalba. Calcined titanium dioxide.

Titanole RMA. Sodium alkyl aryl sulfonate; textile wetting agent.

Titanolith. Titanated lithopone; pigment.

Titan Decitrene. Alkylated aromatic sulfonates; textile wetting agent.

Titanellow. Titanium oxalate.

Titanox A. Titanium dioxide; white pigment.

Titanox B. Mixture of titanium dioxide (25%) and barium sulfate (75%); pigment.

Titanox C. Mixture of titanium dioxide (30%) and calcium sulfate (70%); pigment.

Titanox L. Lead titanate.

Titanox M. Titanium magnesium silicate; pigment.

Titanox RC. Rutile calcium; pigment.

Titanox RC-HT. Rutile calcium; high-tinting pigment.

Composition of Trade-Marked Products

Titascour. Sodium salt of sulfonic acid mixed with a liquid; textile wetting agent.

Titazole A.F. Sulfated monoglycerides; wetting agent.

Titazole S.A. Sodium alkyl naphthalene sulfonate; textile wetting agent.

Titazole T.A. Sodium octyl sulfate; wetting agent.

Titazole T.N.I. Fatty alcohol sulfates with a solvent; textile wetting agent.

Ti-Tint. Tinted titanium dioxide; pigment.

Titol VII. Mixture of methyl cellulose (2), turpentine (3.5) and water (94.5); paper coating (German).

Ti-Tone. Titanated lithopone; pigment.

Tollac solvent. Aromatic hydrocarbon solvent; toluol substitute.

Tombac. Copper-base alloys, with 70 to 92% copper, remainder essentially zinc; tin optional up to 3%.

Tombak. See Tombac.

Tombasil. Brass containing about 14% zinc, 5% silicon; used for wear-resisting products.

Tonalon. Basic aluminum chloride.

Toncan iron. High-atmospheric and corrosion-resistant iron with about 0.03% carbon, 0.5% copper and 0.07% molybdenum.

Toncarine. Methyl coumarin; flavor.

Tonephen. Posterior pituitary extract; used in medicine.

Tonox. *p,p'*-Diaminodiphenyl methane; rubber antioxidant.

Tonsil. Acid-treated clay; used in petroleum refining.

Tophet A. Alloy consisting of nickel and chromium.

Tophet C. Alloy consisting of iron, nickel and chromium.

Toplast. Synthetic tar-acid resin.

Toralit SM18. Copolymer of sty-

Composition of Trade-Marked Products

rene, methyl acrylate and acrylic acid.

Tornesite. Chlorinated rubber.

Toro. Quebracho extract; tanning agent.

Torridex 85. Sulfated tallow; textile softener.

Tortaloid. Cellulose acetate plastic.

Toxaphene. Chlorinated camphene; insecticide.

Trabuk. Tin-base alloy with approximately 5% antimony, 5% nickel and 2% bismuth.

Tracel. Boron, copper, manganese and zinc compounds which dissolve slowly in the soil and supply the necessary nutritional elements to the plant.

Tragantol. Potato starch with a small amount of sodium silicate; used in textile printing (German).

Tragasol. Aqueous jelly containing carob-bean gum (about 4%); thickener.

Tramolin. Sulfonated vegetable oil; wetting agent.

Trancor. High-silicon steel; used for magnetic and transformer purposes.

Transote. Refined coal-tar creosote; wood preservative.

Transparit. Transparent foil similar to Cellophane.

Transpex I. Unplasticized, polymerized methyl methacrylate; used in lenses.

Transpex II. Polystyrene plastic; used in lenses.

Transphalt. Unsaturated coal-tar derivatives; used in rubber compounding.

Trapineol. Pine-oil emulsion; antifoam.

Trasentin. 2-Diethyl aminoethyl diphenyl acetate; antispasmodic.

Tratex. Egg albumen.

Traumaticin. Solution of gutta-percha in chloroform; used in dentistry.

Composition of Trade-Marked Products

Trefoil. Paper, fabric or asbestos bonded with Bakelite.

Trefolia. Amyl salicylate; used in perfume (German).

Trek. Methanol; antifreeze.

Treopax. Zirconium oxide, silicon oxide, sodium oxide and aluminum oxide; opacifier for enamels.

Tri. Trichlorethylene.

Triad E. Stabilized trichloroethylene.

Triafol. Cellulose triacetate film (German).

Triapon M. Cationic emulsion of refined mineral oil; fiber lubricant.

Triapon W. Cationic, paraffin wax emulsion; textile lubricant.

Triasol. Mixture of trichloroethylene and ethylene dichloride; solvent.

Tribase. Hydrous, tribasic lead sulfate; stabilizer for vinyl plastics.

Triclene. Trichloroethylene.

Tricin. Trinitroresorcin; explosive (German).

Tricol. Brown-sugar syrup with 76% solids.

Tridee. Vitamin D_3 in corn oil; used in foods and drugs.

Tridione. 3,5,5-Trimethyl oxazolidine-2,4-dione; drug.

Tridite. Mixture of trinitrophenol and dinitrophenol; explosive in bursting charges.

Trienol. 8,10,12- and 9,11,13-Octadecatrienoic acid; drying oil.

Trigamine. Buffered aliphatic amine; emulsifying agent.

Trigamine stearate. Buffered aliphatic-amine soap of stearic acid; emulsifying agent.

Trigemin. Dimethyl aminoantipyrine butyl chloralhydrate; medicament.

Trilene. Trichlorethylene (British).

Trilon. Sodium salt of $N(CH_2COOH)_3$; used in water softening.

Trilon A. Sodium salt of aminotrimethyl carbonic acid.

Trilon B. Sodium salt of ethylene diamine tetramethyl carbonic acid.

Composition of Trade-Marked Products

Triluxe. Trichloroethylene.

Trimene. Mixture of triethyl trimethylene triamine (55%) and stearic acid (45%); accelerator.

Trimene Base. Triethyl trimethylene triamine.

Trimethylol. Aminomethane fatty acid soap; wetting agent.

Trimonite. Mixture of trinitrophenol and mononitronaphthalene; explosive in bursting charges.

Tri-Ol. Mixture of sulfonated castor oil, sulfonated olive oil and white mineral oil; base for soapless shampoos.

Tripen. Hexachlorobutadiene or hexachlorobutene.

TRI-SO. Trisodium phosphate.

Tri Sol. Mixture of chlorinated hydrocarbons (45%) and petroleum solvent (55%).

Triton B. Tetraalkyl ammonium hydroxide; cellulose solvent.

Triton F. Aqueous solution of dimethyl dibenzyl ammonium hydroxide.

Triton NE. Aryl alkyl polyether alcohol; wetting agent.

Triton B-1956. Polyglyceride of a glyptal resin.

Triton E-40. Salt of sulfonated and sulfated ether; surface-active agent.

Triton E-79. Ammonium salt of alkyl sulfonated ether alcohol; wetting agent.

Triton K-12. Cetyl dimethyl benzyl ammonium chloride; surface-active agent.

Triton K-60. Aqueous dispersion of cetyl dimethyl benzyl ammonium chloride; surface-active agent.

Triton M-25. Sodium salt of an organic ether acid; wetting agent.

Triton N-100. Aryl alkyl polyether alcohol; detergent.

Triton S-18. Salt of oleic and palmitic acid with an aryl alkylated amine; wetting agent.

Composition of Trade-Marked Products

Triton S-51. Sulfonated long-chain aromatic amine.

Triton W-30. Sodium salt of aryl alkyl ether sulfate; wetting agent.

Triton X-100. Polyethylene glycol alkyl aryl ether; emulsifier.

Triton X-155. Alkyl phenoxypolyethoxyethanol; emulsifier.

Triton 720. Sodium salt of aryl alkyl polyether sulfonate; wetting agent.

Triton 770. Sodium salt of alkyl phenoxypolyether sulfate; wetting agent.

Triton 773. Sodium salt of alkyl phenoxyethyl sulfate; surface-active agent.

Triton 812. Condensed sulfonated ether; surface-active agent.

Tritox. Trichloroacetonitrile; insecticide.

Trivitan. Synthetic vitamin D.

Trolit. Cellulose acetate with plasticizer; used in plastic molding.

Trolitan. Phenol-formaldehyde condensation product; used in plastic molding.

Trolit BC. Cellulose benzoate plastic.

Trolitul. Polystyrene-resin plastic.

Trolon. Synthetic tar-acid resin.

Troluloid. Copolymers of vinyl chloride with acrylic esters or vinyl acetate; plastic (German).

Troluoil. Petroleum naphtha solvent.

Tromete. Trisodium phosphate.

Tromex. Trichloroethylene; solvent.

Tropicalizer. Ketoalkyl monoxymercurobenzol; fungicide.

Trostol. Mixture of natural fats and resin acids; emulsifying agent.

Trukon. Emulsion of paraffin wax with a solution of aluminum formate or acetate; waterproofing agent.

Truline. Pulverized rosin; core binder.

Trypticase. Dehydrated peptone

Composition of Trade-Marked Products

prepared from casein by pancreatic digestion; nutrient for microorganisms.

Tuads. Tetramethyl thiuram disulfide; rubber accelerator.

Tubize. Viscose yarn.

Tuc-tur. Copper-base alloy with 21 to 29% zinc, optionally up to 15% nickel and up to 18% tin.

Tuex. Tetramethyl thiuram disulfide; accelerator for sulfurless rubber vulcanization.

Tufnol. Phenol- or urea-formaldehyde laminated plastics.

Tufor. Liquid containing the amine salt of 2,4-D (40%); weed killer.

Tufor 40. Solution of 2-4D (40%); weed killer.

Tungo steel. Low-alloy steel containing approximately 2% tungsten, 1.5% chromium, 0.25% vanadium, 0.50% carbon; used for tools.

Turbax. Synthetic tar-acid resin.

Turgum. Blend of products obtained from crude pine gum; softener in synthetic rubber.

Turgum S. Rosin-turpentine blend; softener for rubber.

Turkelene. Terpene glycol higher fatty acid partial ester; emulsifier.

Turpenol (Detersol; Tetrolin). Soap with hydrocarbon solvents; boil-off assistant.

Turpyne. Wood turpentine; solvent.

Tutocaine. *p*-Aminobenzoyl dimethyl amino-1,2-dimethyl propanol hydrochloride; used in medicine.

Tween 20. Sorbitan monolaurate-polyoxyalkylene derivative; emulsifying agent.

Tween 40. Sorbitan monopalmitate-polyoxyalkylene derivative; emulsifying agent.

Tween 60. Sorbitan monostearate-polyoxyalkylene derivative; emulsifying agent.

Tween 61. Sorbitan monostearate-polyoxyalkylene derivative; emulsifying agent.

Tween 80. Sorbitan monooleate-polyoxyalkylene derivative; emulsifying agent and detergent.

Tween 81. Polyoxyalkylene ether of sorbitan monooleate; emulsifier.

Tween 85. Polyoxyalkylene derivative of sorbitan trioleate; emulsifier.

Tygon. Vinyl chloride and vinyl acetate copolymer.

Tylose (Coloresin). Sodium salt of cellulose oxyacetic acid; aqueous thickening agent.

Tylose HBR. Cellulose—O—CH COONa; used with synthetic detergents.

Tyramine. *p*-[β-Aminoethyl] phenol; used in medicine.

Tyron. Rayon yarn, cord and fabric; used in tires.

Tytrovon RZB. Salt of a high-molecular-weight sulfoacid; detergent.

UAL-A urea-ammonia liquor. Solution of urea in aqueous ammonia; used in mfg. fertilizers.

Ubatex. Water dispersion of plasticized polystyrene.

Ucenol LT. Sulfated fatty alcohol; detergent (Belgian).

Ucepon E. Higher fatty acid with blocked carboxyl group; detergent (Belgian).

Ucon LB. Water-insoluble mixture of highly polymerized polyethylene glycols and ethers; lubricant.

Ucon 50-HB. Water-soluble mixture of highly polymerized polyethylene glycols and ethers; lubricant.

Uformite F-301. Alkyd-modified urea formaldehyde.

Uformite F-200-E. Urea-formaldehyde resin solution.

Uformite MM-55. Soluble melamine formaldehyde.

Composition of Trade-Marked Products

Uformite 430. Concentrated urea-formaldehyde solution; adhesive in the manufacture of durable plywood.

Uintaite. Gilsonite.

Uliron. 4-(4'-Aminophenyl sulfonamido)-phenyl sulfondimethyl amide; used in medicine.

Ulmal. Alloy of aluminum with 10% magnesium, 1% silicon, 0.5% manganese.

U-Loy. Corrosion-resistant copper-bearing steel.

Ulto. Zinc dithiocarbamate; rubber accelerator.

Ultracut steel. High-sulfur free-cutting steel.

Ultradie steel. Alloys with approximately 13% chromium, fractional percentages of vanadium or molybdenum.

Ultralin. Mixture of rosin and higher fatty acids; used in emulsion paints.

Ultralumin. Alloy of aluminum with 4.7% copper, 0.75% manganese, 0.2% nickel.

Ultramin. Polyamine-glyceride condensation product; used in textile finishing.

Ultranate. Petroleum sulfonate.

Ultranate No. 2. Sodium hydrocarbon sulfonate (50%).

Ultranate No. 6. Calcium hydrocarbon sulfonate.

Ultraphan. Cellulose acetate film.

Ultrapole Oil. Sulfated castor oil; dyeing aid.

Ultravon. Sodium sulfonate of 2-heptadecyl benzimidazole or an analog; neutral detergent.

Ultravon K. Sodium salt of a sulfonated condensation product of stearic acid and *o*-phenylene diamine; surface-active agent.

Ultrawet. Sodium sulfonate of petroleum hydrocarbons; wetting agent.

Ultrawet 30E. Aqueous solution containing the sodium salt of polyalkyl benzene sulfonate (25%); surface-active agent.

Composition of Trade-Marked Products

Ultroil. Sulfonated castor oil; wetting agent.

Umbrathor. Liquid containing thorium dioxide (25%); used in X-ray diagnosis.

Umbrex. Hydrogenated fatty acids.

Unemul. Alumina gel; emulsifier.

Unicel. Diazoaminobenzene; blowing agent for making sponge rubber.

Unicol. Sodium lauryl sulfate; detergent.

Unilith. Lithopone.

Uniloy steel. Series of high-chromium steels with 5 to 30% chromium, optionally up to 12% nickel, fractional percentages of other elements, 0.07 to 0.60% carbon.

Union Thinner. Series of petroleum solvents.

Unitec. Mineral oil; rubber plasticizer.

Uni-temp Grease. Synthetic hydrocarbon and a lithium soap; lubricating grease.

Unitex. Sodium salt of an alkylated aromatic sulfonate; wetting agent.

Unitexol. Highly sulfonated vegetable oil; used in textile finishing.

Unitol R. Refined tall oil.

Univan steel. Low-alloy cast steel with approximately 1.5% nickel, 1% manganese, 0.10% vanadium.

Unoba. Barium soap-base petroleum lubricating grease.

Unyte. Thermosetting urea-formaldehyde resin.

Urac. Urea-formaldehyde resin; adhesive.

Uradal. Bromodiethyl acetyl urea.

Ural. Chloral urethane.

Uraline. Chloral urethane.

Uralium. Chloral urethane.

Uralloy. Urea-plasticized green wood that can be bent and shaped.

Uramon fertilizer compound. Com-

Composition of Trade-Marked Products

pound containing urea nitrogen (42%); fertilizer.

Ureka. Blend of diphenyl guanidine and 2,4-dinitrophenyl thiobenzothiazole; rubber accelerator.

Ureka Blend B. Similar to Ureka, but with a portion of the diphenyl guanidine replaced by Guantal; used in rubber curing.

Ureka C. Benzothiazyl thiobenzoate; vulcanization accelerator.

Uresin. Condensation product of urethan and formaldehyde; plastic.

Uresin B. Butyl urethan formaldehyde; used in lacquers.

Urite. Urea-formaldehyde resin powder with or without hardening catalyst.

Urocitral. Theobromine sodium citrate.

Urol. Urea quinate.

Urolac. Urea-shellac compound.

Uropac. Disodium N-methyl 3,5-diiodo-4-pyridone 2,6-dicarboxylate.

Uropurgol. See Helmitol.

Uroselectan. See Iopax.

Urotropin. Hexamethylene tetramine.

Uroxin. Alloxantin.

Uscol. Sodium and zinc sulfoxalate formaldehyde; dyeing assistant.

Utanol. Crude asphaltic petroleum from Utah.

Uteramine. Tyramine hydrochloride.

Utica steel. Low-alloy steel containing about 1.5% tungsten, 1.3% carbon, fractional percentages of chromium and vanadium.

Utiloy. Iron-nickel-chromium alloy.

Uversol. Metallic naphthenate, e.g., zinc naphthenate; paint drier.

Uzolene. Cresylic acid compound; antioxidant.

Vacatone. Soluble extract of fermented molasses.

Vacatone 40. Vitamin B_2 concentrate with riboflavin; used in animal feeds.

Vac-melt. Nickel-base, electric-resistance alloys with 15 to 20% chromium, 7% molybdenum, 3% manganese, 16% iron.

Valex. Concentrated vanilla-bean extract; used in flavors.

Validol. Menthyl valerate.

Valisan. Bornyl bromoisovalerate.

Valite. Thermosetting phenolic resin made from bagasse.

Valone. 2-Isovaleryl 2,3-indandione; insecticide.

Valonex. Powdered valonia extract; tanning agent.

Valyl. Diethyl valeramide.

Vanade. Aqueous dispersion containing sorbitan stearates (35%); used in baking.

Vanadiset. Crystalline petroleum pitch; used in rubber compounding.

Vanaldol. Ethyl vanillin; used in flavors.

Vandex. Finely ground selenium; special vulcanizing agent in rubber.

Vanlite. Water dispersion of polyoxyethylene partial stearic acid ester of sorbitol (30%) with benzoic acid (0.2%); emulsifier.

Vanolith. Lithopone.

Vansulite. Whiting.

Vapoline. "Soluble" mineral oil; wool lubricant.

Vapoline Extra. Blend of mineral oil and higher fatty acid amides; textile lubricant.

Va Pon. Powdered valonia; tanning agent.

Varcum resins. Phenol-formaldehyde base resins; used in plastics and varnishes.

Varene. Liquid terpene polymer.

Varnex. Specially processed linseed oil; used in varnish.

Varno Spirits. Mineral spirits.

Varsol. Petroleum solvent.

Varsol 1. Petroleum solvent.

Composition of Trade-Marked Products

Vasite. Liquid stripping agent of the hydrosulfite group.

Vasogen. Oxygenated petrolatum; used in medicine.

Vatrolite. See Lykopon.

Vatsol OS. Sodium salt of alkyl naphthalene sulfonic acid; wetting agent.

Vatsol OT. Dioctyl sodium sulfosuccinate; wetting agent.

Vatsol OT-C. Dioctyl sodium sulfosuccinate and an inert organic diluent; wetting agent.

Vectolite. Compressed powdered iron oxide and cobalt oxide; used for light-weight permanent magnets.

Vee. Polyvinylidene chloride; synthetic resin.

Veegum. Magnesium-aluminum silicate gel.

Vegamine. Acid-hydrolyzed protein of wheat and corn; soup flavoring.

Vegifat. High-titer vegetable oil.

Vegol. Vitamin E concentrate.

Vejin. Vegetable lecithin.

Vel. Coconut-oil fatty acid glyceryl sodium sulfonate; detergent.

Velan PF. 1-Octadecyl oxymethyl pyridinium chloride; used to give finishes resistant to washing.

Vel-A-Tex. Quaternary ammonium compound; textile softener.

Velatrum. White petroleum wax.

Velofilm. Precipitated calcium carbonate.

Velon. Vinylidene chloride fiber.

Velsicol. Commercial mixture of polymethylated naphthalenes; solvent for DDT and other insecticides.

Velsicol AR-40. Methylated naphthalenes rich in monomethyl naphthalene.

Velsicol AR-50. Mixture consisting principally of mono and dimethyl naphthalenes.

Velsicol AR-60. Mixture consisting chiefly of di- and trimethyl naphthalenes.

Velsicol AR-70. Mixture consisting chiefly of tetramethyl naphthalene.

Velsicol 1. Petroleum thinner.

Velsicol 1068. Naphthalene hexachloride; used in insecticide sprays.

Velsicol resins. Polymerized petroleum-hydrocarbon resins of high iodine number; used in varnish.

Vel-Tox. Chlorinated hydrocarbon; insecticide.

Velveteen. Silica.

Velvetex. Carbon black; filler in rubber compounds.

Velvetol T. Compounded sulfated vegetable and animal oils; textile softener.

Velvo. Sulfonated tallow; used in textile finishing.

Velvoray. Sulfated vegetable oil; textile softener.

Velvosheen. Highly sulfated olive oil; used in textile finishing.

Velvril. Mixture of nitrocellulose and nitrated castor oil or linseed oil; substitute for gutta-percha.

Venalloy. Vinylidene chloride polymer; filaments.

Ventox. Acrylonitrile; fumigant.

Vera Blanc. Calcium carbonate; extender pigment for paints, adhesives.

Veramon. Aminopyrine diethyl barbiturate; sedative.

Verdite. Selected and processed greens and zeolite; ion-exchange medium.

Veriloy. Steel containing about 21% nickel and 11% chromium.

Veritol. *l-p*-Hydroxyphenyl 2-methyl aminopropane.

Vermonite. Acrylic plastic.

Vernonite. Mixture of acrylic resins; used for dentures.

Veroc White. Whiting.

Verodigen. Amorphous gitalin; used in medicine.

Composition of Trade-Marked Products

Verol. Monomethyl *p*-amidophenol sulfate.

Veronal. Barbital; used in medicine.

Vesipyrin. Phenyl acetyl salicylate.

Vestasol. Sulfated neatsfoot oil; emulsifier.

Vesterine. Mixture of edible gelatin and glyceryl mono and distearates; ice-cream stabilizer.

Vetivenol. Vetiver oil; used in perfumery.

Vextram. Compound containing vitamins and iron; flour enrichment.

VGB. Acetaldehyde-ethylene diamine compound; rubber antioxidant.

Vibrin. Thermosetting synthetic resin.

Vicafol. Polyvinyl carbazol; plastic film (German).

Vicalloy. Magnetic alloy of iron, cobalt and vanadium; used in permanent magnets.

Vicrtex. Vinyl-resin coated fabric.

Victor wetting agent 35B. Sodium salt of octyl tripolyphosphate.

Victor wetting agent 58B. Sodium salt of capryl tripolyphosphate.

Victron. Polystyrene resin.

Videne. Vinyl-resin film and sheeting.

Vigantol. Synthetic vitamin D_2.

Vigopas. Tar-acid resin (German).

Vigorol. Phenol-formaldehyde resin; used in making pressed board.

Vigorit. Tar-acid resin (German).

Vimlite. Sheets of cellulose acetate in which 14-mesh wire screening is embedded; used in place of glass in chickenhouses.

Vinal. Synthetic vinyl resin.

Vinarol. Polyvinyl alcohol (German).

Vinarol A. Aqueous dispersion of viscous polyvinyl alcohols (12%); used in textile sizing (German).

Vinethrene. Vinethene; anesthetic.

Vinidur. Hard polyvinyl chloride.

Composition of Trade-Marked Products

Vinifol. Chlorinated polyvinyl film (German).

Vinko. Solution of zinc-calcium stearate in volatile solvents; used in paint.

Vinnapas. Polymerized vinyl acetate; used in colorless varnishes.

Vinnapas B. Low-viscosity polyvinyl acetate.

Vinnapas D. Polyvinyl acetate plastic.

Vinnapas V. Infusible polyvinyl acetate.

Vinnol. Polyvinyl chloride.

Vinoflex PC. Chlorinated polyvinyl chloride.

Vinoflex PCU. Polyvinyl chloride.

Vinoflex S. Relatively low-molecular-weight polyvinyl chloride (German).

Vinol. Polyvinyl chloride.

Vinoplex MP 400. Mixture of vinyl chloride (73%), vinyl isobutyl ether (25.5%) and methyl acrylate (1.5%); used in lacquers.

Vinsol. Black residue left after rosin is extracted with petroleum solvents; used in insulating.

Vinsol Ester Gum. Glycerin ester of Vinsol resin.

Vintox. Sodium arsenite solution; insecticide.

Vinyarn. Polyvinyl compound; synthetic fiber.

Vinycol. Series of products consisting of pigments dispersed in Vinylite resins; used for coatings.

Vinylite. Polymerized vinyl thermoplastic resins.

Vinylite A. Polymerized vinyl acetate resin.

Vinylite Q. Polymerized vinyl chloride resin.

Vinylite V. Copolymerized vinyl chloride and vinyl acetate resin.

Vinylite X. Polyvinyl-butyral synthetic resin; interlayer for safety glass, adhesive.

Vinyloid. Synthetic vinyl resin.

Vinylseal. Solution of Vinylite A

Composition of Trade-Marked Products

resin (35%) in acetone; adhesive.

Vinyon. Synthetic textile fiber consisting of a vinyl chloride and vinyl acetate copolymer.

Vioform. 5-Chloro-7-iodo-8-hydroxyquinoline; antiseptic.

Violite. Phosphorescent or fluorescent luminous pigment.

Vipla. Polyvinyl chloride plastic (Italian).

Visca. Flat-filament viscose rayon treated to simulate straw fibers.

Viscacelle. Regenerated cellulose film.

Viscogen. Calcium sucrate.

Viscol. Polyacrylic acid-plastic film (German).

Viscol. Sulfurized oil; elastomer.

Visco resin. Series of polymerized iso-olefins.

Viskoplus. Aluminum naphthenate; used to increase the viscosity of oils.

Viskord. Monofilaments of vinyl resins, vinylidene chloride or their copolymers.

Vistac. Polymerized olefins.

Vistanex polybutene. Synthetic rubber of polymerized isobutylene.

Vistra. Viscose staple fibers (German).

Vitafilm. Vinyl resin film.

Vital. Alloy of aluminum with 1.15% zinc, 0.6% silicon, 0.9% copper, 0.15% manganese.

Vitallium. Stainless alloy of cobalt, chromium, and molybdenum; used in surgical fastenings.

Vitreosil. Pure fused silica; used in laboratory ware.

Vival. Alloy of aluminum with 1% magnesium, 0.5% silicon, 0.5% manganese.

Viveral. Desizing agent based on pancreatic substances.

V-meth-L. Methyl chloride; refrigerant.

V.M.P. naphtha. Petroleum distillate; used for varnishes.

Composition of Trade-Marked Products

Vocatone. Spray-dried molasses.

Vodol. Corn-oil commercial lecithin.

Vogan. Natural vitamin A.

Volclay. Impure aluminum silicate; thickener.

Volite. Volcanic ash of low lime content; abrasive.

Voltex. Conductive channel carbon black.

Volumin. Mixture containing urea (53 parts) and magnesium chloride (35 parts); used in textile processing.

Vondedrine. Phenyl propyl methyl amine; medicament.

Vream. Hydrogenated oil; shortening.

Vrest. Commercial glyceryl monostearate; used in mfg. ice cream.

Vuelite. Cellulose acetate embossed sheet.

Vuepak. Cellulose acetate; packaging material.

Vulcaflex. Substituted secondary amine; rubber antioxidant.

Vulcafor. Zinc diethyl dithiocarbamate; vulcanization accelerator.

Vulcalock. Thermoprene cement; used for cementing rubber to metals.

Vulcanex. Acetaldehyde-*p*-toluidine-aniline condensation product; rubber vulcanization accelerator.

Vulcanizate. Vulcanized rubber.

Vulcanoil H. Vulcanized vegetable- and animal-oil mixture; used in preserving leather.

Vulcaplas. Organic polysulfide; synthetic rubber (British).

Vulcastab C. Aqueous paste of sodium fatty alcohol sulfate (30%); latex stabilizer (British).

Vulcazol. Hydrofuramide; vulcanization accelerator.

Vulcone. Ethylidene aniline formaldehyde; rubber accelerator.

Vulkacit AZ. Condensation product of mercaptobenzothiazole and di-

Composition of Trade-Marked Products

ethyl amine; vulcanization accelerator (German).

Vulkacit FD. Anhydroformaldehyde *p*-toluidine.

Vulkacit TH. Tetramethyl thiuram disulfide.

Vulprene. Elastomers made by converting triglycerides to dimer acids and then esterifying with polyhydroxyalcohols.

Vultac. *p-tert*-Amyl phenol sulfide; rubber vulcanizing tackifier.

Vultamol. Sodium salt of the condensation product of β-naphthalene sulfonic acid and formaldehyde; adhesive.

Vultex. Rubber latex vulcanized in liquid form; used in mfg. adhesives, dipped goods, for coatings.

Vycor. Borosilicate glass containing about 96% combined silica.

Wagum. Synthetic rubber made by polymerizing butadiene and styrene with an organic sulfide.

Warco. Mixture of sulfated vegetable, mineral and saponifiable oils; finishing agent for textiles.

Warcocide No. 1. Dispersion of *o*-phenyl phenol (25%) in water containing a small amount of solvent.

Warcofix. Quaternary ammonium salt; used in textile finishing.

Warcosan. Alkyl ester sulfate; textile softener.

Warcosol. Sodium alkyl naphthalene sulfonates; wetting agent, emulsifier.

Warcosol 60-S. Alkyl naphthalene sulfonate; used in textile finishing.

Warcosol 897. Hydrocarbon sodium sulfonate and solvent; surface-active agent.

Washine. Sodium hypochlorite; antiseptic.

Waterlite. Synthetic tar-acid plastic.

Waxol P. Wax and tallow emulsions; used in finishing textiles.

Composition of Trade-Marked Products

Weberite. Plastic made from waste citrus peel and pulp.

Webril. Non-woven fabric made by blending thermoplastic fibers into a cotton web and applying heat and pressure.

Weedanol M1 Conc. Solution of 2-4D (40%); weed killer.

Weedicide Conc. Solution of 2-4D (50%); weed killer.

Weedone. 2-4D acetic acid solution; weed killer.

Weedox. Solution of 2-4D (9%); weed killer.

Weed-Tox. 2-4D compound (60%); weed killer.

Weed-Tox 40. Solution of 2-4D (21%); weed killer.

Weipul. Commercial sodium lauryl sulfate; wetting agent (German).

Weircoloy. Galvanized steel sheet.

Weirite. Hot-dip and electroplate tin on steel.

Weirzin. Electrolytic zinc-coated sheets and strip steel.

Weldalene. Mixture of silica (60%) and aluminum oxide (24%); welding flux.

Weldwood. Urea-formaldehyde resin; adhesive for plywood.

Welvic. Plasticized polyvinyl chloride.

Wenjazit. Synthetic tar-acid resin.

Werkrite. Neutral tallow soap; mold lubricant.

Westron. Acetylene tetrachloride.

Westropol. Special soft soap with a considerable amount of trichloroethylene; used in cleaning leather.

Westrosol. Trichloroethylene.

Wetanol. Modified sulfated fatty alcohol; surface-active agent.

Wetonite. Sulfonated ester; surface-active agent.

Wetsit Conc. Alkyl aryl sulfonate combined with terpenes; penetrating agent.

Composition of Trade-Marked Products

Wetzout. Sodium lauryl sulfate; dyeing assistant.

Whelco steel. High-alloy nickel-chromium and stainless steels.

Whitekote. Hydrated lime; used for making plaster.

Whitene. Calcium carbonate whiting of low oil absorption; used in paint.

Whitex. See Whitene.

Wiedolastic. Mixture of butyl acrylate (24), white pigments (26) and water (50); adhesive (German).

Wilkinite. Bentonite.

Winter-Flo. Essentially methanol with a rust inhibitor; antifreeze.

Witcarb. Precipitated calcium carbonate.

Witcarb R. Fine-particle size, precipitated calcium carbonate; used in paint.

Witcogum. Polymerized vegetable oil; rubber substitute.

Witresin. Petroleum hydrocarbon resin; rubber softener.

Wolfatite. Phenol-formaldehyde condensation product; cation exchange base.

Wolfco Solvent. Saponified fat with solvents.

Wolline. Mixture of trichlorpropane (60) and light naphtha (40); spot remover (German).

Wolman salts. Mixture of sodium chromate (about 3 parts), sodium fluoride (2 parts), sodium arsenate (2 parts), dinitrophenol (1 part) or equivalents; used in preserving lumber.

Wompco. High-strength cast iron, with 2.90% carbon, 2% silicon, 0.75% manganese.

Woodfil. Wood flour; filler.

Wooline. Mahogany soap; wool-scouring agent.

WYEX. Channel-process carbon black; used in rubber.

Wyo-Jel. Bentonite.

Wyrol-HX. White mineral oil; used in ointments.

Composition of Trade-Marked Products

Wytase. Natural enzyme preparation; used for whitening bread-dough.

Xeroform. Bismuth tribromophenate.

Xerol. Glyceryl monostearate; emulsifying agent.

Xerol S. Glycol stearate; emulsifying agent.

Xpando. Enzymatic diastatic syrup; used for baking.

Xplo. Carbon black; used for explosives.

Xylanon. Monochloronaphthalene with dichloronaphthalene; wood preservative (German).

Xylonite. Pyroxylin plastic.

Xynocol. Sulfated fatty acid amide; wetting agent.

Xynomine. Sulfated boramide ester of a long-chain aliphatic compound; wetting agent.

Xynomine Softener. Sodium fatty acid amide sulfate; used in textile finishing.

Xyno Pigment White. Titanium dioxide dispersed in an aqueous solution of gum arabic; textile printing paste.

Xyno Resin AA-40. Aqueous dispersion of vinyl resin; used in textile finishing.

Xynoset. Imidazoline compound.

Y alloy. Aluminum alloy containtaining about 4% copper, 2% nickel, 1.5% magnesium; used for aircraft and piston castings.

Yelkin C. Water-dispersible lecithin; surface-active agent.

Yelkin T. Mixture of lecithin (60–70%) and soybean oil (30–35%); surface-active agent.

Yelkin T-X15. Lecithin compound; surface-active agent.

Yellotone. Salt and sulfur; cattle-lick.

Yellow Cuprocide. Yellow copper oxide.

Composition of Trade-Marked Products

Yestamin. Purified, dried, debittered yeast containing vitamins B_1 and B_2 and protein (40%) (British).

Yocoline. Mixture of mineral oil, soaps, sulfonated oil; used for leather finishing.

Yoloy. Low-alloy steel containing about 2% nickel, 1% copper, 0.2% carbon.

Yumidol. Concentrated sorbitol syrup; substitute for glycerin.

Zamak. Series of zinc-base alloys, with up to 4% aluminum, about 1% copper, fractional percentages of magnesium optional.

Zellan. Plastic cellulose derivatives (German).

Zenite. Product consisting of the zinc salt of 2-mercaptobenzothiazole (90%) and hydrocarbon wax (10%); vulcanization accelerator.

Zenite A. Product consisting of zinc benzothiazyl sulfide (87.3%), inert hydrocarbon (9.7%), tetramethyl thiuram monosulfide (3.0%); vulcanization accelerator.

Zenite B. Product consisting of Zenite (90%) and di-*o*-tolyl guanidine (10%); vulcanization accelerator.

Zentralin. Dimethyl diphenyl urea.

Zeobromal. Ethyl dibromohydrocinnamate; used in medicine.

Zeo-Dur. Green sand; softener.

Zeogel. Treated colloidal clay; suspending agent in oil-well drilling.

Zeo-Karb. Carbonaceous zeolite; ion exchanger.

Zephiran chloride. Aqueous solution of high-molecular alkyl dimethyl benzyl ammonium chlorides; germicide.

Zephirol. Aqueous solution of a mixture of alkyl benzyl ammonium chlorides of high molecular weight; bactericide.

Zerlate. Zinc dimethyl dithiocarbamate; fungicide.

Zerok. Polyvinyl chloride-plastic coating.

Composition of Trade-Marked Products

Zerolate. Zinc dimethyl dithiocarbamate; herbicide.

Zerox. Litharge containing small amounts of hydrocarbons, carbon, inorganic materials; used in storage batteries.

Zicol. Mixture of Decalin (60) and light mineral oil (40); textile-spool lubricant (Swiss).

Zilloy. Zinc-base alloy, containing 1% copper and fractional percentages magnesium.

Zimate. Zinc dimethyl dithiocarbamate.

Zimco. Synthetic vanillan.

Zinol. Mineral spirits containing zinc resinate (65%) and rosin; used in varnish.

Zinox. Hydrated zinc oxide; pigment.

Zintox. Basic zinc arsenate; used in agricultural sprays.

Zipacel. Piperidinium pentamethylene dithiocarbamate; rubber accelerator.

Zircofrax. Zircon-base refractory.

Zircopax. Zirconium and silicon dioxides; used for opacifying glazes.

Zircotan. Zirconium sulfate.

Zircotan N. Basic zirconyl sulfate; used in tanning.

Zirex. Zinc resinate; used in paints.

Zirkonal. Alloy of aluminum with 15% copper, 8% manganese, 0.5% silicon.

Zirkonalba. Zirconium oxide.

Zirkosil. Zirconium silicate.

Zirmet. Ductile zirconium.

Zirnu. Zirconium sand; used in foundry molds.

Zirox. Zirconium dioxide; pigment.

Zito Chromate. Zinc tetroxychromate; used in anticorrosive metal paints.

Zitro. Zinc resinate.

"Z" nickel. Age-hardenable nickel alloy containing 98% nickel.

Z-O. Copper zeolite; fungicide.

Zonite. Sodium hypochlorite solu-

Composition of Trade-Marked Products

tion containing 0.9% available chlorine; disinfectant.

Zonolite. Expanded vermiculite; used in thermal insulation.

Zopaque. Titanium dioxide; pigment.

Zorite. Electric-resistance iron-base alloy containing approximately 37% nickel, 16% chromium, 2% manganese, 1% silicon, and 0.5% carbon.

Zote. Resilient cellular rubber compound.

ZTO chromate. Zinc tetroxychromate; rust inhibitor in metal paints.

Composition of Trade-Marked Products

Zulu Colors. Phthalocyanine colors; pigments.

Zyklon Discoids. Hydrocyanic acid absorbed in cellulosic discs; fumigant.

Zylonite. Celluloid.

Zymezate. Enzyme-hydrolyzed yeast protein; used in predigested food products.

Zymino. Enzyme-hydrolyzed proteins of casein and yeast; medicinal nutrient.

Zymol. Specially treated linseed oil; used in mfg. varnish.